LIFE IS A FOUR-LETTER WORD

'This is the state of man: today he puts forth
The tender leaves of hopes; tomorrow blossoms,
And bears his blushing honours thick upon him;
The third day comes a frost, a killing frost,
And when he thinks, good easy man, full surely
His greatness is a-ripening, nips his root,
And then he falls, as I do.'

SHAKESPEARE, *King Henry the Eighth*

VOLUME II

BREAKING OUT

NICHOLAS MONSARRAT

LIFE IS A
FOUR-LETTER
WORD

VOLUME II

BREAKING OUT

CASSELL · LONDON

CASSELL & COMPANY LTD
35 Red Lion Square, London, WC1
Melbourne, Sydney, Toronto
Johannesburg, Auckland

© Nicholas Monsarrat 1970

First edition August 1970
First edition, second impression February 1971

First published 1970

I.S.B.N. 0 304 93461 5

PRINTED IN GREAT BRITAIN BY
EBENEZER BAYLIS AND SON LIMITED
THE TRINITY PRESS, WORCESTER, AND LONDON
171

CONTENTS

ILLUSTRA-TIONS

FOREWORD

There used to be a legendary, one-story *raconteur* whose one story concerned a shooting accident. It was a story he had to tell. During any suitable pause in the conversation, he would crash his fist down on the table, and exclaim: 'Great heavens! Was that a gun? That reminds me of a story—'

He was, naturally, a suspect witness as well as a figure of fun.

I feel the same way about beginning this second slice of autobiography with a war-story of thirty years ago. But for good or, mostly, for evil, a war—any war—is tremendously important in a man's life; it is, like all violence, so cruel and stupid, so odious a breach of love and hope, such a defeat for sweet reason (and there *is* such a thing), such a triumph for the ape in man, that it can make or break him, just as it makes or breaks a nation.

So it must loom large enough to prove the point, though not more than that.

For me, the war started in bad earnest when I was thirty-one, and thus fits in with the pattern of five-year leaps which I set when I began this long accounting with the hero at the age of one.

There was, and is, lots more after the war. But just a minute! Great heavens! Was that a gun?

N.M.

IT *WAS* CRUEL
(1941)

1.

Who remembers the old fights? Who wants to? Who really remembers the bomb that took the house next door, the charnel tanks cremated in choking sand, the hideous night-sky over Berlin, the convoy so mauled that it seemed to be bleeding to death? Who really cares—not in boozy annual reunion, but with deep feeling, and sorrow, and the rare edge of triumph?

I used to talk about the war at sea, for a year or so afterwards; and then it became a bore, and peacetime grew exciting and much more important. I wrote about it eighteen years ago, but not again. Yet even now, a great wheeling quarter-century later, it is still vivid, still awful, still a scar of sorts, however handsomely healed.

It is still, in memory, a wild excitement as well, a testing-time never to be matched until the last enemy comes calling again. So there must be a place for it in the life-and-times; a small place, but still to be filled with the taste and smell, the sight and sound, of men trying to kill each other, or to save each other, or to run away and hide from both endeavours.

I kept the middle watch, all that year of 1941; one of the tied tenantry of a corvette's open bridge, along with two look-outs, a helmsman, and a messenger; on guard, sometimes for seventeen days on end, from 12 o'clock until 4, a.m. and p.m., in the black box of night or the wine of clear sunlight; to and fro across the Atlantic or down to Gibraltar, zigzagging endlessly at slow convoy speed—which was six and a half knots.

A corvette, if harried by the Chief Stoker, might well provoke its push-pull engine up to a shuddering fourteen knots; but we never did fourteen, unless we were chasing a U-boat contact or, blessedly, slipping home for a boiler-clean and the five days' leave which went with it.

On our escort job, we had to match the speed of the slowest member, like a House of Lords procession; and some of the ancient crocodiles in our charge drifted along like seaweed on the tide, as if their very barnacles were asleep.

At the beginning, even a slow old ship, a creeping convoy, a cottonwool fog, a whole night at action stations, a week of merciless weather, had been exciting; the novelty had been all. Now we were getting into the second year of it, and nothing was new any more. It was merely the longest sweat of our lives. No optimism touched our ship, nor any other, so far as we could tell; no one now sang that 1939 fool's favourite, 'We'll Hang Out the Washing on the Siegfried Line'; no one whistled 'Run, Rabbit, Run' while contemplating the bust of Hitler.

Already, in dull endurance, we were thinking of ourselves as 'hanging on'. If we had known that this grotesque Allemande was to continue, with increasing fury, with the flow of blood beginning to match the tidal sea, for nearly four years more, we might well have had some perilous second thoughts.

My father had once said, of his old, wicked, gory Salonika war: 'All I could think of, at the time, was keeping going when we were all dog-tired.' Now there was another war, and this time it was mine instead of his. But the deadly weariness, shot through with fear, was the very same.

I had gone to my war as a gentleman should (in 1940), by answering an advertisement in *The Times*. Just as Lord Reith, the generative giant of the B.B.C., had laid the true foundations of that splendid organization by applying, via the *Morning Post*, to the 'Chairman of the Broadcasting Committee', who in 1922 was looking for a General Manager, a Director of Programmes, and a Chief Engineer (Reith inclined towards the latter), so I had been tempted by an equally low-key piece of bait, which invited 'Gentlemen with yachting experience' to apply for commissions as Temporary Probationary Sub-Lieutenants in the Royal Naval Volunteer Reserve.

IT WAS CRUEL

My father had cut out the advertisement and sent it to me (I was still loyally bound to the *News Chronicle*, and would not have been seen dead with *The Times*, even as bedclothes in Hyde Park) ; and after thinking it over I sent in my application. Apart from yachting experience, which I could reasonably claim, the time was ripe, in many other ways.

Our trouble, in early 1940, was inaction—inaction, doubt, and dismay.

So far I had spent seven months, from the day before the first day of the war, in suspended valour: first as a humble stretcher-party driver, and later as the boss, of an Air Raid Precautions depot in Harley Street.* Taking this non-combatant job had been a matter of conviction. Though we were at war with Germany, I was still an ardent pacifist, war or no war, and this, I decided, was as far as I could go.

It did not seem at all shameful, nor cowardly. At that time, we were all certain that London, at least, would be bombed and burned to cinders, on the first evening of Day One, and that we, as well as succouring the wounded would be catching the bombs with our bare hands.

Yet nothing at all had happened, for weeks and then for months. In Harley Street we had nothing to do but splint and bandage each other, diagnose and treat suspected epilepsy (piece of wood between the teeth), build practice-scaffolding to prop up tottering buildings, and queue up at the canteen (run at first by comedian Douglas Byng) for tea, hot saveloys, and egg-and-chips. After a few months of this, total boredom had set in.

This wasn't what we had volunteered for, even at £2 18s. 5d. a week. What was the point of it, if no one was going to drop any bombs? And what had gone wrong with the war outside Harley Street?

So far there had been complete stalemate on the Continent, where by rights all the men-at-arms ought to be cutting each other to ribbons, and all the battle honours should be adding

* A fellow-stretcher-bearer: Clarence Paget, later Chief Editor of Pan Books.

up to total annihilation of the hated Hun. As a matter of sad fact, it seemed that we hadn't the strength even to march up to the Siegfried Line, much less use it for our laundry.

What had started out in confusion, not least in the Press (the *Observer* was violently pro-Italian, the *Daily Mail* had long ago come out flat-footed for Fascism and Sir Oswald Mosley, the *Evening Standard* had promised 'There will be no war' a short day before the fried egg hit the fan) seemed to have stalled before it started. Of course, we were standing by. We were ready for any sort of knavish trick. We were digging for victory, rearming for total war, and queueing for egg-powder and corned beef. But we weren't doing any fighting.

On our side, no one was in action. Indeed, it sometimes seemed that by far the best turn of speed had been shown by the poet-novelist team of Auden and Isherwood, who, ardent in their guardianship of culture, had taken off for California in the spring of 1939, later announcing that they had no intention of coming back till the war was over—a unique demonstration of how swiftly dreamy intellectuals can become men of decision, while the band plays 'God Save Our Skins'.

Apart from that, and the equally lively leap by Wimbledon tennis-star H. W. ('Bunny') Austin, who also took off for America in December 1939 in the interests of Moral Rearmament, and had been concentrating on such superior weaponry ever since—apart from that, not another mouse stirred. In a London strangely empty of children, who had been issued with miniature gasmasks and re-christened 'evacuees', we had come to call this puzzled trance the phoney war. But that was a blinkered verdict. It wasn't in the least phoney for other people. What had 'gone wrong' with our war had in truth gone wrong for most of the rest of Europe.

The Soviet-German pact, the crudest piece of dog-mathematics in modern diplomacy, had taken care of Hitler's back door. Italy was now preparing to come in on the German side. Russia had jumped on the Finns with both her iron-shod boots and ground the tiny nation into the snow. We could do noth-

ing about that, even if we had wanted to. Hitler then overran
Poland in about three weeks, occupied Denmark without a cross
word on either side, and invaded Norway.

We could do nothing about that either, though it seemed
that in this case we *did* want to. When we counter-invaded,
with what was described by the then Minister of War, Major
Oliver Stanley, as the best-equipped expeditionary force ever
to leave these shores, we were kicked out again in a matter of
weeks.

But not to worry about that, old boy! The evacuation,
though not actually *planned*, had it seemed been conducted with
supreme skill by Major-General B. C. T. Paget; and military
commentators, of whom there was no shortage, now assured us
that 'Paget's Withdrawal' would go down in history as a classic
example of the art of war, one of the brightest pages in the
annals of British arms. We were also assured that we really
were on top of the job, actually: pretty well running this latest
show: firmly set in the saddle; that Hitler had missed the bus
(Mr Neville Chamberlain); that it could only be a matter of
time.

In this connection, there was further comfort from another
slogan:

> It may be long, it may be short,
> It all depends on Viscount Gort.*

and from another news-item—the Germans were already
making coffee out of acorns! So it *couldn't* be long now!

Yet it could not be disguised, even from idle, yawning,
strategically-minded stretcher-bearers, that everyone in the
war was doing something useful or valiant except us, the stockstill British; and among 'us' was me, and I was as bad as anyone.
The only action I had seen so far was to assume the uniform of a
St John Ambulance Brigade sergeant, and 'line the route' on the
Horse Guards Parade for the triumphant march of the crews of

---

* Field Marshal Lord Gort, in command of the British Expeditionary Force in
France.

H.M.S. *Exeter* and *Ajax*, on their return from sinking the pocket battleship *Graf Spee*. Armed with iodine and sal volatile, I was there in case any ladies fainted.

Other events now marched on with gruesome speed; they were no longer a joke, or good for a Windmill Theatre song-title, or even 'part of our overall plan'. While I had been waiting to hear whether I had answered that R.N.V.R. advertisement correctly, Hitler swallowed Holland and Belgium; while I was still under training at H.M.S. *King Alfred*, learning how to salute and how to respond in a seamanlike manner to the Loyal Toast (don't stand up), and studying an ambiguous manual called *Street Fighting for Junior Officers*, France collapsed and Dunkirk happened.

The suggestion made at the time, that the only way out of our grim plight was to appoint the Duke of Gloucester as Supreme Allied Commander-in-Chief ('He would rally the whole nation!'), seemed to hint that we were still not taking this very seriously. But *I* was serious enough, because I had now turned my full somersault, shedding ideals like post-nuptial confetti.

Drunk or sober, sad or boastful, I could bring it down to one simple equation, in three sentences. Pacifism was useless in wartime. Once the thing started, you had to win it as Nelson or Wellington, and then, if you chose, begin all over again as Jesus Christ. *Ergo* (Lat., therefore) *everyone* must get into the fight.

So now, after the months of waiting and the years of nothing much, I was a naval officer, just the way Mother had planned it, back in 1918. But it was only just: my rung on this ladder scarcely cleared the ground. Starting life as a Temporary Probationary Sub-Lieutenant, at an income bracket of £20 a month, I had now come up to Lieutenant (£26 a month, plus £2 6s. 6d. hard-lying money); and I was earning it as a watch-keeping officer in a corvette plying the North Atlantic.

It really was a somersault, and I knew it even then. Discipline, order, a sense of hierarchy and service—all the

Winchester virtues or constraints had come flooding back again, as good as new after more than a decade in the attic of derision.

As well as being scared to death a lot of the time, and unspeakably tired always, I was also very proud.

There was a catch-phrase on board. 'A corvette would roll on wet grass'; and its ring of truth had swiftly turned sour indeed. Corvettes were abominable ships to live in, in any kind of weather; already cramped, wet, noisy, crowded, and starkly uncomfortable, they pitched and rolled and swung, with a brutal persistence, as long as any breeze blew.

To fight in, with any kind of spirit, they were worst of all. The first enemy and the last, the eternal bully, was the atrocious sea; and when we had come to terms with that, we still had to tackle the men who were trying to burn us, or maim us, or blow us up, or hunt us down, and strangle us with the sea's own noose.

Our personal shield, our own tin lifeboat, was H.M.S. *Campanula*, the eighteenth corvette out of many hundreds soon to be built in a crash programme designed to meet the swift and violent threat to our convoys, the early prime thrust of the enemy. Even in the slow-starting first month of the war, we had lost forty-one merchant ships; in the first year, this had swelled to the fearsome total of 617.

Campanula was Clyde-built, which meant, in those days, that she was as sound as salt; but her size—203 feet long, 900 tons— and her design—an old-fashioned whaler-type hull, with a well-deck often awash with tons of sluicing sea-water—could not make her anything but a storm-tossed lemon, as far as the North Atlantic was concerned. By some ludicrous stroke of policy, all corvettes bore the names of gentle and delicate flowers; in *Campanula's* escort group there were also *Bluebell*, *Zinnia*, *Hyacinth*, *Aubretia*, *Convolvulus*, and *Coreopsis* (the latter ship was to be met again, years later, in extraordinary circumstances).

Some names, it was obvious, were preferable to others; we would rather have had our own, even with its elective pronunciation, than *Wallflower*, or *Periwinkle*, or *Daffodil*, or *Meadowsweet* (their Lordships of the Admiralty, with man-of-the-world delicacy, had excluded *Pansy* from the list of possibles).

But the ships, however prettily christened, were all the same: bare platforms for a four-inch pop-gun and a huge clutch of depth-charges, and wallowing cages for eighty-eight men, subjected to every kind of insult from the sea, surviving, with a dull endurance which for the rest of our lives we were to find incredible, a world of shock, fatigue, crude violence, and grinding anxiety.

Dr Samuel Johnson, that quarrelsome old landsman, gave it as his view that 'Being in a ship is being in a jail, with the chance of being drowned'; and, substituting the word 'probability' for 'chance', the two-hundred-year-old verdict must stand, as far as a minor ship-of-war in our wringing wet corner of the world was concerned. There was one other item which Dr Johnson would doubtless have appreciated: our jail would not keep still.

On the job of convoy escort we simply had to point ourselves in the right direction—due west for the New World, and after that due east for the battered Old—and then get going; convoys, at this crucial moment of the war, when an average of three precious ships a day were being sunk, and yet supplies had to be brought in to keep the island fighting, to keep the island fed, to let the island survive at all—convoys could not wait upon the weather.

We had to bash our way through, and come home with whatever we had left—a percentage of the stake-money, in terms of blood and treasure, men and ships: a percentage, like a fuel-oil return, of strength remaining: a percentage of spirit for the next time.

During the first few convoys, in mid-1940, when our officer-complement had been set by a short-handed Admiralty as a

Captain, a First Lieutenant, and two green-as-grass Sub-Lieutenants, we had to keep watch-and-watch at sea—four hours on, four hours off, for day after day until the voyage was over, which could be more than a fortnight later.

It meant that sleep was sliced up desperately small, and often cherished sleep itself would not come to a fluttering brain or a fearful man; or else it was shattered by these hateful clanging bells which, drilling the thin skull, yanked us up to action stations and the astonishment of smoke and flame, and then to sunk ships, half-drowned survivors, and dead men leaking their loathsome salad-dressing of blood and oil into our virgin scuppers.

After about six months of that watch-and-watch nonsense, it had become obvious that we were likely to drop dead ourselves if we had to go on with it. Representations were made, throughout our harassed fleet; some kind soul in the Admiralty did a little sum and came up with the right answer; and presently we were given, first one and then two more officers.

After that, we spent four hours on watch and eight hours off; and even though we lived like pigs, three in a two-berth cabin and the fourth man in a hammock in the pantry, at least (apart from occasional whole nights at action stations) we got the sleep which was our nearly-crying need. But the job itself remained awful.

The nights, of course, were worst of all: the nights when anything, no matter how murderous or vile, could always happen; when even without the jostling of the enemy we stood our watch under sentence of misery, clamped to a wing of the open bridge (made of canvas laced to the stanchions), taking the worst of the wind and spray upon a very tired body, and keeping station on the nearest ship in the convoy, an only friend who was never more than a now-and-then black spectre in a howling grey gloom.

For our own protection, we did the best we could. Like all the others—and we certainly knew each other's wardrobes, in that mean slit of a cabin—I wore two vests, thick long pants, third-best uniform trousers, big clumping seaboots, a sweater and a fisherman's jersey, a duffle coat, a towel and a woollen scarf round my neck, sheepskin gloves from blessed South Africa, and a Balaclava helmet also donated by faraway, loving hands.

By now I had, in addition, a long curly beard. It took care, at least, of half the face. And who wanted to shave, in this wilderness? We weren't *going* anywhere.

Strait-jacketed in this clownish rig, one endured the cumulative blows of a four-hour watch. In bad weather—North Atlantic winter weather—great icy dollops of salt water found their way everywhere: down the neck, up the wrists, into the trouser-legs and seaboots. I used to stand there like a sodden automaton, ducking behind the canvas 'dodger' as every second wave sent spray scudding over the compass house; and then I straightened up to face once more, with eyes raw and salt-caked and streaming, the horrid enmity of the sea. Twice already, in my middle watch, we had had the windows up on the bridge smashed in, by a giant sea which curled up and broke right on top of them.

Mere armoured glass could give up; the man standing in front of it could not.

He had to stay where he was, an amateur Ahab defying the screeching elements, and do three things: run his watch properly, cherish the ship and its ninety-strong boxed cargo of wakeful or sleeping men, and—without benefit of radar, a blessing still unborn as far as corvettes were concerned— maintain station as a link in the escort screen.

I kept a diary, or rather a kind of smudged jotting-book, all that year, in defiance of the regulations, because I was quite sure I was going to be killed (the other certainty that, if this happened, the diary would end up fathoms deep in the same soggy bundle as myself, still did not discourage). Though I didn't know it, the resulting book (*H.M. Corvette*) was to be published next year, with the blessing of Their Lordships, and there were to be two more like it before the war was out, later compacted into one volume.*

But at that time, the hurried first-hand scribbling was just a spill-over of fear and exhaustion. Of the station-keeping chore I wrote, with cold wet fingers:

When you are in convoy, station-keeping at night becomes an endurance test, a matter of staring without respite, concentrating on a little blurred image far ahead or abeam which may be the right ship—or a smudge on one's binoculars. If, in poor visibility, a zigzag is ordered, it has to be worked out on time instead of on distance, and becomes a sort of qualified guesswork: you run the outward course for so many minutes, until the convoy is right out of sight, and then you turn and run back till you meet them again; the whole manoeuvre is a recurrent act of faith.

There is tremendous difficulty, sometimes, in hanging on for hours to a ship which seems to fade devilishly to nothing if you relax for a moment. She may be so blurred by darkness and rain that her outline, even close to, is no more than a dubious smudge in the gloom; and that is what you have to hold on to for four long hours, under orders to remain at an exact bearing and distance from it. And all that time the weather can best be summed up in the Coxswain's phrase: 'Dark? You couldn't see a new sixpence on a sweep's arse!'

The compensations of watch-keeping at night are few, and tremendously realized: the comfort of a small, wavering stern-light, of a big ship easily seen and recognized; of a duffle coat: of a cup of near-solid cocoa half-way through the watch. They are the things you count on and cling to, the

---

* *Three Corvettes* (Cassell, 1945: Panther Books, 1957). This trio of short books was the first writing of mine that attracted any sort of attention. Parts of them were serialized in the *Daily Telegraph, Harper's, Toronto Star, Daily Dispatch, Sunday Express,* and *Maclean's Magazine*; they were published in America by Lippincott, and bits of them were read on the B.B.C. In peacetime all this would have been wildly exciting; in H.M.S. *Campanule* and later ships, it was a brief flicker of light in a very long tunnel.

things that seem to be on your side against the enemy. You grow, almost, to love them.

And again, of that crucifying watch-and-watch system:

Strain and tiredness at sea induce a sort of hypnosis: you seem to be moving in a bad dream, pursued not by terrors but by an intolerable routine. You come off watch at midnight, soaked, twitching, your eyes raw with the wind and with staring at shadows; you brew a cup of tea in the wardroom pantry and strip off the top layer of sodden clothes; you do, say, an hour's intricate cyphering, and thereafter snatch a few hours' sleep between wet blankets, with the inflated life-belt in your ribs reminding you all the time that things happen quickly; and then, every night for seventeen nights on end, you're woken up at ten to four by the bosun's mate, and you stare at the deckhead and think: My God, I *can't* go up there again in the dark and filthy rain, and stand another four hours of it. But you can, of course: it becomes automatic in the end. And besides, there are people watching you.

But when you are working in three watches, and have eight hours off at a time, there is luxury in coming off watch: the luxury of relaxing, smoking, putting on bedroom slippers, turning on the electric heater and feeling your face thawing and losing its stiffness; all with no sense of hurry. It can be comforting below: one *can* forget all the menaces outside. So far I have been lucky in having only one acute attack of nerves—lying down, strained, alert, unable to sleep, just waiting for those shouts, that rush of water, that iron clang. . . . But that was in the middle of a rough party, when another corvette had been sunk, and I don't imagine I was alone.

But, whether one was awake or asleep, wet or dry, fearful or (come daylight) merely drained of spirit, that perpetual rolling

went on for ever, through a hideous lurching arc which sometimes reached forty-five degrees on either side of upright, as if
one were lashed to a pendulum endlessly powered, poked, and
nudged by some idiot god.

Once again, wedged in a corner of the wardroom with a leg
crooked round the table, I made my dutiful, hopeful, compulsive
survey of the odds against:

Apart from the noise it produces, rolling has a maddening
rhythm that is one of the minor tortures of rough weather.
It never stops or misses a beat, it cannot be escaped anywhere.
If you go through a doorway, it hits you hard: if you sit
down, you fall over; you get hurt, knocked about continuously, and it makes for extreme and childish anger. When you
drink, the liquid rises towards you and slops over: at meals,
the food spills off your plate, the cutlery will not stay in place.

Things roll about, and bang, and slide away crazily: and
then come back and *hurt* you again. The wind doesn't howl, it
screams at you, and tears at your clothes, and throws you
against things and drives your breath down your throat again.
And off watch, below, there is no peace: only noise, furniture
adrift, clothes and boots sculling about on the deck, a wet and
dirty chaos.

Even one's cabin can be a vicious cage, full of sly tricks and
booby-traps: not a refuge at all, rather a more subtle danger-
spot, catching you relaxed and unawares and too dead-tired to
guard your balance. Sometimes, at the worst height of a gale,
you may be hove-to in this sort of fury for days on end, and all
the time you can't forget that you are no nearer shelter than
you were, twenty-four hours before: you are gaining nothing,
simply holding your own: the normal rigours of the trip are
still piled up, mountains high, in front of you.

What to do about it? I once wrote out the recipe in detail, in a
letter home. But it was really a directive to myself, never to be
forgotten for a moment:

Hang on to something always: give no chances, secure everything movable including the armchairs in the wardroom, clear your desk and wedge your books in the bookcase. When you are eating, watch with constant care the food and drink, which at any moment will dart for your lap. When you turn in, have your back against the bulkhead and crook your knees so that your thighs lie athwartships: this may keep you in place.

But above all, if you don't want to be hurt, hang on to something, even if you're only taking a couple of steps: even if you are leaning against the bridge-rail having five minutes' inoffensive think-of-home.

To that I added, on a well-informed note:

Our measure of rough weather is domestic, but reliable. Moderate sea, the lavatory seat falls down when it is tipped up; rough sea, the radio-set tumbles off its bracket in the wardroom.

I remember, to this day, that even as I wrote that, *Campanula* did achieve that extra swinish roll, the wardroom radio did tumble off its bracket, and I was flung bodily out of my armchair, finishing up against the opposite bulkhead, with a cracked rib, among a mixed heap of other forlorn rubbish.

A great slop of dirty seawater then came through the ventilator and cascaded on to my head, by way of final blessing.

We were the smallest warships on regular convoy escort in the North Atlantic, armed trawlers being gradually phased out after the wicked winter of 1940; and we were very proud of the fact. We were also very glad to give up and go home again, after our own eternal pasting by the elements.

The first shore-light we saw at night, when nearing home, was likely to be a dearly-loved friend on the island of Inishtrahull, off Northern Ireland; it would arc across the black horizon like the promise of Christmas. Our first daylight landfall would be the fair coast of Scotland, running down to the Mull of Galloway. Near land, the porpoises and the seagulls played sea-games round the ship; the porpoises seemed to be racing us home with great laughing leaps, the seagulls criss-crossed to and fro under our stem, skimming close, planing upwards suddenly if they met another player coming round the other way.

Presently we would be under the lee of the Isle of Man, and there the sea gave up. From the bridge one noticed the first patch of drying deck below. It spread outwards; it meant peace. Then the Bar Light Vessel, guarding the approach to Liverpool, loomed up like a rusty-red signpost to our haven.

It was the prelude to a whole range of delights about to be showered on us: sliding through the dock gates towards our berth, getting the first heaving-line ashore, then the head-rope, then the stern-wire: ringing off the engines—their first respite for perhaps four hundred hours: the curious warm silence which fell on the ship as the mail came on board and was doled out: the first guaranteed night in port, first drink, first undressing for a fortnight, first bath, first good sleep.

The trouble was that this blessed peace never lasted beyond a bare twelve hours. Even in our home port, safely buttoned to the dockside, we had very little rest during those five-day spells in harbour.

A duck-sized warship such as the one we were blessed with still needed a lot of day-to-day thought and care, to keep her (in the naval phrase which was now an oppressive part of my life) on the top line. First—because we might have to go out again in a hurry—we had to be refilled with everything we had spent on the last brave voyage, which meant making requisitions for, and then taking delivery of, a steady stream of crates, boxes, parcels, drums, and wicker baskets, which flowed up the gang-way in tidal tribute from the Department of Naval Stores.

There were the consumables we lived by—the bread which

lasted five days before it had to be soaked in milk and water, heated up again, and thus 'reconstructed'; the fresh vegetables which last a week, the tinned stew which lasted for ever, the choice cuts of meat which finished up as a tired frieze of cinders on the galley stove, the rum with the colour of Nelson's blood and the taste of sweet fire itself.

There were tons of fuel oil with that hateful acrid stink which filled the clean sea air every time a ship in convoy was lost; now it poured on board through filthy gurgling hose-pipes which fouled everything they touched. There were the depth-charges which we had dropped so sourly, and the anti-aircraft ammunition we had merrily and futilely tossed into the air.

There were the medical stores—splints, and bandages, and morphia under my own lock-and-key, and contraceptives which were called 'condoms' (issued free to all comers), and the wretched little tubes of tannic acid which melted into a man's face like raindrops on the crust of a burnt-up desert.

There was gin for the wardroom ($2\frac{1}{2}$d. a tot), and mile after mile of toilet paper for everyone, and 'bosun's stores' (paint, wire rope, scrubbing brushes, canvas buckets, Lysol, beeswax for splices), and duty-free cigarettes, and the suggestive-look-ing roll of pipe-fill known as 'prick tobacco'—a corruption of *perique*, which first saw the light of day in far-off Louisiana.

While all this to-and-fro was going on, and the stuff was being counted, and signed for, and stowed away, we had to clean up the terrible mess left by the sea—all the soaked bedding, smashed benches, weeping rivets, bent stanchions, ruined carpets, scarred paintwork, and hammocks which had burst their lashings and spilled their innocent cargo on to the iron deck.

While all *this* was going on, we, the expendable lieutenants R.N.V.R., took turn-about as Officer-of-the-day, a twenty-four-hour duty which made us the target for every bad-tempered sally issuing from the captain's cabin, and every other stupid or laughable crisis which might blow up from anywhere else. All that happened to the O.O.D. was inevitable, unavoidable, to be borne with the dumb-ox patience which was the very fabric of war.

He had to be on tap all the time, like an over-exploited butler —indeed, a very stupid butler who had signed an acre of small print without bothering to read it. The 'day' started at 5.30, with a call (now known more accurately as a 'shake') from the quartermaster, a cup of tea, a quick shave and dress; and the first action was at 6 a.m , when one had to take 'Hands Fall In —Wash Down', involving a cold windswept deck, the bleak charms of a Liverpool dawn, and a guarded stare at a muster of nineteen seamen who, shivering in their working rig, stared reproachfully back.

At this first grisly encounter, the day's work was doled out and then supervised: hosing down, scrubbing decks, storing, painting, practising lifeboat drill, and depth-charge loading drill, and gun-drill, and fire-drill, and damage-control drill, and the drill for throwing overboard all the Confidential Books when the ship was judged to be sinking.

There were times when I knew that if I had been ordered to drill for oil, I would have started to rig a derrick, without further question.

The long day ended at 2300 (the hour of 11 p.m. had vanished with the civilized past) when the last of the liberty-men stumbled down the quay, stumbled up the gangway, arranged themselves in a tousled wavering line, and were, after scrutiny, allowed to go below. This inspection was not an item of vile slave-tyranny. Mild drunkenness did not matter: but incapacity—i.e., falling headlong down a twelve-foot ladder and earning a broken neck at the bottom—was too expensive to be allowed, if a searching glance could take care of it.

The Officer-of-the-day had done his job if the ship settled down peacefully by midnight. He had failed if someone got hurt in a fight, or hurt himself on his way to sleep. There were marginal areas, often summed up in certain formal charges to be preferred next morning: 'Able Seaman Briginshaw did create vandalism in the galley,' or 'Did urinate in the stokers' mess-deck,' or (a charming phrase) 'Did poke bravado at his superior'. Any of this meant that the O.O.D.'s searching glance had not been searching enough.

The light at the top of the gangway was not always good.

Between that 5.30 shake and the respite of midnight (though if the ship was at anchor out in the stream, one would be standing an anchor-watch on the bridge for the rest of the night, or, for that matter, one might be in charge of dusk-till-dawn fire-watching, since Merseyside was taking a recurrent pasting from the *Luftwaffe* all through the early months of 1941)—before the respite came at midnight, one was a natural dog's-body, a true beck-and-call-boy.

Tending the shore wires, calling taxis, pouring drinks for visitors and often signing for them, keeping an eye on men working aloft, watching the gangway in case an admiral turned up—the poor butler never had a moment to himself. *Campanula* also had to take her turn as Guard Corvette—which was not some noble task of watch-and-ward while the rest of the fleet slept, but meant supplying quay-sentries, and berthing parties for incoming ships, and a signal link for all ships in harbour; keeping the dockside clear of anything which might get in the way of the cranes—for, if thwarted, the dockers could get terribly angry, and lay down their tools, and (choosing the moment carefully) march off to the nearest pub a convenient space before it closed; and seeing that the rubbish of half-a-dozen ships was properly disposed of, and that no vulgar fish-heads, pigs' entrails, nor chicken feathers sullied the sweet waters of the River Mersey.

It was the Officer-of-the-day of the Guard Corvette who bore the brunt of this manly housekeeping. But in H.M.S. *Campanula*, whether she was Guard Corvette or not, he also had one more hazard to put up with.

It could come, at any moment, in the form of a brawling voice which rang out with a particular, raucous, prison clang:

'Monsarrat! I'm going ashore!'

Or: 'Monsarrat!' (I had never realized that my name could sound so like the bark of an Alsatian.) 'Where's that bloody steward?'

Or: 'Monsarrat! That stern-wire's slack again! Hop to it!'

Or: 'Monsarrat! There's too much noise over my cabin!'

Or, on one memorable occasion: '*Monsarrat*! I've been calling you for ten minutes!'

'Sorry, sir. I was in the lavatory.'

'Don't go to the lavatory! Bake it!'

This was our captain, on whom my present peace of mind and future prospects entirely depended.

One thing we all had to do, as soon as we came back to harbour, was to catch up with the latest amendments and additions to our twin bibles, *King's Regulations & Admiralty Instructions* and *Admiralty Fleet Orders*, which contained page after page of directives on anything under the sun or moon: new types of life-saving equipment, new rules about the length of our hair (if too long in the fringe, it might leak oil into our eyes when we were torpedoed, with consequent loss of vision); new rules by which humble R.N.V.R. officers could qualify for a full Royal Navy watch-keeping certificate, and thus escape from their humility (I took damned good care of that one); new dress regulations (badges of rank should now only extend half-way round the sleeve, to conserve gold braid, which was in short supply); reminders about saluting officers of the other services, who were to be accorded the 'normal courtesies', just as if they were members of the human race; and brusque directives on the size of the mesh in our scrambling nets—the rough-and-ready circus job by which survivors hauled themselves on board.

K.R. & A.I. and A.F.O.s, as we called them, had to be watched very carefully; they could trip you up if neglected, or you could miss some tiny crumb of comfort which might later make life bearable. Chart corrections came into the same category, and had to be dealt with on an immediate basis, for obvious reasons: it was a finicky chore, rather hard on the

2

patience and the eyesight: corrections to depth-of-water soundings (now who, unluckily stuck on the putty, had found *that* out?), altering buoys from 'Flashing three every half-minute' to 'Flashing two every ten', and wreck buoys, wreck buoys, wreck buoys all over.

The other task, exclusively for me, was to catch up with fourteen days' weight of the ship's correspondence.

Just as I was in the Navy because I had raced a 14-foot dinghy from the age of fifteen, and crewed in boats as big as four tons, so I was the Correspondence Officer because I had written four novels and a play.

It was a painstaking, dreary job which regularly dropped into my lap at the very moment when all I wanted to do was sleep. I answered letters, and filled in forms, and typed out requests for more of this and not so much of that. I checked through the Stores Lists, with their occasional delicate social distinctions—

Pots, Chamber, plain:
Pots, Chamber, with Admiralty monogram in blue:
Pots, Chamber, fluted, with royal cypher in gold, for Flag Officers only:
Pots, Chamber, round, rubber, lunatic.

and made out all those interminable requisitions needed to top the ship up again for the next convoy.

I prepared memoranda on lice infestation (known below stairs as 'mechanized dandruff') and the possible advantages of using wrapped bread. I gave my considered judgement (or rather, the captain's considered judgement) on the most acceptable kind of 'ship's comforts' (South African sheepskin jerkins *marvellous*, knitted Balaclava helmets not too popular— they got wet and stayed wet).

When my eyelids began to droop, I would give up, and stick on a few 'Official Paid' stamps, and consign the batch to the postman. But there would be another batch tomorrow. And I still had to make out a return of defaulters and their crimes ('Did abandon his post as bridge-messenger without reporting to the Officer-of-the-watch, contrary to good order and naval discipline'—i.e., the poor bastard was seasick) during the past fourteen days at sea.

There was only one sure cure for seasickness, some hard-hearted fellow once told a sufferer: go and sit under a tree.

There were other jobs assigned to me, and there was often a good enough reason for this—or, at least, the same kind of eerie logic to back up the choice.

I was the Censoring Officer, like my mother before me (if I could write, I could presumably read, especially between the lines). There was no such thing as a private letter leaving any warship; they all had to be read, however sketchily, before they went into the mail, on the off-chance that they might somehow give aid and comfort to the enemy. In fact, there was only one thing I was meant to look for—any information about the ship's movements, where she was going, when she was sailing, where she had been on the last trip, plus anything which might have gone wrong with a convoy.

But we all knew the rules, and my censor's scissors never sliced off more than half-a-dozen items in the eighteen months I had the job.

One minor point of interest, as far as I was concerned, was in the choice of the code-word scribbled on the back of the envelope; among these were SWALK ('Sealed with a loving kiss'), HOLLAND ('Hope our love lasts and never dies'), BOLTOP ('Better on lips than on paper'), and the more urgent BURMA ('Be undressed and ready my angel'). Why these messages, which were common currency on board, were not written out *en clair* in the letter itself, I never discovered; certainly I did not need to be shielded—I had ceased to be shocked by any aspect of a sailor's yearning for home, after a small incident on the bridge when I was Officer-of-the-watch.

Through the windows of the wheelhouse I noticed the stand-by quartermaster opening a matchbox and showing something inside it to the man at the wheel. Since I did not want the latter's attention to be distracted (he might start 'writing his name astern', which was our slang for bad steering), I broke up the colloquy and asked what it was all about.

The man with the matchbox, not at all abashed, exhibited his trophy again. Inside the box, enshrined in a tuft of cotton-wool, was a small—a very small—curly hair, of unmistakable origin.

'Just to remind me of home, sir,' he explained. Possibly some private remnant of innocence showed in my face, or perhaps he was certain that all officers must lead sheltered lives, for he added: 'Wilson's got *three.*'

As I left the wheelhouse I heard a mumbled voice behind me: 'All different colours, I'll bet.'

Since I had once tried to be a B.B.C. announcer,* and must therefore have the right kind of voice, I took Divisions on Sunday (the naval version of Church Parade), and read the service.

This had to be prefaced by an order which was awkward to pronounce with any kind of naval precision. Just as, long ago, it had been difficult to rip out the command: 'Empty water-bottles!' at the end of Winchester College O.T.C. 'field day', so now it was not easy to combine authority with religious tolerance in the words: 'Fall out, the Roman Catholics!' But it had to be done; tradition, or more probably K.R. & A.I., had so laid it down.

Thus every Sunday, at this command, half a dozen men

---

* I failed, in curious circumstances, just before the war. After a complicated, two-hour, four-language test with three other short-list candidates, I was told that I would have been accepted, if it were not for an apparent difficulty in pronouncing the letter 'R'. Perhaps I could do something about that, and come back later? I took six elocution lessons which I could not afford, given incidentally by a man who had one of the worst speech defects I had ever heard, and returned for a do-or-die interview with Professor Lloyd James, whose imposing title was Professor of Phonetics and Secretary of the B.B.C. Committee on Spoken English. After half-a-dozen sentences, during which I rolled my 'R's' like demented dice, he told me in a rather offhand way that he was sorry I had been t-r-r-oubled, and I departed, disappointed and penniless as ever, never to darken their doors in such circumstances again. It was a matter of morbid interest to me that, two years later, Professor Lloyd James murdered his wife by hitting her on the head with a hammer and then stabbing her with a carving fork. 'We were so happy,' he said at his trial. 'I wanted her to die while she was like that.' Verdict: Guilty but insane.

would turn smartly right, and double away behind the funnel, leaving us to our heretical rites.

The rites were mine to choose, and, with a free hand, I made up the pattern myself. We recited the Lord's Prayer together; and then I read that marvellous 23rd Psalm which could still ring a gentle carillon of bells within the most agnostic skull:

The Lord is my shepherd; I shall not want.
He maketh me to lie down in green pastures; he leadeth me beside the still waters.

Ah, those still waters. . . . Then came the Lesson for the day; then the 'Naval prayer' which started so splendidly: 'O Lord God, Who alone spreadest out the heavens'; and then we sang that hymn which could still bring me near to tears, even at the age of thirty-one, even after a hundred crude scenes of slaughter, a hundred burials:

Eternal Father, strong to save,
Whose arm hath bound the restless wave,
Who bidd'st the mighty ocean deep
Its own appointed limits keep;
O hear us when we cry to Thee
For those in peril on the sea.

By God, we meant it!—or I meant it, and I hoped the spark might catch. But did I really believe, even in the face of fear? I didn't know then, and I don't know now. It seemed to me that religion was at its most hideous when it went to war: whether it was the Crusades (kill a Moslem for Christ) or the Armada (slaughter the English for Holy Mother Church) or the late Italian invasion of Ethiopia, with full Apostolic blessing, or our own gloss on history (God was on our side, the Huns were brutish barbarians), or my private feeling that such an award as the Military Order of Christ (Portuguese, this time), was true blasphemy, if blasphemy were real, and not the last illusion.

Perhaps I was not alone in doubt, or even derision. To that

tune of 'Eternal Father, strong to save', where it came to the
lines 'O, hear us when we cry to Thee, for those in peril on the
sea!' there was, I knew, a sophisticated back-row choir which
sang, *sotto voce*:

> The working class can kiss my arse,
> I've got the foreman's job at last.

The trouble was, I hadn't yet made up my mind about that
breach of taste, either. But discipline, or at least its public
framework, could be restored by another Sunday morning
traditional, the reading of half-a-dozen excerpts from the
Articles of War, perhaps the most threatening reminder of the
rules ever framed. As I rolled out the fate of the mutineer and
the coward-in-the-face-of-the-enemy—'Shall suffer *Death*, or
such other punishment as the Lords Commissioners of the
Admiralty shall decree'—it sometimes sounded a little rough
for Sunday worship. But then I thought of Nelson, and was
confident again.*

After that, we all went below for the first drink of the
Sabbath morning—christened, by some wag, the thirst after
righteousness—and then I shed my ghostly cassock and got
back to the paperwork.

Since my father was a surgeon, and the captain, who came
from Liverpool, knew this, I was also appointed the ship's
Medical Officer within a few hours of reporting on board. This
was the worst of all my jobs, the most moving, the most ugly,
the most calculated to make me wish that I could revert to an
innocent child again.

At first it meant nothing much; I landscaped a few ingrowing
toe-nails, and bandaged a few scraped elbows, and dealt with a
few cases of that minor venereal infection known as *Pediculosis
Pubis* (or, as a proper ship's doctor was to translate it later,
Little Pattering Feet on the Private Parts). But then *Campanula*

---

* When queried about the hanging of some mutineers on a Sunday, he snapped
back: 'I would have hanged them on Christmas morning!'

went to sea, and then to war, and then to violence and blood-shed; and after that my patients were all survivors from ships torpedoed in convoy, and the worst horror-film of my life began.

Survivors, climbing on board with gasping lungs, or hauled over the side like oil-soaked fish from the scrambling nets, or hoisted up with a rope to torture anew a shattered body, could be suffering from anything, no matter how terrible. They could have swallowed mouthfuls of that corrosive fuel oil, and be coughing up their guts until they died; they could be shuddering in the last bitter extremity of cold and exhaustion; they might have sustained gross wounds, and the shock that went with them; they could be screaming with the pain of deep, hopeless burns, and broken limbs, and bodies half-flayed by a rough ship's side as they slid down into the water.

But good or bad, bad or unspeakable, they were all mine; and when they were brought below, or, too anguished to be moved, were propped up gently in the lee of the depth-charge rails, I had to pick up my little black bag, and attend their sorrows.

I got used to it in the end, after a season of near-vomiting fear: I grew hardened to the loathsome sights and sounds, and per-haps more skilful in rough-and-ready treatment, and less guilty when, in all compassion, I hurt a writhing man until the watching ring of his shipmates, and of mine, seemed likely to break their appalled silence at this butchery, and snatch the knife or the needle or the probe from my hand, and drive it into the back of my skull.

But if anyone had told me, when I first answered that *Times* advertisement for gentlemen with yachting experience, that as a result I would soon be stitching up a gashed throat without benefit of anaesthetics, or trying to coax a dangling eyeball back into its socket; or if I had known that a man with a deep stomach wound, spread-eagled on what seemed like the very rack of Christ, could actually *smell* so awful, like an opened drain, I might well have kept my yachting experience as secret as the grave, and settled for the Army Pay Corps, or for prison, or for shameful defeat itself.

First, mine was butcher's work, and then, all too often, dustman's. To tidy up my medical practice, and because it was probably all my fault anyway, I was assigned to take charge of all burials, and to see the bodies—noted in the log, with raw finality, as 'Discharged Dead'—tipped over the side for their long dive.

I came to know that burial service by heart. I could easily have closed the book on '*Man that is born of woman hath but a short time to live, and is full of misery,*' and run right on through the 'Stop engines' signal to the bridge, and '*We therefore commit his body to the deep,*' and finished strongly on '*Blessed are the dead which die in the Lord; even so, saith the Spirit, for they rest from their labours,*' without a written word to help me.

But I did read from the text, for fear of making a mistake, and also because the words were so beautiful, and deserved this reverence. Yet true feeling—loss, bereavement, a sense of wastage and futility, even with men who were all strangers, who might never have drawn a living breath on board our ship—true feeling had itself wasted away to cold routine, to nothing.

Sometimes I felt that it would never return, even at the grave of my father, or my wife, or my son if I ever had a son.

Just as with my crude doctoring, so with this allied task: one grew hardened to it; it was almost in the realm of paperwork— the most important thing was that the figures should add up correctly at the end of the voyage, and that the Coxswain's 'victualling sheets', swelled by these chance visitors, should be shown to have been diminished by the moment of this leave-taking. A tidy disposal was all.

Once—it was at the dawn of my thirty-first birthday—I buried eight men before breakfast: five we had picked up dead, and three more who had died at the end of my watch. Eight men, eight sailors, eight comrades in this fearful enterprise—I should be in tears, I should be wearing a mourning band round my very heart. . . . But all it meant was that the exercise took a little longer than usual; I still found a ready appetite for the fried bread, the powdered-egg omelette, and the thin brew of coffee essence which was our reward, an hour later.

'The grave opens in sleep,' said the man who could use the English language like a cutting sword or a kiss. But whether waking or sleeping, this our grey Atlantic grave was open all round us, all the time. Let it only gape for others. . . . All I could really feel, as I spoke the words: '*In the midst of life we are in death*,' was the avid hope that this only meant other people; and a secret, heartless joy that the man, friend or enemy, sprawling at my feet, the ungainly canvas package due for delivery to the mortuary deep, was not me.

Finally, to round off the long list of things I was doing to bring the Germans to their knees, I was the Depth-Charge Control Officer: not the skilful fellow who operated our asdic set* to decide when the depth-charges should be dropped, but the man who actually rolled them over the stern or splayed them out from the throwers; and that job, at last, suited me fine.

As a lapsed pacifist, I was still glad that I didn't have to fire guns, which could shed blood and were terribly noisy anyway (even our modest 4-inch peashooter, which was boldly dated 1913). Depth-charges were quite different, as all the world knew. They didn't really kill people; they just sank U-boats, metal objects which were trying to kill *us*. The convention that whereas we had submarines (noble and skilful), the hated Hun actually used U-boats (wicked and treacherous), was still a persistent gloss on history, continued from 1914.

Depth-charges exploded with satisfying violence, an almighty WHOOMP! which shattered the surface of the sea, brought the middle depths to the boil, and, when adroitly used in coastal waters, could supply all hands with a prime fish dinner. The D.C. Control Officer had an inevitable link with the Correspondence Officer. I had to keep an individual case-history of every

---

* This was our U-boat search weapon, christened from 'Allied Submarine Detection Investigation Committee'. The Americans preferred to call theirs 'Sonar', and so in the end did we.

single one under my charge—or rather, of the numbered detonator-pistols which set them off: the date they were fired, the depth setting, the type of pattern, and the performance. Then the empty boxes, all of them also listed in detail, had to be returned to Naval Armaments.

It might not do any damage, I sometimes thought, as I cast my mighty missile into the sea; but by God I had its right number!

So Monsarrat—sailor, surgeon, scribe and sexton, all wrapped up in one harassed parcel, tied with the tarry twine of naval discipline—so I confronted the enemy. Or rather, all the enemies. First there was the sea, undeniably hostile. Then there were the Germans, violently and successfully so. Then—not last at all, often near the top of my private list—there were the people who were supposed to be on my side: certain of my ship-mates and superiors, the small string of putrid albatross which never left my neck.

Who remembers the old fights?—not with humour, but with the blood-chilling anger which they provoked at the time? *Campanula* was a miserable ship in which to serve, under the discipline and submission to which I had sworn; and I used to curse the day, and the stroke of ugly luck, and the very admiral who had assigned me to her odious wardroom. Now, like love or acne, it does not matter. But then it was awful—a Winchester afloat, a jail swine-fevered for ever; and to this horrid coop I was committed, without a single idea in my head of how to get out.

Let us start at the top, and perhaps end there, for there the tune was set.

The captain, a long-term professional sailor in the R.N.R., thought nothing—less than nothing—of us, the pink-cheeked amateurs; and the various ways in which he made this clear, not less than seventeen times a day, ensured that the feeling was mutual. It stemmed, without doubt, from the traditional, stupid, and childish feud between the R.N.R. and the R.N.V.R. —and anyone who doubts that lack of one initial could make such a whale of a difference, should take a parallel alphabetical rift, between the R.N. and the R.N.R., and try it on for size.*

At any rate, we became aware of this attitude from the moment we reported on board: an attitude soon frozen into a surly discontent with everything we did or tried to do. The rules had been pre-packaged several generations before we were out of the egg; the axiom was the R.N.R. were the pros, and knew it all, while the R.N.V.R. were the yachtsmen, the play-boys, the rich men's pampered brats who would never know, nor ever learn, a damned thing which would be of any use to anyone.

There was apparently an ancient catch-phrase—not of my coinage, but that made no difference—that while the R.N.R. were sailors but not gentlemen, we were gentlemen but not sailors. Doubtless the idea had rankled, somewhere within a narrow brain, for decades of plodding sea-duty, and now was the time to square the account.

It reminded me of another fixed attitude of long ago, of the well-established difference between the three major public schools, Eton, Winchester, and Harrow; and I could remember, at the age of sixteen, being entirely convinced of its authenticity, just as the captain must have been sure of his own myth.

Mine was enshrined in a brief story about a girl who comes into a room in which there is a representative from each of these three academies. The Etonian says: 'I say, someone ought to get her a chair!' The Wykehamist fetches it, and the Harrovian sits on it.

There we were in *Campanula* anyway, caught for ever in the same kind of immutable class aspic. Just as our own 'Hostilities Only' sailors were always known on board as 'Hostiles', so we were automatically branded as incompetents, fools, bloody nuisances who were fouling up a real sailor's ship.

---

* To sort out all these initials, for people who have never heard such rubbish
R.N. is the Royal Navy proper.
R.N.R. is the Royal Navy Reserve (professional merchant seamen).
R.N.V.R. is the Royal Naval Volunteer Reserve (bare-foot paddling tots like me).

It always pleased me—it pleases me now, without reservation —that I was in fact given command of a corvette within two and a half years of standing my first watch at sea, and of a frigate (two hundred men, twelve officers) six months later.

It seemed to compare very favourably with *other* people (sniff! sniff!) who needed a professional lifetime to make this grade.

But this reassuring accolade lay in the happier, distant, blessed future. Now I was stuck with the present; and the present was punitive.

One must give the man his due, however much it chokes the throat or hits the sore spot of recollection. He was a superb seaman and shiphandler, one of the best I ever met; and his navigation was spot-on accurate, every day of every convoy. In his hands, our funny little ship, our bouncing dot on the enormous ocean, was safe, and we all knew it, and were grateful for it. But as well as making *Campanula* safe, he also made her very unpleasant.

He was surly, and ungenerous, and (except when he came in contact with a senior officer, when he turned rosy-red and glowed all over) as rough and rasping as sandpaper. Of course we, the amateur help, were greener than new-mown grass; of course we didn't know how to take a star-sight from a heaving bridge, or launch a lifeboat into a bucking sea, or bring in six cables of anchor-chain in a hurry, or run the wardroom accounts, or give orders to fifty-year-old petty officers with thirty-five years' service behind them. *Not to begin with.*

Certainly this fresh-faced ineptitude must have irked him, while giving him the pleasure of constant rebuke. But we *were* trying our best, and learning as quickly as we could, and we were as willing as pit-ponies, or typists on probation, or novice priests for whom Christ was forever king.

Our chosen Christ was the Navy. But if the Navy was like this—*Christ!*

Not a day passed without sizeable scoops of this unearned

excrement flying round the ship; never (as far as I was concerned) did a four-hour watch go by without the rancid voice of
authority, sparked by a heart as big as a mint, invading the
bridge and pointing out, in a mumbled snarl, just what I was
doing wrong and how even the simplest things seemed to be
beyond my grasp.

I put up with it because I didn't appear to have any choice;
and because I had signed up for total discipline; and also,
probably, because of the Winchester training, which had
instilled the belief that the man—any man—set above me
would naturally be a disagreeable tyrant.

'We are but warriors for the working day' seemed to be the
idea to cling to; and the disconsolate yet hopeful mine-sweepers'
song (to the tune of 'Holy, Holy, Holy! Lord God Almighty!'):

> Sweeping, sweeping, sweeping, always bloody well sweeping!
> Lord, send the day when we bloody well sweep no more!

though I could certainly have done with a stanza of 'Where
seldom is heard a discouraging word,' to sweeten servitude.
While my politics told me that we were all brothers, I longed
unceasingly for more congenial company.

What, in fact, was I doing in this rancorous zoo? How could
I escape? Wasn't there a regiment called the Artists' Rifles?
Could I not arrange a smooth transfer to that, and stroll to war
with an orchid stuck in my gun-muzzle, and hear only gentle-
voiced Colonel Rembrandt or Major Michelangelo asking me if
I were entirely content?

There was, as it happened, one tiny blessing on board
Campanula; the fact that we were Liverpool-based, and to some
extent Liverpool-manned. There were some splendid characters
on board, from the Coxswain (the senior rating) downwards,
who all came from my own fair city; and it was comforting to
hear the Liverpool accent again, that hoarse adenoidal twang
which had scarcely been out of earshot from the day I drew my
first Rodney Street breath to my twenty-first birthday.

To meet again such homely nursery phrases as 'We had one, but the wheel fell off,' or 'Look what the cat brought in!' or 'Cloth ears!' or 'Shut your mouth—there's a tram coming'; to know that the dripping condensation in the mess-decks was called 'Bulkhead lager', or to hear the scornful 'He's wood from the tool up!': to listen to a man pleading at the galley hatch: 'Give us a jam butty, love,' and the obliging chef answer: 'Will that manage you?' as he handed over the prize—this was a brief but secure bliss, minted like gold from tons of rubbish.

Sometimes, on awful nights when my middle watch, and the ship herself, was a screaming, rocking shambles, the Coxswain would climb up, step by step, hand over hand, from the petty officers' mess to the open bridge, and hand me a mug still half-full of cocoa. 'It's got a bit of lead in it, sir,' he would reassure me. 'Good for the pencil.' Then, with a grin, he would duck down again.

The 'lead' was a tot of his own rum, and neither the drink, nor the thought, nor the voice could have been more welcome, if it had been served in a jewelled cup by Greta Garbo.

It was moving, and astonishing, to know that on board this absolute sod of a ship there beat a heart like this one—unshrivelled, strong, friendly, humorous, and kind.

The last convoy of March was one of the most terrible so far, completing the toll of an awful month which had started with the loss of twenty-nine ships *in one week*; from the atrocious weather, and then from the enemy, we took such a mauling that my private graph (Are we winning? Are we losing? How will it all end? Watch this space!) made its steepest nose-dive of the war, far below the horizon of hope. A scudding wind was bashing us against the pier as we began to make ready for sea; the familiar summons in the familiar accent: 'Hands to stations for leaving harbour! Special sea-duty-men—close up!' sounded like the chaplain's call for a dawn hanging.

There were snowflakes in the navigation lights as we went down river. They swirled against us, and then with us; they were very beautiful, a sort of magic—for who but God or the Officer-of-the-watch could command red snowflakes, and green snowflakes, and then red snowflakes again, as if performing some gigantic conjuring trick with a child's chemistry set? But for sailors who had given up the wonders of nature for the duration, the foreboding trick was only a trick.

So it turned out. The wind was westerly, hard westerly, as we butted our way outwards from the Bar Light Vessel into the Irish Sea, and set course for Chicken Rock, off the Isle of Man. We had twenty ships under our wing, the Liverpool portion of the west-bound convoy; and for many long hours we cherished them, and chivvied them, and joked with them, and told them to make less smoke and crack on more speed. Then, rounding the last light of England, we turned north, and began to roll and shudder in good earnest.

Very slowly we drew past places which we only knew as labels, the names of lighthouses and headlands and forbidding cliffs; places we would never visit, places we might never see again. But we had learned them all by heart now, as one must come to know a necklace of significant stones; the pretty names alternated with the rough ones—Mull of Galloway, Mull of Kintyre, Islay, Skerryvore, Tiree, and Muck; and then, after a distant glimpse of two truly strange retreats—the Sound of Eigg and the Sound of Rum—we went rolling rolling rolling up through the Minches, with more names to ring more bells.

This was our own branch line on our own suburban spur: Barra Head, Eriskay, Benbecula, Dunvegan, Shiant, Stornoway, Point of Stoer, Butt of Lewis, and the fearful Cape Wrath. On passage, we picked up ships like anticipant girls—some of them very old girls; gradually we drew together a vast acreage of sixty-five merchantmen which, with us, was trying for the tenth or the twentieth or the fiftieth time the fearsome passage from the old world to the new.

Cape Wrath was our last sight of land; its grim outline, thrashed by centuries of giant rollers, blurred and blasted by spray, faded astern as we turned north-west again for Iceland,

and into the teeth of an Atlantic gale, enough (said our Leading
Signalman, a noted phrase-maker) to blow the balls off a bull.

The convoy was in fighting shape now, in spite of all the
elements against it: a huge blunt fortress of ships, ranged in
eight columns and more than two miles wide from flank to
flank: with six scurrying corvettes as outriders, and an elegant
old V & W destroyer* to keep the whole thing in line. The fact
that the convoy stayed resolutely in this pattern was something
I never ceased to marvel at, and to admire.

In the next six howling days and nights, with visibility anything from poor to nothing at all, it still remained a convoy:
keeping good station, preserving discipline and order, turning
when it was ordered to turn, showing no lights, making no
betraying smoke. These were men, it should be remembered,
whose first instinct on sighting another ship was to keep as far
away from it as possible: to whom collision was the ultimate
disaster; who truly hated such close company.

And yet, in this awful weather, which made a big ship almost
unmanageable, and a small ship a wildly bucking hazard, they
still agreed to crowd together and to obey the rules; and on the
bridge of the Commodore's ship the man in total charge was
probably a retired admiral, not less than sixty-five years old,
who had left a Sussex garden or a Chelsea flat or a fireside of
grandchildren to take on this grinding sea-duty again.†

I could never forget, and I did not forget now, that while we
took pride in our little blue suits and little brass buttons and
little bits of gold braid, and zigzagged about and turned on a
sixpence and dashed off towards the nearest horizon, there were
other sailors—thousands of them—who had to stay faithfully in
convoy, and keep their unwieldy ships in line, even in this
wallowing turmoil; who trusted us to guard them while they
plodded onwards at a speed grotesquely less than their best;

* So christened because of their names: *Wolverine, Walker, Vanoc, Vortigern,* etc.
They were designed, and some of them saw service, in 1917.

† Among their honoured ranks was the man with the longest name in the Navy
List: Admiral the Hon. Sir Reginald Aylmer Ranfurly Plunkett-Ernle-Erle-Drax.
He was a sprightly sixty-three when he took on the job.

whose ships were often *the* target—slow-moving, slow-turning, large, violently inflammable.

Yet, when one met them ashore, elbow-to-elbow in a dockside pub, they were quiet men in quiet shabby suits, in whose quiet voices the enormous tensions of this shared ordeal could not even be guessed at.

Our battering continued, for watch after watch and day after day; *Campanula* had deteriorated to her usual ugly shambles, with water sloshing about in the mess-decks, and one of the wardroom armchairs thrown against a bulkhead and smashed to splinters. The food had gone the same way as the ship; for three days we had been reduced to a changeless menu, at all meals, of tea, soup, and corned-beef sandwiches. Nothing more ambitious could be made to stay in or on the galley stove.

There was one comforting thought, to help the eternal strain and tiredness; it was too rough for U-boats, which would have given up the hopeless task of taking aim, and be comfortably riding this out, in the still calm of six fathoms down.

But there was another thought, not so comforting, which went with this, as the ship took her endless punishment and successive tons of sea-water came roaring over the fo'c'sle and thudded down on to the well-deck. If it was too rough for U-boats, might it not be too rough for us? Small ships, hammered too fiercely, rolling too far under a solid top-weight of water, could sometimes lose their stability, and the heart that went with it, and give up altogether.

Within sight of Iceland it was bitterly cold ('Brass monkey weather,' said the Leading Signalman, whose mind seemed focused on one tender area of suffering). The black forbidding land loomed up briefly, and was lost in the scud again; later on, high above it, in one clear patch of night, a fantastic spread of northern lights, changing shape and colour every second, flickering ten miles high in tongues of cold flame, gave the scene a fearful beauty.

We shed a few ships for Reykjavik, and wished above everything that we could have been one of them—anything for peace,

anything for a dry ship and a deep sleep—and then we turned
southwards again, groaning and labouring, for our meeting
with the east-bound convoy, the one we were, at long last, to
take home with us.

Luck, and naval navigation, and skilful planning by slide-rule
men on those faraway east and western shores, gave us a perfect
rendezvous—correct to within five miles, in an ocean which
held thirty-one million square miles of salt water, all of it in
total disorder. The change-over was without dramatics: we
gave them our lot, and took over theirs, and then settled down
in station again.

But turning in the teeth of this gale, bringing the ship round
with agonizing slowness, wallowing helplessly in a long succession of huge wave-troughs, and then starting to run before
a wicked following sea which often lifted our stern higher than
the top of our funnel—that set the pattern for another two long
days of torture.

Running before a wind so strong was hell for everyone, not
least for the arm-weary helmsmen, who had to wrestle with a
ship which simply would not keep in one straight line. We
yawed wildly from side to side, and buried our nose deep into
grey-green water, and shouldered that off, and then felt a fresh
blow of malice, an iron thudding as the next huge wave crested
without warning and broke over our stern.

Sometimes, for a treacherous change, the sea seemed to
explode under our bows: an enormous pile-up of water would
collect itself, and come to the boil, and hiss, and roar, and then
burst outwards with a hammer-blow and a mad phosphorescent
smother of foam. After forty-eight hours of this, the wind
unbelievably took on an extra edge of frenzy, and the wise
Commodore signalled us all to heave-to—which meant turning
our raw faces into the storm again, with the same painful slowness, and settling down with the wind on the port bow, and the
bare revs to give us steerage-way and keep us balanced there.

Sadly, despairingly, we had turned our backs on home, and
were going the wrong way. But at least we were doing it very

slowly; and perhaps the whole ocean itself, under this violent attack, was moving eastwards for England, taking us with it as it went.

We were imprisoned thus for a day and a night, and then, at the second dawn, there came a sudden lull. Our world fell silent; the rigging and the signal halyards and the funnel-guys gave up their screaming, and slatted idly in the sulky air; the waves no longer broke, but butted us, and each other, with lumpish ill-humour. While it lasted, we waited in this stillness, suspecting it, uneasy at such swift respite.

It might mean peace at last, or else this was the eye of the storm, only waiting to spring another trap.

The battered convoy, seizing the chance, drew its ranks together, came quickly round, and headed eastwards with hopeful readiness; and then, with no more notice than a distant sighing, the wind itself whipped round, and picked up its surging strength, and began to blow savagely against us again. It was now a north-east gale, straight from Siberia; the other side of this treacherous coin; and there was now a vile cross sea, baffling, coming at us from all angles, to make it viler still.

But this, it turned out, was only a quick, two-day piece of spite; presently, after a pitch-black howling night, it really did ease off, and once more we pulled ourselves together coaxed the convoy into tight shape again, and set a fair course for home. It was the sixteenth day already, and we were still in 28° West, a thousand miles from safety; and very soon, as if to make the point beyond doubt, the radio began to chatter, and from Commander-in-Chief, Western Approaches, using his magic box in faraway, much-loved Liverpool, the first U-boat reports began to arrive.

In the better weather, they had come up for air, and for us.

It was an established sequence: the wolf-pack pattern which the Germans were now bringing to a grisly peak of efficiency. One U-boat must have spotted us (the convoy had made quite a lot of smoke when it put on speed again, and in clear weather smoke could be seen from fifty miles away). He had called up all his chums, strategically placed across a hundred miles of the known convoy tracks, and waiting for this sighting report; and within twenty-four hours, as the diligent Admiralty signalled, there were 'up to seven U-boats in your area'.

The familiar sick feeling took hold of *Campanula*—or at least it took hold of me, a good average coward, and I did not mind owning to it. The odds were rough indeed; if we had had double the number of escorts, seven U-boats could always get through the screen. All it needed was for two of them to show themselves, or make some kind of diversion (firing a distress rocket was a favourite) ahead and astern of the convoy; corvettes had to be sent away to investigate; the convoy's flanks were thus left with gaps literally a mile wide, and through these the other U-boats slid, and went to work.

It was a middle watch attack, as usual, starting with an underwater thud reported by a stunned asdic operator, and then a huge sheet of flame, topped by acrid smoke billowing black against the stars on the far side of the convoy. It could only be an oil-tanker. . . . I pressed the alarm-bell for action stations, but already I could hear sea-boots, of men in a hurry, men in fear or expectation, drumming and echoing along the iron decks. It was not a night for sleeping.

It was in fact the start of a desperate, three-day, running fight with the enemy, during which we lost eleven ships and got nothing in return. I do not want to fight it again. But there were certain highlights, or lowlights, or moments of special ugliness and terror: successful snapshots in the odious album of war, the ones that came out, and because of their quality stayed out, and have never faded.

These did not always happen when 'Darken ship' was piped: when the deadlights were dropped and screwed home over the portholes, and canvas screens were rigged across all entrances, and the wheelhouse shutters were put up: when no single chink of light showed, and we settled down to wait for the first blood of the night.

One torpedo scored a hit in broad daylight, on what must

have been an ammunition ship; we had noticed her earlier, because she carried a packed deck-cargo of armoured cars and medium tanks, and aircraft with folded-back wings, stuck on to the upper deck like presents on a Christmas tree.

She went up with a great roar, disintegrating from end to end at a single stroke; and after that her place in the convoy was marked only by huge spray-filled splashes as that precious deck-cargo fell back into the sea, item by item.

The U-boats sank two more tankers, to add to the first victim. They were only small ones, but death in burning oil must always be just about the same size.

Not all the news was awful. We had an old friend with us, a big bluff tanker called *Narragansett Bay* which we had escorted many times before. The U-boats got the ship ahead of her, and the ship astern, but they didn't get her.*

While we were collecting the aftermath of this considerable mess, just after dawn, a Sunderland flying-boat (known to us as a steam chicken) flew over on its patrol. She signalled, on her Aldis lamp: 'What happened?' The captain was fed up, as usual, with other people's stupidities, and for once I didn't blame him. He sent back: 'Everything,' and we got on with the task of tidying up a most squalid corner of the sea.

We had with us what was known as a CAM-ship, the initials standing for Catapult Aircraft Merchant: an ordinary freighter, but specially equipped to launch a Hurricane fighter-plane from a monstrous steam-catapult on the fo'c's'le. When the pilot had finished his job, he ditched his aircraft and parachuted down; it was an expensive, even madcap exercise, but it was aimed at doing something about a new breed of German reconnaissance plane called a Focke-Wulf (at least, some called them that) which was currently plaguing our convoys.

One of them was plaguing us now; the Hurricane took off in a cloud of steam and a whirl of salty spray, chased its quarry and lost it, and the R.A.F. pilot then jumped, according to the

* Not till nearly four years later, when in the last months of the war she went up in flames. I was in mourning that day.

drill. But a cross-wind carried him into the middle of the convoy, which could not stop for such heroics; and while we waited
astern to pick him up, his parachute got entangled in the
propellers of a small, intent, persevering merchant ship which
also could not leave its station, nor alter course, nor slacken
speed, nor cut him loose; and he was towed away to a dog's
death—but slowly.

The third night was the worst; we lost five good ships, and
uncounted men, and we never came to grips with a single one
of the enemy. Struck with the guilt of sailors who should have
done much better, who should have warded off at least some
part of this slaughter, we did the only thing left to us—stopped
engines, and waited, dead in the water, to pick up survivors.

We were not the only dead in the water. By the light from a
ship burning handily nearby—which incidentally gave *Campanula* a wonderful silhouette for any marksman in the outer
ring—we could see the usual rubbish of disaster: crates, planks,
baulks of timber, coal-dust, doors, rope-ends, a dead cat, odd
bits of clothing, empty life-rafts, and wallowing corpses—all
floating in inch-thick stinking oil, all part of the wrecked jumble-
sale which was the only souvenir of a wrecked ship.

But presently it became the familiar seascape with figures.
Men lived here. There was a lifeboat coming towards us, with
creaking oars; there were dozens of little lights clustered
together—the small bulbs, clipped to life-jackets, which gave
men still swimming their only chance of being seen in time for
rescue.

There were the sounds of men thrashing about in desperate
terror; shouts of 'Don't go away!' shouts of 'Help me!' shouts
of 'Christ!' There were the other sounds, of men dying, cold to
the bone but still showing a last hot anguish for life; and the
particular throaty gurgle of men swallowing oil instead of air,
and trying to cough it up through a scalding gullet, and failing,
and giving up life instead.

We did the best we could. Among the lolling dead who
drifted alongside and were hauled in with the rest, there was

one extraordinary object: like a dummy figure, like a caricature of a man, grossly swollen, with a great pink face which, by the light of a torch, might have been part of some obscene carnival.

Staring down at it, I had visions of a new weapon, a decoy-man which, like a decoy-duck, lured others to their doom. Still slow in the uptake, I called down to the leading seaman clinging to the foot of the scrambling net, who was trying to get a line round this bobbing balloon:

'What on earth is it?'

He looked up at me. His face in the torch-light was the colour of putty. Then he was sick. Then he called back 'It's an old one.'

We did the best we could, on that night as on the other nights. We picked up a total of 180 survivors in the three-day action; the crowding, and the stench of oil all over the ship, the groaning and the retching, the patient agony and the trembling terror, gave *Campanula* a foretaste of the very marrow of hell. There were twelve Norwegians and Danes and Poles, some bare-footed, some in rags of uniform, quartered in the wardroom; 168 Malays and Chinese and Indians in the crammed messdecks. 'There's a big raffle on, sir,' said my friend the Leading Signal-man, who was helping me. 'First fifty winners get to the heads.'

It was worth a thin laugh, but not much more. I was a busy man, on that last night; and I was down in the messdecks my-self, seeing how the poor lived, ten feet below the water-line, ten feet from the barest chance of safety. It had been crowded enough with eighty-eight of our own crew; now, with another 168 men added, it was chaos.

The survivors filled every available space: asleep on the steel deck, on benches, against bulkheads: sitting at tables with their heads between their hands: talking, shivering, wolfing food, staring at nothing. Some of them were half-naked, wrapped in blankets; some had wretched little cardboard suitcases clutched between their knees. There were puzzled black features, pinched yellow ones, bleary white masks, oil-streaked blurs of the human face.

There were men praying, and weeping, and laughing on a
cracked note of hysteria, and crooning as they cradled their dead
friends; and other men struck dumb, but screaming with their
eyes.

This was my surgery, on that busy night. Here were the men
waiting to be helped, and other men waiting to be buried.

I did the best I could, with the Coxswain to bear a hand, and
the Leading Signalman to hold the first-aid kit, and a telegraphist who had once been a vet to give me a second opinion.
But how did one set a broken thigh, when this, wrenched askew
by the strongest muscle in the body, simply would not come
straight again? How did one tell a burnt man, while staring
straight into his jellied eyes, that he would be feeling better
soon? What did one do for the tortured lascar with the mortal
oil seeping down into his gut? Say 'Choke up, chicken!' like my
mother before me?

Often I willed such men to die, even while I tended them;
and sometimes they agreed. The sound of their dying was not so
wide as a church door, nor so deep as a well, but by God it was
enough, it would serve. Yet when the longed-for silence did
fall, when they became acquainted with death, that was the
worst moment of all.

Then, sometimes, the whole awful picture blurred to nothing, as compassion, the enemy of manhood, came flooding in
uncontrollably. Then the Coxswain would say: 'Your eyes are
running, sir. Must be the smoke. I'll wipe them off.'

He wiped them off, while men, like death, looked stolidly on.
He knew all about my running eyes; otherwise the cotton-
waste would not have been so handy.

One of my father's odd bits of old wartime slang had been to
say, when a man was killed in the trenches, that he had become
'a landowner in France'. Now, in my turn, I could greatly
improve on this; the moment had come when I could confer on
these lost warriors the vast freehold of the Atlantic.

I was unspeakably tired as I stood balanced on the swaying
quarterdeck in that pale and miserable dawn, and prepared to

wind up my accounts. My face was stiff with cold, my sea-boots had leaked a clammy mixture of God-knows-what which I could feel between my toes; there was blood on the sleeves of my duffle coat, and my hands were begrimed with oil. I had been up all night, and we had been at action stations for nearly all the past seventy-two hours. I felt light-headed, and realized I was vulnerable.

I cut the service as short as I could, knowing, as soon as I had stumbled over the 'Off caps!' order, that the performance would not be too good. Fancifully, I seemed to hear a spectral voice, borne on the mourning wind, echoing its complaint about Ophelia's 'Maiméd rites'; calling me a churlish priest; asking me 'What ceremony else?'

Just for once, I did feel that burial as a loss, as a truly sad moment. I *did* want some ceremony else, not for the dead but for the living, for the small bunch of bedraggled survivors, and our own burial party, who had come aft for the committal.

I wanted—God! how I wanted—to say something true about the grey anonymous canvas oblongs ranged at my feet: how they had been sailors like us, how lonely and cold was their grave, how it could happen to any of us at any moment, how it was a waste and yet a hopeful payment, how I wanted us all to remember this, because, because . . .

But there was really no time; and probably the words would not have come to a stumbling tongue, in any case. I might have managed 'Dry sorrow drinks my blood,' and then turned away in fresh tears. That was no way to behave, even in this watery desert.

So I cut it short, and at an early moment they were tipped over, and slipped down into the great shroud of the sea: the final act of a short, bad play which had started lyrically enough with:

> Oh shipmates, help me up!
> For I'm drifting with the tide,
> And I'm sinking in the Lowland sea,

and ended now with this sullen splash.

But it was still the cleanest burial of all—and even at that

moment I remembered a slightly drunken conversation, years
earlier, with a man belonging to the Imperial War Graves
Commission, who had just come back from Flanders. He had
been busy transferring World War I bodies from a small
cemetery to a larger one, in the interest of economizing on
real estate, and to appease the French.

'There are never any coffins left, *as such*,' he had told me,
importantly. 'No uniforms either. Just a skeleton, and some
buttons, and the socks. Always the socks.'

Always the socks. . . . I put on my cap, saluted, and turned
away, and climbed up to the bridge to enter my own graveyard item in the deck-log. Then I went below to the messdecks.
There were so many things to do, at the dawn of another day,
and I had to be on watch again at noon.

But nothing lasted for ever, not even murder at sea. It was
the R.A.F. who eventually came to our rescue, not for the first
time; they sent out two of their new flying-boats, called
Catalinas, and then two more, on a round-the-clock search-and-
strike patrol which really worked. The planes kept the U-boats
below the surface by day, and scared them down again with
flares at night; gradually the convoy was able to draw ahead,
and slip out of danger.

Catalinas were remarkably graceful in flight, and remarkably
hardworking also; some of these patrols lasted up to seventeen
hours, which was a lot of time to spend flying round a bunch of
matelots who couldn't look after themselves. We blessed them
as we made our escape, and plodded slowly home with what
we had left.

This was quite a lot of ships, in fact, though it hadn't felt like
it while the convoy was taking its thrashing; we still had fifty-
four deep-laden merchantmen on our books, and as we led the
Liverpool portion up river we began to feel happier. There
was something about this safely delivered consignment, steaming slowly in line ahead up the muddy Mersey River, which was
exciting and satisfying, in spite of past miseries.

We had been brothers-in-arms for so long, across a thousand miles of wicked ocean; there were gaps, of course, and some sad backward glances at the losers, but there were plenty of winners also, full of arms, full of food, full of all the things so bady needed, and here they were, coming into harbour like champions.

The finish did not seem too tame, nor too depressing. It was even, on a minor key, triumphant. There was still this solid array of ships; there were our 180 survivors, now crowding the rails and looking at the shore-line as if it were part of Eden instead of the distant prospect of Bootle. I had not killed too many men. And we still had, somewhere down the queue, the good old *Narragansett Bay*.

The finish was enlivened by an incident which was not tame at all. Steaming past the Bar Light Vessel, we touched off a magnetic mine, and this could really be called a near-miss; it exploded with a shattering bang and a huge column of dirty water, about thirty yards astern of us. There was no damage, except to our nerves; but we reported it swiftly to the shore signal-station, in case it was one of a cluster.

Perhaps we made it sound worse than it was. Their immediate acknowledgement came in the form of the most heartless signal ever to reach us from Western Approaches Command. It was the simple directive:

'Do not sink in the swept channel.'

Campanula scraped the knuckle of the dock as we came into harbour, and it was my fault; in charge on the quarterdeck, I misunderstood one of those mysterious whistle-blasts, and held on to the back-spring too long. The ship lost a bit of paint, and I some poise. '*Monsarrat!*' came the expected roar from the bridge. 'What the hell are you playing at?'

But he could not really harm me now. We were cue for a boiler-clean, and at last it was my turn for leave—five days of blissful relief from the violence of all my enemies. This could not be stolen from me either: not without an injustice so barbarous that even my fellow-officers would have to take note of it.

2.

I had got married on 7 September 1939, four days after war broke out, as a matter of clear necessity (though this should not be misconstrued: our son was not born till 1942). But the enormous confusion and uncertainty dictated by war, the severance of so many accustomed ties, the massive breaking of rules, all seemed to make such a step inevitable; a loving marriage was the answer, the anchor, the rock, restoring the comfort and security which war was robbing from almost every other nest.

Her name was Eileen Rowland; we had been engaged for about six months, in the face of tepid enthusiasm on the part of her parents. I was manifestly a poor prospect, a *cul-de-sac* in the tunnel of love; her mother took a dim view of my inward nature ('Bolshy!') and my outward appearance, especially my only pair of shoes, which were of grey suede scuffed down to the bone. Her father was dubious about my financial prospects, candidly admitted to be nil.

Since he headed a company which made such a large proportion of the world's abrasive instruments that they could call themselves, accurately, Universal Grinding Wheels, with a factory about half a mile long to be seen as one's train drew into Stafford station, he was uniquely qualified to judge this particular field.

But I liked him, and he was always nice to me, though I was aware all the time that he could tell a fortune-hunter at a very considerable distance, just as Eileen's mother could spot an 'actor fellow,' as I had promptly been labelled, the moment he slid his dusty boots on to the high-gloss drawing-room parquet.

However, the fearful deed had been done, at Marylebone Town Hall (best man, senior witness, and champagne pourer, my friend Norman Pearson from darkest Nottingham); and we had set up house in a tiny flat in Church Street, Kensington, conveniently sited over a grocer's shop (London flats were very easy to pick up, at that doubtful moment of history). We lived frugally on my stretcher-bearer's pay of £2 18s. 5d. a week, plus Eileen's dowry of £1 a week from her parents. Since my working hours were twelve on and twelve off, changing to night-duty every other month, married life was disjointed; but we were very happy, independent at last while conducting some singularly tight housekeeping based on a black japanned money-box with seven labelled divisions: Rent, Coal, Food, Gas, Electricity, Sundries, and, unbelievably, Savings (5s. 6d. a week).

We never went out: we didn't want to, and we couldn't afford it, and the time-schedule, with sleep to be regained, made it impossible anyway. In eight months our only dinner guest was a life-long friend called Morrice James, then stuck in what he called a dreary job, and his superiors labelled an Assistant Principalship, at the Dominions Office.* He was currently itching to enlist in the Royal Marines, and he did so about the same time as I joined the Navy.

For dinner, Eileen cooked us a modest, staple stew called Skirts of Beef *en Casserole*, and we also had a bottle of Algerian claret from the grocer downstairs. It made a considerable dent in the 'Savings' section of the money-box, but it was worth it.

Marriage had seemed important when it happened, under the first impact of war. Now, two and a half years later, it had become essential, involving reason itself. I knew already (and it did not need blood, squalor, nor the miserable pricks of authority to drive the point home), that I would never survive this particular prison sentence without her; and the debt remained, never to be repaid, long after the war was won and the tender magic had been swallowed by it, or destroyed by me, or lost in a post-war, duller-than-dull detergent wash.

---

* The Dominions Office became, successively, the Commonwealth Relations Office and then the Commonwealth Office. As Sir Morrice James, K C.M.G., he became permanent head of the latter twenty-eight years later.

Women, I found, were marvellous at war—in their bravery, their disguise of emotion, their careful ignoring of time. They could fashion out of mundane sticks and stones a centre of warmth and peace, giving it their whole care although they knew, better than anyone, that it could only be enjoyed for a short while. This they maintained secure, against all the aching odds, under the very shadow of dispersal. They spent themselves to the limit while one was there, knowing that the next zero-hour, the next circle of the clock, meant bankrupt solitude again.

War was inevitably a matter of saying good-bye, usually in grisly circumstances: on black winter mornings, in grimy railway stations, outside dock-gates in the rain. It was made more grisly still, for both of us, by knowing exactly what lay in store as soon as the bell tolled: I was headed for my particular menu of cold, exhaustion, boredom, and fear, while she went back to her empty lair, to find, on the mat, a fresh sheaf of directives from the Ministry of Food. But we had managed to give this whole process a lift by renting a small cottage in Gateacre, a village just outside Liverpool, and there setting up house.

It was only a bungalow, as shabby, run-down, and draughty as a bottom-of-the-garden shack; but it was the rock-cave I had to have, and Eileen swiftly fashioned it into a longed-for home. I had already invested in a motor-cycle, a $2\frac{1}{2}$ h.p. Frances-Barnett, as a means of getting about when public transport was curtailed or, under threat of an air-raid, had given up altogether; and this was my home-coming chariot, my link between Albert Dock in the gruesome heart of Liverpool and the rustic solitude waiting for me outside.

It did a lot of sea-time, that motor-bike: up to the Clyde, across to Northern Ireland, and down to Gibraltar, among other brave voyages. But its best voyage of all was the seven-mile chugging run out to Gateacre, when *Campanula* came into harbour at the end of a convoy.

As I crashed the gears and twirled the twist-grip throttle, I would be almost singing, even with a mouthful of rain or a great squelching splash of mud over my uniform trousers. Home was the sailor, home from the sea. . . . The sad reveries of mid-Atlantic, the longing exactly expressed in that four-line verse which had so excited me at the age of sixteen:

> Western wind, when wilt thou blow,
> The small rain down can rain?
> Christ, if my love were in my arms
> And I in my bed again!

—these lonely thoughts from abroad no longer ruled. The reality was coming true again. Indeed, it was just over the next hill, if $2\frac{1}{2}$ h.p., rationed petrol, and chain-drive persistence could only make it.

We did nothing at all in that funny little house, except eat and sleep and make love and, as far as I was concerned, uncoil the fearful spring which a seventeen-day convoy could tighten almost beyond endurance. We had one prime blessing, a treasured gramophone which I had bought second-hand, for £13, on the first day of the war, as a gesture in the face of all that was plaguing us, or was going to: an E.M.G. with a monstrous papier maché horn, and needles made of small slivers of bamboo which had to be sharpened after each record.

This singular contrivance, correctly used, could produce a tone so perfect, so dry and resonant and true, that later hi-fi jobs, with all the aids of tweeters and woofers and thudding bass notes, never seemed able to match it.

We listened, with deep content, to our music: Mozart piano concertos, Beethoven quartets, the simple rites of Telemann and Purcell. I read *War and Peace*, the current target of all those who had never managed to buckle down to it, and after that *Crime and Punishment*, and then, with a backward glance, *Remembrance of Things Past* again, and then the doyen of all the great novels, *Vanity Fair*. Eileen knitted *matinée* jackets for her pregnant friends, while I wore slippers for sixteen hours a day.

We ate with relish, occasionally with elegance. But some of

our meals were spare indeed, and guiltily enjoyed. What we were swallowing was not food but coupons, the rarest of all the wartime treasures. The ration-book was the real required reading, not a lot of rubbishy old novels; and coping with this drab, day-to-day puzzle was now her destiny, whether I was there or not.

Like every other housewife in the land, Eileen was having the worst of the war. Civilian Britain was now ruled by rationing; and rationing, even when backed by pious cries of 'Fair shares all round!' was an undoubted ordeal.

The total organization of one's life by authority was then something new; and the later heirs of this nappy-empire, the citizens who expected Council, or the Town Hall, or the National Health, or simply Them, to take care of everything, whether it was a leaking tap, a missed period, or a runaway horse, were only just being born, and not yet measured for their crutches.

But already people seemed ripe for the embrace, or resigned to the joys of aldermanic rape; already the catch-phrase 'Don't you know there's a war on?' excused everything from a drought of beer to a late-arriving, drunken plumber, and it was beginning to condition the public will as well. Within a few months, people had come to accept dictation: to be organized, ordered about, clamped into categories, fed with minutely calculated packets of food, and animated by slogans designed to make them jump through one numbered hoop, and one alone.

The trouble was, there were so many rules to keep in mind that even the most compliant and loyal subject could lose track of the footnotes.

Women had to deal with almost all this burden; and war on the home front, theirs to endure, was just about as dreary and dispiriting as it could possibly be. 'Don't you know there's a war on?' hung like a tatty embroidered text on every kitchen wall. It certainly hung in Gateacre's.

While, on board a ship of war, we were never short of eggs, butter, and meat (and one might argue that we were entitled to a

small extra dividend, since we brought the stuff over). Eileen
was short of every damned thing in the kitchen calendar, from
the new-fangled American triptych of Spam ('Spiced ham
flavoured with sugar'), Treet ('A kind of mince-meat'), and
Mor ('Chopped pork shoulder-meat tasting like ham'), to the
sinister artefact compounded of soya beans, bread-crumbs, and
chopped windpipe which had now usurped the place of the
British sausage.

Rationing started, as it should, with Lesson One: 'How to
Register'; and this itself was enough to take away a good deal
of the appetite. But as long as she kept her head, the average
housewife could presumably work her way through such guide-
lines as:

> When the new ration-books come into force, you must
> register with one retailer, whether you have changed shops or
> not. You should register as follows: 'Meat: *yellow* book,
> page 13. Butter, margarine, and cooking-fat: yellow book,
> page 13. Sugar and preserves: yellow book, page 16. Bacon
> and ham: yellow book, page 13. Cheese: page 25. Eggs:
> page 20.'

But there were more complicated directives waiting over the
horizon:

> YOU MUST write a large C on the *yellow* meat counter-
> foil which you fill in for your child, if the child has a *green*
> ration-book. For butter, margarine, and cooking-fats: DO
> NOT write on the counterfoil for cooking-fats. YOU DO
> NOT have to register separately for cooking-fats, but they
> must be bought from the same shop as your butter and mar-
> garine. DO NOT register for sugar and preserves separately;
> they must be bought from the same shop. For Cheese: if you
> are entitled to the special 8 oz. cheese ration, DO NOT use
> this counterfoil. Take your ration-book to your local food
> office during the next twelve days.

3

Only manual workers got that special, even sensational 8 oz. cheese ration. The normal allowance was *one* ounce per person per week; and an ounce of Cheddar, which it usually was, measured 1¼ x 1¼ x 1 *inches*.

Sometimes, to keep the housewife right on her toes, they changed the rules in mid-term:

A new system of point-rationing is to be introduced to cover certain types of canned food, including canned meats, canned fish, and canned beans. The term 'canned meats' includes corned mutton, corned pork, tongue, brisket, Australian canned rabbit, Eire stewed steak, and U.S. luncheon meat. This will involve the distribution of an entirely new range of *pink* ration books. A date will be announced shortly.

Yet all this massive and detailed organization still left one hungry. The April meat ration, the month I was home, was 1s. a week, which included 2d. worth of corned beef; and the fact that we lost 106 ships in April (more than 3½ a day, the fraction being appropriate because so many of them were sunk in pieces) made that Sunday joint seem precious indeed. Certainly one could eke things out by eating in restaurants, but even these were now curtailed to 'one-dish meals', and unless you were a son-in-law, or extremely quick off the mark, that one dish was almost certain to be a rissole.*

The jam ration ('Jam, marmalade, syrup, and treacle') was 8 oz. per calendar month, which was one small pot, 2½ inches high.

There was a shortage of macaroni and herring, though eels were plentiful. There was a shortage of onions: the allowance was now 2 lb. per person *per year*, and you could take the whole lot, at one gulp, at 5d. a lb. The egg ration had also been

---

* Though under labels of greater consequence: e.g., Pojarskis, Kromeskies à la Russe, Croquettes, Chevapchichi, Salisbury Steak, Boeuf Britannia, and Savoury Balls.

reduced, to two per ration-book per week, and the household egg had now been promoted to a new status, a 'shell egg'. Otherwise it had already lost its shell, and a lot more besides, and came in packets as domestic dried egg powder.

Whisky had leapt to the disgraceful price of 17s. 6d. a bottle, and you had to register for that, too; though unless you had known the retailer for several years your chances of getting a bottle were as slim as the cork.

But in all these troubles and frustrations, there was still plenty—even a glut—of one particular item; and the Ministry of Food had gone overboard for it, and wanted us all there as well. It was the potato.

They ran a far-reaching range of advertisements for the potato, featuring a helpful, confiding, even cosy fellow called Potato Pete. But Potato Pete was not really a reassuring character: he was in fact a roly-poly shapeless ball of near-humanity, and this, we felt, was how we were all going to end up, if we played the game his way.

Yet the exhortations were persuasive, the hints helpful indeed:

'Why stop at serving potatoes once a day? Have them twice or even three times: for breakfast, dinner, and supper!

'Here's a new way to make use of orange peel! Grate it, and mix a little with mashed potatoes. The potatoes will turn an exciting pink colour!'

'Give the family Surprise Potato Balls! Put a teaspoonful of sweet pickle inside, and wait for the reaction!'

There was a good deal more to come, for the Amazons on the Home Front. After food and drink and Potato Pete and the whole scrotum of savoury balls which now ruled the kitchen, there was also clothes rationing, subject to another minutely detailed rule book in which the fine print was chopped even finer.

Clothes rationing had begun with beguiling simplicity. It was to cover clothing, cloth, footwear, and knitting wool. One was given sixty-six coupons, to last a whole year; and sample coupon-values were set out as:

Woollen dress:	11 coupons
Pair of trousers:	8 coupons
Pair of socks:	3 coupons

2 handkerchiefs ⎫
1 collar ⎬ 1 coupon each
2 oz. knitting wool ⎭

But then, as was inevitable, the system began to take root and branch out. A small library of clothes-coupon books soon became an essential item in every household; and this was presently backed up by a whole series of handbooks, designed to lead the hesitant shopper, step by step, through a very considerable maze.

The clothing-coupon list was now sub-divided into forty-six different categories. These ranged over a wide area indeed, and included such specialized items as: a bust bodice, a modesty vest, a bolero, and a bedjacket: one-piece shelter-suit, apron with or without bib, cotton football jersey, galoshes, rubber bootees, plimsolls, and a pair of cuffs, leggings, gaiters, or spats.

There was, naturally, a special sub-division for the kiddies, with its own intimate vocabulary: *matinée* coats, leggingettes, pantettes, breechettes, buster-suits, waterproof knickers, and bibs or feeders. A bib or feeder cost one-third of a coupon.

It might have seemed ferociously complicated, at a casual glance. But broad gleams of light showed through, nonetheless, and proud Authority pointed these out from time to time to a mouth-watering public. Certain items were to be coupon-free! You could actually walk into any shop, plonk down your money, and walk out again with the following substantial armful: an abdominal belt, specially designed solely for use in the following conditions: hernia, sacroiliac disease, spinal abnormality, or enuresis; an abdominal belt specially designed for post-opera-tive use, including a supra-pubic drainage belt; and a generous mixed bag of industrial clogs, artists' canvas, ballet shoes, jock straps, knee-caps, and academic robes.

All this codified harness was reinforced, in its turn, by constant exhortation, which ranged all the way from the wheedle, the coax, the frown, and the command, to the threat direct. We were ordered to 'Dig for Victory!' and 'Save Waste Paper!' We were warned that 'Walls Have Ears!', that 'Tittle-tattle Lost the Battle', that 'Careless Talk Costs Lives!' (with a picture of a palpably sharp-eyed spy eavesdropping on some stupid sailors in an innocent British pub). We were assured, so ambiguously that the fact was even mentioned in the House of Commons, that 'YOUR courage, YOUR resolution, YOUR skill, will give US the victory'.

There seemed to be a notable shortage of paper (though not of official advertisements, posters, handbooks, and leaflets), and you had to bring your own contribution to the shops if you wanted your purchases wrapped up. Even chocolates could no longer be wrapped, nor be cushioned in those tiny, individual, crinkly nests of their own. Cigarettes were to be sold in loose handfuls—sorry, no cartons. There were no longer any labels on jars of jam: whatever the jam was, its ancestry was to be written on the top of the jar, and nowhere else. There were to be no more Christmas cards.

'Save every piece and bundle it for the dustman!' was the command. The social pressures were fierce: to discard any 'salvageable waste' such as wrapping paper, cardboard, newspaper, or even matchboxes, was to be branded as the owner of a Fifth Column Dustbin. Envelopes had to be sealed and resealed with a specially-designed official sticker, and used until they dropped from the stamp.

There were curt official orders, sometimes softened by a plaintive 'What do I do?' introduction: 'What do I do when I hear the gas-rattle alarm? *I do not look up!*' There were frugal household hints: 'Rinse out your milk bottles with one or two tablespoonfuls of water, and use the liquid in cakes or puddings.' There were truly reassuring directives: 'What do I do to make sure of getting my letters, if my home is destroyed *I fill in Card No. P 2216B.*'

This last one was linked, in its heroic disregard of the odds, with the somewhat sniffy notices now being circulated for display in pubs, restaurants, hotels, and boarding houses: 'There is NO depression in this house. We are NOT interested in the possibility of defeat, and we do NOT discuss it.'

This, for once, rang a true bell. Years earlier, I had seen it, displayed as a piece of genuine Victoriana (*circa* 1899, which was the middle of the Boer War) embroidered on a handkerchief in the civic museum at Helston, in Cornwall.

Other people on the outer, non-official fringe were also contracting the exhortation habit. Already we had: 'How to Win Your War of Nerves: Take Sanatogen Tonic Food!'* 'Sell Your Car and Help the War Effort' was a transparent piece of eyewash, directly geared to the post-war racket in second-hand cars, which was to make a few sharp-witted dealers very rich indeed. 'Civil Servant pays 70 shillings for a suit, puts balance saved into War Loan' was not a patriotically-slanted news item, but an advertisement for a firm of cheap multiple tailors.

There were more direct trangressors, and authority brought them to our attention from time to time. 'Remember, Black Markets exist for Black Sheep!' cautioned the Ministry of Food. 'There wouldn't be a black market if there weren't customers for it.' They then went on to announce, none too subtly, that since the war started they had obtained convictions in 22,356 cases of offences against rationing and food control.

Among these there was at least one lady of consequence, the Countess of Onslow, who was convicted of obtaining meat in contravention of the rationing order: £44 worth of meat, in fact, for £19 worth of coupons. (Fined £5.)

There were cases of people who licensed all four of their cars, obtained petrol coupons for each of them, and then kept one car only on the road. (Sailors were bound to feel angry about this, having seen and smelt some of the precious petrol which failed to get through.) There were cases of bookmakers who were allowed a special petrol allowance for travelling to their

---

* *Cf.* 'Strike-worn nerves need building up: Take Ovaltine!' during the General Strike of 1926.

place of business—which was Newmarket racecourse. There was at least one good story about a would-be shortage-beater.

> Lady: 'I'd like some cod, please.'
> Fishmonger: 'I'm sorry, there's no cod today.'
> Lady: 'I'm sure you've really got some, haven't you?'
> Fishmonger: 'There's *no* cod today.'
> Lady: 'Are you certain? Aren't you keeping some under the counter?'
> Fishmonger: 'Lady, *we haven't any cod.* No C-O-F-D—cod!'
> Lady: 'But there's no F in cod.'
> Fishmonger: 'That's what I'm trying to tell you.'

Cheerful flashes of news pierced the gloom. There would soon be plenty of whale-steak ('Tastes like certain cuts of beef'). South Africa was sending us tons of a tasty local fish called a *snoek*. There were other entirely new fish coming on the market: among them were dog-fish, monk fish, and roker. A number of offals, including liver, heart, and kidneys (but *not* ox-skirt) were now off the ration entirely.

Bad news occasionally balanced these promised delights. The Ministry of Food confessed, sadly, that during the first eight weeks of egg control 'probably 17 million bad eggs had been delivered to retailers.' ('Probably' seemed a delightful word to use in this connection.) And, to remind us that all this was part of a pretty serious subject, a new pamphlet was now available: '*Invasion Hints for All*'.

There was one other piece of light reading with which Eileen could pass her long winter evenings: another official guide-book called the Clothing Coupon Quiz. This was written in the form of a simple question-and-answer series of paragraphs, though she would have needed some very close study to become word-perfect.

> Q. 'Are coupons required for hand-knitting yarn?'
> A. 'All yarn suitable for hand-knitting now requires

coupons. The standard rating is one coupon for two ounces, but as a temporary measure to clear stocks the following reduced ratings have been fixed: Yarn containing not more than 16% by weight of wool, one coupon for 8 oz. Yarn of any kind sold at not more than 4½d. per ounce retail, or 4s. per lb. if sold to a trader, one coupon for 8 oz. Yarn measuring less than 100 yards per oz., one coupon for 8 oz. (To find out the number of yards in a skein, measure its length when laid flat and multiply by double the number of strands in the skein.) You must also bear in mind that "wool" means fibre whether or not subjected to any process of manufacture or recovery from the coat or fleece of alpaca, camel, goat, hare, lamb, llama, rabbit, sheep, vicuna, or yak; it also includes angora wool.'

But there was an easier one:

Q. 'May coupons be given to friends?'
A. 'No.'

And one for the thrifty housewife:

Q. 'If I get my old costume turned, do I give up coupons?'
A. 'Only if you have a new lining will you surrender coupons according to the yardage used.'

Finally, one very good question, No. 92, to round off the evening:

Q. 'What happens when the number of coupons to be given up includes a fraction?'
A. 'Coupons must in no circumstances be cut into pieces. The fraction should be made up to the nearest whole number above, if it is half or more. If it is less than a half it should be ignored, except that where the number comes to less than one it counts as one, e.g., $5\frac{1}{2}$ or $5\frac{2}{3}$ count as 6; $5\frac{1}{3}$ counts as 5; but one-third counts as one. For the purpose

of finding exactly how many coupons should be given up, all purchases made at the same time should be added together, e.g., a yard of 54-inch wool cloth sold at the same time as a large handkerchief makes $4\frac{1}{2}$ plus a half which equals 5 coupons.'

Clear as a bell.

I came back from that treasured leave to find, on board *Campanula*, a superior break in the clouds. Suddenly I had an ally, someone I could talk to; instead of the zoo-like grunting and snuffling which had ruled us so far, actual sentences were now to be heard, with verbs and all.

My rescuer was a man called Jim Harmsworth—or, more correctly, Lieutenant St J. B. V. Harmsworth, R.N.V.R., a Dead-End Kid like myself (there were an awful lot of lieutenants R.N.V.R. in the Navy, chained forever to their oars), whose cheerful disposition did much to dispel the gloom of our non-advancement as well as the sub-zero temperature of *Campanula* herself. He had been a barrister, and hoped one day to return to practise 'when all this inconvenience is over'.

Sometimes he mentioned, without emphasis, 'my cousin Esmond'. As a small ex-snob from Liverpool, I was very impressed. Cousin Esmond was Lord Rothermere, a man of such power and prestige in Fleet Street that his principal toy, the *Daily Mail*, had no need to be either consistent, accurate, nor discerning. It was simply successful.

Jim Harmsworth, as well as his distinguished name, had the added glamour of having been torpedoed, in an armed merchant cruiser called *Patroclus* which went to the bottom off Bloody Foreland in November 1940.

'Oh, I simply swam about,' he said, when questioned about this. 'There were various people looking after us, and they came round to me before too long. But I may say that Bloody Foreland was christened with tolerable accuracy. Quite apart from the snow, the water was *extremely cold*.'

3*

He had also established, though God knows how, that *Patroclus* had been sunk by U.*99*, under the command of one of the three top German aces, Captain Kretschmer. Kretschmer had been taken prisoner, after finally losing his U-boat, about a month earlier, and was now languishing on the Isle of Man.

'I must confess that I opened a bottle of fizz when I heard about it,' was Jim's comment on this. 'And I did *not* remember him at Christmas.'

He was a Harrovian, the man who traditionally sat on the chair which I, the Wykehamist, had fetched; but he could have chopped up that chair for firewood, as far as I was concerned, so welcome was his arrival. At that moment of history he had grown a large red beard,* though the effect was appealing rather than imposing, like a Father Christmas known to be only Daddy after all. As an officer, he was easy-going, and famous on board as an undeniably soft touch, from the disciplinary point of view.

Once, when an infuriated 'Hostilities Only' able-seaman, hauled before him by the hard-breathing Coxswain, burst out in a sudden snarl of revolt: 'Well, I'm buggered if I'm going to be buggered about by a silly old bugger like this bugger here!' Jim's comment was: 'You are in some danger of becoming monotonous.'

I was glad to note, many years later when he was a magistrate at Great Marlborough Street Police Station, and dealing with a substantial traffic in student protest, that things had tightened up considerably in this area.

We enjoyed—well, I enjoyed—one occasion of singular charm, when *Campanula*, in common with the rest of our escort group, was inspected from stem to stern by a member of the C.-in-C.'s shore staff. This was Commander J. E. Broome, a man

---

* Our entire wardroom, save for the Captain, was now heavily bearded. A *News Chronicle* photographer who made a trip with us observed, on first seeing us: 'Christ, that's quite a drop of horticulture you've got there!' We were glad he was so seasick.

of keen eye and tireless curiosity whom, like the corvette *Coreopsis*, I was to encounter later in unusual circumstances.

He toured the whole ship at the head of a comet-tail of nervous officers, with the Coxswain, the Chief Bosun's Mate carrying the traditional storm-lantern, and the uninvited, inquisitive ship's dog bringing up the rear. Commander Broome, equally inquisitive, asked questions about everything, from the First Lieutenant's anchor cables to my clutch of depth-charges; from the wardroom wine accounts to the state of the galley stove (indifferent, it seemed).

We were all grilled, in a thoroughly seamanlike manner. Finally came Jim Harmsworth's turn to be put on the rack.

Commander Broome rounded on him suddenly. 'What's *your* job?'

Harmsworth was relieved to be on safe ground. 'Barrister, sir,' he answered promptly. 'I'd been in practice about five years when—'

'I meant, your job in the ship,' Broome interrupted, with a 'Bloody clot!' look which would have stunned a less assured man.

'Signal Officer, sir.'

'Oh. How many ten-inch projectors do you carry?'

'I think they're all four-inch, sir,' said Harmsworth, courteously enough.

'*Four-inch?* Nonsense! There's no such thing. You couldn't see it at fifty yards! How many *ten*-inch projectors?'

I realized what had happened; Jim, mishearing the question or being confused, at this testing moment, over the difference between a projector, which was a signalling lamp, and a projec-tile, which was what came out of a gun when the button was pressed, had picked the wrong one. This was confirmed when he answered: 'I'm not sure, sir. And I'm afraid the Gunnery Officer is on leave.'

Commander Broome steered clear of this *impasse* by ignoring it; he might already have arrived at what judges called 'a certain conclusion' about my friend. We moved on, in thoughtful silence, up to the signal bridge, and there, by bad luck, there came a sudden cascade of high-speed morse transmission from inside the Wireless Telegraphy office.

The Commander swung round again. 'What's that?' he demanded.

'W/T office, sir.'

'I know *that*. But can you read it?'

'No, sir.' We had men on board who could read high-speed morse, but Jim was not one of them. Nor was I.

'Pity about that. You could intercept the German broadcasts.'

The idea of Jim Harmsworth, who even then preferred to make a measured appreciation of every move, reading German morse at the rate of about two hundred words a minute, was an affecting one, and I had to turn away and stare at some nearby paintwork before I had properly mastered it. Behind me, I heard him making a last try for justice.

'I'm afraid it's rather too fast for me.'

'I thought you said you were the Signal Officer!' said Broome, as if he could scarcely believe his ears.

'Well—*faute de mieux*, sir.'

'What's that?'

'*Faute de mieux*.'

'Oh . . . .' A suspicious glance frosted the air between them. '*Faute de mal*, I should think you mean.'

In spite of the wayward French, it lost very little in translation.

Yet Broome was not the kind of 'shore type' one could seriously resent, except as a professional disciplinarian in avid search of our amateur shortcomings; and in any case he was only coasting between jobs as a destroyer captain in charge of an escort group, which was a superior sailor indeed.

Jim and I had more satisfaction, however, with the other kind of shore-based sailor, who spent large amounts of time on board *Campanula*, performing such modest tasks as twiddling two small knobs on a Lewis-gun mounting, saying 'That should be all right now' (it had been all right before), and then settling down in the wardroom to drink our gin, cadge our cigarettes, and bewail the fact that he was 'stuck ashore', instead of performing prodigies of valour on the bounding main.

A few such visitors were genuine in this ambition, and a universal condemnation would have been unfair; a ship had to have a base, a base had to have specialists, and people so categorized had to stay where they were and do the dull jobs instead of the exciting ones.

But some of these jobs were minimal as well as dull; the softer the billet, the more tenacious the incumbent limpet; and at Liverpool, teeming with hard-driven ships and men, we had one or two such talented loafers, fluent and condescending, intent on making us feel that we were merely the salt brawn of the Navy, while they were the brains. But ah, if they could only be posted to sea. . . .

There was one, nicknamed the Lieutenant-Soprano, whose strangled, hot-potato voice constantly enjoined us to keep up the good work—the 'good work' being such demanding tasks as making *regular* returns of all canisters of red lead expended above the mean average for our size of ship, since this involved forward planning at staff level. This water-fly haunted the ship whenever we were in harbour; and as it was his custom to arrive promptly at 11 a.m., and remain languidly at anchor in the wardroom until he had to be invited to lunch, we came to know him well, and to loathe him accordingly.

Luckily, lunch was usually so awful (especially our basic diet of galley-hard hash with a rubber fried egg vulcanized to the top) that we could well feel that we were striking back. Jim's manner—not quite sarcastic, not quite artless—of saying 'Do have some more of this delicious *ragoût!*' was alone worth the money. I hadn't heard the word *ragoût* since I read my last Victorian novel.

There was another of these recurrent pests whom we finally routed. This was an electrical expert whom the advent of a new type of mine had brought into action, in order to ensure that the ship's magnetic field was either positive, or negative, or

neutral—in spite of qualms, I had lost track, quite early on, of
the explanatory lecture, and I did not know, nor would ever
understand, what it was (apart from being made of wood), which
would make us safe.

He was, like the Lieutenant-Soprano, a frequent visitor and a
most determined stayer; he had a voice of almost liquid pom-
posity, and his favourite theme (apart from the hazards of the
magnetic field) was his wish to serve afloat.

'You know, I really envy you chaps,' he once said, taking his
ease in one of our few remaining armchairs. ('Us chaps' were
still thawing out our frozen toes after a winter gale which had
pursued us to the very threshold of the dock.) 'Actually going
out on convoy. . . . And here am I, just because I have certain
specialist qualifications, assigned to the C.-in-C.'s staff for what
looks like the duration. I can assure you, I would do anything—
anything—to get to sea.'

I became aware that Jim Harmsworth, sitting quietly in one
corner, drawing on a cigar, had decided to strike. He said,
using an early blend of the judicial and the influential:

'That might be arranged.'

'Really?'

'I will have a word with Noble.'

Our visitor's assurance suddenly lessened. 'How do you
mean, Noble?'

'Sir Percy Noble,' Jim answered. 'Commander-in-Chief,
Western Approaches. He is some sort of connection of mine.' (I
knew this to be a lie, but it was a lie in a very good cause.) 'He
would certainly never stand in the way of any young officer who
preferred to serve in corvettes rather than on his staff.'

The effect was swift. Indeed, I had never before seen a man
contract hay-fever before my very eyes. He coughed, he
spluttered, he lay back gasping; he wiped his streaming eyes
before he managed to say:

'There *is* another reason. . . . I don't talk about it much, but
there it is. . . . It's my infernal bronchial trouble. . . . That's
really why they put me ashore in the first place. . . .'

'You mean, you might not pass the medical?'

'I *know* I wouldn't.'

'What very bad luck,' said Jim. 'Do let me know if there is any change.'

We had to have a *little* fun.

Actually we had quite a lot of fun in Liverpool, on a different plane. Liverpool was now, more than ever, a sailors' town; night after night, month after month, sailors by the tens of thousands, from a dozen escort groups and a hundred merchant ships, came rolling ashore, intent on drinks and girls and perhaps a good brisk fight at closing-time; and the fact that these licensed marauders, turning the place upside down, were still welcomed and forgiven by the sober inhabitants, made me more sure than ever that the city of my birth had a special quality, a special spirit, which nothing was going to quench: not the weather, not the Germans, not even us.

It was wonderful to walk down *Campanula's* steep gangway, free of the farmyard at last, and traverse the jetty on my faithful Frances-Barnett: past the nose-catching dockside lavatory where, I knew, a shaky hand had chalked the inscription which had so delighted me at the age of thirteen: 'This is where the knobs hang out'; past the indulgent customs men (indulgent over a pot of jam or a tin of corned beef, not at all indulgent about cigarettes or anything in a bottle); past the tall policeman who always said: 'Enjoy yourself, lads!' and out on to the wide cobbled freedom of Pier Head.

Ashore, we left the salt grime behind, and wore spotless suits of warranted, superfine, No. 1 doe-skin, and high-gloss ankle boots from Gieves, and pigskin gloves, and, by edict, the prime nuisance of the war, our gas-masks. The target was always the Adelphi Hotel, that splendid monument to heavyweight Edwardian charm, built when no one would dream of using a brick where a stone would do, or a stone when a slab of mottled marble was just the ticket.

This was the mecca where, ten years earlier, I had daily surrendered my bowler-hat and gold-topped Malacca cane, and taken Afternoon Tea in the lounge (3s. 6d., for choice of tea-cake or muffin, a whole cornucopia of sandwiches, iced cakes or a wedge of Dundee from the trolley, and an orchestra to play selections from *The Student Prince*). Now, as we went through the revolving door in search of the same sort of gilded relaxation, it was marvellous to find the welcome as assured as ever.

There, *en route* for Gateacre, and peace, and Eileen's blessed cooking, and the first appetizing meal of the day, we besieged the American bar and got mildly plastered. There we gazed longingly at the permanent frieze of beautiful Wrens, though (even if we had not both been happily married) these flowers were not for us to pick; they were reserved for the base staff, against whom we would never have stood a chance.

These insidious shore-types were *there*, while we were not; they could lay a long-term siege while we had a bare three or four days to complete the mating dance; they could creep adroitly back into bed while we crept past the Mull of Kintyre.

There I once saw Vivien Leigh, more ravishing than ever, walking through to the grill room for an early dinner before she went on stage and entertained the troops. She gave me a wave and a gorgeous smile; then she turned back to her escort. He was a Rear-Admiral. What a hope!

There we once saw Mr Winston Churchill, who had come north to cheer the city up after a bad blitz. He wore his Trinity House uniform, and looked like a good, dependable, sea-faring man; he also looked a very rock of confidence. Crossing the foyer, he gave us a beam and a victory sign, and we, having rocketed straight out of the bar, returned him an identical salute.

At that moment, I felt the same warm uplift as did the rest of the Western world whenever they caught sight of this lion among men, or heard his rallying snarl on the radio. In spite of firm principles, I could even forgive him his awful remark, when goaded in the House of Commons by Aneurin Bevan (whom he labelled 'a squalid nuisance'): 'I am told that one cannot get into the underground shelters because of the Socialist sewer rats who are there already.'

Conservative or not, he was the man we had to have, and even a brief glimpse was enough to prove it.

There, one evening, Jim Harmsworth and I caught a German spy.

We had stayed longer than usual in the bar; Eileen had somehow procured—probably from her parents, who lived in the country and had access to all sorts of rarities—an actual whole ham; and to this unheard-of luxury, which might never come our way again, she wanted to give the sort of preparation and the scrupulous cooking which it deserved. We were not expected until nine.

We stood up at the American Bar counter, surveying the agreeable scene with tolerant good humour. Presently a voice at my side said:

'Have you lads just come in?'

I turned on one elbow. It was a stranger in a dark suit, a small, fifty-ish man with a lean face and friendly eyes. He looked all right—not a nuisance, not a homosexual. I did not mind the direct approach; I did not mind us being addressed as 'lads'; at that stage, I did not mind anything.

'No,' I answered. 'As a matter of fact we've been here quite a long time.'

The man smiled, with great good humour. 'I mean, just in from your convoy?'

'Oh. Yes, we got in a couple of days ago.'

'Rough trip?'

'Not too bad.'

At my back Jim Harmsworth, like me at peace with all the world, asked:

'Who's your friend?'

The stranger, changing places adroitly, stepped round until he stood between us. He murmured a name which I did not catch, and then said:

'How about a drink?'

We were not in the mood to say no; and as far as I was concerned, gin-and-tonic at Adelphi shore-prices did not suit my
lieutenant's scale of pay. Before long, we were a companionable
trio. But there was no doubt that the third man was inquisitive.

'I work down at Gladstone Dock,' he told us presently.
'See a lot of you chaps coming in and out. What are you in?
Destroyers?'

'Corvettes,' I said.

'What are they like to live in?'

'Awful.'

'But you get quite a long time in harbour, don't you?'

'Four or five days.'

'Then I suppose you'll be off pretty soon.'

I was about to say 'Tuesday', and then I thought: 'No, damn
it!—I'm not supposed to say that,' and I answered instead: 'It
all depends.'

He seemed to switch subjects very quickly. We turned—*he*
turned—to ship repairs ('Of course, I'm interested, working at
Gladstone'), and how well they were being done, and what the
Liverpool dockers were like, and all the new kinds of equipment
coming in.

It must have been at exactly the same moment that Jim and I,
exchanging alert glances, decided that this man was an obvious
German spy, and that we were being tempted into gross
indiscretion. The moment was when the stranger asked:

'I suppose you've got huff-duff?'

'Yes,' said Jim, after a thoughtful pause. 'We had it for
lunch.'

There was a merry laugh. 'You know what I mean. HF/DF.
Those bloody great aerials. I think I've seen one or two of
the corvettes fitted with them. It must be a great help. *If* it
works.'

'Why shouldn't it work? What are you hinting at?'

The man, meeting Jim's keen and formidable glance, seemed
to back away. That in itself was suspicious. . . . 'Well, it's new,
isn't it?'

'But what does HF/DF *do*?' I thought this question of mine was a very clever ploy; it switched the ball right back into his court, putting him in danger of betraying himself. Jim and I could certainly take care of this.

'I'm not an expert,' the stranger countered. 'I leave that to you chaps. Some sort of direction-finding, I suppose.'

'Talking of that,' said Jim, 'I really must go and wash my hands. Then we must be off.'

'So early?'

'In point of fact it is late.'

'Come back and have another drink.'

'I would prefer not.'

Jim could be very stiff when he cared to, and this was one occasion. The man reacted:

'Well, you needn't be like that about it!'

Gone was our warm friendship; vanished the easy masculine companionship of the past hour. We were practically declared enemies; this was almost certainly one of the people on the warning posters; tittle-tattle might easily have lost this battle if we had not been so prudent, so vigilant.

'As a matter of fact,' said Jim, 'I don't like your attitude.'

'I don't know what you're talking about! I haven't got an attitude!'

'That's what we don't like.' It was my turn for the brilliant, telling dialogue. 'Confidentially, do you think we're winning the war?'

'How should I know?'

'Ah! Alarm and despondency!'

'If I were you,' said Jim, with enormous emphasis, 'I should be extremely careful in the future.'

We then roared away into the black of night on the Frances-Barnett. Our headlight with its slotted cardboard cover was masked down to nothing: Jim swayed to and fro on the pillion-seat: the red beard and the black streamed in the wind, while the road curved and dipped, and the front forks wobbled like a pair of jellied eels, and God spared us. Shouting above the uproar, we decided that we had been more than a match for that insidious, traitorous swine.

Looking back on it, it seemed likely that the man was either a natural gossip, or a lonely character who actually did know a thing or two about our ships, or else one of our own security officers, trying to find out whether careless talk had infected the Navy, and if so, how deeply. I chose the latter, and I would have dearly loved to have read the transcription.

Though full of patriotic resolve, we did not report the encounter ourselves. Eileen's glazed ham, adorned with hoarded sugar and inherited cloves, was much too good to spoil; and next morning, as on every other next morning, things seemed quite different, as soberly explainable as the sunrise.

There was one special reason why it was so good to be back in Liverpool. The war had, by fantastic chance, brought us all back to our native city, to flog our guts out at a crucial moment in its history: the 'all' being my father, my brother Denys, and myself.

My father, who was now well into his seventieth year, had assumed a dull title (Group Officer, Emergency Medical Service) and an appallingly demanding job: the disposition of all wartime casualties, over a large area, from the first bang to the last dismissal to the grave.

This was at a time when Lancashire, whether from its own air-raids, or from hospital trains from other harder-pressed areas, or hospital ships from thousands of miles away, was at the receiving-end of a steady, mounting tide of sick, broken, half-dead or wholly dead fellow-citizens.

He discharged this task throughout the war, for six years on end, working through the boredom and pettiness of the waiting period, the fearsome casualties of the Liverpool blitz, and the gross seepage of wounded and dying from the new fronts in France, Africa, Italy, the Atlantic, and France again. It was the compassionate crown of a lifetime of looking after the wounds of other people.

I found, on one occasion at least, that he could still find the patience to look after my own.

I had told him, between one convoy and another, how awful I found my absurd appointment as Medical Officer in *Campanula*; how it sickened me, how I hated and feared it, how it was the one thing about the Navy which I was not sure I could stand.

'If it is any comfort to you,' he answered, in a memorable lecture, 'I felt exactly the same way when I was approximately the same age as you—and don't forget, this was my chosen profession, the way I was going to earn my living and spend the rest of my life. I can tell you *now*' (did he think I had suddenly grown up?) 'that the prospect appalled me. The worst moment was here in Liverpool, at the Northern Hospital.

'I was on duty in the casualty department, and my very first job was to be called down to the docks, in the ambulance, to do something about a stevedore who had been caught by a cargo-sling. The hook had gone through his mouth, and come out just below one eye. He was still hanging from it when I got there. I had once seen a fish like that—foul-hooked, we called it—but that was all. . . . Try to remember that these are only bodies, like your own; they are human, they are sad in suffering, but they are *material*.'

He said 'material' in a very special way, as a tailor might say 'cloth', or an artist 'paint'; it was clear that he had come to work unconcernedly with such material; he had touched it, shaped it, used it, liked it, perhaps honoured it; but above all he knew it, and he wanted me to know it too.

'Try to remember,' he said again, 'crude as the idea may seem, that a piece of the human body is like a piece of raw steak. You are not shocked by cutting up a raw steak. Do not be shocked by raw human flesh. Be gentle, be precise, be ruthless if you have to, but do not be sick.'

I was still sick, now and again, but at the worst times I could always think of that cargo-sling, and know that I was not alone.

My brother Denys, in contrast with my father's dedicated life-time, had now achieved, at the age of twenty-seven, the

first worth-while job ever to come his way. Things had gone
wrong for Denys, rather too early on the private road of life.
He had wanted to be a doctor, to my father's delight, but could
not pass even the preliminary examinations; he had left Oxford,
after two years, without a degree, because of those failed
exams, and also because—this was 1933—my father had found
himself very short of money after the catastrophic stock-market
crash, and Denys, unfairly, inevitably, became one item in the
grim process of 'cutting back'.

It was a time of unemployment, which steadily engulfed successive millions of men; a time of hunger and misery, wretchedly
pared-down wages, brazen promises, ebbing achievement, and a
wolfish search for work. It was not the time to pick and choose.

Denys had taken the first job which offered, in a dental
mechanics' factory-office in Nottingham. He lived at home,
which was now near Newark, with Mother and my sister
Felicity; he drove fifteen miles to work every morning, and
fifteen miles back at the end of the dental day; and he must have
regarded the future with an early injection of despair.

The only thing which had gone right was his rugger-playing.
He was a spectacularly good full-back, skilful and cool; and in
this lonely, limelit position he played, first for Nottingham and
then for the combined three-counties team of Nottingham-
Lincoln-Derby. But the trouble with being a rugger-player was
the trouble I had noticed when I worked in Nottingham myself;
it was off the field, it was the gang of beefy, beer-swilling clods
who became his natural companions, and with whom, when play
was over, he thronged the Black Boy bar and dutifully knocked
back the noggins.

He was a sensitive and disappointed young man; neither
aspect of Rugby football, however well he played or however
many pints he swallowed, could have made up for the stalemate
and the bleak future. From all this, glorious war had rescued
him, as it rescued a melancholy and shameful proportion of
young men caught in the same trap, the gross human swindle
which was the fag-end of the Thirties.

He had joined up straight away, enlisting as a private in the Royal Artillery; as with my father, twenty-five years earlier, he was that sort of young man. The dead-end job, the lapse of promise, might have had something to do with it; but I think he could claim to have seen the thing more closely and urgently than I did, from the very beginning.

As I clung to the rags of pacifism, and fooled around as the man in charge of a stretcher-party depot which was not to be put to the test until a year later, Denys was already sweating away in khaki, and learning a really effective, professional job.

We had only met once, during that suspended period, when we foregathered in Nottingham for Felicity's wedding to a solicitor, Hilary Armstrong, who was also a newly-minted soldier. Denys looked tough and competent, with, already, a Lance-Bombardier's stripe on his sleeve; technically I out-ranked him, in the foreboding black uniform of a St John Ambulance Brigade sergeant.

When we greeted each other, he noticed that I carried a steel helmet, which he himself still lacked.

'We can't get those things for love or money,' he protested. 'Why on earth do they issue them to you chaps?'

'But,' I said reproachfully, 'I might have to go out in a blitz.'

He blinked, and said: 'How perfectly horrid for you.'

He was a gunner in an anti-aircraft battery.

His own marriage soon afterwards, to a girl called Meryl Wardle on whom he had been concentrating ever since he returned to Nottingham, took place when I had just joined the Navy, and was totally dedicated to the task of learning to salute.

But I saw the wedding photographs; everyone looked very cheerful, and Denys's sergeant's stripes were well to the fore. By the time we met again, he had risen another important peg; the single pip on his shoulder proclaimed him a Second Lieutenant, and it was the A.A. job which had brought him to Liverpool, in charge of a battery which was part of the port defences. I was part of the port itself, as was my father, and we were very glad to have him there.

When *Campanula* was in harbour, he used to come over to Gateacre on a large and brutal-looking khaki motor-cycle which made mine look like a half-starved chihuahua, and there, while Eileen cooked the dinner and Meryl helped her, we relaxed, and compared our brave deeds, and, the present being so uncomfortable and the future so doubtful, talked mostly of the past.

It seemed then more likely that I would be killed before he was; and once, when we said goodbye on my sailing day, he used a foolish phrase: 'Don't forget to sell your body dearly!' to acknowledge the fact. This was the closest we had ever been to each other, after the brotherly fights and feuds of the past; and it came at the most welcome moment of our joint lives.

I suppose he could picture me on the bridge of *Campanula*, when the darkness was suddenly split by flames; and I could certainly picture him on his frosty gunsite—the up-turned face, the eyes watching the sky, the ears straining, and at his side the pointed fingers of the gun-barrels, also probing a black roof which might at any moment let loose the hurtling splinters of war.

I once said that this waiting for the heavens to fall couldn't be much of a job. He answered: 'Oh, I don't know. It's better than a poke in the eye with a burnt stick.'

I decided that he must have been mixing with Australians.

There we all were, anyway, united in this hazard; the surgeon (the real surgeon), the sailor, and the gunner, all doing our best for King and Country and above all for Liverpool. But were we winning? It was, as we got deeper into 1941, very hard to tell. As the spy had protested in the Adelphi bar, how was I to know? How was anyone?

Certainly there were nuggets of good news. The pongoes, as we called them, were always bashing away in North Africa, where the desert war continued in a strange ebb-and-flow which kept enthusiasts for sticking pins into maps phenomenally busy. We had captured a sort of joke-town called Sidi Barrani, and another called Bardia on the Libyan-Egyptian border; we had gone on to capture (or was it recapture?) a town called Tobruk, a much-disputed prize which General Wavell had now wrested from Marshal Graziani, with a surrendered garrison of 100,000 Italian prisoners.

'Some of them,' a friend of mine on the spot reported, 'were the most depressed-looking little sods you ever saw, with sweaty green uniforms and crinkly cardboard jackboots and drooping cocks' feathers on top of their helmets. They were all about five feet tall, including the dust. They said they were called the Wolves of the South.'

We had won a spectacular naval victory near Cape Matapan, off the southern tip of Greece, where Admiral A. B. Cunningham, in command of three warships which were actually veterans of the Battle of Jutland (1916), the *Warspite*, *Valiant*, and *Barham*, had stalked, cornered, and demolished a luckless Italian force of thirteen ships, including four 10,000-ton cruisers and three destroyers.

It was, we were presently told, the first use of radar in gunnery. Radar was then known as radio-location or R.D.F. (radio direction finding), 'A system of rays, which are unaffected by fog and darkness, sent out far beyond the limit of our shores.' Its inventor, however, indubitably belonged to our shores—Mr Robert Alexander Watson-Watt of Brechin, Angus.

Putting two and two together, we decided before very long that the famous R.A.F. fighter pilot, nicknamed Cat's-Eyes Cunningham, who could shoot down German planes because he could see in the dark, owed this gift to radar rather than to the six raw carrots which, according to the current fable, he always munched before he took off.

But would small escort-ships ever get this R.D.F.? Think of the difference it would make in station-keeping, in convoy, in spotting surfaced U-boats. . . . It was rumoured that one or two of our destroyers had already been blessed. Would corvettes ever get it?

'*Corvettes?*' our captain pronounced, in scornful dismissal. 'We're sucking on the hind tit!'

But however we were placed at the udder of invention, we were at least getting some substantial nourishment from elsewhere. America was now sending us enormous amounts of war material, under the all-embracing title of Lend-Lease; and there was tremendous pressure within the United States to see that the stuff arrived safely, instead of being sunk or blown up on its journey across the Atlantic.

Henry Stimson, their Secretary of War, had declared: 'The American Navy must safeguard our arms shipments to England. We cannot permit these sinkings;' and, by a generous interpretation of the word 'neutrality', they were already operating Neutrality Patrols 2,000 miles out into the Atlantic, which was more than half-way over. Presently they were escorting their convoys all the way to Iceland, at which point we took over; and one of the first friends we met, and talked to, in this exchange system was a U.S. destroyer called the *Reuben James*, which was itself the first U.S. warship to be torpedoed on this generous mission.

While a gifted namesake, Myra Hess the pianist, was initiating the National Gallery lunchtime concerts, one of the prime, intimate blessings of the war, Rudolf Hess, Hitler's own Deputy Führer, took off on a strange flying mission which, starting at Augsburg near Munich, ended when he baled out in southern Scotland.

On arrival, he said that he was on his way to visit the Duke of Hamilton, 'who would conduct him to King George,' with a view to arranging a peace settlement. The Nazis, more factual, said that he was suffering from hallucinations and had been forbidden to fly. On balance, this very odd escapade was one to us.

Another one to us, much more certain, was the death of Lieutenant-Commander Gunther Prien, probably Germany's top U-boat commander. In October 1939 he had brought off the most spectacular and daring *coup* of the war, by penetrating the intricate system of defence-nets and guard-ships at Scapa Flow, negotiating the sunken wrecks and the vicious rip-tides of that part of the world, and sinking the battleship *Royal Oak*, with the loss of 833 men.

At anchor inside Scapa Flow, *Royal Oak* had been a sitting duck. But only a brave and skilful man could have got such a prize within his sights, fired four torpedoes at it, stopped to reload, and fired three more. Prien, in U.47, had now been sunk by our own comrade, the destroyer *Wolverine*.

At the other end of the scale, the ex-Kaiser Wilhelm II, who (at least in our history books) had started all this bloody nonsense, died at the age of eighty-two. A genuine German spy who parachuted down with a lot of expensive spying equipment, plus an identity card, ration-book, clothing coupon book, plenty of money, and a supply of wedding-rings (it was difficult to determine his primary target) was caught, sentenced to death and shot in the Tower of London. Six others had previously been hanged.

Then there was news which was good and bad mixed. We sank the German battleship *Bismarck*, brand-new and hugely powerful (45,000 tons), after a tremendous sea chase which spanned the Atlantic from the north-west corner of Iceland to the latitude of Brittany. But it cost us another of our own prized warriors, the twenty-five-year-old battleship *Hood*, very early in the action.

H.M.S. *Hood*, first hit at an extreme range of about twelve miles, was finally and swiftly dispatched by what must truly be called a lucky hit, though certainly aided by prime naval gunnery. She blew up, in total destruction, when struck in a single vulnerable spot at a range of over seven miles One fateful 15-inch shell from the *Bismarck*, forged in an evil hour, apparently bounced off her fore-deck and went down an open magazine hatch.

This was the gambling equivalent of hitting Zero at the roulette table, not within the confines of the wheel itself but from across Trafalgar Square. The fearful stroke needed no further advertisement save its casualty list, starkly set out at 1,416 missing, presumed killed. The sole survivors of her huge ship's company were three: a midshipman and two ratings.

Then there was one of the biggest surprises of the war, at

least to simple sailors: the cancellation of that cynical pact of
eternal friendship between Germany and Russia, by the most
effective means available—a massive German attack across a
1,800-mile front which advanced like a swift steel arrow to
within eighty miles of Moscow. It was nice to see our enemies
falling out so decisively. But was this good news, or bad?

Certainly we now had millions of brand-new allies, the gallant
lads of the Red Army, who last week had been our sworn foes.
The Germans were now engaged on two fronts simultaneously,
with lengthening lines of communication, which all the military
pundits told us meant instant disaster.

But suppose the military pundits were wrong again? (They
had scored practically 100 per cent in this area so far.) Suppose
the Germans actually rolled up the Russian army, as quickly as
their devouring advance promised? Suppose the bloodthirsty
tyrant of the Kremlin—no, that was wrong, for a start: suppose
the kindly, benevolent heir of the brutal Tsarist regime, Josef
Stalin, collapsed in a heap of blood and snow, leaving the Germans free to concentrate upon us, backed up by all the food and
all the factories in Russia?

Would this somehow mean that Hitler had missed the bus
again?

There was another example of military activity nearer home,
the Case of the Naughty Captain: an excellent *News of the
World* type of story which enlivened our somewhat morbid
breakfast-time reading. The (possibly) under-employed captain
was charged as follows:

'That he recounted improper stories to an A.T.S. corporal;
that he said to a civilian girl clerk that he wished he were
abroad so that he could meet oriental women; that he asked an
A.T.S. telephone operator how she would respond to passionate
kisses; and that he kissed a civilian girl clerk against her will.'

By way of defence, the captain maintained that the whole
thing was a diabolical plot, and that he had once had to
reprimand one of the witnesses because she had adjusted her
stockings in his presence. He was acquitted.

Finally, in this good-bad, light-and-shade area of endeavour, there was the curious affair of Mr Robert Boothby, Member of Parliament for East Aberdeenshire and Parliamentary Secretary to the Ministry of Food. He got into deep trouble over the disposal of certain Czech financial assets in this country: the offence (whether technical or not) being that while working hard to have these unfrozen and released, he did not disclose that he had a direct interest in the matter, which involved some £24,000. In fact, when asked if he had such an interest, he misled the House.

This has always been taken seriously, and Mr Boothby's case was no exception. A Select Committee inquired into his conduct in the matter, and didn't think much of it; and Mr Winston Churchill, moving the adoption of their report in the House of Commons, came rolling out with one of his best pieces of fatherly advice:

'One can only say that there are paths of service open in war-time which are not open in times of peace. Some of these paths may be paths of honour.'

Mr Boothby took the hint, resigning from the Ministry of Food job (though he hung on to his seat in Parliament) and joining the R.A.F. (which was the inspiring part of the story). The path of honour did in fact re-open for him in peace-time, with a knighthood in 1953 and, in 1958, a Life Peerage under the style of Lord Boothby of Buchan and Rattray Head. We happened to know Rattray Head rather well: a murky corner of Scotland not at all liked by sailors.

Then there was what had to be classed as the really bad news, without benefit of happy ending. There seemed to be an awful lot of this, as 1941 unrolled; that April figure of 106 ships lost at sea set the tone for all sorts of other places as well.

While the North African campaign swung to and fro, events in another nearby battle-area, Greece, were only swinging one way, and that was smack in our face. Greece was being steadily overrun by the Germans, and we with it; already we were fighting a rearguard action, described on 30 April in an

ominous phrase as 'a fight to the last inch in Greece'. In fact, we
evacuated our forces two days later.

We then retreated a hundred miles south-east to Crete; and
from *there*, less than a month later, after a twelve-day, very
heavy attack by German parachute troops, we also withdrew,
with a mere handful (15,000) of our surviving soldiers.

The facts were bad enough, even to sailors who also had to
retreat, gathering up whatever they could salvage in the process
and licking their wounds as they steamed away. But what was
disturbing was the sunshine gloss, the pure banana oil which
was still being spread over our wounds, even in the twenty-first
month of the war.

The *clichés* still had the snide ring and the sour smell of
Dunkirk and Norway; and by now, everyone except parlour-
patriots, saloon-bar storm-troopers, and the bright-eyed,
bushy-tailed, nut-secreting squirrels at the Ministry of Information, knew this perfectly well.

Thus the *Daily Telegraph*, commenting on the merciless
bashing we had taken in Greece, sought to comfort us, and to
improve the occasion, with a dose of good old Brand X cough-
syrup, under the heading: A GREAT FEAT:

> 'Remarkable' is a modest word for the long fighting march
> and embarkation which have brought four-fifths of the Empire
> Forces from Greece. The Prime Minister prefers understate-
> ment of good news. . . . To evacuate at least 48,000 of the
> 60,000 British and Dominion troops from Greece is on its
> scale an even finer feat of arms than the Dunkirk conflict.

In any context save a match to see who could whistle
loudest in the dark, this was not a fine feat of arms at all; it was
the tail-end of a thrashing—another thrashing, in a hell of a long
series. The comment recalled one which the same paper had
made when we were slung out of Benghazi: 'In pursuance of the
policy so successfully adopted at Sidi Barrani, of waiting to
choose our own battlefield, we withdrew.'

All the newspapers were now down to six pages, occas onally even to four, which was a single sheet folded. Sometimes even this seemed too generous. Sometimes the realists seemec better company, in this dark hour: Virginia Woolf, for example, who (Afraid of life? Afraid of the desolation of war? Afraid of Virginia Woolf?) drowned herself in lonely death; or P. G. Wodehouse, the funny man who, by way cf easing the *ennui* of internment, was now doing regular broadcasts to America on behalf of German radio, from a comfortable lair in the Aclon Hotel in Berlin.

Yet even the Greek and the Cretan and very soon the North African bad news had its single bright side: that reminder about 'Empire' or 'Dominion' troops. At this desperate hour, they had all come flooding in to help us, sometimes across half the span of the world—Australian and New Zealand fighting soldiers, South African and Rhodesian airmen, the Royal Indian Navy, and cheerful Canadian sailors sculling to and fro in their own corvettes, built on the shores of the St Lawrence River.

They were to fight for us on every ocean, in every navigable sky, on every battlefield from Burma to Normandy. Already they were there when they were wanted, not waiting for a plaintive hail; and they had a solid, heart-warming, two-year start on the Americans, who, in the end, scooped the prestige pool.

I belonged to a party which had consistently derided the whole imperial concept, from the plumed helmets to the white man's burden of sweat, and I had done my fair share of making fun of this improbable structure myself. By now, I was sure that I had been wrong.

It was an emotional conversion, under all the pressures of a hard-fought war, but perhaps the Commonwealth, as it was presently to be labelled, was an emotional concept itself. In cold logic, it did not exist at all, except as a pattern of trading pre- ferences; and these were bargains between merchants rather than ties between friends.

Yet the ties were there, strong as a New Year handshake, at this moment of history: ties of blood, of like thinking, of loyalty to 'our' idea rather than to 'theirs'—theirs being the German, which if it succeeded could bring the curtain down for the longest night of our lives. We needed help, and the help came, not with the sound of dragging feet—nor of dragging chains either—but with a guileless readiness only to be forgotten by the very priests of ingratitude.

Not even those prudent squirrels at the Ministry of Information could fudge or obscure the news about German air-raids, since their bombs were now cascading about our ears with almost continuous loud explosions, and such things got about. This was the beginning of the 'Baedeker Raids', so nicknamed from the old German guidebook founded by Karl Baedeker in 1839, which set out the prime architectural treasures for the tourist to concentrate on.

Baedeker's highest praise was: 'Not to be missed'. Now our tourists were keen-eyed young men in Heinkels and Dorniers and Messerschmidts who, their lofty guidebooks in hand, made the very most of their visits. They hardly missed a thing.

Apart from the obvious, worthwhile ports like Liverpool and Plymouth and Southampton and the Pool of London, there had in fact been a curious concentration of spite upon cathedral cities: Bath, Canterbury, and Norwich were among them. The list of these Baedeker targets in London itself was formidable, by any standard.

They hit Buckingham Palace. They hit the House of Commons, destroying St Stephen's Hall and damaging the Members' Lobby roof. They demolished our treasured Queen's Hall, where Sir Henry Wood and the Proms had taught me all I knew and loved in music. They bombed Westminster Abbey, St James's Palace, the London Museum, Lambeth Palace, the Old Bailey, St Clement Dane's Church, and, spreading their religious favours impartially, the headquarters of the Salvation Army in Victoria Street.

They scored a gruesome hit on the Café de Paris, the glittering night-spot near Leicester Square, so smart and expensive that I had only been there half a dozen times, by courtesy of

Cambridge friends or later patrons who picked up the bill. The single bomb went through the roof and fell smack on to the bandstand, killing almost all the orchestra in mid-tune and a large number of people circling the packed dance floor.

The first thing which the rescue squads and the firemen saw, as their torches poked through the gloom and the smoke and the bloody pit which had lately been the most chic cellar in London, was a frieze of other shadowy men, night-creatures who had scuttled within as soon as the echoes ceased, crouching over any dead or wounded woman, any *soignée* corpse they could find, and ripping off its necklace, or earrings, or brooch rifling its handbag, scooping up its loose change.

It was not the first air-raid looting I had heard of, but for some reason it seemed the worst.

Another sad air-raid casualty was the premises of my new publishers, Cassell's, who had chanced their arm on my first full-length (250,000-word), worthwhile novel. *This is the Schoolroom.** This had taken me nearly two years to write, and had been scheduled for publication four days after war broke out, on 7 September, 1939, when no one was giving much thought to books or to anything else not directly geared to war.

Though they had held it over until October, it still sank without trace, and had earned, by the war's end, in England and America, £164 4s. 7d.

Now Cassell's themselves had almost been sunk without trace. In 1940 their Watford warehouse, containing two million books, had been gutted; now it was the turn of their cherished headquarters, La Belle Sauvage, at the foot of Ludgate Hill and rather too near St Paul's Cathedral. Here they lost all their records, as well as priceless manuscripts and archives incorporating the *memorabilia* of such writers as Charles Dickens, Robert Louis Stevenson, Oscar Wilde, Thomas Hardy, W. E. Henley, and James Barrie.

The sad fact—as related to me by Desmond Flower, then a soldier but later, after his father Sir Newman Flower retired,

---

* *This is the Schoolroom:* Cassell, 1939; Alfred Knopf, Inc., 1940; Pan Books, 1960.

4

the chairman of this phoenix-rising firm—was that Cassell's itself was not even directly hit. Other buildings in La Belle Sauvage were; scourging fires started all round them; since the faithful Thames was at low tide, the firemen could not get any water for their hoses; and the whole precious corner went up like a torch.

Other bombs even scored a hit on the august, venerable British Broadcasting Corporation. They demolished, among other things, a popular weapon of entertainment called the B.B.C. Theatre Organ; giving us, at least, one of the more superior jokes of the war: 'The last thing played on the B.B.C. Theatre Organ was the hose.'

But in the main it was an exhausting and terrifying ordeal, for half the nation at least; hardly to be relieved by promises of retaliation on Berlin, nor by such brief tonics as that cheerful Adelphi wave from Mr Churchill, nor the brave words with which he concluded one of his matchless evening broadcasts:

> And not by eastern windows only,
> When daylight comes, comes in the light;
> In front the sun climbs slow, how slowly,
> But westward, look, the land is bright.

The reference was, of course, to America, which one day, it was hoped, would match her armaments with men and get us out of this hole. But for me the words rang another sort of bell, and when I looked them up, it was my old friend Arthur Hugh Clough again, the Liverpool poet whose plaque on the wall of No. 9 Rodney Street was still unmatched by one on the wall of No. 11, where I was born myself.

Yet the first four lines of that poem, remembered from school, had been:

> Say not the struggle naught availeth,
> The labour and the wounds are vain,
> The enemy faints not, nor faileth,
> And as things have been, things remain.

and these I found much more depressing, because of the doubts
they raised. Who could, with real confidence, say *not* to the
suspicion of futility, at such a moment? Who could really
prophesy that the enemy would suddenly start to faint and fail
—and if so, why?

It sometimes seemed that the labour and the wounds *were*
going to be in vain; that we had started a job which we could
not finish, and that the price of trying would bankrupt us, in
blood and treasure, long before that westward sky brightened
into daylight.

As if to point up this morbid doubt, Liverpool, early in May
and three days after the Churchill broadcast, suffered the most
ferocious punishment of its life, from a week-long series of raids
which altered its pattern and perhaps its spirit for ever.

I recorded it in my notebook, day by day, as it all happened,
because *Campanula* was in harbour, in the heart of the docks,
throughout that fearful week.

Liverpool, the hub of the Western Approaches command,
was a target well worth hitting. There were never less than a
hundred ships in harbour, loading and unloading; plus their
tugs, and the oil-storage tanks, and eleven miles of docks with
their cranes and ammunition barges and ship-repair yards and
warehouses and dock-gates and the whole network of rail-
linkage which bound it to the rest of England. Worth hitting,
it was now hit, with relentless accuracy, for eight nights on end.

The sustained, continuous bombing started huge fires, laid
waste acres of the town, and killed hundreds of people. The
fires, indeed, were one of the principal features; at dusk, each
evening, there were always one or two of them still burning
from the previous night's onslaught, serving as a pointer to the
heart of the city from a hundred miles away.

Waiting on board in the middle of the dock area, the main
target, we cursed those betraying fires, though without much
conviction. We were for it, anyway; there was not much wrong
with German air navigation, if they could hit us so hard in the
total blackout of Day One.

In fact the docks often fared better than the main part of the
town, and especially the crowded slum areas of Bootle and
Wallasey, on either side of the river; but where the corvettes
were berthed, three abreast along the quayside of Albert
Dock, it was certainly bad enough. One night the bonded
warehouse alongside us was set ablaze, and we had to land a fire-
party to help put it out, expecting all the time that the whole
flaming structure, glowing scarlet like a runaway oven, would
crash down on to the upper deck.

Since corvettes weren't built for that sort of thing, we always
warped ourselves out into the middle of the dock after that;
it gave us, at least, an additional twenty yards' margin of
safety.

The waiting, each evening, in the absolute certainty that the
raids would go on for at least another night, was the finest
exercise in patience, nervous control, and the avoidance of
heroics, I had ever had; it also kept the sweat-glands in
admirable trim. We were all nervous, and we all knew it; this
was not our proper element at all: we should have been hundreds
of miles out at sea, on one of those nice safe convoys. Sitting in
the wardroom with a row of monster whiskies and sodas standing at ease in front of us, we did not bother to keep up even a
token conversation.

It was always a relief, though a queasy one, when the sirens
sounded, and we could leave the wardroom, pick up a steel
helmet from the rack in the lobby, and go out on to the upper
deck to man our modest guns, assemble our futile babyish
sand-buckets, and tend the fire hoses. Action was the only cure
for the acute nervous tension which had been gradually tighten-
ing since midday.

Each night had the same crude pattern: after the warning, a
pause, and then the far-off guns, the near ones, the whistle and
crash of falling bombs, the noise of buildings in dissolution, and
men and women in pain, and the ring of fires which gave
us, towards midnight, a daylight horizon all round the dark
compass.

As we waited on the upper deck, wondering sometimes where the last bomb of an approaching stick of five was destined to fall, hearing the steel splinters clatter and clang on nearby ships or on *Campanula* herself, watching the sky with the rapt attention which was our twentieth-century substitute for star-gazing, I thought of Denys, somewhere out on the perimeter defences, and hoped that he was wide-awake and that his shooting would be up to standard. Even if he discouraged *one* enemy plane out of the swarm above us, it bettered our chance of survival, and we could go off to sea again, and be torpedoed.

Campanula herself came nearest to dissolution from a huge land-mine which, floating down by parachute and silhouetted impressively against this bombers' moon, fell into the dock-basin with a gentle splash about twenty yards astern of us. Not knowing what sort of activity could touch this sneaky weapon off—it might be noise, electrical interference, temperature change, a certain pattern of vibration, or the simple lapse of time—we closed down everything we had, from the bilge pumps to the radio set, and, moving on tiptoe and talking in whispers, pulled ourselves out of the neighbourhood with our own strong arms. The mine went off next morning, killing nine men on a barge and blowing away a substantial section of the nearest building.

The Germans dropped a lot of those delayed-action land-mines; after the worst raid, on 6 May, they kept going off all the next morning, as if to assure us that we were not forgotten. I lost count at thirty-three. It was on that morning that I drove through the city on my way to Gateacre, to see if Eileen was all right.

There was no public transport, even if there had been negotiable streets on which to ply; but I had the Frances-Barnett, the only means by which I could have traversed the torn, rubble-strewn acres of the city. As I made my way up from the docks, forced into a dozen slow detours, it was impossible not to feel the poignant contrast between being alive on a lovely May morning, and moving through the newly-ruined

streets of my birth-place, where billowing black smoke fouled
the air, and smuts and wood-ash and charred paper, drifting
on the wind, bore the reek of destruction across the whole
county.

Poor Liverpool. . . . The Overhead Railway (nicknamed the
Dockers' Umbrella), directly hit at James Street station, had
collapsed into the street below, in a tangle of wood and metal,
stone and trailing high-tension wires. From the docks up
to Lime Street and Bold Street, great fires were still burning,
their smoke filming the sun with an orange pall; other buildings
lay sprawled in the roadway, surrounded by their familiar wartime ant-armies—the rescue workers digging and shoring, the
ambulances waiting, the firemen sorting out their tangled
hoses, the onlookers lining the kerb in dull attendance on
disaster.

James Street, Castle Street, it was all the same: buildings
seared and scarred by flame, heaps of rubble which had yesterday been shops and offices: sagging overhead wires, a litter of
splintered glass, crumbling brick, and torn woodwork defiling
every street. A gaping front window in a tobacconist's bore a
brave scrawled notice: 'YES WE ARE BLASTED WELL
OPEN!'

The whole of one side of Lord Street had been destroyed;
further up, near the damaged Adelphi Hotel,* two big stores
were shattered and in flames. The streets which I had known so
well as a boy, the walks which Felicity and Denys and I had
taken, were now in confused ruin; here and there, even in this
familiar and loved town, I did not know where I was, so
complete was the obliteration.

I remembered the iron safety curtain which used to be

---

* Jim Harmsworth had dined at the Adelphi one night earlier in the week, when
the hotel itself was near-missed, a man killed by freak blast on the fourth floor,
and all the lights in the restaurant put out. That was the end of dinner, of service,
and apparently of diners as well. Jim went back next morning, like a good citizen,
to pay his bill. The restaurant manager, against a tawdry background of shattered
glass and boarded windows, shook his head. 'Compliments of the hotel, sir. No
one else in the whole restaurant bothered to pay.'

lowered ('By command of the Lord Chamberlain') between the
acts at the Playhouse Theatre. It had borne an inscription which
had become curiously memorable: 'For Thine Especial Safety.
Hamlet, Act 1, Sc. 2.' Liverpool could have done with that
curtain, between such acts as these.

At some street intersections there were soldiers on point-
duty, directing the traffic and shepherding the wandering, aim-
less crowds. The fact gave rise, later, to the foolish slander that
Liverpool had been so demoralized by its ordeal that soldiers
had been drafted in to keep order and prevent 'mutiny'. This
was nonsense of a wicked kind, shaming a proud record; the
truth was that so many ghoulish fools had driven into town
to see the fun that troops were called on to help the police with
traffic control.

Eileen was all right; we had been equally, and unnecessarily,
anxious. (Yet bombs, dropped a little early, could miss docks,
and hit villages seven miles away; dropped a little late, they
could reverse the process and disqualify the breadwinner.) But
our own village now bore a disconcerting and sometimes pathetic air; thronging the sleepy lanes, brushing past the first dusty
buds of spring, were bombed-out families from the slums of
Bootle and dockland Liverpool, brought out by bus and lorry
and Good Samaritan car and dumped upon us, for both sides to
make what they could of their total upheaval.

The refugees went from door to door, lugging suitcases and
parcels, with staring, grey-faced children in tow; they were
hungry, and very tired, and as desperate to go to the lavatory
as I had ever been in the heyday of my denial, but they were also
strangely undismayed by the violent uprooting. There was no
anger and no bitterness, though these would come later: at the
moment it was just the air-raids, just bloody Hitler—there'd be
another dose that night, for certain, but with luck, out here in the
country, they would miss it.

We did what we could, like everyone else; the school was
opened and turned into a makeshift dormitory; the police-
station, for once in its life, was crammed to the roof. And tea,

the only available balm for history's malice, flowed in rivers, as hot and sweet and comforting as the revenge we might one day enjoy.

On my way back into town I called at my father's office in the Medical Institute, which had been shaken by a near-miss and lacked some windows and a lot of plaster from its ceiling. In the centre of this dusty discomfort, my father was completing the grim balance-sheet of last night's raid. He looked very tired; in fact he looked nearly seventy, for the first time in our joint lives. He had had no proper sleep, and no meals that were not snatched off a desk-corner, for several days and nights.

I learned later that one of his minor problems, a footnote to his profit-and-loss account, was that a bomb, with grisly precision, had hit a warehouse containing his reserve stock of coffins—all two thousand of them.

As I came in he looked up and asked: 'Ship all right?' and when I answered that it was, he said: 'Denys just rang up.' Then he bid me good-bye again, with the kind of brisk authority which still came very easily.

Campanula went down river at last, in the dusk of the eighth day, and we were damned glad to be going with her. At anchor near the Bar Light Vessel, waiting for our convoy, we had a grandstand view of the last heavy raid on the port. Now at last one could feel detached, like a prompter in the wings, with a word-perfect cast, watching from the shadows the progress of the play, enjoying—without having to suffer—the full benefits of stage lighting.

Occasionally a turning German aircraft roared over our heads, shaping up for another run over the target; but all one's attention was for the noise and the astonishing display of fireworks ashore—star-shells, flares floating down like mellow Christmas candles, tracer-bullets from ships, the pin-point flicker of the barrage, the crash of bombs, and the great gouts of flame which followed them.

It was sickening, it was awful. But there was always the ignoble thought—even with my father, my wife, and my brother still there, somewhere under this fiery canopy—which was the identical, ignoble thought of my quarter-deck burials. The dead were lying over *there*. I was still standing *here*.

3.

We were transferred to the Clyde Escort Force—same job, with a different starting-gate—early in the summer, which meant good-bye to Liverpool and all our cherished contacts ashore, and hallo to a city which, for a dozen reasons, I held in less esteem.

The Clyde had engraved some sour memories for me already. It was here that *Campanula* had been born, up an oily creek at Fleming & Ferguson's yard in Renfrew, attended by the ear-splitting midwifery, the iron uproar of hammering, punching, drilling and riveting which went to make a ship.

It was here that, ordered by my draft-chit to report to Admiral Superintending Contract-Built Ships, I solemnized my marriage to the Royal Navy by knocking on the door of a dock-side hut labelled, ambiguously, 'NAVAL OFFICERS KEEP OUT'. The notice had been posted by our first First Lieutenant, an Australian who was to demonstrate, before he left us, a high-grade talent which could have supplied the text for a most saleable book, short-titled *The Hundred Best Ways of Being an Objectionable, Uncouth, Workshy, Snarling Sod.*

It was here that our captain sized me up, wearing the expression I had once seen on the face of a referee just before he disqualified *both* boxers for not trying. It was here that I had saluted Colours at sunset for the very first time, and hoped, against all belief, that the Navy could meet even half-way my enormous pride and pleasure in belonging to it, and my hope of achievement in the future.

The best thing about that part of the world was the approach
4*

to it, particularly after the strife and stress of our job outside. The Firth of Clyde was and is one of the fairest sea-gateways in the world; from the moment we rounded the Mull of Kintyre, chugged past the strange gaunt cone of Ailsa Craig, and set course northwards for Holy Island, and Garroch Head, and the Great and Little Cumbraes, and the blue-grey hills of Rothesay and Hunter's Quay, we were on peaceful passage past a most marvellous coastline, which the sun could turn into a golden riot of bracken and heather, and the clouds to a misty nobility, with lowering patches of black shadow racing across green sheep-pastures.

Coming up the Mersey River, however much one welcomed the landfall, was like plodding up a dirty alleyway leading to the back entrance of an iron-works. Coming up the Clyde was like beginning a sweet-water holiday.

But soon, alas, that fair approach petered out, and we were back in the alleyway again, with muddy shoes and, usually, a clammy wet raincoat as well.

Our home port was now Greenock, a small, unlovely collection of brick and granite terraces, well-run docks, dirty streets, and shops with flyblown cardboard advertisements designed, seemingly, to drive the customer elsewhere at the fastest clip he could manage. For the moment the town had borrowed a certain professional consequence, being dominated by the vast upper-works, the steel elegance, of H.M.S. *Repulse*, which was in dry-dock for a refit before setting sail for eastern seas again.

Further down the coast was another town, Gourock, of the same drab, mean quality, though it had a hotel, the Bay, held in high esteem by rollicking sailors and presided over by a lady whose universal nickname, Two-Ton Tessie, was never a subject of dispute. Such were the delights which awaited us ashore.

But *Campanula* was hardly ever alongside, in any case. The corvette and destroyer anchorage was about a mile off-shore, at the Tail-of-the-Bank, and here we lay in isolation, swinging to our anchor cable, served by supply and liberty boats which, being converted herring drifters built like wooden tanks and crewed by stalwart Scots fishermen who liked to signal their arrival with a good solid thump, were a constant menace to paintwork and plating.

Downstream from us was the vast pool of convoy shipping which was there one night, gone next morning, and replenished with scarcely a half-day's delay as the traffic ebbed and flowed. Among them—another touch of quality—were two French liners now soberly camouflaged for their job of troop-carrying: the graceful *Pasteur*, which had a flaring bow like a very rich man's yacht of the vintage of 1900, and my old friend the *Colombie*, on whose maiden voyage I had sailed from Havre to Bordeaux, *en route* for my hot solo walk over the Pyrenees in happy, innocent 1936.

Between us lay a day-and-night reminder of how irretrievably that innocence had been lost.

This was a wreck-buoy, painted green, flashing green every five seconds—green for the colour of grisly death. It marked the grave of an ill-starred French destroyer, whose mast and funnel still showed above water, whose crew still lay imprisoned within. Her story had been one of the brief, early horrors of the war: an explosion on board had been followed by a fire, and the ship quickly became one vast incandescent torch, fled by a few leaping men, before the sea surged in and snuffed it out for ever.

Now she lay there, as our nearest neighbour, a rusty, weed-washed charnel house; and many times, as we came up river at dusk, looking for our anchorage, and drew near to the green winking eye, I could not help projecting my mind below the surface of the water, and trying to picture the details of the horror below, and what it was our anchor saw as it plunged down and came to muddy rest.

Sometimes the feeling persisted long after we had swung and settled down. 'You are alive,' the green eye accused me, every five seconds. 'We are dead, very dead. We are charred, swollen, abandoned. There are scores of us down here, within a few hundred feet of you.'

At a certain level of tiredness or despair, one could imagine without too much fantasy that Death, waiting for us outside, had left this pale green calling-card, appropriately French, *pour rappeler.*

It was said, by someone who had met a diver ashore, a diver who claimed to have inspected the wreck for the prospects of salvage, that out of one of the portholes there still wallowed and lolled the head and shoulders of a skeleton, trapped for ever in the frenzied act of escape.

Twenty miles away there lay in wait for us a trap of a different sort: the grimy maw of Scotland's pride and joy, the City of Glasgow.

Perhaps it takes a Scotsman to love Glasgow, or even to put up with it; if so, I remain defiantly proud of owning allegiance to Liverpool, and nowhere else. To me Glasgow seemed uncouth, filthy, and complacent, all at the same time; and on Sundays it added a fourth element, a God-fearing pursed-mouth piety which closed the cinemas and pubs and spread an additional layer of gloom over the whole grim city.

Though this, at least, gave the pavements outside a breathing-space after Saturday night's vomit, it meant a dreary Sunday indeed for sailors tempted to explore the dark interior of what the natives called, without a trace of sarcasm, Bonnie Scotland.

Of this mecca they sang: 'When I've had a couple of drinks on a Saturday, Glasgow belongs to me,' before collapsing in a maudlin heap under the nearest railway arch. Of themselves, they hiccuped 'Here's tae us! Wha's like us?'* as they ogled themselves in the saloon bar's happily distorting mirror.

Here, as the rain coursed down the raddled tramlines of Sauchiehall Street, civic patriots roared 'Scotland for aye!' and shouldered aside all lesser mortals.

It has been said that the name Glasgow means 'Dear green place,' and was so christened by St Ninian (*circa* A.D. 40) 'the

* It gains little in translation: 'Here's to us! Who is like us?' The comforting answer: Not too many.

scope and extent of whose work,' according to the encyclopaedia, 'are the subject of much controversy'.

Between convoys, such was my choice of relaxation ashore; Glasgow's brawling crudity (though, to be fair, there was one excellent restaurant with the good old Scottish name of *La Malmaison*): Greenock's pubs or cinemas, and Gourock's Two-Ton Tessie, all to be prefaced by a bracing trip ashore on the open deck of a herring drifter.

I found that, soon, I always stayed on board *Camparula* when we were in harbour, volunteering to take over Officer-of-the-day like some toadying boy scout. Robbed of those delicious quiet evenings at Gateacre, it seemed better to swing round the buoy off the Tail-of-the-Bank, and to opt, like any other deprived pensioner, for the wireless.

Gratitude for relief in hard times should last for ever, and mine has done so. We were wonderfully served by the B B.C. during the war; the imprint of quality and the range of endeavour remained steadfast, even though the prime author of these, Lord Reith, had now relinquished the helm and had been side-tracked into the job of Britain's first Minister of Works, concerned (among other things) with managing the Royal Parks and administering the Ancient Monuments Acts.

But his most recent monument was now doing more for our morale than any system of communication had ever done before.

Like the rest of the crew, I had my special favourites among the radio regulars, and was lucky enough to catch them in generous measure, not only between convoys but sometimes— when harbour-time was over and we were hundreds of miles out to sea—with the aid of the Petty Officer Telegraphist, who could girdle the earth and tune in these magic voices like Ariel himself.

Two of them were visiting Americans, who that year had come over to see what was going on and had stayed to hearten us all. First was the unusually named Raymond Gram Swing, the Mutual Broadcasting commentator whose gravelly voice was possibly the roughest public product since the invention of the cement mixer. His persistent message, designed for

America but also relayed to us, was that we were going through hell but would never give in. This, at certain moments of stress, was a substantial and believable comfort.

His team-mate in this American support-group was Quentin Reynolds, a *Collier's Weekly* man with an even snarlier voice and a nice taste in adjectives. I heard two of his broadcasts, and they were sensational in their sustained invective and their transparent hatred of the two men he was admonishing on our behalf—Führer Adolf Hitler, and the truly odious German propaganda chief, Josef Goebbels.

Adolf Hitler—addressed throughout as Mr Schicklgrüber, which was his original name—was told flatly: 'Your greatest mistake was to wake the dead here in England.' This came after a ferocious series of air-raids on Plymouth and the South Coast, and our honoured dead were Sir Francis Drake and Lord Nelson.

Goebbels—'Herr Doktor' to Quentin Reynolds—was assured that when all this was over, fate would catch up with him and he would be hanged for his manifold crimes against humanity. The prophecy proved false, though unimportantly. Goebbels, at the appropriate moment of retribution, killed his wife and seven children and then committed suicide.

Mr Winston Churchill could also snarl, and he snarled to good effect during all this dispiriting time; his very pro-nunciation of our enemies' detested label as 'Narzies' was enough to raise the national temperature to a hopeful level. He was at his very best in his June 1941 broadcast following the German invasion of Russia, during which, after suitable side-swipes at the evils of communism, he simplified the issue thus:

I see advancing upon all this [the Russian homeland] in hideous onslaught the Nazi war machine, with its clanking, heel-clicking, dandified Prussian officers, its crafty expert agents fresh from the cowing and tying down of a dozen countries. I see also the dull, drilled, docile, brutish masses of the Hun soldiery plodding on like a swarm of crawling locusts. I see the German bombers and fighters in the sky, still smarting from many a British whipping, delighted to find what they believe is an easier and safer prey.

Behind all this glare, behind all this storm I see that small group of villainous men who plan, organize, and launch this cataract of horrors upon mankind.

Last in this sustaining gallery of champions was the novelist J. B. Priestley, whose 'Postscripts' after the 9 p.m. news were, in their content, tempo, and timing, some of the best broadcasting we had ever heard. There was no snarling here: just the bluff Yorkshire accent, highly unfashionable, yet wonderfully persuasive in its humanity, and needing nothing else to touch our hearts.

What he gave us, besides a dose of good cheer for our current woes, was a look into the future, the years ahead for which we were fighting: his vision of a better world—an equitable, hopeful, *Good Companions*, 'Let the People Sing' sort of world— which, though not yet within our grasp, was *there* all the time, waiting for us after our fearful labours were over.

He was criticized at the time for being 'too Left Wing', and it was widely supposed that this was the reason for his being taken off the air by a prudent B.B.C., or a B.B.C. reacting to formidable pressures from above. Priestley was to recall, later, some of the letters he received which made this point clear, and in particular one from the most fundamental (and anonymous) of his critics, which contained nothing but a sheet of used toilet paper.

After these lions and tigers came others less serious, but heartening and healing in the same sort of way. Their very names sound foolish now, as unlikely to raise our spirits or inspire us to fresh endurance as The Scaffold or The Marmalade or Screaming Lord Sutch; but then, they were as much a part of the fabric of morale as the World War I, ever-potent magic of *Chu Chin Chow*.*

* A favourite West End musical comedy which started in August 1916 and ran for 2,238 performances.

Who would suppose that Vera Lynn, with the daunting title of 'The Forces' Sweetheart' (and she really was, by universal acclaim), could move millions of people almost to weeping with such trite lyrics as:

> There'll be bluebirds over
> The white cliffs of Dover,
> Tomorrow—just you wait and see!

which dug even deeper into the tear-ducts with:

> And Johnny can go to sleep
> In his own little room again,

or:

> We'll meet again,
> Don't know where, don't know when,
> But I know we'll meet again
> Some sunny day.

Who would suppose that two mature cross-talk comediennes (the traditional billing was inevitable) called Elsie and Doris Waters could, as 'Gert and Daisy', so establish themselves in our affections as to become an essential part of the weekly listening scene?

Who would suppose that a four-letter emblem, ITMA (standing for 'It's That Man Again'), could excite such affection, such a universal appetite of enjoyment that, every Thursday night at half past eight, all other worlds including Hitler's came to a total halt for it?

ITMA meant Tommy Handley, Liverpool boy turned national institution; and his weekly show gave us all a lift so enormous that it was difficult to exaggerate it. It would have been difficult also to exaggerate the lunatic rubbish of which these programmes were composed; and especially the catch-phrases which we speedily came to know by heart, which would scarcely stand repeating now, but which then excited us to hilarious giggles as soon as they were telegraphed to the audience.

There was Mrs Mopp, the lewd charwoman, ('Can I do you now, sir?') who always had to be signed off with 'T.T.F.N.' ('Ta-Ta For Now!'). There was Colonel Chinstrap the army drunk ('Don't mind if I do.') There was Signor So-So the excitable Italian ('I go—I come back!'), and Sam Fairfechan the wily Welsh introvert; and Funf the Spy ('This is Funf speaking,' and he was speaking into a tumbler to increase his spy potential); and Ali Oop (dirty Egyptian postcards); and Sam Scram the U.S. operator ('Gee, boss!') and Frisby Dyke, afflicted by such a prime case of Liverpool adenoids that the crew of *Campanula* could feel at home, wherever we were.

Undeniably foolish, totally inspiring, ITMA was to run for ten years, and to die only when Tommy Handley himself died in 1949.

Some of these B.B.C. programmes—notably Churchill's and Priestley's—strayed into the realm of 'war aims', though not so seriously or definitely as the later efforts of the Army Bureau of Current Affairs, designed as a morale-booster but by then largely unnecessary. In 1941 it did not seem to matter much why we were fighting, as long as we won; the idea that a man fought better because of some crystal-clear conviction of right— or, to bring it down to the fine detail, that the gun-layer on our four-inch cannon took more trouble with his sights, or I saw to it that my depth-charge primers were more lovingly greased, because we felt ourselves to be the fist of democracy in action, because of our 'ideals'—this was strictly a novelist's conception of stimulus, and one could not go more wildly astray than that.

We were fighting for a whole jumble of reasons, none of them either heroic or inspired. We were fighting because everyone was fighting; it was now the law of the land (I had happened to volunteer, but I would have been conscripted a few months later in any case).* We were fighting because a uniform

---

* In fact I received my call-up papers for the Royal Tank Regiment when I got back from my first convoy. Sadly missed by all at Alamein.

was the current social passport. We were fighting to win because it was clear that the Germans would have our guts for *sauerkraut* if we lost; and somewhere far down the list, because of a certain national pride, long dormant, long derided—the idea that we could beat these buggers if we only hung on: the idea that they had started the whole dreary business, for the second time, and that we, at last thoroughly provoked, would now finish it for them.

But the governing motive was far from reputable. At sea in *Campanula*, we kept a very sharp look-out because we did not want to be killed. After that, the convoy; and after that, the war.

The war took us on three more summer convoys (though the North Atlantic had not yet been notified that it was summer), and then came a real treat: a refit, and the six weeks' lay-off that went with it. Better even than that, we were to go into dry-dock in Liverpool; and best of all, I was now the heir to the latest of a wonderful line of inventions, which, starting with the motor-car, and building up via the aeroplane, the telephone, the radio, the talkies, television, and the contraceptive diaphragm, had now topped off the process with the finest blessing a sailor could hope for—a radar set.

Radar was still such a Most Secret secret that, bound as I was to the blunt end of the ship, I never heard anything about its arrival until I noticed that a curious, round, opaque glass cylinder, like the top third of a lighthouse, had been hoisted up and clipped to our mainmast. It had arrived under heavy guard, I learned via the galley wireless, the rumour-mill which mixed truth and fantasy as skilfully as it turned out our favourite cheesy-hammy-eggy, and had been unpacked in strict security below decks; two scientists *in very dark clothes* had remained closeted with the captain for over an hour while all this was going on.

We were now told what it was, and instructed to return 'evasive replies' if asked about it. The most popular evasion was that our impenetrable new structure would be used for growing fresh tomatoes at sea. Perhaps this would have been a better idea, at least to start with, because it was a long time before we could get this embryo model to work. But presently, with the aid of an entirely new crew member, a Leading Radar Mechanic who was also a demon bridge player, it shed its teething troubles and settled down.

It was to work wonders for us, that precious radar set. It made station-keeping at close quarters a safe and exact science. It found lost convoys, and wandering escorts, and headlands hidden in the murk of a Hebridean summer day. It could pick up channel buoys as we went down river in fog; and ship's boats whose survivors might otherwise have been left to die; and rain-squalls just over the horizon which, an hour later would blot out everything except the vague grey hump which was our own windlass; and off-shore fishing-boats careless of their riding-lights.

Best of all, it could find surfaced U-boats and, with the help of an ingenious plotting device, betray their plans. Though radar would never supplant seamanship and skill and watchful commonsense, yet it aided them all so enormously that we were left wondering how we had ever survived two years of convoy-escort without it.*

But before we could be equipped with this paragon, and bene-fit also from certain other alterations and improvements (some dry-shod wizard of the drawing-board had at last decided to abolish the corvette's principal plague-spot, the well-deck, and allow us actually to make our way from the fo'c's'e to the bridge without being maimed, drenched, or drowned in the process), we had to survive six weeks in a Liverpool dry-dock.

The executive order for this was 'H.M.S. *Campanula* will

* Among the many myths surrounding this magic instrument was one to the effect that close contact with it rendered the operator sterile—a rumour so widespread that it had to be countered by an official pronouncement that there was no ground for any such fears, and that radar operators should be assured that, no matter how long they worked on the set, it could not affect their capacity to have children. Whether this was good news or bad was, even then, a matter of dispute.

basin at 0800 hours' (what on earth had happened to the English
language while we were in Scotland?) In due course we basined;
the vast groaning gates swung shut behind us, divorcing us
from the sea; finger-flipping men in bowler hats spread-eagled
us dead-centre on our enseamed bed as the water-level dropped,
and enormous oily baulks of timber shored us up, to preserve
what was left of our poise.

With the ship dripping dry, we were presently able to walk
down and inspect the prime collection of marine life clinging to
our hull—waving green weeds, crusty barnacles, torpid sea-
snails, tiny crabs, and the doomed wriggling shrimps which were
the most unwilling of all the gifts from the sea; and then
Campanula, the orphan of many a storm, began to lose the name
of action.

Since two out of the three watches had gone on leave, and I
was left in sole charge of the wardroom, the ship would have
been something of an echoing iron cage in any case; with the
boilers blown down (no heating) and the humming generators
silent for the first time in half a year, she seemed somewhat
spooky as well. When, preparing for evening rounds, I walked
out on to the shadowy quarter-deck which had seen so much
mortuary service in recent months, I could not help feeling that
we must surely have collected quite a lot of poor drowned
ghosts already.

Campanula quickly grew derelict, and cold, and uncomfortable; the assistant cook's meals were so terrible that I
knew he must be pining for his peacetime job in the pickle
factory; the necessity of using the dockside lavatory instead of
our own was an awkward nuisance, with undertones of squalor.

At night, the steady drip of water into the great stone grave
below did nothing to lull me into easy sleep. After-dinner
drinking did not help either, though I gave it a good try.

But each morning the ship came alive again, in a way I grew
to dislike even more than the night's loneliness. From 8 a.m.
onwards we were invaded by an army of major and minor
technicians concerned with our refit: riveters, welders, joiners,

plumbers, painters, electricians, carpenters, caulkers: boiler scalers, funnel sweeps, plain crash-and-bangers, tea-maker's mates. . . . They trooped on board in a snuffling, untidy, foot-dragging, shambling throng, and took over the ship; and the ship, lately so disciplined, so taut, so keyed up to its job, began to suffer from it.

Each day *Campanula* became a dirtier shambles; soon she was no longer a ship-of-war in working trim, but a kind of run-down factory hard hit by the depression, and only waiting for the rats to take over. All the decks which we had kept scoured and scrubbed since the day we commissioned became a barnyard of cigarette ends, cartons, crates, wood-shavings, oily rags, slices of metal, strips of welding, bits of wire: bottles, cans, half-eaten sandwiches, and gobs of prime Liverpool sputum.

At first it made me angry, and then sad, and then resigned. The sight of a filthy raincoat dangling from a gun-barrel had, on Day One, seemed scandalous and insulting. Presently it became a natural part of the infected scene, an item of our squalid camouflage. And commonsense told me that a major refit must inevitably turn the place upside down, and propriety with it.

But there was another aspect of the invasion where anger did not ebb away, nor give place to commonsense. Most of these people 'concerned with our refit' were hardly concerned at all. They were not working very hard. Some of them, as far as I could judge, were not working at all. The first time I came on a school of card-players snugged down in the captain's sea-cabin at ten o'clock in the morning, I was furious, and shoved it. I remained furious on all later occasions, but I was officially told not to be, and above all not to 'interfere'.

There might be a strike. . . . It seemed to me entirely grotesque that the strike-weapon, or the threat of it, could still be used in war, but it was so, and we were instructed to live with it.

Yet it remained wildly, disgustingly unfair that, of two men fighting the same war for the same stake of survival, one of them could enjoy home life, and high-grade pay, and still refuse out-right to work unless he was given more, while the other, con-scripted at a wretched wage-level, put into a blue suit, and sent far from home and headlong into danger, could have been shot out of hand if he tried the same tactic.

Our able seamen, working like galley slaves in sub-human conditions, got their keep and four shillings a day. An eighteen-year-old fitter's mate ashore who kicked up a row about his 'conditions of employment' was found to be earning £13 a week. These contrasting oddments multiplied as time went on.

In a debate on 'voluntary absenteeism' in the war factories (we were even disinfecting the language, in the interests of national solidarity), this habitual Monday morning truancy was blamed on 'the application of income tax to the incomes of manual workers'.

Mr Ernest Bevin, the Minister of Labour and National Service, when accused in the House of Commons of having initiated a 'Slacker's Charter' by introducing legislation which forbade certain workers being sacked for any malpractice short of sabotage, fought back stoutly on their behalf. In July, a member of the Boilermakers' & Iron and Steel Shipbuilders' Society (there must have been a whole gang of them on board at that very moment) had been fined £3 by his union's board of discipline for working too hard.

At certain factories suffering from persistent mechanical breakdown, there was said to be a light-hearted variant of one of our patriotic slogans: 'Give us the job and we will finish the tools.'

My own reaction to this discrepancy between dream and event reached a certain personal peak of disgust when one of these visiting potentates, tilting up his welder's mask with an agile thumb, offered me 'all the petrol I liked' for my motor-cycle, without the formality of coupons.

For me, as for all other sailors, a petrol coupon was not a grubby slip of paper; it was a man, an actual mother's son with

frying hair, swimming away from a burning tanker and failing
to make it. It was a life. God damn it, it was *my* life! I felt bound
to tell him, sniffily, that I was all right for petrol.

After that, I stopped being angry, though I could still be
surprised; I stopped thinking that I must be in the wrong job,
and knew, sanctimoniously and proudly, that I was in the right
one. Yet watching all this going on—or not going on; seeing it
at first hand, observing these privileged idlers spinning out
their day's quota and fouling up the whole ship in the process, I
had my first, my very first suspicion, instantly suppressed for
reasons of loyalty and political conviction, that my dead certainty about socialism was not going to prove as certain as all
that.

There was a faint misgiving here, a tiny doubt no bigger than
a man's hand of cards slapped down on *Campanula's* chart-table,
that, given lots of money, life-long security, and guaranteed
social protection, people *perhaps* would come to lean on their
spades a little longer than was necessary, in the course of their
arduous daily toil.

It was to return later.

Across the quay from us, in the twin of our own dry-dock,
was another ship also going through this mill. She was a French
'submarine chaser', about the size of a small destroyer, called
the *Commandant Dominé*, manned by 'Free French' sailors*
who had bravely brought her across Channel at the fall of
France, and were now integrated with our own Navy.

I used to walk over and enjoy their hospitality as often as I
could, firstly because her captain was a delightful man, secondly
because the food was excellent, thirdly because I then had a taste
for *Caporal* cigarettes, and lastly because there was a wine issue

* They were re-christened 'Fighting French' towards the end of this year, at the
suggestion of General de Gaulle, the French leader-in-exile whom we had rescued,
revived, restored to hope and indeed created from nothing. It was thought that the
term 'Free French' had connotations of sexual prowess which, though very likely
true, contributed a certain alarm and despondency among British servicemen.

on board the *Dominé* instead of a rum issue, and bottles of this acceptable brew graced the table at every meal.

I had to explain privately to her captain that, though he was welcome to drink our gin and whisky till France was whole again, I was reluctant to invite him or his wardroom to one of *Campanula*'s meals. (Visions of French naval officers, having lunched exquisitely in their own ship, dining in ours and picking their way through warmed-up soused herring and bread-and-butter pudding, were too shameful to contemplate.) The captain of the *Commandant Dominé* said that he entirely understood— and I was ready to bet he did.

But I often found myself wondering about these polite, good-natured, civilized exiles, even as I enjoyed their hospitality and revived my lagging French. What could it really be like, to be in their place? In spite of naval integration, the *Commandant Dominé* must always be on her own: she was an idea as well as a ship, the golden idea of honour and freedom, the idea of which tarnished France had been robbed, and which these men now maintained in lonely hope.

The ship—and she wasn't really much of a ship, despite the devotion within—was all that was left to them of their native land, taking the place of their homes and families and lost friends: the only world they could now depend on.

Some of them seemed largely adventurous, drawn to this cause by love of excitement, by boredom, perhaps by private betrayal. Others were more serious, more single-minded, and more sad; they were fighting only to get back home again, the home of which they had no news—save of the shameful farce of Vichy France, collaborating France, dishonoured France—for nearly two years.

Others knew, or feared, that when they returned, it would be to nothing. But they still had this ship, and their uniform, and their idea; and they were fiercely jealous of all three, as a man must always be jealous of his very last possessions.

One could only feel envious of such desperate, outcast dedication, even while prudently content to be fighting on home

ground, under a banner of admiralty which had watched over
British sailors since Samuel Pepys decided to codify the rules, in
the hopeful spring of 1672.

I wondered also what, in their urgent spirit, their impatience
to fight back, these Frenchmen must be thinking of Britain's
finest craftsmen, the argumentative bloody-minded rubbish who
were conducting their refit at the pace of clapped-out snails.

Their captain had once told me who the actual Commandant
Dominé was, or had been, but I forgot soon afterwards. Doubt-
less he was a naval hero whom the ship's name honoured, like
Admiral Hipper or Graf Spee, John Paul Jones or Nelson.

But in literal French, Commandant Dominé could readily be
translated as 'the dominated captain', or the captain 'under one's
thumb'. No wonder I was envious.

'H.M.S. *Campanula* will unbasin at 1400 hours' was the word-
ing of our release order; and as I read the signal I remembered
the precise chord which this hideous piece of jargon set a-twang-
ing—the phrase 'Battalion will de-bus, negative haversack
rations' which had sometimes occurred when the Winchester
College Officers' Training Corps embarked on its Field Day.
(The haversack rations—one meat-pie, one corned-beef sandwich, one packet sweet biscuits, choice of apple, orange, or
banana—were not to be picked up until later, so as to thwart
our lust to devour them at 9 a.m. instead of noon.)

H.M.S. *Campanula* duly unbasined. But the melancholy word
enshrined a cleansing process which a sailor could only welcome;
after the six weeks' ministration of our dockyard maties, the sea
at last came to our rescue, and sluiced away the grime of
foreign hands, and baptized us under the honest name of ship
again.

I leant over the quarter-deck guardrail and watched as the
dry-dock crew began to run the bath-water. The incoming tide
sucked and swirled round the baulks of timber which had been
cradling us for so many days; on its way it picked up a horrid
chaplet of wood and rubbish and filth, topped by a grimy slick

of coal-dust and oil, as the level rose and climbed step by step
up the side of the dock. The gangs of men in waders, stationed
far below us, collecting the shores and wedges as they floated
free, soon began to retreat in a widening circle, leaving us to
our own element.

Presently the good salty Mersey water was climbing up our
own side, lapping the fresh paint higher and higher with successive happy tide-marks. One by one our props lurched free, and
drifted off, and were retrieved with eighteen-foot boathooks by
men now reaching out from the edge of the dock.

There was a long hopeful pause, while the whole basin
swirled and filled; then the last timber floated sluggishly up
and away, and became the last prize for the shore-gang; with a
maidenly tremor, not too convincing, and a small stagger to
celebrate her liberty, *Campanula* was released; and thus, on the
next tide, we returned to our war.

4.

I had thought that the punishing March convoy was likely
to be the worst of that war. But I was wrong, and was smartly
proved so, as soon as we had spring-cleaned the ship and rejoined
the Liverpool Escort Force; we now embarked on the most
horrible voyage of all, made especially foul by the fair weather
which blessed us throughout the trip.

This time our run was south to Gibraltar, to calm blue seas
and hot sunshine, and to the longest gauntlet of murder we were
ever likely to encounter.

As with the March beating, there is no temptation to fight
this one again, particularly as we lost it so brutally; but there
were such contrasts, astonishing and appalling, in that convoy
that memory remained infected for ever, and can stand an
airing, if only for pity's sake.

We were routed far westwards, in a great arc which started from our usual North Channel exit and curved out for hundreds of miles into the Atlantic, so as to take us out of bomber range of the French coast. The weather, as the smoky hills of western Ireland faded astern, and we made the latitude of the Bay of Biscay, grew peerless: the sort of 'sunshine cruise' conditions which, even in the mid-thirties, the advertisements had no trouble in selling at a guinea a day.

We were all in good heart, after the long lay-off. We liked our newly-furbished ship; we had the radar to fiddle with; above all, there was this canopy of sky and carpet of calm sea which, after the snuffling gloom of Liverpool, seemed far out on the profit side of paradise. There was a new, sensual pleasure in that southward journey which seemed to take the whole ship away from the war and into the simple warming joys of being alive and afloat.

We passed whales, and basking sharks, and once a lone turtle, paddling manfully westwards towards its first and only landfall—Florida, four thousand miles away. Flying fish were reported; in the dog watches the hands sun-bathed, displaying shameful tattoos and snow-white legs; naked stokers, laid out like half-cooked bullocks on the after-deck, listened to the mouth organ before they told the organist to pack it in, and dozed off again.

On my twelve-to-four afternoon watch, nothing happened, and nothing was wonderful. The water slid past under our keel; station-keeping and zigzag were both as simple as marshalling a toy flotilla on a pond; the convoy kept its shape like the flock of good sheep they were, sheep who trusted their good shepherd; *Campanula*'s mast rocked to and fro across the blue, as gently as a frond of seaweed, through a tiny five-degree arc of movement.

All I had to do was to maintain the zigzag pattern by the clock; to answer 'Very good' as the look-outs changed at the half-hour, and the helmsman was relieved; to keep up the deck-log (our course and speed); and translate the weather pattern into the required officialese: 'Wind light, variable: Sea smooth:

Cloud nil: Corrected barometric pressure in millibars, 1002.'

Sometimes the Coxswain, totally unemployed in such a benevolent world, came up to the bridge to gossip with me. He
would begin with a formal salute, continue with a confederate
grin, and, invariably, fire off one of his awful jokes:

'Did you hear about the sultan's ninth wife, sir?'

'No, Coxswain, I don't think I did.'

'She just got the hang of it.'

'Coxswain. . . .'

But in fact I welcomed the variation; I thought it was going
to be: 'She had it pretty soft,' or 'She got it twice weakly.'

Sometimes there would be a signalman washing out his flags
and pendants in a bucket of suds at the back of the bridge, and
the Coxswain could never resist a comment.

'Eh, Bunts!' 'Bunts' was short for 'bunting-tosser': the Coxswain pronounced it 'Boonts': either way, it sounded agreeably
rude. 'Eh, Bunts! You're making a proper snake's honeymoon
of that lot!' Then he would turn back to me. 'You don't know
whether to laugh or cry, do you? How are we going on, sir?'

'All right. Pretty slow.'

'Slow all right.' He looked across at our drifting convoy, and
astern at our gently furrowing wake. 'Six knots and a Chinaman,
I'd say.'

This was a new one to me. 'What on earth does that mean?'

'Old sailing ship yarn.' He was always glad when I asked a
question, because he always knew the answer. 'Like, there was
this Chinaman streaming the log to find out how fast the ship
was going. He dropped it over the side, and the line ran out too
strong for him, and jerked him overboard. Never saw his little
yellow botty again. The captain says to the mate: "How fast
are we going?" and the mate says: "Six knots and a Chinaman."'

The joke, totally good-humoured, totally heartless, seemed
just right for our own secure voyage.

At night, in my middle watch, I was alone above a sleeping
ship. On the open bridge, in the calm darkness, one could hear

everything: the thresh of a propeller from the nearest merchant-man, the ripple and thrust of our own bow-wave. Sometimes there was even the beat of a seabird's wings, unseen, flailing the water as it fled our advance; sometimes we moved through a bath of phosphorescence, and that bow-wave could actually be seen streaming away into the darkness on either side, joining the rippling pattern of the other bow-waves of all the ships in company, which each had this faint luminous line from stem to stern along her waterline.

Sometimes porpoises played at being submarines in this phosphorescent world, darting towards the ship's side at right-angles, passing underneath our keel in a swirling glow—a glow always good enough for a missed heartbeat, until the April Fool torpedo proved its innocence by circling swiftly and doing it all again.

The sixth dawn came, on this magic voyage; the luck seemed good, the life wonderful. Dawn was never quite included in my middle watch, even at high summer; but I always stayed on, at the back of the bridge, to watch and wait for it, until at fifteen or twenty minutes past four o'clock the longed-for miracle happened. The change was always swift: at one moment the sea was silvery, the sky black, the stars brilliant, and then, when one next looked round, the colours had all turned pale grey—the grey which was the day's first signal.

Campanula's outline took shape with swift decision, along her whole length; the men on the bridge became faces and figures instead of shadows or voices unseen. The duty steward climbed the bridge ladder, to forage for the plates and cups of the middle watch's picnic. It was the best hour of the twenty-four. We were all still alive, and safe, and 168 miles nearer harbour; the barometer was rock-steady, and the sun on its way —and then, even as I turned to go below, one of the new look-outs sang out 'Sound of aircraft, sir!' and within a second or so I had got it myself, and the sick fear that went with it—the steady hateful drone, somewhere out on the pale fringes of the dawn, which meant that we had alien company.

Some finger, prompt and itchy on the trigger, was already pressing the alarm bell, and *Campanula*, lately so sleepily content, jumped into urgent action. My place of duty, instead of snug between the blankets, was now the anti-aircraft gun-turret aft, where there was newly installed a four-barrelled 0·5-inch pom-pom, nicknamed a Chicago Typewriter. (A Chicago Piano had eight barrels.)

The gun's crew of five was there almost as soon as I was: five young men, steel-helmeted, their faces puffy with sleep, the white tops of their sea-boot stockings standing out in the faint light of dawn. We closed up round the gun, and tilted its multiple snout skywards, and waited: watching, listening to the snarling anonymous intruder, peering about as the gaining light gave us more to peer at, for a full hour; and then there was a sharp call on the bridge voice-pipe—'Aircraft, red four-five!'—and we all swung round, to find, far away on the port beam, the author of our harassment.

It was not a true enemy, but a spy—yet the worst spy we could wish to see: one of the Focke-Wulf long-range reconnaissance planes, circling round and round the convoy, far out of range even of a destroyer's guns.

We had been discovered, and beyond doubt reported; and before long the cutting edge of war sliced our brief paradise to bloody rags. The last warning for action was signalled to us, in a disgusting way, that same afternoon: the sighting of some fresh human excrement on the surface of the water, where no honest ship had travelled for many a long day. U-boats. . . . As dusk fell, violence began to split our whole universe.

We lost fourteen merchant ships in the next five days: fourteen of our small stock of twenty-one—a percentage so appalling that the cold print seemed almost worse than the sights and sounds of action. We lost four tankers, and that was 'I can give you all the petrol you like' in full colour. We lost a small cargo-liner called the *Aguila*, which had on board the first draft of Wrens going out to Gibraltar. We lost the rescue-tug which, the previous night, had picked up the last four or five surviving girls.

We lost a Norwegian destroyer, full (like the *Commandant Dominé*) of orphaned exiles far from home. We lost one of our own cherished sisters, a corvette-in-arms for more than a year, H.M.S. *Zinnia*.

Zinnia was commanded by a tall, friendly, capable man called Cuthbertson, whom, as an occasional visitor to our wardroom, I liked very much, if only by reason of contrast; and when I saw her go up in one quick stab of flame, far out on the wing of the convoy, and knew it could only be her, I was saddened and sickened far beyond any ignoble thought that at least it was only them, and not us. What a waste, what a waste. . . . The extent of that waste was made apparent next morning, when as soon as we could be spared we were sent back to pick up the bits.

There were only fifteen men alive: Cuthbertson himself (picked up by another ship) and fourteen wretched members of his crew of ninety, and corpses a-plenty. I was in charge of the scrambling nets aft; it was my pride and privilege to yank from the water half a dozen shipmates of this admired man, this oily, half-dead master mariner, as I found him to be when he came on board at Gibraltar.

He had nothing much to say then except thank you: what man could have had anything to say, who had just lost seventy-five of his crew and a corvette which, turning under full helm, was hit below the boiler-room and broke in half while those left alive on the upper deck were still shocked and staring? I could only tell him that I had looked after his stunned survivors, and buried his dead: those rows of sailors like ourselves, their badges proclaiming their faithful service, their wide-open eyes attesting their last surprise.

Cuthbertson may have forgotten all this quite soon, but, movingly, his mother never did. She must have been, even then, quite an old lady; but when my own son was born she sent a message of congratulation, and for years afterwards, punctually on his birthday, a card arrived, for me as much as for him, sending her best wishes, still saying thank you.

Lieutenant-Commander Cuthbertson occurred later—I made

him occur later—when, like the corvette *Coreopsis* and Commander J. E. Broome, the past drew together in one extraordinary flight of fantasy. But on that day in Gibraltar he was only a shrunken hostage from the sea, one of the witnesses to the last act of this rotten play when, with the tatters of our convoy—our seven remaining ships—we beat our retreat.

Faced with reports of 'U-boats joining', and old and new enemies still waiting astride our route to Gibraltar, we fled the scene. We took what was left of our flock, and led them up the River Tagus towards Lisbon, within the safe neutral prudent waters of Portugal—as bitter an act of surrender as could ever come our way. Then—only a clutch of escorts in line abreast, not a convoy any more—we made all speed for Gibraltar, past Cape St Vincent and other honoured names, to tell our wretched story.

The last entry I made in the deck-log, on my last middle watch, was: 'Cape Trafalgar bearing due east, twenty miles.' We were thus crossing the very shoals where lay all the iron shot of 1805, and the bones of the French 74 *Redoutable*, from whose cross-trees a sharp-shooter had taken aim on an admiral's emblazoned coat; where Nelson, dying, yet hearing with a sailor's faithful ear the surf growling under *Victory*'s lee, had given his last recorded order: 'Anchor, Hardy! Do you anchor!'

But that had been *Victory*, victory.

We were barely past the Straits of Gibraltar, with Spain on the port hand, Morocco on the starboard, the scorched smell of Africa in between, and a distant view of the Rock to lure us homewards, when we were told to turn round again and start a two-day 'anti-submarine sweep' through the waters of our defeat: perhaps to teach us the virtues of discipline and fortitude, or to recall a long-ago signal: 'England confides that every man will do his duty,' or to drive home the disgrace of still being afloat.

We felt we knew enough of all these things already.

It must be admitted that most of us were a little cracked, in all senses, by the time we were finally released: by the time our last landfall, the lighthouse on Europa Point, blinked and gave in to the sun, and we made harbour. It had all gone on too long; we had been nearly a week at action stations, missing meals, missing sleep, with nothing to show in return save a shameful tally of lost ships climbing past the 60 per cent mark.

Indeed, we had done nothing more martial than to kill, with a depth-charge, some diving seabirds which, with wings outstretched, bowed to us, flat upon the water, as we passed. Yet Gibraltar proved a healing balm, in a way I would never have thought possible.

There was literally nothing to worry about here, except keeping a look-out for Italian midget submarines which were rumoured to be trying to break into the harbour. There was nothing much to do, especially since the official mail had not caught up with me, and could not do so. The sun shone all the time; we wore the Navy's tropical kit—white bush-jackets and shorts, white stockings and shoes—which was itself a tonic, though white shorts topped by a bushy black beard must really have looked very odd.

With Jim Harmsworth for agreeable company, I swam in what truly seemed a rich man's playground, Rosia Bay, not quite shadowed by the Rock, in the warm Mediterranean water which really could caress an exhausted body. We travelled round the town by gharry, a light, springy, slightly crazy four-wheeled cab topped by a linen awning. There was no black-out. We took our *apéritif*—Tio Pepe sherry—on a balcony overlooking Main Street, crammed with the eddying to-and-fro of the evening parade. We dined *à l'espagnole* off onion soup and *paella* and dripping melon and roughish Algerian wine, while at our back the bristling honeycombed fortress of the Rock stood guard, and seemed by its very name to restore our honour.

Gradually the war faded from this blessed scene. We could not quite forget *Zinnia*, but we began to forget all the rest. We could even recall, with laughter instead of embarrassment, an

5

answer which our captain had sent to another corvette whose signal he had not understood. It had been: 'Snow again. I don't catch your drift.'

Then, we had all felt very ashamed. Now—and certainly by the time we reached the brandy stage, out on that suspended, honey-coloured stone balcony again—we could agree that certain of the minor horrors of war were minor indeed.

Campanula was berthed in the very shadow of *Ark Royal*, the huge towering aircraft-carrier which was the target of two angry air forces, German and Italian, as long as she was in harbour, as well as of U-boat spite whenever she put to sea. It must have been strange to serve in such a notorious 'hunted ship', but it seemed that her crew were inclined to relish their notoriety, as an extra source of pride.

They used to listen to Radio Hamburg, and especially to William Joyce (hanged for treason, 1946) who, like John Amery (hanged for treason, 1946) earned his luxury brand of daily bread by making regular broadcasts urging his British compatriots to give up the fight before it was too late. William Joyce, whose curious, fake upper-class accent had earned him the nickname of Lord Haw-Haw, specialized in announcing bad news about our convoys; in a rasping raven croak, instantly recognizable from the moment he said 'Chairmany calling!', he took such sour and savage delight in our losses that he positively rolled the tonnage-figures off his tongue.

When he mouthed the phrase 'Gross registered tons' he could actually make it sound lustful, as if part of a perverted appetite for dead and dying ships.

Latterly he had taken to asking, over and over again, on a menacing snarl: 'Where is the *Ark Royal*?' and in the *Ark Royal*'s messdecks they took an answering delight in roaring back: 'HERE!'

In fact, William Joyce must have known very well where the *Ark Royal* was; or, if he did not, some little man just down the corridor could certainly have told him. For we knew all the time that Gibraltar was totally open to the spying eyes of the enemy; across the bay in Algeciras, five short miles away, the complacent Spaniards, our coward foes, had allowed German agents in the guise of diplomats to set up batteries of high-powered telescopes which kept a round-the-clock surveillance of all shipping entering or leaving the harbour.

The Spaniards prayed devoutly for our defeat and, as far as they dared, worked for it. We knew that we had no friends at all in this part of the world, save for Fortress Malta down the street. Here the Rock was everything, and fortunately it was more than enough.

The war—the real war—did come back to us for one poisonous half-day, when the cruiser *Manchester* docked to dis-charge her cargo. Her cargo was human, or, by then, something less; they were the week-old, oil-and-water-marinated corpses of thirty-eight of her crew, trapped below decks when she was hit by a torpedo, and necessarily left to their wallowing, sealed-up grave until she could make harbour.

Opened up, *Manchester* stank like an abattoir where the power had failed and the staff had walked out in despair. She was berthed just astern of us, and through the windscoops fixed outside our portholes, designed to catch any air that moved, we caught an air so infected that we were forced to seal everything up again.

Later that morning, the liquid dead were trundled past us on push-carts, manhandled by ratings who wore masks tied across their nose and mouth, and transferred to another corvette for burial at sea.

A notch or two of seniority saved us from this horrible task, which fell, thank God, to the 'canteen boat', the junior corvette which was always landed with the overload of odd jobs cropping up from time to time. She could not have had a worse assign-ment than this.

It took nearly eight hours to load her quarterdeck with these putrid bundles, which had to be sprayed down at intervals to make their company even bearable. Then she left harbour at dusk, with her leaking burden, and when she came back next morning, she was still stinking to high blue heaven, and so remained until we sailed again.

We were losing too many sailors.

5.

We were losing too many everything.

The Americans, stung to action by that 'day of infamy' at Pearl Harbor, when most of their Far East fleet was destroyed, and more than two thousand men killed, by the century's most treacherous stroke of war, joined us at last; a gain to our side of incalculable proportions, a lowering of the average time it took them to spring to arms, in two world wars, to two and a half years; and an end to a ribald song which had lately been going the rounds (to the tune of 'Let's Go Out to the Ball-game'):

> There'll be lots of banquets and parties,
> Lots of parties and balls:
> As President Roosevelt has said before,
> That's the way to stay out of the war:
> There'll be lots of banquets and parties,
> Lots of parties and balls:
> There'll be banquets and parties and parties and banquets
> And balls, balls, BALLS!

But apart from that turn of fortune, 1941 closed with a cataract of bad news: unbelievably bad, crowning a disastrous year. It came thudding down, in successive blows which tumbled all our hopes and seemed to be tumbling all the world as well. Things were all over the place in North Africa. Malta was being first strangled and then crucified. The whole of the Far East was going up in flames—other people's flames. In November, a single torpedo took the *Ark Royal*; and at last we could tell Lord Haw-Haw where she was—only twenty-five miles from Gibraltar, but forty fathoms down. We lost, in quick succession, seven other big warships.

For sailors, the darkest hour (apart from the 371 Allied merchant ships sunk in three winter months) was the demolishing of two great capital ships, the *Prince of Wales* and our Greenock friend the *Repulse*, in one single Japanese air-strike. But this was topped, for all of us, by the loss of Singapore six weeks later, with 95,000 prisoners taken during the brief campaign—the worst capitulation of British arms in British history.

Guns pointing the wrong way! Christ, wouldn't you know it! And now they were calling such antics 'battle fatigue . . . . It seemed, unjustly, a typical soldiers' balls-up, only to be expected from what we had come to call, with savage, selfish derision, the Gabardine Swine.*

But as well as blaming the bloody pongoes, we were now looking round for other scapegoats—anyone but ourselves, in fact; and in the process we were beginning to fix the blame, with equal lack of charity, on another identifiable sector of British life, the bloody Conservatives. Our successive misfortunes and retreats now seemed, to a great many people, to be Chamberlain's fault, and before him Baldwin's, and the fault of the droves of beefy company directors, the right-royal fat-heads who had passed for Conservative M.P.s in the corrupted Thirties.

They had got us into all this mess. . . . Churchill's massive defeat at the polls in 1945, and everything that followed in its train, was, unfairly, inevitably, being forged now.

Campanula ran eleven convoys that year: two of them awful, two featureless,† and the rest so-so, yawing between bad and

---

* The R.A.F. were, more affectionately, Intrepid Birdmen. We our elves were Blue Jobs.

† We missed one with a unique feature of its own. When the Canadian corvette *Chambly* rammed a U-boat, its captain jumped out of his conning-tower and landed on the deck of the corvette, leaving his crew to sort things out for themselves. His rank, appropriate to the very last moment, was Korvetten-Kapitän.

not too terrible. But at the end I was still alive, though occasionally astonished by the fact—and home for Christmas!

At that season ('That season . . . so hallowed and so gracious . . . wherein our Saviour's birth is celebrated') there was indeed much that was moving, for all sorts of reasons. We still found things to be happy about. My father was less vilely overworked; Denys and Meryl were with us; and an American friend, who could scarcely have imagined what fantastic largesse he was sending our way, slipped me a tinned package-deal consisting of a boned turkey, a segment of sage-and-onion stuffing, and a little tube of cranberry sauce to pour on top. Such riches. . . .

At that season, in the oak-panelled bar of the Black Bull Hotel at Gateacre, I said good-bye to Denys, destined by my guess for a landing in North Africa; and that was the last I saw of my friend and brother. At that season my son Max was, by inference, conceived. But Hong Kong, almost our last bastion in the tormented Far East, fell on Christmas Day; and on the cold morrow I went back to sea.

SIX

LET'S BEAT IT
(1946)

1.

Though the first year of peace started with the longest
New Year Honours List ever issued (six viscounts, seven
barons, 119 knights, plus the only worthwhile award, the
Order of Merit, to commend and console Mr Winston
Churchill), yet gloom hung over us, as thick as the fog itself
which, together with ice-bound roads, had affected 13,000
square miles of Britain. London was awful, like the rest of the
country: a dull drab dreary mess of raincoats and head-scarves,
shabby clothes, filthy weather, eternal queueing, balloon-cloth
shopping bags, half-empty shops and foul tempers.

Suddenly, it seemed, there wasn't any Britain any more, so
brave and enduring and united for six long years. Such
generous comradeship had died with victory, or had choked on
it. Now there were just a lot of people snapping and snarling at
each other, waiting and hoping for what never came, stealing
and cheating to try to beat the game—but all in slow motion
because, like me, they were all dog-tired.

Caught in a clamp of natural misfortune, of record gales and
storms, of snow, rain, hail, and flood which never ceased to
plague us, we were short of everything which might have made
the punishment tolerable. Houses and flats were stone cold, factories were dim and draughty, shops were lit by candles,
because there wasn't enough coal, coke, or anthracite—the output continued to drop owing to that euphemism which was now
a permanent factor on the industrial scene 'voluntary absenteeism'. London coal merchants never had more than an average of
one week's supply in hand. Not even the Bevin Boys—young
men who opted to work in the mines instead of doing two years'
military service—could improve our lot

There wasn't enough electricity, for the same reason. Power cuts came unannounced, just when one needed the stuff; heaters faded to a pale nothing, stoves cooled at noon or 6 p.m., meals were ruined. Shops were not allowed to leave any lights burning at night in the front of the window; that would be advertising, a wasteful crime.

Naturally there wasn't enough gas, which was always 'under low pressure', even though troops were often called in to help with the gas-holders. Petrol was still severely rationed. Pubs ran out of beer long before closing time. Even trains ran out of railway lines—three rail crashes in a single week indicated that a large number of locomotives and wagons were breaking down, and that repairs or replacements were long overdue.

You couldn't get anything else repaired, either; electricians, plumbers, and carpenters seemed to be holed up in some haughty limbo of non-availability. There were either 'no spare parts', or 'no labour', or 'no time'. The dreary excuse, 'Don't you know there's a war on?' had been supplanted by a simple variant: 'It's the war, you know.' Strikes multiplied, particularly in the car industry, vital to our export life and grimly needed at home; Ford's had an 'unofficial sit-down' (a new expression) involving 10,000 men, and had to close its factory at Dagenham, while on the same day 4,000 men walked off the job at Humber's in Coventry, and another 1,000 at the Austin works at Longbridge.

There were 'spivs' all over London, sharp fellows with padded shoulders to their overcoats, and wide-brimmed hats, and black suede shoes: stationed at every street corner, they flogged unheard-of luxuries such as nylons and elastic and petrol (12s. 6d. a gallon, take it or leave it). A Conservative M.P. of some naïveté complained that when he walked down Oxford Street he had seen a street vendor 'selling combs at *seven times* the controlled price!' (Sensation in the House.)

No wonder the 'war brides' had taken wing and left us.

These were the girls who had married United States servicemen, and were now being shipped to America in 'war bride liners' to rejoin their husbands. But if the destination was America the rules on board were British indeed There was a total ban on fraternization between the girls and the sailors who made up the crew during the voyage. However, the latter were told, grudgingly: 'If you are approached by a passenger and asked a question, you may make a formal reply.'

But at least these bonded charmers were voyaging towards a new world. We were stuck with the dejected Old. Victory, in fact, had for the supposed winners already turned sour

Though the carnivorous sheep who were the Germans had been led to their own slaughter; though France had been rescued and General de Gaulle safely installed in Paris (but what did the chap really want?—he had just resigned from the presidency in a lofty huff, declaring that he had had enough of this nonsense and was retiring from politics for ever); though the Japanese had been taken out of the match in two moves, two swift atomic strokes at Hiroshima and Nagasaki—though all these good things had come our way, there didn't seem to be any profit from them.

To begin with, we were not the glamorous conquerors, galloping to the rescue of an enslaved continent—that was the Yanks. Britain was the limping partner, worn to shreds and demonstrably broke. There wasn't any money in the till, and we could measure our war-debts by the ton.* There wasn't anything to buy, even if one had the money. There wasn't any *spirit* left—we were walking about like the ghosts of Christmas Past, pale as soap, feeble and spindly as day-old pups.

---

* We had, in addition, squandered nearly all our dollar assets when, at certain crucial moments between 1940 and 1942, we had to buy ourselves a breathing-space at any price. Among these, we had sold our vast holding in Courtaulds, the international textile firm, for a modest dollar credit, only to see these shares resold at a prime profit within a few months. We had also granted 99-year leases on naval and air bases in Newfoundland, Bermuda, Bahamas, Jamaica, Antigua, St Lucia, Trinidad, and British Guiana, in exchange for fifty antiquated, dead-beat destroyers which we had to have, in order to fill the gaps in our escort-screen: which proved entirely useless in service, and which I had myself seen achieve a sixty-degree roll before they shipped water down two of their four funnels and were towed home for repairs. In war, many hard bargains are struck. This was probably the hardest.

5*

Indeed, there weren't even any ex-enemies left; it seemed that we hadn't beaten any determined foes, only a lot of misunderstood people who had really wanted to be friends.

Certainly there weren't any Nazis (would you mind spelling it?): just some jolly, middle-of-the-road democrats who had never cared for Hitler and hadn't known a thing about extermination camps for the Jews. There weren't any little yellow animals beating their captives to death: just smiling sons of Nippon bowing and scraping before General MacArthur. The argument about the atom bomb was still raging; and the percentage of people who maintained that we ought to be ashamed of ourselves for dropping it mounted all the time.

For myself, I had no doubts then, and have never had any since. One had to weigh against each other those two monstrous strokes of surprise: the careless murder at Hiroshima against the iron hatchet-blow at Pearl Harbor. Both hideous, both vile, they could hardly be separated in violence or cruelty, only in motive. But Pearl Harbor, a great crime, and the more sustained obscenities of Japanese treatment of their prisoners on the Burma Road and elsewhere,* were part of a calculated effort to conquer, to terrorize, and to enslave. Hiroshima was retribution, and a quick end to the war as well.

If the Japanese, briefly and locally lords of creation, were now a lickspittle lot again, I did not care how the benign process had come about, as long as it had.

The idea that these horrific bombs had been dropped because the Japanese were 'only Asians' was a late-flowering weed of dialogue, when consciences then unborn emerged as tender as new-hatched tits. One could as well have argued that 'only Asians' would kill 2,000 men in a surprise dawn attack, using soft smiles for camouflage and the best weapons then available for teeth.

However, this was no more than war talk, and I was sick of

---

* When the Japanese overran certain villages in Sarawak, they killed all the adults and then sent the children up to roost in the trees. Then they shot these small game-birds down, one by one.

that already; especially when I heard it in a certain ex-officers' club, where it seemed that the drone of reminiscence was only just building up an agreeable head of steam. This old-boy, dated drivel was to continue for at least fifteen years; apart from selling each other life insurance, it seemed for most members the only topic on which they felt at ease.

Already, whenever I heard 'Do you remember that time. . .?' I felt my cringing-gear creep into operation. All I could personally contemplate was the fearful cost of my slice of the war, my own Atlantic corner, which the actuaries had now calculated at 3,000 ships sunk, and 30,000 sailors blown to bits or drowned.

To balance that, 780 U-boats had been sunk. But even this huge total could not restore anything. It could not, for example, restore the summer paradise of Trearddur Bay, where the small tally of our private dead left gaps as wide and deep as the Atlantic itself.

By a coincidence which moved me strongly at the time, I had returned briefly to Trearddur Bay, as a sailor, very near the end of the war, when we had almost won the thing (in the conventional sense) and I had at last begun to think I was safe, and to dream a little of a peaceful future without feeling either guilty or stupid.

At the end of another Gibraltar convoy, we had taken a small clutch of ships into Barry Roads, the last harbour on the left before one got to Cardiff; and then we were routed back to Liverpool, independently, by way of the Welsh coast, and Cardigan Bay, and Anglesey, and therefore by way of Trearddur Bay, the beloved seaside village where I had spent every summer of my life from age 0 to age 29.

There was time to spare, and when we had a good fix on South Stack lighthouse I made a circle into the bay itself, where I had spent uncounted hours sailing, and racing, and fishing, and doing nothing, in the blissful summertimes of the twenties and thirties.

I was the boss at last, and I could do this; in fact, if my

frigate decided to take a close look at some inshore lobster-pots, that was exactly what she would do, without any comment from anyone. Barring a new-laid minefield (and who would dare to do that to *my* playground?) there was no hazard here that I had not known for more than twenty years.

But though I had been cherishing the idea, and the moment, ever since we had laid a course to cross Caernarvon Bay, it was desperately sad after all. Trearddur Bay—especially Trearddur Bay by moonlight—had too many ghosts. In fact, it had become a ghost itself.

I saw Ravenspoint first, the 'big house' where the fabulous Grayson family had lived; its vast luminous façade stood out as sharp as print, dominating and dwarfing our own Hafod next door. From the bridge I stared and stared at the small cottage where we had spent such a magic string of summers, where my brother Denys, heavily veiled, had been brought when he was a few weeks old.

No lights showed; there was just the pale face of the house, and the gash of shadow under the roof of the veranda—no, Mother said it was to be called the *loggia*, and the *loggia* it still was. In front, the garden sloped gracefully down towards the sea. It all looked the same, but of course it could not be; Hafod didn't belong to us any more, we would not go there again, and many of our summer callers would no longer be going anywhere.

We made our slow circle into the arm of the bay. There were a few scattered lights, and once a car with masked headlamps topped the rise of Big Bay Hill; but otherwise we moved through a motionless, mourning silence—our curling bow-wave, and the surf breaking inshore, were the only things that stirred.

There was something important missing, and I was searching for it—and it was the windward racing-mark off Porth Diana, which had been taken up at the end of the last sailing season, and never put down again. When, our circle completed, we passed the Commodore's house, and the tall façade of the Cliff Hotel, there was nothing left of Trearddur Bay except the picnic cliffs of Porth-y-Post, and South Stack lighthouse again.

I had forgotten the sailing club boat-house, and when I looked for it we were too far off shore, and I didn't want to go in again. Why should I? Inside it were all our boats, *Clytie* among them, dried out and mouldering away as they had been for five years and more. By the time we got back to Treardour Bay (and that suddenly seemed unlikely) there would be nothing left of them but salty, shabby planking, and turkey-red sails bleached to rotted ribbon.

There would not be much left of some of the owners, either. Too many people had died, between the bright 'then' of 1939 and the doubtful 'now' of the war's end. Peter Munro, who had taught me to sail: Nigel Wood, who had been my all-powerful crew for years, and had *made* me win races: both Lancaster boys, the Vice-Commodore's sons: Beth's brother Bill—these were among the lost ones, lost to the rest of us, lost to Trearddur Bay.

Beth herself, widowed before the war, had been widowed again by Dunkirk, though she had to wait for years, under the shadowy sign 'Missing, Believed Killed', before the last of the returning prisoners killed hope as well, for ever.

Last of all, there was Denys, who had survived that North African landing with the American First Army, and a year of desert warfare, and had been accidentally and foolishly finished off in a jeep accident. For him, burial in Algiers was the nearest he would get to Treardour.

There was still time for me to be killed, too. . . . I had the feeling, as we set course to clear the South Stack headland, that whether that happened, as it had happened to Denys and the others, or whether, by some unfair spin of the wheel, I survived this crude gamble, I would not be coming here again, nor would I want to.

But who, in their senses, would want to come back to peace-time London?—that was now the depressing, dominant thought, as one read the morning paper—on any morning, and in any paper—and digested the latest list of things which had gone wrong or, even more discouragingly, were going to stay exactly as they were.

All the old plagues were with us, without the prick of danger or that warming all-in-the-same-boat feeling to make them seem bearable; and there were other powerful strains of virus, newly dreamed up by doctrinaire authority to keep our noses to the dusty grindstone of 'postwar rehabilitation'.

The Ministry of Food still issued their weekly advertisements, headed 'Food Facts'; and the facts about food were uniformly awful. A top price of five shillings had now been set on all restaurant meals, though this restriction was widely evaded, by such expedients as making a cover charge, or calling each course a separate meal, entitled to its separate bill (you can't help it if a man wants two meals in quick succession, can you?) or charging God-knows-what for the ultimate cup of coffee.

We had, in fact, just begun the long corrupting process of mass-evasion of the rules, of somehow sliding and wriggling round the law, which was to set the pattern of British behaviour for ever afterwards, and turn us into pious cheats instead of people.

That five-shilling restaurant meal was not likely to be particularly palatable, whatever it cost; just as had happened five years earlier, if you arrived late and didn't know the management, or had neglected to make some prior arrangement, the meal was still the basic rissole, or else a solid slice of Spam (I must have over-imported Spam, in the course of my other efforts: the country was now nearly sinking under it) covered with a good imitation of pale chocolate sauce, and lashings of wretched little button mushrooms like luke-warm eyeballs.

If encased in dried-egg batter, this prize was likely to be described as Chop Toad Americaine.

The list of food in short supply was also announced at regular intervals, like the form-sheet of runners and non-runners in the sports pages. In February, the schedule of nearly-unobtainable items was officially given as: tinned soups, cereals, onions, bacon, biscuits, sausages, offal, rabbits, suet, and fish.

We were further warned that the allocation of domestic dried eggs (just try and get a shell egg!) would have to be discontinued because we could not afford to buy them from America. 'But we import thousands of dollars' worth of films from America!' said an angry M.P. 'Why not egg powder?' (No answer.)

We were also warned (we were always being warned, nowadays) that the fat ration would soon have to be reduced, and that owing to a cut in wheat imports we were going back to the wartime loaf (a grey-brown artefact, like superior cardboard). But as usual the Ministry of Food was comforting, though still stern, over this:

'Can you personally do anything to help? Yes! Don't buy any more bread than you can eat. In canteens and restaurants, don't ask for bread unless you intend to eat it. Bread means lives! Don't waste a crumb!'

I tried, and failed, to work out how bread could mean lives, in the ninth month of peace.

In mid-February, Sir Ben Smith, the Minister of Food, charged into the House of Commons with a whole new armload of bad news. There would now be a return to wartime conditions of austerity. There would be a reduction in the ration of butter, margarine, and cooking fats, from 8 oz. a week to 7 oz. Rice could no longer be imported at all; cereals were to be drastically cut. There was no hope of any more bacon, poultry, eggs, or meat (the latter allocation now varied between one shilling and 1s. 4d. per person per week). Stringent soap rationing would continue indefinitely.

But one luxury consignment must have slipped through, before they plugged the dyke against all such threatened indulgence. In the same month, a child aged two years and ten months died after eating, perhaps too fast, four bananas, a fruit she had never in her life seen before.

Clothes rationing and control now seemed to have come into full flower, at a point when one might have expected a gleam of freedom and colour to cheer us all up. Clothing coupons were naturally still with us (just as we were still being exhorted to 'Save Waste Paper!'); and embedded in this structure there was now the new concept of 'Utility'—utility clothes and utility furniture, of standard pattern, sternly dictated quality, and of course controlled price.

But Authority was watching out for us all the time, we could be sure; they offered us every possible crumb of comfort, while still seeing, or trying to see, that no one got away with such a garish concept of liberty as the freedom to pick and choose.

The realm of corsetry, for example, was to be slightly eased. Production of roll-on corsets, which had not been manufactured for four years, was now being resumed. There were absolutely no restrictions on the amount of elastic which could be used, either. But watch those prices, now! The maximum retail price had been fixed at 5s. 6d. for a one-way stretch, 7s. 5d. for a two-way stretch.

Then, in mid-March, came a real break-through, announced, with that wealth of intimate detail which had become common-place in Whitehall, in a series of benevolent directives.

As from now, embroidery and beading would be allowed on women's and maids' outer-wear overcoats, jackets, skirts, dresses and blouses. There would be no restriction on the number of pleats, pockets, or buttons; and fur and velvet trimmings could once again be used on coats. Tucking and smocking would be allowed on infants' and girls' wear. The limitation on pockets and buttons, the restrictions on width, and the ban on belts, were now lifted from men's, youths', and boys' overcoats. Boys' and youths' suits might be double-breasted, and have turn-ups to the trousers, as well as unlimited pockets and buttons. Men's, women's, and children's raincoats and rubber-proofed coats would no longer be restricted as to double-breasts, pockets, buttons, width of skirt, tabs, buckles, or straps.

In the world of footwear, the limitations on the height of the heel, and the ban on sandals, brogues, bootees, and sports shoes would end on *April 1st*. (Exact timing was now very important

In theory

THE WELL-DRESSED NAVAL OFFICER

. . . and in practice

CORVETTE, WITH CHRISTMAS ICING

H.M.S. *CAMPANULA* ON WET GRASS

THEN A SOLDIER
My brother Denys in 1941

GENERAL SMUTS, Prime Minister of South Africa
At the summit of Table Mountain

THE BIG HOLE
Kimberley Diamond Mine

EILEEN AND MAX
At the War's End

THE TABLE MOUNTAIN CLIMBERS
From the top: General Smuts, Patrick Duncan, Morrice James

BEFORE THE STORM
Left to right: N. M.. Seretse Khama, Ruth Khama, Resident Commissioner
W. F. McKenzie, C M.G., C.B.E., at Serowe

INTO EXILE
Seretse Khama and escort waiting for the plane to take him out of Bechuanaland. Commissioner McKenzie on left

THE CRUEL SEA
A *DAILY MAIL* CARTOON BY ILLINGWORTH BORROWS A CATCHY TITLE

AFTER A SHORT DROUGHT
THE RAINS CAME

indeed.) Embroidery, appliqué, tucks, or frilling could be put on women's and maids' underwear, as from *April 5th*, and from *June 1st* double cuffs and unlimited tail-lengths would be in order for men's shirts. We might also have pockets on our pyjamas.

Thus accoutred, after very careful inspection, we faced the constricted present, while the future was being minutely plotted for our delight.

In due course, announced Mr Herbert Morrison, Lord President of the Council, there would be nationalization of the iron and steel industries. (A bill to nationalize the coal industry had already been introduced in the Commons.) Free medical, specialist, hospital, and dental treatment was to be provided for every man, woman, and child, irrespective of means. It would cost the huge sum of £152 million a year, or £3 per head of the population.*

'Can we afford to have it?' a few anti-social doubters asked, perhaps perturbed by the current trade figures, which showed that in a sample month Britain had exported 32 million pounds' worth of goods, but imported 93½ million pounds' worth. 'Can we afford not to have it?' was the customary telling answer, which quelled all argument. The unworthy critics were further hammered into limbo by Mr Aneurin Bevan, another prime enthusiast in this area, who assured them that the cost would decrease with the passage of time, as the general health of the public improved.

Sir John Anderson, former Chancellor of the Exchequer, warned us that we must expect three years of economy. Prime Minister Attlee, a cautious man, expressed his hope that during 1946 we would get half-way back to pre-war standards in consumption goods. In the next two months, for example, we would be importing 20,000 tons of Canary Islands tomatoes,

* This was one of the earlier bad guesses. Eighteen months after its introduction, the National Health Service was costing £388 million a year; in 1969, the figure had risen to £1,850 million, or £33 a head. The record for a single-item estimating boob should go to the Concorde aircraft, which soared in almost-vertical take-off from £180 million to £730 million.

enough to provide 1 lb. per head for the entire population of the British Isles.

I was not too thrilled by the prospect of tomatoes, even on such a lavish scale, but one of *my* 'consumption goods' was whisky or gin, and here the deprivation was fierce. One had to register for such supplies with the nearest wine merchant, and even for fully accredited customers the likely ration would be two bottles a month.

Wine merchants were now men of great consequence, courted like whores in the Klondyke spring, and they were very ready to show it. I never quite forgot one of my early attempts, in this happy post-war world, to buy myself a bottle of gin in Notting Hill Gate. Was I a registered customer? I was asked, as soon as I approached the communion rail.

I said, No, because I had only just moved into the district.

The man behind the counter closed his face as if it were a slit in one of his own shutters. 'In that case, there's no gin available. I can't take on casuals, can I? I've got to look after my regulars.'

'But I couldn't have registered with you.' For heaven's sake, had I become a casual? 'I couldn't have registered with anyone. I've been living all over the place for five years—Liverpool, and Glasgow, and Harwich.' His look of disbelief stung me. 'Damn it, I'm in the Navy!'

'Ah,' said the man, 'that may be. But it's not my fault if you keep dotting about, is it?'

I was beginning to have certain doubts about all this; indeed, since politics remained something of a religion, they could be classified as Doubts, the kind that tortured Victorian divines. Was this the brave new world we had been promised, which we had promised ourselves? Was this the nation of which Richard Aldington, my admired favourite of long ago, had reminded me so movingly:

> We are the far-off future
> Of the distant past,
> We are the noble race for whom they dreamed and died.

Was this, in fact, *really* the new Britain I had voted for?—the one I had even tried to fashion myself, as a member of Parliament?

I never became an M.P.; in fact, I never got as far as fighting a parliamentary election. But I did try hard, and it must have been a near thing, if simple arithmetic counted for anything in politics.

Though still in the Navy, I was suddenly taken in the spring of 1945, with a lust to enter Parliament. Party politics still meant a great deal to me, though I had hardly given them a constructive thought for five years; except when, as commanding officer, I had to render a monthly report on any evidence of subversive activity on board the vessel under my command— and if that bare statement contravenes the Official Secrets Act, by which I am bound till the day I die, then I apologize.*

But now was the moment to get moving! Peace was on the way. Labour was what I believed in. A really worthwhile job was what I would soon need. . . . I wrote the necessary letter of application, through the accustomed naval channels: starting with the quick-fire word 'SUBMITTED', declaring that I wished to seek political office at the next General Election, asking for permission to indulge in such activities, and expressing my continued humility and obedience towards their Lordships of the Admiralty—which was undoubtedly true.

In accordance with the generous Service custom at that time, I was given this permission without delay, plus all the leave I might need in order to make my bid. But first I had to get myself adopted for a constituency—any constituency; and here I found that I was already late on the scene. Almost every conceivable hole had been filled by the rush of prospective pegs.

When I said that I would take *anything*, I was offered Winchester.

---

* A disgruntled stoker, in a letter which he thought would elude censorship, once wrote from a ship which I will not identify to a friend in Scotland: 'The officers are a lot of twerps! Roll on the revolution, Jamie!' I let that one go by, the name 'Jamie' disarming me.

Even that is an exaggeration. I was offered an uncertain stab at Winchester, which had been true-blue Conservative since King Alfred burned the cakes in A.D. 878 (a statue at the bottom of the main street commemorated his reign). For Labour, it could only be the most forlorn of hopes, since it boasted this eternal, thumping Conservative majority, and an electorate (academic, ecclesiastical, agricultural, shop-keeping, sober), which was highly unlikely to make any dramatic change, no matter what happened to the rest of the country.

But *if I liked*, I was told, with the look which accompanies 'Of course you can come back to the flat! My husband the all-in wrestler will give you a drink!', I could go down to Winchester, as one of the short list of three prospective candidates, and have an interview with the local Labour Party committee, and try my luck.

It was also hinted that the fact that I had been at school at Winchester, a Conservative establishment since 1382, would not necessarily weigh in my favour.

But I was still, in the contemporary phrase, thrilled to bits. I was going to get into Parliament! . . . I went down on the appointed day, and it was all very exciting, very daunting, very educational, and, at the end, very disappointing.

There were three of us in that contest, as I had been warned; the others were Mr X (a local citizen, never got his name), and a man called George Jeger. I could not fail to notice that Mr Jeger was brought down to the interview by the great Morgan Phillips, General Secretary of the entire Labour Party, whom I had once seen for about five seconds when this excursion, and my possible candidature, had been fixed up.

At the time I thought: how very nice of Morgan Phillips to bring Mr Jeger down. He's probably shy, and needs the company. . . . Certain pockets of fresh innocence still persisted; in fact, I was still splendidly naïve.

We were summoned before the committee in turn, for a brief statement of our faith ('Why do you wish to represent Winchester in the Labour interest?') followed by a reasonably acute cross-examination. (Sample question: 'Would you like to see Winchester College abolished?' Very difficult: they should have asked me while I was there.) Mr X went in first. I was next and demonstrated, I hoped, a certain sweating eloquence in my plea that now was the time for a new deal all round, and that I was the ideal man to bring it to this particular corner of Hampshire.

Then Morgan Phillips, giving me a nod more distant than one might get, or even expect, from some ex-girl-friend newly-engaged to the Aga Khan, led in George Jeger. After a brief interval, it was announced that George Jeger had been adopted as the candidate.

There were handshakes all round. There were smiles, in spite of bitter disappointment. The best man, I declared, punctually on cue, deserved our unanimous best wishes. There were counter-declarations from the chairman, of how hard a decision this had been, and how impressed they had been with us losers. A committee-man, whom I thought had been sneering at my uniform and its modest row of ribbons throughout the inter-view, said: 'We liked you, lad. Wasn't easy. Better luck next time!'

Then I went back home, defeated before I started, vaguely suspicious, mortified, humble as humble could be, and still a naval officer.

But God damn it, George Jeger won that election! He got in! In 1945 Winchester voted Labour for the first and last time in its sheltered life; and he stayed there as its M.P. for five years, before the constituency swung back to its time-honoured allegiance (Jeger, having by this time found his way around unaided, had switched to the more fertile industrial climate of Goole in Yorkshire, the terminus of the entire British canal system, just in time, and was not affected by this local over-throw).

It could have been me, if I had started a little earlier, and known a little more about how things were done; if I had realized that politics started from the very beginning, with the nuts and bolts of minor patronage, and not half-way through when, on Amateur Night, they let in a few show-off children to get a glimpse of the footlights.

It could have been me. George Jeger, a dedicated Labour back-bencher for the next twenty-five years, was not such a glittering comet that only he could have won Winchester; otherwise he would never have been landed with this long-odds chance in the first place, which a hundred other bright-eyed tryers must have looked at, and sniffed at, and given up as hopeless before asking for something better.

It could have been me. Years later, when I told this story to Norman Pearson, he said, with careful emphasis and that touch of disparagement appropriate to a top-ranking businessman: 'A member of Parliament is a very good thing *to have been.*'

The sophisticated, long-range verdict was possibly accurate. But at the time the defeat seemed mortal, and the setback the worst since—-well, there was just no yardstick for such an inglorious rout.

I voted Labour, of course, like everyone else—and though that is factually inaccurate, only a massive percentage of 'everyone else' could have given Labour 394 seats and an overall majority of 186. It was my mood at the time, and the mood of twelve million other people; domestically, it had been spearheaded, not by the *Daily Herald*, which never managed to spear-head anything sharper than a wet loofah, but by the radical *Daily Mirror*, which for a year had been running a campaign, aimed principally at its women readers, on the simple theme 'VOTE FOR *HIM!*'

'Him' of course was their man overseas: the man linked only by his yearning, disgruntled letters, fed up with the war, still a lance-corporal, mucked about by his twerps of officers, sick of taking orders, footslogging while others rode, loathing all authority, and particularly that authority which had summarily sliced five years off his life, stuck him where he could easily get killed, and still expected to be returned to power as soon as this lot was over.

'Vote for *him*,' and all the other pressures of the time, produced a massive landslide in favour of a better deal: an instinctive determination not to let 'them' botch things up again, but
to take a muscular personal grip on the future, and never let go:
a resolve gently yet perfectly summed up by the poet John
Pudney's *For Johnny*:*

> Do not despair
> For Johnny-head-in-air;
> He sleeps as sound
> As Johnny underground.
>
> *
>
> Better by far
> For Johnny-the-bright-star,
> To keep your head,
> And see his children fed.

The sentiment of those last two lines, the idea, the aim, all
seemed crucially important. So I voted Labour, in spite of those
fornicating Liverpool dockers, and the fact that it meant reject-
ing Winston Churchill, beyond question the heroic architect
of our victory. I 'voted for *him*', as the *Mirror* instructed me,
and as the low-life and times of the Thirties practically dictated; and I voted for me; and I think I was right.

The Labour victory shifted the entire spectrum of British
politics and British attitudes, leftwards, for ever; but this was
overdue—we had been congealed in our rigid class-aspic for too
long. It was also the signal for a decade of dreary 'austerity'; in
our current fix, that had to happen too, though it earned for the
Labour Party, which had to execute the verdict of events, and
particularly for Sir Stafford Cripps, President of the Board of
Trade and later Chancellor of the Exchequer, a lasting public
dislike and also a reputation for a grim, anti-fun, misery-loves-
company attitude which stuck for ever.

But Stafford Cripps himself was a necessary, an inevitable
man. Britain really was broke; our affairs were in a chaotic

* From *Collected Poems* (Putnam & Co. Ltd.), by permission of the author.

mess: the idea of 'fair shares all round', which in practice meant
damned little for anyone, was a matter of hard necessity. If the
Conservatives had got in, instead of Labour, they would have
had to turn off just as many taps, fix just as many clamps round
our necks, and try to keep us just as poor, frugal, and honest as
the non-Conformist conscience itself.

Tories might have done it in more style, with rounder
phrases, a fruitier voice, and more practice at hectoring the
tenants. But done it had to be, and, on balance, Labour were
probably the right people to do it. So on that triumphant day of
26 July, when we rolled back the carpet with such a hefty thwack,
such a giant stirring of dust, and gave Mr Attlee—probably
the most unlikely successor to Mr Churchill which even a com-
puter could devise—the helm, I rejoiced, with the majority of
my fellow Britons.

I was very sad at not being an M.P., particularly as a lot of
friends and contemporaries had turned the trick. Winchester,
also moving slightly leftwards, sent in Richard Crossman,
Douglas Jay, and Hugh Gaitskell to join Sir Stafford Cripps for
Labour, as against Kenneth Younger and Douglas Dodds-
Parker for the opposition; and I could recall all these as medium-
sized boys in little straw hats, all going through the same
small-grinding mill as myself.

Harold Wilson got in. Christopher Mayhew got in. Petty
Officer J. Callaghan got in. A particular friend from the old
Nottingham days, Henry Usborne, got in for Acocks Green in
Birmingham; and when I called to congratulate him, told me a
rather good story about the ethics of electioneering.

It concerned a question which the Labour Party candidate in
a nearby constituency, after weighing all the factors, decided
not to ask the Conservative candidate in public. The question, to
be bawled out from the back of the hall at any appropriate
meeting, was:

'May I ask the candidate who is his eldest son's godfather?'

The answer, rather too emotive for the times, had to be:
'Mussolini.'

In face of strong temptation, decency prevailed. Besides, said Henry, who seemed to have matured overnight, you never quite knew what the other lot might have up *their* sleeves.

The feeling of being on the outside looking in, and completely excluded from this triumphant turn of events, still rankled after three or four months. Though I had been left behind by all these new-risen stars, there must be *something* I could do to join the march of progress. . . . I ferreted about a bit, in my new home area of Notting Hill, made closer contact with the local Labour Party, got myself chosen as a candidate at the forthcoming Borough Council elections, fought the seat, and won it.

Thus for a dizzy half-year I was Councillor Lieutenant-Commander Monsarrat, North Kensington civic figure, and junior member of two worthwhile committees—welfare and housing. But the Royal Borough of Kensington (North and South were amalgamated for local government purposes) was understandably Conservative; we were very much the minority faction, which might have been exciting if I had not come to the conclusion, before too long, that party politics were hardly relevant at all to civic administration, and that Kensington was being perfectly well run by its solid Tory majority and its titled Mayor.

In fact, local politics were *not* very exciting, and the contrast between being a borough councillor, arguing about rates and rats and rubbish disposal, and being a genuine Member of Parliament, concerned with the very fabric and pattern of Britain, was too great, and too ludicrous.

I began to feel bored with the whole idea; and there was now another area in my life which was also not very exciting, and this, unlike politics, was entirely my own fault.

Eileen and I had, sadly, grown apart during the later war years, instead of together. The birth of our son had been a significant milestone; indeed, it had been never more significant than at 6 a.m. on 23 September 1942, when the matron of Heswall Nursing Home in Cheshire rang me up and said:

'Congratulations, Lieutenant Monsarrat: you have a daughter!'

I had already dispatched all the necessary telegrams, and was toying with the name Nicola, before an important correction was telephoned through.

But after that—I don't know. Perhaps the dissolution had begun long before. I seemed to be away all the time; leaving Liverpool, I had been posted back to Greenock, and then to Londonderry; then *Campanula* was attached to a Canadian escort group, and I spent more time up the grim creek which was the harbour of St John's, Newfoundland, than on our own side of the Atlantic. It was no longer possible for us to have a house in my home port.

Then I was transferred again, this time to Harwich on the east coast, and after that, getting my first command was an event so exciting and important that for a long time it swallowed every other emotion. The ship and the job were all, leaving no room for anything but driving hard work and a certain amount of self-conceit.

The process of division was accelerated by nearly seven months' absence in America, when I was standing by a newly built frigate in Providence, Rhode Island—a frigate which, as soon as she could be made to work, would be my own pride and joy. But she had been built at lightning speed, together with twenty-three others, by Henry J. Kaiser; and I was never surprised to learn, not many years later, that the Henry J. Kaiser car was no bloody good, because the Henry J. Kaiser frigate was no bloody good either.

Mine was called *Perim*, after the tiny island-colony near Aden (there was another one called *Montserrat*, but they wouldn't give her to me), and in *Perim* we ran fourteen sea-trials, thirteen of them resulting in significant damage to our main bearings, before a little man from Tyneside was flown out, put his stubby finger on the trouble, and got the programme moving again.

Meanwhile, along with my crew of 212 (multiplied by twenty-four, to cover the crews of all the other sick and rejected

ships, which incidentally cost five million dollars each), I was
marooned for months and months on these highly hospitable
shores, first in Boston, then in Providence, and then in New
York for a refresher command course in convoy tactics.

Any married man who has spent over six months on the
eastern seaboard of the United States during wartime, when it
was a patriotic female duty to welcome the fleet aboard, and
who still retained his virtue, must have been either queer, or
singularly ugly, or a man of so saintly a character that the Navy
could have no billet for him in the first place.

I did not behave at all well, in this exotic climate of disengagement, such a long way from the war that we might have
been on another planet; the indulgence proved habit-forming,
since now, back in London, I was not behaving at all well either.
I had no doubt that this was obvious; and it reminded me, with
guilt and cheap amusement mixed, of a parallel situation
between my own parents, when my father decided, at the age of
sixty, that total separation would suit him best, and Mother,
announcing the astonishing news, told us:

'I knew it all the time! I knew what was happening, as soon
as he bought a two-seater! It was so he could go off by himself,
without Hollywood [the chauffeur] knowing, without having
to keep the Daimler waiting outside. I could see Hollywood
smirking, every time your father ordered his own car! He
smirked!'

I didn't have a two-seater, nor any other kind of give-away
transport; no chauffeur smirked at this master's solemn subterfuges—or suspected subterfuges: the evidence seemed, even
then, circumstantial to the point of farce: though my father
might indeed have fallen in love, it could have been with a new
car, thus anticipating, in 1926, what is now a humdrum liaison.

But part of the present decaying pattern was the fact that
Eileen had been staying in the country for a long time, while I
camped out in a bedsitting-room in Ennismore Gardens; and
that we now lived in guarded domesticity, under a newly bought
roof in what I liked to call my constituency, Notting Hill.

I was still, six months after the war's end, in uniform; but already I had been put ashore, and the shore I landed on was the biggest stone frigate of them all, the Admiralty at the top of Whitehall. I had loathed the idea of shore duty, had resisted it, argued about it, and tried for something better. But there was no doubt that the all-disposing man in Appointments was right.

After five ships, four and a half years of sea time, more than a hundred long and short convoys, I was desperately tired. Tired sailors of thirty-five belonged, in wartime, somewhere else than on the bridge. There were now lots of younger chaps coming along, who deserved their chance and who *wouldn't* make mistakes.

The Admiralty was not the gloomiest official building in London, but it was no mean runner-up, in an area of hot competition. Outside, layer after layer of grey grime, shading to black at exposed points, covered the ancient weathered stonework of this monument to three centuries of sea-power; within, the beige corridors stretched, orphanage-wise, as far as the shadowed eye could reach.

Upstairs, of course, were men of great consequence, in my world and in Britain's also: admirals, sea-lords, directors of operations in five oceans, forward planners, naval intelligence experts, and superior authors of strategy. Well down at ground level, occasionally sinking to the basement, was the Department of Naval Information, to which I had now been assigned, because it was my turn for a shore job and I had written three books about corvettes.

Entering, passing the security check-point, walking down a murky tiled corridor towards God-knows-what area of obscurity, one knew instinctively that the last breath of salt sea air had finally been breathed.

But to start with, the Information Department was great fun. I found myself sharing a room with two delightful men, one of whom I had known before the war, the novelist John Moore: the other was an oldish, grey-bearded man of infinite courtesy and consideration, John Scott Hughes, who had been the yachting correspondent of *The Times* since 1934.

I was very glad to meet John Moore again. He was, like myself, a put-ashore sailor, who had survived an exciting term as a pilot in the Fleet Air Arm; a job which had included service in aircraft-carriers and flying, on torpedo missions, those terrifying little aircraft which the navy called 'Stringbags' (I would hate to think what the Fleet Air Arm pilots called them.*)

It must be admitted that John Moore had scored an even greater hit, as far as I was concerned, by giving *Three Corvettes* a marvellous review in the *Observer*, a review so eminently quotable that we were using it on the dust-jacket a quarter-century later. He was a good friend then, and he remained one for the next twenty-three years, when, after dedicating his last book to me, he sadly died.

There we were, anyway, happily and companionably installed in an obscure room which was, to our continuing pleasure, very hard for anyone else to find. We did little official work. Some of us did none at all. We talked, and pondered, and smoked, and jotted things down, and occasionally said 'I don't think so' on the telephone, and took hours off for lunch.

It reminded me all the time of Cambridge, and that 'fatigue of idleness' which was phrase-maker Edward Gibbon's excellent contribution in this sphere of endeavour. But we all agreed that we were entitled to the respite. The war by now was nearly won, partly by us. Let the fresh-faced boys do the mopping up, while the men rested on their arms. We felt free to dream of the future, and even to do a little work on it.

John Moore was correcting the proofs of his new book, *Brensham Village*, and muttering to himself 'It's not right! But

* Officially these were Swordfish torpedo-bombers, whose top speed of 148 m.p.h made them almost theatrically vulnerable to anything pointed in their direction. It was Swordfish from the *Victorious* and *Ark Royal* which scored the first vital hits on the *Bismarck*. But in a later English Channel action against the battle-cruisers *Scharnhorst* and *Gneisenau*, six of them were flown off and six were shot down. For this brave try, a posthumous Victoria Cross went to Lieutenant-Commander Esmonde, the flight-leader, who had also led the *Bismarck* attack.

it will be!' On Christmas Eve he led us all in chanting his private carol: 'Noël! Noël! All book reviewers go to hell!' with a malevolent fervour I was not to appreciate until many years later.

I was scribbling down two different sets of notes; the first for a book about my brother Denys, who seemed to deserve one, if only as an act of piety; and another, highly tentative, for a *possible* novel about the Battle of the Atlantic, which also seemed to merit someone's attention.

John Scott Hughes was drawing up sail-plans for the ideal contender for the America's Cup, and saying: 'Of course, all I really want to do is to go back to *The Times*.'

It is worth recording that all these things came true. *Brensham Village* was one of John Moore's bigger successes, after *Portrait of Elmbury*; I did publish, three and six years later respectively, both the books I had been dreaming about; and John Scott Hughes did return as yachting correspondent to *The Times*, and stayed in that agreeable niche for another thirteen years.

But at the time, they both seemed to have a clearer view and a much tighter grip on the future than I had, or was ever likely to; and it was beginning to worry me.

Meanwhile I did what I could, in this climate of sloth, to go on earning my pay, which was now £66 a month, without benefit of living free on board ship. I wrote the articles I was asked for: one on 'Fine Qualities of the Navy's Little Ships' for the *Imperial Review*: one on 'Sea Power in Action' for the *Round Table*: one on the blessings of radar for *The Trident*: and one on 'The Royal Navy Fights Japan' for general consumption.

I did an occasional B.B.C. broadcast about the deeds of other brave men, in a weekly afternoon feature on the Navy. Once I got bored, and asked the man on the next floor up if I could be sent somewhere—anywhere—which might yield some usable material. He took me at my word.

I was promptly driven down to Dover, put aboard a motor-gunboat which roared across Channel to Dunkirk, in the roughest bumpiest ride I had ever endured (better six knots in a corvette than forty-six in a gunboat, any day); driven 150 miles in an Army jeep to Eindhoven in Holland, and then attached to some Royal Marine Commandos who were conducting nightly forays across the River Meuse, in preparation for the crossing of the Rhine.

The commandos invited me to join in that, too; but I said I had to get back. I liked them very much, and it had been fun (of a certain kind) to swab my face with black boot-polish and wade ashore from a small dinghy into enemy-held territory; fun to fly in a plane called an Auster, about the size of a motor-cycle and sidecar, just out of range of anti-aircraft shell-bursts, to try to plan something interesting for tonight; and fun to spend that night in a derelict windmill boldly marked on our captured German map ('Much better than ours'), waiting to surprise an enemy patrol which *might* try some counter-offensive action.

But good heavens! This was Germany! The bullets were real! I was too old for this sort of caper! Crossing the *Rhine?* . . . I went back to Dover in a nice, slow, empty tank-landing craft, scuttled into Whitehall, and told the boys all about it instead.

But all *they* could talk about was the latest crop of 'Buzz-bomb' or 'Doodlebug' stories. Everyone in London had their tale to tell. It was the time of the V1 and the V2, Hitler's last violent effort against a side which was so obviously winning that only a lunatic would go on struggling.

This final try came in the form of a series of bombs and rockets, a short sharp flurry of murder with which the Germans, in desperation, were trying to subdue our civilian population. V stood for *Vergeltung*—retaliation. The V1 was the worst, and the most effective.

This unnerving, soulless, and cruel weapon, aimed almost entirely at Greater London and anyone who might be working or sleeping there, was a pilotless, jet-propelled flying bomb which crossed the Channel at 400 m.p.h. and steered itself towards its huge, sprawling target.

One could hear it coming; presently, when it was somewhere

overhead, its engine cut out, there was a silence, and we waited. Then it fell, and the solid ton of explosive in its warhead went off. In its short career the V1 destroyed or damaged three-quarters of a million houses, and killed 6,184 people.

Its companion piece was the V2, a breed of long-range rocket, each weighing twelve tons, which approached in total silence from a peak height of fifty miles. These poisonous arrows killed another 2,700 people before our advancing armies pushed their launching bases out of range.*

But those advancing armies (not pongoes and Yanks any more, but liberation troops, or even simply brave soldiers) were doing all sorts of other things at the same time. Presently, on a day of wild triumph, the war—or at least the German part of it —ended. A long-awaited VE Day—V for Victory, E for Europe —dawned on 8 May 1945, five years and eleven months from Day One.

The war ended, for me, on a most moving note. All officers above a certain rank in the Naval Information Department had to take their turn as acting 'Duty Captain' during the night hours—the proud title meant no more than standing a telephone and signal-watch, as the wakeful link between the outside, land-or-sea world and the people who really did the work, but who preferred, if nothing important was happening, to get some sleep at nights.

I was acting Duty Captain at the Admiralty, charged (on this sub-contracting basis) with Britain's entire naval destiny, on the last night of our war.

Even inside the massive building, one could hear the tremendous noise from nearby Trafalgar Square, which, when I had come on duty at 8 p.m., was already packed with a cheering,

---

* All this last-minute misery and bloodshed was inflicted by courtesy of Wernher von Braun, the German scientist who, as 'Technical Director, Liquid Fuel Rocket and Guided Missile Centre, Peenemunde', for eight years, masterminded both projects. Since we provided this valuable target practice, Britain does perhaps deserve a tiny Mention in Dispatches, at the very end of the screen credits, for the moon landing (via Saturn rocket) twenty-four years later. This also was by courtesy of Wernher von Braun, now a staunch American citizen.

roaring, dancing, swaying crowd: a crowd sampling the magic taste of the first evening of peace.

I carried the enormous happiness of that moment, the choking relief, with me into the Admiralty, where everyone else I met was happy, because, at least from the Atlantic and the Mediterranean, there would be no more news of U-boats ('Up to nine in your area'), no more terrible tidings of disaster ('Following six ships in convoy sunk last night'), no bells tolling across a thousand miles of the worst widow-maker of them all.

I would have given big money (well, medium-sized money, suitable to my station), for a celebration drink on this night, but no such facilities were on tap in our humble area. Instead, I said 'enjoy yourself' to the fortunate man whom I had relieved, leafed through the last hour's signals, and settled down in the consequential armchair normally occupied by the Duty Captain.

But by midnight the crescendo of noise and cheering, the blaring of horns, the fireworks (hoarded for this moment?), the sounds of amateur music-makers, were very hard to resist. My telephone had not rung for the past hour. The signal-log was almost bare. Nothing was happening, because we had won the war.

On a guilty impulse I deserted my post, and climbed up the devious stone pathway to the top of Admiralty Arch.

The view from there was marvellous: backwards down the Mall towards Buckingham Palace, forwards to Trafalgar Square and the tall honoured pillar with Nelson a-top, a sailor who, at this particular moment, would have been feeling as joyful and as proud as anyone within ten square miles of the Admiralty But one's first reaction was one of astonishment—not at the crowds, but at something else.

There were lights! There were lighted windows, unmasked headlamps, gaping doorways stripped of their black-out screens. Both Buckingham Palace and the Admiralty Arch itself were floodlit. There were actual lights, for the first time in nearly six gloomy years. Apart from victory itself, there could have

6

been nothing more moving than this simple freedom, this blessing.

I stood there for quite a long time, listening to the crowds, laughing at them and with them; leaning against the parapet which was like the bridge of a ship, except that in front and below me was not the sea, calm or cruel, peaceful or murderous, but an ocean of people with its own surging wave-pattern, its *life*. Then, on a half-turn, I became aware that I was not alone, on top of the Admiralty Arch.

There was someone standing within five yards of me, also staring down at the crowds, and oblivious of close company for the same reason as I had been—because we were both entranced by the magnet of what was going on below. With that perceptible twinge of nervousness which had been built into my life for so many years, I recognized, first the rank and then the man.

The massive display of gold braid told me that he was an admiral, like his brave and lonely brother on top of the column. Then I realized that this was a very superior admiral indeed. I counted one thick band of gold, and *four* thinner ones. He was an Admiral of the Fleet—the highest any sailor could go.

In fact, I suddenly recognized, he was *the* Admiral of the Fleet. The man in my company was the First Sea Lord and Chief of Naval Staff, Admiral Cunningham.

Andrew Browne Cunningham—one remembered the initials, and what they stood for, as one remembered in boyhood the admired labels of great cricketers, jockeys, prefects, even writers. (H. G. Wells was Herbert George; Thackeray was also William Makepeace.) Cunningham had been a legend with us all for years; he was in command at the Battle of Matapan, and Commander-in-Chief of the Mediterranean when, between the onslaught on Malta and the brutal ebb and flow of the North African campaign, it was an ocean which had to be cleansed before we could make any headway at all.

He had done that, and then moved on. In fact, he had probably done more for our side than any other living sailor.

Cunningham, we knew, had joined the Navy at the age of fifteen—in 1898. He had trained in sail. He had been a destroyer-captain at Gallipoli in 1915. But now, in our own inherited war, he had carried this tremendous load for years on end, and all his plans, all his patient, brave, and faithful service had borne fruit. We had won. *He* had won It must be quite a moment for him.

It was. I watched him surveying the raucous happy crowds. Then he looked up at Nelson. Then he leant forward, his knuckles planted squarely on the parapet. The movement brought his face into the floodlights shining from below, and I saw, in one bare, glistening fraction of a second, that he was crying.

I returned to duty forthwith.

The duty I returned to had now taken a swift nose-dive. Both John Moore and John Scott Hughes had left, en route for the blessings of an assured or at least a planned future; I was now isolated in a new and darker cave, a cellar-room next door to the cafeteria, where I was obviously the Tail-End Charlie of the Department of Naval Information.

There was even less to do than before, and a wise man would have got out; but I was as far as ever from being a wise man, and I clung to office like any other minor limpet. The war really was over; now there was 'only Japan' to be dealt with, and the Americans, conducting an island-hopping exercise across the whole breadth of the Pacific with the greatest skill and bravery, hardly needed our help at all. Japan, in fact, folded within three months of our own VE Day, and after that, peace came down like a dusty, rusty, final curtain.

But, unbelievably, I stayed where I was for another six months, playing at being a sailor, playing at being gainfully employed, playing *tout court*. Immured in my little cellar, I enjoyed an occasional gossip-session with a charming senior officer, Captain Taprell Dorling, who, under the pen-name of 'Taffrail', had written a whole string of books about the sea, and was now compiling a historical account of the Battle of the Atlantic (so someone else must already have latched on to this good idea).

Occasionally (everything was now occasional, like sunshine on the south coast), I was visited by a beautiful Wren, a driver from the Admiralty Motor Pool. She had, as a lustful sailor would say, all the right ideas. At every possible opportunity she would dodge down to my sordid lair (though it had been sordid long before I got there), and say: 'I've got half an hour. Can I drive you anywhere?'

The answer was always: 'Just round the bend.'

Since our furnishings were not of the best—one desk, two chairs, one filing cabinet—the misuse of twelve square feet of low-grade Admiralty carpet was inevitable.

By way of recuperation we used to dine at Siegi's, off Berkeley Square, a day and night joint where they had inexhaustible supplies of real steaks and tender lamb chops; or else at Hatchett's in Piccadilly, where a talented band-leader called Chappie D'Amato sang for us, and for a hundred others, his oddly moving version, to the tune of 'Lili Marlene', of 'The Gallant 8th Armada', a kind of doggerel recital of the battle honours of the 8th Army. It ended, in reference to the current shortage of almost everything:

> Their job in Europe's finished, the boys'll soon be here,
> You'll meet them in the local, queueing for 'NO BEER',
> But that's all been sent to Germany, to Germany, to Germany,
> No beer for the 8th Armada, the gallant 8th Armee.

The vinegary taste of victory could not have been better summed up.*

Sometimes duty called, and I was told to write something, and then summoned upstairs to withstand the scrutiny of the

---

* Copyright 1944 by Major Bob Crisp, D.S.O., M.C., and Chappie D'Amato, 3rd London (Fulham) Battn., Home Guard: both late of the Royal Tank Regiment. The full text of this deplorable, wildly appreciated *chanson de guerre* will be found in Appendix A.

Commander R.N. who now seemed to be charged with my
destiny. This humourless fellow, who after all these years was
still intent on teaching the R.N.V.R. a thing or two about the
Navy, used to keep me stationed in front of his desk for anything up to half an hour, while he leafed through my efforts and
digested at his leisure whatever article or broadcast or news-
release I had laid before him.

He reminded me of my housemaster at Winchester, another
petty tyrant set in authority, another man whose pleasure it had
been to nail me upright in this penitential stance while he took
his own sweet time over the current inquisition. But now, the
tiny edge of rebellion had a little more body to it.

I felt entitled to be angry and mutinous, even though I might
have just levered myself up from my beautifully embroidered
carpet, and be looking forward to the next free-style dive. Here
was this fattish, pinkish nonentity, who could keep me standing
for twenty-five minutes while he read, frowned over, blue-
pencilled, and finally tossed back my draft for a B.B.C. broadcast.

He might, I thought, have asked me to sit down, without any
gross violation of naval discipline; there were sumptuous
chairs all round the room, no doubt reserved for his superiors.
God damn it, I had been at sea for nearly five years; I had been
captain of a frigate. . . . As I waited, in fuming impatience, I
used to wish I could have Chappie D'Amato singing off-stage,
especially for me:

> Now landsmen all, whoever you may be
> If you want to rise to the top of the tree,
> If your soul isn't fettered to an office stool,
> Be careful to be guided by this golden rule:
> Stick close to your desks, and *never* go to sea
> And you all may be rulers of the Queen's Navee!

I have no doubt at all, now, that this could well have been an
unfair judgement, and that Commander X had probably fought a
good hard war before being put ashore, like me, and into a job
which he hated as much as I did.

But it was this sort of occasion, imposed by this very man, which decided me against staying on in the Navy, at a moment when there was a real prospect that I would do just that for the rest of my working life.

Various kinds of official bait were being held out. Various promises, which now seem laughable, of interesting and rewarding employment for wartime naval officers who wished to stay on, were going the rounds. It seemed that they still wanted the R.N.V.R., though as it turned out there was to come a time, not many years ahead, when they could not axe their own people quickly enough, and if you, as a regular officer, would kindly leave the Royal Navy well before you were forty, you would be rewarded with a handsome present.

But though I was tempted, because I loved the service and the pride and discipline which went with it, it was not too hard to work out the odds against. As a temporary officer, I might have to revert to lieutenant. The competition for command, in a shrinking Navy, would be fierce. There would be very little sea-time, which was the only kind of time worth spending. Perhaps, once a year, one might be lucky enough to cruise down to Gibraltar, or across to the coral strand of Bermuda, where *Perim* had worked up.

For the rest, it would mean a desk job, and men like this plaguey commander, with all his affectations and false frowns, sitting squarely on my neck for the rest of my career; it really would mean polishing up the handle of the big front door, and, in one's spare time, dancing social minuets with admirals' wives, those formidable brass-bound creatures who could, I already knew, match their husbands, broadside for broadside, on any day of the week; who wore the stripes as other women wore the trousers.

The answer was No; and it was still No, even after a chance re-encounter with a man who had done more for me in the service, and taught me more in a short time, and had left me wiser—had left me, in fact, knowing at long last what the Royal Navy was all about—than any other human being in the whole six years of war.

He had a long label in the Navy List—Lieutenant S. R. Le H.
Lombard-Hobson, R.N.—and he had been captain of my new ship
when I finally winkled myself out of *Campanula* and was posted
to another corvette, H.M.S. *Guillemot*, as First Lieutenant.

Sam Lombard-Hobson was tall, austere, highly efficient,
totally self-disciplined, and devoted to his chosen career. He
ran his ship, which was the best-kept, best-drilled, best-behaved
corvette in the Harwich Flotilla, with an unrelenting grip. But
his aim was obviously to teach. Above all—as I could tell from
the moment I reported on board—he believed that the R.N.V.R.
were teachable.

He only disciplined me once, fairly enough, though at the
time I thought him every kind of a bastard for the way in which
he did it. It was my own fault. I had failed to call him on one
occasion when something might have gone seriously wrong:
when *Guillemot*, in close convoy, was being crowded down on
to a wreck-buoy by a wandering merchant-ship which was having trouble with the cross tide. I thought I could deal with it
myself without waking him up, and I did so.

But he had heard, with that captain's inner ear, the quick
flurry of helm orders and the sudden rise in engine revolutions,
all indicating a moment of crisis, and he was up on the bridge
before I had finished. To start with, he did nothing, and said
nothing. Then, when it was over, he turned on me.

'First Lieutenant!'

'Sir.'

'You are relieved of the watch. Go down to my cabin and
bring me the file of captain's standing orders.'

When I returned he said: 'Open it, and read me number
twenty-three.'

We were out of earshot of the quartermaster and the other
men on the bridge, as custom demanded, but they knew
damned well what was happening.

So did I. I asked: 'All of it, sir?'

'Yes.'

I read, in a voice just this side of protest:

The Officer of the Watch is to call me, without fail, in the following circumstances:

(a) On sighting or hearing an aircraft not identified as friendly.

(b) On obtaining an Asdic contact.

(c) On sighting any vessel which is either (1) suspicious or (2) likely to interfere with our intended course (e.g., a destroyer on patrol or a minesweeper on our own side of the channel).

(d) On sighting flares or star-shell at night.

(e) On a change in the weather or visibility.

(f) If a buoy or light-vessel is not sighted at the expected time.

(g) On an escort or ship in convoy leaving its proper station.

(h) On any ship (escort or merchant ship) joining the convoy.

(i) If the presence of other ships nearby seems likely to force us off the swept channel, or on the wrong side of a wreck-buoy or other dangerous obstruction.

(j) In any doubt or emergency.

It was obvious which one he was going to get me on, but being a perfectionist he had to drive the point home.

'Read me paragraph (i) again.'

When I had finished, he asked: 'Is that absolutely clear?'

'Yes, sir.'

'Then why was I not called?'

I knew that he should have been. *Guillemot* was his ship, and his alone. If I had made a mess of things, and hit the wreck-buoy or the wreck itself, it would have been his responsibility, his fault, and his neck.

'I'm sorry, sir. I thought I could deal with it myself.'

I wanted to say that it was only because of all that he had taught me that I had this sort of confidence, but that would not have been an argument. Also it would have sounded awful.

He said, as harshly as before: 'First Lieutenant, you will not do that again.'

'No, sir.'

'Now take the file back to my cabin.'

It was a wretched, shaming moment, and I was wildly angry. Christ! if I couldn't get the ship out of a minor tight corner without calling for help, what the hell use was I anyway? . . . But at breakfast, an hour later, he was his unruffled, generous, all-competent self again. He called me 'Number One instead of using that threatening formal title. He asked me to *please* leave him some of the fried potatoes. . . . I knew that only if I had turned sulky (and there was a lively urge to do so) would he have kept up the pressure.

He could always outlast me—that was one of the perquisites of his rank, and a lesson hammered home long before I had wet my second stripe. So I did not turn sulky. I also remembered, in tranquillity, that though a brilliant ship-handler himself he had *not* taken over the ship from me the moment he reached the bridge. If he could resist such raw temptation, so could I.

He could still surprise me in other spheres as well. Many times during the eight months we were shipmates he had talked about the R.N.V.R., and what they were doing for the Navy. Though a dedicated professional, he had no illusions about our contribution, which he thought had proved itself absolutely essential.

'It's shaken us up a bit, as well,' he once confided. 'Broadened our ideas. You people have come from so many different jobs. The average naval officer doesn't *know* enough.'

I received a curious confirmation of this opinion when, returning from leave, he asked me, in exactly the same voice as he used when discussing boat-drill or harbour exercises:

'Tell me. If one has a miscue on the doorstep, what are the chances of having a baby?'

Already I prided myself on being a resourceful, even a damned good First Lieutenant.

'Absolutely nil. Well, let's say a million to one.

6*

'Thank you.'

I appreciated that he was inquiring for a friend.

It was a sad day for me when Sam Lombard-Hobson was promoted, and given command of a Hunt Class destroyer, and sent down to the Mediterranean where the action was. But he recommended me for command, and I got it promptly, and I stole and carried away with me his personal rubber stamp which said 'Lieutenant-in-Command', the proudest rubber stamp that ever came my way.

Having learned from him how to run a ship, how to handle her in any weather, how to get the best out of tired men, including one's tired self; how to deal with defaulters, how to talk to valued petty officers, even how to walk up and down the quarter-deck in private contemplation, I had been eternally grateful ever since.

He was never made an Admiral, against all my confident predictions. Surviving the Korean war as well, he finished up as Captain S. R. Le H. Lombard-Hobson, C.V.O., O.B.E., and Naval Attaché in Rome. But if any man could have signed me up for the Navy for another fifteen years, this was he; and meeting him by chance again, even outside Charing Cross Station in the rain, was one of the prime delights of the post-war world.

He was then a commander, 'shopping for a job', as he put it, though the phrase only meant that he was concerned with his next posting in the Navy. I was also shopping for a job. But I had, by then, no such frame of reference.

In fact, what on earth was I going to do now?

I was thirty-six—almost over the hill already. I wasn't going to be a sailor; and by now it seemed that I wasn't going to be a writer either, if the figures were anything to go by. Simple arithmetic was against me, among a formidable array of other things.

In thirteen years I had made £1,647 out of writing eight books; the modest balance sheet read as follows:

Think of Tomorrow	£30
At First Sight	30
The Whipping Boy	30*
This is the Schoolroom	164
Three *Corvette* books	1,213
Depends What You Mean by Love	180

£1,647 in thirteen years worked out at £127 a year a living wage for a starving dog, but not much else. In fact, it worked out at failure. The only theme which had even looked like clicking was the 'Corvette' series, and this was now dead for ever. I would do the book about Denys because I wanted to; and I *might* try that Battle of the Atlantic idea. But neither of these was likely to keep me alive.

Meanwhile I would need, very shortly, a living wage of my own.

I played with the idea of trying for the B.B.C. again, but it had much less appeal now. Announcers were still men of consequence who wore evening dress when on night duty; and if they had to intone 'Hallo, Twins!' when they sent out birthday greetings on the Children's Hour, they did it with unimpaired style and dignity.

But the organization as a whole seemed to have entered a rather precious phase. Everyone was now called Ronnie, and those who weren't had developed a new, annoying fad for souped-up names with a single initial in front of them—T. Ambrose Jones or M. Jackson Smith.

As far as I could see, the only man in this curious category who ever made good, in or out of the B.B.C., was J. Walter Thompson.†

I needed something more serious, more orderly after the years of naval discipline, I still wanted an embrace of similar severity and good repute. I could never go back to that pre-war 'freedom' which had been wonderful in one's mid-twenties,

---

* This was the standard pre-war advance for beginners.
† Well, there was J. Paul Getty.

but seemed sloppy and second-rate when one was shaping up for forty. Also, there was a continuing need to serve. . . . Then I heard about a new thing called UNRRA (the United Nations Relief and Rehabilitation Adminstration) which was just setting up shop. It was going to help with the reconstruction of a war-torn world. To start with, it was going to the aid of Austria, where there was an outbreak of typhus. Was that the sort of thing?

I discussed it with Eileen, who came back with one of the most perceptive comments she ever made. Though entirely good-humoured and tolerant, her verdict was:

'But isn't that just your picture of what Nicholas Monsarrat ought to do after the war?'

I answered, sourly enough, 'I suppose so,' but I knew that she was right. The idea *was* part of a show-off pattern of 'doing good', which though sometimes effective in action was often deeply suspect in motive. I needed something more than to strike ill-paid attitudes of selfless benevolence.

Then Morrice James, not for the first nor the last time, came to my rescue.

Morrice had returned from the war as a lieutenant-colonel in the Royal Marines, and was now back at his desk in the Dominions Office. All sorts of adventures had come his way, principally in North Africa. He had even met Evelyn Waugh, who had also enjoyed a short spell with this prestigious corps before transferring to the Royal Horse Guards.

'What was he like?' I asked.

'Not wholly admirable.'

From a Dominions Office man, this was serious disparagement.

'But he's such a marvellous writer!'

'Oh, I agree. But that is not always enough.'

I gathered, in the course of later conversation, that Evelyn Waugh had proved himself a snob of some magnitude as well as a crotchety companion, with early signs of a disease which we christened Creeping Infallibility. But having just read, in quick succession, the entertaining *Put Out More Flags* and then the masterly *Brideshead Revisited*, I could forgive Evelyn Waugh anything and everything.

Morrice James and I spent a lot of time talking. Though glad to be alive, neither of us was entirely decided on what to do with the extension of life. He was still hankering after something more exciting than spending the next quarter of a century as a slow or fast-rising civil servant. He talked of writing: in fact, at that moment of time he was a civil servant who wanted to be a writer, while I was a writer who wanted to be something else—even a civil servant.

For relaxation we patronized a theatre club of which he was a member, and where probably the best intimate entertainment in London was available: the Players' Theatre, mysteriously situated under one of the arches carrying the suburban traffic from Charing Cross, where an elegant and delicious riot called 'Ridgeway's Late Joys' was presented nightly.*

This, an irreverent re-creation of Victorian music hall, had Leonard Sachs as its all-capable chairman and master of ceremonies, and a cast which included such young-men-with-a-future as Bernard Miles and Alec Clunes. Here we sang the choruses of 'Little Polly Perkins of Paddington Green', and those weepy ballads where virtue succumbed to evil designs well advertised by a villainous black moustache; here Archie Harradine and Joan Sterndale-Bennett led us in praise of tempestuous Spanish beauty:

> She sang like a nightingale,
> Played the guitar,
> Danced the cachucha,
> Smoked a cigar.
> Oh what a form! Oh what a face!
> And she did the fandango all over the place.

* I am indebted to Mr Leonard Sachs for information on the curious parentage of this title. The establishment started life, in the 1860s, as Evans' Music Hall in Covent Garden; but since the building had originally belonged to a Mr Joy, it was billed as 'Evans', late Joy's'. When Sachs and Peter Ridgeway revived it in 1938, they compacted this neatly into 'Ridgeway's Late Joys'.

Here a fantastically talented young man, Peter Ustinov, (who had first performed there at the age of nineteen), regaled us with three marvellous impersonations: one of an ancient Wagnerian *prima donna* soprano called Lieselotte Beethoven-Finck, giving one of her never-ending 'final performances'; another of a humourless old bore of a Russian professor who, while holding forth in praise of his own published works, dismissed Tolstoy as 'a *farceur*!'; and a hilarious third, the ageing Archbishop of Limpopo giving a talk on pygmies to the boys of St Paul's.

Once, when we arrived late, and I was moving somewhat prominently to my seat, Leonard Sachs called out: 'Just the man we want! Look at that Adam's apple!'

I huddled well down.

But after one of these spirited evenings, when we were having a last drink at the slum end of the Café Royal, Morrice said:

'We may not be having many more of these, I'm afraid. I'm going to be posted.'

'Where to?'

'South Africa.'

'Oh.' I felt bereaved already. 'But what as?'

'Assistant Secretary. On the High Commissioner's staff.'

'Who's the High Commissioner?'

'Baring.'

I felt I should have known the name and the man, but of course I did not. While I was still considering this brusque turn of events, which would leave me orphaned, without anyone to talk to, Morrice went on:

'They're planning to open the first British Information Office there. It will be part of the High Commission, but in Johannesburg instead of Pretoria. It's concerned with British propaganda, really, except that propaganda has become such a tainted word. Let us call it—' I could tell that he was quoting from some prudent memorandum '—the dissemination of information about all aspects of the British way of life. Anyway, they're looking for a director to take charge. Why don't you try for it?'

'But I don't know enough about it, do I?'

'Oh, I wouldn't say that. You've had a year at the Admiralty. You've been dealing with the Press and the B.B.C. You can write, damn it!' He grinned at me over his glass of lager. 'I can assure you, your application would look perfectly adequate on paper.'

I had an idea that, as a helpful friend, he might already have mentioned my name; and this was confirmed, in a roundabout way, when he said:

'Of course, there are one or two other factors. For example, did you ever actually join the Communist Party?'

I had not known, till then, how sharp his glance could become.

'No,' I answered, truthfully. 'I nearly did once as you know. And I used to sell the *Daily Worker* in Piccadilly.'

'Please!' He held up his hand. 'Spare me the horrible details. Then you never actually joined?'

'No. When the time came, I found I didn't believe in it any more. Spain took care of that. Too much political killing. . . . The nearest I came to it—' I searched my pre-war archives, 'was to join the Friends of the Soviet Union Sunday Film Society.'

'*Potemkin*,' said Morrice, whose memory was always excellent.*

'Exactly.'

'I think we can overlook the battleship *Potemkin*. And of course you must have had naval clearance. Well, there it is. If you like, I'll put your name forward.'

The mad idea suddenly took shape. South Africa? Actual *sunshine*? Lots of butter and meat? British propaganda? A responsible job on the staff of the High Commissioner? A regular salary? Why ever not?

'I think I'd like that very much.'

* *The Battleship Potemkin*, Sergei Eisenstein's 1925 film about revolution and the Russian Grand Fleet, was a perennial favourite with progressive audiences, and a masterpiece in its own right.

The keen glance, which might have been more daunting if I had not developed one myself, for sea-going use, bore down on me again.

'Naturally you'll have to behave yourself.'

'Oh, I think we both will.'

I wasn't going to take too much of that daunting glance. For Morrice James himself, an energetic bachelor of thirty with a set of rooms in Albany, this was not a bad moment to move on to South Africa, either.

We had known each other a long time.

After that, things advanced very quickly, giving the lie (for the first and last time, as far as I was concerned) to the idea that the pace of the civil servant was the pace of the world-weary snail, something like six feet for each cup of tea. I was interviewed by a succession of grave men in progressively darker suits. Finally I was interviewed by the Permanent Under-Secretary of State for Dominion Affairs, Sir Eric Machtig, who was in black.

A week later, I received a letter offering me the job of Director of the United Kingdom Information Office, Johannesburg (still to be established). The appointment, in the first instance, was to be for a term of two years; and the salary, *not* subject to an annual increment and *not* carrying a housing allowance, would be £1,250 a year.

It was more than I had ever earned, or was likely to, and nearly double my naval pay.

I talked over the whole thing with Eileen, and found that she was as tempted as I was; it was a big step, but attractive for many reasons, and there was between us, unspoken, the idea that a new country and a new job might give us a fresh start in other directions as well. Against that, there was the feeling, absolutely genuine and valid, that we ought to stay where we were, as loyal British subjects, and sweat it out; if not for the pride and pleasure of sharing national hardship, then for the experience itself.

While we hesitated, a cracking blizzard ('the worst since

1939', just like everything else) hit the entire British Isles: and as if that were not enough, there were fresh warnings of reduced rations, and a news-item from the Ministry of Food not at all calculated to improve the appetite:

'We have a squirrel pie recipe which has not been generally issued to the public, but is available to applicants. The ingredients are: 1 squirrel, 1 large chopped onion, 1 rasher of bacon, 1 oz. of flour, seasoning, and water. *Instructions* Wash the squirrel well in salt water, cut in small pieces, roll in flour, place in a pie dish, and bake.'

Free cartridges would be supplied by the local pest officer to shoot the squirrel with.

That did it. I sent my letter of acceptance to the Dominions Office, and began a swift round of visits concerned with briefing me for the new job. I went to the newly formed Central Office of Information, and talked to its first boss, Robert Fraser. I went to Buckingham Palace to talk to the Press Secretary, Captain Lewis Ritchie, who wrote sea stories under the pseudonym 'Bartimeus'.*

I went to the Board of Trade to talk about imports and exports, to the Treasury to talk about money, and to the Foreign Office to talk about their policy—now *my* policy. I saw Mr Francis Williams (now Lord Francis-Williams), lately editor of the *Daily Herald* and now the Prime Minister's Adviser on Public Relations. I paid a courtesy call on the South African High Commissioner.

Within the Dominions Office itself, they gave me their views on what the new Information Office organization should be, and also a crash course in everything important that was going on which might affect my job. This came in a series of succinct directives.

PALESTINE: Shiploads of illegal immigrant Jews were trying to reach Tel Aviv; we would have to keep them out, having undertaken (to the Arabs) to limit the growth of the new state. Watch that—lots of Jews in South Africa.

* After the blind beggar in the Bible. Ritchie had one eye.

UNITED NATIONS: the first Secretary-General had just been appointed, Mr Trygve Lie (after General Eisenhower had turned the post down). Watch that: General Smuts, Prime Minister of South Africa, was very keen on the United Nations.

COLD WAR: a series of grisly confrontations was just starting between Mr Vyshinsky, Soviet Vice-Commissar for Foreign Affairs, and the American and British U.N. delegates, on such varied topics as Greece, Persia, Yugoslavia, and Indonesia. Mr Gromyko, Russian delegate to the Security Council, had just staged his first walk-out. Mr Winston Churchill, coining the new phrase 'iron curtain', had warned an American audience, and us: 'The dark ages may return on the gleaming wings of science. Beware, I say! Time may be short. A shadow had fallen on the scene so lately lighted by the Allied victories.' Watch that: it was bound to get worse.

THE NUREMBERG TRIALS: the latest evidence was now being given by Goering, Hess, and Ribbentrop, and before long there would come the inevitable verdict. Watch that: a very large body of opinion in South Africa had been pro-German during the war, and was anti their punishment now, even taking into account the well-documented horrors of Belsen, Auschwitz, Sachsenhausen, *et al.*

'Don't get into any arguments' was the general theme of all this briefing. There were two sets of people in South Africa, English-speaking and Afrikaans-speaking, Briton and Boer (the old phrase was apparently still appropriate); they were almost irreconcilable—always had been, always would be. Monsarrat with his little Information Office wasn't going to alter any of that. But he needn't make it worse. He should talk about what Britain was doing *now*, and was trying to do, and leave it at that.

Above all (and this was added in a voice from which every inflexion save that of politeness had been rigorously excluded) —above all, *pas trop de zèle.*

A perceptive fellow, the top expert on South Africa, added that General Smuts (pro-British) was probably on his way out, and would be succeeded by an Afrikaner Nationalist Party government, traditionally dedicated to hating Britain's guts. This might make my job more difficult. But anyway—have a good time.

Suddenly the tempo rose; all the waves curled, anc were about to break. We did our packing, and said our good-byes. As a last gesture in the direction of socialist brotherhood, I let the Notting Hill house, furnished, to an impecunious Reuter's journalist for £4 a week—about one-third of the current rate. (No capitalist landlord I.)

I tried, and failed, to sell my naval uniform and bridge-coat ('No market for this sort of stuff.') Instead, I went up to the R.A.F. depot at Uxbridge, and selected my free demob outfit: 1 suit, 1 shirt, 1 tie, 1 pair each of socks, shoes, and traces, 1 pork-pie hat, and (on the way out) 1 packet of Liquorice Allsorts.

Finally I collected my Navy gratuity (£134 for s x years' watery slog) and we took off.

2.

We took off in a cargo liner called the *City of Madras.* our second choice of ship after a preliminary skirmish in which I bravely stood up for my rights, like any other Labour Councillor. Originally, the Dominions Office had booked passages for Eileen, Max, and myself in a troopship: a troopship, moreover, not going direct to Cape Town, where I was due to meet our High Commissioner, but through the Mediterranean, the Suez Canal, the Red Sea, and the murderously hot East African route down to Durban—a four-week voyage which would land me about nine hundred miles from where I wanted to be.

I did not think much of the idea, but, as the newest of new

boys, I was prepared to do as I was told. Then I read the agreement which had to be signed before we could go on board, and decided that it would not do at all.

It came in the form of a document which was as discouraging for the intending traveller as anything since Noah started loading the Ark.

This was headed 'Conditions of Travel in Troop Transports', and set out the prospect before us with commendable precision.

It must be stressed that conditions of passage will be austere in the extreme when judged by peace-time standards, and attention is directed to the following points:

1. No particular type of sleeping accommodation can be guaranteed: accommodation may be of the kind used for troops.

2. Bathing and toilet facilities will be of a limited nature, and not necessarily within easy access of sleeping accommodation.

3. Meals will be on an austere scale, but the quantity of food will be adequate. It is not guaranteed that it will be possible to serve meals to all passengers in the Dining Saloon, nor that there will be sufficient stewards available. In this latter event it will be necessary for passengers to wait upon themselves.

4. Passengers may have to keep their own quarters clean.

5. Public rooms are restricted.

6. Passage must be accepted on the implicit understanding that no question of refund of passage money will subsequently be entertained.

7. It must be understood that passengers will be subject to ship's discipline administered by the Master (and Officer Commanding Troops, if any).

I fully understand that my passage has been granted by troop transport in accordance with all the above mentioned conditions, which I accept; and that a passage ticket will not

be issued until this form is signed and returned to the
Shipping Company.

Signature. . . . .

They would get no signature from me. . . . Austerity was all
very well, and we had come to accept it, and live with it, and
even to see its point, for years on end; but this latest example
seemed well over the limit. Eileen had recently been ill; Max
was three and a half, and had never known any heat worse than
75 degrees. Both of them would have to have yellow fever
inoculations, which could be a knock-out. They would be
travelling in squalor for twenty-eight days instead of the normal fourteen.

Meanwhile, I would be making my own bed, fetching my own
austere meals, eating them in the nearest alley-way, queueing
for a faraway lavatory, and doing as I was told by Officer
Commanding Troops. No, sir!

I said that I was sorry, but it was impossible, and set out my
reasons in a long, carefully composed letter (I was better at
letters than at interviews, where I could always be baffled and
buffaloed and persuaded that things were all for the best). I
included a daring last thrust, that if my new job was of so little
consequence that I could be offered this kind of travel facility,
then etc. . . . Finally I had to ask, sir, with due respect, that
something better should be arranged.

Junior civil servants in their first week of employment do not
write this kind of letter; luckily I did not know this, and I am
sure that certain benevolent men in authority appreciated the
fact, and let me get away with it instead of hammering me into
the ground under six feet of Dominions Office carpet. There was
a silent pause, while I pondered, and re-read my letter, and
waited for the lightning to strike, and trembled at the possibilities—I was unemployed, we had already let the house, I had
£130 in the bank and no prospects of any kind.

Then I was informed, without further comment, that our
passage had been re-booked in the *City of Madras*, which would

be leaving two weeks later and going direct to Cape Town. She
sailed from Tilbury on the morning tide, and I took damned
good care to be on board.

We heard ITMA, for the last time, as we went down
Channel.

The *City of Madras* was a handsome, newish ship, handily-
sized at 9,000 tons and carrying twenty-four passengers. Even
with this small complement, we were still crowded (twenty-four
was probably double her planned capacity), and the sexes were
rigorously separated. I was in a cabin with three other men;
Eileen and Max shared another with two very old ladies, an
arrangement which did not make for harmony.

They were subject to various ailments (as they had every right
to be) but this made them fractious, and adamant about
draughts; the portholes had to be kept closed, up to the
equator and beyond. The disparity of seventy years between
Max and the older of the old ladies was a generation-gap which
could never be bridged. When Max, clambering out of his upper
berth, landed on a much-prized morning cup of tea below, the
severance must have seemed complete.

I had my own troubles, with a late-night conversationalist, a
drunk, and a dedicated snorer. (This was all one man.) But to
such accommodation we were committed for the duration.
Eileen and I were thus parted, not long after sundown each day,
like an engaged couple under strict family surveillance. It was
not the best basis for refashioning a marriage, though the rest
of our voyage into sunshine was so blissful that perhaps the
repair work was being done in other ways.

There was only one uneasy day, on the whole of that 6,000-
mile southward journey, and this was when, after crossing the
Bay of Biscay in one of its good moods, we sailed down the
west coast of Spain, where so many of the sailor dead lay—
abandoned by me, beginning to be forgotten by the world.

With a little less luck, I might have been down there with
them, one of a multitude of wet and weaving corpses. Now I
was turning my back on all they had fought for, all I had fought

for myself, and making my escape, in a way which only selfish
Conservatives were meant to do.

But then the weather warmed, and such thoughts lost their
edge, and faded astern like our own trailing wake. The guilty
feeling that we were deserters was presently forgotten. I was
going to work for my country, after all. . . . Why not—
fantastic thought!—enjoy this good turn of fortune?

We began to do that. The process was helped, as far as I
was concerned, by a wonderful feeling of irresponsibility, for
the first time in years of sea-going. This wasn't my ship! I
wasn't the captain, nor even the junior midshipman of the
watch. Other people were taking the load: if something went
wrong, if we ran aground or sailed slap through a fishing fleet,
someone else would face the mournful music, and explain to the
Board of Inquiry that everything had been perfectly all right
when he left the bridge at midnight.

The most violent noise in the dark hours could only be a
dropped tray.

With a coward joy I became, at long last, a passenger. As
such, all I had to do was to gamble daily on the ship's run, play
deck games of such absolute futility that it was a pleasure to
lose, run a General Knowledge Quiz which infuriated three-
quarters of the participants ('Man, he must think we're bloody
intellectuals!' said a muscular young South African, on whom I
would have cast no such slur), and eat!

How we ate: four-course breakfasts, five-course lunches, six-
course dinners, with actual butter on the table and five kinds of
meat a-carving on the sideboard. And how we drank: free of
wartime rationing, free of that servile touting for an extra half-
bottle of gin, we laced into the drinks as we laced into the
food, with the gross appetite of prisoners set free.

Max, with a smaller share of such urgent yearnings (the
Ministry of Food had done wonders for wartime children, and
with the aid of special allotments of fruit juices and other
restoratives, he was in better shape than any of us)—Max
probably came off the worst. Apart from the constrictions of

cabin life, he was often in marine trouble; he fell down a ladder twice in one day, shaking himself badly and bruising his back; and the small amount of rough weather we had was an inexplicable misery.

It was difficult to keep track of him all the time, as I explained to the captain when, after the second of these accidents, I was summoned to his cabin to explain our neglect. The captain, mentioning that he had children of his own ('But not on board, thank God!') agreed with me. But at the same time. . . . I promised to do better in future, thus involving Eileen at least in some round-the-clock supervision. (Fathers always had more important things to do.) But the fact that Max was the only child on board, and pampered on that account, meant that she had some sporadic help.

The more important things I had to do did not make up a very impressive list; I was secure and satiated in our floating haven, shedding cares and burdens like cold-weather clothes. But I found time for some necessary reading from the clutch of files I had brought with me, and a lot of slightly dreamy planning, and a little covert inspection of the South Africans on board, random samples of my future customers.

They were not altogether reassuring. The idea that I was journeying to a new, dynamic, go-ahead country, jumping up and down with raw energy, bursting at the seams with fresh injections of forward planning, would have to await further evidence. The odds against this were, by early shipboard calculation, 3–1 against, or, to be exact, 6–2.

There was also an early whiff of bigotry, of set attitudes, of a thick-skulled refusal to learn from anyone or anything, which took me a long way back in pre-history—for example, to my own sixteen-year-old true-blue horror at the very idea of the 1926 General Strike.

On the profit side, there was one delightful South African woman on board, an undoubted beauty of such glowing quality that, though there was every reason to suppose that she was over forty-five, she need not have been more than forty-six. This civilized creature was concealed under the dull label of Mrs Hugh Bairnsfather (*née* Cloete), softened by a melodious Christian name which I was allowed to use.

An hour in her company, whether attended by mid-morning sunshine and chicken *bouillon*, early evening twilight and what I was already calling a sun-downer, or after-dinner star-gazing and Cointreau, restored both the grace of the past and the hope of the future.

I need hardly add, though in all the circumstances I will do so, that on such occasions I was always decorously accompanied by Eileen, with Max (by official edict) never far away.

The second person in the plus-account was Mr Coetzee, who had been working with the South African Information Service in London and was now returning to take up another similar job. We had met briefly in London, as part of my early indoctrination; and now, he was being extremely helpful and co-operative with the mass of queries (some of them ludicrously naïve) and the widening range of doubts which I was beginning to have about the job ahead.

The first item of information he volunteered was that Mrs Bairnsfather ('She's a real peach, eh?') lived at a place called Alphen, near Cape Town, and that this was the most beautiful house in the whole of South Africa. I was not at all surprised.

But at that point the good news stopped, as far as the *City of Madras* was concerned. The South African representation now continued with four bone-headed young men, all dazzling white shorts and gleaming brown thighs, who ran the deck games, won them all, and looked round for the applause. In the afternoon, they monopolized the swimming pool, merrily ducking any intruder; in the evening, they sucked down South African brandy, talked about *kaffirs* and niggers and the yids who ran Johannesburg ('Watch out for them! They'd steal the tickies off a dead man's eyes!'), and sang, interminably, one sad song called *Sarie Marais*, and another, more cheerful, about a sugar-bush.

It was the leader of this quartet who had been heard to complain about my General Knowledge Quiz, in which a sample question was:

Who wrote: (a)   *War and Peace?*
              (b)   *Pride and Prejudice?*
              (c)   *Sons and Lovers?*

and a sample answer was a blank space.

Then there was an older South African, a spry sixty-year-old so intent on proving himself continuously spry that, when leaning over to retrieve a deck-quoit, he did a full Knees Bend—Down! Up! Hup!, like some blasted P.T. drill sergeant—instead of the more indolent male curtsy with which one retrieved a dropped handkerchief.

It was he who, shortly after the scandal of that highbrow General Knowledge Quiz, cornered me in search of the facts. He had heard some rumours about me, he said, not at all on a friendly note. Something about giving out information. Like in a school, eh? What exactly was I planning to do in South Africa?

Using the innocuous formula of the Dominions Office, I returned a soft answer to a suspicious man. No, it would not be like a school at all. I was coming out to open a British Information Office, because we wanted the world in general, and South Africa in particular, to know what Britain was saying and doing and thinking, at this moment of history. The information office would produce the facts, and answer questions about them. That was all.

Old Mr X was still suspicious. He gave an energetic hitch to his white linen slacks. 'But you're going to teach us. Is that it?'

'No.'

'Better not try it!' The determined eyes took on a crocodile ferocity. 'One thing South Africans don't like, is people telling them how to run their country!'

I assured him that I would not be trying to do anything of the sort.

But perhaps he had not been satisfied. I knew already that Mr

X had a friend, a travelling companion, called Mr Y, also an old man but not spry at all; rather a gnarled, rheumaticky patriarchal man who sat motionless in the sun all day, wearing a vast khaki bush hat and staring with pale blue eyes at the sea, or the sky, or sometimes at the antics of his fellow-passengers.

He seemed to prefer the sea. I was therefore astonished when, that same evening, he beckoned me to his side. I felt favoured, even flattered, since he really was a figure of some authority. But the summons, it turned out, was only to give me a second gruff grilling, this time about politics, racial politics. Was I, he asked, a Liberal?

He had used the word as if it stood for something very disreputable indeed. But I felt that I could answer no, with a clear conscience. I had never been a Liberal.

'That's good,' he said, and nodded several times at the distant horizon. His face, close to, was something like a map of Africa itself: gaunt, eroded by time, craggy here and there, burnt down to the bone, but enduring. 'Too many of you Englishmen coming out, you're no better than Liberals! You want to tell us what to do with our own country. You want to put the *kaffirs* in charge. But that's not God's will, is it?'

'I don't know.'

'Don't you read the Bible, boy?'

'Certainly.'

'It's all there in the Bible. They often read it out in our church. What you would call the D.R.C. In your English Bible it goes: "The sons of Ham shall be hewers of wood and drawers of water for ever." That's God's own word! You can't deny it.'

A spectral, Dominions Office voice was reminding me across three thousand miles, not to get into any arguments particularly this sort of argument. But I went so far as to say that the Bible was always open to interpretation; that things did change, that ideas changed, that people changed, that the world itself changed all the time. A million years ago—

I was interrupted promptly and forcibly. 'Six thousand years ago!' And as I looked at him, uncomprehending: 'Six thousand

years ago! That's when God made the world! In seven days!
It's in the Bible!'

'But scientists——'

'Ach, those damned fools!' Mr Y really was provoking himself to a noticeable pitch of vehemence. 'Such blockheads don't
know anything!' For a moment he was pondering, busy with
the horizon again. Then the pale blue eyes and the fierce bushy
eyebrows came round to me. 'What was the name of that
rooinek who said he had sailed round the world? Back in the old
days?'

'What sort of—er——' I wasn't going to try to match his
reverberating pronunciation of a unfamiliar word. 'I mean,
where did he come from?'

'From America! Where else?'

'Oh.' Here was some familiar ground at last. 'You mean
Joshua Slocum.'

'That's the rascal!' A gnarled fist came down on a thigh which
withstood it manfully. 'Did you know when he reached South
Africa, he made a visit to see President Kruger himself?'

It was a long time since I had read *Sailing Alone Round the
World*, or thought of the lonely *Spray*. 'I'd forgotten that,' I
answered, dishonestly.

'Well, I can tell you, that *skelm* Slocum never forgot it! He
paid this call on the President, and he said: "Mr President, I
have sailed round the world." Or maybe it was: "Mr President,
I am sailing round the world." Do you know what Kruger
answered him?'

'No.'

'He said: "You cannot sail round the world. The world is
flat!" What do you think of that for an answer?'

The Dominions Office directive was proving a severe test.
'Well——'

But old Mr Y did not really want an answer from me, only
from President Kruger.

'Ach!' he said, and infused a great deal of delight into this
unlikely syllable. 'He was *slim*, that one! He was smart all right!'

'Who was smart?'

'Oom Paul!'

Later I took all this to my friend and sheet-anchor, Mr Coetzee, who was kind enough to unravel some of the skeins, with details which came easily from a fellow information expert now daily drawing nearer his own home ground.

It was true, he told me, that President Kruger (1825–1904) had believed that the earth was flat. But, said Mr Coetzee, an Afrikaner with his own pride of race, Kruger had been clever otherwise. He had been more than a match for the British, eh? He had indeed been 'slim'. The word meant crafty or cunning, and the gift was still held in high esteem.

The D.R.C., he went on, in answer to further queries, was the Dutch Reformed Church. They preached that the whole of the Bible was literally true, word for word. If it said that the world was 6,000 years old, then they believed 6,000 years. It was the same with the sons of Ham.

'The D.R.C. says that God made the white man superior. They say He put a curse on the black man, the son of Ham, and made him a servant. They say it is in the Bible, so it must be true. Most South Africans believe in the idea, anyway. They don't need the Bible.'

'But a servant for ever?'

Mr Coetzee, a man of humour, intelligence, and compassion, who had been exposed to foreign travel, gave me the sort of smile which came as a certain relief.

'That's the big question, eh?'

I had a few more questions of my own. 'Tell me, what's a *rooinek*?'

He corrected my pronunciation. 'It means a red neck, literally. Because of the sun-burn in the Boer War. The British nearly went mad! Now it means any foreigner.'

'And *skelm*?'

'A good-for-nothing. A loafer.'

'And Oom?'

'That's "uncle". We call anyone we like who is old, Oom.

So President Paul Kruger was Oom Paul. Now you'll find people calling General Smuts "Oom Jannie".'
'And what are tickies?'
'Three pennies. What you call threepenny bits. You'll hear a lot about tickies in Johannesburg. On the Stock Exchange. Anyone who settles for a quick profit, they call a tickey-snatcher.' The sound of young voices, raised in mournful praise of *Sarie Marais*, came to us faintly from the bar. But we were on the boat-deck, under a glowing moon, surrounded by a tropic night and the gentlest breeze I had felt for many a year. Perhaps it was this happy division, this distancing of art from nature, which prompted Coetzee to say:
'Make no mistake. We are funny people. We are *different* people—different by thousands of miles. But you will love South Africa, I can tell you. It is the most beautiful country in the world.'

Thus we sailed onwards, for a total of seventeen days, days which slipped by like the quicksilver moon itself. Thus the *City of Madras* made her appointed passage—solid, stable, safe, the size of ten *Campanulas*. Finally, after a season of such dreaming indolence as I had never hoped to live again, we rounded smoothly into Table Bay, and the Tavern-of-the-Seas which was Cape Town Harbour; and there, at sunrise, with the wakening town dwarfed by the massive grey backcloth of Table Mountain, and noble smoky-blue hills beyond, and a sparkling green sea behind us, to prove that we had voyaged 6,000 miles instead of turning a single page in a picture book, there we came to rest.

It was the end of what was to be my last holiday for two and a half years. But then, I did not know that. All I knew was what I saw and felt, as the mooring hawsers snaked ashore and were secured: the warmth, the sunshine, the bright colours, the excitement, and a view of what Mr Coetzee had called the most beautiful country in the world.

At first glance, I saw that this could well be true.

We found a heartening reception committee waiting on the dockside, just the kind one needed when taking the last step down the gangway and the first into a world absolutely new and strange. There was an energetic, bearded young South African called John Bold, who had been the lone Information Officer on the High Commissioner's staff for the past few years; and Ian Maclennan, the First Secretary—the same age as myself, but with an early crop of luxurious grey hair which made me envious; and Patrick Duncan, then the junior member of the High Commission staff.

This was, though we did not know it then, an assembly of very diverse talent. John Bold, who stayed on as a most useful Press Officer in the new organization, finally decided on a more individual career, which was to invent, develop, and popularize one all-embracing native language.

This, destined to be the *lingua franca* for the whole of Southern Africa, he christened Fanagalo. It was a devout dream, but Fanagalo never prospered, and the multitude of tribal languages remains intact.

Ian Maclennan, climbing a lofty ladder, was to be High Commissioner in the Rhodesian Federation and in Ghana, our Ambassador to Ireland, and High Commissioner in New Zealand.*

Patrick Duncan, a cheerful young man in spite of a severe and painful limp, the product of some early parental confidence in Christian Science, made his own pathway of honour. Son of a former Governor-General of South Africa, he became

---

* Since, during my short term in South Africa, the High Commission staff also included Morrice James (High Commissioner in Pakistan, the last permanent head of the Commonwealth Office before it was merged with the F.O., and High Commissioner in India): David Scott (High Commissioner in Uganda): David Hunt (Private Secretary to both Attlee and Churchill, High Commissioner in Uganda, Cyprus, and Nigeria, and Ambassador to Brazil): Arthur Clark (High Commissioner in Cyprus): Edward Beetham (Governor and Commander-in-Chief of the Windward Islands and later of Trinidad and Tobago): Roland Turnbull (Governor of North Borneo): and John Wakely (Ambassador to Burma), the South African contingent turned out to be quite a stable, with knighthoods running very close to 100 per cent.

disenchanted with the country when it was reshaped under
Nationalist rule; he resigned from the public service, and teamed
up with various inter-racial and thus outlawed groups; and he
went to gaol at least once, in a courageous one-man attempt to
stem *apartheid*, before he died.

But then, this was just a trio of cheerful young men on the
quayside at Cape Town, against a background of market-stalls
crammed with marvellous flowers which I had never seen before
—cannas, chincherinchees, poinsettias, bougainvillaeas, and
tiny sprigs of wild orchid the colour of pale olive stones—with
that whopping great monolith of Table Mountain on top of
everything.

Meeting them was one hesitant newcomer, wrongly dressed,
nervous of authority even one notch above him, and knowing as
much about starting up an information office as they did about
running a tourist ballet company in Peking.

Yet confidence returned, as we were wafted through Customs
with a few diplomatic finger-snaps, and then driven in the High
Commission car up to the Mount Nelson Hotel, a splendid
monument to colonial rule which had survived to become a Cape
Town showpiece and a centre of old-fashioned opulence. There
we settled down, in guilty luxury; forgetting a starving
Europe, forgetting our dear ones far away, crouched over their
squirrel-pie as the gas pressure faded to nothing; transplanted
at a stroke into careless paradise.

After a pre-lunch drink under the trees in the garden, we
took our places in a sunny corner of the dining-room, with a
matchless view of the slopes leading down to the harbour, and
made our selection from the menu. This was a noble document
listing some fifteen items, with a footnote: 'The limited menu
is in accordance with the restrictions imposed by Gov. Reg.
1945'. I hoped there would be many more Gov. Regs. like that
one.

We feasted off paw-paw, and a new fish-dish called Fried 74,
and meat such as we had not tasted for half a decade, and
crêpes suzettes, and (for me) a cigar, regretfully the smallest they

had available, a Corona-Corona for which the going price in London, even if obtainable there, would have been 15s. Here it was 2s. 6d., and here, thank God, I was smoking it.

There was another High Commission man staying in the hotel, a superior character with the memorable name of Hercules Priestman (one took, I thought, a certain chance with such a christening, almost equal in valour and daring to calling one's daughter Venus). Luckily Priestman, who perhaps had been a huge baby, had grown up to be a huge man.

He was sketchily introduced to me as the Chief Secretary for B. B. and S. The initials, which stood for the three High Commission Territories of Basutoland, Bechuanaland, and Swaziland, were to prove a load of trouble in the near future.

But on that day they were simply initials, and Hercules Priestman a most engaging companion, though his sense of humour did not always accord with my tender anti-colonial conscience—as when he said, of a formidable woman, an ex-proconsul's wife whose husband had just retired to Basutoland: 'Never had the earth been so liberally bedewed with Basuto sweat as when her ladyship started replanning the garden.'

Next morning I had my first interview with the boss, High Commissioner Sir Evelyn Baring. The session completed a twenty-four-hour induction as inspiring, hopeful, and reassuring as it could possibly have been.

Baring, son of an earl (Lord Cromer) who had transformed Egypt from a slum into a country at the turn of the century, and the grandson of a marquess, was the first aristocrat of achievement I had ever met, as distinct from the aristocrats of indolence with whom I had wasted so much time at Cambridge, and a couple of aristocrats of tailored incompetence I had met during the war.

He was still under forty-three, and had already carved himself a distinguished career in the Indian Civil Service; he had just completed a term as Governor of Southern Rhodesia, and ahead of him still lay the Governorship of Kenya during the worst of the Mau Mau era, and the chairmanship of the

Commonwealth Development Corporation, with £160 million a year to distribute as wisely as possible.

He was tall, he was friendly, he had been at Winchester; and I was an admiring member of his staff for the next five years. He was a wonderful man to work for, while demonstrably working like a demon himself: the first of two High Commissioners (the other was Archibald Nye in Canada) who had what seemed to me the perfect attitude towards the men on the payroll beneath.

This was to teach them, control them, praise them when appropriate, blast their stupid heads off when they made a mistake, *but*—and this was the biggest 'but' in this area, widely neglected by other practitioners of authority—always to draw the mantle of personal responsibility over the battlefield, when something had gone wrong.

One could depend on the fact that any mistake one made was, in the last accounting, a High Commission mistake, covered by a tough protective screen which was the screen any good ship's captain was always ready to use. Underneath it, all sorts of disciplinary fists might be flying—anything from 'I'm afraid this won't do' to a speedy passage home and a dusty bowler hat awaiting the culprit at Southampton. But it was the High Commissioner who, locally, picked up the bits and rearranged them tidily.

I was to have two prime examples of this—examples not too awful, but awful enough for me: once when I got into a row with some professional Zionists in Johannesburg, whose local newspaper then clamoured for my recall; and once when we were banishing a chief, Seretse Khama, from Bechuanaland, for what seemed good and sufficient reasons, and I made some ill-phrased comments to the assembled newspapermen on the strong-arm tactics of his supporters.

Each time, the outcome for me was the biblical 'The tongue is an unruly member—guard it!' kind of lecture, followed by a soothing telegram to London, making the point that Monsarrat was doing his best in difficult circumstances, and still enjoyed the High Commissioner's full confidence.

Baring might have been stretching a point, each time; but the full confidence was there on the record, and from my own side it was there in the flesh and the spirit. This process of private and public loyalty started now, in Cape Town, with our first meeting and first mutual measurement, and if it ever lagged, it never did so with me.

Baring, agile and energetic in spite of indifferent health, now and then used to climb to the summit of Table Mountain (3,550 feet), in company with the Prime Minister, General Smuts, who at the age of seventy-six regarded Table Mountain as no more than a pleasant, slightly uphill walk. Members of the High Commissioner's staff were always welcome to tag along (Morrice James was one who did so), though my own severe war wound (1940: thrown out of bunk: cracked rib) unfortunately prevented me from volunteering.

But this ascent somehow symbolized for me the section of ladder which now faced me, and the climate of behaviour which my first interview with Evelyn Baring signified. This was a world of strict endeavour, efficiency, good conduct, and the honourable discharge of duty. It was like the Navy, except that now the ranks were vague, and the uniform non-existent. The uniform, in fact, was the civil uniform of service. I wore no other for ten years, and when I lapsed from it, only a selection of glad rags took its place.

Later that day he found time to take me round on a series of visits—and here again the idea was to start me, and the new office, off on the right foot, by giving us his personal seal from the start.

We called on the editors of the two English-language newspapers, the *Cape Times* and the *Argus*, who were cordial in their welcome. We had sessions with the South African Bureau of Information, the Ministry of External Affairs, and the South African Press Association, which under its short title SAPA-Reuter was the principal export-import agency for all news from this part of the world, and all news from outside.

We sat in for a dull half-hour at the House of Assembly, now in mid-session, which, by contrast with the young, new-style ferment now rising at Westminster, seemed incredibly old and tired and bored. We had reviving drinks at the two clubs, the Civil Service and the City, of which I was now an honorary member: clubs so comfortable, leisurely, solid, and important that I knew I had at last gone up in the world.

Then I went back to the High Commission Office (there was no doubt that this was a working day), and continued, with the help of the registry, making my selection of the files which I either wanted to read on the spot, or take with me when I went up to Johannesburg.

But there was plenty of time to look about, during the ten days in Cape Town, and looking about was depressing.

Though this was a handsome city, with some splendid Cape-Dutch buildings and a magnificent harbour, all guarded by the bulk of Table Mountain and its attendant Devil's Peak and Lion's Head: though strange fruits and gorgeous flowers grew like luxuriant weeds: though the surrounding coastline, where the Atlantic met the Indian Ocean, was as fair as the Firth of Clyde, with guaranteed sunshine as the essential bonus: though people were fantastically hospitable and welcoming, and food and drink as lavish as at some banquet of all the nations, yet there was poison in the Cape air.

It was not an undeniable poison, nor a poison beyond argument, nor poison so mortal that it could never be another man's meat; but it was poison for the man I still was—the compassionate socialist with strange and lasting injections of naval discipline, the mixed-up do-gooder who wanted everybody to be happy, on the basis (equally mixed up) that we were all God's creatures, sharing the same huge and bountiful pie, and that if we could not be generous enough, and wise enough, and nice enough to make a fair division of such bounty, then we did not deserve the label, nor the pie either, and would lose the lot on the garbage tip of history.

The poison was, of course, the colour bar; and though in theory I knew all about this (it had been Item Number One in my briefing, under the implied heading 'None of your business'), yet to see it put into practice surprised and disgusted me— particularly as South Africa still marched towards its destiny under the banner of General Jan Christiaan Smuts, one of the prime architects of the United Nations which, at its inauguration at Lake Success, had made such valiant declarations of universal brotherhood.

Only later did it occur to me that Smuts had been so busy with his star billing on the global stage that he had neglected his own back garden; that while he beamed and bloomed in the heady sunshine of world acclaim, his own country staggered towards ill-fortune and a mean, un-Christian, rigid, permanent division into Have and Have Not.

This lack of application, I came to believe, was why he was slung out of office two years later, to be succeeded by men who *had* been cultivating their own garden, with a pruning hook as sharp as a serpent's tooth, and weed-killer which went down to the very roots; and why Smuts deserved his dismissal. Vanity, the enemy of commonsense, and pride, the worst of sins, destroyed what hopes he might have had of the future, and made of his neglected country an orphan among her friends, and a polecat for her enemies.

To his intimates and relatives, General Smuts was indeed 'Oom Jannie', as Mr Coetzee had told me and as Ian Maclennan was able to confirm.* But to the rest of his country he was the *Oubaas*, which could be translated without inaccuracy or malice as the Old Boss.

The label had good connotations as well as bad: 'Boss' did not have to mean slave-driver, any more than 'love' necessarily meant lust in action.

But this was an old boss who did not boss—not where it was really needed. He was coasting, in a preferred climate of

---

* His wife also had an affectionate title, *Ouma* Smuts—i.e., Old Mother or Grandmother. But she was less affectionate towards our side than one might have wished. When in labour with her first child, she had insisted that the bed should be covered by the *Vierkleur*, the old Transvaal republican standard, so that the child should not be born under the British flag.

adulation; he was enjoying an enviable run as Friend of the Great, and Neglecter of the Poor. Within two years, history was to catch up with him, when, in 1948, the Afrikaner Nationalists rode in, spurs a-jingling, whips poised, to take over the whole restless camp and coin the brand-new word *Apartheid*.*

They were never to ride out again: not in twenty-two years, perhaps not in thirty-two, or a hundred and thirty-two, or until a vast shedding of blood washed all the good and all the bad, all the love and care and hatred and mean conceit, down the same drain, which had already served a tormented continent for half a million years.

Correction: 6,000 years.

But that is a 'now' judgement, with all the sad erosion of the recent past to make it seem valid; then it was 'then', in April of 1946, when all I had to go on were the eyes and ears and the pursed lips of a new arrival. Then, all these rules were new to me, and horrid in their implication, and traitorous in their denial of the last six years.

I had just fought a war—and unless we were all blind-bull idiots, led by the century's most spurious nose-ring, we had *all* fought a war—dedicated to the proposition, happily victorious, that there must be no master-race; that a Jew was an equal man, and a Pole an equal man, and all the other slaves of the Thousand Year *Reich* were equal men.

This *must* mean that a black man was an equal man, with two of everything except where it counted most, where we were once again all equal: that a Cape-Coloured man was just the same: that one could not kill Hitler, and hang his guilty aides,

* In 1949. It meant nothing more sinister than 'apart-ness'. It was first set down in print in 1950, when the Congress of the Dutch Reformed Church adopted a resolution calling for 'full territorial *apartheid*'. It still remains the most uncompromising and therefore the most honest term for social and racial discrimination, preferable to all other evasions, glosses, and sneak short cuts to segregation.

One would rather hear *apartheid* thus proclaimed, loud and clear, than the contemptible sneer 'Fine old Scottish name!' applied to a Jew, or the slightly more endearing Liverpool label, 'Smoked Irishman', for a Negro. With the one, you know where you are; with all the others, you know where you are but you won't admit it.

and cleanse the infected air of his dream of race-slavery, and
then emerge smiling into the sunlight, to inherit all the oot of
violation for which we had just fought him to a standstill.

Yet as soon as one stepped out of the Mount Nelson Hotel,
and walked easily downhill through the Gardens towards the
High Commission Office, this was what one was supposed to
accept, without question.

It came in the form of notices, which were displayed everywhere, even in Cape Town's most quiet retreat, where in the
cool shade there was an aviary, and strange trees whose
twisted bark followed the turning track of the sun, and an endless succession of warnings: 'Europeans Only'—'Non-Europeans
Only'—'*Blankes Alleen*', from one end to another of this small
Eden.

Down town it was the same, except that there men and
women carried these signs in their eyes as well—or perhaps it
was that malady of short sight which I came to know very well,
the literal colour blindness which ensured that on the streets
and in the shops and at any public gathering, one did not see a
black man or a coloured man or any man who did not belong to
the white totem.

One looked straight through him; or, shortening the focus,
saw him as a dark blur, a grey ghost, a shadow in the path, a
near nothing in the white world of everything.

First the brain turned aside, and then the eyes, and then, if
necessary, the feet. But this last need scarcely ever happen.
Already, in 1946, the coloured man took to the wall or the
edge of the pavement, or the gutter, or the dusty hedgerow, as
the white man passed.

On a short train journey down to the beach at nearby Muizen-
berg (which those horrid young South Africans in the *City of
Madras* had called, with a smirk, 'Jewzenberg'), the fact of the
separation of man from man was made even plainer.

Here the labels multiplied until they were a permanent
frieze of denial; they were on every railway carriage, and every
lavatory; on every bench of every station; at every ticket-office,

and every shelter, and at every entrance and exit; at every bus-
stop outside, and on the wind-blown beach itself, where one did
not stray 'down there' because that was the coloured section,
generously labelled, and They certainly did not stray 'up
here', because they knew a bloody sight better than to try it
on.

Blankes Alleen was the only ticket to have. Anything else was
comfortably counterfeit.

I supposed—indeed, I knew—that if one had grown up with
it, from blond childhood, it would certainly have been acceptable, like the pox in the Middle Ages, or the later, dirty
travesty of democracy which allowed a teacher of the young to
tell them that violence was 'relevant'—i.e., a permissible way to
get what you wanted.

But to an innocent stranger it was a shock, just as sharp as it
must have been to a country boy who walked for the first time
into the city of fifty years ago, and there read, with astonished,
ashamed eyes, the crude notices which commanded him: 'Do
Not Spit'; 'Keep Off the Grass'; 'Adjust Your Dress'; 'Commit
No Nuisance'.

Until then, he would have had no thoughts of spitting, or of
treading on anything which grew, or of not buttoning up, or of
urinating anywhere except behind the nearest, thickest privet
hedge in sight.* Now, under the new urban rules, he had to
watch his every step, in case he grew careless, or was corrupted
by such evil communications.

Of course, the poison in this air *was* one man's meat; it was a
lot of men's meat; it was these men's meat, and as neutral
visitors we could only watch them enjoying it. It was none of
our business, as Ian Maclennan and all the others had been
trained to assume automatically on their arrival, whatever their
private thoughts, and as they taught their comrades and
successors.

This was South Africa, and nowhere else; it was *their*

---

* 'Privet', first noted in 1542, is labelled 'origin unknown'. I still like to think that
the derivation is from '*privatus*'.

country, not ours; we were not there to change it (that chance
was long gone, with the wind of change itself, which blew as
strongly from the south as it blew from the north). We were
only there to observe, to report privately, and to maintain
polite and firm contact with an ex-colony which we hoped would
not become an ex-Dominion.

That (with a short pause for uncontrollable laughter) was
why I was there: to set up our own shop-window, to talk and
write about Britain, to preach the virtues of the Commonwealth.
but never, except by the mildest implication, to draw any comparison whatsoever.

Occasionally, very occasionally, it was pleasant and preferable not to draw any comparisons, because one would have
been on the losing side. Certainly my admired mother-country
had nothing to offer like Alphen, in the Constantia Valley,
where we went for lunch on my last weekend in Cape Town.

Such shipboard invitations, even the most insistent, usually
dropped into the dock as one walked down the gangway and all
the firm fourteen-day friendships dispersed along with the
friends. This one had not done so, and it proved a blessed
exception. Mrs Bairnsfather not only confirmed our lunch-date,
but sent a car to collect us.

It was a memorable day, starting with a beautiful drive
which wound all the way round Table Mountain towards the
green wooded slopes which were the foothills of the Constantia
Mountains. This was wine country, among other things
(Alphen itself was a well-known South African *marque*); the
vines marched in orderly procession up the hillsides. the sunlight filtered through interlaced branches, and fell gently on the
backs of men and women bending to their work, on children
who waved and dogs thumping their tails on the hot earth.

Alphen itself was not large: a small gem of a place built in the
Dutch-Colonial style in 1753, and the handsomest house I had
ever seen.

Every piece of it, we were told, every stick and stone, had
been brought from Holland or the Dutch East Indies, and much
7*

of the furniture too—furniture polished by loving or industrious hands for nearly two hundred years, so that their surfaces, of satin wood and ebony, *imbuia* and yellow wood, oiled
teak and burr walnut, served as mirrors for all the other riches
of the house, and for the ancient glaze of blue Batavian tiles.

We had approached Alphen slowly, by its long avenue of
oaks, themselves as old as the house, which wound past the
vineyards; and the first sight of it—its gleaming white walls,
its flagged courtyard and the twin white-washed columns of its
first and last 'slave bell'—were enough to catch the heart, and to
eassure all doubts.

Whatever else might be going on in South Africa, here everything was noble and peaceful.

Having come to stay, in 1750, these men had built to endure;
and even a transient heir of such lasting beauty, as I was myself,
could draw unassailable comfort and pleasure from the fact.

At lunch we enjoyed our first genuine South African cooking
(the Mount Nelson menu, though extensive, catered for
travellers who did not want any nasty surprises), and everything
we drank—sherry, dry white wine, and an exquisite liqueur—
came from just outside the house, where our view through the
open top half of the 'stable door' was a lovely square of sunlight, the yellow and red leaves of the huge oaks, more of those
flowers and shrubs I had never seen before—jacaranda, protea,
flame-of-the-forest—and in the hazy distance the vineyards
industriously climbing the hills.

Afterwards we walked round those vineyards, and through
the cellars, where vast vats, holding up to 2,200 gallons each,
were readying the next year's brew. Life in this beautiful
corner of the world must have been enchanting. Of course, as any
fool could divine, without benefit of social conscience or a
reformer's beady eye, it was founded on cheap labour, in plentiful
supply: labour which stayed put, from the first generation to the
one now in occupation, and bred its own successors.

But that labour must have been well cared for, and protected,
and still content—if smiles, and open-handed greetings, and no

single sullen glance from five hundred assorted people, meant contentment. There was no evidence that they wanted to leave, or to change places with anyone outside; and if this was due to ignorance, or lack of ambition, or dutiful acceptance of the established order, yet it worked, here, without question.*

The superb house, the people in it and around it, the feeling of a huge family *enclave*, where all were fed, the sick cared for, and the children schooled, was such an antidote to the poison of *Blankes Alleen* that I now felt much better, in a thoroughly sentimental way. Already I saw myself as an expert; already. I thought, I could have been half-way through writing one of those travel books occasionally to be found in antiquarian booksellers, with long rambling titles which left nothing to chance:

BONA SPERANZA: The Cape of Good Hope described; with some observations on the Bushmen, Hottentots, Boers, Uitlanders, and Cape Malays; Copiously illustrated with sketches of the Flora and Fauna, and a Prospect of the Harbour from the Heights of the Devil's Peak; All by AN OFFICER (late His Majesty's Royal Navy), and Dedicated by gracious permission to the Most Honourable the Marquess of . . .

Half a day later, I was in the train (four to a sleeper, taking thirty-five hours to cover a thousand miles) on the way north to Johannesburg.

That journey, the longest I had ever made on land, was also one of the most fascinating. I had been prepared for the size of the country, but not for its novelty; from the first mile to the last, there was scarcely anything to be seen which I had seen before, scarcely any natural or man-made object of which I

* A cynical friend in Johannesburg, an Afrikaner, was soon to give me his version of this Cape-Coloured 'contentment'. It was, he maintained, based on the 'tot system', by which part of their wages were paid with a massive daily ration of fortified wine. That, as he put it, kept them 'gently weaving, feeling no pain', throughout their working life. He had served with the R.A.F.

could say: 'I saw something like that in Spain', (or Hungary, or Fife, or Massachusetts Bay). It was all new, all foreign, and all intensely watchable.

My companions were John Bold, who continued to act as a useful guide and chaperon (he had already rescued me from the solecism of straying into a Non-Whites' lavatory on Cape Town station); and two strangers, two tough young men from the Government Forestry Department on their way to a conference in the capital, Pretoria.*

They were cheerful, talkative, individual, and self-reliant; one of them had been in minesweepers during the war, which, as training for survival in any peacetime hazard, could hardly be bettered. But I could not help noticing that they were both extraordinarily adolescent, even childish, where women were concerned, and this, perhaps, would prove to be the one peacetime hazard they could not cope with.

They kept ceaseless watch for anything which came into sight; in the restaurant car, they were hardly in our company at all, so intent were they on 'the goods' (as they called any girl between fifteen and forty-five). Careful survey, detailed speculation, fiery glances, attempts at a pick-up, always followed. They reminded me of stamp-collectors whose greatest fear was lest any envelope, however unpromising, might be discarded before it had been checked for possibilities.

But what they hoped to do about it, in a sleeping compartment already crammed to bursting point with four men, was beyond my comprehension. Over my dead body. . . .

When talking to each other, they spoke Afrikaans. It sounded basically Dutch, as Yiddish sounds German. It also

---

* Pretoria, in the Transvaal, was the administrative capital of South Africa, and Cape Town the legislative capital, where Parliament was convened annually. Twice a year, on the agreed date, a vast migration took place, when train-loads of civil servants, secretaries, and filing-cabinets, plus the entire diplomatic corps (which had to maintain dual establishments), were transferred from one nesting-place to another. The seasonal exchange coincided with the cooler weather awaiting these transients at either end of the country; though the intensive, highly competitive house-hunting which the move imposed took most of the edge off this dividend.

sounded ugly and slipshod, a kind of guttural baby-talk. I knew, even then, that in spite of the best intentions I would never learn it. But the way they could reel off the mysterious words of Southern Africa—high-veld and low-veld, hinterland and *kraal, wildebeeste, uitspan,* and *aasvogel**—was an excitement in itself.

There was one local custom I could have done without, on that stirring northward journey, and that was the early morning cup of coffee, which was compulsory. Promptly at 5.30, there was a menacing crash at the door; the lights blazed up, and a tray of cups, sloshing over as the train rocked, made a brisk circuit of the assembled company.

When we had swallowed this offering we did our best to settle down again (we had only stopped drinking a fierce brew of brandy called Commando about four hours previously). But hardly had sleep returned when the door crashed open again, the lights repierced the eyeballs, and the tray reappeared. It was the man for the empties.

After that, realizing that South Africa was a young, energetic, early-rising nation, I stayed awake: staring out of the window at the railway embankment which sped past, rising and dipping like water sluicing past a porthole; a view which gradually widened, and receded, and drew away until it reached the skyline of the eastern horizon.

Presently this turned pale, and then began to glow. It was the sunrise, making me free again of a country which seemed to have every variety, from ugly to beautiful, from dull to unbelievable.

We had been climbing, through the great escarpment of the Swartberg range, all the time since we had left Cape Town; now we were 3,500 feet above sea-level (the exact figures were proclaimed at every wayside station) and travelling through the Great Karroo Desert—which even my patriotic companions dismissed as 'miles and miles of bugger all'. But the exhausted Karroo was fascinating, nonetheless.

* Just a vulture.

We passed limitless stretches of low scrub, cactus, and stony wasteland; we crossed dry river beds with the bleached bones of animals marking their own last graves. We saw a few sheep grazing ('Average, one to an acre,' the tree men volunteered), and a few alert springbok on the horizon; and all round this horizon were the eroded hills, like flat-topped slagheaps, which contained this arid landscape, and seemed to set an absolute limit to it. But of course they did not. This was Africa.

The Karroo, I had once read, was the oldest part of the earth. Within the memory of man it had been fertile; now a brutal drought (no drop of rain for three years), and steady soil erosion, and a parching wind, and the baking sun had all but destroyed it. Even the lone, high-wheeling vultures must be going through a very bad patch.

The few farms, widely spaced out, were of enormous acreage: 'As far as a man could ride, from sunrise to sunset, in the old days,' John Bold told me, setting out the ground-rules with a romantic gleam in his eye. Each farmstead was surrounded by a private troop of a dozen small windmills, manfully pumping water to sustain some sort of fertility—and to keep alive those lonely sheep which, I already knew, produced mutton and lamb of miraculous succulence.

Sometimes there was no house, nor farm, nor animal, nor man to be seen, as far as the eye could reach. Only a wisp of smoke on the horizon, the kind which used to betray a convoy at sea, but which was here a precious landmark for the traveller, promised that one might find human company at the end of the long day's journey.

The lonely life produced the lonely landscape; and the lonely landscape had a harsh beauty, a pale-yellow, skeletal authority which proclaimed, all the time: whoever first carved out even a bare sustenance in this wilderness, they must have been men; and whoever now lived there were men of the same breed, not likely to surrender, not disposable without a fight of African ferocity.

The wayside stations were strung out along the railway line,

with names so varied that the next one could never be foreseen
—Worcester, De Doorns, Touws Rivier, Prince Albert Road,
Beaufort West, Nelspoort, Three Sisters, De Aar; they were
for the most part only halting-places for our train to pick up
water.

But I was voyaging all the time towards the High Veld, and
the parched yellow was changing to verdant green again. . . . It
was irresistible to step down from the train at every opportunity
to walk, to stare about, to buy grapes or apples or water-
melons from an ox-cart manned (the word was inescapable) by
some of the biggest women I had ever seen.

'Afrikaner women are all big,' said one of the Forestry boys,
when I commented on these reigning Amazons, squatting tent-
like on fecund haunches, like the Albert Memorial with a frilled
and faded sunbonnet on top. He did not sound at all displeased.
'Lots of kids, eh?'

From these wayside stations, grouped round the huge
dripping water-tank which must serve as our life-blood for the
next stage of the journey, countless sandy roads as straight as
rulers led off into the blue, and disappeared over the far
horizon, in hope, or despair, or brave endeavour.

The men and the women who had first trodden them out, the
people of the Great Trek—only a hundred years earlier—had
never stood still, and never compromised themselves or their
hungry faith. At nightfall they had outspanned their oxen from
the creaking wagons, and slept within the *laager* like tired
giants; at each dawn, they had yoked up again, and set off in
search of the dream once more.

Put down in this dry wilderness, they did not sit in sorrow
nor lie about in soft stupor, waiting for help. They broke out
and away, at a hard right angle to the trodden path, and discovered what was over the farthest hill, and the one beyond
that; and when they found exactly what they were seeking—a
sheltered green, a spring still running, a bare chance of fruitful-
ness—there they stopped, and made it their own.

I was already half in love with this whole continent.

Now we were beginning to move through and into the pages
of history, some of them having proud links with the past, some
unhappy and best forgotten. At dusk we left the vast Cape
Province behind, and crossed the Orange River into the Orange
Free State, so named a hundred years earlier by those same
wandering *Voortrekkers*, whose turning wagon wheels were not
to be stopped, even by the Orange River in spate.

But they still had to fight the climate, the Basutos, the British,
and the hordes of diamond seekers flocking in from every
corner of the world, before their new stake in Africa was
confirmed.

This was over the half-way mark of our own trek. Next came
the Modder River, which stood for ancient frontier battles just
as memorably as did the Delaware, in that other frontier-
country across the Atlantic. Then, when I should have been
getting ready to sleep (but who could ever be ready for sleep, on
such a journey?), we came to Kimberley.

'Four thousand feet above sea-level,' proclaimed the first
light falling on the first notice-board. But there were thousands
of other lights to mark the thriving town, to remind the
traveller of its violent and colourful history, and of the men who
had scooped (and were still scooping, though in a more genteel
way), diamonds by the million-pounds' worth from Kimberley's
peculiar pride and joy, the biggest man-made hole in the world.*

* Later, after a conducted tour of the whole vast operation, and a look into the
frightening depths of that enormous hole in the ground, into which we were
encouraged to throw stones and then listen for the faraway splash as, after what
seemed like five minutes, they finally hit water a thousand feet below—later I
could never read the slightly suave advertisement in the *New Yorker* and *The Times*
with the same sense of opulent wonderment.

The slogan 'A diamond is forever' (misty-eyed bride, fond husband with plenty
of juice in the bank) kept translating itself into an army of greedy human ants
clawing endlessly at this succulent patch of muck: clawing hundreds of feet down at
the end of rope-pulleys, until the slip-and-slide operation became impossible even
for the most agile fortune-seeker, the greediest ant of all, and more sophisticated
burrowers took over.

The farm on which all this started had been bought by farmer De Beer for £50
in 1860, and resold, when the strike was made, for £6,300. In the next seventy-
five years alone, it yielded £90 million in forever diamonds.

It was never a time for sleeping. We crossed the Vaal River in the middle of that night; in the old days, this had been so important, such a decision to make, such a step into the unknown, that anywhere north of that point was called the Transvaal, and still is.

Now we forked right for Johannesburg, instead of left for Mafeking, another ominous name in this ground-plan of history; and at 6.45 a.m. we steamed at last through the frieze of strange-looking sand castles which were in fact very grown-up toys—the mine-dumps, the yellow dross of forty years' frantic boring for gold—and stopped with a shriek and a shudder in Johannesburg itself.

The city was just waking up, and so—lightheaded, sleepless, and enthralled—was I.

3.

I had left Eileen and Max behind in Cape Town with no more sinister motive than the true one—freedom of movement, which would leave me unharassed by the thought of the little woman pining away at home, while the pitiful orphan boy cried out for his daddy before merciful sleep etc.

I now had to become briskly mobile on several fronts at once; an acting bachelor could deal with such short-term pioneering without regard to time-table; and Eileen was better off in Cape Town anyway, where she could await a summons from the frontier-breaking breadwinner from the preferred vantage-point of the Mount Nelson Hotel.

In Johannesburg, I had to find, as the very basis of existence, an office, a secretary, a telephone, a house, and a car; and it had to be done in that order, to justify the new-found status and the lavish salary.

I dived right in, free of all encumbrances, and with a zest— sparked by the sunshine, the thin clear air of 6,000 feet, and half a dozen other blessings—such as I had not felt for seven long years; and, like any politician, I could point with pride to the fact that within three days I had collected the nucleus of everything I needed.

I was greatly helped by a newspaperman who later became a very good friend, John Shannon of the *Rand Daily Mail*. This large convivial man, who fuelled on brandy and talked as gently as mother's milk, did an interview with me on my arrival, during which we both seem to have said all the right things:

> Monsarrat has a lot of confidence in Britain and thinks that many people have the wrong impression that she is down and out. England, he said, was going through a difficult period, but there was still a spirit of cheerfulness and optimism underlying the drab monotony which was most people's lot.

It sounded like a nice sunny day in Johannesburg. . . . But after this right-thinking preface, John Shannon turned to the difficult period which Monsarrat himself was going through. He had nowhere to work, poor chap. He had nowhere to live. He had no staff, no telephone, nothing. Poor chap indeed! Help him, someone!

Help him they did. Offers for everything I wanted began to flood in, starting at breakfast time and continuing all day. By noon I had acquired half a large office, by courtesy of another good friend-to-be, T. C. Robertson, editor of a magazine called *Libertas*. I could share their telephone until I was fixed up with something better.

In fact, the first U.K. Information Office was already in being —even though it was still only me, John Bold, and the dust on the floor. This fact was not lost on one of our earlier job-seekers, a challenging young woman who bounced in with the words: 'Good morning! I was in the Wrens!'

I had always liked the Wrens—in fact I used to like four or five of them a great deal; but I knew I would never like this one, a grim-looking hybrid from my favourite female service. I could tell very well that she had been a tyrant officer, chivvying her wretched girls around like a bad-tempered turkey hen; and that the prettier they were, the nastier she was to them, because she was rather ugly herself, and no badge of rank could ever free her of this handicap.

Such were the wayward, non-director-like thoughts which rattled round my brain as the girl, looking about our shabby roost, said tartly:

'I don't see anything very British about this! Why don't you have a few placards or something?'

I explained that we were only just getting under way (I thought the nautical expression might appease her), and that I did not want to hang out any signs until we had something tangible to offer.

'No harm in making a bit of a splash, is there?' She glanced at our small table on which were displayed *The Times*, the *Telegraph*, the *Daily Herald*, and the *Spectator*. 'You haven't even got the *Tatler*!'

It was clear that she had already decided not to work for this crummy outfit, thus beating me to the point of decision by a few seconds.

But engaging even one good secretary had already proved a problem. By agreement with the South African Government, the High Commissioner's Office could only pay its local staff at the same salary rates as the host government itself, thus preventing too much poaching by richer countries which might be able to advertise unheard-of salaries, and so ruin the market.

My office came under the same arrangement; and the best I could offer a qualified shorthand-typist (they were called 'stenos') at that stage was £16 a month, which was approximately £8 to £10 under the market rate in ordinary commercial offices outside.

But luckily (there was a lot of luck floating round Johannesburg in May 1946) I found a gem in Miss Pybus, an older woman of great competence and firm character, who said that the salary did not matter, who took me well in hand from the start, and who ran the other office-girls (soon there were six of

them) with the kind of motherly authority which reminded me—
well, of Mother.

She was to stay with us for nearly seven years—Miss Pybus
of U.K.I.O.; though towards the end, she did become slightly
disenchanted with the Director. By then I was conducting a
torrid love affair with a young woman in Cape Town, involving
an exchange of scorching telegrams two or three times a week:
telegrams which for some reason always arrived at lunch-time,
when I was out, and had to be read by anyone brave enough to
open them, and then lay them, in all their non-official candour,
on the Director's desk.

Miss Pybus was always brave enough. But I could not help
noticing that her lips, firm even at normal moments, became
positively strip-welded as this long-continuing fling progressed.

However, that was in the scarlet future. Now, on Days One,
Two, and Three of my endeavours, she was a rock of competence, and I could get on with the rest of my searching, without worrying about stray callers or hot-shot stationery
salesmen.

By the second day, from a big selection, I had rented a
furnished house in a suburb called Northcliffe, about six miles
outside the city. It faced north (in our topsy-turvy continent,
that was where the sun was), with a terraced garden and a
superb view round three-quarters of the compass towards the
Magaliesburg Range and the true high veld. Its rent was £25
a month (this was not yet a fashionable place to live); and the
wages of the Zulu cook-houseboy were £4 a month.

Finally, there was the car. Cars were the one thing almost
unobtainable in South Africa at that time; there had been no
imports for nearly five years, and no home-made brands to help
out; the old crock market was now a ferocious one, with cut-
throat competition to buy anything which moved, and an
equally fierce contest to patch up, wire together, re-paint, and
somehow galvanize every last fugitive from the wrecker's yard,
and unload it on to any customer who had to have a car at all
costs.

I had already gathered, from cautionary friends, that selling secondhand cars in Johannesburg had now superseded the retail trade in gold bricks, fresh out of the crucible, as a profitable line of endeavour.

But I was one of those who had to have a car at all costs; though 'all costs' must not exceed £200, which would be everything I had in the world, plus most of next month's salary, plus some savings from my Tropical Clothing Allowance which I was still clinging to.

For the time and the place and the money, it wasn't such a bad car, when I finally found it and wrestled it to my bosom. It was a 1937 Plymouth, 23 h.p., price £200; and certainly there was no lack of competition to acquire it.

I had snapped up the afternoon Johannesburg *Star* as soon as the paper appeared on the streets; flipped through the 'Cars For Sale' section until I found a possibility; noted the address, jumped into a taxi, and driven three miles eastwards along the Reef Road to a garage which, like the car, had seen better days.

Within ten minutes of buying the paper, the deal was clinched, with a deposit, by cheque, of £50. Then the customers, arriving by slower taxi, by tram, and on foot, started to hammer on the door. There were eighteen of them altogether; many would not believe that the car had been sold already, and one of them, fingering my cheque disparagingly, said he would pay the full price, there and then, in cash, if the garage owner would just tear up 'this bit of paper' and forget all about it.

But by then I had a signature, and John Bold as a witness; and the car—shabby grey, rusty, with springs peeping through the upholstery, a groaning transmission, and an electrical fault which administered a small six-volt shock every time one changed gear—the car was mine.

I drove nearly 2,000 miles by its faked speedometer before the front axle broke, and the Plymouth, subsiding gently on to its sump, slid to a last halt in the heart of Pretoria. But good or bad, it was the first car I had owned for twelve years, and it gave us our first coupon-free spell of simple 'driving around' since 1939.

On Day Five, which was a Monday, I engaged an office-cum-messenger boy (the word 'boy' did not concern age in South Africa, only racial status) with the charming, the irresistible name of Motorcar B. K. Ratshiko. At midweek, Philip Birkinshaw, who was to be my deputy-director, arrived from England, with gruesome tales of travel by troopship but an undiminished cheerfulness which, in the same circumstances, I could not have matched.

At the week-end, a girl with another euphonious name, Martli Malherbe, a South African who had once worked at the Cabinet Office in London, arrived from those far-off Magaliesburg Hills which I could see from my own mansion, and began to set out her wares as Films Officer.

Now we had to get moving.

I still knew nothing about running an information office. It was like the first week at Winchester, or on board *Campanula*; a crossword puzzle in an unfamiliar language, a tiny personal clearing in a forest of doubts; except that here, no one else apart from John Bold knew anything about it either, and now I was the headmaster, or the captain, and everyone was looking at me.

I had been given £20 by the Chief Accountant in Cape Town as a 'contingency fund' (the manager of the Standard Bank on Commissioner Street was able to keep his head as I opened our account with this significant sum), but I wasn't too sure what it was meant to cover. For example, I wanted to buy a wastepaper-basket—and I hoped that this would not be the first reaction of our customers as well.

But was this a contingency? Or should I send the bill to the H.C.'s office? Or refer the whole thing to Whitehall? Or spend £1 on a phone call to Cape Town to find out, and perhaps face charges of squandering public money?

I realized already that I had not asked enough questions while the questioning was good.

There were more important problems. 'We want,' I had said in my very first interview, 'to give the people of South Africa as

true a picture of Britain and of its hopeful future as possible.'
How did one really set about that?

The office had been vaguely planned as a 'British shop-
window'—though not literally so, on the ground floor of a main
street; that would have been too expensive. But we hoped to set
ourselves up in a modern, down-town office block, and be
'accessible', and boldly labelled for what we were.

In fact, the sooner we found permanent quarters, the better—
one of the basic problems, since the post-war building boom was
only matched by the post-war demand for office space, and the
frugal standards of the Office of Works, by whom all such leasing must be approved, were lagging some way behind
Johannesburg's gaudy yardstick of accommodation.

But once installed, we had laid plans for a very good
reference library; and a public reading room with as many newspapers and magazines as the budget would stand. (We never
managed the *Tatler*, but we did have five daily newspapers and
eight magazines, ranging from the *Economist* to *Time & Tide*.)

We were to have a film library, lending out British documen-
taries (which were then very good) free of charge; a features
service (articles from the Central Office of Information, to be
made available to newspapers, without too much favouritism);
a photograph library, run on the same basis—everything from
the routine royal poses to the latest British hearing-aids; and a
telephone information service—that was Philip Birkinshaw,
except where politics were concerned, when it must be me.

In addition, I was to make speeches, broadcast as much as
possible, get around and meet people, and be on terms of the
closest familiarity with newspaper editors, radio notables,
librarians, civil servants, politicians, mining magnates, and the
common man.

The common man would always be white—this was South
Africa. But my office, and all its facilities, were to be available to
any man of *any* race. This was my own strong inclination, in
any case. But it could mean that we might be ostracized by the
very people we wanted to reach—the undecided Afrikaners, still

prepared to give Britain a hearing if Britain was still worth it. Once the word got round that all you ever saw at the U.K.I.O. was a bunch of bloody *kaffirs*. . . .

Once again, it was my problem—and it was only a tiny part of this same problem of adjustment, which was to plague Eileen to the very end, and myself until I surrendered to the local facts of life: until, using an early pair of soiled bootstraps, I climbed swiftly above it, seduced by friend and foe alike into borrowing, accepting, and swallowing alive the total philosophy of life at the top of the heap.

But in the innocent beginning, with memories still raw of blood and suffering, poverty and self-denial, sharing and caring, the dilemma was rooted in a feeling, deep in the gut of conviction, that South Africa was all wrong. How could a man of goodwill (the Thirties phrase* was still potent) think otherwise? Had I really come all this way, to smile and smile, to take, eat, and never deny, even for the first time, the idea that the sons of Ham were hewers of wood and drawers of water for ever?

The answer turned out to be yes. But in 1946, the country into which I had thus been pitchforked, with instructions to make friends and influence people, to accept things as they were: *not* to criticize, *not* to argue, *not* to quarrel about anything more important than art or boxing: *not* to strike any attitude save that of a chummy neutrality; yet at the same time to preach the liberal, tolerant, British way of life—this country, and its mainspring the City of Johannesburg, seemed at that crucial point of time and instinct to be the most awful place in the world.

It showed itself in little things as well as big; in the small insults, the minor cuts and smarts which one set of people could inflict on another set not allowed to answer back, as well as in the massive prohibitions and roadblocks which, even in the benevolent days of General Smuts, had already set an unscaleable barrier between black and white South African.

---

* Forever enshrined, for us dated innocents, in *Les Hommes de Bonne Volonté*, by Jules Romains.

I was a foreign civil servant, not free to comment on this. Indeed, I was not always inclined to, because the pattern of injustice had to compete with an environment damnably beautiful in every respect.

I thought then, and I still think, that South Africa, with all its riches of nature and its embellishment by man, its variety, marvellous climate, and stunning impact, was and is the most beautiful country in the world. But as the sentimental allure of retreats like Alphen faded, it was succeeded by an astonished disgust at what men could do to such a paradise when they really got their claws into the place.

I was ready to believe, as John Bold had once said, that race-relations in Cape Town *were* far better than in the Transvaal and the Free State; that people down at the Cape—*all* the people down at the Cape—were modestly content with the way things were. But even if this were true, did the contrast have to be so awful that a traveller from another frontier began to be ashamed of his own borrowed lordship?

The whole of this beautiful country seemed to me to be poisoned by politics, by race, and by a built-in cruelty and meanness such as I had never expected to meet again, once I had escaped from Winchester. That might not seem a high standard of evil; but it was still mine, and I still found the re-encounter vile.

To begin with, there was a gulf, longstanding already, between white man and white man; between people of British stock (lumped together as *rooineks* or 'fortune-hunters' by those who did not like them), and those whose roots and language and instincts were in Afrikanerdom (dismissed, with the same kind of blanket contempt, as Dutchmen, squareheads, Boers, even white niggers).

The old hatreds were still alive, and frenziedly kicking; large numbers of Afrikaners had prayed (and how they could pray!) for a British defeat in the war; there had been open treason, and covert sabotage. Even now, the Nationalist Opposition leader, Dr Malan, was the subject of an official Parliamentary inquiry into allegations that he had tried to negotiate a separate peace-settlement between South Africa and Germany, involving 'conversations with enemy agents' while the fighting men's backs were turned.

Dr Malan was cleared of the charge. But the fact that it could be brought, in full Parliamentary session, was a measure of this internal hatred and suspicion. Worse still, a lot of people believed it to be true, and would accept nothing to the contrary.

Some Afrikaners never referred to the British flag except as the 'Union Joke'. The Oppenheimer family, and all other such indispensable citizen-builders, were the Hoggenheimers. The British had won the Boer War by torturing women and children in concentration camps, far worse than anything the Germans ever did.

They had denied them all medical aid; even the Red Cross had confessed to being British spies. They had fed their prisoners bully beef with powdered glass in it, meat with embedded fish-hooks, poisoned water, maggoty bread; and there was a 'Concentration Camp Museum' down at Bloemfontein to prove all these things beyond a shadow of doubt.

On the other side—and this was the side I was on, as an occasional violent telephone call made plain—a patronizing ridicule was the only reaction. It centred, to a large extent, on the Afrikaans language, of which Afrikaners were perhaps inordinately proud. A poet of some stature in South Africa, Uys Krige,* had told me when we first met that Afrikaans was 'more beautiful than French'. Another poet, Roy Campbell, had committed himself even further:†

> The Afrikaans language is full of adventure for the bold and daring . . . and unique among contemporary tongues for youth and freshness. It has the sinewy simplicity and beauty of tools, the lean bleakness of arms. . . . Would

* He had also been a soldier in our honourable cause, and his 'escape' novel, *The Way Out*, recounting his experiences on the run from the Germans in Italy, was a most attractive book.
† Chambers Encyclopaedia (1950 edition): Vol. XII, p. 763.

the language as spoken by the comfortable burghers of Amsterdam have sufficed the needs—practical, emotional, or devotional—of the Voortrekkers? Certainly not! The language had to express a new life more intense and poignant. Greater economy of time was required—words that were hammers of iron, rims of sturdy wheels, words that were cruiser-prows of ploughshares, cutting the white-baked clay with crimson wakes . . . words that asked no sanctions of profes-sors, but exploded spontaneously into life as they were needed, amputating unnecessary limbs from the mother-tongue. Coarse and healthy as a young colt, Afrikaans is just now in such a state as was the English language when Marlow first snaffled its jaws with thunder.

English-speaking South Africans, if they had ever read Roy Campbell, or heard of him, or could distinguish him from Rob Roy, or *The Campbells Are Coming*, or even Campbell's Soup, would have found such fulsome propaganda incomprehensible, and therefore ludicrous.

They would have dismissed the admired language as 'Tram-drivers' Dutch'. They would have enjoyed a little bawdy fun with 'sinewy tools'. Then they would have cited the Afrikaans translation of *Hamlet*, in which the Ghost's doom-laden 'I am thy father's spirit' came out as: '*Ek is jou poppa se spookie*', (literally, 'I is your daddy's spook'), or the Biblical 'Gird up your loins', which must be rendered as '*Mak toe jou broekies*'.

These, and other gibes at 'kitchen-*kaffir*' and its users, were always good for a dinner-table laugh; and a dinner-table laugh, whether at the high table or the low, was often the only regard which Afrikaners earned from the other side. For the rest, they were 'all right as farmers'; they must be kept out of commerce and industry because they would never understand it and they couldn't be trusted because, unbelievably, after all these years they still hated the British.

Can you imagine that, old boy? Well, when you think that they have to translate nuclear fission as '*nuklear viesjoen*', I'd believe anything of that lot. Have another brandy. Donkey manure.*

So much for white man and white: hating each other, fearing and jeering, wishing each other out of the way so that South Africa could be 'free': running in blinkers which should have disappeared, at the very latest, when the first tractor turned the first Free State furrow. But beyond white man and white there loomed the giant shadow of white man and black; and there, give or take a few thousand liberals who apparently saw nothing wrong in white girls bearing a bunch of little black bastards—there was where the two white races clasped hands in agreement.

The English preferred to be 'nice' to natives; the Afrikaners thought this was going too far. But they were in entire agreement on the black man's role, now and in the future. It was to be down there.

General Smuts, prophet, preacher, architect of humanity, and eagle among statesmen, who had recently drafted the preamble to the United Nations Charter, had included in it the following slice of high-flown sentiment:

> We the peoples of the United Nations, determined . . . to reaffirm faith in fundamental human rights, in the dignity and worth of the human person, in the equal rights of men and women . . . and for these ends to practice tolerance and live together in peace with one another. . . .

In answer to which one could only exhort him: Look homeward, Angel! But Smuts did not really need the reminder, nor deserve it either. He must have known—since he was an architect of South Africa also—that there were disgusting things going on in his own backyard which made rubbish of such pious nobility.

On any bright morning, one could always see, befouling any public park in Johannesburg, small bands of tramps known as 'sherry gangs': filthy drunkards, spitting, vomiting, shouting obscenities, urinating at will, and pestering passers-by for money.

* A merry mispronunciation of *Dankie meneer*—Thank you, sir.

They were, in any context, the very muck of humanity. Yet the obscenities they shouted, being mostly directed at Negroes, were taken for granted; since any sherry-gang type was automatically superior, because he was white, to any native, no matter how modest, unassuming, or hardworking the latter might be.

They could, and did, shoulder all such black trash off the pavement and into the gutter; and so, using a more subtle type of wrestling, did everyone else.

In South Africa, roughly two million whites were playing host to nine million non-whites; to redress the balance, to preserve a decent superiority in such a threatening jungle, the pressure had to be unrelenting. The native population, as well as being generally insulted and ignored, was inexcrably clamped and confined into menial jobs.

They were also being pushed further and further away from the city centres and into 'native townships'—wretched squatters' villages, with one tap to a rutted street, and a bus service so inefficient, overcrowded, and offensive to all the senses that, as the only link between white master and black servant it also came into the category of permanent insult

My friend Motorcar Ratshiko, as dependable, honest, and hardworking as anyone I had ever met (quite as good as the Trearddur Bay postman, and better than a thousand Liverpool layabouts)—Motorcar had to join his Orlando bus-queue at 5 a.m. in order to be in the office at eight, when we opened.

Even there, there were things I did not like, but hesitated to check because even this might be interpreted as unwarranted interference by an outsider. Any native, calling with a message or collecting a consignment of films, would always be addressed as 'John' by our first receptionist. It was an automatic reaction, like that sherry-gang superiority. A white man had a name, and a welcome. A native boy was John, and 'What do you want, John?' his only greeting.

At home, even in our liberal Northcliffe household, Eileen bought meat for us and 'boys' meat'—God knows what leaky bundle of chopped gristle and string—for the cook-houseboy, the gardener, and the nursegirl who now made up our modest staff (total cost, £10 15s. a month).

If anyone had asked me what the hell I, a medium-grade civil servant with £30 in the bank, was doing with three permanent servants, who shared two huts and a lavatory consisting of a hole in the ground shaped something like a violin, the only possible answer was: 'I'm living in South Africa.'

Perhaps this first feeling of guilt was purely, parochially English. It was to disappear, like any other unwanted corpse, with time and corruption. But then it was strong, and so were lots of other feelings, as I surveyed the scene and the temper around me, and found both of them odious.

An African, any African, had to have a passbook—just like the white man's passport, except that here it conferred nothing save a miserable internal tyranny. He must carry it at all times, even if he stepped a foot beyond his own fence; he could be stopped and asked for it by any roving policeman, and if he did not have it on his person, he went to jail for that night, and stayed there until he was bailed out by the *baas*.

Adam, our forgetful Zulu (Adam, the first man!), had to be thus rescued four times, and his £1 fine paid, before we found the answer. Eileen made him a leather wallet, which was stapled to his only belt, and since he could not leave the house without his belt, because his trousers would have fallen down within six paces, even Adam the first man had to realize that there was something amiss.

The police, in this and almost every other area, were brutal.* Anyone who had seen a passless native, trying to argue his case,

---

* They were once fairly brutal to me too, perhaps because of my 1937 Plymouth with the fringe of rust on top. When I made a doubtful, certainly arguable crossing on a yellow-light traffic-signal, I was stopped by a large blond cop with an effective snarl. 'Didn't you see the robot, you *pampoen?*' *Pampoen*, I knew already, meant pumpkin; but robot puzzled me. While I looked round for Martians, the policeman took out his notebook. Robot, it transpired, was a traffic-light. (Case dismissed: diplomatic immunity, which we were not allowed to plead without very good reason.) The temporary bafflement recalled John Bold's first friendly invitation in Cape Town: 'Would you like to come to the bio? It's Deanna Durbin in *Can't Help Singing*!' 'Bio' was bioscope, the somewhat dated term for cinema.

arrested on the street: his arm twisted, his back savagely kneed as he was shoved into the police car—any casual witness to this, black or white, knew very well who was the *baas* and who the *kaffir*. He was meant to.

The courts reflected this savage discrimination between man and man. Two cases, reported almost side by side in the *Rand Daily Mail*, established the balance of justice accurately enough. A thirty-year-old native was sentenced to death for raping a European girl aged seventeen; while a forty-six-year-old white farmer was given five years' hard labour for an identical offence.

The term 'imprisonment with spare diet' for an African convicted of common assault was thus spelled out by the sentencing judge: 'That on three days out of every seven he should be locked up in solitary confinement, without anything to ea except a little rice, and the water in which it was boiled.'

Parliament itself supplied its own back-echo to such illiberal practice; demonstrated by a motion introduced by a Nationalist M.P. that any war pensions given to natives who had served in the armed forces should be halved in relation to white soldiers' pensions. They might have been warned of this a little earlier, in the blinding heat or under the shared stars of the North African desert.

I had thought Johannesburg itself an absolute nut-house, almost from the moment my train drew into the station with that 'shriek and shudder' which was soon to seem so appropriate; and as time went on the verdict only gained in validity. It was a a money-mad, raucous, pioneering town, wildly happy when the stock market was up, dejected beyond belief when it was down; a sixty-year-old mining camp* still flexing its muscles and hacking out a rich living from the baked earth—some of its citizens with picks and shovels, others with honest brains, some with crooked fingers, and all with an avid devotion to the mountain of gold we were sitting on.

* Lord Milner, when Governor of the Transvaal, had called it 'the university of crime'.

My arrival had coincided with a brand-new, fabulously rich gold-strike in the Free State at Odendaalsrust, which I had passed on my way north. Even without this, Johannesburg would have had enough fables already, and enough crazy energy to stock the biggest Bedlam in the world; with the Odendaalsrust strike the city took off on a new, dotty extravaganza of rumour, riches overnight, and the ruined hopes of those who had guessed wrong.

Odendaalsrust (for connoisseurs of South African mining shares, it later became the Free State Geduld mine) sparked off a vast new complex of gold mines which ensured the area a glittering future; it was, to quote Sir Ernest Oppenheimer, the doyen of all the experts, 'the most significant in South Africa since the discovery of diamonds in Kimberley and gold on the Witwatersrand.' Here on the Witwatersrand, it set Johannesburg alight as well.

The total fascination of everyone—cab drivers, men on both sides of bar-counters, poor-white lift attendants without a penny in their pockets, rich men with millions, wealthy women with alimony to burn, widows in sole control of the dear departed's life-time loot—was really extraordinary. A short feature film about the new gold-strike was received, on the night I saw it, with the Oohs and Aahs and the rapturous acclaim usually reserved for royalty, Frank Sinatra (then at his warbling peak), or crude sex.

The film itself was a positive monster of inverted values. The close-ups of the assayed gold, of the borehole, of the very drilling rig itself, set the whole audience drooling. Foolish faces flashed on to the screen; among them the owner of the farm where the strike was made—'She has been farming this land for forty-two years,' said the commentator, as if those forty-two years were worthless, a life-time only redeemed by this new, gilt-edged annunciation.

Then came the men who had actually made the strike, the surveyors who had followed them up, the speculators who were now preparing to rip the little village apart: all paraded like so

many Olympians, while the audience exclaimed and whispered
and yearned over them.

Pictures of farmland, of sheep grazing, of innocent pastoral
occupation, were bashed off the screen by a forest of probing
derricks—'Soon,' the man said, as if he could not wait for it,
'all this will be a thriving gold-mine city.' A final roar of
applause signalled the prevailing approval. To hell with sheep
and wheat, cattle and people. *This* was the stuff one could really
eat.

Inside the cinema, and outside also, I seemed to be the only
man who was not impressed: the only man in Johannesburg who
had not made £5,000 over the weekend, and was confident of
making plenty more. Such lack of enthusiasm was a blasphemy
in this town, where the success sign, in drinking circles, was to
crash a fistful of loose silver down on the bar and say: 'Take it
out of that!'

There was one curious perversion. In this city of greedy men,
there was a virulent anti-semitism. Oppenheimer was Hoggenheimer; Johannesburg itself was Jewburg. It was the anti-
semitism of a collection of people, themselves as acquisitive as
tearing vultures, who feared they might be out-smarted at their
own game. If they did win, it was brains. If they lost, it was
those bloody Jews again.

Such was this grotesque city, whose interest I had to capture.
It was going to be hard. It was hard enough already. A 'Victory
Parade' through Johannesburg, by South African soldiers who
had fought across Africa and up the cruel spine of Italy, was such
a flop that even the well-disposed *Rand Daily Mail*, under a
cross-heading 'Admiring But Silent Spectators', had to admit
that 'the Johannesburg crowd was the most restrained of all'.
(They had previously marched through Cape Town, Durban,
and Pretoria.)

It was better summed-up by O.C. Troops, an on-the-spot
realist, who said: 'I have seen more enthusiasm at funeral
services.'

The enthusiasms were not for anything so vague as memory;

8

they were more sharply focused altogether. Money came first; then a great deal of determined drinking, in which I presently joined, helped by the altitude which was a sovereign cure for hangovers; and then an enormous level of casual fornication— with which, at this, the first prim stage of my lease, I was not connected, even as a knowing spectator.

After that, the major and minor lunacies took over. Where else but in Johannesburg, I thought, as I toiled in my office, sub-editing a piece about 'British Breakthrough in Plastic Ovenware' which just would not do at all: where else but in Johannesburg would core-samples (that was the stuff which was supposed to come out of a drilling-for-gold rig) be so liberally laced with added precious metal that shares went sky-high before the culprits (trapped by gold-dust in their trouser-turnups) were hauled off to jail?

Where else would there be 'fishing-pole burglars'—smart fellows who, angling through open bedroom windows, hooked out coats and handbags and dresses and trousers, sometimes with lovers inside them?

Where else would window-shopping at night be a pleasure absolutely unknown, since no one with any regard for their safety would walk the streets after dusk? Where else would there be no bottles of liquor on display in any bar or lounge (even in a private club) where women were admitted, since the weaker sex was not allowed to see drinks poured out or corks drawn in public?

Where else, when the ladies had left the gentlemen for coffee after dinner, would a shattering report from the drawing-room be followed by a reassuring: 'It's all right, darling—we were just comparing revolvers.'

Where else would the faked titles assumed by some visitors be good for at least a month's free board and lodging, before it dawned on people (aided now and then by my reference library) that 'Sir Jock and Lady Strappe' lacked the authentic ring of aristocracy? Or a woman who claimed to have spent soul-searing years at the Belsen concentration camp have indeed done so—as a wardress? Or a delicatessen shop of a most superior type, advertising asparagus tips, cream cheeses, plump smoked salmon, rich ripe salami, palm kernels in olive oil, *pâté de foie gras*, caviare, stuffed Spanish olives, smoked oysters, and Parma ham in aspic, go by the name of Fatti's?

Where else but at Turffontein, the Johannesburg racecourse, would a horse break its leg in a scuffle opposite the winning-post, and be put out of its misery by a spectator who, vaulting on to the course from the ten-shilling enclosure, drew a revolver and shot it stone-dead?

For a writer—even though I had stopped being a writer—all this was irresistible, and I made reams of notes, mostly on Dominions Office stationery which was good, durable stuff of a superior quality. But the sad parts outweighed the mad ones, by far more than that $4\frac{1}{2}$–1 black-white majority; and thus the novel I wrote about it, nineteen years later,* came out sad— sad and angry.

In one passage I tried to string together all that I had thought and felt at the time, about Johannesburg and South Africa and the hideous pattern of inequality which was coming to be the hallmark for both. My protagonist was an excitable and rather drunk young Englishman (Jonathan Steele) quarel-ling with some rich people in a night-club; so it could hardly be me (well, I mean to say!). But the bitter reaction was mine, and the wish to voice it also:

'You can't do that [improve your racial economic status] in South Africa,' said Jonathan Steele. 'There's a line between the Negro and the white man, and the Negro can't cross it. There's a wage-level dividing the Negro and the white man, and the Negro can't rise above it. There's an educational barrier between the Negro and the white man, and the Negro can't climb it. You've got the poor bastards ham-strung, and you're going to keep them that way.'

* *The Pillow Fight* (Cassell, and Wm. Sloane Associates, 1965; Pocket Books, 1966; Pan Books, 1967).

'And a bloody good idea, too!' said Bruno van Thaal, who had his own notion of paradise, and was not ashamed of it.

'Of course it's a good idea, from your point of view,' said Steele, 'but I'm talking about *real* people. . . . That means that you have a permanent slave economy in South Africa, something unique in the twentieth century. Do you wonder that the rest of the world thinks of you as barbarians?'

And a little later on:

'The net result is a criminal mess!' Jonathan Steele burst out. 'Good God, don't any of you use your eyes as you walk about? You're living on top of the worst ghetto in the world. . . . It wouldn't be so bad, in a way, if you made something worth while out of your slave state, like Athens did, or Rome—something handsome, creative, cultured, to justify all the misery at the lower levels. But all you make is money.'

'That's bad?' asked Bruno sarcastically.

But Steele couldn't be bothered with the fleas on the body politic. 'The same goes for women,' he said, though not looking at Kate Marais. 'Here they are, with unlimited servants, unlimited leisure, unlimited opportunity to make something out of their lives. What do they do with it all?—just bridge teas, gossip, triviality, love affairs, a six-hour siesta every day. They're the laziest, most expensive harlots in the world.'

'Come on, Steele,' Kate Marais said suddenly, edgily. 'You haven't said a damned thing yet. . . . What else don't you like about us?'

His eyes came round to hers, very straight, very direct; she decided that he wasn't drunk at all, just explosively keyed up, bursting with things he had wanted to say for a long time, to the people he thought deserved them.

'The way you treat your natives,' he said, as if reciting from some inner rubric. 'The way you just don't *see* them, on the street or in a room. . . . The way old natives can be barred from using the lifts, and have to walk up eleven flights of stairs. . . . The way servants, regardless of sex, are herded together in the sleeping quarters at the backs of houses, like a kennel full of mongrels. . . . The "Whites Only" labels on benches, trains, lavatories, shop counters. . . . The brutality of the most degraded poor whites, tramps, the sherry-gang type, towards *any* black man, regardless of his worth. . . . Johannesburg, especially, is just an appalling square mile of jungle, surrounded by black civilization.'

Gerald Thyssen burst out laughing. 'Now I've heard everything.'

'You've heard it,' said Jonathan Steele, 'but you haven't listened to it.'

It was clear to me within a few months, as it had been to Jonathan Steele, that I could never love this city nor this country; in spite of all its innocent blessings—the sun, the dry warmth, the champagne altitude of 6,000 feet (though my nose did begin to bleed as I climbed the stairs of the *Rand Daily Mail* to call on the editor, Rayner Ellis)—in spite of all this, and a lot of good people who became good friends, I did not want to be exiled for longer than I could help, in a country which seemed to impose an absolute denial of all I had come to believe in, after thirty-six years of trial and error, of chopping and changing, of the reading, writing, and basic arithmetic of man's hoped-for humanity to man.

If I had known that I was to spend the next seven years in Johannesburg, in charge of the same information office, I would have voted against it, firmly and conclusively. But luckily the job itself quickly became so absorbing and so seemingly worthwhile that I could concentrate on that, and give the bleeding heart the most effective tourniquet of all—a conditioned neutrality.

By mid-year U.K.I.O. really was a going concern. We had taken a floor of a new office block, happily named London

House; and there we had our reference library, our film library, our photograph library, our poster service, our regular supply of feature articles and trade news, our gramophone-record lending library, our telephone information department, and our link with the British Council and the B.B.C. Transcription Service.

We also had my private pride and joy: the reading room, the only place in the Transvaal (except at the rival U.S. shop up the street) where a Negro could sit down next to a white man, and read *The Times* or the *New Statesman* in peace. Now, it might sound nothing: just the common currency of civil right. Then, I hope and believe, it was a new and crucial blessing for a great many people.

The studious calm which ruled the whole room, from opening time onwards, was all I needed, by way of endorsement.

As a back-up job to this small viable empire, I started running round in various circles; and, over the months, called on everyone of any consequence whom casual contact, or the High Commissioner's superior hot-line, made available.

Most of them are now only names; sometimes only names on gravestones, with all their energetic lives gone to dust. Then, they were the people to know, and so, putting on the airs appropriate to the Chief of British Information in South Africa, I came to know them.

Many of them were United Party politicians (a bad bet, since even the United Party itself was shortly to go to dust, and to stay there for a solid quarter-century of opposition); men like Dr Colin Steyn, Minister of Labour, a roly-poly old charmer who once told me, accurately enough: 'If you stay more than two years in Africa, you will never want to leave'; Henry Gluckman, Minister of Health, with whom I was later to share the reins of South Africa's foremost charity, the War Memorial Health Foundation; Marais Steyn, the Transvaal U.P. leader; Major Piet van der Byl, Minister of Native Affairs, whose title of the best-dressed man in the House of Assembly certainly marked the peak of his career since he rowed for Cambridge in 1911; Harry Lawrence, Minister of Justice; J. G. N. Strauss,

Minister of Agriculture and later the leader of the Opposition for many heart-breaking years; and A. E. P. Robinson, city councillor, fellow-member of the local Brains Trust, and later (lots of things were to come later) Sir Albert Edward Phineas Robinson, High Commissioner for the Rhodesian Federation.

There were other kinds of politician: notably Colin Legum, Labour Party leader on the Johannesburg City Council and chairman of the Housing Committee; Bertha Solomon, as talkative a female M.P. as ever stopped talking to cook *gefül te fisch* as it should be cooked in heaven; and Bernard Friedman, the M.P. for Hillbrow, who, since he was another Jew with lots of brains, was naturally known as the Member for Highbrow. There were also sportsmen—Alan Melville, the South African cricket captain, and Bobby Locke, one of the last golf champions still addicted to plus-fours.

There were professional thorns in the flesh (as all Christians inevitably came to be, in that part of the world), like the Reverend Michael Scott, just working up to his first jail sentence as a 'passive resister'; and Father Trevor Huddleston, trying out his wings in the same angelic league; Réné Caprara, the last civilized Director-General of the South African Broadcasting Corporation (after that, S.A.B.C. became a bare-faced factory for Nationalist propaganda); R. F. Kennedy, the City Librarian, and one of the nicest of that high-class breed I ever met; Dr J. D. Rheinallt Jones, with a hard row to hoe as the director of the South African Institute of Race Relations; and Chooks Dawson, editor of the *Sunday Times* (South Africa went in for funny nicknames: 'Chooks' could be matched by another friend, 'Pot' Steward of External Affairs, and by the bearers of such male endearments as Hennie for Hendrik and Fanie for Francis).

Last came a couple of financiers, though they were set a certain distance apart: John Martin, the legendary head of Central Mining and Investment, the holy calm of whose office was a good deal more impressive than many a cathedral; and Norbert Erleigh, a multi-millionaire whiz-kid who shortly had to turn his back on his losing race-horses and winning wife Olivia to serve a jail sentence (four years, plus a £40,000 fine), for whatever such whiz-kids did on their precipitate way to the top.

Add John Schlesinger (5ft. 6in.), who owned all the cinemas, and Adrian Berrill (6ft. 5in.), chairman of the Central News Agency, which sold all the newspapers and magazines; and the introductory list was long enough, and varied enough, to keep a newcomer forever on his wary toes.

After these stars came the people without a specific label save that of their main preoccupation: social people, drinking people, bedding people, working people; art people, Press people, racing people, poker people; stockbrokers, heartbreakers, gold-brickers, born suckers.

In Johannesburg, one need never stop mining such lodes. But in the first year, I could only scratch the crawling surface, with finger-nails manicured to a polite length by protocol, a lingering British reserve, and a salary of £104 a month.

I was now doing regular broadcasts on a Brains Trust type of programme called Listener's Forum, though inhibited by the rather large number of topics I could *not* talk about—among them South African politics, religion (unless disguised as ethics), race relations, sex (the British Government had no official views on sex), and divorce, which was a popular sport in Johannesburg but the hottest of hot potatoes in the vast Bible belt outside.

I could never forget, also, that one of my most dedicated listeners was the Deputy High Commissioner, now only forty miles away in Pretoria, who was a *pas-trop-de-zèle* man of the deepest conviction.

I also did some undercover book-reviews for the Johannesburg *Sunday Express*, and began to make a lot of speeches.

For these there was an unlimited range of audience: chambers of commerce, women's clubs, ex-servicemen's organizations, schools, universities, and Rotarians, whose female contingent, sad to relate, called themselves Rotary Anns. Looking down on the bald heads, or the earnest faces, or the blurred after-dinner

moons, or the sea of millinery which distinguished those most
daunting gatherings, women's luncheon clubs, I dutifully fired
off my Set of Variations on a Noble Theme—the theme being
Britain, her Manful Past, Energetic Present, and Bright Future.

I believed in this with conviction, even with passion; I
believe in it still, though the speech-sample I now quote sounds
like the longest, most forlorn echo of shrivelled hope that ever
lasted for a quarter of a century: a bell tolling endlessly down
the years until everyone concerned—ringer and hearer, disciple
and carping critic, even the very bell itself—were all slightly
cracked.

Once again, from the *Rand Daily Mail* (and once again the
date, 1946):

> Britain was not the country which would now fall down on
> the post-war task of producing goods of the quality and
> quantity that the world needs so badly, said Mr N. Mon-
> sarrat, Director of the United Kingdom Information Office, at
> a luncheon which followed yesterday's annual general meet-
> ing of the Northern Branch of the British Manufacturers'
> Representatives Association at the Hotel Victoria.
>
> Mr Monsarrat said that the British were putting up with
> controls which were irksome, simply because they believed
> them to be necessary to safeguard the future. They did not
> like controls. But they liked the alternative boom-and-slump
> which followed the First World War even less, so they
> wanted to avoid its repetition in this way.
>
> Statistics showed that the 1946 production figures were
> three to five times those of 1938.
>
> Agricultural machinery exports were three times as high as
> in 1938, aluminium and brass goods five times higher, and
> Britain was now building 52 per cent of the world's ships—
> five times the total of the United States.
>
> Britain's colossal war-debt had to be paid off, and only
> healthy trade could do this.
>
> Mr Monsarrat did not want people to buy British out of

8*

mere sympathy with Britain. He wanted the selling point to
be simply that British goods were the best, and he praised the
vitality of a country which was still building into its products
that high pre-war standard of excellence.

The chairman, in thanking Mr Monsarrat, mentioned 'A
certain concern' among members of his association over the
late delivery of British goods and the failure to meet contract
dates.

One of my audience at that speech—indeed, a head-table
guest, as befitted a solid citizen with diplomatic overtones—was
Bill Hamilton, head of the United States Information Office and
my opposite number in the current polite tug-of-war for
influence—or, as we sometimes phrased it to each other, in
moments of enlarged vocabulary and diminished responsibility,
the wrestling match for the soul of South Africa.

Hamilton was a robust, charming, immensely capable ball-of-
energy; the kind of chap the British ought to have had, as head
of *their* information set-up, if the very idea had not been so
terribly un-British.

He was the first and the last man with whom I once shared
twenty-two whiskies before lunch. He could shatter party protocol with a single, resounding, mid-Western belch, and then
disarm the company with an equally outrageous: 'Sorry, folks;
it must be the cooking.' His wife once told mine: 'If Bill even
looks at me, I get pregnant!' (So *that's* what women talk about,
I thought sourly, surveying my single son.) He had a wonderful
story to tell about his recent arrival in Cape Town, when, faced
with an immigration form which demanded: 'State whether you
are European or non-European', he had boldly, naïvely, yet
accurately answered: 'Non-European'.

Hours later, he had been rescued from the appropriate dockside shed, along with the rest of the incoming rubbish, by a
member of the American Embassy.

Maddeningly versatile, he could talk to South African
farmers about hybrid wheat, whatever that was, and tell them,

sneakily and winningly: 'We have just the same problem in
Oklahoma.' He could talk to newspapermen about off-set printing, photogravure, and flongs. He could talk to women, and fill
their little ears with easy-flowing trans-Atlantic molasses. He
could certainly talk to me.

'Nice going,' he told me after the speech, when we had
adjourned to the underground Goldfields Bar (it was only 3
p.m.) and got stuck into the brandy. 'There's nothing I like
better than to hear a man with a funny accent whistling in the
dark. And what was that crap about building five times as many
ships as the United States?'

I was sure of my ground. 'It's true,' I said. 'It was in the
brief.'

'What brief was that?'

'From the Board of Trade.'

'Tell them to throw it down the toilet. If they have toilets in
jolly old England. I can let you have a *real* set of figures.' Bill
Hamilton drank deep, as was his custom, looked round the bar
which was full of the after-lunch dross of Johannesburg, and
the men for whom this was lunch itself, and said: 'I wouldn't
have guessed that your Board of Trade was still speaking to
you.'

The comment stemmed from another recent speech of mine,
when, seeking to drive home the new dynamic thrust of industrial Britain, I had quoted, and then sought to deny, a merry
quip on the subject of our official lassitude.

'You may have heard,' I had begun, 'the story of the man
who had two brothers living, and one in the Board of Trade.'

The joke, though cheerfully received, had not gone down
well with the British Trade Commissioner, who was a guest of
honour and, from that moment onwards, a formidable thunder-
cloud hovering about four feet away from me.

'But it was only a joke,' I told him, when brought to book
later.

'In very bad taste, I must say,' the Trade Commissioner
answered. He was one of those men whose necks could

apparently swell out at will, and the trick was now working at
full pressure. 'We're not going to make much headway here,
if you chaps—' he made me sound like one of a troupe of down-
at-heels jugglers, going 'Yip yip!' as the balls fell all over the
stage '—if you chaps let the side down like that.'

'But I went on to say that it wasn't true—the very opposite,
in fact.'

'Ah! But by then the harm was done, wasn't it?'

Bill Hamilton had not missed that one, either.

At the moment he was having an easier time, professionally,
than I was; America seemed to be getting everything right,
while most of the things we did were either wrong, or unpopular, or dull. His was now the top nation, beyond any doubt. It
was thriving before our envious eyes; and the Marshall Plan for
aid to a troubled Europe, the most imaginative and generous
effort ever made by any country in the search for a better
world, proved that the thriving was not selfish, and that the
derided Yankee Dollar could do many other things besides
glitter and boast and provoke.

Meanwhile, Britain had imposed bread rationing, for the very
first time in her recorded history ('Not even in the darkest days
of the submarine war!' Mr Churchill thundered); there was an
allocation of one egg per person per week; the O.B.E. was
awarded to the four-foot-high Liverpool comedian, Wee
Georgie Wood; an unholy mess began over the stopping by the
Royal Navy of wretched immigrant ships trying to get to
Palestine; and the rules for people attending Ascot races were
thus set out:

> Women in the Royal Enclosure are not permitted to bet;
> nor to smoke; nor to wear pearls [pearls being the only
> jewellery worn by the women-folk of the Royal party].
> Guests should not watch the Royal family too closely. No
> cameras or sketchbooks may be carried. No divorcées can be
> admitted.

Bill Hamilton, cutting the item out, sent it across to my office with a scrawled: 'Do they let *horses* in?'

For an awkward month, he himself had something not so easy to deal with: the American atom bomb tests in the Bikini Atoll in the Marshall Islands. These had become very unpopular, long before they started; though no one except about fifty Japanese fishermen had ever heard of Bikini Atoll before, it certainly looked a beautiful place, and the idea of blowing it to pieces with those damned bombs, which already seemed destined to be the curse of all our lives, was almost sacrilegious.

In the event, the accounts (and photographs) of this innocent Eden reduced to sudden blinding turmoil; of huge throw-away ships like the *Saratoga* and the *Arkansas* pulverized in a single orange flash; of the 8,000-foot mushroom-cloud of sea water which turned to boiling vapour with a layer of ice on top. of tidal waves sweeping far and wide across the Pacific; of the macabre victims of this inferno—particularly the wandering sacrificial goats, wearing asbestos waistcoats, which had been left behind to test 'survival technique'; and the fact that the awesome weapon itself, the first Bikini bomb, had a picture of Rita Hayworth 'in a low-cut gown' pasted on to it, together with the chalked word 'GILDA' (her latest film)—all this was rather hard for a war-sick world to appreciate.

'If it's any consolation,' I wrote to Bill Hamilton 'we were great note-swappers in those days; Motorcar Ratsriko, our intermediary, must have been thinking all sorts of things), 'Nostradamus, sixteenth-century prophet and seer, forecast the dropping of the Bikini bomb in 1588, so you could hardly have got out of it. Quote: "A revolutionary form of sea-warfare shall be initiated. A ship from the west by a great flame bright as day shall be ruined in the mist." The mist must be that radio-active cloud.'

'I suppose Nostradamus was British,' Bill said grumpily, when next we met.

'No, he was French. You know—Notre Dame.'

He brightened. 'Notre Dame is American!'

Pronounced like that, it certainly was.

I missed him very much when, following a ruthless Congressional economy drive, they closed up the U.S. Information Office and sold off every single item in the building—only to re-open it again, about a year later, at enormous expense (the carpet in the reception hall alone cost more than our total annual rent). Bill Hamilton went on to bigger and better things in the State Department, but I can personally guarantee that he was doing all right in Johannesburg.

He had an expression—new at that time, slightly uncouth, explicit—with which he used to close some of our sessions, when even Chiefs of Information had to go back to their offices and sign a few letters: it was 'Keep your nose clean'. Exiled in South Africa, half in love with it, half revolted by a whole frieze of the most disgusting human violation, I kept my nose clean, occasionally in demanding circumstances, for several months. Then I got into a big row myself.

Foolishly, it had nothing much to do with South Africa. It was Palestine.

As befitted a city where the Jewish community had worked so hard and contributed so much, since the day, sixty years earlier, when the first hopeful pedlar had pitched his first tent, Johannesburg had an influential Zionist organization, and was taking a strong interest in what was, and was not, happening in Palestine, the 'Jewish Home' which had still to be labelled Israel.

Locally, this was sparked and spearheaded by the Chief Rabbi, Professor L. T. Rabinowitz, who operated under the auspices of the United Zionist Revisionist Party.

Rabbi Rabinowitz, a dedicated, attractive, and ferociously energetic man whom one chance encounter established as an enemy instead of the friend he was later to become, had, or thought he had, a lot to work on, as far as Palestine was concerned. He was dramatically, professionally furious about the whole thing.

He could point to the fact that the entire might of the Royal Navy seemed to have been deployed to intercept and turn back the stream of leaking, broken-down immigrant ships which were currently trying to run the blockade and bring East European Jewish refugees to their only safe harbour.

God knows they had suffered enough already, under murderous persecution first from German then Polish, then Russian spite. So why could they not be allowed through? (Answer: There was an Anglo-American-Arabian accord which limited the Palestine intake to 100,000 per annum, in order to avoid total chaos on the spot. Simple arithmetic could prove that for one incoming Jew, there was likely to be one displaced Arab. Both of them, under this tidal drift of humanity, could starve to death.)

The rest of the dispute was a hideous mixture of charge and counter-charge: the small lie supplanted by the big one, the genuine tear by the crocodile: the honest soldier shot in the back by the honest patriot: the crooked referee lynched by the virtuous crowd. Still saddled with the tail-end of their mandate, the British had to hold the ring.

Against them was ranged the Stern Gang, self-styled 'Fighters for the Freedom of Israel', and unlicensed murderers in any language, who once hanged half a dozen British soldiers in an orange grove, as sad and sunny a death as could be devised. There was another terrorist organization called IRGUN, which kidnapped five British officers from their club in Tel Aviv; and shot two others in Jerusalem; and then, in the same city, blew up the entire King David Hotel, the British military headquarters, leaving 106 dead (including girls from our Auxiliary Territorial Service).

From our point of view, we *had* to impose a stiff military rule. It was our duty as the appointed custodian. From the Chief Rabbi's, however, the best thing we could do would be to get out, stay out, and let Palestine forge its own destiny. In protest against our continued presence, he had recently discarded all his British military decorations, and sent the lot back to Buckingham Palace. Now he invited me to take part in a public debate on the whole issue.

I might, he said, with a certain menacing honesty which I found difficult to resist, be the only one who would support the British side.

By now, it was thought that I was grown up, and I had a free hand in accepting or declining all such invitations. Perhaps I should have been more wary, in this threatening climate. But some of the things which were being said about us—particularly at an anti-British rally attended by the Mayor of Johannesburg, Mrs Jessie Macpherson, where we were firmly branded as fascists, as anti-semitic tyrants 'worse than Hitler'—got under my skin.

The childish business of the Chief Rabbi's medals clinched it. If he thought he had a lot to work on, so did I. I accepted, put on my best suit and a Royal Navy tie, and went down into the arena.

I had been prepared for the fact that the final score might well be Lions 6, Christians nil; but the ferocity of the occasion was a genuine surprise. It developed into a real old-fashioned slanging match; and I might have been playing the bagpipes in a high wind on top of Mount Carmel, for all the progress I made.

All our past efforts were derided or forgotten, up to the moment of 'now'. Now, it was repeated, we should get out and stay out. We had no business in Palestine, anyway; not even to have our soldiers murdered in the pursuit of liberation. There weren't any arguments on our side. There was only our guilt, our certain humiliation, and our duty to leave the scene in favour of those who were properly entitled to deal with it.

There was one man whom I could talk to, who even paused to listen, on that so-called panel; the rest might have served as fully paid-up members of the Holy Office, conducting a standard inquisition with the faggots noisily piling up in the background. This was a lawyer called Louis Pincus, a gentle character who was soon to sell up his practice and actually go to Palestine, where he became a member of the Cabinet.

So he was all right: an honest man prepared (as Bill Hamilton would have said) to put his money where his mouth was. The rest of them, safely out of range of the real action, were baying for blood; anyone's blood. Mine was the nearest supply on tap; and mine it was.

At the end I did the best I could, by way of fighting back. After listening to every kind of insult and misrepresentation of the British role in Palestine, with side-swipes at my own effrontery in even daring to answer back, I said that I wanted a couple of minutes of uninterrupted time, to put my point of view. Aided by Louis Pincus, I finally got it.

I then said that we were in Palestine because it was our duty, from which we were not going to run away, however loudly the dogs barked and snapped at our heels. If people were going to call the British names, then they might as well get the names right.

'Fascist' was not a suitable epithet to apply to a nation which had expended enormous efforts and a great many lives in rescuing Jews from a miserable tyranny, and were now in the process of half-starving themselves in order to send food to Middle Europe.

If it had not been for Britain's ultimate challenge to Hitler, there would not now be a Palestine for the Jews to reach, nor any Jews to go there.

The hissing uproar which this provoked was well reflected in the next day's issue of the Zionist newspaper, which carried as slanted an account of my efforts as I had ever read, outside my last school report. I had insulted the entire Jewish community. I had called them dogs. Clearly, out of my own mouth, I was an anti-semite of the deepest dye. The best thing, the only thing, the British government could do now was to recall me forthwith.

All such mistakes and strokes of misfortune—indeed, *all* mistakes and misfortunes—are one's own fault; that is the lesson of life, whether one realizes it early, or late, or goes whining to the grave still shrouded in a sense of injustice.

On this occasion I should either have presented my views deep-fried in diplomatic batter; or kept silent; or preferably not been there at all. The silly part was that I was probably the least anti-semitic person in the whole of Johannesburg.

I had already come to the conclusion that the Jewish community—who actually read books, bought paintings, supported the theatre and the symphony orchestra, and gave money to charity with open hands—were the only people who redeemed Johannesburg from its squalor; and I admired and honoured them for it.

Later, when I came to know Harry Oppenheimer—son of the fabulous Sir Ernest, brother of that Frank Oppenheimer who had been a fellow-member of the Lucullus Club at Cambridge—and saw his new mine down at Welkom in the Free State, where he had established unheard-of living conditions for his mine-workers in the face of ferocious opposition from authority; and listened to him as an M.P., and a Cabinet Minister, and the controlling brain of a huge empire of half the world's diamond, gold, and uranium supplies (all this at the same time), I grew more convinced than ever.

His was a blue-print of accomplishment which made nonsense of race or religion; demonstrating just how much one man, with vast inherited wealth, great talent and ability, and an outlook, a code of ethics, which it would be insulting to call Christian, could do with such assets.

But already, without benefit of Harry Oppenheimer or any other particular star to convince me, my feelings were such that the charge of anti-semitism was baseless. To hell with Rabbi Rabinowitz, I thought, as I read of my misdeeds and awaited the inevitable summons to Pretoria. To hell with such a far-off freedom fighter who could condone murder without a splash of its blood to soil his pious hands.

There were far better Jews, far better citizens, far better men. One had only to seek, and one found them; and I had discovered this already.

In this row (which quickly petered out, like the fake hurricane it was) as in every other crisis, the High Commissioner's Office was a marvellous supporter all the time. Ian Maclennan was the link-man, dealing faithfully with my silly questions and bailing me out if I had already given the wrong answer; and Morrice James, when he arrived towards the end of the year, was also a tower of strength—although his first announcement was to the effect that he had bought an American car, and hoped that this would not compromise my position.

The way in which they, the pros, suffered the hopeless amateur was continually encouraging. Until I found my way about, my civil service crimes multiplied. I bought myself a desk which was almost three feet wider than the one to which my rank entitled me, but somehow I was allowed to keep it. I used to write my minutes in red ink! (Only the High Commissioner himself could use red ink, or even pencil.)

I also got into a hopeless tangle with the Information Office estimates, which had to be broken down into about thirty different categories, from wages to stationery supplies, from cleaning costs to the probable freight charges on our exhibition material.

How could I possibly forecast how much I would spend on postage and telephones between July 1947 and June 1948? Well, Ian Maclennan thought he knew, and by God he was just about right. Who could say just how much corrugated cardboard, wrapping twine, and gummed labels we might need in the next six months? 'In *our* experience,' Morrice James began his helpful answer, using the right colour of ink (though whether he was speaking for the High Commissioner's Office, or for himself and God Almighty in concert, was luckily beyond my need to determine), 'this sort of expenditure usually bears a precise relationship to—etc. etc.'

In the event (and soon I was beyond surprise at such divination) we never ran short of corrugated cardboard, nor did the newly christened Commonwealth Relations Office ever run out of money.

4.

The rest of that jumpy year went like the wind, with the office steadily building up to the point when it was taken for granted as part of the scene—though there were some things we simply could not deal with, as when one admirer, complimenting us on our Monthly Diary of Events, wrote: 'I would like to receive your Monthly Diary every week in future.'

My errors, for the moment, were mainly social, and included one whopping misdemeanour which followed me around for some time. As with every crossroads, big or small, it was only a matter of having said Yes instead of No; but, fresh from the tangle with the Chief Rabbi, I should have had more sense.

There was at that time a murderer in England by the name of George Neville Heath, currently being tried and then hanged for two revoltingly sadistic murders involving women whom he had stripped, bound, stabbed, raped, mutilated, and generally bashed about in the pursuit, presumably, of pleasure. He had been married during the war to a South African girl, and everyone in Johannesburg knew it.

It really was quite a talking point, in a society which had not a great deal to do besides enjoy such light chit-chat. Speculation centred on one intriguing aspect: if George Neville Heath took his pleasures so devoutly, what had it been like to be married to him?

I knew the girl, and her new fiancé, a serious and compassionate young man transparently dedicated to her welfare. At a dance which they bravely attended, they asked me—no, she asked me, while he listened—if people were talking about herself and her late husband. Being in the business of accurate information, I was fool enough to answer: Yes, of course they were. Then, what, she asked, were they saying?

Leaving out certain monstrous expressions of curiosity, I told her that too.

Tears followed, public distress; grim silences; and then a
swift withdrawal of patronage which presently left me at an
empty table with my innocent and faithful wife, who up till
then had been enjoying herself, and with—God damn it—the
bill.

'You really *are* a fool!' Eileen said, when I gave her the
details. 'Why didn't you tell her, No, no one knows anything
about it?'

'But she asked me!' I had been taken aback by 'Fool', which
coming from Eileen was extremely rare—perhaps too rare for
my own good. 'What else could I say? One has to tell the truth.'

'Oh, God!'

It could have been a direct salutation, a recognition of a new
role, but somehow it didn't sound like it.

We had some very welcome visitors to look after, often
imported with the help of the British Council; among them, in
that trial year, were Solomon the pianist, George Formby the
funny man with the ukelele, and Malcolm Sargent, who did not
need any instrument to make him a rousing success.

He was a fantastically alive man; a great talker, a polished
wit, and of course a musician with that marvellous knack of
communicating pleasure and understanding to people hitherto
hardly touched by either.

As part of our modest promotion (modest because he did not
really need any help), we showed to an invited audience a film of
him conducting—as well as talking, analysing, expounding, and
generally doing for music what Sir Kenneth Clark could do for
art, or Julian Huxley for science. It was a great success. When
the lights went up, Malcolm Sargent was seen to be applauding
vigorously.

I somehow bought myself a brand-new car, the first one of
my life, and that too was subverted to the uses of propaganda.
'FIRST POST-WAR RILEY ARRIVES ON RAND', the headline proclaimed, above a substantial news-item which said that
the car would be on view over the weekend, by courtesy of Mr

Monsarrat, and how it had a 1½-litre engine (58 brake horse-power!) and four-wheel brakes, and the new torsion bar sus-pension, and four jacking points 'so that wheel-changing and home lubricating present no difficulty to the owner,' and fine craftsmanship throughout; how it could go 80 m.p.h. . . .

All true. I did not do too much of that home lubricating; but the Riley could manage a genuine 80, and with its sleek lines and leather top looked handsome indeed—a small gem of a car which carried me in turn down to Cape Town, and through the Valley of a Thousand Hills to Durban, and along the Garden Route to Port Elizabeth, and across to the Game Reserve near the Mozambique border, and once up the entire length of Bechuanaland, from Mafeking to Francistown, where the Karroo Desert was out-matched by the far more cruel Kalahari, and the most comforting thing a man could tell the traveller was: 'You'll get through all right—the road's just been ploughed.'*

Indeed, even in South Africa, much of this voyaging lay along awful ox-cart roads still waiting to be paved, as they had waited since the *Voortrekkers* first urged their wagons through the clogging yellow dust, and carved the first rut into an unmarked plain.

But above all it was Africa, real Africa; the innocent part, the part one could love, without guilt and without mastery either.

Back to U.K.I.O., and modern propaganda, and modern transport. . . . Though B.O.A.C., successor to Imperial Air-ways, was still operating a flying-boat service from Durban to England (total time, five days, with overnight stops) we were now able to publicize the opening of an entirely new run. This was by the latest Skymaster, which carried forty-four passengers, and could fly them from one country to the other in under thirty-eight hours. Travellers could have breakfast in London on Saturday, and dinner in Johannesburg on the following Sunday night!

* A seasonal method of making such roads passable, by ploughing up the centre hump to fill in the washed-out edges.

The world was growing smaller, and we could point with pride to the fact that part of the shrinking was being done by us. I had to preserve a lofty silence when Bill Hamilton said: 'What's a Skymaster, for God's sake? That plane's a D.C.4! It's American!'

But just over the horizon was something which *really* ought to give our side a lift: the projected Royal Tour of South Africa, planned for early in 1947. The King, the Queen, and the two princesses would arrive at Cape Town in the battleship *Vanguard*, 42,500 tons, the biggest in the world, and just launched at a cost of £11 million.

I had been invited to serve as a Royal Tour commentator by the S.A.B.C., and was allowed to accept the job if I did not use my own name. I therefore appeared as 'Nicholas Hamilton', an information service compromise.

Somewhere in the background of this visit there was hovering an enigmatic figure who was rumoured to be a suitor for the hand of Princess Elizabeth. He was Prince Philip of Greece, soon to be stripped down to the bone and reconstituted as Lieutenant Philip Mountbatten, R.N. There had already been a question about him in the House of Commons, when he had applied for British citizenship.

Mr Chuter Ede, the Home Secretary, said that such an application would be given priority. 'On what grounds?' a sanctimonious Labour M.P. queried. What was this all about? Were the rumours of a forthcoming engagement true?

The questioner (who did not get an answer) was Mr George Jeger, the man who had usurped my seat at Winchester. Now if Monsarrat had won Winchester, I thought primly, that was one silly question which would never have been asked.

Bill Hamilton, cradled in republican America, refused to be impressed by my touring royalties. 'O.K., your majesty,' he said. 'Who else have you got coming?'

'Air-Commodore Whittle.'

'Huh?'

'He invented the jet engine.'

'That was Lockheed.'

Nettled, I asked him: 'Well, who have you got?'

'H. J. Heinz.' I knew about H. J. Heinz. 'And after him, Jim Farley.'

'Who he?'

'Jesus, don't you know anything? James A. Farley. He used to be Postmaster General. Now he's chairman of Coco-Cola.'

'Whoopee!'

Bill Hamilton grinned. 'Well, it's a start. You wanna Coke?'

'No. You wanna Scotch?'

'Yes.'

But a new plane service, and a beautiful new car, and a royal tour in the world's newest and biggest battleship, and sunshine speeches about Britain's dynamic will to work, could not really compete with the stuff we had to put out, or to read. Perhaps, as Bill had said, I *was* whistling in the dark, and I might be out of breath long before dawn.

The news from London continued to be depressing, and lifeless except where it was bad-tempered: more and more rationing, more and more strikes: homeless squatters moving into empty luxury flats, fuel cuts 'in preparation for winter': and Minister of Food Sir Ben Smith thundering: 'I still hear of wasted bread, porridge, and potatoes! Waste is a capital crime! We must tighten our belts!'

One of the latest news pictures which my office had to distribute was of the new 1¾ lb. British loaf, which had replaced the previous 2 lb. job in the interests of economy. It was backed up by a quote from Dr Edith Summerskill, Parliamentary Secretary to the Minister of Food,* who, hitting an early streak of volubility, cut loose with the following:

Take the case of a woman whose husband is a manual labourer, and whose three children range in age from three to

---

* As Baroness Summerskill of Ken Wood she was, fifteen years later, one of the first beneficiaries of a curious new idea just advanced by Lady Violet Bonham-Carter, that there should be life peers and life peeresses.

twelve years. First she must see that her husband applies through his employer for cards known as BUX and BUY, giving him the extra units to which he is entitled. Then she must apply to the local food office for a BUX card which entitles adolescents to four more bread units a week. Then she consults the ration scales, and finds that children under four get five units, children four to eleven get thirteen, and she herself gets nine units a week.

In the adult ration book she will find pages marked L, M, and G. The L page had 52 squares, each worth one bread unit; the M and G pages also have 52 squares, though these are worth two and six units respectively. Page G of the adult book is replaced by page F in the children's book, and by page J in the adolescents' book.

Having worked out the maximum number of loaves to which her family is entitled, the housewife then registers with a baker, stating firmly on which days she will need bread, and how much, having borne in mind that three units must be surrendered for one pound of flour, and two for one pound of cakes, buns, pastries, trifles, fruit loaves, and other supplies grouped together as flour confectionery.

Small loaves require two bread units, large ones need four.

Someone else in Johannesburg had my kind of doubts, and was able to voice them publicly—or, to be exact, *not* able to voice them but to see that they attracted wide attention. This was a man called Bob Crisp, an ex-tank commander and one of South Africa's principal war heroes, along with Sailor Malan the airman; the same Major Bob Crisp, D.S.O., M.C. who had apparently written some of the words for Hatchett's 'Lili Marlene Gallant 8th Armee' extravaganza, and must accept the burden of their copyright.

He was one of my earliest friends in Johannesburg: a large, commanding, restless man, disdainful of all non-fighters, non-leaders, non-heroes, who was obviously finding peace-time dull and second-rate compared with the recent past; a man who had not, and perhaps never would, come to terms with the fact that wars finished, and guns fell silent, and the proudest flags were lowered and laid away; and that even the most exuberant fighting animal must at last grow tame, and sheathe its claws, and only bare its teeth for a smile—or else be disciplined by the prudent, peace-loving mice who would be setting the rules for the rest of its life.

At the moment he was selling insurance, and writing articles, and doing occasional radio broadcasts. But he had recently been back in Britain, and I knew what he felt about it; it was therefore no surprise to read in the *Rand Daily Mail* one morning that he was having a stand-up row with the South African Broadcasting Corporation, which had censored one of his talks off the air and wouldn't even give him back his script so that he could get it published elsewhere.

The S.A.B.C. had excused themselves on the ground that the talk 'might cause ill-feeling'. That was probably true; professionally speaking, it should have caused some ill-feeling with me. His theme, as it was now summarized in print, had been the laziness of Britain when compared with South Africa.

Britain, he said (or had wanted to say), seemed to have lost its sense of direction and purpose. The people had become very rude. They had lost their pride in workmanship, and were generally idle and bloody-minded.

From a mixture of motives, I kept well away from that one. But I felt able to tell Bob Crisp that as far as I was concerned he could hang on to his medals.

Max, son and heir and only child (I seemed to have lost the knack for the moment), was now four: a small, bright, blond boy who had thrived on British rosehip syrup and cod liver oil in the past, and was now thriving on South Africa's lavish spread of all other items in the larder. Full of energy but inclined to conserve it, he went everywhere, even to the lavatory, by tricycle.

I could not see much of him, except at weekends. But it was

nice to know that my ancient nursery jokes still went down well:
that the old riddles ('Why is five o'clock in the morning like
a pig's tail?' 'Because it's twirly!') were still considered
uproarious, and that a brand-new one ('What's the difference
between a sick elephant and a dead bee?' 'One is a seedy beast,
the other a bee deceased,') was, after a little explanation,
equally successful.

He had a song to sing me, just as I had had one to sing for my
father. It was never my first choice, but it was certainly his It
was called 'Shoo-Fly Pie and Apple Pan Dowdy'.

When Max laughed at a joke, there was always some
delighted laughter echoing in the background. This came from
Victoria the nursegirl, a loving black shadow who never seemed
to be more than ten paces away from him, and was the most
devoted attendant he was ever likely to have.

Like all natives—like Adam in the kitchen and Simon in the
garden—Victoria was sweetness and gentleness itself with
Max, and with any other white child who might be around.
Though it was obvious that these privileged children must one
day grow up to be privileged tyrants, like all the rest of the
white adult world, yet no trace of this foreboding knowledge,
this absolute certainty of duress, ever showed in their manner,
their voices, their smiles, their infinite patience, as they took
care of the rulers-to-be.

Thus it was painful, it was almost disastrous, to note that
Max had already picked up, from God knows where, the
instinct of lordship over Victoria and the others. He bossed them
around, argued with them, ordered Victoria to fetch his toys, or
to collect them at the end of the day, plagued her to carry him on
her broad back, demanded hand-outs from the kitchen, and,
when punished as he had to be for such nonsense, took it out on
the victims in any way he could, and always resumed the habit
of command.

Where had he got it from? He did not go to school. He would
never have learned such arrogance from our own almost morbid
solicitude for any native we dealt with. Certainly he played with

other children, but they were the children of imports like ourselves, not yet in tune with white South Africa and never likely
to be.

Yet in a short half-year he had contracted the disease already.
We decided that it must be in the very air—that divine, rare,
benevolent air which, for all its seeming purity, carried a horrid
contagion as well.

Since everyone in South Africa talked politics all the time;
since everything had a political slant, from *Boeremusiek*
(Country and Western, in thumping jig-time) to beards (the
upper lip unshaven denoted an ardent Nationalist); there were
plenty of people I could talk to about this sort of thing, in spite
of the general climate of *baasskap* and the care I had to exercise
not to get publicly involved.

Uys Krige was one; though a proud Afrikaner he was
violently opposed to the Nationalist philosophy which was now
on the march all round us, and was thus thought of as a traitor
by a large majority of his race. (Also, he had fought for the
British against the Germans. *Skandaal!*) Another was Sarah
Gertrude Millin, a delightful woman whose book, *God's Step-
children*, could teach one more about the wretched plight of the
Coloureds (mixed-blood) in South Africa than anything short of
actually living in their community.*

Also in this category of safe confidants was T. C. Robertson
of *Libertas*, our first landlord, a hard-core political journalist who
knew more about 'the Nats' and their wartime intrigues—
intrigues to the point of treason and beyond—than certain
Nationalists could bear to contemplate. So was Councillor Colin
Legum, who now had a delicious new title, Chairman of the
Jubilee Committee (Johannesburg was currently celebrating its
sixtieth anniversary as a city).

His jolly label hardly accorded with the sour future; Legum

---

* However, one could learn a little of their wry sense of humour in conversation. I
knew an old Cape-Coloured teacher who sometimes came to our reading-room.
Once he said: 'Our great trouble is, we all arrived after the white man,' and when
I asked how long afterwards, he said, with a wonderful sly look: 'Nine months.'

was not yet set in the mould of the know-it-all pundit, as bred
by the *Observer*, with all the answers to all the carefully loaded
questions. Then, from my liberal, give-and-take point of view,
he was all right, and excellent company anyway.

We did enjoy one spectacular dinner-party at his house, when
much more than the food and the conversation was memorable.
It was early in December, and therefore high summer; Johannesburg was undergoing one of its rare summer storms (they happened every two or three years), when forked lightning was
playing along the whole length of the Reef, and reports were
coming in over the radio of hailstones certainly as big as the
traditional pigeon's egg crashing through the equally traditional corrugated iron roofs.

Since Colin Legum's house was thatched, another popular
design thereabouts, we all felt safe. But after dinner, which had
been punctuated by a series of shattering thunder-claps, just as
Colin had said something rather rude about a politician called
Ebenezer Donges,* and I had remarked: 'I suppose if the Germans had won he would have been your local *Gauleiter*,' our
impiety was swiftly punished. The house was struck by
lightning.

There was a crash, a cascade of bricks down the chimney,
and then an acrid smell of burning wood. When we ran outside,
the roof was already in flames.

I like to think that we all kept our heads. Mrs Legum rushed
upstairs to rescue the baby, and Eileen after her to collect its
wardrobe. I rigged a hose from the kitchen tap, and, leaning out
of one of the dormer windows, tried to play it on the flames;
but when a piece of burning thatch missed my ear by inches on
its way down, I decided to stop being a hero and join in the
salvage operation. After that, our reactions were swift, and
curiously personal.

I lugged out the radiogram, and Colin's very respectable
collection of records. He concentrated on his filing system, and

* Later Minister of Finance. His daughter Una once applied for a job in my office.
The answer was a diplomatic No.

then on his books. Anton Hendriks, a South African artist of repute, saved all the pictures. Oliver Walker, of the Institute of Race Relations, went for the carpets. Uys Krige, with a poet's logical inconsequence, salvaged the fire-irons. Then, within half an hour, the whole roof fell in, and that was that.

On the lawn outside, at that grisly moment, the flames showed, among other collector's items, a bottle of gin, a teddy bear, a heap of candlesticks, and some charred posters proclaiming, in both official languages: 'COME TO JOHANNESBURG THIS EXCITING YEAR'.

There were some tears as well, understandably, and it was hard not to share them. This had been a house-warming party; the house was barely six weeks old, and they had only just moved in. A lot of the furniture, newly-bought, had not yet been insured.

I had that demanding job, and through it could compensate for the shortcomings and imperfections of all around me. Eileen had no such sublimation available, and was much less happy. The freedom to buy a dozen eggs, ten gallons of petrol, a tub of butter, a *sack* of oranges, could not mask the glaring lack of other freedoms, which nagged, or should have nagged, at the conscience and the instinct of decency without giving either of them a moment's rest.

We were both stuck in a cage of demonstrable misery and distress. I could look the other way, for quite a lot of the time. She could not.

But in the world outside, who was happy, towards the end of 1946? One peered about, like a sociologist or a lost sailor, and wondered. Where was the good news?

Ah yes, the Aga Khan must be happy, quite near to us, in Dar-es-Salaam. On his annual visit to his faithful Moslem subjects, he had been weighed against a matching mound of diamonds, and had turned the scale at 243 lbs. (17 stone, 5 lb.). This offering cost £350,000, which was given to the poor.

But happiness, otherwise? . . . *Not* in Britain, under a blight of

austerity which would have taken the heart cut of a prize lettuce.
Not in Greece, where a civil war, of brother against brother,
was boiling to a crescendo of merciless blood-letting *Not* in
India, split and crucified by religious rioting which left the
streets of Calcutta and Bombay littered and reeking with
corpses—up to a hundred a day—for the vultures to pick over at
their leisure.

Not in nearby Basutoland, where five Basutos, led by the
late Paramount Chief's son, were up on a medicine-murder
charge (lips, eyebrows, and ears sliced off, to make good
strong medicine; then the head wrapped in a cloth and buried
under the floor of the hut).

Certainly *not* in the dock at the Nuremberg trials, where
after 227 days of evidence and summing-up the death sentence
had been passed on thirteen top Nazi war criminals. Thirty
picked men from the British prison service, plus a special consignment of rope, had been flown from London for the occasion.
At last we were doing something constructive.

Among the more prominent condemned men were Goering
(who contrived to commit suicide), Foreign Minister Ribbentrop, Hans Frank (the chief exterminator of Polish Jews),
Kalterbrunner (who had specialized in prisoners-of-war and
shot-down airmen), and the odious Jew-baiter Julius Streicher
who, propagandist to the last, went to the gallows shouting:
'Heil Hitler! Now I go to God on the day of the Feast of Purim,
a Jewish Festival! The Bolshevists will hang you too some
day!'

By contrast, Dr Hjalmar Schacht, President of the Reichs-
bank, a wily money-man who up to the moment of war had kept
the whole Nazi machine in top gear by the most superb
financial juggling, was acquitted. Perhaps the fact that his full
baptismal name was Hjalmar Horace Greely Schacht had some
weight with the American members of the tribunal.

I felt absolutely hard-hearted about all this; like Nelson, I
would have hanged the lot on Christmas morning. The Nazi
war crimes were forever summed up, for me, by a small piece

of evidence which came to light at the Belsen concentration camp trial.

There, one of the Belsen guards explained virtuously that he could not have been present on some particularly horrific day of slaughter because he had been in hospital with a scalded foot. 'Scalded? How scalded?' 'In fat, hot fat!'

Two more questions revealed that it had been human fat, which was being run off from the crematorium.

Where, indeed, was the good news? *Not*, once more, in South Africa, where a white farmer, having got a black girl pregnant after a brief encounter *under* his parked car, killed her, beheaded her, and then disembowelled her of the tell-tale foetus, which he thought might reveal its pale origin. His wife, equally concerned with social pressures, held the lantern for him to work by.

There were moments when the fullest office day could not drop a curtain anywhere near large enough or thick enough to take care of South Africa. Now and then I knew that if I had been a Negro in Johannesburg, I would have become *anything*— thief, liar, murderer, rapist, revolutionary, medicine killer, political assassin—if it would have improved my lot by half-a-crown a week, or let me get level with even one of my oppressors, whether a tough, head-cuffing policeman, or an indolent white missus.

One particular day in the company of Michael Scott confirmed this.

5.

The Reverend Michael Scott was an Anglican priest who had become one of the most prominent and controversial figures on the South African scene. Rather frail (he had been invalided out of the R.A.F.) and strikingly handsome, he had originally been appointed the priest to one of the Negro community's churches, and lived in a *rondavel*, a small thatched hut, on the edge of Sophiatown, a miserable plague-spot of a native location, intolerably overcrowded with 36,000 people.

He had a notable ally in another brave man, Father Trevor Huddleston, who ran a mission in the same kind of ghetto; but Scott himself was at that time drawing nearly all the fire.

He had first headed an organization called the Campaign for Right and Justice which, as so often happened in South Africa, soon became so poisoned by politics that he had to withdraw from it. Then he had refused to pay his taxes, as a protest against racial prejudice, and sent the money instead to the Indian Passive Resistance Movement in Durban.

Presently he had linked himself more directly with the Indians, who were trying to fight the harsh economic restrictions placed on them by a recent act of Parliament (a Parliament in which they were not represented), and had gone down to Durban to take part in one of their demonstrations. This involved no more than sitting quietly on the ground, in company with other patient and determined men and women; refusing to move when ordered; and inevitably being carted off by the police. However, the police were by no means over-zealous or prompt in their interference. They usually let the white population have a good bash first.

The Indian passive resisters, and Scott with them, were nightly the target of organized violence and brutality at the hands of roaming bands of youths, who circled round them, then suddenly invaded, kicked the unresisting bodies, and beat many of them insensible. Scott, in his white cassock, was never actually assaulted; but he was vilely taunted, particularly by young girls, who screamed 'Coolie guts!' at him, and sometimes 'Curry guts!'—surely one of the strangest taunts anyone could devise.

After several nights of this barbarous ordeal, of eventual arrest and later release, Michael Scott was actually brought into court, and given three months in jail. When he had served this, he came back to Johannesburg—not to fold his hands, but

9

to try to do something about the native locations there, which
were as miserable as anything to be found in Durban, and as
much in need of Christian care and compassion.

He was thus preaching Christianity, which made him very
unpopular with almost every white in the country (one of the
more generous comments I heard about him was: 'Of course
he's a saint! But it's so bad for business!') He was also living
Christianity; hence the series of collisions with the police. But
in the process he had become an undoubted hero, a seeming
saviour, to thousands of Negroes in Johannesburg and beyond.

When he asked me if I would like to have a look at a new
native township called Tobruk, where he was now living and
working, I took a day off from the office—indeed, from my
whole career—and went with him.

Tobruk was an organized, self-run shanty town which had
been started by returning servicemen, who were devoutly, passionately eager to prove that such a community could be made
to work. It was a curious choice of name, since 'Tobruk' was
still synonymous with a somewhat spectacular defeat suffered by
the South African army in 1942, when it had garrisoned the
desert fortress, allowed it to be overrun by Rommel, surrendered
it within twenty-four hours, and marched out into captivity more
than 25,000 strong.

For some time after that, South African soldiers were known
to the ill-natured as Tobruk Harriers.

The new Tobruk, established in such bright hope and brave
ambition, had gradually become an overspill area for the
crowded locations all round it, and thus one of the outlaw communities which defaced the hills overlooking Johannesburg. It
had a bad name already, for many reasons. Close to, it was the
most awful place I had ever seen in my life.

Most of the huts were a pitiful patchwork of corrugated iron,
rusty old oil drums, planks and barrel staves; some were
hessian shacks, with walls of cardboard cartons, floors of
trodden cow-dung, and a leaky bucket for sanitation. The
'streets' had grown out of the tracks which criss-crossed the

hillside; they were rutted, littered with refuse, and served as
open drains for slow-moving sewage. Filthy goats, half-starved
dogs, coal-black innocent children patrolled them in company,
like some small nightmare army of mixed conscripts.

Over all was a corrosive smell of fouled earth and wood-
smoke and excrement; and over *that* a choking, enveloping
ochre dust, a pall which was the true pall of defeat and death.

I followed Michael Scott as he made his rounds: sick at
heart, proud to be with him. For there was no doubt of his
stature in this terrible place; as soon as he came into sight, a
crowd gathered, and the word 'Scott. . . . Scott. . . . Scott'
exploded in whispers all round us.

He answered a few questions, and hailed a few friends, and
then we began to walk, to tread the disgusting streets of
Tobruk. We went into some of the huts: knocking on rusty iron
doors which drooped from their hinges, drawing aside tattered
hessian curtains. Outside was the sun and the filth; inside, a
noisome darkness to match the worry, the apathy, the despair
which were on almost every face. Only the naked children
smiled, and opened wide their bright eyes. They would learn,
they would learn. . . .

Scott was asked, many times, if it was true that soon they
would all have to leave Tobruk, that they were to be rehoused
in a new place, Moraka. Must they really give up these, their
only homes?—or was it true that if one had a certain paper from
Ethiopia, even the police could not touch them?*

Michael plodded on, up one filthy street and down another;
in his dusty cassock and cracked boots he might have been a
latter-day Christ on the Mount of Olives, compassionate, wise,
and observant, suffering for all who suffered. But he was an
angry Christ also.

'Ethiopian passports!' he exclaimed at one point. 'That must
be Khomo again. . . . The worst thing about a place like this,' he

---

* Currently there was a brisk trade in 'Ethiopian passports' (five shillings each)
in which the Lion of Judah declared that This His Beloved Subject was exempt
from the South African pass laws, and could live anywhere he chose

said, staring round him as if he would have given his life for one
chance with a magic wand, 'is that even here they prey on each
other, like hyenas. . . . Tobruk is a terrible place at night—they
steal, they get drunk on that horrible *skokiaan* that the women
brew, they beat people up, they extort food, they burn a man's
hut if he won't pay protection money.'

'Who is "they"? And who is Khomo?'

'A wicked man.' Michael would never have used the word
without good cause. 'He has gone now, thank God—' and I
could tell that he really was thanking God for some deliverance.
'Khomo was one of the ex-soldiers who started Tobruk. Then
he decided to take it over. He set up his own police force—a
band of drunken, lawless thugs—then began to rule it. The
whole thing became a racket; it still is. Protection money, rent
money, water money, roof money—he and his police preyed on
this place like gangsters. In fact, they *were* gangsters.'

'But you say he's gone.'

'Yes. He finally ran off with all the camp funds. But I think he
still rules this place, from outside. I can tell that, from their
faces. . . . There is fear here. I can smell it.'

For me, it must have been lost in all the other smells. 'But
what about the police—the real police?'

'They always looked the other way. Khomo saved them a lot
of trouble. He kept order, of a sort. . . . I used to have a church
here,' Michael went on, as if he were talking of a golden age.
'Just a wooden shack with a tin roof, and a yellow pine cross
over the altar. The night before Khomo left, his chaps broke into
the church. They hacked the cross down, and stole the altar
cloth, and then they burned the whole place.'

We had finished our tour, and were walking towards my
car. Many people waved, and smiled, and shouted good-bye;
the children crowded round the car, as wide-eyed as fauns.
Michael smiled back, and called greetings, yet I could tell that he
was horribly disappointed, and unhappy, and fearful of the future.

'I'm afraid it's true that they will have to leave Tobruk before
long. Even this place is wanted for something else. Or it has to

be kept empty, to fit in with somebody s plan.' He sighed.
'The master plan for the master race. . . . So they must move on.
Even from here. And I have to answer a summons, next week,
for living here at all.'

'Why?'

'The Native Urban Areas Act says that I mustn't.'

We left Tobruk, and its miseries and poisonous air and
loathsome denial of humanity. We drove off in my beautiful
new Riley, with its walnut dashboard, its real leather upholstery,
its chic disengagement from all that was crude and vulgar.

What, on God's good earth, could one do about South Africa?

6.

Being a civil servant with deep though underlying political
convictions, I had my answer ready. South Africa, clearly, must
be acquired and administered by men of good will; it must be
rescued, refashioned, set on the right path, and kept firmly to it.

Thus it was now time for my third invention; after the Automatic Gear Change (1921) and Perpetual Motion (1926) must
come South Africa Reconstituted (1946).

Obviously I would have to take the whole place over; or
rather *we* would have to take it over—'we' being me and my
praesidium of the wisest in the land. Over Christmas, I drew up
my master plan; and here, in all its naïveté, its good intent, and
its inherent bossiness, is the text of that blueprint, forever
enshrined in Copy No. 1 (there were no others) in the only
SECRET archives which have survived from the past.

Outline of: THE SOUTH AFRICAN PARTNERSHIP

South Africa needs reorganizing, from top to bottom, within the next ten years: it needs a political, commercial, and
ethical spring-cleaning. Already out of date, it is heading for

political repression of the worst sort, and ultimate disaster—
the fate of ALL police states. To find a cure, seven million
natives have somehow to be fitted into the political and social
scheme: they cannot be ignored or repressed indefinitely:
sooner or later they have to become full and valuable citizens
of the Union.

Our aim must be, progressively, to work towards:

    (a)   A contented labour force, without which this
           country will grind to a full stop and a consequent
           blood-bath.

    (b)   A full black-white partnership, making of this
           incredibly rich country a model nation and a most
           successful one.

Our beginning should be on these lines: first and foremost,
to raise the standard of living of the Natives: save them from
being gypped by Indian traders, European adventurers and
opportunists, and their own worst elements: feed them
decently and cheaply, clothe them decently and cheaply, give
them something to do in their spare time, keep them
healthy; and generally make them feel that they are REALLY
being looked after by their own natural protectors.

Starting with the four essential provisions—something to
eat, something to wear, somewhere to live, and something
to do—this is our basic outline of progress:

Establish:

1. Native department stores.
2. Native cinemas.
3. Community centres—meeting places for natives,
   comprising a concert hall, rest-room, information
   and advice bureau, and sports ground.
4. Health centres.
5. Cheap transport to and from their work.
6. Schools.
7. Adult education centres, native training for jobs,
   native apprenticeship schemes, native trade unions.
8. A first-class native Press.

We must make a start with the first four items on this list, which with seven million customers cannot help being a tremendous financial success. That, of course, isn't going to be the point of it for us, but we need money for power, and especially for Press backing. We should make a start up on the Reef, South Africa's prime problem and plague-spot, where most of the misery and injustice of this continent is concentrated: our first venture should be to establish three of these centres (north-east, north-west, and south of Johannesburg), comprising a department store (two-storey, mainly clothes and food, native sales-staff, white supervision until they are educated to take over), a cinema, a meeting-place, and a health centre, grouped together into a single entity (say, round a courtyard) which will be trusted, respected, and automatically repaired to by the vast majority of the natives in its district.

Notes on the above—the first nuclear units of the South African Partnership:

(1) DEPARTMENT STORES. Our stores must sell cheap food, cleaning materials, clothes, fuel, radios, and prefabricated houses. (Natives will buy the ready-made parts, assemble them themselves, and pay for them over a period of years. This in itself would solve much of the misery, discomfort, frustration, and violence at present making hell of the Johannesburg locations.) With an enormous turn-over, we need only a marginal profit, and can under-sell anyone else with purely commercial ambitions.

(2) CINEMAS. We must show them the best entertainment films (not cut-of-date trash, as at present) and selected educational shorts, with dubbed native language sub-titles if necessary. Later we must commission films with all-black casts: there is no earthly reason why they should not see their own people acting their own stories.

(3)   MEETING PLACES. If you give natives something
to do in their spare time—whether it's organized
games, sports to watch, art-and-craft classes—it
will cure much of the crime-wave overnight. All
they need is space, privacy if they wish, and
expert and sympathetic direction. They must
also play, sing, and act for themselves: there is
unlimited talent. We must also have group-
listening to a genuine Third Programme, a
Bantu one with plenty of audience participation.

(4)   HEALTH CENTRES. These are vitally necessary:
education and advice on (a) maternity and child
welfare, and (b) dietetics, are prime require-
ments in this field. We must co-operate with the
War Memorial Health Foundation, whose head
man, Paul Anning,* has all the right ideas on
this subject. As a sideline, the Health Centres
could train and turn out really good nurse-girls.

If this start in Johannesburg is a success, progress and
development in the rest of the country will follow naturally:
immense political power will result, and in the end we can
dictate our own policy. The forces behind us, financial and
political, are prodigious: they only need controlling and
canalizing on the true lines of progress. The main point is
this: we are NOT in it for money. To start with, we need to
borrow about £600,000, cheaply, using in the first instance the
bait of a stable native population, which clearly pays its own
dividend. A man such as Harry Oppenheimer with (a) mining
interests demanding a contented labour force and (b) a social
conscience seeking an outlet, might be persuaded to finance
the whole thing at nominal interest. With no burden of debt
to be serviced expensively, and no thirst for inflated profit,
we can defeat any purely commercial competitor; and while
we are establishing ourselves we will have the political back-

---

* I had the privilege and the good fortune to succeed him as chairman five years
later.

ing (for a variety of reasons which do not matter) of the
strongest forces in this country and (important) the approval
of Great Britain. In the end we can reorganize TOTALLY
the whole political and social life of South Africa, and make it
the most influential, socially-minded, and worthwhile country
in the world.

It is idle to pretend that natives are now deserving of full
partnership with Europeans: they are not within a hundred
years of it. But they MUST be set on the right lines, instead
of being frustrated or ignored; and above all they must be
made to feel that the white man is prepared to back their
development with complete honesty and unselfishness.

On its present course, South Africa could destroy itself
within a generation; on the basis of an eventual full black-
white co-operation, it can be invincible.

N. M. Christmas 1946

Greatly daring, taking an enormous chance with all sorts of
hazards, I showed this manifesto to a few South African friends.
The reaction was mixed, to say the least; perhaps it was that
first sentence, which took too much of their friendship for
granted, and was a shade on the arrogant side also.

But I believed in it; and I believed deeply in the idea of a
partnership in Africa. Certainly one should make the Negro a
full citizen. But why throw out the white man, the forerunner,
the contributory brain, at the same time? There was room in
Africa for both, and a crying need for them too.

A sketchy attempt at such a policy of partnership was tried,
seven years later, in the Rhodesian Federation: tried, and abandoned after ten years as impossible, or futile, or Not Wanted
on This Voyage. But that Christmas of 1946, when I mapped
out the first timorous beginnings, all was real, and true, and of
good repute, as far as it concerned me.

Perhaps it was the last year, the last moment, free of corruption: the last season of innocence, of other-love, of belief.

9*

FORTY

THE BOOK THAT LOST
ITS HEAD
(1951)

1.

For the first time, though happily not for the last, I was waiting for a divorce.

Eileen had gone back to England in 1948, when my contract as director of the Information Office came to an end, and I was asked to renew it for another two years. I wanted to stay on, very much; Eileen did not; it was a mutual acknowledgement that the end of this road had been reached, that she did not like the compromise of values which living in South Africa entailed, whereas I had come to accept them, and even to enjoy them.

There had also been a further complication, only just over the domestic horizon: the beginning of the Cape Town love affair which turned at least three lives upside down, and continued to do so for another twenty years. Now, three years later, I still had the same prized job; I still wanted to marry the girl; and I was still waiting for things to sort themselves out—waiting in nervous, almost tremulous indecision, for two very good reasons.

The first was that Directors of Information didn't get divorced, any more than ambassadors or bishops or candidates for the U.S. presidency; this was a sensitive area of propriety, diplomatic, fully lime-lit on an old-fashioned apron stage. The second was that the girl herself, tired of waiting, or of me, or of the way I had turned her own life upside down, had taken off again, and immured herself in Cape Town.

For more than a wretched year, no telephone calls reached their target, no letters were answered, no appeal got further than the blank wall of denial. So, even if the divorce came through, I would still face two questions which had the power to destroy: would the Commonwealth Relations Office stand for it, and would the girl be there to make sense of victory?

Thus deserted, thus miserable and alone, thus taking ferocious advantage of Johannesburg's counter-attractions, I had written a book.

It was that Battle of the Atlantic novel which I had been dreaming about, ever since the war ended and I had found myself in the Admiralty cellar with nothing to do except my round-the-bend female friend. Five years of living that war, three years of thinking about it, two years of writing it, had at last produced the result, for whatever it was worth.

It had been written alone, every single night after the long office day, after the current girl had gone, after the whisky had blurred the edge of tiredness and the sad mourning for the girl who wasn't there: after stillness had fallen on the house and the city, and silence and peace and solitude were all guaranteed. Now I had finished it, and sent it off to Cassell's in London and Alfred Knopf in New York.

It was 200,000 words long. There was not a paragraph in it which had not been written and rewritten four or even five times. Into it had gone more alcohol, sweat, semen, hopeless misery, sad music, and grinding determination than anything in my life before. It was my twelfth book, and I had been writing for eighteen years. Now I was waiting to hear if it was any good.

But I was waiting in circumstances which, give or take a few heart-aches, headaches, aches of high-strung conscience and low-slung genitals, suited me down to the ground. For now I really liked Johannesburg, and I didn't want to live anywhere else in the world.

I had the flat in Parkview, just north of the city, part of an elegant house owned by Leon Levson, a talented and highly fashionable portrait photographer, whose wife Freda Troup had written a very worthwhile book about the trials, miseries, near-triumphs and near-misses of Michael Scott.*

With the flat went a well-cultivated garden (cultivated by

* *In Face of Fear* (Faber & Faber, 1950).

Leon, not by me), a handsome view down a valley, and all the
benefits of a *cul-de-sac* where no traffic could pass, disturbed only
by the occasional plodding slurring feet of natives using the
short cut up and down the hillside; natives whom the curfew, or
fear of those pass-hungry policemen, drove off into limbo very
early in the evening.

With the flat went my ancient and faithful houseboy, whose
name, White, adorned one of the blackest Africans in the whole
of the Transvaal; whose footfalls were like thunder, whose
cooking was so-so—roast beef on Sunday, roast veal on Wed-
nesday, roast lamb on Friday, with mounds of roast potatoes
on top and all around, and tinned fruit salad enticingly labelled
'KOO' to follow*—and whose patient loyalty was something to
marvel at.

To help me on life's journey, which had become a wild
mixture of sad solitude, miserable jealousy, laughter, self-
indulgence, and the most exhilarating sexual marathon ever
likely to come my way, I had alcohol, which (in the true tradition of Johannesburg) was beginning to have great charm by
day, and becoming a necessary drug at night; and I had music,
blessed music to comfort the dark hours.

Taste had not altered nor progressed much here, except to
include César Franck; the Mozart piano concertos were still a
staple joy, the Brahms Clarinet Concerto and the Double
Concerto were prime favourites, and opera a pleasure yet to
come. But I had one sad song, gloriously sung by Kathleen
Ferrier, which suited the times so exactly that it did heavy duty
for many months: the *Orpheus and Eurydice* gem, 'What is life
to me without thee?'

The second line of that song was 'What is left when thou art
gone?'; and what was left to me when she was gone was the
remarkably robust life of this city, catering generously for all
the appetites, and all the moods save tenderness and compassion.
Johannesburg was a male town; my off-duty life was now based
on poker, racing, boxing (spectator only), cracking 100 m.p.h.

* Not for years did I discover that this was short for Kooperativ.

in the 2½-litre Riley which had now succeeded the 1½-litre ladies' model, and a little minor gambling on the stock exchange, where the gold-share market was currently enjoying a prime fit of the staggers.

Racing was the Saturday sport, and I went every week; the guaranteed sun and the extremely good amenities out at Turffontein made it a tonic occasion, even though I hardly prised a cent out of the bookies. This was particularly true when I worked up to owning a half-share in two four-year-old race-horses, and dutifully paid their feed-bills, and watched them run, and said 'Bad luck' to the trainer afterwards.

They were ungenerous crocodiles both; one was called Noted Fox, the other True Measure. God knows what Noted Fox was noted for; it certainly was *not* for winning races, which it never did in its life; and the true measure of True Measure was that it was no earthly good on the race-course either, and once off it, might well have originated the phrase 'Eating like a horse'.

But what of it? I owned race-horses! Practically a string of them, like Lord Derby or the Aga Khan! I had my own colours! I could stand in the middle of the paddock, and talk to my trainer and my jockey, and look as if I could tell a forelock from a fetlock! Marvellous!

Johannesburg was a big boxing town as well, with two fistic idols (and they were actually called that, at least in print); one was a heavy-weight from Bloemfontein named Johnny Ralph, the other a Lebanese lad from Cape Town, Vic Toweel. Johnny Ralph, the South African champion, was doing all right until he was unwisely matched against two ironclad British cruisers in quick succession, Freddie Mills and Bruce Woodcock; after which he virtually stopped doing anything.

Vic Toweel, extraordinarily quick and strong, had a better run and stayed at the top for a long time. All these fights were refereed by my tailor, Mr William Corner, whose curious spare-time hobby this was. Whenever I called in to see him after a fight, he used to say: 'I think I took their measure correctly'—a pretty good tailor's joke.

But poker was the greatest pleasure of all; the taste I had
developed for it at Cambridge, and lost in the serious-minded
Thirties, had returned again, stronger than ever. We had
virtually the same poker-school all the time I was in South
Africa, seven years altogether; it was strictly captained by
Johnny Whitehouse, who worked at the Central News Agency
and had one of those moustaches one occasionally sees in
cartoons denigrating the British Raj.

For our weekly ritual we wore dinner-jackets, started
punctually at 8 p.m. and played until 1 a.m., were fined five
shillings a time for bad language, kept strict accounts, and
enjoyed ourselves thoroughly every Saturday night. Our trades
ranged from stockbroker, Lloyd's agent, gambler, business
executive, and newspaperman all the way down to information
director. But we were all united in our one devotion, to what we
fondly called the Green Baize.

We played 'straight' poker, with none of those horrid
American and Canadian variations of seven-card-stud and high-
low and half the pack wild. Play was not high—certainly not by
Johannesburg standards. I once won £126 (four kings against
four jacks), and once lost £70.

Over the seven years, I was £84 down altogether, in
approximately three hundred games, which meant that the
majority of the other six were probably better players than I
was, and also that this cherished pastime—the best in the world
for skill, luck, deception, intuition, patience, observation of one's
fellow human beings, and all the perils of poor judgement and
bad guesswork—that this paragon of games was not wildly
expensive.

However, it was habit-forming, in more ways than one;
hallowed catch-phrases were coined, and persisted to the end.
Even in the seventh year, Johnny Whitehouse still gently
stroked the broad black ribbon of his monocle when deep in
thought; and Bob Crisp was still saying 'I've got the biggest
pair in Africa', when laying down his two aces.

Soli Ornstein, my wild Balkan friend, still commanded: 'Open your legs!' when he meant 'Show your hand', and Jack Hyman, a stockbroker who had married the widow of dam-buster V.C. Guy Gibson, still said: 'I must go to the office' when he needed time to think.

Whenever I was holding good cards (this I was told, but naturally not until the end) I always put on a special expression of disgust which would not have deceived a drunken child of five.

There was one other Johannesburg ritual, for our pleasure and occasional profit; and that was a five-times-a-week lunch-time session at the Waverley Hotel.

They were just lunches—long, lazy, talkative, greedy, geared to gambling, sex, and idle gossip; they suited us, and Johannes-burg, and the golden times in which we lived, and if that was a measure of our idleness, greed, proneness to gossip, and sexual preoccupation, then I would not argue about it for a moment, nor want to change it either.

The Waverley was a small hotel with good food and service, and a semi-secret, semi-legal back bar presided over by Nick the Greek (in Johannesburg, all Greeks were called Nick, as all natives were called John); and there we gathered punctually at 12.30 each weekday, to down an average of six drinks (four on Monday, eight on Friday), and then—slightly wearing, pro-nouncing our final decision on who was going to win the big race or the big fight, the medium murder-trial or the small divorce—we sat down to lunch.

After that, gambling took over, as it took over almost every-thing in Johannesburg, from a game of golf to that heads-or-tails juggling with paternity known as Catholic Roulette.

This time the game was called Queen Bee, and it some-times needed a full hour and a half to complete, with suitable pauses for eating. It was based in its turn on the game of Matches, where one guessed how many matches the other man had in his closed hand, added one's own, and declared the result; a game which, elevated from the nursery where it must have started, could reach extraordinary peaks of ferocity, skill, and inspired guesswork.

Queen Bee was in two parts. First everyone played each other, to determine the first-stage winner, the Queen Bee himself; and then the Queen Bee played each member of the party in turn, for the total price of the lunch. Thus, no one could lose more than that price; but if the Queen was in form he could win all the way round the table.

Lunch for six or seven people cost about £5; and so, on a really triumphant day, the winner might take home something like £30, plus a free lunch, plus the infuriating grin of smugness and superiority to which he was entitled.

The care with which I have described this ludicrous pastime illustrates the importance which it had for us. Lunch was no fun at all without Queen Bee; and to it we brought, every day, all the rapt attention and the ruthless greed of children at a party—in fact, the very spirit of Johannesburg.

The guiding hand at the Waverley belonged to an elderly Italian called Cavagna; a smiling man pale as a slug, full of solicitude for his clients, a very good restaurateur indeed. He was always helpful. He could even be too helpful.

On one occasion, when Queen Bee had been lost and won, we started arguing about sweetbreads. What exactly were sweetbreads? Some said one thing and some another—and some of the things they said were not nice at all. I had always thought that sweetbreads were part of the cow's interior gut, like tripe. Soli Ornstein went higher up—'Between brain and heart!' he said, almost lyrically. Others definitely went lower down.

We summoned Cavagna, as we always did, whether to anoint a salad or cash a cheque. He was helpful as ever, but his English was not good. At first he thought we were slandering his sweetbreads. 'No, they *not* come from there!' he said, scandalized. Then he told us the answer, but it was in Italian, and sounded terrible, and we were not satisfied. Then he thought that we wanted to *see* sweetbreads. He trotted off, and came back with a kitchen bowl.

In it, swimming in blood, was a great mound of grey-green

THE BOOK THAT LOST ITS HEAD

raw flesh, veined in scarlet like diseased marble, fronded at the edges, seeming not quite dead.

'Sweetbreads!' said Cavagna, beaming. But we had lost interest already.

Yet not for long, as far as I was concerned. What was the good of running an information office if it couldn't produce information? I had always been proud of my reference library, and I was proud of it now.

One had, it seemed, a choice of sweetbreads. Throat-sweet-breads came from the thymus gland. Belly-sweetbreads came from the pancreas. They both came from a calf, not a cow.

I spent some time telephoning people with the good news. Naturally there had been a lot of betting on it.

Cavagna, firm friend and blessed host, came to a sad end—one of the saddest ends I ever witnessed. He died. His funeral was listed in the *Rand Daily Mail*. I went along—not to the Catholic church, where I was always scared of making mistakes, but to the graveyard.

It was that rare thing in Johannesburg, a rainy day. It was also mid-morning in a working week. Yet Cavagna had served thousands of people, and made hundreds of personal friends on the way. I expected to see a lot of them at this farewell.

But by the graveside there were exactly eight people: six of his waiters, myself, and the priest. The rain dripped down, weeping briefly on the coffin before it vanished in the thirsty earth. I held the umbrella over the priest's head. It was my turn to be a waiter, and I was privileged to take it.

But that was only one sad and heartless day, out of a thousand which, as far as the Waverley was concerned, brought nothing but the pleasure of its company. Even walking back after lunch, between the two tall men who were my friends— Soli Ornstein the bookmakers' darling (until he reformed, and became a pillar of industry, Soli had only to get within a mile of a race-course to go berserk), and Bob Foley, Lloyd's man in South Africa, as imposing and aloof as an R.A.F. Group Captain (he had been an R.A.F. Group Captain)—even this idle stroll back to work was part of the enchantment of living.

After-lunch was my favourite time of the day, except for the one which would assuredly come later, in a city which had emerged as an undoubted favourite. The shadows were lengthening, the caverns of the street growing cooler as the western side was thrown into shade. But the scene was never less than lively, the spirit restless, the mood a challenge to hope and vigour and survival.

The first edition of the *Star* was being snapped up at the street-corners, where people who looked as though they didn't have a penny in the world thumbed through the noon stock-market prices, the race-results from England and Australia, the sweepstake draws, the rare investment opportunities, the ten-roomed houses for sale in select northern suburbs.

But most of the faces were black. There were women selling lemons and pears and limes and pawpaws; women with sleeping babies strapped to their backs; women in gaudy clothes, the *élite* from the native brothels. The black men were office-messengers like Motorcar Ratshiko, grimy mineboys trudging in convoy to and from the railway station, herded by a native policeman with a polished, lethal knobkerrie swinging from his wrist; legless beggars squirming on the pavements, loafers, possible pickpockets.

Shabby, gentle old clergymen from the Bush Baptist league looked sideways as they passed the knots of young *skelms*, patently on the alert for the unlocked car, the suitcase forgotten on the back seat, the handbag hanging open, the chattering American tourists who were fair game for anyone.

From the groups playing dice at the street-corners came an occasional pungent drift of *dagga* smoke—the homegrown marijuana which gave courage, or brief happiness, or enough resignation to endure this iron jungle. I did not mind that, either.

On the sunny side of any street, the colours were still bright and glaring; in the shade, we walked in a cool early twilight. When we said goodbye, at one street-corner for Bob Foley and at another for Soli Ornstein, who always said: 'Walk one more corner! I have schemes, big schemes!' we were all three on our way to an honest afternoon's work, since Johannesburg was a working town, a pressure-hive of diligence as well as all the rest.

But soon would come the idle hours, and then (speaking only for myself) I would be home again: At Home, in fact, (though I dispensed with the old-style engraved invitation) in my own little hive, to whomever had been mutually laid on for the evening.

I was now a bachelor, a Johannesburg bachelor. We did not sit about twiddling our thumbs. In fact we hardly sat about at all.

Something in the altitude, or something in the lordly, beyond-all-censure men, or something in the over-leisured women, had made South Africa, like Kenya, wonderful screwing country; and everyone knew it, and took advantage of it, and made of this hothouse a place of cool yet avid misbehaviour.

Like the cynical Quebec election slogan which I was soon to encounter: 'Vote early! Vote often!' there was in Johannesburg an impolite sexual version of this command, which gave to all connoisseurs the freedom of the city, and the urge to prove that our civic motto, *Fortiter et Recte*—Strong and Upright—was no idle boast.

I joined the club, with the same quiet determination, the same preference for private action over public discussion, which was later to emerge as one of the most crucial marks of the generation gap. My own slogan was simple. If I could not have the one I wanted, then I would have all the rest.

Outrageous fact calls, not for gamey reminiscence but for detached prose. It is worth a try.

What was available for this flourish of swordsmanship had all the marvellous, beckoning variety of a really good *delicatessen*. There were other men's wives, though such shop-lifting could be dangerous. Lovers often came to a sticky end in Johannesburg. My favourite restaurateur (after Cavagna died) had half his head blown off by a jealous husband with a good aim, a shot-gun, and a clear view down the drive.

On the other hand, husbands could also provide wonderful insurance. Many of them did not give a damn what was going on, as long as there wasn't too much noise. They were busy enough themselves, wandering the same sort of track. Yet they held the title-deeds, so one could not get stuck with the suddenly vacant mansion. Short of saying: 'I'll have a spare latch-key cut,' they could not have been more co-operative.

There were other men's sisters, but this posed no problem. When they said: 'I'd like to see Martha settled,' they usually meant 'Settled for next week'. There was nothing worse than a sisterly shrew in the house. There were other men's daughters; but the younger generation were such skilful liars that Daddy scarcely had a moment's worry.

Then there were what one could only call (borrowing from the world of popular music) the Old Standards. These were mature ladies, trained in Cape Town convoy work during the war, but still active and willing, seemingly embalmed in rejuvenating fluid. Sometimes a glimpse of steel-grey pubic hair would serve to date them, as accurately as any other relic. Such energetic hags were two a penny, and, like pennies, quickly spent.

One or two of them shared with older writers a highly critical view of newcomers. '*This* is the proper way to do it,' they used to tell me, demonstrating some positive circus-act of applied gymnastics. 'Don't you *know?*'

But one had to work through the list. It was like being presented at court, in the old days of social protocol. There could be no such thing as a debutante who had not passed all these hallowed portals.

There was one very finicky lady who asked: 'But haven't you a *spare* room? I always think that's nicer, don't you?' Another, a precipitate volunteer, reminisced: 'Do you remember how one always made straight for the sleeping-car as soon as the train left Victoria? One didn't want to waste any time!'

Then there were girls, just girls. Girls who came tripping to my lair with shining eyes, to admire the eiderdown and then the ceiling. Girls who took me to their own nest, and said: 'I'm sorry it's so narrow.' Girls who preferred the open air, to match their legs. Girls with a mother or a husband on the alert, who were only available at lunch-time, and thus imposed the strain of conflicting loyalties. Between Queen Bee and this private hive, who could really choose?

There was one girl who was very beautiful, and knew it. Once the imminence of seduction (to misuse an honest word) had been established, she stripped like an athlete who hears the first bell, and stood in front of me—stark naked, supple as snakeskin, formed for love as an apple is formed for peeling, a sheath for a sword.

'Flawless,' she said, turning towards the flattering, caressing lamplight. The dark would have been light enough, but I could not complain, nor disagree. She *was* marvellous: glowing in the bedside light, creamy dark like the last peach of the harvest, promising warm ecstasy at the first bite, and the next, and the next.

Yet 'flawless' had been for me to say, not for her. In a way it had been a command, not an invitation. She was in charge of this invasion; she would give the time as well as the place. She was also too critical altogether.

Her last lover had been French; she could not forget this, nor let me escape comparison. '*Mon amour!*' she said as she prepared to clinch the deal, composing those truly gorgeous limbs for a carefully calculated orgasm—and I felt like the male spider, good enough for the working web, soon to be eaten.

'*Mon amour!*' . . . I was only from Liverpool, and I knew I would not last.

There was a girl with a husband, a garden balcony, and a watchboy who might also have been trained in French farce. I had to park my car down the road, tell the watchboy to watch it, climb the balcony as if all the Montagues and Capulets in hell were after me, and climb down again before the husband came back from his Chamber of Commerce meeting. It was nice work, but too athletic for my age-group.

There was an Afrikaner girl, rarely beautiful, recently widowed, who always wore black stockings, the mark of mourning among her compatriots. She would never take them off; though this doubtless stemmed from feelings of delicacy, the lickorish effect was unimpaired.

There was a curious, almost unexplained girl with a dead-white face and slightly mad eyes. It was like making love in the House of Dracula. There was another girl who was appropriately shacked up at Hotpoint House; this was only a block of flats built round an electrical showroom, but (perhaps for the very first time) the medium was the message. There was a newspaper girl, agile as quicksilver, always eager for that late extra. There was a mother and daughter duet, not at all harmonious.

There was very nearly a queue. Among them must be numbered, in the interests of statistical accuracy, the girl who changed her mind—not on a single coy occasion, but three times in succession. At one moment she would be poised on the diving-board; at the next, she was leaving the pool in a flurry of protest. It really was a case of Now you see it, now you don't.

'I should have warned you about her,' a confederate friend told me. 'I thought everyone knew.'

'But *why?*' I was feeling more deprived than any off-white orphan in the land. 'Damn it, she said yes!' Or had it been maybe? 'And you know how she dances.'

'She always dances like that. Once she said to me: "Darling, they're playing *our* tune!" And you know what it was?— *Stone Cold Dead in the Market*! I can tell you, I gave up years ago.'

If my friend had given up, that was indeed a definitive verdict. 'You mean she's a virgin? Even with all that come-on stuff?'

'That's part of the fun. Perhaps it's *the* fun. Power without responsibility.' He must have read Rudyard Kipling on harlots. Or perhaps cousin Stanley Baldwin on Lord Beaverbrook.

'Actually Jack Hyman put it better, as usual. He said: "She twirls your nuts, and bolts".'

But that was a rare bird indeed. Almost without exception, this was a season which Marcel Proust had labelled for me already, twenty years earlier in the wet and pallid wastes of Nottingham, as *A l'Ombre des Jeunes Filles en Fleurs*.

I never improved on that record, nor did I want to; there was only the craving need for it, then the pleasure of notching it up and forgetting about it. *Palmam qui meruit ferat*, as my old schoolmaster-friend Mr Sutton used to say, when talking of the Winchester examination: Let him who deserves it, bear the palm.

I bore my palm right until the end, right into the private solitude which I could count on, which I had to have; right into the refrigerator . . . For months and years on end, after such exertions, I had climbed out of my bed, or her bed, or any old bed I had happened on, and regained my solitary lair, and poured out a whopping whisky and soda.

Then I settled down at the typewriter again, to rewrite page 100 or page 300 or page 579 of *The Cruel Sea*.

Now I was waiting to hear. Presently, clear and persistent noises in the wings indicated that I had, incredibly, written a best-seller.

It was incredible because, apart from this last forlorn try, I really had given up writing as a bad job—or as a good job which I just couldn't do. The last book, *My Brother Denys*, had been the usual flop; it had made £366 in three years; I could do better at poker (that wasn't exactly true either, but the line of thought seemed clear).

I had a good job already, which I loved. The killing sweat of being a writer, the animal spark of creation which had been living and writhing somewhere within my gut for at least twenty years, were leading me nowhere. Better to give up, better to fold my spare pair of hands and let the real ones fashion whatever career lay in front of me.

I *could* be head of the C.R.O. Information Service (I was now their senior overseas director). I *could* even be a High Commissioner, somewhere where it didn't matter, if the present trend of treating information personnel as Gentlemen instead of Players continued.

But that writhing spark, or whatever it was, had lived just long enough for 200,000 words of narrative to emerge in one piece, one shape, one entity, one compact book. Suddenly, of this book—my very last hostage to enemy fortune—Desmond Flower, chairman of Cassell's, wrote:

'I have just finished the manuscript of *The Cruel Sea*. It is a wonderful book, one of the finest ever to come into the Cassell list, and you are a great writer.'

Few letters like that ever come an author's way; none had come mine, and the morning I read that letter was the brightest and happiest I could remember, for a very long time. I stepped as lightly as the dry warm air all round me; I ate through the office work with twice the appetite of yesterday; I drank uncounted extra martinis; *I won at Queen Bee.*

Soli Ornstein, perceptive as a gipsy, asked: 'What is it with you, Nicolai?' and when I told him, with bursting pride, he said: '*Fabelhaft!*'—one of the many words which this generous man used to indicate his pleasure in another's good fortune.

But there was more to come, much more to come . . . Cassell's advance royalty, I learned a fortnight later, was to be an unprecedented £275. From across the Atlantic, Alfred Knopf also indicated his satisfaction, in the guarded terms appropriate to a pillar of the publishing establishment who had introduced Thomas Mann and André Gide to the other half of a waiting world. Knopf's advance would be £430!

The snowball—a very rare thing in South Africa, and even rarer in my own life—gathered speed and size. A fantastic cable from London told me that *The Cruel Sea* was to be a Book Society Choice. The Book Society! I could remember the very first Book Society Choice being unwrapped by my mother, a founder member, in 1929. It had been *The Love of the Foolish*

Angel, by Helen Beauclerk. If only *The Cruel Sea* could do half as well as *The Love of the Foolish Angel*.*

Hardly had I taken in that cable than there was another from Alfred Knopf in New York. The book was to be a Book-of-the-Month Club choice in America. Then it had been bought by the *Atlantic Monthly*—a stupendous accolade. Then it was to be serialized (for fourteen weeks!) in the *Sunday Chronicle*. Then it was an *Evening Standard* Book-of-the-Month in London.

There was one film approach, then a second, then a third (from Ealing Studios). The South African Argus Company (Johannesburg *Star*, Cape *Argus*) also wanted to serialize it. Finally *Reader's Digest* made an unheard-of offer (unheard-of by me) for their million-by-million readership of Condensed Books.

All this avalanche of good news came winging, swinging, toppling down on me, four months before the book was to be published.

For that reason alone, all this avalanche, in so short a span, hardly seemed real at all. I wasn't a writer; that question had been settled, in progressive sad stages, via eleven unread books and eighteen years of literary endeavour and literary nothing. Only *this* world was real: the United Kingdom Information Office in Johannesburg, shortly to be expanded to include Cape Town.

This was my real creation. The fly-by-night progress of *The Cruel Sea*, before it had even seen the public light of day, could only be a kind of phantom pregnancy, beyond all credence, suspect from the first surprise swelling.

I had my baby already, and the little bastard was really a-growing.

It was, to say the least, an interesting time to be conducting British propaganda in South Africa. Our ally General Smuts

* Thirty-nine years after that first Book Society nomination, a novel of mine called *Richer Than All His Tribe* was their last 'Choice', before the Society died its sad death.

was dead; he had been decently mourned at a state funeral in
Pretoria, and then consigned to oblivion within a few months.

The United Party was out—out of office, out of power, out of
juice altogether; and the Nationalists, with a secure majority,
were beginning also an anti-British rampage which was to
reach its peak ten years later, when they took their country out
of the Commonwealth for ever.

The new Prime Minister was Dr D. F. Malan, who by a
rare coincidence came from the same tiny *dorp*, Riebeeck West
in the old Cape Colony, as his predecessor Smuts himself.
Daniel Malan was an austere character; indeed, his moral
rectitude was a by-word throughout the land. It had been well
summed up by a nice dead-pan caption to a photograph of him
and his family, at the time he took over the premiership: 'Dr
D. F. Malan, the new Prime Minister,' it said 'with his wife and
children. Dr Malan is noted for his strict code of behaviour. He
does not drink. He does not smoke. The children are adopted.'

Many of his followers were the same—tough, humourless,
dedicated; and one of the things they were *all* dedicated to was
a South Africa run by Afrikaners for Afrikaners, with the
English-speaking section relegated to the very back-alleys of
power. The *Engelsman* could work, but he was not going to
manage or control. Britain was not going to manage or control,
either.

In this vastly changed climate, the U.K. Information Office
did its best to present Britain as a fair, broad-minded, well-
conducted, co-operative friend.

Our output of every kind of material—news, photographs,
and films about British politics, fashions, trade, inventions,
finance, theatre, cinema, art, music, cars, ships, anything under
the pale sun—had been stepped up until it was a steady spate.

I made a weekly excursion to Pretoria, to discuss and settle
any problems with Evelyn Baring, still the High Commissioner,
and his new Deputy, who under the slightly daunting name of
Horace Algernon Fraser Rumbold concealed both a prodigious
industry and an unfailing kindness and helpfulness towards me,

my office, my prudent and imprudent efforts, and my occasional lapses.

(I *still* could not master those bloody estimates. And I could not help feeling guilty when I faced these admirable men. They were so nice to me. They behaved so well themselves. We were all walking a tightrope of protocol in which reputation, manifest integrity, were paramount. What was going to happen when the divorce story broke?)

I also made my technical contribution to Baring's occasional dispatches on the state of things in South Africa; dispatches which, addressed to the Secretary of State, ended on a note of charming courtesy: 'I am, My dear Sir, With every truth and regard, Your most obedient servant.'

We had been given more money for putting on exhibitions and film shows, and for importing visitors—lecturers, concert performers, occasional actors. I had even been given a little more money myself—a rise in salary, and a rent allowance—following a visit from a charming old gentleman called Sir William Clarke, head of the Clarke Commission, which was touring overseas posts to see how we were getting on financially.

It was important to make the point that we were not getting on at all well. Dressed in our oldest clothes, borrowing broken-down cars for transport, serving frugal meals on cracked plates, bringing sandwiches to work—we went through all the motions of an abject poverty quite unsuitable to British representation abroad.

Sir William, a wise man, could not have been deceived on the scale we hoped for, nor perhaps deceived at all. But the result, for me at least, had been a combined salary-jump to the dizzy height of £2,200 a year.

As visitors, we had Paul Rogers and Douglas Campbell in *Macbeth*, which they played in red beards and hideous pinkish-green kilts. We had the ballet stars Markova and Anton Dolin, with a thin piano-and-drum accompaniment which could not quite cope with the thudding footfalls and the excusably heavy breathing. We had Hugh Casson, who came out to architect our

British Pavilion at the Cape Town Exhibition, and stayed on
to lecture with the utmost skill and charm.

We had Sir Eugen Millington-Drake, a tall sixty-year-old
ramrod of an ex-diplomat who had been the British Minister to
Uruguay at the time of the Battle of the River Plate, and had
been instrumental in seeing that the crippled German battleship *Graf Spee,* which had taken refuge in Montevideo, neither
overstayed her welcome, nor spirited her crew ashore to confederate Argentina in order to escape internment, but put to sea
again, there to scuttle herself under the guns of the waiting
British warships.

We had Sir Paul Dukes, who had been a secret agent in
Russia, and lectured on international affairs spiced with a little
espionage, but seemed at his happiest when he was demonstrating his favourite Yoga positions on his hotel carpet, after
lecturing was done.

But the most interesting import of all, that year, was Mr
Patrick Gordon Walker, Secretary of State for Commonwealth
Relations, who came out to pick up the bits and trim the edges
of the Seretse Khama affair.

I had campaigned with him a year earlier in Bechuanaland, in
those strange and occasionally baffling goings-on which cul-
minated in Seretse's banishment for five years. From that time
on, he was a man I never ceased to admire.

Chief Seretse Khama was a public relations headache of the
first order. He was a rather fat, self-indulgent young man of
twenty-seven who was the paramount Chief-Designate of the
Bamangwato tribe, the most powerful in Bechuanaland; educated in South Africa and at Balliol College, Oxford, he was due to
return to Bechuanaland to pick up his inheritance. Just before he
came back, he married a white girl, Ruth Williams.

The marriage occasioned some scandal among his fellow-
countrymen, who did not like their future chief straying from the
racial-purity fold; it precipitated an uproar in South Africa,
where the opposition to a mixed marriage, though different in
kind, was certainly a great deal more ferocious and vocal.

One had to look at the map, as Baring was to say later. South Africa was a next-door neighbour, with plenty of leverage; much of Bechuanaland's prosperity, and all her communications, depended on a smooth working relationship. But Bechuanaland, as a High Commission Territory, was our baby, and we did not want any outside interference in a family row.

However, the problem was there, the crisis undeniable. The tribes (eight in number, all beginning with the letter B, all posing problems of pronunciation—Bakgatla, Bakwena, Bangwakatse, Bamalete, Bamangwato, Barolong, Batawana, and Batlowka) were fundamentally split on the marriage question; South Africa was making ugly faces just over the wall; we had to decide whether, in all the circumstances, Seretse would make an acceptable chief. British Government opinion was hardening towards the decision that he would not.

We dived right in; Sir Evelyn Baring in the van, Patrick Gordon Walker later paying two visits to try to patch things up; and Monsarrat trailing along behind, to deal as best he could with the regiment of pressmen from all over the world who flocked in to watch the fun.

We ran into trouble straight away. A great tribal *kgotla*, or gathering, called by Baring at Serowe, the 'Native capital', was totally boycotted; not a man turned up, not a dog barked, as I waited at one end of the police telephone link to advise the High Commissioner whether it was worth coming down.

Obviously it was not, and I had to tell him so. Then I walked out, across the dusty deserted *kgotla* ground, towards the crowd of pressmen and photographers waiting under a tree.

They were obviously enjoying our discomfiture; indeed, some of them had done a certain amount to bring it about, by a persistent policy of deriding every effort and every move we made, and flattering the malcontents and dissidents who had been drawn towards this murky brew.

One of them, Noel Monks of the *Daily Mail*, in search of a story—any story—which might embarrass us, had already provoked a first-class fake incident by taking Seretse into a

'Whites Only' bar, demanding a drink, and waiting for the resulting scene to reach its natural peak.

I was thus in a bad temper, for a variety of reasons; and the white uniform, white helmet, medals, and sword which I had donned for the great occasion seemed ridiculous. They were also very hot. I then made my second big public relations boob.

I was met by a rapid quick-fire of questions, the kind I had become used to during the last few days. But this time they seemed to have an extra edge to them, and I was fresh from our undisguisable defeat.

'What's happening?' asked the friendliest of the newsmen, who was working for *The Times* and had a grasp, somewhat rare, of what was involved in this tangle. 'Is the meeting going ahead?'

'No. It's cancelled.'

'Why?'

'Well, obviously—because no one turned up.'

'Why not?'

'There's a boycott. You know the situation. The tribe is split.'

'If the tribe is split, why didn't some of them turn up?'

'They were—discouraged.'

'You mean, kept away?'

'Yes.'

Pencils were now very busy. 'Who by?'

'People who wanted the *kgotla* to be a flop.'

'But what people?'

'I can't give you their names. We don't know for certain. But there is a section of the Bamangwato who were determined that no one should attend the *kgotla*.'

'How did they keep them away? Did they use force?'

'They threatened to use force.' There was abundant evidence of this from the police.

'Have you got any proof of that?'

'We have police reports.'

'What's going to happen now?'

'The High Commissioner will hold a Press conference at twelve o'clock.'

'Is he going to announce a change of policy?'

'I don't know. I shouldn't think so.'

'Is he angry about this?'

'He doesn't get angry. Of course he's disappointed. He wanted to tell as many people as possible what the situation is. Now they won't know, or they'll get the wrong story.'

There was some additional sniping on this topic. Finally:

'Can we hear some more about the people who are supposed to have used force to stop the *kgotla*? You say you don't know their names. What *do* you know about them? What kind of people are they?'

'A sort of strong-arm gang. Some of them aren't much better than thugs.'

That did it. I had been provoked into using a much too quotable word which, though absolutely accurate, looked very unpretty in print. It reached the headlines. It certainly reached the Commonwealth Relations Office, which fired off a remarkably prompt telegram suggesting that Monsarrat should 'refrain from further comment'.

To my enormous relief, Sir Evelyn Baring came to my rescue, with equal swiftness. An answering telegram drafted by Arthur Clark, the Chief Secretary, and approved by the High Commissioner, said that I had been doing my best in trying circumstances, that I had been of great help during the past difficult week, and that I enjoyed the High Commissioner's full confidence.

God bless all honest men . . . Baring was going through a tortuously difficult time himself; the boycott of the *kgotla* was, in its context, an atrocious personal insult; my 'thug' remark could only have served to complicate the issue for him when he had more than enough troubles already.

It was in fact a stupid lapse in self-control. Yet he found time to back me up, when many a lesser man might have tossed me to the Whitehall wolves.

An irredeemable I.O.U. was involved there.

That of course was not the end of the Seretse Khama affair; in fact it was the beginning of a long-drawn-out series of skirmishes in which the British Government, faced by a barrage of hostility from almost the entire world's Press, held firmly to their belief that there could be better men than Seretse, with his white wife, carefree habits, and tendency to indolence (he had trouble with his Bar examinations—in fact, he was beginning to sound more and more like me) to rule a divided and restless nation.

That tenacity of purpose belonged to Patrick Gordon Walker, with a rebellious House of Commons forever on his back. The day-to-day campaigning fell on Sir Evelyn Baring's enduring shoulders. Coping with the Press was still my job, and, with all its rough edges and smooth betrayals, I would not have had any other.

For me, there were three more journeys to Bechuanaland before it was over. One of them was made in my cherished Riley, and that was an error of judgement also. I had done the trip once before, when time didn't matter and everything went right. Now I had an appointment to keep, I was the bearer of an important Order in Council, and everything went wrong.

I later wrote an account of this excursion for the Automobile Association's magazine *Drive* (well, where else, for God's sake?) and here is an extract, strictly from the motorist's point of view.

Road maps of this part of the world, which includes a stretch of the Kalahari Desert, are very sketchy; the distance from Mafeking to Serowe looked to be about 400 miles, along a road marked by the thinnest red line I had ever seen. For the second time on this particular run, I was told: 'You'll be all right, it's just been ploughed.' But that wasn't the problem. Then, it had been the end of the rainy season. Now it was high summer.

The heat, the dust, the bumpy ride, and the sheer hard

work of that drive have stayed in my memory until this day. The Riley left behind it a towering yellow cloud of dust, but the stuff was everywhere—eyes, ears, nostrils, hair, and neck-band. It was unbelievably hot—105° in the non-existent shade. Towards dusk on the first day, I ran over an enormous boa-constrictor which was slithering across the road. Anyone who has ever driven over a twelve-foot snake in a low-slung car will know how I felt.

Towards the end of the second day, when I was nearly there, everything suddenly went wrong, in the space of five seconds. I hit a section of the middle hump, which the plough had missed, and fearful groaning noises came from the transmission. Then the brakes failed, and I ran gently into the ditch.

There was no traffic; just the dust, the heat, a few vultures weaving overhead, and a car which would never go again without major repairs. I was stranded on the edge of the Kalahari. All I could think of was that boa-constrictor.

Then, far down the road, a smaller cloud of yellow dust appeared, with a tiny blur at the base of it. It took an hour to reach me. It was an ox-cart, driven by an old old man who raised his bee-hive hat with great courtesy and then, without a word, set to work to pull me out. After that, he towed me the last nine miles into Serowe.

If anyone is making out an itinerary, a span of eight oxen towing a $2\frac{1}{2}$-litre Riley with no brakes and a broken transmission does $1\frac{1}{2}$ miles an hour.

On one of his visits, Patrick Gordon Walker also convened a *kgotla*, and this time, after laborious groundwork and some careful sounding of opinion, it turned out a success. There had been a very slow movement of support towards our side, and Mr Gordon Walker made an excellent impression. At the end there was a formal presentation. Six of the Serowe headmen appeared, bearing between them the most magnificent lion-skin any of us was ever likely to see.

10

A gasp, and then an excited murmur, went round the *kgotla* ground as the gift was displayed. It really was a matchless trophy—hugely beautiful, tawny-yellow, its shape and its markings perfect. It must have been at least ten feet long; fearful when alive, it was still good for an awed shudder now.

Patrick Gordon Walker beamed as he accepted it. Then he prepared to make his speech of thanks.

The Bamangwato, to whom the lion was royal, may have had some vague idea that the skin was destined, if not for the palace of the King of England, then at least for some noble council chamber in the heart of the Commonwealth Relations Office. But Mr Gordon Walker had no such delusions.

'On behalf of myself *and my wife*——' he began.

I had very little doubt where that lion-skin was going to finish up.

After a long and wearing tug-of-war, both in Bechuanaland itself, and in the House of Commons, where Mr Gordon Walker held his ground in an acrimonious series of debates, the final decision was taken. Seretse was to be banished from the chieftainship, and from the Bamangwato Reserve, for five years.

I was the 'conducting officer', detailed to see him and his wife safely off the premises.

They could not fly from Johannesburg, which was the obvious take-off point; the Nationalist Government would not have this race-shame horror on their sacred soil at any price. The only way to make the transfer was by a Royal Air Force plane from Bechuanaland to Livingstone in Northern Rhodesia, where no such nonsense ruled.

From there they could catch the BOAC flying-boat to London. BOAC had no funny rules either.

The operation, which was now my responsibility, was not without drama. A well-disposed pressman, the *Star* correspondent from Johannesburg, passed on to me 'for what it was worth' the information that there were strong rumours of a kidnap plot, to prevent Seretse leaving.

The airfield, which was a single strip of brown earth trodden flat by that most efficient instrument, the human foot, was to be invaded. A car would be standing by. Seretse would be seized, by force if necessary, and then driven off into hiding.

Well, it was possible . . . Fearing to use an open telephone line, I spent half the night coding up a message with this dramatic tip-off. It was—it had to be—taken seriously.

Early next morning the little airstrip was surrounded and patrolled by all the policemen we could drum up. No one— not the most loving relative, the most respected tribesman, the most enthusiastic flag-waving child—was allowed past the boundary. The aircraft itself was ringed by R.A.F. guards.

We took off without incident, and headed northwards for Livingstone. After the sad farewells, both Seretse and Ruth Khama were glum, as I would have been myself. I walked forward to the tiny cockpit, and had a look at the chart. It showed that, with a very small alteration of course, we could fly directly over Serowe, the capital, and Seretse's own birthplace.

I went back and asked him if he would like that. The answer was Yes, and we spent ten minutes circling the vast spread of mud huts, maize patches, herds of cattle, and dusty tracks before getting back on course again, and steering for the swirling cloud of spray, a thousand feet high, which marked the point where the Zambezi River thundered over the Victoria Falls.

At Livingstone the Khamas were taken over by the District Commissioner, while I was quartered in the local hotel. My unequivocal orders were to see that they caught the flying-boat at eight o'clock next morning.

The last-minute delays, after all that had gone before, were somewhat trying. The flying-boat (which only flew once a week) was prompt to the minute; Seretse was not. When I called in the car to pick him up, he was just sitting down to breakfast.

I think he liked his breakfast; he was certainly enjoying this one, and it was not to be hurried. I could not really blame him; he had me by the tail anyway, and my impatience as he worked his way through the mealie porridge, the eggs and bacon, the soft rolls with chunky marmalade, the cup after cup of coffee, must have been laughable—especially as it was the last laugh he was going to enjoy in this part of the world, for a very long time.

By courtesy of our faithful ally, BOAC, I managed to hold the flying-boat until the last crumb was disposed of, and there was no egg left on anyone's face. Then Seretse caught his plane.

I telegraphed Arthur Clark, in our agreed code: 'EXIT'. Then I had *my* breakfast.

It hardly needs to be added that Seretse returned to his country at the end of the banishment period: first as a private citizen, then as a councillor, then as Prime Minister, and finally, in 1966, as Sir Seretse Khama, Knight Commander of the Most Excellent Order of the British Empire, and first President of Bechuanaland, now the independent Republic of Botswana.

Back in my old home town, and outside the flourishing office, I had taken on a huge amount of other work, and was as busy as I had ever been in my life. There was nothing like rejected love, I found, to give a man an appetite for all the other kinds of love, and a matching lust to fill every available hour of every day with something—anything—which would forestall the miseries of brooding unemployment.

I made lots of speeches; the theme now was not so much Resurgent Britain as the Buoyant British Commonwealth— another idea which I believed in strongly, but which in South Africa was beginning to go the way of the Union Joke, fluttering downwards into the mud.

Steering clear of obvious traps, hewing closer to a line of such topics as the United Nations, planned economy, and the need for cultural exchange. I volunteered readily for discussion-groups and public panels; and on S.A.B.C. I was one of the regulars on 'Listeners' Forum', a recorded show from which any smart-alec opinions could be excised later.

I now did five book reviews every two weeks; two for the

Sunday Express, two for the Central News Agency on the new commercial radio channel, and one, at noon on Sunday morning, for S.A.B.C. The necessary reading took up what spare time there was, and it was often a hard squeeze.

But I was serving an excellent market. People really bought and read books in South Africa; the bookshops actually flourished, instead of eking out their existence on a diet of greeting cards and Scotch tape.

Then I took on another weekly radio show, as Question Master on that old standby, Twenty Questions, which had just started on S.A.B.C. This also flourished, with the biggest fan mail they had ever had, though I got into occasional trouble with 'objects' like 'an erotic zone' and 'what a Scotsman wears under his kilts'. (The correct answer, Nothing; but a sample awkward dialogue: 'Is it a space?' 'A sort of space.' 'Is it a hole?' 'Well . . .' Protests flooded in.)

Then finally, and with that 'astonishment of command' which had seized me, ten years earlier, I was elected chairman of the National War Memorial Health Foundation, after four years as a committee member.

The Health Foundation was a very big and very worthwhile charity which I was proud to work with, and prouder still to lead. We collected money, in a single annual fund-raising drive of battle-field proportions, which could rake in half a million pounds in a good year; and then we spent it, after very careful costing and comparison, on what seemed the next good thing to do, within the terms of our charter. We kept administrative expenses down to a cheese-paring six per cent.

We built community centres in half a dozen native locations, from Johannesburg all the way down to Cape Town. We had a children's holiday camp on the Indian Ocean, near Durban, and another at the planning stage up in the Northern Transvaal. We ran crèches for working mothers, and modest libraries for anyone.

We paid the wages of various essential people—health visitors, nurses, carpenters to patch up houses, midwives, sports instructors, people who could write letters for people who couldn't write letters.

We ran soup-kitchens, and distributed clothes and blankets, and planned babies' diets, and gave people what we hoped was the right advice on their problems, and tried to cheer them up in a harsh world.

Naturally, most of the money went to help the poorest in the land, and there was damned little doubt who they were. Thus we had to survive a variety of gibes—that we were communist, that we were pampering the Natives, that we ought to be bloody well ashamed of ourselves . . . But we managed to steer a fairly adroit course, and to retain our Government grant in the face of back-bench sniping.

In this I was greatly helped by three people: Henry Gluckman, the ex-Minister of Health and our permanent president, a tough and durable politician who knew how to get things done; by Father Trevor Huddleston, who (now that Michael Scott was concentrating on other nearby miseries in South-West Africa) was the foremost conscience-in-action man to be met anywhere, and gave me lots of skilful advice as well as friendship; and by Phyllis Lean, the National Secretary, an admirable woman who did all the work and gave me all the credit.

My progress in this area was watched with a certain anxiety by the High Commissioner's Office. There were obvious political hazards if Monsarrat Boobed Again. But the fact that they let me accept the job, with their blessing, was the best example I ever met of officialdom taking a chance on a dubious enterprise, and I was lastingly grateful for it.

On my way back from the weekly committee meeting, I used to pass Johannesburg City Hall. On one of the civic pillars was a chalked inscription which survived for many weeks, and was the most succinct expression of hope in adversity, perhaps of stubborn pride, perhaps of rebellion, I ever read.

It was: 'GOD IS BLACK'.

When Margaret Bourke-White, the top-flight American photographer, called at my office and asked for suggestions as to what she should photograph in Johannesburg, I told her about GOD IS BLACK. She sped away before it could be rubbed out. Students of the back numbers of LIFE Magazine will find it there, forever enshrined, forever true for the man who wrote it and for the majority of those who read it

Thus I was busy, busy all over. Sometimes, in moments of self-esteem, I laid claim to being the busiest man in South Africa. When my friend Soli Ornstein heard this arrant boast, he said: 'Not true, Nicolai. Come with me tonight. I will show you the busiest man in South Africa.'

'Where?'

'At the circus. Where else? I went last night. Come with me again.'

'All those elephants?'

His eyes gleamed. 'I will show you elephants *plus!*'

He would tell me no more, but I broke a date with a girl who was developing signs of proprietorship (I didn't want the freehold, just the short lease, with absolutely no dilapidations) and went with him.

It was not a very good circus. We sat through interminable high-wire performers, jugglers, sad dwarf clowns; 'Arabian steeds' which waltzed about as well as I had done myself, after my first dancing lesson; a sea-lion which played the trumpet, a camel which plodded round on spongy feet, as arrogant and bad-tempered as the Second-Best-Dressed Woman in the World.

Then there was a fanfare and a roll of drums, and by God it *was* elephants!

'Only wait,' said Soli.

Elephants always do it, whenever I go to the circus. Perhaps they save it up for me—and judging only by volume this could well be true. I did not have long to wait. Presently the last elephant hesitated in its stride, gave a delicate shudder, and delivered itself of a series of enormous, gleaming clods of excrement.

There was the usual impressed murmur from the ringside

But Soli positively sighed with pleasure. 'Now you see the busiest man.'

A tall native leapt into the arena, and ran like lightning across to the mess. He had only one arm; the other was a stump, which ended just above his elbow. He bent down, as swiftly as a really good slip-fielder, and with his bare hand began to scoop up the colossal steaming turds, each about the size of a small football.

He tucked two of them under his stump, and put a third in his right hand, with a fourth balanced on top of it. Then he darted back the same way as he had come, at a bounding gallop. The whole wild-fire operation could not have taken him more than fifteen seconds.

Though horrid stains appeared under his armpit, and disgusting fluid dripped from the maimed arm and the other laden hand, he was grinning all the way there, and all the way back.

The crowd cackled, and cheered him.

God *must* be black.

Then the dam burst, and *The Cruel Sea* flooded over.

2.

Who remembers the old best-sellers?—not as an item in a library catalogue, or even as a brand-name after nearly twenty years, but with the sharp appetite and the wild, explosive excitement of publication day itself? Who wants to? Well, the author wants to, and no one is going to stop him.

The Cruel Sea was scheduled for publication on 6 August in New York, and 31 August in London, and in view of what had happened to the book already both Alfred Knopf and Cassell's had invited me to come over and enjoy the fun. I had months of leave due to me, having served in South Africa for five

straight years, and the idea was very attractive. But there was
a little question of money.

At the moment I hadn't any. Keeping two homes going, as
well as other excesses, had brought me very low.

Even with the air-fares paid, I would need all sorts of expendable cash on a free-ranging trip like this. For some reason,
some vestigial trace of the author's awe of his publisher, I
didn't like to ask for a further hand-out before more royalties
were due.

After thinking about it I wrote to my bank, told them that I
had a successful book in the works (it had been widely publicized
in South Africa already), and asked if they could possibly let me
overdraw to the extent of £500.

Bank managers may believe in civil servants, whose salary-
cheques they know down to the last penny. But this one
obviously didn't believe in writers. The answer was a firm No.
There could be no overdraft without satisfactory security, or a
guarantor. In passing, they drew attention to a debit of £8 in
the account already.

Mortified, I took my intimate problem to Soli Ornstein. I
realized that, what with one thing and another (both of them
horses), he hadn't any money either. But he did know about
banks and guarantees and credits (none better) and he might be
able to advise.

'You *pampoen*!' he said, on an immediate note of friendship
and support. 'You don't *write* for an overdraft! You go and see
the man!'

'But I don't know the man.'

'Then you should.' He sounded distinctly bad-tempered, as
if no one could possibly be so stupid after five years of his close
company. 'Have you any securities to give them? Any shares?'

'No, not yet. But damn it—the book's bound to earn at least
£10,000! The Book-of-the-Month Club alone——'

'Promises, promises . . .' He must have noticed my scandalized look, for he softened his reaction. 'Nicolai, you are babe
in the wood. You are *wood* in the wood! You know the book will

10*

make money. *I* know the book will make money. The *papers* all
say the book will make money. But the bank doesn't read the
papers. It doesn't believe the papers. It writes its own papers.
All it believes is security.'

'But I could show them all the letters.'

Soli shook his head, like a teacher who, even after a solid
hour, hasn't taught the class a damned thing. 'Letters are not
security.'

'Do they think I *forged* them?'

He said something in Rumanian, which was the language he
had been born to. When he saw my puzzled face, he translated:
'I said, "It would not be the first time".'

'*But good God!*——'

He cut short this childish dialogue. 'Would you like me to
guarantee your overdraft?'

'But Soli, how *can* you?'

'I know the man, and he knows me.'

I got my £500 the same afternoon. I also got yet another
item to add to the long tally of things I didn't understand, and
never would. The idea that Soli Ornstein . . . Ah well.

There was now another new invention to add to my lengthening list, the pure-jet engine; and it was in the brand-new,
highly publicized, much admired Comet One that I flew to
London on the first leg of my journey.

This was my introduction to long-range flight; the prestige
aircraft, in which so much hope was placed, seemed the very
last word in luxury and sophistication; and to fly, as we did at
one point of that magical night, eight miles high above the
black Sahara Desert, and then to see a blood-red moon rising
below the plane, was like a foretaste of all the other kinds of
magic which must be just over the horizon.

It was this same plane which was later to break up and crash
near Rome, killing among other people Chester Wilmot, the
foreign correspondent who had just scored a big success with
his book *The Struggle for Europe*, and also killing the Comet
programme stone-dead for at least five years.

I only had a few hours in London before winging on my way; long enough to hear that things at Cassell's were positively steaming (their first print of 60,000 copies would barely cover the subscription orders from booksellers), and to see the giant coloured posters announcing that only in the *Sunday Chronicle* serial, just started, could one get a preview of that sensational new novel ('The Scoop of a Generation—Most Moving Story Since *All Quiet on the Western Front*') *The Cruel Sea*.

With this swift glimpse of good fortune to come, never dreamed of in all my modest philosophy, I took off for New York.

Once again I was enshrined in luxury. BOAC had just started their 'Monarch Service' to and from the United States, and were falling over themselves to make it outshine all competitors. Their plane had a lower deck with a spiral staircase and a small bar; after sampling their free champagne, free martinis, free everything, we dined off spotless napery decked out with real silver, and were served from an ornate silver trolley which glided to and fro along the centre aisle till we had all had enough of everything, from the caviare and turtle soup to the Bombe Surprise, the Stilton, the complimentary liqueurs and the cigars.

Then we—or at least those of us who were travelling at the expense of rich American publishers—could retire to our sleeping-berths to sleep off all the compliments.

That was the theory, at least, and most of it came true. But headwinds and foul weather spoiled our schedule, and we were seventeen hours between London and New York, stopping off in Iceland for fuel and a change of crew. In those seventeen hours I ate, in swift series, dinner, supper, breakfast (Iceland), breakfast (airborne again), and a 'light repast' (*canapés*, cold salmon, and champagne) before landing.

Stewards had hovered over me with bottles throughout the voyage. There were times when I felt more like taking a sleigh-ride on the silver trolley than sitting in my 'full-length reclining *chaise longue*'. By the time we arrived at New York,

I was in a high old state of happy benevolence, with strong
undercurrents of exhilaration and alcohol—in fact, in a mood
exactly suited to this marvellous city.

I knew it, and had been strongly attracted to it, already,
though in a minor wartime key; roosting in a single slot of a
room, on British naval pay, at the Barbizon Plaza Hotel, where
a packaged breakfast, like a Nineteen-twenties 'lunch basket'
as supplied by the London, Midland & Scottish Railway, was
delivered at 7 a.m. in a cardboard box pushed through a flap
in the door, was not quite the same thing as being installed at
the real Plaza, in a huge, delightfully old-fashioned suite, as
comfortable as superb service could make it, with a wonderful
view northwards across the whole of Central Park.

Obviously the life of Riley had begun. I could not really
believe in any of it, but one did not have to believe in order to
enjoy. I had my suite at the Plaza. I had a book which seemed
all set for a thunderous success. I had an agent and a publisher,
both of whom were obviously going all out for the book and for
me. I had two photographers to meet me at the airport.

Though it could not possibly last, it would certainly last
out the week.

My agent was Willis Wing, who handled such consequential
clients as Somerset Maugham, Nevil Shute, Robert Graves, and
Erle Stanley Gardner, and who was later to be president of all
the literary agents in America. He had an office, the kind of
cramped, almost excessively modest office which only men of
undoubted prestige could afford, appropriately sited on top of
the Morgan Guaranty Trust Company's bank on Fifth Avenue;
and there I went, after a second light lunch fully in keeping with
the style of living I had suddenly been born to.

We had not seen each other for nearly seven years, when
he had sold two of the *Corvette* books to Lippincott's, and there
had been precious little in subsequent books to encourage him
to waste time and effort on a rather shadowy British writer. But
he had stuck to me, and I to him; and he was still the same rock
of a man—in energy, in physical strength (in spite of the

crutches which had borne him for many years), in integrity, in his absolute sureness of touch in anything concerned with his job.

He also had an undoubted charm which made instant friends, and must have cost many publishers instant sums of extra money.

Now, after the minimal greetings, he jumped straight in, according to custom.

'It's a fine book,' he said, 'but I've told you that already. Luckily lots of people hereabouts think the same way. Knopf have done a first print of 35,000, but they reckon that will go in about three weeks, so there's a reprinting on the way. I hear the *Times* Book Review are giving it the front page. The Book-of-the-Month are doing 180,000. *Reader's Digest*—well, they never give out any figures, but I guess that should be worth about $17,000 later on. I've got eight serials lined up in local newspapers, here and in Canada, as well as the *Atlantic*. So—' he spread his hands across the desk, and gave his alarmingly attractive grin, '—this thing is really moving, and just for once it's something that deserves to. Incidentally, do you want any money now?'

'It's always nice to have,' I said, with British reserve.

'How much—a thousand dollars?'

So much for my credit in *America*. 'That'll be fine.'

'There'll be a big cheque coming from Knopf at the end of the month.' He glanced down at the scribbling-pad in front of him. '$24,640, to be exact. And of course there'll be a lot more later on.'

I swallowed. It was no good trying to be blasé about this. $24,640 was nearly £9,000. 'That's fantastic,' I said. 'I can hardly believe it.'

'It's wonderful what you can get used to . . . Now, about the programme. The Book-of-the-Month are giving you a lunch. So is the *New York Times*. So is Alfred, of course. I guess you'd better see the Knopf office next. In fact I made a date for you there at four o'clock. They've fixed all the interviews and the

TV and the radio. I think they've got Harvey Breit of the *Times*
waiting already. They want you to go to Boston, too—they sell
a lot of books in Boston. And of course the *Atlantic* people are
there, all ready to pounce.'

'Pounce?' I had memories of a wartime indiscretion in Boston,
when I had got rather drunk at a dinner party given by Edward
Weeks, the editor of the *Atlantic Monthly*, and had treated the
company to my closely argued lecture on geo-politics, forecast-
ing two giant land-masses, Russia and America, which would
carve up the post-war world, leaving Britain a tiny nothing
in the middle. It had been a forecast absolutely correct, but
currently treasonable in terms of the British war effort—and too
long, anyway.

Willis Wing noticed my expression, and as usual could
pinpoint its origin. 'Don't you fret. All is forgiven. They're
giving the serial a terrific play. And Ted Weeks doesn't like
stuffy Englishmen, in any case.'

'God knows I wasn't stuffy.'

'So I hear . . . Now, how do you want this money? Or shall
I send you a cheque to the Plaza?'

Next stop, the Knopf offices on Madison Avenue, where
vulgar commerce was excluded from publishing altogether,
and money never mentioned except in terms of artistic acceptance, which *might* lead to a certain number of books being sold
—or rather, absorbed by the reading public on terms agreeable
to both sides.

Alfred Knopf, long the General Montgomery of the publishing world, was well on his way to becoming the Charles de
Gaulle. Tall, distinguished, urbane, and beautifully mannered,
he had at the same time such a lofty disdain of the rat-race
indulged in by the lower orders of publishing, that one could
scarcely believe that his firm published lots of books and made
lots of money out of them.

They did both; and when I met him in his office his guarded
references to the 'favourable reception' now being accorded to
The Cruel Sea showed that this latest venture—not a typical

Knopf book at all, a slice of straight story-telling rather than a work of art—was being handled with the skill and drive which were, somewhere well out of sight, always at the heart of this remarkable firm.

They had made a beautiful production of the book—Alfred was *the* typography expert, and all his Borzoi books were a delight to see and to handle. I did not like the jacket at all, which showed a sort of *Boy's Own Paper* version of a corvette at sea, gaily decked out with signal flags, turning its back on some ships in trouble on the horizon. But that was the only flaw; otherwise the book, the prospects, and my own reception were alike uniformly encouraging.

It had been established quite early on that I was very fond of cigars, and he produced from a massive cabinet in his office a rare specimen, a Montecristo about as long as a very long pencil. When I commented on its excellence, he answered: 'It has been maturing for four years. That's the very minimum, don't you agree?'

At the end of our session, he glanced at his watch and said: 'I had planned to select some more cigars this afternoon. Won't you come along?'

I liked 'select', which was not at all the same thing as buying. We strolled sedately up town to Dunhill's on Fifth Avenue, took the tiny lift to the Cigar Humidor, and entered the very temple of this particular worship.

It was a small room lined from floor to ceiling with tiers of cedar cupboards, each labelled with the name of the tenant. Some of the greatest names in politics, the arts, the financial world, and show business were among this formidable array. Did Bennett Cerf really care so much about cigars? Did Alfred Lunt? Did someone called Vanderbilt? Apparently they did, and so did Alfred Knopf.

Deeply impressed, I watched while four boxes of Belindas were carefully handed down from his private retreat, examined, approved, and put on one side for dispatch. I bought some Romeo and Juliets myself, of a quality suitable for customers who, though not permanent lessees, yet had taste enough to patronize this establishment.

Outside on Fifth Avenue again, Alfred Knopf sighed.

'So much for pleasure . . . Apart from our lunch for you, I shall see you at Purchase at the end of the week . . . Some of the first reviews should be out tomorrow.'

'I'm keeping my fingers crossed,' I told him.

Alfred looked as though he did not approve of that sort of thing at all. 'They would be very foolish not to praise your excellent book.'

I went back to the Plaza, where four preliminary interviews for radio and television had been arranged for the early evening, in great good humour. I really must have one of those cedar lockers at Dunhill's . . . Awaiting me in my suite were some flowers from the management, two bottles of marvellous Bourbon whisky from Harold Strauss, chief editor at Knopf, an invitation to enjoy the delights of Sardi's, and Willis Wing's hand-delivered cheque for $1,000.

Writing suddenly seemed a very agreeable profession indeed.

It continued to be so. The reviews which now began to flood in were astonishing, both in quantity and in what they said about the book.

We had our front page in the *New York Times* Book Review* and another in the Chicago *Sunday Tribune*. We had three columns in the New York *Herald Tribune*, and three more in the *San Francisco Chronicle*.

We had a man in Milwaukee calling it 'soaring and vivid', another in San Francisco who labelled it 'the finest volume on war afloat ever written', and a girl in Washington (Mary McGrory) proclaiming it 'one of the finest chronicles of action at sea to come out of this, or any other war'.

* It was a good review ('A fascinating story, and a compelling one,') but not all that good. It was written by W. J. Lederer, an ex-U.S. naval officer; a fact which prompted Alfred Knopf to publish a counter-advertisement headed 'Isn't there a critic in the house?' and to wonder out loud whether the *Times* would have assigned Dante's *Inferno* to Billy Sunday for review. Billy Sunday (1862–1935) was an early model Billy Graham,

MOIRA LISTER AND DIRECTOR CHARLES FREND TALK ⁻OVER AT EⱯLING STUDIOS

H.M.S. *COMPASS ROSE*, ex-*COREOPSIS*, STEAMS INTO THE
LIMELIGHT

MORNING, WITH CORPSES—AND DONALD SINDEN

JACK HAWKINS ON THE BRIDGE

JACK HAWKINS AT THE BAR
Launching 'The Nag that Lost Its Head' to become 'The Cruel Sea' pub
in Hampstead

ARRIVING FOR THE NEW YORK PREMIERE

WITH MR AND MRS OSCAR HAMMERSTEIN II

WITH MR AND MRS PAUL GORE-BOOTH

WITH THE RT. HON. LESTER PEARSON
then Secretary of State for External Affairs, later Prime Minister
of Canada

THE FIRST OF THE XK JAGUARS REACHES JOHANNESBURG

ANTHONY, MARC, AND SHAGGY DOG
(aged 2, 3 and 13)

IN DARKEST NORTHERN QUEBEC
Caricature by Bob Hyndman

JOAN CRAWFORD, HEATHER SEARS, AND ROSSANO BRAZZI
in *The Story of Esther Costello*

We had sixty reviews in the first rush, many of them syndicated ten or fifteen times. We had one absolute sinker, and this, unhappily, in my very favourite magazine, the *New Yorker*.

One had to make a choice between Clifton Fadiman: 'Who touches this book touches men deep in desperate enterprises,' and that nameless *New Yorker* scribe's verdict: 'A dismal tale by a dull writer.'

One had to make a choice. I certainly made mine.

The book had already climbed into the best-seller list (it was to be No. 3 in its third week), though I could see that the competition ahead was going to be fierce. The top incumbents at the moment were *The Caine Mutiny, From Here to Eternity,* and *The Kon-Tiki Expedition,* and two real star-quality jobs, Salinger's *The Catcher in the Rye* and Rachel Carson's magnificent *The Sea Around Us.*

Meanwhile, I was manfully working my way through the nine-day programme set up by Knopf's. Into that short space, as well as sixteen assorted interviews, were crammed six broadcasts and two television appearances.

Television was absolutely new to me; I had only seen it once before, in the embryo version of 1936; South Africa had hardly heard of it; and the idea of my actually appearing on it was remote as the moon . . . The highlight, as far as I was concerned, was the Dave Garroway 'Today' show, for which I rose at 5 a.m., presented myself for rehearsal and make-up at six, went on the air at 7 o'clock—and 8 o'clock, and 9, in repeat performances which grew progressively more unreal.

It was no more than that run-of-the-mill, routine event, the celebrity interview programme, which has now become commonplace, even *passé*. But Dave Garroway, a charming host (even at 6 a.m.) who had obviously read the book, had a taste for variety, and I was only one of three star performers in a most curious Hall of Fame.

The other two were Mrs Eleanor Roosevelt, who spoke passionately and at machine-gun speed about human rights, and

a talented though sullen chimpanzee called J. Fred Muggs, a
nation-wide favourite which opened *its* performance by taking
a brisk side-swipe at my friendly, outstretched hand.

'You shouldn't have done that,' said the trainer (owner?
partner? cousin?) afterwards. 'Fred is *very* highly strung.'

As with the old joke about the concert pianist ('What do you
think of his execution?' 'I'm in favour of it,') I could have
wished that to be literally true.

Thus, between Mrs Roosevelt on human rights, J. Fred
Muggs all over the studio, and salvo after salvo of advertising
breaks, I did my best to plug a book about British sailors at war.
I had an early morning hangover. The coffee, unexpectedly, was
terrible. The old-style lights were positively grilling.

After our third and last performance, Dave Garroway said:
'It has been a real privilege to meet you.' But even he was
sweating, and his orange make-up was cracking like a dried-
out mud lake, beneath which mysterious forces bubbled and
stirred inexorably.

The realization that, while he survived—and must even have
enjoyed—jumping through this hoop five days a week for
fifty weeks of the year, I was an exhausted clown after three
hours of it, gave me an early hint that writing, and only writing,
was the reputable way of life for writers.

All else—particularly all the rubbishy 'television personality'
cult—was either show-off, or squandering of precious time, or
admission of failure.

It remained a permanent conviction ever afterwards.

Then I made that quick trip to Boston, another city I liked
very much. I had already spent quite a long time there during
the war, waiting for the American-built frigate which was so
bashful about putting to sea.

It was a strange, lively, Irish-orientated town (though the
Boston Brahmins would give you plenty of arguments about
that); a community so permissive that a popular mayor could be
re-elected while he was still in jail; so friendly to British sailors
that there might never have been either a Boston Tea Party or

a Battle of Bunker's Hill; a city so handsome that even to sit on
a bench in the middle of Boston Common and watch the passing
scene was a delight, yet with areas like Scollay Square which
could rival any dockside jungle in the world; and so bigoted,
here and there, that a Roman Catholic priest could be allowed to
say, without rebuke: 'Our only enemies are those damned,
Mary-hating Protestants!'

There I had met Edwin O'Connor, who started life as a boy
from Woonsocket (there were some odd, Indian-based names
hereabouts), served his time as a radio announcer and a sailor,
and was soon to bring his undoubted gifts to flower with *The
Last Hurrah*.

There I met Sergei Koussevitzky, the Boston Symphony
Orchestra's conductor, and listened avidly while we sat in his
study in the middle of a forest, and he talked of every musical
thing under the sun.

There I had made a little extra money on the side by doing
book reviews for the *Herald-Traveler*; and watched raw bur-
lesque at 10 a.m. with one of their energetic, scallywag repor-
ters, James Kelley; and enjoyed a memorable *Othello* with a
matchless pair of stars, Paul Robeson as the man himself and
José Ferrer as Iago.

This time it was a quick, crowded trip. Visits to bookshops,
where, for once in my life, a man could come forward and say:
'It's really selling!' and look as though he meant it. Autograph-
ing a toppling stack of books already sold. A celebration lunch
with Ted Weeks and Charlie Morton of the *Atlantic Monthly*,
and being diplomatic about their hideous cover, which showed
the author of *The Cruel Sea* with liquid brown eyes and a ship
going up in flames by way of a halo (but then, they had once
been diplomatic about *me*).

A party given by Alice Dixon Bond, *doyenne* of literary editors in this area, an old friend who had been kind enough, in her
review, to couple the book as 'enduring literature' with *War and
Peace* (no arguments from me, though certain interior doubts);
a party at which a very old lady with patrician features and an

immense flowered hat had assured me: 'Now I *really* know how to escort a convoy.'

A short night at the Ritz-Carlton Hotel (where else, where else?), an early morning plane caught with the help of loyal, sustaining friends, and I was shovelled back into New York, ready for the second round. Now it was mainly social. There was a lunch-party for twelve given by Alfred Knopf, at which I was seated next to a columnist from the *New Yorker*, who talked affably of everything to do with the written word except the merits and demerits of *The Cruel Sea*.

I decided that I could be just as affable, with an upper lip as stiff as that poisonous *New Yorker* review.

There was a smaller lunch given by the Selection Committee of the Book-of-the Month Club, which, seeing that they were in the process of making my fortune, posed no problems of any kind except moderation. One of the board members was a formidable, pint-sized old lady called Amy Loveman, the very prototype of all those other old ladies who bought books by the hundred thousand and could make or break an author, from the financial point of view, across the length and breadth of America. (Alice Dixon Bond was another, though she was larger, and an undoubted ally.)

Miss Loveman had a sweet face and a beady eye, and I kept a very sharp watch on both.

Then, best of all, with the greatest sense of occasion for me, was a lunch given in the boardroom of the *New York Times*, attended by all the top brass of the editorial staff, publisher Arthur Sulzberger and editor Lester Markel among them. It was another moment when, like my first meeting with Sir Evelyn Baring, I felt I had at last come up in the world.

Sitting, eating, talking, listening, in the very heart of the world's best newspaper, was an undoubted treat which I remembered ever afterwards. There was also a surprise at the end; when the table was cleared, the cigars alight, the brandy comfortably at hand, a sudden silence fell, and Arthur Sulzberger said: 'We'd like to hear from you about South Africa.'

Feeling nervous, I made the point, first, that I was a civil servant in a diplomatic post, and must talk off the record; and then felt immediately ashamed of the warning—these were not the kind of men who would betray anything except betrayal itself. Then I did my best.

The questions which followed showed me that, even after five years' residence in the territory, much travelling, much covert observation, and free access to all the men who were doing things and all the other men who were trying to stop them, I was often only a bare half-step ahead of what the *New York Times* knew already.

It was a sobering and a reassuring discovery.

Now there was only one more day and night left of my American dream. Spurred on by intensive Johannesburg training, I made it a mixture of the sacred and the profane.

There could be no doubt about the first: Sunday lunch with Alfred Knopf out at Purchase, the setting for his country house about twenty-five miles north of New York, was like a highly enjoyable extension of Divine Service. Once outside the city, Alfred, like many New Yorkers, shed the urban life as if it were unwanted make-up; but it seemed that he only did so in order to assume another disguise, another brand of *maquillage* —*Caresse Paysanne* instead of *Vie Soignée.*

In this luxurious charade, he did not wear English tweeds— the sun was far too hot. But the English tweeds seemed to be there, nonetheless: part of a phantom, rather endearing country-gentlemanship which affected even the way he walked and talked. Alfred cutting a rose for a button-hole, and Alfred cutting a book critic down to size, were two almost violently different people.

The ease of the transformation was not the least impressive part of it.

I could not complain; I would not have dreamed of doing so. As an urban publisher he, like the Book-of-the-Month Club, had been strenuously concentrating on my interests for many months past; now, as a weekend host, he gave me one of the best lunches

I ever enjoyed, conjured up by a food and wine *expertise* without parallel in this part of the world.

It was topped off by one of those exquisite Belinda cigars which I had seen at the very moment of its resurrection from his private mausoleum—and all in surroundings which one could not fault, for comfort and taste and the kind of easy magnificence which had vanished from England with the death of Edward VII.

All made out of books, I thought, in a small moment of assessment, as I sat on a sun-drenched patio, in a chair which might have flattered Cleopatra's reclining limbs, and surrendered to the last stages of all these varied delights. If I could ever do half as well . . . If I could ever do a quarter as well, after another twenty years . . . It was a pity this place had to be called Purchase . . . Inheritance, perhaps? . . . Accolade?

'I think you will like this liqueur,' Alfred said, at the appropriate moment. It was my introduction to *Marc de Bourgoyne*, of which I had never heard, nor tasted its rough, jolting, savage splendour until that day in August 1951. I had thus wasted forty-one years and five months.

In all this indulgence we had been skilfully supported by our hostess, Blanche Knopf. I had been told that the lady was formidable, and report had not erred. Clockwork precision was always at work here; one could not escape the feeling that, for her, entertaining was an intellectual exercise, like skimming the cream from a manuscript, like translating bad French into good English, like making a double-acrostic come out exactly right, like the music of Bach which must have an exact beginning, an ordained middle, and a scrupulously tailored end.

In fact, with life as with art, the pattern was all, the pattern was sacred, and this included Sunday Lunch.

But if the result was this lunch we had so much enjoyed, who could quarrel with the recipe? Certainly not I, who had found this small, supercharged creature alternately stimulating, daunting, and deeply impressive. She was the vice-president of A. A. Knopf Inc., and a perceptive and watchful hostess at the same time. She was in total command of all her surroundings. Indeed, I could only detect one small weakness, and it was blessedly female.

She was the only human being I ever met who, as a Chevalier of the Légion d'Honneur (as well as a Cavaliera do Ordem Nacional do Curziero do Sul, doubtless a Brazilian cavalry version), had the red-and-white ribbon of the former order seemingly attached to her entire wardrobe. I had noticed it on a town suit earlier in the week. Now, at lunch, it had been sewn onto her cardigan.

Blanche was *not* the sort of woman whom one could ask about her nightwear.

Back now to New York, where at last I had an unequivocal date. It had been gently simmering for a week, since I had always had something more important to do than enjoy love from a stranger—at least, more important from A. A. Knopf Incorporated's point of view. But we both knew it was all fixed, if we could just get round to it.

One-night stands are probably the best version of the string-less love affair, as long as the rules are set out beforehand: no prologue, no epilogue, just the significant bit in the middle with a blank margin on either side. She was Jewish, blonde, laughing, alive. She was also a candid prospect. 'Have you got your eye on me?' she had asked, earlier in the week. There could only be one answer; it had become obvious already. 'Well, when you can just quit being the Great British Author . . .' I quit on Sunday night.

We had twelve hours at the most. First we wandered the town a little, window-shopping down one side of Fifth Avenue and up the other. Saks beckoned us, and Cartier's, and a shop selling freakish male fashions, and then Doubleday's Bookshop, where a superb display of the book was topped by Leon Levson's suave photograph of the author.

'You look older already,' she said.

'A year older.'

'Better slow down . . .' She put her head on one side,

appraising the photograph under the bright lights within. 'He
made you look rather Jewish, too.'

'Perhaps he could foresee the future.'

'That isn't the future.' She sighed, and laughed almost at the
same moment. 'That was a hungry sigh, in case you're nervous.'

'Then we eat.'

We dined at a pitch-dark, elegant retreat called the Barberry
Room, and drank champagne, and held hands, and hoped that
all the other couples were lovers too, poised on the edge of
happiness. Then, at the end, we became practical.

'We could go back to the suite,' I said. 'But I don't know
what the Plaza rules are.'

'The Plaza rules are the same as everybody else's rules. Don't
do it in our hotel. Please go somewhere else. Otherwise we
might *just* knock on your door.' But she was alive and alert,
beneath all the softness and the compliant glances. 'I positively
refuse to worry about a thing like that. You come back with
me.'

All lovers should wake, just once, on a tenth floor high above
the East River; and look down on a metropolitan dawn, and
watch the tugs and the barges and the police boats threading
their way upstream until they were lost in a mist pearly grey at
the edges; and then turn to another window, with a view down-
town across the whole spread of Manhattan Island; and hear the
traffic begin to growl, and decide regretfully that it was time to
move, and leave a sleeping girl in a memorable bed.

Innocent once more, light-headed for many good reasons, I
walked all the way south, from 100-and-something street to the
chaste portals of the Plaza, fifty lonely blocks away. Normally I
should have been knifed or robbed five times over on so foolish
a journey, but this was my fortunate sunrise, as it had been my
fortunate night.

No one at the Plaza seemed at all put out that my bed had
not been slept in. Probably they preferred it that way.

At mid-morning I made a last call on the Knopf office, and
talked to Harold Strauss and to some salesmen, and heard only

good news. Then I had a farewell lunch with Willis Wing at the University Club on the corner of Fifty-fourth Street and Fifth Avenue, a club so solid, so monumental, so well-conducted, so secure, that it could have put the Athenaeum to shame.

We talked no more of copies sold and royalties to come (that had all been disposed of), but only of politics, and music, and the future, and a possible novel about Africa, and the shadows under my eyes ('Hope we haven't been working you too hard,') and the way the world was going to hell and the way that people could, might, *must* somehow do something to stop it.

The *decrescendo* was just right, the sign-off perfect. Half dead, and exquisitely alive, I said good-bye to Willis in the hot turmoil of Fifth Avenue, taxied out to Idlewild, and caught the 1630 plane back to London.

Though there were still three weeks to go before British publication, the snowball which had never stopped a-rolling was now gathering real speed. Details of the New York reception had preceded me; indeed, I had already had three trans-Atlantic telephone calls from newspapers, inquiring at enormous expense (it seemed that newspapers could invent more ways of wasting money than the people who ran the Groundnut Scheme in East Africa) what it felt like to be successful.

The most amusing contact was with Eve Perrick, the high-rated columnist of the *Daily Express*, whose quiverful of wasp-stings fairly screamed their way across the Atlantic. After warming up, in a disbelieving voice, with 'How many hands have you shaken?' 'Will you go on writing about the sea?' and 'How much do you know about love?' she had weighed in briskly with a little slice of the past: 'In that play of yours, *The Visitor*,' (now how on earth had she heard about *The Visitor*—no one else had, in the entire British Isles) '—you once said that money took away a writer's character. How are you standing up to an estimated £30,000?'

In Eve Perrick's trimmed prose, my answer came out as: 'It is probable that since devaluation, money takes away less character than it did before. I am doing my best to withstand the weight of it, and the Income Tax Authorities are very much on my side.'

I cannot claim that this dialogue rings absolutely true, but there was no quarrelling with the sentiment.

The final Q and A was reported thus: 'What do you look like—or am I to take the fanciful description "Rake-hell adventurer's face and the brow of a poet" as your own opinion of the Monsarrat appearance?'

This was the first I had heard of this 'fanciful description' (it was certainly fanciful), and my own opinion of the Monsarrat appearance inclined more to the Civil Service image. I seemed to have done my modest best with: 'From my photograph you will see that "brow of a poet" refers obviously to a receding hair-line.'

But now the range had closed. By a strategam which must take up a great deal of radio-traffic time, and could legitimately infuriate the normal traveller, all other passengers were held back until, first off the New York plane, I had made a carefully posed appearance in the doorway, waved to imaginary adorers, and descended the steps ('Not too fast!') towards the waiting photographers.

Then I was borne into town, by courtesy of the Daimler Hire Company, and intensively interviewed on the way by a reporter from the *Sunday Chronicle*, which seemed to have established a lien on my arrival.

They certainly had a vested interest, as was explained to me a couple of hours later when I called on Cassell's, and talked to one of their directors, Bryen Gentry, already a long-term friend.

'The orders are still rolling in,' he told me. 'In fact, we're more likely to run out of paper than anything else. The *Chronicle* serial is giving us a marvellous run-up to publication. Just what we want. It hasn't done their circulation any harm, either.'

'But shouldn't that affect the book sales?'

'Normally it might. But this thing isn't normal. We're up to 84,000 copies already, and I've got a feeling that it's only the beginning.' He smiled at me. 'I've been reading your cuttings What's it like to be so successful?'

'I wish you could think of a really good answer to that one.'

'Is it true there are nine translations fixed up?'

'Something like that.'

'Christ, you're not getting *blasé* already, are you?' He looked down at some papers on his desk; everyone now had papers on their desk when they talked to me. 'We've got a hell of a programme mapped out for you, but it can't start for another ten days. Why don't you take a holiday?'

'This is all a holiday.'

'It doesn't look like it. How was New York?'

'Wonderful. A little bit of everything.'

'That's what it looks like . . . But seriously, it wouldn't be a bad idea to drop out of sight till the fun starts. Visit relatives or something. How *are* the relatives?'

I knew what he was talking about. 'Just the same.'

'Is it going to be all right?'

'I think so.'

'I've been worrying a little about that. I mean, a divorce in the middle of all this——'

The line between publicity and public relations suddenly emerged, sharp and clear. 'There won't be one. It's still hanging fire.'

'Good . . . You take a holiday,' Bryen said again. 'But get back here on the 25th. That's D-day, as far as we're concerned, and you're on "In Town Tonight".'

By one of those coincidences which either sweeten or poison life, according to the outcome, the promise of a holiday, a drop-out-of-sight, now landed smack on the floor in front of me. I learned that, if I really wanted it, I could have another date— a real date, *the* date—there and then, in Rome.

I really wanted it. I wanted it so much that there was never the remotest question of anything save instant compliance. For pride's sake, I might have said no; but there was no pride here, only love, the other mortal sin.

It was to cost me, in the end, about a quarter of a million pounds.

In those less sophisticated times, it was easier to move quickly; though the impudent nonsense, the tyranny, of 'travel restrictions' had already been dreamed up, by people who did not want to go abroad themselves, or had the Ministerial privilege of unlimited junketing, yet the allowance was a comfortable £100, and, for anyone coming from South Africa, £200.*

Within half a day, I had hired a Jaguar (for speed rather than elegance); driven down to Lympne on the south coast, hopped across the Channel in a twenty-minute wave-top arc, by a shuddering plane in which the cars travelled first-class and the drivers sat on a wooden bench in the tail section; landed at Le Touquet, cleared customs, bought lots of francs, and begun to burn up the road towards Paris and the south.

In preparation for the basic 1,000-mile dash, across all France and most of Italy, which had already provoked a giant mood of exhilaration, I slept that night in Paris and then got on the road bright and early, aiming to break the journey at Avignon on the banks of the Rhône. The first day took me swiftly through the very heart of France: Dijon for the spirit of wine, Lyons for the power-house of heavy industry, the Route Napoléon for the sheer pleasure of travel.

Avignon, ruined bridge and all, was mysteriously beautiful; in the quiet dusk, the ancient ramparts and the castle which had sheltered a dynasty of Popes more than six centuries ago, carried even a flashy Jag driver back into the noble past. But that bridge had a foreboding air, all the same; it started with such huge confidence, so beautifully, so bravely, as if the very stones were proud to lie one on another, and then ended

---

* As far as Britain was concerned, it fluctuated with our fortunes, financial and political: from a high of £250 (Conservative) in 1959, to a low of £25 (Conservative) in 1952; from the lowest point, *nil*—no money at all, stay where you are, don't leave the country (Labour) in 1947, to the end of a mucked-up quarter of a century with a happy free-for-all, the only restriction a £300 limit on foreign exchange, with no limit to the number of journeys (Labour again), in 1970.

nowhere, thrust out into limbo and imprisoned there for ever.

I should have read the lesson right, or listened to *Sur le Pont d'Avignon* for the mourning beneath the melody. But I wasn't reading anything that night except the *Guide Michelin*, the menu, the wine-list, and the arrows pointing to the marvellous future; nor listening to any tune except a singing heart.

Day Two was a harassing one. There were Cannes, Nice, and Monte Carlo to be negotiated, with all the rich folks in their whopping great chariots, all the lumbering lorries which proclaimed their ownership of the road by driving slap down the middle of it.

There was the Grande Corniche, a-swarm with those maniac drivers in Fiats and Ferraris and Alfa Romeos, charging past or through all the opposition, one foot on the accelerator, one hand on the horn, one burning glance for all other mortals, one ruthless ambition. I did not compete. I wanted to reach Rome more than anything else in the world; but I also wanted, very much, to stay in that world, and live . . .

After that, the journey tailed off into sunlit pleasure, and a necklace of towns like a small history lesson: Genoa, the handsome sea-port whence Columbus sailed, on his way to discover Fifth Avenue for me: Pisa (once round the Leaning Tower and away, away!); Leghorn where Nelson refitted a battered ship but could not save a battered eye, and at last the Seven Hills of Rome.

Two days flat . . . I was proud of myself as I made a final traffic arabesque and drew up outside the Hotel Excelsior on the Via Veneto; proud, tired, and silly with happiness.

We were not in this city, the world's most beautiful, for reasons of piety; but Rome and piety went hand in hand like another generation of lovers which had outlived everything except gentleness, and peace, and tranquil meditation

Whatever one might do within the polished, un-Roman shell of the Excelsior Hotel, the hallowed stones outside guaranteed pardon for it, forgave all straying pilgrims their sins, and guided their feet to God. Since I seemed to have lowered all other guards, even this instinctive one did not matter any more. The most determined infidel—Jew, Moslem, accursed Turk, circumciséd dog—could here be taken by the throat, could here believe.

We wandered Rome, like children, like lovers, like penitents. Love was in the very air, clinging to the warm stone: love of God, love of man and woman, love of the unassailable past and the enchanted present, love of love.

Love even of proud priests, the *élite* who should have been humble; of thronging nuns, gabbling and gawking like any other women's club outing; love of the fetid slums of Trastevere, the elegant fountains of Rome, the cascading Spanish Steps, the holy magic of St Peter's Square, where love of Bernini could almost supplant the official target.

We even wandered through the Colosseum by moonlight, gliding in and out of the shadows like a myriad other ghosts, or the scores of pick-pockets, robbers, sexual stalkers, mean assassins who also haunted hereabouts. Once again, we should have been knifed or robbed, but innocence protected us, even in this temple of much blood, of Christian flesh mauled by real lions, of the cruelty and splendour and concerted wickedness which must cling to these ancient, evil walls.

Just so did love cling to the sheltered humility of the Vatican, and forgivable pride to the statues of the great emperors, good or bad; the vanished, ever-present ghosts of Nero and Caligula, Claudius and Hadrian, Constantine, Tiberius, Trajan, Augustus: and the Latin text-book man who was here only a neighbourhood celebrity, Caius Julius Caesar.

Popes could be called Pius; Popes could be called Clement; Popes could be called Leo, Urban, Benedict, Felix, Deusdedit, Innocent, and Celestine. They could even be called Nicholas the Great. They all lived in these parts. The wolf still suckled Romulus and Remus, the darling twins who had founded all this wonder . . . One could get purely drunk on the gentle turmoil of

history: the stirring past, the barbarian rape, the quiet, holy,
heart-embracing present.

All lovers, we agreed, should be lovers in Rome; and whatever outlandish breasts had kept Romulus and Remus alive,
eight hundred years before Christ, Rome in A.D. 1951, the
Year of Everything, had brought matters up to date: under the
banner with the strange device—Excelsior! Excelsior! (four-
star hotel)—Romulus and Remus, in drowsy afternoon siesta
or under the acute spur of night, tumbled the wolf from its
brazen pedestal, and suckled love itself, and were heavenly
twins again.

Obviously one could be drunk all the time, without a sip,
without a swallow. Yet vulpine teat, flowing Tiber, fountain of
Rome, hot and cold holy water—they were all there, and we
must have sipped and swallowed without noticing: still believ-
ing like innocents, like popes innocent, like damned fools, that
we did not need another man, woman, or dog in the world to
help us.

Presently we realized that we must watch the calendar, and
obey it.

I had driven down, like a lusty Roman charioteer, in forty-
eight hours; now we returned as tourists, spreading the journey
over a full week, choosing our stopping-places by the clock,
the speedometer, and our own indolence.

A day in Florence, with respectful calls on Mantua and
Verona, was succeeded by two at San Vigilio, a minute fishing-
village on the shores of Lake Garda, where the sunlight and the
water matched each other for warmth and gentleness, and the
tame trout beneath the balcony were fat from bread-crumbs and
tossed chicken bones.

Then came a determined Alpine dash across most of Switzerland; then Dijon again, Paris again, and London at last; London,
where there now waited for me a happy, headlong plunge into
another kind of turmoil; a turmoil not Roman, not geared to
the bloody past, not in the least historical except for us, the only
people who mattered, and especially for me—emperor, pope,

clown, bond-slave and bonded lover, and Liverpool boy made
good.

My faithful and energetic agent, Christine Campbell
Thomson, who had been furiously busy throughout all this—
negotiating translations from Norway to Japan, serials from
Gibraltar to New Zealand, and a film deal with Ealing Studios
which was coming swiftly to the boil—had still found time to
rent a flat for us, on an open-sided mews, with a reassuring view
of Brompton Oratory pointing the way, like St Peter's itself, to
a heaven still available for sinners.

There we settled down, in under-cover domesticity, and
there, as a first shot in the campaign, Kenneth Tynan came to
interview me.

Tynan was then an innocuous and even agreeable young
man, nervous, stuttery, blinking when directly addressed
(which could not have been very often). He was earning a little
extra bread by writing 'profiles' for the *Evening Standard*; the
ripe savour of a later personality, the rumble and squeak of his
portable lavatory wall, were not yet in the public domain.

He wrote a flattering piece—'The man who has leaped to
fame with one book'; talked of its 'cruel nobility'; and signed off,
after comments on my former pacifism which drew total agreement from me, with: 'He is that rare and disquieting creature, a
sincere, intelligent, and civilized human being who is at his best
in mortal combat.'

The last six words of this I thought true, and sad for what
they said about the mean shortcomings of our world, but
not basically dishonourable; lucky was the country which,
pitch-forked into war, could count on its amateurs to turn
professional, to be warriors for the working day and then,
when all was over, go back to the minor chores of citizenship
again.

I was less enamoured of the few side-swipes which Tynan
felt bound to include: 'Rather a weak mouth, pursed generally
round a cigar . . . A gardening sort of man, you would say, with

the deep judicious appraising voice of a cricket commentator
. . . From the neck up he looks saturnine, from the neck down,
baggy.'

Weak mouth? Gardening? Cricket? *Baggy?* . . . Even my
best friends had never told me. My father was particularly-
indignant. 'Who's this fellow Tinnan?' he demanded. 'I can
assure him, he's talking through his hat! If he knew the trouble
I had to get you anywhere *near* the garden!' And the number of
callers who rang up and asked to speak to Baggy was wounding
indeed.

But the real start of this gorgeous circus was the launching
party—almost literally a launching party—given by Cassell's.
This consisted of a nice boozy trip down the Thames to the Pool
of London and back again in the good ship *Abercorn* (detached
from her normal sight-seeing, day-tripping rôle), with a cargo
of newsmen, booksellers, envious publishers, a few human
beings, and the biggest floating bar which ever shoved off from
Westminster Pier in the shadow of the House of Commons.

Such extravaganzas should never be described seriously; the
straight face does not belong in this gallery. The best account of
this very odd, highly effective event was given by Patrick
Campbell, later to be all sorts of things including Lord Glenavy,
but then, like Kenneth Tynan, hacking out a blameless living
by writing, in his case for the magazine *Lilliput*.

Patrick Campbell was a funny man to talk to, and an even
funnier man to read. He treated it just right:

On the principle that nothing is more interesting than the
work of public relations officers, press agents, publicity
advisors, and all who seek to gain favourable comment in a
national daily for a good cause, we went along the other
evening to the Motor Vessel *Abercorn*, moored at Westminster Pier, where a party was being given for Mr Nicholas
Monsarrat, author of the best-seller *The Cruel Sea*.

To hold a party on a river for a man who had written a
book about the sea seemed to us a rather special example of

II

the press agent's art, and we were eager to see how it would work out.

We arrived early, fearing to miss even the smallest detail, and had to wait for nearly ten minutes while a party of some 200 sightseers disembarked from a river steamer across the Motor Vessel *Abercorn*'s deck. Things were so far from being ship-shape and Bristol fashion that we were glad Mr Monsarrat had not yet arrived.

He is an ex-Naval officer, accustomed to the rigid discipline of the silent service. We thought he might have been distressed to see the *Abercorn*, chartered in his honour, laden to the scuppers with nervous elderly ladies, and children at work on boiled sweets.

When the crowd had cleared we went below, to find the cabin laid out with cocktail party appurtenances, and three waitresses in neat black uniforms putting small sticks into sausages.

A Mrs Davidson introduced herself, as a representative of Mullally & Warner Ltd., the press agents involved. 'I can't,' she said, 'stop these carnations leaping about.'

There were what we estimated to be about 30s. worth of carnations in a silver vase on one of the tables. The vibration of the engine was indeed causing them to leap about. We told Mrs Davidson not to worry. 'Mr Monsarrat,' we said, 'has probably seen much worse things at sea.'

He arrived himself shortly afterwards, a youngish man with singularly deep-set eyes, a comfortable, but costly-looking green tweed suit, touches of grey at the temples and what smelled like a very good cigar. He seemed tired, but set to with a will to provide drinks for the guests, nearly all of whom were unknown to us save for two elegantly dressed young women whose names we have never discovered, but who seem to attend nearly all these affairs. We suspect that their purpose is to promote good will.

It was some time before we could draw Mr Monsarrat away from his duties. We put the question to him without delay. 'Mr Monsarrat,' we said, 'what do you think is the purpose of giving a party on a river launch for a man who has written a book called *The Cruel Sea*?'

He considered it carefully. 'I've been trying to work it out since this morning,' he said. 'I think that the fact that we're in a boat serves as a reminder that I have written a book about the sea. I'm afraid I can't narrow it down for you,' he added, 'much further than that.'

We asked him how his health was standing up to the publicity campaign in which he had been involved since his book was published in America, and immediately leaped into hundreds of thousands in sales.

'I had nine days of it in New York,' he told us. 'Lectures, interviews on the radio, two television appearances. I must tell you frankly, I found it very agreeable.'

'What kind of questions did they ask you in the interviews?' we inquired. 'How you do your work—that sort of thing?'

'Yes,' said Mr Monsarrat. 'Actually, I do it straight onto a typewriter. I like writing. I'm already half-way through a new novel. Will you excuse me? There are some friends of mine here—discussing democracy—I think perhaps I should ——' He gave the word 'democracy' a slight yet obviously ironic emphasis. He meant that conversation on a high intellectual level was taking place, and that it was up to him as a writer, and as the guest of honour, to join in and do his share. We gained the impression that Mr Monsarrat was a very very nice man indeed.

As we moved away we noticed for the first time that Mr Mullally, who wears a beard and is normally one of the sharpest dressers in the West End, was now encumbered with a not very pretty bandage round his neck. We tracked down his wife, Miss Suzanne Warner, who is the other half of the firm, and asked, directly, if it was boils.

'Ingrowing hair,' said Miss Warner promptly 'His hair is very curly at the back, and one of the hairs grew inwards. He had to have it lanced.'

That seemed to us to be the most astonishing revelation of the evening.

Mullally & Warner were indeed the 'press agents involved' in the brave voyage of the *Abercorn*. They had been hired by Cassell's, in a display of enterprise almost unheard of in publishing circles at that time, to put the book and its unknown author on the map, and to keep them both there until natural momentum had taken over from initial energy.

Frederick Mullally was the man, complete with beard and ingrowing hair; Suzanne Warner was the girl—and one of the most ravishing, rarely beautiful red-heads I had ever seen in my life. They had a consequential office in Hay Hill, just off Berkeley Square, and they did a very good job indeed.

The man who actually shepherded me around was David Davidson, husband of that Mrs Davidson who had been so concerned about the leaping carnations. He was a small, bald, forceful man, highly skilled in his somewhat dubious profession. He seemed to know everybody who could be of the slightest importance to me at this crucial moment of time. He fixed interviews, fixed broadcasts, fixed meals and drinks and transport, and also fixed me with a watchful eye at parties, never relaxing his gaze for a moment.

He was essentially a realist, as he made clear very soon after our first meeting.

'People are already asking about that dedication in the book. You'd better tell me what it's all about. We don't want any surprises.'

I cut a few corners, as, with David Davidson, it was very easy to do. 'We're hoping to get married.'

'Not too soon, though?'

'No.'

'But that's the girl I met in the flat?'

'Yes. Should I say anything about it?'

'Christ, no! Just leave it blank. Who knows about this, anyway?'

'My publishers. My agent. A couple of people in Johannesburg. That's all.' But how could I be sure? And how could I
tell Davidson that my real worry was not about the book at all,
but about the High Commissioner's Office in faraway Pretoria?
'Do you think anybody else knows?'

'Maybe. They will damn soon, anyway. Did you *have* to put
in that dedication?'

'Yes.'

'Oh well . . . What about your wife? Will she——' his right
hand, which was expressive, described a flurry of widening
circles in the air.

'No.'

There we left it; in fact, there we left it for ever. It was, to
me, truly remarkable that not a word was ever printed about the
estranged wife, the deserted child, and the next candidate cosily
installed in Ennismore Gardens Mews, though by the time I
left London the whole situation must have been transparently
clear, and the topic tailor-made for comment.

It was possibly the most striking compliment that *The Cruel
Sea* ever earned. No one wanted to spoil it.

London was now in the thick of the Festival of Britain, our
first post-war effort—seemingly forlorn, actually an undoubted
success—to inject a bit of spirit into our lagging self-esteem by
sprucing things up, slapping on a few layers of paint, hoisting a
lot of flags, and putting on a show which would persuade visitors and natives alike that nationally speaking we were not
quite dead.

The focus was on the south bank of the Thames, where a
huge funfair and cultural exhibition centre had been established (to replace the ugliest frieze of derelict wharfs and warehouses ever to befoul a capital city); it was here that, from an
embryonic Festival Hall, I made my first timid essay into
British television. But I could not help feeling that the Festival
of Britain itself was really part of my book promotion: a mounting build-up which was a repeat of New York but, astoundingly,
just about double the size.

My festival meant the window displays all over town, not only in the bookshops but in stores like Selfridge's, Harrods, the Army and Navy, Barker's: window displays which centred round a life-belt (by courtesy of the Royal National Lifeboat Institution), and pyramids of the book itself, distinguished by a plain, unadorned, instantly recognizable jacket featuring a marine painting of a rolling sea.

It was, ironically, a German picture, which had hung in Sir Newman Flower's study for many years. Now it had changed sides, or at least become neutral, like the Atlantic itself.

My festival was the acres of reviews which were now beginning to pour in, reviews which would have warmed the heart of a dying Christmas cracker riddle-writer. I took as my personal text the one from Compton Mackenzie (Compton Mackenzie!): 'In this book can be heard the surge and thunder of the Odyssey.'

It was certainly the proudest tribute of my life: it had to be offset by a sniffy verdict from Liverpool, my own home town, where the *Post*, after dwelling on 'cheapening episodes' and 'woeful' shortcomings, said that a really good book about the Battle of the Atlantic was still to be written.

Some of the adverse comments were much more entertaining than the friendly ones. There was a disturbing query from Mr J. P. W. Mallalieu M.P. (author of *Very Ordinary Seaman*, later Minister of Defence, Royal Navy), in the *Daily Express*: 'Will women understand *The Cruel Sea*?' The *Glasgow Herald* pounced on two slips; I had described River Clyde pilots as wearing bowler hats (they did not), and Glasgow pubs as permitting dart-playing (dart-playing was *not* permitted on these blameless premises). The *Oxford Mail* complained that: 'The sociological asides are sparse and superficial' (well, I should bloody well hope so).

Mr John Betjeman in the *Daily Telegraph* produced a tetchy inaccuracy, sucked from God-knows-what overworked thumb: 'His dislike of those who speak and write makes one wonder why he was so inconsistent as to write a book himself.'

I had just completed my fifth year of unrelenting support for any writer or speaker who could be persuaded to bear a hand in our good cause, whether his subject was art, economics, ship-design, or British bloodstock lines.

Finally I suffered a lofty blast of disapproval from an admired man, Admiral of the Fleet Sir Philip Vian, G.C.B.:

'There is a note, disagreeable to a naval reader, of un-warranted fear. The crew of the *Compass Rose* were hunters, not the hunted; and to suggest that hounds were afraid of their fox creates an impression as demoralizing as it is false.'

Ha!

There was a little extra fun to be derived from the 'local tie-up' angle. One of these came from Nottingham, where my claim to fame was as 'Grandson of a former mayor'; another, more detailed, recorded that 'Mr Monsarrat's father, a noted Liverpool surgeon, was at one time on the staff of Nottingham General Hospital. His aunt, Lady Readett-Bayley, is shortly taking up her residence in the Old Rectory, at Langar, the one-time home of Samuel Butler, author of *Erewhon*. Mention of Samuel Butler reminds me . . .'

In Stafford I was 'Stafford Author: Son-in-law of Mr William H. Rowland, joint managing director of Universal Grinding Wheels.' In the *Cumberland and Westmorland Herald* I 'revived old memories for Mr Charles L. Emmet, clerk at Kirkby Stephen (East) Railway Station, who formerly worked as a coder in two of H.M. frigates commanded by Mr Monsarrat.' In a *Rand Daily Mail* leader I was 'Local Boy Makes Good'—and very nice too.

My festival was a very funny song* included in a revue called *Intimacy at 8.30* at the Criterion Theatre. It was entitled 'Business in Great Waters', written by David Climie, and sung by a trio of duffle-coated naval officers, whose attitude of stiff-upper-lip correctness alternated (according to the stage direc-tions) 'with a kind of asinine jocularity'.

The middle verse is enough to give its immediate flavour:

* See Appendix B.

We're three rollicking literary sailors!
Writing of the things that sailors do.
While patrolling our Dependencies some psychopathic tendencies
Were shown by certain independent members of my crew.
I said, 'Go on and mutiny—I don't care what you do to me—
It's what I need for Chapter Three.'
I can't forget the fateful day a Channel port we took;
I hoisted up a signal as we sailed around the Hook—
'England expects this day that every man will write a book'—
A book about the Cruel, Cruel Sea!

>   I must go down to the sea again,
>   To the lonely days and the nights;
>   And all I ask is a small advance
>   And the *John Bull* serial rights!

My festival was Cassell's, having sold every book in the
building in the first five days, now running out of printings
one and two (120,000 copies) before the autumn leaves had
begun to fall. Edwin Harper, then their able publicity manager
put it to me, man-to-man:

'I'm afraid we've got troubles.'

It was the first time I had heard the word for months.
'*Troubles?*'

'Paper! We've run out of paper! We might even run out of
ink! We can't print it fast enough! We're printing another
40,000 in Australia. That won't last till Christmas!'

Though this particular log-jam, studded with Edwin's ex-
clamation marks, eased in early October, as his *Bookseller*
advertisement showed,* it continued to be one of the world's
happiest headaches for the best part of two more years. I bore it
—we all bore it—as best we could. In the meantime, there were
a number of other worries, real ones, concerned not with paper
and ink but with people.

I had three and a half other preoccupations during the six
weeks in England: divorce, my son, my father, and the future of
the job.

* See illustration facing page 131.

Eileen, I found, had done nothing about a divorce, though it was three years since she had left South Africa and two since I had asked for what I then called, without irony, 'my freedom'. There was really no reason, from her point of view, why she should have taken action; the ethics of the betrayed wife could never be clearly defined, cut-and-dried, hard-and-fast, nor even in accordance with local custom.

They were determined always by individual circumstance, with the million variations to which men and women in this fix were both entitled.

Thus she had decided to wait and see; a perfectly reasonable tactic, but, for me, the worst possible answer to my own dilemma. *She* could wait and see. *I* could wait and see. The third party was not going to do either, and that was the one I was worried about.

I put on the pressure as best I could, though to do so in the present circumstances made me feel even more than normally guilty. Success deserved to be shared, if only by reason of a shared past. But a conviction of guilt was not going to stop me; it had never stopped anyone or anything once they were set on course, whether a thief, a blackmailer, a mad dog, or a runaway horse.

Presently she agreed—she really agreed—that our position was not retrievable, and that the time had come for dissolution.* With that out of the way, we were able to travel down and take a joint look at our offspring, now at school in Oxford.

This really was a separate operation, without strings. Children do not save a tottering marriage; in fact they are more likely to ruin it for ever. At the lower level, it is the noise and the nappies a man longs to be quit of, just as much as the nagging voice, the slattern's housekeeping, the woman he has

---

* We were divorced about a year later: my own adultery being proved, and discretion exercised in her favour. The action was heard before His Honour Judge Leon, better known to the world as the writer Henry Cecil (*Brothers in Law, Alibi for a Judge, Settled Out of Court*).

II*

grown sick of, long before little Charlene came along to complicate things. At the higher, the child is just something else to
be rid of, another item in the clean break.

Both such levels are ignoble. But the idea that tiny fingers
can curl round an errant heart and make it better again is a soap
opera dream, just as the idea of a double bed as the answer to all
marital discord is the dream of the celibate priest. A man lured
into this supposed cure for a quarrel is left with a resentment
more fierce, a loathing more terrible, than if he and his wife had
slept at opposite ends of a warehouse.

All he knows is that he has been swindled again; the glorious,
healing balm of sexual intercourse has turned out to be the same
old push-pull mechanical contrivance; the burden round the neck
remains, and Christ! there might be another snotty kid to add to
it.

Thus Max, last seen when he was six, now a sprightly nine,
did not unite two lonely hearts. But for both of us he was still a
beloved feature of the human race; and for me a surprise—the
kind of surprise felt by children themselves when the gift-doll
came to life on Christmas morning.

It walked! It talked! It could say Mama—and, if kicked hard
enough on its little rump, Papa as well! It was almost human
. . . Max was now at a prep school called Summer Fields, and
we went down to see him on Sports Day—a sports day in which
he did not seem to be in the least involved.

'I forgot to put my name on the board,' he told me, as wide-
eyed as I had been myself, thirty years earlier, when I had told
my father transparent lies about my own lack of success. I supposed that he had been eliminated in the preliminaries, several
days before we arrived on the scene. It did not matter.

Summer Fields was not at all to my taste, and no doubt this
was mutual. Years later, Dick Usborne, last met as one of the
proprietors of *London Week*, the entertainments magazine which
had kept me alive for over two years in the hungry mid-Thirties,
invited me to contribute, as a 'Summer Fields parent', to a book
he was editing about the school.

I could not summon up more than a morsel of the enthusiasm which perhaps he was looking for. But I did my best—and since my contribution never earned me a cent, I feel entitled to steal it back again, on the same basis, though with due acknowledgement.*

Dear Dick,

Thank you so much for your letter, which (to dress the stage) finally reached me on the small Canadian island where I live and work in the summer. Your letter suffered in transit between the island and the mainland (to be frank, it fell overboard), and it has not been too easy to decipher. But it seems that you want me to write something about the Dragon School.

Alas, I know nothing at all about it, except that my son Max was incarcerated there about ten or twelve years ago. During that time, I was toiling for the British Government in South Africa (in the sense that I was on the High Commissioner's staff), and I never set foot on *your* mainland for seven long years. Max never wrote to me (quite correctly; I do not encourage my children to write: it is something one should only do for money), and I never really gathered whether he was happy or unhappy, hard-working or lazy, or even fat or thin. However, I paid the bills regularly. They were much too high. Carpentry was extra.

I know that they did not educate him well enough to get him into Winchester. But this may have been Winchester's choice, since I had been there myself earlier.

I did pay one brief visit to the Dragon School while Max was there. This must have been about 1951, when I was in England on leave. I think it was a Sports Day, or Parents' Day, or something like that. I didn't enjoy it, anyway

At a first glance, the school seemed to me to be tumbling down, though this may have been the teaching staff, not the

* Reprinted from *A Century of Summer Fields,* ed. Richard Usborne (Methuen, 1964), by kind permission of the publishers.

actual buildings. Max not only did not win any races; he did not run or jump at all; he explained that this was because his name had never been put down for any of the events. I took this at its translation value—i.e. that he had been knocked out in the preliminary heats. Anyway, there was nothing to cheer, and damned little to eat, and nothing at all to drink unless one had some sort of Private Entrée, which I had not.

Though it is about thirteen years ago now, I remember that I thought this must be a rather snobbish school. Parents were obviously graded, like show cattle, and treated accordingly; a perfectly odious woman with some sort of title was the centre of attraction. As a medium-level civil servant (£1,425 a year, plus overseas allowances), arriving in a rather old, hired Jaguar with a label on the windshield saying 'Welcome to Britain', I was low man on the scholastic totem-pole. The fact that I had just written a best-selling novel was far from being a credit entry. Writers, it was well known, made scenes, got drunk, left their wives, and passed the port the wrong way.

I was wearing suede half-boots, and a suit which had seemed rather subdued in Johannesburg, but was obviously, in Oxfordshire, part of their image of *Guys and Dolls*. Scarcely anyone spoke to me, though one of the older boys asked me to move my car, to accommodate a $4\frac{1}{2}$-litre Bentley.

I met *you* there (I think), and Norman Pearson, and a master (name forgotten) who could not have been more off-hand if I had been an unsatisfactory member of the catering staff. When I asked him how Max was doing, he said: 'Yes.' This struck me as so unusual a piece of dialogue that I later incorporated it in a book. But my publishers asked me to delete it. Too *avant-garde*.

So much for the Dragon School. I wish I could be more helpful, but I never really got through to the place, and *vice versa*. However, it is worth remarking that Max did emerge from it as a rather likeable young man, who still does not write letters. Instead, he wants to be a farmer. I do not know if this odd ambition should be attributed to this particular establishment.

Yours ever,

P.S. On re-reading your letter, I see that you asked me to write about Summer Fields, not the Dragon School. How extraordinary! It was my *brother* who was at the Dragon School; Max was at Summer Fields. Yes, yes, I remember it all clearly now! But I do hope that I have not confused you. Would it help if I asked you to substitute 'Summer Fields' for 'Dragon School' throughout?

Dick Usborne gave a qualified welcome to this letter, doubting whether it was quite what the Governing Body of Summer Fields, the prime movers in the project, had in mind.* But he was kind enough to recall, in passing, the sum-total of sex-education he had received from official sources at school: 'Keep your hands out of your pockets, or you'll never be any good at games.'

I decided that this was probably enough for Max, at the age of nine, to be going on with as well. But I was giving rather more attention to some other aspects of his future. He had been entered for Winchester (at least, I thought he had been entered, having filled in all the regulation forms on the stroke of eight years old), though the decision had been a hard one.

If Winchester were currently anything like it had been in the Twenties, then I would as soon have sold him to the nearest glue-factory. But my contemporaries who now had sons there assured me that it was not. Beating was out—or at least the enthusiastic, nightly lust for it which had so inspired the prefects of my time was no longer fashionable. Politics were more liberal. Boys were sometimes even known by their Christian names, without shame.

My grateful admiration for a true classical education had

* It also left unresolved his query (under the general heading 'So far there is almost no good salacious stuff'): 'Did Max have anything to do with the maids?' I believe not.

grown with the years. Snobbery tipped the scale. I put his name down for my old house, and hoped for the best. His school reports were encouraging enough; certainly not as daunting as one which, a generation later, attracted my attention.

The subject was five years old, and the verdict: 'Peter is not really mature.'

The third family call was on my father, now in his eightieth year. Mother had died four years earlier, in 1947: a sad death, alone and undiscovered, during a brutally cold blizzard which had isolated her small cottage for several days. He had then, at the age of seventy-five, and to the accompaniment of cheers from me, married an 'old flame' (the language was his), and he now lived with my step-mother in a Cotswold village near Woolstone, which needs further identification as being near Faringdon.

The village lay in the shadow of a hill, into which was carved a most attractive, beautifully stylized, galloping 'white horse'— the famous Uffington White Horse, in fact, which had certainly been in existence prior to 1084 and was traditionally ascribed to Alfred the Great, who thus commemorated a battle won in A.D. 871.

My father's cottage could not claim this antiquity, but it could certainly claim enough of it—upwards of five hundred years, with all the authentic draughts, discomforts, head-denting beams, and tortuous stone stairs to match.

I am sure that he loved it, and must have found my reluctance to negotiate rope banisters, worn stone steps, whistling winds and icy temperatures in order to go to the bathroom, effete and unworthy. But it was good to see him so happy, so pre-occupied over the reception of his latest book, with its unlikely title *Human Desires and Their Fulfilment*, and so well cared for by a loving companion.

The old cottage was not the only thing which linked him with the past. He still clung to certain attitudes, accepted and prolonged certain traditions, which bound him comfortably and firmly to a Victorian childhood.

'We have *darkies* next door!' he told me, as soon as I arrived on this visit, and he pronounced the key-word almost gleefully, as perhaps Cecil Rhodes or Livingstone or even Marco Polo might have used it, to denote total mystery, a strangeness scarcely fathomable, a bizarre and alien strand in a pure English thread.

Darkies in Uffington. . . . That same evening he said: 'Come with me a moment,' and led the way outside. We peered through the bushes into the next-door garden. '*There's one!*' my father exclaimed suddenly. There was indeed a black man mowing the lawn, using skilfully a very businesslike rotary mower of a pattern unusual, indeed unobtainable, in rural England. He was certainly Negro, and strong, and personable. Presently he rested from his labours and, in the cool of the evening, put on his jacket.

When he saw us watching, he waved cheerfully. He was a United States Army Air Force colonel.

There was one thing, and one thing alone, which I did not like about my father's changed and happy circumstances. He had already found it necessary to excise the past, and to rewrite it. For very many years his entry in *Who's Who* had recorded, accurately and perhaps proudly, his marriage in 1898 to 'Marguerite, d. of Sir John Turney, Kt'.

Now all detail had suddenly been expunged, and a marriage-tie of forty-nine years had been shrivelled down to: '*m.*; one s. one d.; *m.* 1947, Marie, widow of etc.'

Such maiméd rites. . . . I did not think, and do not think, that a work of honest reference should thus become garbled, for any reason whatsoever.

Finally, of all the things which lay outside the turmoil of Topic A, there was the big question: whether to stay, or not to stay, in what I still regarded as my real job, the Information Service. Suddenly and obviously, it became important.

I had been offered Establishment, that formidable word which meant that one was assimilated into the permanent civil service, with certain perks such as an annual salary increment, a tiny chance in the Honours List lottery, and a foot on the ladder leading to a modest pension, instead of being part of the help hired in the yard outside. Someone had decided, at long last, that information work was worth doing, and information personnel worth incorporating in the machine.

I agreed with this; and certainly I loved the job, and the feeling which went with it of being, in however minor a degree, inside instead of outside the corridors: the satisfaction of reading the political telegrams, knowing what was going on, and understanding why certain things were being done one way instead of another.

It had always been exciting, in that respect; there was even an instance of this now, while I was in London, when Patrick Gordon Walker, who had to make a further statement and answer some questions about the future of Seretse Khama and Bechuanaland, asked that I should be included in the small back-up team from the Commonwealth Relations Office which attended him in the House.

We sat in a little box, just to the right of the Speaker's chair, and listened, and (as far as I was concerned) hugely enjoyed the feeling of consequence. During a pause, Mr Gordon Walker came across and asked me something. It could not have been very important, but good heavens! I felt as though I were actually advising my Minister! Talk about the power behind the throne. . . .

Even when the superior C.R.O. man next to me dismissed it all with the jargon phrase: 'Well, I think he made the right noises,' I still had that warm thrill which came from sudden involvement in great affairs.

'I had to go down to the House,' I told an interested party, with the correct touch of *ennui*, when explaining my absence; and I thought: How about *that*?

I still had some of the same silly feeling next morning, when I went for my 'establishment' interview.

This was a friendly occasion; I supposed that the High Commissioner had given me the required backing, for which I was very grateful; but I had the impression that the selection board was rather sceptical about me. Did I (I was asked, in different ways, at least three times), *really* want to stay on, now that. . . . The 'now that' was never exactly defined, but it was sufficiently obvious.

I had heard the same question from countless people outside Whitehall; sometimes it seemed to be the first thing that anyone thought of, when they met me after five years of hardly knowing whether I was alive or dead.

'I suppose you'll give up your job,' was the recurring key-phrase, as if everyone always loathed their job, and prayed daily for release, and I must be one of the majority; as if I were a lavatory attendant suddenly endowed with a colossal win on the pools—except that the lavatory attendant always answered: 'Of course I'll stay! Might have a bit of a holiday. Might even buy a little bungalow. But I'll stick with it, mate, don't you fret! I like it down here!'

The interviewing committee seemed to have the same sort of doubts as most of my friends. Then, when I said that I also liked it down here, and was certainly serious about staying on, there was some talk about my future, which was likely to lie in Canada, or India, or both—the two information posts which were at the top of the heap.

I raised a gentle query about jobs outside the information circle—ordinary C.R.O. appointments, in fact, which might take one up the ordinary ladder of promotion towards reputable positions *en poste*. The answer was non-committal, in a way which told me that the matter, or at least the theory of it, must be under discussion.

I thought of mentioning John Buchan, who had survived being a writer to become Governor-General of Canada. Then I thought better of it. After all, John Buchan had been a *real* writer. . . .

For I was still deeply sceptical myself, on the opposite side of the fence. The book was a fluke to me, an enormous fluke. I seemed to have been reinstated as a writer again, but how long would that last? Certainly I had lots of ideas for books—fifteen, at least—but I had had lots of ideas before all this, and look what had happened to that early crop.

An idea took shape as I left the C.R.O., bowed (in spirit only, since there were policemen about) to the doorway of No. 10 Downing Street, where my modest hero Mr Attlee was still installed, and set course along the fringe of St James's Park. I had been in the job for five years, and I did like it. C.R.O. had always been nice to me. Opposite the Horse Guards Parade, I took an oath to stay on for another five years at least, and then to think again. That would see me through until 1956.

Topic A returned, swiftly enough, with a Savoy lunch given by Sir Michael Balcon and the completion of the film deal with Ealing Studios.

Everything about the film of *The Cruel Sea* was tremendously exciting, from the early, tentative interviews with Charles Frend, who directed it, and Eric Ambler, who fashioned its distinguished script, to the first night at the Leicester Square Theatre, twenty months later, and the subsequent queues which had to wind twice round the block before they could start to pour their money into the till.

Most of the story does not belong to 1951; film-making takes time, while a year can only take twelve months. But it was all of a piece with the glittering explosion, the first and last astonishment; and all of this piece it should be.

It had been obvious for a long time that a film was going to be made of the book; we had had two American offers which, with all those noughts, certainly looked wonderful on paper. But for all sorts of reasons I did not want it to be made in America.

The hallowed jokes about Errol Flynn winning the Battle of the Atlantic single-handed were not really the point (though Humphrey Bogart had already expressed a keen interest in playing the leading role of a corvette captain). But I did want a film specifically British-flavoured because I thought we deserved it, and need not be ashamed to say so.

I also wanted my own way with the script, and a genuine say

in the casting. In America, it seemed, unknown writers who asked for this sort of thing were directed to the tradesmen's entrance, and tripped up on the way. But presently word came from Sir Michael Balcon at Ealing Studios that they would have no objection to any of these ideas. Of course, they could not offer me an awful lot of money. . . . Would I like to meet the man who would, if I agreed, be directing it?

This was Charles Frend, whom I knew by name already, as the director of *Scott of the Antarctic*, an excellent piece of reporting, faithfully accurate, with some marvellous photography. The omens were good. We met at a party arranged by my agent Christine Campbell Thomson.

To start with I was seriously impeded by the large number of people, men and women, thirsting to expound those twin themes which are the bane of authors—which are to authors as stoats are to rabbits: either 'I have a marvellous story, but I can't write. Will you write it, and we'll go fifty-fifty?' or 'I could write a best-seller too, if only I had the time'.

Then Charles and I, who had been eyeing each other warily across a murky waste of smoke, noise, and potato chips, managed to get together in a corner. He was diffident, and nervous: too nervous indeed to say anything except what was in his mind.

He said: 'I *would* like to make a film of it,' on a note of such extraordinary wistfulness that I knew this was the man for me.

We adjourned to a nightclub at the lower end of Bond Street, where we became so engrossed that at 2 a.m. we left without paying the bill. Bright and early next morning, the waiter who, according to the house rules, had got stuck with £3 11s. 6d. worth of bad debts, appeared on the doorstep of the wrong house—up in Notting Hill Gate, where Eileen and Max were still installed.

'I've called about an oversight,' he began.

'Ennismore Gardens Mews,' said Eileen, and gave the number. She had never needed many clues.

After that it was just a matter of bargaining about percentages, which Christine Campbell Thomson took up with zest,

and the contract with the Great Seal of Ealing thereon embossed, and a final clinching session with Sir Michael Balcon.
Michael was like a really charming ferret, a ferret with lots of
taste who appeared to have mastered film finance—that boiling
reef which had wrecked successive generations of British losers
since the turn of the century.

I signed for £12,000, and a slice of the profits. It was
approximately a quarter of what I could have got from other
sources, but one of the best bargains I ever made. I then became,
from Ealing's point of view, their ideal author: 6,000 miles
away, and debarred by civil service regulations from any prospect of return for thirty months. But once again—and perhaps
this could only have happened with Ealing, and the honest men
I was involved with—it did not matter at all.

Eric Ambler was always in close touch over the script.
Charles Frend gave me a running commentary on the filming
itself. Michael Balcon delivered Mosaic tablets from time to
time, announcing that they had found just the man to play the
second radar operator in that telling scene off Cape Wrath. He
always turned out to be right. It was delightful (and, I gathered
from other toilers in this field, absolutely astounding), to be
treated by film-makers as a reputable human being.

Since it was a big book—well, let us not debase the language:
since it was a *long* book—it took Eric Ambler five months to
make a film-script out of it. His first version would have needed
four hours to screen. He trimmed and pared this down to two
and a half hours, and this was as far as he or anyone else was
prepared to go, at this stage.

He sent me his successive drafts; I made about twenty minor
suggestions altogether, and of these, eight took root or made
some sense. This was not my area of endeavour, and I knew it;
reducing a book of 416 pages to a two-hour film was a matter of
special expertise; Eric had it, I did not, and it might have taken
me another twenty working years to learn the new techniques
of a new job.

Charles Frend's information was mostly of snags, including

the biggest one of all—finding a corvette to play the star. The Admiralty had none on their books; in fact, though unsparingly helpful, their reaction was almost 'What's a corvette?' so outmoded had these funny little hookers become.

Leslie Norman, the producer, scoured the seven seas in vain. Most corvettes, he found, had either been broken up or converted to small freighters now plodding to and fro across the China Seas. Four were doing duty as weather ships, and too busy to be spared.

The Greek navy still had two in commission; so had the Norwegians, so had the Irish. None of these could be spared either. Then at last, after eight frustrating months, Leslie Norman tracked one down. She was still afloat and, like any other ageing actress, at liberty.

She was one of the Greek navy ones, now abandoned and on her way back home to be broken up. She had been lying for five months in Grand Harbour at Malta: old, battered, rusty, and already being steadily stripped and cannibalized by the shipbreakers. She was manned, when Leslie went on board, by one Maltese tea-maker. But he went on board with the eye of faith. 'Just what we want,' he declared, in face of all the evidence.

The corvette's further death was postponed, for as long as Ealing would need her, and she was towed home to Devonport to be patched up. (First job: clearing the olive stones out of the voice-pipes.) She had been masquerading since 1943 as His Hellenic Majesty's Ship *Admiral Kreizis*. But she was, incredibly, the old *Coreopsis*, one of my own group from the Liverpool Escort Force of 1941.

There was another very strange coincidence concerned with the filming, also announced by Charles Frend in one of his newsletters:

'The Admiralty,' he wrote, 'are being absolutely marvellous. They've promised to lend us a frigate as soon as I've sunk the corvette. They've also given me a most useful line onto two naval advisers. One of them is a retired R.N. captain called

Jackie Broome, who will be in charge of *Coreopsis/Compass Rose* when we put to sea. He says that he knows you.'

Well he might. This was the same Commander J. E. Broome who had made that well-remembered inspection tour of *Campanula*, also back in 1941, and had dealt such death and destruction all round. Now he would be manipulating my destiny again. . . . To Charles Frend I expressed the hope that the end-product would be an improvement on his report of ten years earlier. Happily, it turned out that it was.

Coreopsis and Captain Broome were two-thirds of a very curious link with the past. The other had been forged already, by my own hand. The character of Lieutenant-Commander Ericson in the book was based, as far as looks, achievement, and reputation were concerned, on Lieutenant-Commander Cuthbertson, the corvette captain whose survivors we had fished out of the water when *Zinnia* was sunk, on that wretched Gibraltar convoy; the man whose mother still thanked me, via those yearly birthday cards to Max, for this half-forgotten gift from the sea.

I wished—how I wished—that I could have stopped being a civil servant, even for a couple of months, and taken part in the filming, which sounded like one long, hilarious marine picnic with plenty of complications to prevent its ever becoming dull.

The crew of forty-three, ex-sailors and trawlermen recruited (sometimes from safe shore-based jobs) all round the coast, from Hull to Glasgow via Liverpool, performed manfully; so did Captain Jack Broome, who proved as stern a disciplinarian as I had remembered him.

Once Charles Frend brought on board a naval officer friend who was interested in what was going on. As they gossiped on the upper deck, Charles became aware of what he described as 'a still presence' nearby.

It was Captain Broome, who broke an awkward silence to demand: 'Who is this man, and who gave him permission to come on board?' Charles (who was after all in charge of the whole operation) explained.

'I am the captain of this ship!' Broome thundered, and that was the end of the visit.

He was inclined to regard most of his crew as 'scallywags'; it was certainly true that when *Coreopsis* approached Plymouth of an evening, a crow's-nest lookout was posted to keep watch for policemen who, it was said, wanted to interview some of those on board (charges unspecified) and were following their progress up the Sound on bicycles.

Charles himself had trouble with one of the cooks, a memorable character who volunteered his services at the start of filming.

'I asked him, very reasonably,' Charles told me, 'if he was a good cook. "Never mind asking stupid bloody questions!" was all the answer I got to that one. "You said you wanted a *cook*. And that's what I am. A *cook!*" It turned out that he was not, and those he was cooking for came ashore with a very good appetite for dinner.

'Once we took him to see the "rushes" of what we had filmed the previous day, at the local Odeon. It was late, long after licensed premises had closed, and he fell asleep. When he woke, the showing was over, and the sound-recordist was running through his own contribution again, without the picture. All that appeared on the screen was a wiggly, worm-like black line which climbed continuously to the top of the frame and down again.

'The cook surveyed this for a long time, then turned to me. "Well, all I can say is," he declared, "you been all round the Eddystone Light, and all down the coast, and all the way back again, day after day, and what I say is——" he pointed to the wiggling worm, "if that *there* is what you want, well all I can say is, that's what you bloody well *got!* Good night all!" '

It may have been this disgruntled individualist who, at noon each day, put out the following announcement on the public address system: 'Hands to dinner! Film unit to luncheon!'

There were various mishaps. Once *Coreopsis* suffered a steering breakdown, and had to be towed home by the tug which

housed the second film unit. Most of the time the sea was
uniformly flat—about as cruel as luke-warm melted cheese, in
fact, and not at all what was wanted for the picture.

Towards the end they astonished passing ships by appearing completely iced over (plaster of Paris) in the flat calm of a
midsummer day. But on the very last available morning the
wicked race off Portland Bill started to perform, the light-
house-keeper signalled to them, and they got all the vile
weather stuff they needed.

Coming back into Plymouth Harbour, they were in collision
with the destroyer *Camperdown*, which was lying alongside,
band-box fresh from a long and expensive refit, and sliced half
her fo'c'sle open as neatly as any sardine tin. ('Card-playing in
the engine-room' was Captain Broome's verdict, after ringing
for full astern and not getting any of it.) Later, slinking into the
nearest hotel bar, Charles Frend met the *Camperdown*'s First
Lieutenant.

Charles apologized profusely. They had, he believed, been
all ready for sea after a stem-to-stern refit; now they would be
delayed indefinitely.

'I *know*,' said the First Lieutenant. 'Isn't it bloody marvellous?
What will you have?'

On the last night (this was Captain Broome again), a small
deputation of two ex-commandos waited on him in his cabin, at
the appropriate hour of midnight. The ship, they reminded him,
still had her 4-inch gun, and plenty of ammo. How about shoving off and trying a bit of piracy? Broome's cut would be fifty
per cent. The crew would be with him to a man.

However, wiser counsels prevailed, and on the morrow
Coreopsis was towed away towards her honourable grave at the
ship-breakers, and on this delightful note disappeared for ever.

Once again, I wished I had been there.

After this there was a long pause, punctuated from time to
time by small cries of anguish from Charles Frend. Alan
Rawsthorne's promised musical score was lagging far behind
schedule. The difference between the award of a U certificate

(wonderfully profitable) and the restrictive 'Adults Only', was flickering in the balance. And the film was still too long! Sadly, Charles had to trim and trim it, and pare it down finally to two hours and ten minutes. But at last, in March of 1953, it was ready for the public eye.

I would not have been able to come to London for the *première* without bending the rules about overseas leave out of all reasonable shape, except for a fortunate turn of events. Late in 1952, the promised divorce had come through, and I had promptly remarried, my second wife being a Cape Town journalist whom her fellow gossip-columnists, loath to miss a good chance of myth-spinning, had labelled 'The Cruel She'. It was a good moment, a very good moment indeed, to leave South Africa, and I was transferred with equal promptness to Canada.

I still had six weeks' leave to come. Our route could only lie through London. We sailed back in the *Athlone Castle*, broke our journey at Claridge's, and dived head-first into the fun.

Fun there certainly was; it was even more exciting, from the nervous author's point of view, than that first night at Daly's Theatre, seventeen years earlier, when *The Visitor* had exploded on the theatrical scene like a cottonwool bomb and, in spite of Greer Garson's best efforts, fizzled away to nothing in three weeks. Then, I could hardly believe any of it, but now, the omens seemed set and the strong tide running for a rip-roaring success.

There were to be two *premières* in London, a preliminary run for the Press and the corps of booksellers who were still keeping Cassell's busier than they had been twenty months earlier, and the real first night, which had been captured as a charity event by the King George's Fund for Sailors, and for which all 1,750 seats had long been sold out. It was at the Press show that I had my first sight of the film.

It was very moving indeed. I thought that Charles Frend and all the rest had done a wonderful job, and it was fascinating to see what they had made of the book, and to note how new minds, working on what was now, to me, old material, had come up with all sorts of fresh discoveries, which brought the book to life in a way which could still surprise me.

The journey from one medium to another involved a real, vivid transformation, and I would never be too proud to acknowledge it.

However, I could have done without one such new mind, too inventive for me altogether, which saw in the relationship between captain and first lieutenant a strong homosexual tie. 'The film,' we were told, 'deals skilfully with this aspect, which in the book was sadly repressed or ignored, perhaps unconsciously, perhaps naïvely.'

Well, thank you, sir. One never knows what sailors can get up to, particularly when one is writing about them.

I had been very lucky in the cast. Jack Hawkins, the captain and the star (about as homosexual as a hard-boiled egg with its shell intact) might have been made for the part. Stanley Baker as the bastard first lieutenant, Donald Sinden, and Denholm Elliott were all just right.

Moira Lister scored instantly in a tiny part as a bitchy actress wife, waiting for the coast to clear. 'Have a nice trip, darling,' she said to her wretched husband, due to go out on a murderous convoy, as brightly as if he were off to New York on a sales spree. It made one groan for all the betrayed sailors who ever went back, sick at heart, to sea. The rough weather photography was superb.

Virginia McKenna, as a loving Wren, was rather less satisfactory. 'She seemed to be making love in the Service manner,' I said to a reporter afterwards, and then asked him to scratch out the remark, which he obligingly did. But if her cool performance established the point that love and war did not mix, because war must have the priority, then that was all right with me.

It was clear that they had all combined to give me a writer's dream—a film which, far from whoring up the book, had cherished, illuminated, and even honoured it. We waited for the *première* with tremendous appetite. *All* five Sea Lords would be there, and most of the Board of Admiralty. The Duke of Edinburgh would be the star guest, and we would be presented to him afterwards.

There was only one shadow which threatened us. Queen Mary, that marvellous old stalwart, now eighty-five, was very ill. If she died, much of the prestige of the occasion would have to be abandoned.

It was. Sir Michael Balcon gave a party out at Ealing, two nights before the *première*, for the people who had worked so hard and to such good effect. We were having a high old time when the fatal news was announced.

Queen Mary had died peacefully in her sleep. There would be court mourning for a month. The Duke of Edinburgh would have to cancel all his engagements. That included us.

It was a sad blow, for many reasons. But making every allowance for the natural disappointment of those who had set their hearts on building this into a very big event, to crown all their hard work, I was appalled to hear one of my fellow-guests break the silence with:

'Oh God! Why did the old girl have to do it *now?*'

Pop-eyed at the best of times, he was positively bursting with rage. As a sentimental monarchist, I had to answer back, and we quarrelled briskly. I was just as disappointed as anyone in the studio, but if someone like Queen Mary had to die, at the age of eighty-five, after a lifetime of service, it should not be to such an epitaph.

Before long the party melted away—there was a great deal of replanning to be done. Then I was privately taken to task for my stuffy attitude.

I could only answer that if anyone didn't like my stuffy attitude, they could stuffy it uppy. Ah, those days of wine and roses. Ah, early signs, broad hints, of multiple strife to come. Ah wilderness, and ah, my head.

Yet in spite of this subdued atmosphere, and the downgrading of what should have been a great occasion (I was very sad myself not to meet the Duke of Edinburgh, a much respected man who would know at first hand what *The Cruel Sea* was all about), the *première* was quite an evening. In fact despite the tantrums of one lady and the death of another, it was terrific.

With two wives, one son, one father (aged eighty-one), one stepmother, one sister, King Hussein of Jordan in a horrid little pin-stripe suit, Jack Hawkins, Lord Winterton, Jim Harmsworth, and eight ex-shipmates from *Campanula*, *Guillemot*, *Shearwater*, and *Perim*, the assorted company nearby had its complications.

But the film, most moving in itself, received the kind of absorbed attention—a true participation by everyone watching and listening—which at the end left me almost shaking with emotions long buried, long forgotten.

I knew then what it meant to feel drained—and there was only one cure for a drained man. We gave a party afterwards at the slightly haunted Cafe de Paris, where the bomb had fallen and the orchestra, the dancers, the waiters, and Ken Snake-hips Johnson fell with it.

That night, some smaller bombs fell on me, as the corks popped and triumph was prophesied. Though I patched it up with the man who had made the Queen Mary remark, I had a secondary row with his wife who, being American, thought my accent was the funniest thing since George III. My own wife, in sultry mood, was giving the general impression that marriages should only last about three months.

But by then I didn't give a damn. By God, that book still lived! . . . And it was marvellous to meet, for the first time, so many beaming admirals.

I was to see that film fourteen times altogether, in various parts of the world, before I decided that an occasional glimpse on late-night TV would be enough in the future. A week after London, we returned briefly to Johannesburg for another very considerable charity bash (Colosseum, 2,200-seat sell-out). This was followed by a *première* in Ottawa, attended by Mr Lester Pearson, another in Toronto with a multitude of sea-cadets, and a third in Montreal, where I inspected a naval guard-of-honour bare-headed and wearing a dinner-jacket. It cannot be done in any sort of style.

In New York the film broke the house records at the Fine Arts Theatre, and I was honoured to sit between Oscar Hammerstein and the banjo-eyed comedian Fred Allen. In Washington the occasion was stage-managed by Paul Gore-Booth, later to be head of our Foreign Office (and after that a Life Peer) but then my opposite number as director of British Information Services in America—in fact, little better than a humble, card-carrying information officer.

So it could be done, I thought later, as I watched his sky-rocketing career. But perhaps it could only be done by Paul Gore-Booth.

In Washington my next-door neighbour was Senator Estes Kefauver. He had recently been photographed wearing a Davy Crockett coonskin cap, and the spectacle had become a popular subject with cartoonists. When I brought it into the conversation, I had the impression that it was no longer his favourite topic, if it ever had been.*

There was one other curious tailpiece to this comet-ride across and across the film world. Some time in 1956 it was decided to rename a pub in Hampstead 'The Cruel Sea' (it had previously been called 'The Nag's Head', which made for quite a change of scene), and Jack Hawkins and I went up to open it.

Neither of us had declared a pub open before, though we might have closed one or two in our time; and when the moment arrived to do so, I could think of no more suitable phrase than the executive naval command: 'Sink everything in sight!'

The occasion was then happily swamped by large numbers of opportunist sailors who, having heard rumours of free beer all round, flocked in from far and wide and converged upon the bar.

The free beer concession had to be withdrawn after an hour.

---

* It was still pursuing him, bushy brush and all, when he went down to defeat as Mr Adlai Stevenson's running-mate in the 1956 presidential election

Back in my proper space-time pattern of 1951, with no notion of the real scale of what was to come, I was already sufficiently stunned. What was happening to me was what every writer prays for, whether he will admit it or not: whether he keeps on trying, in face of all the odds, or gives up and becomes a critic or a television person; and that is, to do his very best with a book, and then to see it take off vertically into the clouds.

What makes tens of thousands of people suddenly decide that they want to read one particular book, and no other, and that they won't be happy until they have bought it and taken it home, is a mystery which has baffled publishers, beyond despair and into bankruptcy, since books were first printed and bound and launched into the market-place.

It does not baffle writers in the same way, since (unless they are harlots or computer-boys) they will always write exactly what they want to, and take a chance on success, or failure, or a drawn game.

I had written exactly what I wanted to, and was already stupefied by the result.

But I knew, even then, that an enormous amount of luck had been involved. Nothing had happened to me in the war which had not happened to a hundred thousand other sailors. But it had meshed in with every other factor in my life so far—including the basic one of being born in 1910, so that by the time I was called on to fight I was young enough to have the energy for war, and old enough—just old enough—not to be destroyed by it.

I had already learned my trade as a writer. I had not been killed, nor maimed, nor driven mad, nor brutalized. When I got out, I had a marvellous story to tell: the same as everyone else's story, but still so tremendous that it was a privilege to be given the chance.

Finally I had got there first with my version, and at the very moment when, for absolutely no reason at all except that mysterious tides of impulse, choice, taste, and will *do* move to and fro, as chartless and astonishing as the governing moon itself, thousands of people (presently to be millions) decided that they were ready to think about the war at sea again, and to read a book about it.

The book about it they all wanted to read was mine. The tide itself was mine. It could never happen again, in such a conjunction of fortune, if I lived to be a hundred and the world turned back and I beat the Spanish Armada. It was a once-in-a-lifetime miracle. . . . On which sobering thought—and I certainly needed one—I closed the *prima donna* account in London and flew back to Johannesburg and my proper job.

Soli Ornstein met us at Palmietfontein Airport. When I heard him call out 'Nicolai!' in tempestuous greeting across the customs barrier, and then: 'I rise my hat!' I knew that I was home.

3.

It was indeed home, but with a vast difference. In our reversed seasons, when winter was July and Christmas meant eating ritual turkey and plum pudding in the only oven-hot month of the year, a golden spring was now under way, with a golden summer to follow.

I had been enjoying South Africa before. Now, the most beautiful country in the world had become the most beautiful place to live in—which was something quite different, and violently arguable if one still had a taste for argument.

But somewhere on the way, somewhere steering south, somewhere in the swift ascent from humble pie to upper crust, I had lost the will to fly into a passion about the frail rights of man and the wrongs of stony privilege—except in theory, blessed theory, which need not cost a penny-piece in performance.

The still-soft conscience did not preclude the hardened attitude, whether in bed or out of it. One could deride 'Let them eat cake' while still drawing comfort from all that bread in the bank.

Johannesburg had seemed masculine before, with female twanging noises from the world's most subtle instrument only audible after dark. Now it was all feminine, and elegant, and luxurious, and proud. The spare hawk became the homing dove, coming in to rest on golden-slippered claws—the prettiest, most pliant metal on the market. The domestic cushion grew tassels, the hard pillow was gentled to a soft, downy whisper. The fat cat sat on the mat. The dream was cream.

Well, damn all the words for corruption. Bless them, and damn them.

'Domestic' was the new keynote. Though there were signs of legal stirring in London, the promised divorce was still only a promise. Yet in some not too baffling way, I had become a more respectable prospect, a better bet. We therefore settled down together, in scandalous circumstances which, at the Johannesburg level of social acceptance, were no scandal at all.

Our rented nest was a large house in Illovo, north of the city; a house which, with four acres of garden, a swimming pool, seven servants, and a Cadillac in the drive, put me *just* in the ranks of the upper classes hereabouts.

There was no doubt that I had come up in the world, and though a book had done it, it was not literary esteem which had thus jacked me up. It was the twin thrusts of sudden, wall-to-wall money, which was well thought of in Johannesburg, and the social level of those who, when all the smoke had cleared, would constitute the body of my in-laws.

This was a typical South African family of the old school, with connections in mining, racing, finance, alcoholism, slimming pills, energy tablets, lesbianism, uproarious divorce, and, as far as my future father-in-law was concerned, the award of a gold medal at the Olympic Games of 1936, personally presented by Hermann Goering to the chairman of the South African Jockey Club.

It says much for my state of mind that I found all this deeply flattering.

Social life now centred on Sunday lunch, a notable fixture at which the crested club blazer vied with the Paisley silk neckerchief and the reversed-calf pale-green brothel-creepers as acceptable male *décor*, and on the rather more formal dinner party—ours and other people's.

It would be wrong to think of English-speaking South Africans, then or now, as a bunch of expatriate hicks with tons of money and the taste of newly-rich Midlanders or Yorkshiremen or pop-stars or film whores. In this world, largely above race and above politics, there was considerable sophistication and style.

The best entertaining, outside London or Paris or Rome or Washington, was certainly to be found, as standard practice, within the five square miles of this brand-new contender It was often hard to keep up. It was also a great pleasure to try.

Thus, when we sat down to dinner under soft candlelight, with a view across the tiled patio to a moonlit garden with the tiny gleam of the watch-boys' brazier marking one corner (naturally, we had our own small police force); when we sat down to dinner, with a white-uniformed, white-gloved, scarlet-sashed servant to each two or three guests, and sampled the first mouthful of the shrimps in avocado or the *caviare au blinis*, the mood of 'I'm all right, Jack,' took on, at least, a superior gloss.

In these circumstances—brittle, perfumed, worthless, armoured against fate, and highly enjoyable—we entertained recommended passers-by and selected residents.

We entertained Leslie Hore-Belisha, successively Minister of Transport, Minister of War, and Minister of National Insurance (a progress which might have baffled those who were trying to divine the precise course he was steering). Having given to the world the 'Belisha Beacon' which still marked pedestrian crossings in Britain forty years later, he was now turning an astute financial brain towards the problems of private life.

12

For anyone with that particular quest on their mind, the first stop was always South Africa.

We entertained—and were honoured by—Alan Paton, a far better writer, I thought, than I should ever be, whose *Cry, The Beloved Country* had lent poetic significance to the jungle-life boiling and brewing not more than five miles away over our secure garden wall.

We entertained Major-General Sir Francis de Guingand, Chief of Staff to General Montgomery before, during, and after the Battle of Alamein, whose old-boy reminiscences about what he called 'The Recent Contest'* concealed a formidable analytical brain. Indeed, they *must* have concealed it, otherwise we could not possibly have won that particular contest, nor any part of it. It still remained a remarkable piece of camouflage.

We entertained another soldier, the sad United States Military Attaché, Colonel D. W. Maher, and his not-so-sad wife Drue who, after his lonely suicide (handled with stone-faced discretion by the U.S. Embassy), opted for more variety and married Mr H. J. Heinz II.

We entertained another sad man, though a man of such absolute charm, distinction, and shy wit that sadness could often be forgotten: Vyvyan Holland, the younger son of Oscar Wilde. Grey-faced, wary, battered by the past long before the present gave him a second chance, he felt, on one particular evening, free to talk of long-ago nightmares.

But a single sentence, remembered by him from the age of nine—'They told us nothing, except that we were never to mention our father again'—was enough to bring silence down like a curtain: an appalled, almost loving silence in which all the world's sickening cruelties seemed to be hovering just above our heads.

We entertained Mr Claudio Arrau, most gifted of musicians, and cursed the fact that we had no piano. We entertained the Egyptian ambassador, and received an early shock.

* Bulldog Drummond, another well-disguised military expert, used to call it 'The Last Show'.

The ambassador was known to be a hearty eater, and he did not disappoint us. Having demolished approximately half a duck and a small mountain of wild rice, he sat back, and massaged a well-rounded stomach.

'I like your food,' he announced, in a chance conversational pause. 'But it makes me fart.'

This was unusual freedom of speech, even by Johannesburg standards. In the persistent silence, no one seemed inclined to comment, and the host took up the burden like a man—a slightly shattered man. 'Your Excellency,' I began, without the vaguest idea of how I was going to finish the sentence, 'I am so sorry——'

Luckily he interrupted me. 'It makes me f-a-a-t!' he said again, with a slight, crucial change of inflexion. He patted the troublesome stomach once more. 'I tell you, last month I put on ten pounds!'

We entertained South African sugar baron Douglas Saunders, whose habit of switching to Scotch whisky sharp on the stroke of eight certainly inhibited the menu and did damned little for the conversation. We entertained Mr Leif Egeland, South Africa's most notable High Commissioner in London. We entertained my four future sisters-in-law. Charming, utterly charming.

We entertained the semi-resident nest of queers then fashionable in Johannesburg society. They were not at all fashionable with me, but then I was only the dull bread-winner, just good enough for a confederate giggle before the door closed behind me. It must have been then that my anti-homosexual bias was finally forged—and I would maintain such forgery against a whole world of consenting males.

Though they certainly kept the conversation going, and could contribute to any gathering more girlish chatter than a talking-doll factory, I could never forget that homosexuality was not just a couple of pretty boys holding hands in the sunshine, or fooling around with their pocketless trouser pockets. Their freakish sport concerned sodomy: correctly called an unnatural offence, aesthetically revolting, explicitly documented in the

reports of the Oscar Wilde trial, when an embarrassed land-
lady (and why should she not be embarrassed?) had to testify to
the smears of vaseline mixed with excrement which were so
hard to remove from her soiled sheets.

There could be no welcome, from me, for these horrid little
castaways on the Coast of Buggaree.

We entertained a succession of King's Messengers—and let
us not get our characters mixed up, on any account. It was part
of my job to meet these regular voyagers, carrying diplomatic
mail between London, Pretoria, and Lourenço Marques; to
transport them, look after them, afford them the maximum
security, and see them on their way again without delay.

They were mostly ex-Army officers; some were charming
assets to any company, some were wayward drunks, some
arrogant nobodies. But they all liked to come to dinner, and
then be shovelled onto the night train for Portuguese East
Africa.

When one drove a King's Messenger, one was not allowed,
for security reasons, to have anyone else in the car. No friends
marooned at the airport could share this sacred vehicle, no lifts
could be given to wayfarers. The Riley had to remain virgin
territory until the diplomatic pouches were securely locked in
my office safe.

The fact that the girl in charge of the petty cash also had
access to the safe, and was accustomed to open it any time she
needed a 2d. stamp, occasionally worried me. But I could never
quite believe that our diplomatic traffic to and from Lourenço
Marques, where we maintained a consul-general to take care of
drunken British sailors, was really as vital as all that.

Anything important, going either way, was immediately
cyphered up, and would arrive by a new invention called the
telegram, before the King's Messenger could get his elastic-
sided boots on.

We entertained—again, as an inescapable part of my job—
a lot of newspapermen. Some of them, in the best traditions of
Instant British Journalism, flew in, flew round, and flew out

again, all within a week; and all within another week one would read their daring *exposé* of the bestial conditions—mostly viewed from my black-and-white tiled patio—which made South Africa such a stinking ghetto for all right-minded citizens.

Some were less stupid and set in their attitudes than others. It would be fair to say that they varied, like blood-groups or grades of infant-food. A year saw the rise, shine, and set of such luminaries as Sefton Delmer and Frank Rostron of the *Daily Express*; Patrick O'Donovan, already infected by the *Observer* disease (and the papal habit) of infallibility; Bob Stimson of the B.B.C., who had some long-ranging common-sense; and Douglas Brown of the *Daily Telegraph*, who pre-ferred the short-range swipe, particularly where the Informa-tion Services were concerned.

There was also a much-preferred candidate, Vernon Bartlett, ex- of the *News Chronicle* which long ago had formed me, and ex- also of a famous by-election of 1938, when he fought as an 'Independent Progressive' in the forlorn constituency of Bridg-water in Somerset, and won it, on the issue of collective security, by simple merit, simple honesty, and simple principle.*

We entertained also such unclassifiables as Lady (June) Carbery, who Knew All (and said nothing) about a very famous Nairobi murder case during the war, when some unnamed (well, un-hung) miscreant put paid to an amorous lord.

We entertained Michael Comay, then in training as one of Israel's future top-flight diplomats; and a Joel or two; and Mr Garfield Todd, soon to be Prime Minister of Southern Rhodesia, and a stalwart hope of federation before federation was swept under the rug of history, and Messrs H. Banda, E. Kaunda, and I. Smith settled for separate prayer-mats.

Well, it was a mixture, anyway.

* Six years later we met in the Long Bar of the Raffles Hotel in Singapore. He was by then working for the *Straits Times*. I expressed some astonishment at this transformation. 'If you lived in Singapore,' he said, 'you would think working for the *News Chronicle* was a pretty odd thing to do.' At a single stroke, the theory of relativity became much less of a theory.

The mixture, the variety, seemed very important that year. Hands up, those who have travelled from Johannesburg to Cape Town via Alfa Romeo, Battle Class destroyer, bosun's chair, aircraft carrier, and admiral's barge. What, everybody? Ah, but at the age of almost forty-two? Well done, that man!

That man was myself; otherwise I would not be making such a production of it. But there was another character involved in Stage One of this excursion, a polo-playing darling of society called Tommy Charles, one of the few really smooth, really well-tailored, really amusing playboys yet thrown up by twentieth-century Johannesburg.

As well as being a social lion and a talented gambler, Tommy Charles was one of the world's original unruffled men. I shared with him a curious experience at the house of a woman who had better be called Madame X; the very last woman, in fact, to give me a genuine, memorable surprise. All other, later surprises were either predictable betrayals, or happy conclusions to some forward planning. This one had all the charm of shattered innocence.

It happened at one of Madame X's rather superior parties, before dinner, when I was standing with her and Tommy Charles, drinking champagne cocktails and hoping to be fed before too long. It was already nine-thirty, and by now everyone was more or less plastered.

Madame X was wearing one of those strapless, wired up, fore-and-aft-rigged evening dresses, then in vogue, which seemed to defy all the laws of gravity as well as the hopes of the spectators. But on this occasion, gravity won and hopes were rewarded. When she said: 'I really must see about dinner,' and leant forward, the top half of her dress plunged earthwards, leaving her naked to the waist.

I had expected at least a brassière, to veil the mysteries, but there was no such impediment. There was instead a very cunning arrangement, on either wing, of two thin strips of adhesive tape, strategically placed at the correct tension to keep up her appearances.

One learned something new every day, I thought, slightly

bemused. Adhesive tape? *Band-Aid?* The effect was really very charming. But hell! I thought again, as the lady, apparently unaware of betrayal, still lingered before leaving us: hell, these were not my pigeons. I said to Tommy: 'You'd better take care of that—I don't know her very well,' and turned away. When I turned back again the top had been re-hoisted, and Madame X was saying, with exactly the same kind of earnestness: 'I really *must* see about dinner.'

Though there were at least thirty people in the room not one of them raised an eyebrow. When I asked Tommy about it later, he said: 'Oh, she's always doing that. There used to be rather a good story about it. Apparently it once happened at dinner, and the butler spooned the lot back in. Nobody minded much. But the hostess was furious. She said: "James I've told you a hundred times! Use a *warm* spoon!"' Tommy looked round the room, world-weary as usual. 'I suppose we're going to get something to eat *some* time. I must show you the new car afterwards.'

'What is it?'

'Just an Alfa. But rather gorgeous.'

For twenty years T. Charles has always owed me, in theory at least, the sum of £90, the result of a very simple gambling operation known as 'cutting through the pack' at £5 a card on that same night: a mixed-up occasion when I thought we were playing seriously and he (it later appeared) did not. But the debt, if debt it was, has long ago been forgiven, if only for what followed that preview of the Alfa Romeo.

I was due to go down to Simonstown, the British naval base about twenty miles south of Cape Town, to meet Admiral Packer, the recently arrived Commander-in-Chief, South Atlantic. Tommy wanted to try out his new car, an open, two-seater, pale ivory, really beautiful model which had just been run in. One thing led to another. The result was a wild ride together, of 980 miles against the clock, when we thought we would try to break the unofficial road record between Johannesburg and Cape Town.

We were shooting at something like fourteen hours, an average of more than 65 m.p.h., and I had to be extremely careful about it. Tommy was the playboy type, and habitually did things like this; I was a civil servant, and did not. Society might be indulgent to him if caught; but the High Commissioner would rightly take the dimmest possible view if one of his staff was copped for careering down South Africa at anything up to our top speed of 140 m.p.h.

There would be no question of pleading diplomatic immunity. Fines for speeding were graduated at something like £2 for every mile over the official limit of 60. After that, I would find myself on a different kind of carpet—one that really mattered.

However, some spare money and a superior love-affair, soon (I hoped) to be up-graded into a superior marriage, had given me the necessary wilful confidence. I said Yes to everything, which included splitting the fines, whichever one of us was the official culprit.

We started at first light, while the suburban exits were still free of traffic, and drove in two-hour tricks. Most of the way lay along clear stretches of first-class road, with only one major town, Bloemfontein, to slow us up, hardly any other cars to worry about, and (I must emphasize) no one to kill.

We had to stop in Bloemfontein for petrol, and an admiring crowd gathered round the car. With its high-gloss ivory paint-work, scarlet upholstery, and bonnet about as long as a tennis court, it certainly caught the eye. One of the local sophisticates peered down at the radiator, proudly emblazoned with 'Alfa Romeo—Milano', and gave his verdict: 'Jolly good cars, these Milanos!'

Even at that late date, there was still one unpaved section to be negotiated, a two-hundred-mile ordeal of ochre mud, packed down into a country-style byway but often viciously corrugated. Once a month the 'grader'—a kind of sharp-bladed bulldozer with a parasol on top to protect the patient driver—travelled

down one side of it and up the other, scraping off the top ripples
and smoothing out the surface.

This must have been the twenty-ninth day of that particular
month; parts of the road were like the entrance to Dover
Harbour on a bad morning, with the ruffled shirt of the sea
running against us, as ferocious and tough as any old iron.

The only way to avoid being shaken to bits was to rev up and
float across the waves: to press on regardless, as Tommy
Charles, who had been in the Air Force, still phrased it. (I reminded him of another item, dredged up from his wartime
handbook: 'We were stooging around at nought feet,' and he
countered with: 'There was I, surrounded by balloons.' In our
present earthy situation, one pressed on regardless until the
car began to skate sideways, and then pulled back a bit. Tommy
(perhaps it was his polo training) knew the trick, and was much
better at it than I was.

But it was all very beautiful—even that parched, waterless
Karroo Desert prostrate under the burning heat: very beautiful,
and exciting, and largely uneventful. We simply kept going,
reeling off the miles with real, thirsty appetite, exchanging one
horizon for the next, one arc of clear sunlight for another even
more alluring. At one point on a long empty stretch Tommy,
who had been dozing, woke up and glanced at the speedometer.
It was registering 190.

'Steady on, dear boy,' he said, in mild reproof.

'It's all right. It's only kilometres.'

I knew that arithmetic was not his strong point.

We kept up a very good average, better than 60 m.p.h., for
hour after hour, including the necessary stops, those corrugated
iron stretches, and a road-gang which, intent on repairing a
washed-out bridge, were having a lot of fun with their red and
green flags. Obviously they preferred the pace of Africa to the
pace of Alfa Romeo.

We raced a train, and waved to its driver, and left it chuffing
away in the distance like a toy abandoned on an enormous, forgotten nursery floor. There was one dead-straight stretch of

12*

fifteen miles, tenantless, inviting a flat-out surge of speed. Once we did 127 miles in 100 minutes.

But towards the end of the journey we were fatally slowed down by a convoy of army lorries crawling up the long, steep, curling road which climbed to nearly 5,000 feet to cross the Swartberg Range, and with that we lost our chance of a record run. By then, we knew it could not be done—not on that day, anyway.

It was 16¼ hours before we were sliding down into the long shadows of Table Mountain; and against that magnificent drop-curtain I said goodbye to Tommy Charles ('Let's try it again on the way back!') and took off for Simonstown and more sedate company.

Their Lordships of the Admiralty, back in the brave old days of 1814, had certainly known how to look after the Commander-in-Chief of the South Atlantic Station; Vice-Admiral Sir Herbert and Lady Packer, the current heirs of this largesse, lived in very considerable style, and their Admiralty House, Simonstown, was an elegant palace, a white Stone Frigate which really deserved the name, and from which one could survey the naval dockyard below with an appropriate sense of ownership and pride.

Lying off the harbour there was now quite an array of British naval strength, currently in South African waters on a showing-the-flag visit which came as a pleasure but no surprise, since I had put out a Press-release about it a couple of days earlier.

There were two imposing aircraft carriers, *Theseus* and *Vengeance*, and four brand-new Battle Class destroyers, looking about twice the size, and twice as lethal, as any destroyer that had ever come my way in that ancient, long-ago war of 1939-1945.

But at the moment my preoccupation was social rather than maritime. Lunch with the Commander-in-Chief had, for me, such prestige, such immediate glamour, that I became a dutiful junior officer again with my very first step through the solid portals of Admiralty House.

The amateur who never made the grade, summoned into
the presence of the professional who undoubtedly had, could only
worry about the correct manipulation of knives and forks and a
light, deferential touch on the conversational ball.

Though I was also there on a private errand of inquiry, I
doubted already if this would ever come to anything. There
could be few ex-R.N.V.R. officers who would care to ask a Vice-
Admiral, across his own lunch-table: 'Did you, or did you not,
check with the Admiralty to see if I had been lying about my
wartime naval career?'

Yet, having still a few naval friends left in conveniently sensitive places, I knew that this was true. I knew also that my
modest claims had been endorsed as 'Substantially correct'
(what bloody impudence! They were *absolutely* correct, down to
the last humble syllable); and I wondered if the subject would
come up for an airing in lunch-time conversation.

It did so, at one point, and it was brought to light by my
hostess, Lady Packer, when she turned to me and said, with
that sweetly poisonous innocence which only women swathed
in gold braid could get away with, that all this *Cruel Sea* publicity
had been awfully good for the Navy. I really must have made
the very *most* of my time in the Admiralty Information
Department.

I could tell by the confederate smiles and glances from the
staff officers among the other guests that they knew what this
was all about, and that the C.-in-C.'s wife was judged to have
struck home with her first broadside.

Yet Lady Packer was not really like that at all. Nor was the
Navy. This was a curious peacetime backlash to the old days,
when *they* were the only pros, and *we* were the rats and mice of
the service. But there was something here even more curious,
and perhaps more disgusting: the fact that, faced with a real
Admiral, of formidable presence, at the head of the table, and a
ring of watchful sycophants round him, I was once more sub-
missive, still saluting all over.

I returned my hostess an evasive answer. Not even that. I

simply agreed. But at the same time I was very glad indeed that
I had not stayed on in the Navy.

Perhaps, also, this reluctance to engage had something to do
with Lady Packer herself who, though she had to go through
the traditional motions, and might even be enjoying them, was
not in fact the bullying old battle-axe which her role normally
demanded. She was *soignée*, and lively, and unexpectedly warm.
She was also a writer—the salt of the earth as well as the salt of
the sea.*

Never mind, I thought, relapsing into the unco-operative
silence which was the nearest I would ever come to mutiny,
even in face of such privileged insolence. Never mind: I had been
captain of a frigate when these little tight-arsed courtiers were
still wetting their beds. . . . Afterwards I went down to the
harbour to look at the ships; and there, the first man I met was
a tall, rake-thin commander just stepping ashore from his
gleaming motorboat, handled alongside like a jet-propelled
cork.

The commander, I saw at the second astonished glance, was
one sailor who did *not* think of me as the perennial tit marked
'Press' on the wardroom wall. It was my old captain from
Guillemot, Sam Lombard-Hobson.

He was now, it seemed, the captain of *Jutland*, one of those
whopping great destroyers attendant on the carriers. He was
also, thank God, still a firm friend.

'Come round to Cape Town with us,' he said immediately,
when the first surprised greetings (though sailors were never
really surprised at such turns of fate) were over. 'We're acting
as close escort to *Vengeance*. You can stand the middle watch.'
He went even further. 'You can have bacon and banana fritters
for breakfast!'

'Good God!'

But I was in the mood to say Yes. Who, after 930 miles in
the Alfa, and some snide comments from an Admiral's lady,

---

* As Joy Packer, she had already published *Pack and Follow* and *Grey Mistress*
with lots of fiction still to come.

could say No to the promise of sea-time again, in a destroyer like *Jutland* or *Agincourt* lying just across the bay? . . . However, I had my own time-table, like any other conscientious wage-slave.

'When are you due in Cape Town?'

'At six o'clock tomorrow morning. We sail at midnight tonight. Well, *we're* not due in Cape Town. The carriers are, but we're coming back here for night exercises. This old boy is very hot.' 'This old boy' was Admiral Packer, at whose table I had been drooping so despondently, twenty minutes earlier. 'But we can transfer you to *Vengeance*, just off Cape Town.'

'How? By helicopter? I've never been in one.'

'Well—*no*. That would cost rather too much money.' He sighed. 'This is *peace-time*. Do you realize that these days we're not even allowed to ring full ahead without giving our reasons in writing? In triplicate? No, we'll *transfer* you. We'll rig a bosun's chair and a couple of pulleys, and haul you across. Block-and-tackle job—about fifty sailors at each end.' There was now such a gleam in his eye that this could well have been something he had wanted to do ever since 1942. 'It'll be like oiling at sea. But at twenty knots. And it'll be a very good exercise for my first lieutenant. He's never done it before.'

The prospect was irresistible, for all sorts of reasons.

I was delighted to see Sam again; naturally he had a superb ship, run as every destroyer should be; and although our night's voyage was only fifty miles, with what he called some fiddling about in the middle (changing from one screening pattern to another, on the curt order 'Execute!') it was the best night which had come my way for a long time. Even as a passenger, I was proud to be one of *Jutland*'s ship's company.

We dined in some state in the wardroom, with an assembly of sixteen officers many of whom, like policemen, seemed to have hardly finished with their schooldays. Sam and I revelled in utterly boring reminiscence. But there was, I thought a surprised, even respectful interest round the table when I told them of my very first night as their captain's first lieutenant; how we had

stalked and sunk a German E-boat off Lowestoft: how
spirited and swift an action it had been—there was I, in fact,
surrounded by tracer bullets as I stood on the quarterdeck: and
how one of those tracers had surged out of the darkness and
whistled between my legs—the nearest I had ever been to utter
character-assassination.

Perhaps it was just as well that such re-encounters did not
happen too often; otherwise, one would be stuck in an incurable,
life-time groove of reminiscence, with one's listeners (what
listeners?) equally stuck, suspended there for ever like yawns
in aspic.

At midnight, after the customary short nap allowed to middle-
watchers, I went up to the bridge to enjoy our passage at close
quarters.

It was a velvet night, an African night; as we moved out of
False Bay in line ahead, dipping our fore-foot into the last few
miles of the Indian Ocean before it merged into the broad
South Atlantic, that burnt smell of Africa wafting across from
the Cape Flats was all round us, just as it once had been at the
far other end of this colossal continent, in the Straits of Gibraltar
between Tarifa and Tangier.

We set course southwards for the true Cape of Good Hope,
with the carrier *Vengeance* as huge as Africa itself against the
yellow moon.

Even after half an hour on *Jutland*'s bridge, I was very glad
I was only a passenger. She would have been too much for me
altogether. The bridge and the two decks below it were
crammed with complex electronic equipment I would never
understand; within a short spell of ten years, the gadgetry
involved in running a ship like this had gone beyond bafflement
into total mystery.

The best training any modern R.N. captain could have would
have been a degree in applied science, and after that, lots of
reading and plenty of luck.

Sam Lombard-Hobson himself confirmed one aspect of this,
when he handed his ship over to the Officer-of-the-watch as soon

as we were clear of complications, and stayed to gossip, leaning on the wing of the bridge.

'The trouble is, I'm hardly ever up here,' he said 'We never get any fresh air. We hardly even see the sea. If there's anything at all interesting going on, the captain has to be down in the plotting room—it's armour-plated all round—watching a lot of knobs and dials, talking into the intercom. You'll see when we start those screening manoeuvres. There won't be any real ships round me. Just a lot of damn fluorescent blobs on the plot.'

'She's still a wonderful ship,' I said.

'Oh yes. But I'd rather smell the sea.' He nodded towards the vast blur which was *Vengeance.* The night was so still that we could hear the thresh of her bow-wave. 'I'd rather see her up-moon, and *know* I was in station. It isn't any fun the new way. When we're at action stations, there's just one sub-lieutenant left up here. He's to tell me if it's raining Do you remember——'

Thus the night, with a calm sea stretching back to India and forward to Cape Horn, and south to Antarctica, with a mug of cocoa as thick as prep-school porridge when the breeze turned cold. Thus our slow gentle passage round the southern Horn of Africa, and up towards the great iron magnet of Table Mountain. Thus the dawn off Three Anchor Bay. But then it was my turn for all that fun and fresh air, which the captain never had.

I stood on the fo'c'sle-head, surrounded by interested spectators, all seeming to wear the kind of expression one sees when the dare-devil high wire act—'One hundred feet above the arena!—NO safety net!'—is announced with a roll of muffled drums, and watched as we surged alongside *Vengeance.*

A heaving-line went across, and then the first wire, and then a complicated festoon of other wires, which gradually took shape like the top half of a spider's web. I hoped it would prove the strongest spider's web in the world. During long convoys, we used to send fuel pipes across to our supply tanker with this sort of rig. But *people?*

Then, when all was ready, I stepped into a kind of waist-high canvas bucket, wearing a life-jacket, carrying my little brief-case. . . . Between the two ships, keeping pace side by side, the water foamed and boiled; it was twenty feet below *Jutland's* deck, then receding to a forty-foot drop at the other end.

If I had not known that Commander Lombard-Hobson was running this lot, I would have been worried. As it was, it all happened so quickly that I had no time to be scared until I was safe at the other end.

Half the ship's company was now tailing on to various ropes, taking the strain as the bosun's chair rose and fell. I began to move—out from the safety of the deck, into the empty air and a void of swirling water below. Sam, using the loud-hailer from the bridge, called out: 'Good luck, Number One!'—one of the stranger good-byes of my life. Then the heaving and hauling started, and I sped across.

The chair sagged horribly, to within ten feet of the surface, in the middle; a hundred jokes about the cruel sea came to mind as the surging water seemed to be licking at my feet; then I rose up and up in a great curving loop and into a square black hole in the middle of the mountain. The support of the bosun's chair fell away like dropping trousers (rather too appropriate an analogy) and I stepped out onto a blessedly solid iron deck, to be greeted by a midshipman who saluted and said: 'Sir, my father met you in the war.'

After that it was something of an anti-climax. Carriers were too big to be interesting; if one wanted to live like that, a large second-class hotel was better. But breakfast was superior, if fritterless; Table Bay ennobled by a streaky sunrise was as magnificent as ever; and if one had to make a short swift journey from a ship at anchor to the safety of dry land, then an Admiral's barge with its stylized boat-hook ballet at either end was *the* way to travel.

I was happy in love, happy indeed, as who could fail to be when securely installed with a rarely beautiful girl who could also speak, if not with the tongue of angels, then at least with the voice of close command and the barb of wit.

I was also getting away with murder, always a pleasing accomplishment: our nest, even in Johannesburg, had some notoriety, and just down the road in Pretoria was the High Commissioner's Office—not blind, not deaf, not at all inclined to be careless about things like this.

By now I had told them about the coming divorce, but the other subject was never raised—which was astonishing since I was now 'established' and really subject to the whip. Perhaps it was thought that next time round I would settle down into the cosy domesticity—but legal, please—which was the only acceptable norm. Perhaps I was being allowed to be half a civil servant —one wife, two children, one dog, one car—and half a writer— rogue, vagabond, adulterer, swine. Perhaps—I could not even guess.

Meanwhile, and certainly, I was as faithful as any civil servant who wore his marital blinkers from dawn till dusk and dawn again. Normally, the sudden avalanche of money would have meant, at least, that I would be looking round for a better class of woman, and getting it. Now, when it had happened, there was no such ambition.

I was only seriously tempted once, on an ill-humoured morning when a domestic row about something—feeding the dogs, or queers for breakfast, or that bloody silly thing I had said to Bridget Oppenheimer's mother the night before—had sent me to work in a mood to rebel.

There was a very good-looking girl in that town, whose husband had been removed from the scene, and who was thought to be having a fling with a rich if dim young bull from the American Embassy, now known to be holidaying in Switzerland. (My personal information service was just as good as the official one.)

On that morning I was out at Palmietfontein Airport, waiting for the Khartoum plane and another King's Messenger, when the girl arrived, outward bound. She was travelling in considerable

style; the fur coat carried by the chauffeur must alone have
cost enough to set up a rival zoo, and this ravishing creature,
its prospective filling, also looked like a million dollars, from
all the angles freely available.

We both had ten minutes to spare, and we spent them in a
secluded corner of the lounge, with a little mingling of eyes, a
little folding of the hands. She was going to Zürich, presumably
to rendezvous with her American swain and really let him get at
the goodies. But his position, I realized, was still precarious.
The local temperature was rising sharply, within a very few
moments of our meeting.

'Why don't you come along?' she asked me suddenly. 'Meet
me there. It'll be fabulous!'

It was not impossible. Nothing was impossible in those days.
And I was damned sure that it would be fabulous. But it still
didn't make much sense, according to the current form-sheet.

'I thought you were fixed up already,' I said.

'Well—you know.'

Indeed, I did know. It was always a prime mistake to leave
a girl like this loose in Johannesburg, even for twenty-four
hours. That American dip must be nuts. . . . Her alarmingly
beautiful eyes, as deep as the cleavage, as soft as the promised
pillow, told me that the options, like everything else, were still
wide open. (Yes, Virginia, I was an appetizing old codger in
those days, with cash in the bank.) Then the King's Messenger
manifested himself at my side, in a flurry of sealed mail-bags
and rather a bad temper.

He was one of the ones who expected to have his shoes
cleaned, preferably with real spit, as soon as he stepped off the
plane. The luscious moment ebbed, and passed away for ever.

'Sorry,' I said to the girl. 'But have fun.'

'Well, any time.'

Yet I hadn't really wanted to, row at home or no row: only
for a single moment of rebellion, the mood of revenge for not
being loved every minute of the day: only through a casual
vision of those come-on legs waiting for me by the Zürich

lake-side: only when this gorgeous young woman, whom I had once vaguely had in my sights (but she would have been so expensive), suddenly offered free delivery: only in the sunshine of Johannesburg, only at this nutty altitude when the thing you did next was the thing you wanted to, no more and never less, and it was just bad luck, hard cheese, tough tits on the loser.

But in fact, I was securely bound already, give or take an emotional bashing now and then, and ecstatically content with my servitude. Indeed, I knew that I was bound for ever, or until something awful happened. *La Belle Dame sans Merci* had me in thrall.

It might have been a puzzle what to write next, and God knows there was plenty of advice, from interested, disinterested, and plainly malevolent bystanders, to whom the spectacle of a 'best-selling author', that abominably lucky fellow who could not possibly have more than one book in his head, falling flat on his face with its successor, would be a private and public delight.

But I had made up my mind already; this was *my* country, right or wrong, and no bright boy-critic with his little quill dipped in vinegar would ever discourage me. I had a conviction that I was going to be slaughtered anyway, whatever I wrote; the philosophy of 'Build them up, let them stand, tear them down' was as deeply ingrained in literature as it was in the construction business.

If I stayed with the sea, I would be 'repeating the formula'; if I tried something different, then I should have stayed with the sea, which was all I was fit for.

In any case I did not want to be typed as a sea-writer, like C. S. Forester or even Conrad; *Son of the Cruel Sea* might have been wildly profitable, but it would also have been an ignoble exercise in cashing-in. I had all sorts of other ideas. The only thing to do was to write exactly what I wanted, and take the consequences, whether it meant another explosion or a dull thud; a collective back-slap, or a dubious shaking of the head, or a lethal shot of poison in the cup.

I had one idea in particular which appealed to me. Helen
Keller, the blind, deaf-and-dumb, near-genius of communication, had recently toured South Africa, on a fund-raising
expedition which was as moving as it was successful.

On a certain savage morning, reading about her triumphant
progress, I was struck with the thought of how awful it would be,
how vile, how unbelievably corrupt, if Helen Keller or someone
like her were in fact a crook, or was being exploited by crooks;
if she was not blind at all, nor deaf, nor dumb, but simply a con-
summate actress, manipulated by criminal conspirators for
their own ends.

The idea of course was as far from the true Helen Keller
story as it could possibly be. But it was now my story, the one
I wanted to write. To celebrate conception, I invested in a new
typewriter, giving the old one—a veteran of thirteen years,
bought in the honest old days of 1938 when typewriters were
built to last, like cars or light-bulbs—to one of the waiters at
the Waverley Hotel.

He said endearingly: 'You write a book—now I write a book!'
and we both settled down to it. Mine was published two years
later, in 1953, as *The Story of Esther Costello.**

Most curiously, it was banned in South Africa, at the instance of a bloody-minded old clergyman who had been instrumental in bringing Helen Keller to the country on her fund-
raising tour. He now chose to believe that the book referred to
her, and promptly went into action. By way of a first shot, he
wrote me a furious letter which contained the strange phrase:
'If, during Miss Helen Keller's visit, you did notice anything
unusual, I am sure there is an innocent explanation.'

I was absolutely sure already. But when I told him so, and
added that in fact I had never met, heard, nor seen Miss Keller,
even at a distance, he called me, with Christian resolution, a liar.

Running the Health Foundation, which was making strong

* Cassell and Alfred Knopf, 1953; Pocket Books, 1955; Corgi Books, 1956;
Romulus and Columbia Pictures, 1957; Pan Books, 1966.

progress, and (in a secondary sort of way) running the Information Office, were now the only gifts to God. They were the
substitutes for the social conscience which had, in this exotic
climate, dried to a very modest trickle of endeavour.

Politically, South Africa was still enormously exciting; the
tensions and the pressures were mounting all the time. But who
could really grow enthusiastic about the minor cross-currents of
in-fighting which were all that showed above the surface?—the
jokes about block-headed Van der Merwe, the other jokes about
Hoggenheimer and Lord Money-Bags, the vicious charge and
counter-charge, the hopes pinned on a split in the Nationalist
Party which had been threatening to bring them to utter ruin
since 1910?

Who could do anything about the real tragedy, the other
nine-tenths of the racial iceberg? It was a hard fact of life that
the Nats were now installed in the driver's seat for ever, and
that with their generous permission the South African police
were assembling a formidable armoury of power, bristling with
legal weapons and a very tough mood to match.

All one could do was talk about it, which was the interminable rule, because political argument was a never-ending South
African hobby. But it was never much more than idle *fainéant*
gossip: it was talk tailored to those easy-going Sunday mornings, or for dinner parties, or the lavish three-hour lunches at
the Country Club: talk between the dances at the Charity Balls
which were held to raise funds for the Opposition United Party,
which would never get in again until (as earthy Mr Khrushchev
once phrased it) shrimps began to sing.

I no longer wanted to go much beyond this—and had not
Father Trevor Huddleston, that stern upholder of everything
(including his own *corps d'élite*, the Community of the Resurrection), criticized me publicly for my 'pagan morality'? Occasionally I had a little social fun myself by denouncing the cushioned
life which was so much to my taste; by telling my hostess,
between sips of champagne, that South African women were too
rich, too lazy, and too useless altogether.

Just so had Mr John Strachey, the fiercely radical ex-Minister of Food and ex-Secretary of State for War, author also of *The Coming Struggle for Power*, been accustomed to ravage the lecture circuits across the length and breadth of America by lambasting his audience, mostly female and richly furred: making their flesh creep deliciously as he assured them that they all belonged to a doomed, decaying society, that they were no more than the froth on the surface of a boiling brew of hatred and injustice, and that the communists would get them one day, and pretty soon at that!

Shivering with delight, they always gave him an ovation. After all, Mr Strachey had been at Eton. He *must* know.

My own denunciations were less popular. Some of the best late-night rows used to take place at a favourite night-club on Commissioner Street, where Red Webber our Irish host dished out an irresistible combination of high-power charm, iron control, and Polish eggs, and an embryonic Eve Boswell was trying out her vocal wings.

But here, politics seemed ever more unreal: as unreal, in their own peculiar way, as the sign which said: 'Fire Escape. No Exit.' If we were also part of a decaying, doomed society, then it was better to lie back and enjoy it, letting the Nats take the strain, incur all the odium and abuse, and (incidentally) make sure that our decline and fall was slow, affluent, and pleasurable.

Turning one's back on such arid strife, it was more fun to swop the latest gossip, and spice it with a little extra malice; to exchange the trash of politics for a higher quality of rubbish. It was more fun to watch the lovers coming in, rather too soon after making love, their faces still wearing that un-secret, silly joy which was a dead give-away; or, by contrast, to speculate on the relationship of a well-known show-off couple, which spiteful commentators maintained was platonic.

It was more fun to sit in the half-dark, and listen to the dreamy music, and talk to Red Webber himself, that charming and trustful man, and hear what action he took when a cheque persistently bounced (Stage 1, a polite letter; Stage 2, a rude letter; Stage 3, a social call; Stage 4—'But let's not spoil a merry evening,' he would finish, with a grin).

It was more fun to watch Mrs X, the brilliant society hostess with the enamelled face and hay-cart hair, charming her assembled guests at the table opposite, her laughter infectious as dysentery. It was more fun to hear someone say: 'Eleven children?—he must have got his needle stuck!' or someone else propounding a currently popular riddle: 'What is eight inches long, hard as steel, and transfixed by an arrow?' (Answer: Custer's last stand.)

It was more fun to gossip about the energetic performer who from time to time was cautioned by her doctor: 'You should refrain from sexual intercourse with your husband.' Of course, we all knew that she couldn't stand her husband, so *that* was all right.

It was more fun to watch Freddie de Guingand dancing like a Major-General, and Joonie-Woonie Carbery not; to be drawn by a screeching uproar from one of the darker corners of Fed Webber's domain, and to hear him murmur: 'The queers are restless tonight' before strolling across to deal with it; even to hear one of my future sisters-in-law, staunchly Catholic, say of some mishap: 'It's G.P.F.!' which stood, in such circles, for God's Pointing Finger.

It was more fun to gossip about a busy local hairdresser, baptized Larry Skikne, who had made quite a name for himself in South Africa's semi-amateur theatre before taking off, as Laurence Harvey, for England, all points west, and a permanent wave of success.

It was more fun to hear how Jack Hyman had thrown a visiting English noblewoman into total disarray. She was being very gracious about our Game Reserve. But had she visited it? 'Not yet!' she answered, in that deep, contralto, *fête*-opening voice. 'It is a pleasure to come!'

Jack Hyman had clapped his hands together in girlish rapture. '*Isn't* it!'

It was more fun.

In the shadow of Christmas 1951 we made a radio version
of *The Cruel Sea* for Springbok Radio, the commercial step-child
of the South African Broadcasting Corporation, and it was the
hardest piece of sustained work which had come my way for
a long time.

A girl on the Johannesburg *Star* named Margot Bryant—in
unlikely fact, the Women's Editor—produced the script, and a
very good one too; I did the narration myself—introduction,
linking material in the middle, and the sad or exciting bits at the
end; and we taped twenty-six half-hour episodes in twenty-
nine days, rehearsal, sound effects, 200 speaking parts, and all.
We finished with a gasp of triumph on Christmas Eve.

'Taped' is the wrong word to use, and that was part of the
trouble; for some reason connected with the durability of the
material, it could not be taped, but had to be cut directly onto
a master record. For some *other* reason, whenever we made any
sort of mistake, we had to go back to the beginning again.
Apparently there was no way of keeping in the good part, and
picking up again in the middle.

If anyone fluffed his lines on the 26th minute of the recording
—as I did on one ghastly occasion in Episode 22, by which time
we were all getting thoroughly snappish and exhausted—then
Cedric Messina, our talented, infinitely patient producer, said
'I'm sorry, chaps', and we all went back again to the introductory music, the seagulls, the asdic pings, and the sound of
salt water smashing down onto an iron deck, which marked our
fade-in.

Cedric Messina, whose later work with the B.B.C. included
some masterly productions of Verdi and Puccini operas, was a
tower of strength. The whole rather expensive enterprise was
sponsored by the firm of C. C. Wakefield ('Castrol, the
Masterpiece in Oils!') and 'oil on the cruel waters' became a
good gossip-writer's quip.

There was one actor who was outstanding: an S.A.B.C. newsreader and panel moderator called Henry Howell. He was small, bald, and mild; he played the part of Commander Ericson, the 'hero'—large, fully coiffed, and about as mild as Nelson's Blood.

A long listening career provides many examples—almost the whole cast of *The Archers* is a case in point—of actors who don't look anything like the part, but who do sound like it, down to the last semi-quaver. Henry Howell was one, and a real anchor man too.

In the shadow of Christmas I read one absolutely superb novel, *The Case of Mr Crump* by Ludwig Lewisohn, an account of a horrific, murderous marriage which did indeed end in murder. In the shadow of Christmas, I bought myself a small but sensational car, a two-seater coupé Jaguar XK 120, of palest green like shimmering emeralds, which superseded all other cars in my adoration.

Naturally we gave a reception for it, on a rather special Sunday morning. Twelve strong men heated it up and carried it across flower beds, round trees, and onto the lawn in front of the *stoep*, where, with an orchid Scotch-taped to its radiator, it made a glamorous show-piece.

Diamonds and rubies completed the rest of the Christmas shopping.

On New Year's Eve we attended the Party of the Year, a recurrent fancy-dress festival given by a generous man called Eric Gallo. Before very long, I decided, I would be giving the party of the year.

Still in the shadow of the new year, I cast the accounts for the sensational old one.

In the first five months of its wild life, the book had sold close to half a million copies (80,000 in America, where it had notched up fifteen printings and twenty-two weeks in the best-seller list, though perennially second to *The Caine Mutiny*; a huge chunk from the Book-of-the-Month Club; and past the 200,000 mark from Cassell's, where the poor struggling fellows still could not print it fast enough).

The sixteenth translation had just been sold to faraway Iceland, though I was still looking and lusting for an Afrikaans version. I asked Uys Krige if he would like to undertake this. The answer was No. I offered him a flat £1,000 for the job. The answer was still No. (Proud poets are the best.) Then a bi-lingual Nationalist M.P. who must be anonymous volunteered to take on the assignment, if the action could be transferred to the South Atlantic, with 'lots of good Afrikaner names', and based on Cape Town instead of Liverpool. The answer was No.*

I was informed that I would be awarded the Heinemann Prize for Literature, with a Fellowship of the Royal Society of Literature to add to the accolade.

My account book, now a firm second-favourite in the library, showed that I had made £15,000 that year—for me, an unheard-of total. It was to jump to £58,000 in 1952, but by that time it was only money.

---

* This had a parallel in an early German offer to publish, if 'tendentious' references to U-boats were deleted. I did not fancy quite such a slim volume as this.

THE YEAR OF THE STUPID OX
(1956)

FORTY-SIX

1.

There is at least one sizeable chunk of Holy Writ which any alert sub-editor, looking for circulation, would have excised with quick, flashing strokes of his blue pencil. It is the 'Begat' bit, which starts: 'And Cush begat Nimrod: he begar to be mighty upon the earth. And Misraim begat Ludim, and Anamim, and Lehabim, and Naphtuhim. And Pathrusim, and Casluhim (of whom came the Philistines), and Caphthorim. And Canaan begat Sion, his first-born, and Heth.'

It continues thus for nine chapters, 397 verses, and 1,125 named characters, and ends, uncounted generations later, with unquenchable energy:

'And Azel begat six sons, whose names are these: Azrikam, Bocheru, and Ishmael, and Sheariah, and Obadiah, and Hanan; these were the sons of Azel.'

I was reminded of this generative marathon by a letter from Mr F. B. Wickwire, of the legal firm of MacInnes, Wilson, & Hallett (Halifax, Nova Scotia, six partners). Mr Wickwire is the latest, though probably not the last, in my own Begat Series, which started in the long, long ago with Mr Duncan Mactavish, Q.C., of Gowling, Mactavish, Osborne, & Henderson Ottawa, fifteen partners).

Duncan Mactavish (Chairman of the Canadian Liberal Party, later a Senator, and always a good friend, even though on the opposite side of the marital fence, until his death), begat John Mirsky, Q.C., of Mirsky, Soloway, Assaly, & Houston (Ottawa, nine partners).

John Mirsky, before he was killed in a car crash, begat John Brooke, Q.C., of McCarthy & McCarthy (Toronto, thirty-three partners and associates).

John Brooke, on becoming a judge, begat J. W. Swackhamer, Q.C., of Fasken, Calvin, MacKenzie, Williston, & Swackhamer (Toronto, twenty-two partners).

J. W. Swackhamer, on a change of residence, begat Mr Wickwire of Halifax, N.S.

Mr Wickwire, heir to this formidable line of succession, which has been keeping me under inexorable scrutiny and well-tempered pressure for the past thirteen years, recently begat me a letter.

In it, after a reminder, in the customary sharp terms, of some unpaid alimony (the previous nine years' total payment of $177,230 had still proved insufficient to ward off penury), I was requested, in spite of my 'desire to be remembered by posterity', to leave out any reference to my second wife in the next volume of my autobiography.

Ah, posterity . . . It will not be easy. Already posterity seems to be crying out for the facts, more stridently even than that spectral legal firm—Gold, Frankincense, & More!—which still looms as the eternal last enemy, the last Begat. But I will try. Indeed, I try now.

Yet that injunction of 1967, being odd and impudent, would have found itself thoroughly at home with 1956, which must now be down-graded to the realm of chaos: to the *chiaroscuro*— —the light and shade—of true lunacy, of a string of scenes lit by flashes of foolish revealing glare, and then darkened again by the drop-curtain of bad judgement, bad behaviour, bad hopes and bad luck.

1956 must be branded, also, with the conviction that no one I have ever known, nor read about, nor imagined, ever gave or took his half-share in such squalor of spirit, such waste of work and love, such murderous abrasion of one person by another, such a sad longing for peace, or such a clownish butchery of achievement, as was to bring me to the pole-axe in the Year of the Stupid Ox.

On New Year's morning I woke up in the Royal Victoria Hospital in Montreal, and it was pure, unalloyed bliss.

I could safely claim to be a little ill. I had bronchitis, cr—to stretch a point—bronchial pneumonia, or pneumonitis, or a persistent hacking cough which, if used carelessly, could tear a trifle at the lungs.

Laying the groundwork of my duplicity at an appropriate moment, Christmas Eve, I had hacked away like Camille, like Mimi in *La Bohème*, like Robert Louis Stevenson, like Chopin under the baleful gaze of George Sand.

But in fact the symptoms were genuine enough, or excuse enough, for not venturing outside into the 10° below zero weather, which now ruled two thousand miles of eastern Canada, from St John's, Newfoundland, to the shores of Lake Superior. They were good enough for the fateful jargon word, 'Hospitalization'. They were good enough for my confederate doctor.

When I had demonstrated to him, on ample evidence, that I had an important book to finish and that I would never finish it at home, he had dispatched me to Montreal for a 'complete check-up', which in Canada could mean anything from a loaf in bed to the terminal diagnosis of cancer of the rectum.

I would be staying there for three weeks, my medical adviser assured me, or even a little longer if a little longer would suit my peculiar, slightly pathetic circumstances. After that I had better recuperate, preferably in the Caribbean.

It was true that they had drained my sinuses, a painful and rather disgusting operation, and assembled a small library of X-ray photographs, and committed some rude acts with a barium enema. But then they left me alone. Everyone left me alone. The cracking cold outside, the crisp, glistening snow slopes below the hospital walls, the bare frozen trees through which one could see all the way down to Montreal harbour itself (the very road was called *Côte des Neiges*) were all deeply attractive, especially if viewed through double-glazed windows, buttressed by seventy degrees of steam heat and a permanent 'No Visitors' sign affixed to the door of my room.

Thus warmed and protected, in glorious isolation, in blessed, tranquil peace, waking and sleeping only with my typewriter, I finished, at a miraculously fast clip, the last 15,000 words of an 840-page manuscript called *The Tribe That Lost Its Head.*

The book, after three years' sweat, was already four months overdue, and this was the only way left to me; and if I had to lie and simulate and insist and plead, and cough up half my lungs in tune with high C, in order to carve a path towards it, then that was the only way also.

Thus did the poison of deceit infect the new year, from its first tender moment. Thus, with an easy, triumphant mind, did I think less than nothing of such subterfuges. Thus did I close the book at last, and the typewriter, and uncurl my toes, and declare that I was ready to leave.

On a happily appointed day, Angus, butler and mainstay of our household, flew down from Ottawa to bring me some different clothes and to pack for me. I distributed half a dozen books to half a dozen angelic nurses. A hired Cadillac waited upon the halting invalid at the hospital front door. Down town, I cashed a cheque for $5,000 and drove to Dorval Airport, pausing on the way to inspect summer's apple-of-my-eye, the Dragon yacht *Valhalla*, now tarpaulined under two feet of snow at the Royal St Lawrence Yacht Club.

Then I slid swiftly southwards, first to New York on literary business and then to Barbados, for the pleasure, the gigantic relief, of idleness in the sun.

The new, hard-won manuscript flew with me, to be delivered to my new, hard-won publisher, Thayer Hobson of Morrow's.

Splendid elements of farce had attended a recent break with Alfred Knopf.

It had started three years earlier with the book I had been determined to write, as a successor to *The Cruel Sea*, for no other reason than that I thought it was a good story, and I felt like doing it: the slightly ill-fated, murderously reviewed, highly enjoyable (for me) novel, *The Story of Esther Costello.*

Alfred Knopf had disliked *Esther Costello* on sight, very heartily indeed, and the fact had been communicated to me, together with some fatherly advice which did not at all suit a supremely buoyant mood. I decided that I did not want another father-figure in my life, on Madison Avenue or anywhere else. My own father, God bless him, was still alive at eighty-one. Alfred was only sixty. And, come hell or high water, *Esther* was going to be my next book, whoever was its publisher. I made that point as strongly as I could.

Proofs and the usual pre-publication drill went ahead, without further comment. Then someone in the Knopf office was fool enough to submit the book to Helen Keller, presumably to find out if she had any objections to it.

No one told me a word about this ridiculous tactic, which clearly betrayed nervousness and thus gave half the game away before we even started, and I was furious when I heard of it. Sabotage! . . . I was still furious when Helen Keller replied, sensibly and accurately, that the book seemed to have nothing whatever to do with her.

Esther Costello, as written, was then published by Knopf, with such a muted fanfare, such minimal enthusiasm, that it might have been an anonymous pamphlet on the merits of bi-metallism, or that volume which once won a *New Statesman* competition as the title least likely to attract: *How To Ride a Tricycle.*

The Knopf production flopped dismally; a pair of lead water-wings would have been air-borne by comparison. It flopped critically, which I had been expecting, and financially, which I had not. It sold, in America, a net total of 11,000 copies, which in the context of its predecessor was less than peanuts—it was the very *shells* of peanuts, trodden down into the cinema floor.

It was also, in a wider context, a gross reversal of the form. *Esther* did very well in England. It had sold twelve translations. It was going to be filmed. What had happened to it in America? And why?

Hell hath no fury like an author thus fouled-up. If Knopf's didn't believe in the book, they shouldn't have published it. If they did believe, they should have gone to town on it. I felt betrayed, like any decked-out bride left at the church door. But there was another, more weighty item. This bride was pregnant as well.

Already I had another book in the works, a winner, a darling child, and I was absolutely determined that Knopf's would never get their slack hands on it. Damn it, they didn't deserve *The Tribe*! . . . It was much too precious for such prudent mice as these.

The fact that Alfred was possibly right, and myself probably wrong, about *Esther Costello*, only made my resolve the more implacable.

Yet there was a snag here, a familiar snag, a snag with hammer and tongs, teeth and clause. Knopf's still had an option on my next book. They still had the cast-iron right, under contract, to publish the next work of fiction after *Esther Costello*. Even if we were grappling each other by the throat, the right remained.

Baulked, bewildered, and still adamant, I took my problem, as usual, to Willis Wing.

As befitted a man whose integrity was always apparent, even across four hundred miles of New York telephone line, Willis was judicious, unruffled, and supremely fair.

When I told him (as he had guessed already) that I wanted to change publishers, and went on to explain why, he swung me back to the right point of departure.

'How's *The Tribe* coming along?'

'Oh, very well.' This was far from true. There were already days, many days, when I did not think the book would ever be finished. But that didn't affect what I had in mind. 'I'm about half-way through.'

'Still?' But he did not waste time on further comment. 'When will it be ready, then?'

'Well—probably by the Christmas after this one.'

'Christmas *1955*? That's more than a year ahead. You could still change your mind about all this.'

'No.'

'Don't forget, Alfred did do very well for you with *The Cruel Sea.*'

'I know that.' It was something which could never be in doubt. 'But he didn't do so well with *Esther*, did he? Across the humming wires, I could almost *see* Willis' express on, which told me that *Esther Costello* was not *The Cruel Sea*, nor had I meant it to be, and we both recognized the fact. 'It's no good, Willis. I know all the arguments. But I don't want him to have the next one.'

'Very well.' He became an agent again, instead of a wary critic. 'It's your decision. . . . Let's go on to stage two.'

Stage Two, presently put into operation, was to make a formal request to Knopf's that they should drop their option on my next book, and that our contract should then be cancelled, without my having to submit a new manuscript. Not surprisingly, not even unfairly, this was turned down flat.

Stage Three was an exploratory visit to Ottawa by an entirely new character, Thayer Hobson, chairman and boss of William Morrow and its fellow company William Sloane Associates.

Morrow's was the firm I had already picked, tentatively, after some wide-ranging advice from Willis Wing, as my next publisher. They had a good list. More important, it was my sort of list, with a solid basis of books which sold well, and were not thought to be too awful on that account of authors who were popular, yet not despised because of it. Among these were Laurens van der Post, Nevil Shute, Ernest Gann, St John Ervine, Laurie Lee, and (for bulk supplies) Erle Stanley Gardner. Morrow's would suit me fine.

They were also 'very nice people', Willis assured me. Certainly the man who now turned up in Ottawa was a very nice man indeed.

Thayer Hobson was then fifty-seven: a tall spare wiry transplant from Denver, Colorado, obviously capable, an undoubted charmer who, like Willis himself, could combine this with the tough fibre needed to make effective headway in the iron jungle of New York City.

He was a marrying man, as I was; his second wife later married Alger Hiss; and his third essay had been with Laura Z.

13

Hobson, the novelist whose *Gentleman's Agreement* gave an almost definitive account of anti-semitism in North America, from its polite social exclusion to the grosser aspects of the snide, Jew-baiting sneer: a story which, translated into a film with Gregory Peck, had doubled its impact as an interior view of racial obscenity.

Thayer's approach to me, a possible new author for his stable, was correct yet perceptive. He was not poaching. He admired Alfred Knopf very much—and he had never yet met a man in the publishing world who did not. But he had heard from Willis Wing that I wanted to make a change, and I would not be the first nor the ten thousandth author who felt that way and wanted to do something about it.

But when, over a companionable drink at the Rideau Club, with a view of the nearby Parliament Building to remind us of the eternal force of law, we came to 'doing something about it', the basic snag was in the forefront of both our minds. It was that unbreakable option.

We walked round this time and time again, like fellow-gardeners wondering whether a certain tree would live or die— or could be made to live, or made to die.

But in the event, there was only one suggestion which had any substance at all. I had to write for a living. I could not stop writing, and sulk. Alfred Knopf had a firm clinch on the next manuscript. Therefore . . .

'You'll just have to write another book,' Thayer Hobson said finally. 'Before *The Tribe* is ready to be published. It needn't be too wonderful. Just a book. Eighty thousand words, or whatever it is. But it will be the option book. Alfred can publish it, or not publish it, whichever he likes. Either way, that completes your contract, and then you're free to offer *The Tribe* anywhere you choose.'

'But I can't possibly write another book!' I objected, scandalized for all sorts of reasons. 'I'm having the damnedest time with this one as it is. I can't break off now. Anyway I haven't got a suitable idea for another one.'

'There are lots of ideas,' said Thayer. 'I can always give you an *idea*.'

'But how do I write it?'

'Take a month off.'

I looked at him across my glass. He was quite serious. 'I don't write books in a month. You wouldn't want an author who could.'

'I want an author,' he said. 'You. I'll let you have whatever help I can.'

'I still don't think it's possible.' The idea of putting aside *The Tribe*, which really was giving me tremendous trouble already, and writing another whole novel, however lightweight, was so appalling that I could hardly bear to consider it. It was also an immoral project, when measured by the scale of virtues still persisting. Whatever the pressures, if contracts had to be cancelled it should be by more fragrant methods than these. 'We'll just have to think of something else.'

'I don't believe there is anything else.'

There we had to leave it. His visit, though highly enjoyable, ended in stalemate. It was only brought to a precipitate boil again by Stage Four, the fearful saga of the sailing of the liner *Queen Mary*, from New York's Pier 90, on 26 January, 1955.

By then I was due for some leave again, having served two straight years in Canada, and this time we were destined for a return visit to Johannesburg, via London, to show off our first-born son and half of our second to a possibly doting South African grandfather. It meant a break in writing, but I was used to that, and so was everyone who now relied on me for a deadline.

To make the first leg of the journey, a suite—*the* suite, £370 for four and a half days—on board a giant Cunarder romping across the Atlantic from New York to Southampton seemed just the thing for a thriving author. Together with a nurse, a child, a fur-lined carry-cot, and a baffling array of other luggage, we flew down to New York, and moved into the Pierre Hotel for the forty-eight hours before sailing.

I called round to see Willis Wing on the day of our arrival, but only in the late afternoon. It would have been better, far better, if I had done so immediately.

Apart from the subject of changing publishers, which was a continuing cliff-hanger constantly in doubt until the next instalment, I only had one minor query for him: just a little one, a baby, a throwaway line at the end of a long conversation about money, and royalties, and film prospects, and his family, and mine, and snow in New York, and the merits of the Pierre Hotel as against the Plaza, or the St Regis, or the Algonquin which I had never tried.

'What does it mean,' I asked him, 'in the sailing instructions, when it says I have to have a tax-clearance certificate before I can go on board?'

Naturally, he knew the answer. 'That's one of our funnier national customs,' he said. 'Like painting the Fifth Avenue traffic lines green on St Patrick's Day. Like you always have crumpet for tea.' Willis, I was glad to note, still had certain areas of innocence. 'If you leave the States by air, it doesn't matter to anyone. You're just a tourist. But if you go by boat, that could be for ever. You could be skipping the country. So they want to be sure all your taxes are paid up. So anyone who sails needs that particular piece of paper.'

'I hope that doesn't mean me.' But I was not really serious; such solid British burghers as myself could hardly be touched by this vulgarity. Indeed, I was not serious at all until Willis said:

'I think it applies to everyone going on board who earns money in America. But don't you worry. Go down and see them tomorrow. They'll dig out your last tax return, and then give you clearance.'

This was slightly mysterious. 'But I haven't got any tax returns to dig out. Not in America. I've never lived here.'

'All the same . . .' Willis was giving me rather an odd look. 'Haven't you been putting them in every year?'

'No. Why should I? You deducted the thirty per cent flat rate all the time I was in South Africa. Now I pay U.K. taxes wherever I am, because I'm a diplomat.'

He shook his head. 'You still have to put in a return here, if it's above a certain figure. At least, that's my understanding.' He swung round in his agile executive office chair, and took a small tubby book from a shelf behind it. Then he leafed through it, and stopped, and read for a moment.

'Here it is,' he said after a moment. 'Tax-paying made easy. . . . Any alien—that's you—earning more than $15,400 here—don't know why they picked on that figure—has to put in a U.S. tax return anyway. Then, unless there's a tax treaty between the two countries, he probably has to pay a little more than the thirty per cent.' He looked up. 'Didn't your tax people in England tell you about this?'

'No.' My tax person in England had been ill, and sometimes did not answer letters for four months, and he was not quite such a universal overseer as I could have wished. 'Anyway, there *is* a tax treaty between America and Canada, and Canada and England. I pay full British taxes, for my sins. I've been doing it for years. It's all understood.'

'All the same, you still have to put in——' he stopped suddenly. 'How about South Africa? There was no tax treaty while you were there. That was why I had to deduct at source.'

'But you did deduct the full thirty per cent, all the time.'

'That was just the basic rate. I think you'll find that you owe rather more than that. Quite apart from not putting in the returns.'

A slight prickling feeling about my scalp began to make itself felt. We had been having such fun, and there was going to be so much more, in the *Queen Mary*, and in London, and in Johannesburg, and in London again, and now all this blasted rubbish. . . . The extra tax—if there *was* any extra tax—didn't matter much. But the sailing permit——

I said, a little desperately: 'I can't possibly deal with all this in two days! Less than two days.' I looked at my watch; it was of honest gold, bought in South Africa, the country we were talking about. 'Less than thirty-nine hours, in fact.'

'I think you'll find——' there was that cautionary phrase again,

'that they won't let you sail until you've taken care of everything.'

'Oh, well.' It all sounded horribly complicated, but I was still
a respectable person, after all, as well as a dedicated tax-payer
all the way round the globe. 'I'll go and see them. Tell them
I'll pay up in full—*if* I owe them anything—as soon as I get
back.'

'I don't think our tax people——' Willis stopped again. 'It's
my belief you'd better see John McCabe right away.'

He was one hundred per cent right.

John McCabe was Willis's talented tax-accountant, and I
had met him earlier, in circumstances which lacked crisis
altogether. He was now near retirement; a tall thin old man (as
I would have phrased it until I reached his age), grey-haired,
slightly stooping, with a very sharp eye and—most unusual for
anyone in his grim occupation—a sense of humour as well.

He seemed to know more tax jokes, and to tell them better,
than anyone I had met. It was just as well. In the next twenty-
four hours, I certainly needed tax jokes.

He asked me a lot of questions, in a gentle voice which disguised its perceptive probe. He looked closely at the royalty
accounts which I had brought across from Willis Wing. He did
a little figuring, while I listened to the growling downtown
traffic outside his office (it was on Liberty Street, which I tried
to think of as a good omen) and waited.

Finally, he was ready. 'On the face of it, you are delinquent,'
John McCabe told me, and I could only think: Fancy being
delinquent tax-wise as well. All his jargon was very catching,
and now it had caught me. He tapped lightly on the half-page of
figures in front of him.

'1952 is the year they're going to hit you on. They can be
nasty to you for not having put in any returns, but not too nasty,
because most of the time you didn't owe any taxes, and it was
only a formality.' He smiled. 'And of course you were just a
simple Britisher. . . . But 1952 is something else, and there's a
little bit of 1953 involved as well. In 1952 you paid your statu-

tory thirty per cent, deducted at source, but you should have made full returns and paid quite a bit more.'

'How much?'

'As near as I can figure it, $23,000.'

'O.K.' It was an appalling amount of money, but it wasn't the end of the world. Certainly I would pay them $23,000—about £8,000—but I couldn't possibly pay them £8,000 before I sailed, early the day after tomorrow. 'If I agree to all this, and promise to pay when I come back, can you get me a tax clearance certificate?'

He was a wise old man, much wiser than I was, or perhaps would ever be. He knew the odds; I just made the mistakes. He thought for a moment, put down his pencil, and said:

'No. I don't think so.'

The scalp began to prickle again, in good earnest. 'But I *have* to sail!' I almost wailed—and it was true enough. There was a vast amount laid on, in a carefully planned three-months' sequence. The *Queen Mary* trip itself was a long-promised treat. Then there was a whole time-table of meetings and television things in London, the film *première* of *The Ship tha Died of Shame*, a booked flight to South Africa, all sorts of arrangements there, and then back to London and back to New York and back to Ottawa, in time to obey a strictly-ordained calendar of leave.

The best brains in Ottawa's best travel agency had been bashing away at this itinerary for weeks. So had Edwin Harper in London, and Cassell's man in Cape Town. Now it seemed to be in danger of falling to bits.

'First things first,' said John McCabe soothingly. 'Let's say that they agree to our provisional figure of $23,000. Have you the money?'

'Yes. But it's tied up in gold shares in South Africa. It would need at least three or four weeks to sell up and get the money back here.'

'How much could you raise now?'

'Oh—nothing. About a thousand dollars. Travelling money.'

His face creased into its first frown, itself enough to daunt the

least delinquent tax-payer in New York City. 'I guess we'd
better go and see them. It's too late now. But early tomorrow
morning. As soon as they open. And I think I should warn you
—these people have heard everything. They can be *very* tough.'

It was my introduction to a wilder day than I would ever care
to live again.

The Alien Income Tax Section on Lexington Avenue was a
foreboding sort of place, particularly at 8.30 in the morning: a
vast room, astringently clean as conscience itself, full of little
steel desks ranged in long rows, like toy soldiers. Behind each
desk sat an income tax inspector; in front of each desk was an
empty chair, constantly replenished from the cloudy tank of
tax-payers who waited on penitent benches at the side.

A steady murmur—of woe? of pleading? of iron insistence?—
already filled the air.

Could they all be delinquents? It seemed likely, at that hour,
in the mood of anxiety which had steadily been building up
since dawn. When John McCabe, my only serviceable escort,
my frail Rock of Gibraltar, ushered me in, sat me down on one
of the side benches, and began a rangy scouting of this huge
cavern of delinquency, I was ready to concede defeat.

I was ready to concede anything, as long as I could go on
board the *Queen Mary*, one single sunrise from today.

I noticed that even he, a character of unchallengeable probity,
was nervous. Perhaps nervous was the wrong word, unless one
could say that Nelson at Trafalgar, Wellington at Quatre Bras,
or a fighter pilot taking off from Biggin Hill in the late summer
of 1940, were all nervous.

'Keyed up' was probably a better phrase: warily alert for the
dangers, the pitfalls, the chances of disaster. This was his testing time. It was his own familiar battleground. Yet perhaps the
ground was weak? Perhaps this was a day of misfortune, the
stars in a conjunction adverse? Perhaps the case was undeserving,
perhaps I was not such a hot ally after all.

Waiting, I wanted to be anywhere but where I was. I wished
I had not dined so extensively at the Pavillon the night before,

in a mood of such careless indifference to fate that I had invited
the entire company to join us on board the *Queen Mary* for a
champagne party at sailing time.

I wished that I did not feel that I really belonged in this room,
and would belong there for ever, part of the cast of the Alien
Income Tax Section, the longest-running, grubbiest puppet-
show on Lexington Avenue.

John McCabe returned. His shoulders still stooped, but he
was looking a tiny bit brighter. 'There's one I know here,' he
told me. 'A lady. She'll see us next.'

Presently we were beckoned forward. I sat down in the con-
fessional chair, and faced the opposition. John McCabe sat
by my side, on another chair filched from the next desk. The
opposition, as he had told me, was a lady.

That's not a lady, I thought, already flippant in adversity.
That's a U.S. Government tax inspector wearing a skirt.

I rather liked Miss or Mrs Tax Inspector, in spite of a formidable air of competence. She was about forty: slim, blonde, not
bad looking at all. It may have been that she rather liked me; I
was in the same category of the human animal in its middle
years. But the stars were against us from the start. We could not
declare our love. I could only declare my income, and she her
judgement on it.

We told her our tale. The tale was honest enough, yet
inexorably damned by fact. It seemed that I did owe them—
the United States Government—this lady here—the rough sum
of $23,000. It was not altogether my fault, except that stupidity
was always one's fault. Yet my fault remained at $23,000, due
on that day, with further penalties for delinquency yet to be
assessed.

'But I'm booked to sail tomorrow morning,' I told her, trying
on a little British charm. 'If I *promise* to pay as soon as I can
make the arrangements, can't I have the tax clearance, on that
basis?'

I might as well have been playing a broken flute in a boiler
factory. Effete British charm, suspect from the start, came up
13*

against sturdy Yankee grit, wilted like sweet violets, and sank like the expendable rubbish it was.

Sure I could have my tax clearance, and catch my boat. They didn't want to be unreasonable. At this stage, they weren't going to argue about a thousand dollars here or there. Just as soon as I paid up the provisional assessment, in cash, the certificate would be mine.

'My client,' said John McCabe, a watchful spectator in much of this, 'is not in a position to make an immediate cash settlement. But he does have to catch the *Queen Mary* tomorrow. He has gold shares in South Africa, more than enough to cover this. But it will take a little time to realize them. My client also has diplomatic status. He would never consider for a moment——'

It was all wrong, and I knew it; it did not need a mirthless smile from across the table to tell me so. I could read the signs. I could even make up the interior dialogue for myself.

This lady did not have to catch anything so exotic as the *Queen Mary*. Perhaps she never would. In the meantime, perhaps I never would. Diplomatic status? It sounded like part of a familiar swindle. And gold shares? *They* sounded more and more like gold bricks, every time they were mentioned.

The expected verdict was handed down. She was sorry— and perhaps she really was sorry, in a theoretical sort of way. She could afford to be. The figures were there. They were the figures we had presented, the figures she was ready to accept. They showed that I owed the United States Government $23,000 in back taxes. I could only board the *Queen Mary* if I paid up. In barrel-head cash. Before sailing time. It was just too bad, but she had no discretion.

She had everything else, as I realized when, the very shredded wheat of a delinquent tax-payer, I emerged into the pale light of Lexington Avenue.

'I was afraid of this,' said John McCabe, sadly. 'I think I told you, they can be very tough.'

Now I was on my own.

The situation was beginning to be appalling. I was far from

home, on a cold and frosty New York morning. I was $23,000
short, with twenty-three hours to get hold of it. Peanuts!
announced the man on the corner stall, as I flagged down a taxi
to take me back to the Pierre. But he was dead wrong. It was
now ten o'clock, and somehow we had to be on board, with our
tax clearance certificates, minus 23,000 of those peanuts, by
nine next morning.

In the fearful flurry which ensued I had the idea, all the time,
that Soli Ornstein would not have been in the least proud of me.

At 10.15, back at the Pierre, sipping some scalding onion
soup for which I had formed a brief, breakfast-time attachment,
I put through a call to the Bank of Montreal in Ottawa. Thank
God for the Bell Telephone Company, I thought, as the call
came through in less than a minute. They were on my side. If
only everyone else would prove as efficient, as friendly, and as
productive.

My bank manager, John Hobson, was his usual cheerful self.
How was the weather? How was New York? How was that
cute youngster? And the *Queen Mary*? All set?

'Well, no,' I had to tell him. 'There's been a snag John. I
need some help.' I explained all about the unpaid taxes and the
sailing permit, conscious that $23,000 sounded an awful lot of
money, even to an ever-friendly Canadian bank manager: conscious also of a sizeable overdraft already, an overdraft which
must have flicked into his agile mind as soon as he heard my
voice.

'Twenty-three thousand?' John Hobson, in accordance with
his rank, had a good cautionary tone, and he used it now. 'Of
course I'd be only too glad to help. That's what a bank is for.
Isn't that the truth? But what's the exact position with the gold
shares? Who has the actual scrip?'

'The Standard Bank in Johannesburg.'

'M'm. That makes it a little difficult. Of course we would
always extend your loan, against securities like that. But they
would have to be deposited here.'

'There isn't time for that. Look, can't you stretch a point?'

The shares are in South Africa. You know they'll get to you as
soon as I can arrange it. But I need the tax money *now*. Today.'

Already he was regretful. He was also firm, as he had every
right to be. 'Stretching a point' was not bank-speech. It was
loose writer's talk, liable to close scrutiny from every angle.
'I'd have to take a thing like that higher up. It would need a
meeting. There's also the exchange control aspect. It would
mean two or three days, at the least.'

'But John, can you *try*?'

The answer was prompt enough. 'I'll call you back in fifteen
minutes.' He was a good friend. He was also a highly competent professional banker. It was impossible to judge which
would win.

By the time I had finished the onion soup, John Hobson was
on the line again. His answer was definitive, and absolutely
correct. Personally he would like to help me. So would the bank.
For a valued client like myself. . . . But even for a valued client
like myself, the banking norms must be preserved.

My share certificates would have to be in their possession,
and, rather more important, in negotiable form. A dollar loan
against South African sterling, though perfectly feasible, was
not something which could be arranged at such short notice. He
was awfully sorry.

I could tell that he was. Huge banks such as his could be
caught in just the same squeeze as tiny customers with their
shirt tails hanging out of their trousers. Meanwhile, time was
romping on. I said good-bye, and turned to the next idea on my
list.

I put through a call to Johannesburg, at $4 a minute, after
doing a small mathematical wrestling-match with the time-
factor. Eleven o'clock in New York was five p.m. in South
Africa—or was it six? It was six, but the man I wanted was
traced to his home. Once more, good old Bell Tel! . . . I made
up my mind—I swore devoutly—to leave them something in my
will.

The Johannesburg bank was prepared to be helpful, just like

Ottawa. Certainly they could send me the share scrip, within three days, though in its present form it was not freely negotiable. Certainly, as an alternative, the shares could be sold on the Johannesburg stock exchange, and—since they had originally been bought with American dollars—the bank could send me the proceeds. But that would take time. The Exchange Control people worked slowly and carefully Say—a fortnight?

I didn't have a fortnight. Could they not cable me an irrevocable credit of $23,000, against the security of the shares, and then sell them?

Certainly they could do that, also. (Everyone was wonderfully reasonable that morning.) But a cable transfer of dollars, even in such favourable circumstances, still needed Exchange Control permission. The bank could not possibly move without it. They would have to apply formally. Once again, it would take a little time. They could probably put it through in—say, four days?

Four days was, for me, the same as four months—no good. I said another good-bye, across 9,000 miles. Now it was 11.30. I paid a promised courtesy call on British Information Services. Their elegant office on the 60th floor of Rockefeller Centre gave the climber a superb view to the south and west.

Within this sector lay the piers of the Hudson River. Within one of these piers, clear to the naked eye, lay the *Queen Mary*, waiting to sail. The red and black Cunard funnels were an immediate focus.

'I envy you,' said the man.

It was noon. I telephoned Willis Wing. There was only one thing for it. I must ask Alfred Knopf for an advance, against my future books. This would mean—it could only mean—that his options would be extended indefinitely. It could not be helped. Though the money would be repaid within a month, the options would remain, stretching far into the future. That would be the price of accommodation—and, for any quick taker, an unusual bargain.

Willis, asked for his opinion, approved the plan only as a very

last resort. I said that this was now what it was. The squeeze
was on. I was going to catch the *Queen Mary* if I had to mortgage another life-time. 'I'll call you back,' he said, businesslike
as ever.

He called me back. The answer from Knopf was an astonishing No. It was astonishing because, even as a restive author,
I was surely a minimal risk to him. Short of war, or earth-
quake, or my untimely death (readily insurable), what in hell
could go wrong? 'He doesn't want to think in terms of
$23,000,' Willis answered.

It was late lunch-time. I had now been thinking in terms of
$23,000 since the world's first chicken was plucked. Over a
snatched smoked-salmon sandwich in the Pierre suite ('Don't
look so harassed,' I was told: 'there's a man coming from
Hammacher Schlemmer,') I evolved a wild scheme. The
innocent, tax-free parties could go on ahead in the *Queen Mary*,
while I slipped back to Ottawa, untraceable, and then flew on to
London. It was not actually illegal. Only if I left the States by
ship was I forced to pay those back taxes on the nail. I could
easily have changed my mind. . . .

But (some second thoughts here) it would spoil everything!
There went my £870 suite, blown sky-high! And it could also
be made to look and sound extremely odd. I had visions of being
stopped at the Canadian border, haled back to New York, and
manacled in the dock as an income tax fugitive.

'British Dip Skips Tax Probe'—I could see it all. Reluctantly
I dropped the idea onto the Pierre carpet, and, with it, ran out
of ideas altogether.

The phone rang (I really must send some flowers to the
switchboard girl below). It was Willis Wing with a foot-of-the-
scaffold reprieve. 'Thayer Hobson was just on the line,' he told
me. 'He's heard something. God knows how. But he says, can
he help?'

Thus, between that late smoked-salmon sandwich, the tea-
time hour which I no longer observed, and the bottle of champagne which I presently opened, Thayer Hobson of Morrow's—

on the off-chance that he might one day be my publisher—sent across a cashier's certified cheque for $23,000.

There were only two enclosures. One was an acknowledgement of debt to his firm, to be signed 'in case you fall overboard'. The other was a scribbled note: 'We'll take care of the details later. Have fun.'

At five p.m. John McCabe and I hurried down to the Alien Income Tax Section of Upper Manhattan. Now it was a different man we had to see, the man who actually took the money. But he knew the sordid story, and he was not at all impressed: not even by a cashier's cheque for all those thousands of dollars, obtained by an Alien Delinquent at seven hours' notice.

For him, it was only routine. People always had funny ideas about income tax. In the end, they got over them. Today, like any other day, the tax-whip had cracked, and here was the cur with its cheque between its legs.

In exchange for all this excruciating turmoil, compressed into a miserable harassment of time, I received a small slip of paper. It was my Certificate of Compliance, certifying that 'N. Monsarret' (Christ, they even spelt my name wrong!) had satisfied Section 146(e) and (f) of the United States Internal Revenue Code.

There was another for my wife, who had no such problems, and a third for Nurse Katie Nicolson. The child Marc (at seven months) was O.K.

The plural of sequel is *sequelae*. There were a couple of memorable *sequelae* to this affair, one ludicrous, one astonishing: one as early as next morning, and one delayed for three months.

Next morning, we drove down to Pier 90, with bag and baggage, and went through the slow channelled drill which would take us on board the *Queen Mary*. I felt drained of all excitement, and of every other emotion except the exquisite relief of having won through. The colossal black hull of the ship, shapely as sculpture in motion, towered above us. It towered above everything, as if to mark our triumph, with a brave array of flags to salute it.

I came to the last hurdle of all—Customs and Immigration Control, just short of a covered passageway labelled 'First Class Gangway—Up'. I presented all the considerable array of documentation which had now accumulated: the passports, the tickets, the company's boarding-passes, the health certificates, the baggage vouchers, the cabin identification. They were all examined, and approved, and sometimes stamped. I kept my prize, my $23,000 jail-delivery notice, until the last.

Then I put the Certificate of Compliance (Income Tax) down on the counter.

The man, a friendly fellow in a blue peaked cap, glanced at it. 'That's the next window,' he said, and turned. I could see that he was looking at a blank space. 'Joe!' he called, and waited. Then he shrugged his shoulders. 'I guess he's not here this morning,' he said. 'Why don't you folks just go on ahead?'

After that, it was impossible not to enjoy the voyage, though the magnificent ship, at 83,000 tons, seemed so divorced from the sea that we might have been still on Fifth Avenue, with every window bolted fast and every curtain drawn. We were assimilated, very happily, into a curious quartet consisting of Esmond Harmsworth, Jack Buchanan, Hélène Cordet, and the *Daily Mail* man in New York, Don Iddon.

On one very rough night, we stood by a small Greek ship which was in trouble, and took off, by lifeboat, one of their sailors who had fallen down a hatch, and broken both legs and possibly his back. It was a vivid four hours, and involved a remarkable feat of seamanship as well. As soon as it got under way, I said that I planned to call the *Daily Express* later, and give them the story.

But Don Iddon of the *Daily Mail* had other ideas. 'You don't really want to bother with that, do you?' he asked, as bland as cream cheese. 'Why don't you come up to the bridge, and tell me exactly what's going on, and I'll include you in my story. I'll say how you explained everything.'

I did indeed explain everything, from telling Don Iddon which was the pointed end of the *Queen Mary* to describing the difficulties of a very large ship making a lee shelter for a very small one. The handling of our ship's lifeboat came in for special mention.

The *Daily Mail* carried an excellent, first-hand account of an exciting night. Don Iddon, by the sound of it, was practically up in the crow's nest, directing the whole operation. And Nicholas Monsarrat, noted ex-sailor who explained the finer points?

'These things happen,' Don Iddon said later. 'They must have cut you out.'

It was nice to be able to recall that a little earlier I had cut *him* out, and every other soul on board, by scooping up a resounding £498, the 'pool' on the ship's run for the last day of our voyage.

There was no tax sequel worthy of the name; just an anticlimax, the sore place after the honeymoon. The unpaid taxes, on closer inspection, turned out to be about $17,000; the money duly came through from South Africa, in no-strings dollars, and the bill was paid within a month. (But I made very sure of filing my U.S. tax return, often merely formal, for the next sixteen years.) Blessed John McCabe's fee was $1,000. It was the only bill I was delighted to pay, except to give Thayer Hobson his money back, also with some heart-felt thanks.

I could never have guessed that all this was only leading up to the sequel of *sequelae*: Stage Five, the farthest-out chapter of them all.

Stage Five had a second parent, in addition to the Bureau of Internal Revenue, and that parent was anger. Unfairly, because he did have a case, and I had recognized it even in the midst of all the uproar, I was absolutely furious with Alfred Knopf for not taking a chance and lending me the tax money when I had to have it.

Damn it, I had never been in a more desperate fix in all my life! . . . There would be no more books for him, even if it meant going back to lobster-fishing for a living.

Thayer Hobson was in London, and we met. 'Not a bad little place you've got here, not bad at all,' was his comment on Suite 418–19 at Claridge's, thus proving, what I had long suspected, that American understatement was just as effective, and phoney, as the British brand. Still in a sulphurous mood, I told him that I was going to take his advice, and produce that contract-breaking book, thought it would mean stopping work on *The Tribe* and somehow sucking some ideas for another story from a well-worn thumb.

'It just so happens,' Thayer said, 'that I have a pretty good idea for a book. I've had it for years. It's a thriller. It might actually make quite an exciting film. If you want to work on it, you can have it.'

'What's it about?'

'International crooks. Beautiful girls. Mysterious castles in the South of France. Mistaken identity. Near-rape. Clean-cut young American boys galloping to the rescue. There's one scene where——' he checked himself. We were in Claridge's. 'Let me send you a synopsis of the story-line. I've always thought that something worthwhile *could* be made out of it. Anyway, there's a book there.'

He did send me a very full synopsis, and to my surprise I liked it. It had, as he had said, an exciting swing to it. It would certainly do for me. . . .

The book was written at an absurd speed, to shorten the interruption to the other one; 8,000 words a day for about ten days was the ruling rate, practically the speed of speech, a rate never reached before and never attempted since. It was rough and ready; I could not be proud of it; but buried beneath the easy flow there was, as Thayer had said, the germ of a good idea.

It emerged, like one of those old, speeded-up films of a chrysalis turning into a butterfly, as *Castle Garac*; and as *Castle Garac* it was promptly retyped and delivered to Alfred Knopf Incorporated.

It was rough, *but* ready. For good or ill, it was the option book. Still in the same rebellious mood, I put a price-tag on it of $23,000, the amount which, at a crucial moment, had been denied to me earlier: a $23,000 advance royalty, and *no future* options of any kind. I was absolutely certain that it would be rejected out of hand.

After a pause, Alfred Knopf countered with an astounding cable (I was in London again). *He liked the book.* A contract for it was on its way to Willis Wing. He would pay the huge advance on signature, and publish it in the fall. And—*and*—the Literary Guild had just bought it for $30,000. And—*and*—Pocket Books would shortly be following suit, for a sum still under negotiation. Kindest regards.

As Thayer Hobson, who was entitled to take a paternal interest in all this, wrote to me later:

'It's like dropping something heavy, and it floats up to the ceiling and starts singing. It's like somebody walking on his hands, eating with his feet, and putting the food you know where.'

I didn't try to improve on that.

So here I was, almost exactly a year later, with an 8 lb. manuscript, *The Tribe That Lost Its Head*, in my hand, a sense of achievement such as must always have come to any Christian who managed to strangle the lion, and a certain aura of invalid *faiblesse*. I was *en route* for Barbados, where, with great care, taking it very easy indeed, I might just recover a shattered health.

Meanwhile it was a celebration, with all the top brass of William Morrow Incorporated to assist me: Thayer Hobson himself, and a charming man, rather like a young Thayer with hair, named Sam Lawrence, and John Willey, their chief editor. We lunched at a French restaurant, now defunct, called the Chambord,* a restaurant set in such a sleazy area of lower New

---

* Named after the Comte de Chambord (1820–83), a legitimate claimant to the French throne who did not try hard enough. The verdict on his adult life: 'He passed forty years of blameless inertia.'

York that its elegance, and presently its cooking, came as
almost a bigger shock than the saga of *Castle Garac*.

I gave them their manuscript. Their eyes gleamed. I said I
would like *bouillabaisse* for lunch—no more, no less—and when
it came, with a lobster on the side and generous ladlefuls of a
saffron liquid to replenish it, *my* eyes gleamed. We drank a
superior *rosé*, slightly tart, full of body, full of sunshine, served
to us by a mountainous *sommelier* dressed as a *sommelier* should
be—blue smock, buckled leather belt, silver chain of office,
little tasting cup, and all.

Even the serried copper saucepans gleamed, winking down
on a quartet of merry literary gents who felt at almost sinful
ease with each other, and with all the world.

At half-past three, perceptibly rocking, we stood on Third
Avenue outside the Chambord. Third Avenue, run-down, rimed
with slushy snow, and ripe for the breakers, looked like a sunny
corner of the South of France.

'What now?' Thayer asked me. He had the manuscript in an
iron grip under his arm. 'Can we do anything for you? Would
you like to see the office?'

'On my way back would be better. I've got to do a little shopping. After that I should really get some sleep. My plane leaves
in the middle of the night.'

'What time?'

'The bawdy hand of the dial stands upon the prick of—about
six a.m.'

'O.K. What is it you want to buy?'

'Madras cotton Bermuda shorts.'

'Oh, God!' This was John Willey, a sartorial purist.

'And a bow-and-arrow.'

'Abercrombie & Fitch,' Sam Lawrence advised promptly.
'They stock everything.'

Even at that moment, I was just sober enough to wonder
what on earth they really thought of me. This was an English
novelist? . . . But they had *The Tribe*, and I had the beginning of
a marvellous, exhilarating freedom.

Abercrombie & Fitch did indeed stock everything, particularly in the Sports Section, where presently, after several false tries, I found myself.

'I have the wild idea,' I said, breathing God-knows-what mixture of martinis laced with Pernod, *bouillabaisse*, *rosé* wine, Brie, and Armagnac across the counter: 'I have the wild idea of catching fish with a bow-and-arrow in Barbados. Is there such a thing as——'

'Certainly,' said the man, who must have seen many a disgraced, drunken fugitive on his way to big-game slaughter and merciful oblivion in Southern Africa. 'There's *this* one—thirty-five dollars—and *this* one—bigger reel, much longer range, with a nylon line—at sixty dollars. If I were you——' and he could well have been right, 'I would recommend a spare arrow.'

Next morning, thus armed, and with a thunderous hangover, I took off for Miami and points far south.

On that happy, rather wayward journey, my island-hopping plane touched down at a string of half a dozen magic places, like a bee sipping briefly at successive gorgeous blooms in a full garden before it decided, regretfully, that it *must* move on.

It was an unhurried voyage, perhaps designed, certainly chosen by me, for the sensual pleasure of the slow approach; the gradual forgetting of the snow and ice and sub-zero grip of harsh Canada, the gentle melting of the winter spirit, the wooing of the darling sun.

After the big leap across Cuba we took the journey in smaller sips. We called at Grand Cayman, and then at Jamaica. We sped low over Port Royal, where the pirate Captain Henry Morgan, of good and evil memory, had once held sway: averted our eyes primly as we flew past Haiti, where funny things were happening every day and night of this twentieth-century year: sampled Puerto Rico, paid a visit to Ste Croix in the Virgin Islands, exchanged that for Anguilla, and then for Antigua, where Nelson sweated out his 'foul fever' (probably malaria) when he was courting Fanny Nisbet in the spring of 1785.

We passed that old family estate, *my* island, Montserrat:

tasted the ancient French flavour of Guadeloupe and Martinique; and then faced the final stretch of our voyage, southwards and eastwards to the last outpost of them all, Barbados.

At each stop, the air grew warmer and softer, and the quest
more richly rewarded. The flower scents, of hibiscus, and
bougainvillea, and wild orchid, made New York's fume-laden
stench seem like some ancient, forgotten, boarding-house kitchen, left behind in the drab past. Many of the tiny air-fields
were marked out at their edges by rows of scarlet poinsettias.
How else should it have been done, in this soft southern
paradise?

Gradually we shed our coats, our waistcoats, even our ties.
At airport 'shops' which were no more than bamboo shacks, yet
cool under the burning sun, people bought funny woven hats,
wore them selfconsciously for ten minutes, and then, in happy
transformation, looked as though they had never worn anything else in their lives.

At each stop, rum was now the drink, rum decorated with
extraordinary bouquets of mint leaves and orange slices and
pineapple tops and the skins of fresh limes. On board the plane,
rum was now the drink, served by a beautiful, scatter-brained
girl, a slim Jamaican with a skin of palest honey and amber; a
girl with small, shy, perfect breasts, a girl with promise,
a girl who might have turned us all into lecherous wingéd
wolves.

But we did not want her. At least, I did not want her. I just
wanted her to be there.

We were progressively delayed, and began to lag far behind
our schedule. It did not matter. It had started with an earlier
tie-up at Puerto Rico, where the first and last United States
customs post, having planted its flag and staked its claim to
freshly won officialdom, was administered by a small arrogant
breed of new Americans, tasting power—even the nuisance-
power of the hard stare, the rubber stamp, the grubby transit
pass—for the first time.

The delay grew longer with each stop as we flew southwards,

to find the people nicer, and slower, and more concerned with smiling good manners than curt officious tyranny: concerned with a gentle pace of life which had been there before the first intrusive jet-plane screamed in, and would be there afterwards. That did not matter either.

It mattered even less that it was dusk by the time we left Martinique, on the last stage of our journey. We should have been gone earlier, but how much earlier, who cared? We flew low across a dark sea laced with sudden silver ruffles when it crossed the track of the moon. The stars came up, to see us homewards: the Dog Star for mariners, the distant Southern Cross for romantics, the Pleiades ('Canst thou bind the sweet influence of Pleiades?' asked Job, who probably didn't know the first thing about them) for glistening decoration.

Presently we picked up the glow of Bridgetown Harbour, and the thread of lights along the shore-line. I took the last permitted tot of rum at the airline's expense; and then we dropped down from our high heaven, and came to rest in the warm, embracing air of Barbados.

It was eleven o'clock, on a night as soft as velvet. Miami and the rest of the forsaken world were twelve hours astern of me, twelve hours back into limbo. Even though the pace had already slowed miraculously, they could never catch up with me now. Blessed retreat was mine, and solitude, and the most instant love-affair with a few square miles of good earth that I had ever known.

It was a first visit, and the good earth had been chosen for me, in a fortunate hour, by that same doctor-ally who wanted to see me live a little longer, in command of certain essential faculties. (Translation: 'You'd better get away before you go nuts.') Even the hotel itself had been thus chosen, in the knowledge that I had lately developed an odd, embarrassing terror of heights, and that anywhere I lived must be small, and protected, and on no account more than four storeys high.

The final prescription was a modest private hotel called Bagshot House, on the west coast of the island, where a fault in the coral-rock surface had produced, x million years earlier, a slight coastal depression presently to be christened St Lawrence Gap.

When I woke on my first sunrise, and padded out onto a balcony a reassuring twenty feet above a most beautiful, tranquil-as-heaven, azure lagoon, it was to a world of the most blissful innocence and peace.

It was five o'clock in the morning, a time to treasure, a time to make one's own. I wandered down, through just-stirring corridors; patted the yawning dog, saluted the night-watchman, trod softly upon rush mats the colour of pale sunlight; and found myself on the beach, my toes in the warm Caribbean, my head already in cloudy happiness.

The beach formed the inner margin of a small blue lagoon, perfectly shaped, beyond price: the kind one saw in the advertisements, and read about in lying travel supplements, and never found—and I had found it, and it had found me. Its containing edge, three hundred feet away, was a half-circle of coral reef, across which the turning tide was just beginning to thrust—but only gently, as if to say, without insistence, that the sea still had its right of way, even through such a haven as this.

It was bound, by a compact with the moon and the stars, to assert it, twice a day. But then it would retreat again, without staking a claim, without stealing; and that was another compact, another firm promise, on which all beleaguered men could rely.

Soon I was paddling, in and out of the rising tide, and the wavelets as small and neat as pleated silk; wandering like a dog which must explore every single thing in the world; leaving smudged footprints on golden wet sand, just as at Trearddur Bay, and only forty smudged years later. But Trearddur Bay, with all its blessings, could never have shown riches like these.

It had never had delicate double-winged shells (they were called Auroras, I found later: named after the dawn, and as good as the dawn on any morning) in colours ranging from Chinese yellow to royal purple. It had never had six-inch-long flying fish stranded at the edge of the tide-mark, small gasping

orphans which a small boy could, and a grown man did, help
back into their saviour element.

It had never had a morning air as soft as this, and a sea green-
blue like a poor man's emeralds, and ancient drift-wood which
might have haunted this Caribbean strand since the first coral
pushed up, an inch at a time, a foot in a hundred years, and
found the air and light it had always known must be just above
the surface of the sea.

It had never had coral itself, pink and grey and mottled
brown; coral shaped like skulls, like the branches of trees, like
fronded leaves, like the lips of women and the private parts of
men.

It had never had a man, an ancient Barbadian in a terrible
hat, standing waist-deep in the blue water, twirling and casting
a weighted net. Twenty times he poised, and swung, and threw;
twenty times the net whirled through the air, and plunged and
settled in a perfect circle. Then he whipped it in, hand over
hand, and examined it, hand over hand, and put whatever small
trophies he had gained into the dripping sack tied across his
shoulders.

As he waded ashore, I waded towards him. He smiled, but
did not speak. His world was patience, toil, cunning and fish,
not indolent white tourists. But on the beach, he opened the sack
—perhaps for me, perhaps for his own proper pride.

His catch was a hundred tiny fingerlings, silver like minnows,
gleaming like drops of water, black-backed like baby sharks:
the smallest fry of the sea, and his very own.

'What are they?' I asked.

His creased, wizened face came round It was curiously aloof;
the old fisherman, half naked in faded, threadbare, drenched
blue jeans, was still a private man. He was as strong as his own
woven net; the sinews in the spare body might have lasted
seventy years, but they were as good as mine. Better—they
had been put to this testing use, and would be tested again, on
the next tide, and the one after that.

Under the drooping tattered hat, he could have been anyone:

anyone old and wise: anyone from Moses to Captain Ahab, from Chaka the Terrible to Uncle Tom.

'What was that?' he asked.

I pointed. 'What are they?'

'They're fish, man!'

Silly question.

Dreamily I reached the far end of the beach, where an outcrop of rock met the curved arm of the reef. Dreamily I stood and stared, while the land-crabs, which had been scuttling away as I approached, now stood and stared themselves. The hotel, a full mile away, was only a pink dot in the distance, under an arch of sentinel palm trees bending towards the lagoon.

Presently I began to wander back again, through the warm blue water, with the sun already hot on my shoulders. Once a crabby young crab nipped at my ankle. He was welcome to it— and as I jumped I uncovered a marvellous new shell, a pale yellow helmet conch unmarked by time, still flawless after ten thousand tides had rolled it slowly landwards.

From the hotel balcony somebody waved, and I waved back. It was my hostess, Eileen Robinson, slim, attractive, cool in a flowered cotton dress. She had met me at the airport and, at midnight, reopened the bar, the kitchens, everything.

Now she offered me breakfast on my balcony—'Or would you like a rum snap first?'

I had learned already, and appreciated, that rum did not count as a drink in this benevolent corner of the world.

'I'll take both,' I told her. 'What's for breakfast?'

'Paw-paw. Fried dolphin. Flying fish. Corned beef hash, if you like.'

Already I had found all I was looking for.

The island, which a homesick young Captain Nelson, heading his letter 'Barbarous Island', had called a detestable spot, was small, pear-shaped, dry, green at the edges; perpetually brushed, sometimes buffeted, by the north-east Trades, so that the east side was craggy from the attack of the sea, and the west sheltered and gentle.

It was twenty-one miles from end to end; twenty-one miles of a colonial past, bloody and pious at the same time, and of a happy and hopeful present.

Its piety was attested by some of the place-names; all the small counties were known as parishes, even for electoral purposes (their representatives were actually called 'Vestrymen'), and named for a saint. My guardian angel was now St Lawrence, Bridgetown the capital was in the care of St Michael, and so on down, or up, to St Lucy, not a saint whose name sprang to mind in instant recognition.

But this had been cruel slave country, nonetheless; the sugar plantations, still profitable, had been even more so in the past, when 'field hands', bound and shipped like stinking cattle from West Africa, were set down in this alien land to work until they dropped.

A poster in the local museum bore witness to this hateful century: a poster unequivocal, proclaiming a history of pain in clear, terrifying accents:

To be Sold This Day on the Block at St John's:

1 Mulatto Cook-Boy, THOMAS, 30 years old, warranted sound.

2 Field Hands, JAMES & EZRA, from Bankrupt Plantation.

1 BOY, Martiniquan, speaks only French, aged, no warranty.

1 House Maid, SAVANNAH. A fine Clean Girl. Together with two female children (one 4 years, well-grown, one at breast).

Also JASPER, a runaway.

Grouped nearby this catalogue of wares were rusty shackles, worn manacles, oxhide whips, and a leg-iron with a great metal ball attached.

But now all that was gone, and, astonishingly, gone without malice. The slave past, which might have bred a sullen murderous resentment for ever, had left instead the most cheerful people I had ever met, and the best-disposed towards the white men, the successors—often no more than the great-grand-children—of their old tyrant overlords.

Now Barbados, which had never been out of the British clutch since 1627, had its independence, and was doing its best to make it work. Currently there was talk of a federation with nine other islands, from Jamaica in the far west to pint-sized Montserrat nearby; and later it was to be tried, for four short bickering years, until it foundered on certain pockets of selfishness (Barbados was *not* one of them) based on the easy rallying-cry: 'Why should we, big and rich, carry most of the others, small and poor?'*

But at the moment Barbados was on its own, carving out a future and turning its back on the fearful past. One had only to drive into Bridgetown, past the 'Garrison Savannah' which was another reminder of that ancient servitude, to find black and white crowds jam-packed in total harmony.

Another, older historian (1654) had noted Barbados, rather charmingly, as 'One of the richest Spotes of Ground in the world, and fully inhabited'. Bridgetown was still fully inhabited.

There was a main street, called Main Street, which was one solid mass-movement of people, from proud-looking planters in actual coats and ties to proud-looking women selling fresh limes and lemons, by the half-dozen, or the quarter-dozen, or the two, or the one. When the pavements were full, they walked in the road, clogging the traffic which at the best of times moved like an amiable snail.

Lacing this permanent throng were taxi-drivers who handed out their personal cards to all comers: 'Edwards. Drives You Anywhere. Also known as Phillips.' They had to compete with the men selling lottery tickets, and tourist-shop proprietors wheedling from the side-lines, and women in orange head-scarves offering postcards and rush-mats and necklaces of shells,

---

* A local historian told me that in fact the word 'Federation' had always meant, in old-time Barbadian slang, a free-for-all fight in which anyone could join, because of the vicious riots which attended the first proposal for it in 1876.

and grinning, waving children, to whom the whole thing was the biggest joke in the world.

Above all there were the tourists themselves, freshly disgorged from the gleaming cruise-liners which called, from America or Canada or Britain or France or Italy or Sweden, every day of every week.

Tourists were always terrible; shambling hordes of tourists were often monstrous. One glimpse of a bulging woman in scarlet Bermuda shorts, or a skinny girl haltered like a skinny horse, or a three-year-old child in a frilled bikini bra, or a fat—a really fat—man in a striped baseball cap and flowered Hawaiian shirt, girded with cameras, shouting 'Hold it, honey! I must get this!' was enough to make me shrink into the nearest doorway, ashamed of the whole white race.

But Barbadians were not at all ashamed, nor even surprised, nor inclined to cringe away. They might stare a bit, and giggle a bit; but they were the hosts, and these were the guests, and if the guests looked like something dreamed up by a man drunk on paraffin, if the guests were sick on the pavement, or shouted at the taxi-drivers to go to hell, for Chrissakes! or strode down the middle of the road like conquerors or bargained like miserable pack-pedlars, then that was the way the world was, and Barbados could put up with it, and learn to live with it, and in the meantime make all such comers welcome.

Once they had had *camels* here, as they had in far-off British Columbia. Once in every decade they had a hurricane. There had been a hurricane the year before, with people killed by the score, houses wrecked by the hundred, and ruined sugar crops to be measured in thousands of pounds. Compared with that, tourists were nothing—and, in another sense, everything.

Down in the harbour was another sort of chaos—busy, thronging, industrious, colourful with the true colour of the Caribbean rather than the shiny garish dross of affluent strangers. The harbour police—dressed in white duck suits, blue neckerchiefs, and badged straw hats like a musical comedy version of Nelson's own sailors on shore leave—watched and grinned, and occasionally gave an order or stopped some foolish nonsense or directed someone to do something, however urgent, at the pace which suited both parties.

Off-shore, in Carlisle Bay, could be seen the bigger ships, surrounded by clusters of lighters like bees round a hive, loading and unloading all the strange and commonplace cargo which kept an island alive. The lighters congregated almost in midtown, crowding the quays; so did the fishing boats, landing anything from a giant sting-ray to a basket of mackerel; so did the island schooners—and *they* could unload anything from Grenada limes to Dominican red-baked pottery, or (on one fascinating morning) a pair of baby elephants, sick as dogs, destined to complete a travelling circus.

Sometimes the schooners were hand-hauled into the inner harbour, the Careenage, where they were indeed careened— pulled over onto their sides by mast-head tackles, to be scraped, and caulked, and painted for the next year's voyaging.

In the centre, a statue of His Lordship, Admiral Nelson himself, apparently forgiven for his hasty words, surveyed this seascape and seemed to find it good.

I found it very good. As usual, the sea called, with a familiar urgency. One day, I swore, I *must* ship out of here by schooner, and slide from island to island down the trade winds: those winds which blew so sure that not a rope need be tended, nor a sail trimmed, for 500 miles. But it could not be that year.

That year (or this small part of it) was for loafing. In fact I had to wait two years for my mysterious voyage; and then it was by brigantine—the U.S.S. *Yankee*, skippered by Captain Irving Johnson, which called in on the last stage of an eighteen-month, round-the-world odyssey, and obligingly gave me passage from Barbados to Antigua, by way of Martinique.

It was to include one utterly memorable day, when we were at anchor off Basse-Terre in Guadeloupe, and everyone was ashore with the exception of skipper Johnson, super-cargo Monsarrat, and ship's doctor Christopher Sheldon.

'Three old men,' Irving Johnson said. 'Let's take her out!'

The phrase 'Take her out' had so far, for me, involved nothing bigger than a fourteen-foot dinghy, a four-ton sloop or a thirty-foot Dragon; certainly not a full-rigged brigantine, ninety-six feet from stem to stern. Perhaps Johnson, on his seventh and last round-the-world voyage, was in the mood to make the most of it. But it happened.

We hoisted sail—square-rigged on the foremast, fore-and-aft on the main, with a vast staysail in between; then we upped anchor, and away! I steered; Skipper Johnson tended the sheets and saw to the navigation; Chris Sheldon kept lookout, broke out fresh canvas when the wind fell light, cooked lunch, and photographed sea-birds in his spare moments.

The two of them padded up and down the deck like sunburnt, barefoot giants, while I nursed the huge wheel like a little boy sailing his first toy yacht. Three old men. . . .

It was a matter of hard fact that our combined ages were something like a hundred and fifty years; that we sailed the brave brigantine *Yankee*, under her towering white wings, thirty miles up the coast of Guadeloupe and thirty miles down again; that we brought her home on a gentle evening breeze, dropped anchor not fifty feet from the point we had raised it, and were sitting on deck, happy as clams, smug as owls, when the returning shore-party bumped against the starboard ladder in the long-boat.

For the rest, Barbados was rather ordinary, by West Indian standards. Inland, there were the usual dry-as-dust cane-fields, with that pervasive reek of raw sugar which could be smelled fifty miles off-shore; some avenues of wind-swept palms, and roads which suddenly narrowed down and finished nowhere; and then the eastern Atlantic coast, oddly called Bathsheba, a spooky area where the wind blew strong and the rocks stood like great black sentinels; a deserted strand where moving, breathing, hopeful man seemed totally out of place, as friendless and irrelevant as a pop-singer in the Sahara or a goat in Piccadilly.

There was one superb ruin of a house, Farley Hill, dating

from the days of 'plantocracy': built of coral rock, most
elegantly proportioned, and soon to undergo considerable
prostitution at the hands of the makers of the film *Island in the
Sun*, who were quite sure, against all the evidence, that such
houses must always have had giant plaster-of-Paris porticos
over the front door, and great looping outside staircases leading
nowhere, like those inland roads, and vines and magnolias and
coconuts all over.

There was also one very strange discovery.

I had been driving to and fro across the island with Eileen
Robinson, on a zigzag, off-the-track exploration which for her,
as with the Londoner who had never seen the Tower of London, nor even knew exactly where it was, came as a series of
novelties. ('I'm a Bajan, man!' she said, in that lilting West
Indian accent she could assume at will. 'I don't know the bloody
island either!')

We came to a village, deep in the interior, if a country measuring twenty-one miles by fourteen could be said to have such a
thing. It was a curious, derelict place, a scattering of wretched
wooden shacks along the edge of a cane-field. Suddenly I noticed
that the handful of people we met were all white—yet not
white, in the downright cocksure category of the world outside.

They were pinkish, and shambling, and odd. They were
albinos, negroid, very strange indeed, almost fugitive. They
disappeared behind houses at our approach: the children ran
away, and then peeped out again, furtive like mice, looking at
the car as if it were one of those baby elephants, one of those
camels of long ago. But they were all pink, damn it!

'Who on earth are they?' I asked.

'They're Red Legs,' Eileen answered.

'*What?*'

'Red Legs. Haven't you heard of Red Legs?'

'No. Who are they?'

She knew one answer, but no more. 'Nobody knows.'

Someone must know, I decided, and I had to find out, for a
special reason. I had seen people like these Red Legs before: a

single family of fishermen in the Eastern Province of South
Africa, pink and white and odd in just the same way. There, an
admixture of Scottish white blood in a coloured strain had persisted, and strengthened, and finally won a genetic tug-of-war
for ever.

There, it was a freak, if one could use the term gently and
without the smallest malice. With the Red Legs of Barbados,
the truth was much more dramatic, as I presently discovered.

This handful of very strange people had, long ago, been
Cornishmen, men of Devon, born and bred in the West
Country. Their ancestors were those simple country boys who
had joined the Monmouth Rebellion in the reign of James II,
and had supported that sad character, the Duke of Monmouth,
natural son of Charles II, against an equally sad character, soon
to be deposed, but then the lawful monarch of England.

The rebellion ended in the bloody rout at Sedgemoor, as all
the world knows, and Monmouth was beheaded on Tower Hill.
(His last words were possibly his best, and certainly his bravest;
to the waiting headsman he said: 'Here are six guineas for you,
and do not *hack* me as you did my Lord Russell.') Judge Jeffreys,
a thoroughly reliable time-server for the king, was then sent on
circuit to the West Country to punish the losers, and he made a
historic meal of it.

Our Red Legs were the direct and only descendants of men
who, escaping the hangman's noose—something of a stroke of
fortune in that evil year*—were sentenced to transportation for
life 'to the plantations of the Barbadoes', in the Bloody Assize of
1685.

This small piece of research was certainly the most sustained
effort of any kind I made during my stay in Barbados But I did
have one minor social flurry, lasting about a week.

Interviewed by the *Barbados Advocate*, I gave my views—
liberal, hopeful, and (as it turned out) futile—on the prospects
for the West Indian Federation. In passing, I surveyed the

---

* The score: Hanged, 320; Transported, 841; Imprisoned, whipped, or fined, no
count kept.

14

status of the modern novel, with a good solid plug for *The Tribe That Lost Its Head*.

Lured by the radio, I took part in a panel game—it was good old Twenty Questions—and discovered how much easier it was to be the question-master rather than one of the guessers. Aided by the manager of Barclays Bank, I joined the Royal Barbados Yacht Club—mostly drinking—and the Bridgetown Club—all drinking, but a most delightful colonial survival, where the favourite tipple was sangaree (rum, Madeira, and Curaçao), and the favourite game a wild gambling romp, never met before or since, called Cork Billiards.

I ate Pepper Pot, one of the world's hotter stews, at a Planters' lunch, and listened to steel bands which, for all their crude equipment (oil drums left behind by an American Construction Battalion) could still manage a most delicate air, and to a rude calypso singer called Lord Life Expectancy (no man from the Pru, he). I went to one night club to see a girl called Chee Chee, who was well spoken of, and to a second for the Limbo Dancers, and a third, inadvertently, for steak fried in coconut oil.

I visited an elegant hotel, Sam Lord's Castle (Sam Lord was an eighteenth-century pirate turned landowner who, when in the mood, still festooned his palm trees with lanterns to simulate the nearby harbour of Oistins, and did a nice steady trade in the subsequent wrecks), and another establishment called Four Winds, less elegant, delightfully run down, where the lizards outnumbered the guests, and the host, Martin Griffiths, when *he* was in the mood, served possibly the best food in the entire West Indies and, when he was not, told casual callers to go somewhere else, because the hotel had just closed.

I met a few people, some of them Canadians (Barbados was developing as a favourite Canadian playground). I met Campbell Radcliff, who had just bought for me a vast house in Ottawa, for $82,000. I met Manson Campbell, who (though I didn't know it at the time), would be selling me a Plymouth for Christmas, and another man who had involved me so heavily in life insurance that I was, by actuarial estimate, better off dead. Canadians tended to sell things to each other

I met a girl I had once known in London during the war, a girl who used to be one of the girls who decorated the stage, standing stockstill (local by-law) and stark naked, in 'Revuedeville' at the Windmill Theatre off Piccadilly Circus. She had always been a realist.

'—the glamour!' she once told me. 'It was too bloody cold! And all you could see from the stage was a lot of little flickering lights. It was the reflection from the binoculars of all those dirty old buggers in the stalls!'

She was now happily married to a stalwart apostle of normalcy who worked for Cable & Wireless.

I met Barbados' most bizarre expatriate, whose formal label of Lady Brooke disguised her true status—the Ranee of Sarawak, wife of the last White Rajah ever to rule those exotic shores. The Ranee, now living in modest state at a hotel called The Bread-Fruit Tree, was attended by three daughters who had, in certain circles, the rank of princess.

It was difficult to sort them out: we—vulgar Canadian democrats—only knew them as Princess Baba, Princess Nono, and Princess Googoo. One had been married to an old-time bandleader, Harry Roy of the May Fair Hotel, whose band (perhaps under a certain compulsion) had played *I'm Just Wild About Harry* at his wedding reception. Another had grappled in matrimony with an all-in wrestler named Gregory.

But they were universally beautiful, and the Ranee, whose husband included in his *Who's Who* entry some of the most delicious, if dated, phrases ever there inscribed ('Has led several expeditions into the far interior of the country to punish headhunters; understands the management of natives; ruled over a population of 500,000 souls and a country 40,000 square miles in extent. *Address:* 13 Albion Street, Bayswater Road, W.2.') the Ranee was, to quote Baedeker on monuments, well worth a visit.

Then suddenly my little ballet was over. *Jeux d'Enfants* ran for a packed week. Then it was time for *L'Après-Midi d'un Faune*, and I embraced the role with loving appetite.

It involved, like *L'Après-Midi* itself, a sensual daydream, sometimes intensely happy, sometimes sad, because often, nowadays, there were small flocks of mournful questions in the air, like homing geese their compass all awry: doubts as to whether, at the end of the long account, the catalogue of the sad was going to outweigh the small print of happiness.

Yet morbid thoughts were for morbid people; and no one, no stranger thirsting for comfort and reassurance, could be set down in Barbados and not draw solace from it.

Life, tranquil life, centred on that blue lagoon. Every morning, when I woke, it was to one of those dawns which only a very clever painter, and no photographer in the world, could ever catch: lucid as water itself, fresh as young virginity, soft as the feathers on the wings of sleep.

One woke to this pale, yellow-green light with quick pleasure: instantly aware of all one's blessings, and clear-headed in spite of yesterday. As in Johannesburg, the sovereign cure for a hangover was the immaculate air itself.

The new day beckoned; one must be ready for it; ready for anything, and—best of all—ready for nothing again. The lagoon below my balcony was the shrine of all this innocent joy.

I spent hours there, sometimes exploring the tide-mark, sometimes wading out to the coral reef. Anything I saw, anything I found, whether it was the bleached feathered skeleton of a sea-bird, as dry as its sanded grave, as dead as Icarus, or a fronded sea-anemone, still beautiful, still living, still urgent for a promised harvest, was part of the same dream of hope and life.

I would plod a slow, meandering, barefoot course, or bend to look at new treasures (the reef was alive!—alive all the time, with all the magic of creation), or stare seawards towards the deep water, where the sails of the fishing fleet dipped and swung and stood taut against the north-east Trades. Sometimes I fished myself, with that sophisticated, totally ineffective bow-and-arrow: opposing the whole might of Abercrombie & Fitch against the barracuda which, slim as pencils, agile as electric eels, patrolled up and down the reef.

Once the arrow sliced through the only vacant half-inch between two of these prizes; never did it strike home. But this still seemed the least important thing in the world, even when set against secret ambitions to wade back to the hotel with some great gleaming trophy from the sea, and invite the natives to feast. Happily I returned to standing and staring, savouring the only real prizes, the ocean brine and the hot, life-giving sun.

It was in the very air, this climate of disengagement. It was in the tide, washing across the reef like an invader, yet due to disappear in six hours and twelve minutes exactly. I found that I could watch a single wave—watch it swell, watch it break, watch it retreat, watch it die—and think how stupid, how futile, how tiny was all human endeavour. Such thoughts would never produce a book, but by God! they made contented men!

It was in these moments of trance, in this rum-soaked, sun-blessed, sea-circled paradise, that there was a temptation to contract-out for ever; to cast off and sail—by island schooner, by dugout canoe, by outrigger catamaran, by raft—anyhow and anywhere, as long as it was far enough away; to let the awful argumentative world go by; to disappear without trace—and then, if man, stupid man, had to write instead of live to come back five years later with the best book ever written about the tidal influences of the Humboldt Current: with a skin the colour of rubbed mahogany, and nothing to say to the inquisitive except: 'It was heaven.'

At noon I would wander back to the hotel—now my home, my shell, as everything on the reef except the questing barracuda seemed to have a shell of sorts—and taste the delights of Inside Soup and whatever else was available for the beach-combing layabout who had found this submerged, dark-green, urgeless level of contentment. Then I would sleep, fathoms deep, under drugs innocent and insidious at the same time: rum, food, sun, the caress of the sea, the denial of all the built-up world, and of the demanding clock which was the sun itself.

Eileen Robinson, who knew my mood exactly, as she had to know the mood of any other twelve-dollar-a-day tyrant, 'ran interference' for me, as we phrased it in Canadian football circles. She knew that, basically, I was still under that blessed 'No Visitors' embargo. Sometimes she went a little far, though with the best intentions in all Barbados.

'There were some Canadians here this afternoon,' she said once. 'They wanted to see you, but I sent them away.'

'Who were they? Did you get their names?'

'Mr Massey, I think it was. Rather a nice old man.'

It was just the Governor-General of Canada.

At night soft rain fell obligingly, washing all clean again. At night one slept like the infant Jesus, blameless, guileless, sinless, destined for heaven because it had been set down long ago, in sacred, cool, unarguable print. I would live! If I kept very still, and broke no laws, and traded no insults, and tried to do absolutely nothing except float in and out with the tide, I would live.

I had come to Barbados, so my doctor told me, to 'unwind'. It was another jargon word, like hospitalization, like a 'fun' party, like love. Sometimes I thought: unwind from what? But I knew very well. In darker moments, I knew absolutely, down to the last half-inch of the very stinking root of knowledge.

Who can tell how oft he offendeth? Usually one had a damned good idea, and was either sad about it, or proud of such accomplishment. In the present case, I was never more than baffled.

Women are tender plants, like wire wool: soft to a firm hand, harsh to a giving surface, treacherous, surprising, perverse: beyond forecast or concise estimate. I lived—*we* lived—in a world of violence and gentleness mixed, like the best or the worst of Indian curries, where sweet chutney, or bland coconut, warred with a fierce, breath-stopping, bitter infusion from hell's own kitchen.

It was a His and Hers world of Dexidrene and Equanil love and hate, gin and Campari, exhilaration and deadly boredom, admiration and smirking mockery; plenty of both, plenty of all, *enough* of everything to choke an elephant, poison a saint, strike the observer dumb.

Sweet reconciliation could, in a moment, give way to wary neutrality, to fear, to plain cowardice. 'Anything for a quiet life' grew positive toadstools of poltroonery, successive crops of Late Flowering Funk. I had such a fearful amount to lose.

I could lay solemn claim to being the only man in the Province of Quebec whose forehead had been grazed by a box of 50 Dunhill's No. 1 Romeo y Julieta which, having cannoned off his troubled brow, then shattered the neon tube in a brand-new 24-inch television set.

I was certainly the only man who did nothing about it. But I could also lay solemn claim to storing up, within a furious brain, all the exact, gruesome details of this encounter.

I could not forget. No one else seemed to remember.

It was all my fault? I had come to Barbados to do a little thinking, as well as indulge a little self-pity, a little resentful rage against heaven. But Christ stone the crows I was an *angel*! It was all my fault? Perhaps, perhaps. Books came before wives—was that a betrayal? Two children in eleven months—had that been too ardent, too selfish, too silly for words?

My esteemed grocer, Monsieur Vaillant, had been very concerned about this. But only on my account—this was Quebec. 'You will exhaust yourself,' he told me. 'These things affect a man's strength. You must take great care.' But he could add a little Gallic wit—Quebec Gallic. 'However, there are compensations. In this province, when you have had ten children, you get one free.'

Ten children? I did not want ten children. Sometimes I wanted none; usually I wanted the two incumbents, the two darling tenants, plus peace—PEACE, in capital letters, in blood if need be, in solemn compact anyway. These were still early days. We had only been married three years. But already I

could be in despair, in a mood of rueful retreat, in humble
surrender if surrender would only be accepted.

I would wag my tail. I would offer my tail on a golden dish
marked 'DOG'. I would *eat* my tail.

I wanted to love, and I wanted to write. But I could no longer
add the two things up. I could only subtract them, one from
another, taking turn-about to name the loser, like an idiot child
with a grown-up puzzle, in nonsensical, degrading, fatuous
non-arithmetic.

The law of diminishing returns was not only for wooden-
headed, baffled economists. It was for husbands. Already there
were days and weeks when I expected nothing, and the man
who expected nothing gave nothing.

Why should he? Why get your head shot off when you could
cash a cheque and duck out of sight, out of mind, out of life? The
storm-signals, like the shout of 'Wolf!' grew meaningless. The
cries of rage lost their impact. The noisy weeping became
laughable.

But I could not go to hospital every time I had to finish a
book.

Yet I *had* finished the book, against odds which often seemed
insurmountable; now, a stretcher-case with only my little bow-
and-arrow for defence, I was recovering. It was all part of the
same wildly theatrical farce. The farce grew more convincing,
more pleasurable anyway, when the verdicts on *The Tribe*
reached me. Thayer Hobson sent a heartening cable, Desmond
Flower of Cassell's a letter at least as encouraging as the one
which had signalled *The Cruel Sea.*

Yet—had all life come down to that single, cautious, mousy
word?—*yet* the happy issue only reminded me of another pressing problem. There was a firm of money-lenders in Ottawa
called Household Finance. I had no dealings with them; I only
registered their impassioned pleas on the radio ('Bills getting
you down? H.F.C. is waiting for you!') But the two key words
could still strike home to a timid heart.

I had problems of my own, in the realm of Household

Finance, and they then seemed, in my blind and blissful innocence, the biggest problems imaginable. The till, forever replenished, was forever empty.

I read Thayer's cable, and Desmond's letter, on a sunlit balcony. I drank to the future gratefully. It sounded as though *The Tribe* would be published with all available *panache*, and would make a lot of money. But one success could only breed another. It had to, because one success had already disappeared down a gilded drain.

The Tribe would come and go, like the other one. The squirrel's cage would still be there, turning and turning like that blasted 'Wheel of Fortune' song. I was forty-six already, to my shame and regret. Would I still be in the excremental soup when I was fifty-six? *Sixty-six?*

To this problem, and its peculiar setting, I presently returned.

2.

It was, and is, a large house, the house where I was bound. Across the river from Ottawa, and therefore in the Province of Quebec by a technical half-mile, it had been built by a construction engineer for his own enjoyment, in 1931, when high-quality materials were cheap and bread-line labour was cheapest of all; and sold to me by one of the sharper real-estate operators of our time, Shann Sherwood.

Mr Sherwood's starting price was $90,000; mine was $75,000. After a prolonged minuet, where fancy footwork alternated with cries of pain and appeals for justice, mercy, and a reasonable attitude, we settled for $82,000. It could be called a kind of victory; he had come down $8,000, I had only come up $7,000. Plus a little bit more.

'*Not* included in the sale price,' Mr Sherwood wrote promptly, when the preliminary contract was signed, 'are the two cords

14*

of firewood stacked in the basement. These are best quality
trimmed logs. Rather than put you to the trouble of having
them carted away' (now watch that, watch that, Mr Sherwood!
It's not my trouble, it's *your* trouble) 'I suggest a token price of
twenty dollars.'

I paid the token price of twenty dollars, thus making the final
figure leap to a deplorable $82,020. Though the logs kept at
least one room warm for one winter, I still felt outwitted.*

The house, solid as Gibraltar, built of grey stone, oak
panelled inside, with well proportioned rooms (all eighteen of
them), was called, to no one's surprise, Stone House. It was set,
surrounded by huge elms, in sixteen acres, with a view down
to the Ottawa River and the far-off Peace Tower of Parliament
across an unbroken eight-acre lawn—and, for students of time-
and-motion, it takes a writer, working turn-about with a
gardener (old, but sparked by some good Indian blood, and
called, naturally, Dinty Moore) a day and a half to mow and
trim eight acres of prime greensward to the satisfaction of both.

I adored that house, which really was handsome inside and
out, and though I presently grew to loathe it, and threw it back
to the winds—for that profitable $105,000, *minus the carpet
underfelt*—in two years and four months, the early honeymoon
was memorable.

Stone House, when seen in a certain light which was the one
I chose to see it in, seemed to be a bargain: an ex-white elephant
(empty for four years) which suddenly suited an unexpected
owner. If I wanted a monument (and even then I could acknowledge the motive) then this was it.

It cost a fortune to buy, a fortune ($58,000) to furnish, and a
fortune ($2,000 a month) to run. It even cost $3,350 to paint
(double the estimate, but after I had been encouraged to argue

---

* Such marginal losses always inflict disproportionate wounds. When the time
came to sell, the buyer, Mrs Jules Loeb, insisted that the underfelt of the main
staircase carpet (approximate cost, $150) *must* be included in the purchase price
of $105,000. Otherwise, there would be no sale. Outwitted again, I could only
surrender.

about this, it turned out that all sorts of tricky refinements had been added, and I had to back down, with an embarrassed grin and a cheque for the full amount), and $1,080 a year to heat.

Servants were a problem, but only the finding of them; paying for our small regular army (butler, cook, nurse, two maids, a gardener, a girl who sewed all the time, an odd-job man, basically a plumber, who later fell out of a tree, a man to plough the snow and another to lop and prune the elms)—this was mere routine, a writer's little chore, like sharpening his pencil every week.

So was having a secretary, Mrs Macdonell, my most stalwart ally, who among a lot of other things kept the accounts and, being married to a Royal Canadian Mounted Police sergeant, was a paragon of discreet non-comment. So, I suppose, was the £750 which it cost to import one of my sisters-in-law from South Africa; and if she stayed with us for seven months, who but a mean old bastard would even notice the fact?

'Well, it'll cost you!' was the recurrent, cautionary phrase used by people invited to do something, or to sell something, or to change something, or to repair something. 'Well, it'll cost you,' said the man who came to see what could be done about stripping off the jungle-strong ivy creeper and poisoning its roots (and indeed, it did cost $30).

Everything cost me, where Stone House was concerned. All the grotesque figures should have been alarming, but they never were. I loved the house, I liked the life, and as long as I could keep on writing, there should always be enough coming in to cope with the bath-water flow running out.

It cost a fourth fortune to enjoy the place.

I had come back from Barbados to celebrate my birthday, with a carefully planned dinner for eighteen. We just happened to have eighteen Crown Derby soup bowls, big plates, little plates, tiny plates, salad plates, butter dishes, and coffee cups; plus the necessary finger-bowls, cocktail glasses, sherry glasses, champagne glasses, liqueur glasses, tumblers, table mats, and ash-trays; plus the vital fish knives, fish forks, other knives, other forks, big spoons, little spoons, snail tongs, cheese scoops; plus enough salted peanuts and fried onion rings to start things off, and enough coffee-sugar crystals, brandy, Cointreau, Curaçao, Tia Maria, Grand Marnier, white *crême de menthe*, Marc de Bourgogne, whisky, Carlsberg lager and orange juice to round out a modestly hospitable dinner party.

Add: guest towels, Kleenex, cigarettes, cigars, after-dinner mints, flowers, Alka-Seltzer, and monogrammed match-boxes.

N. B. Had I remembered to tell Angus to tell Dinty to switch on the arc lights in the parking area, and to have the Land-Rover ready in case anyone got stuck in the snow?

Answer: No. Sometimes, fantastically, unbelievably in this world of Yes, the answer was No. But it was a superior evening, my forty-sixth, nonetheless.

Among the birthday presents brought by the slightly captive guests were a Visitors' Book from the darling old American ambassador, Douglas Stuart, a Chopin record from Lou Rasminsky, Governor of the Bank of Canada, a bottle-opener from Doug Abbott, lately Minister of Defence and now a Supreme Court judge; another bottle-opener, mink-handled, from George Drew, the Leader of the Opposition, a bottle of beautiful Bourbon whiskey from Giff Scull, the American naval *attaché*, and a three-record version of *La Forza del Destino* from crony and Q.C. Bernard Alexandor—a record which, coming from La Scala, Milan, with Maria Callas as Leonora, and Richard Tucker and Nicola Rossi-Lemeni to complement her rapturous voice, was soon to convert me to opera in general, as the supreme expression of music, and to Verdi in particular as the composer of all composers.

It was a good party, as usual; and, as usual, it was based on a strange, complicated, and vilely expensive operation. The extraordinary fact about it, and about all such parties, was that in terms of dollars to spend on them we had none at all.

I drew my modest salary as Chief of U.K. Information; and a grudging Treasury, before they changed the rules,* allowed me to keep, out of my dollar earnings, $900 a year—rather less than the monthly wage-bill for the staff.

Everything else which went to make such an evening, n such a house, from the champagne and its silver cooler to the tall ivory candles on the table (*and* the table), had to be imported from England and paid for in sterling.

The juggling act was entirely legal. It certainly aided the export drive. But it really was the most farcical exercise I had ever undergone since I was taught how to make Molotov cocktails at H.M.S. *King Alfred* in 1940.

There is a phrase in *Venus and Adonis*, which long ago used to make my imagination smoke a bit: where Venus falls down backwards, and Adonis (who always sounded rather coy, if not queer) accidentally falls on top of her, and it says: 'Now is she in the very lists of love, Her champion mounted for the hot encounter.'

The very lists of love, in my case, were something else again. They came from Lawn & Alder, Gordon & Gotch, Fortnums, the Army & Navy Stores, Harrods, Peter Jones, Cox & Kings, and Saccone & Speed, and many another august firm accustomed to exporting the best of everything to our far-flung empire.

A sample shipment, taken from the Saccone & Speed and Cox & Kings scriptures of late 1955, went like this:

Case No. 1
24 tins Maxwell House Instant Coffee
24 tins Sardines
24 tins Tunny Fish
24 giant pkts Dreft
24 magnum Lux Flakes
48 pkts Kleenex Tissues (200's)
 3 boxes ea. 3 Mammoth Ovals Morny's Sandalwood Soap
 3 tablets Bath Size Imperial Leather Soap

---

* Without telling me. Certain things one finds out too late in life; and too late in life it transpired that this ruling was 'out of date', and that I should have been advised that I could retain the lot.

Case No. 2

4 1lb. tins Earl Grey China Tea

12 lbs. Green Label Tea ($\frac{1}{4}$ lb. pkts)

3 1lb. tins Twinings Ceylon Breakfast Tea

12 tins C & B Asparagus Soup

12 tins C & B Mushroom Soup

12 tins C & B Celery Soup

12 tins C & B Oxtail Soup

12 tins C & B Vegetable Soup

12 tins C & B Tomato Soup

2 No. 4 Tins Sweet Assorted

2 No. 4 Tins Afternoon Tea

4 Biscuit Tins

2 Jars Stilton Cheese

4 No. 4 Tins Cocktail Assorted

2 Biscuit Tins

12 Large Tubes Listerine Toothpaste

2 prs. Ladies Shoes

2 Morphy Richards Irons repaired

Case No. 3

6 1lb. tins Strawberry Jam

6 1lb. tins Raspberry Jam

6 1lb. tins Apricot Jam

6 1lb. tins Blackcurrant Jam

6 1lb. tins Oxford Marmalade

12 1lb. tins O.E. Marmalade

6 bts. Green Label Chutney

12 tins B.L. Mushrooms

6 tins White Shoe Polish, Kiwi

6 bts. Heinz Walnuts

3 large bottles L & P Worcestershire Sauce

3 Airwicks

6 Tins Salted Almonds, $\frac{1}{2}$ lb.

6 Tins Salted Cashew Nuts, $\frac{1}{2}$ lb.

6 Large Tubes Ipana Toothpaste

6 Large Tubes Phillips Dental Magnesia
6 Jars Max Factor Melting Cleansing Cream
4 Large Bottles Omy Bath Salts
30 tins Carnation Milk
21 tins Heinz Baby Food

Case No. 4
 1 Linen Basket
24 Georgian Tumblers
24 Georgian Tumblers
 2 Ice Jugs
 2 Casseroles
 2 Feather Dusters
 1 Banister Brush
 2 Scrubbing Brushes
 2 Brooms
 2 Handles
 1 Grater
 2 Dustpans
 1 Tidy-Bin
 3 Chamois Leathers
 1 Frying Pan
 2 Saucepans and Lids
 2 Saucepans and Lids
 1 Knife
 1 Knife
 1 Serrated Knife
 3 Carving Knives
 3 Car Sponges
 1 Baking Tin
 1 Roaster
 1 Sandwich Tin
 3 Spoons
 1 Frypan
 1 Saucepan
 2 Mats

1 Primus Stove
2 Saucepans

Case No. 5
2 Pyrex Dishes
2 Thermos Jugs
2 Sieves

Even now, I cannot bear to put in the prices.

Sometimes we over-ordered. In the flurry which preceded my retirement from the Information Service, which meant that we had to stock up here and there before I lost the diplomatic privilege of free import, we certainly over-ordered.

The final shipment, of 23 bales of wine and spirits and six cases of household goods, must go down in mini-history as one of the more futile exercises in conspicuous spending. In bald, explicit import-speak it is really too awful to quote in full. But it ended, on a final flourish, with:

12 cases of Lanson 1947 champagne, 48 pots of French mustard, 72 tins of Anchovy Fillets, 48 tins of Tunny Fish, 3,000 sheets of headed notepaper and 3,000 envelopes (Smythsons), and 20,000 Churchman No. 1 cigarettes.

A gruesome analysis of latter-day history showed that such supplies, and others unrecorded, ran out as follows:

The Malayan Curry Mixture: 1960
The Swiss Black Cherry Jam: 1961
The last of the wine (Château Paveil de Luze, 1947): 1962
The Major Grey Chutney: 1962
The Earl Grey Tea (who *was* Grey?): 1966
The Anchovy Fillets: 1966
The Heinz Pickled Walnuts: 1967
The notepaper: 1968
The envelopes: still in strong supply, 1970
The duplicating paper: ditto.

In the garden, the noble lawn outside my study window was a delicious focus for a wandering eye. Across the drive, under the elms, the swimming pool waited for its first spring filling. In the garage, the Land-Rover (sometimes the only weapon which could get me to the office through winter snow) was ready for me; so was the horrid blue Chevrolet; so was the marvellous, run-of-the-mill Rolls-Royce, a grey Silver Cloud bought to replace the Continental Bentley which had been a disappointment.

Rolls-Royce, I found, included a wonderful dead-pan directive in their manual for the new owner: '*Running In:* You should not exceed 90 m.p.h. for the first 500 miles.'

In my panelled study, the great log fire kept me warm while I thought about the next book, and did not find much of an answer. In the immaculate drawing-room, the Will am and Mary veneered walnut spice-cabinet (now accommodating bottles instead) gleamed its welcome. In the sunroom, the wrought-iron furniture from Hammacher & Schlemmer was more elegant and comfortable than any overstuffed alternative.

In the kitchen, Mrs Evans was busy on the roast duck. In the pantry, Angus was polishing the silver. On a distant flower-bed, Dinty Moore was tending the first brave tulips. In the nursery, just over my head, subdued thuds through the solid ceiling indicated that brother was at odds with brother—or was helping him to do something novel and awful: it was difficult to tell.

The phone rang. It was Willis Wing from New York. *The Tribe,* which was being read 'on the coast' (meaning that province of the United States centred on Los Angeles) might possibly be sold as a film to Philip Yordan, who had made such a good job of *The Caine Mutiny.*

At the club, I had overheard someone say: 'That guy lives like a pig with its ass in butter.' Could it be me?

In the nursery. . . . I now had two sons. Indeed, I had three, though Max, the original model, already fourteen, was not in evidence, except when he flew across from London during the holidays. He was now at his public school, Lancing, after a most singular passage-of-arms, and defeat, over his admission to Winchester.

He had been entered for a particular house there, at the correct moment some five years earlier, with that precise regard for the rules which, God knows, Winchester instilled. The application was acknowledged, and I thought no more of it; I was fully employed in South Africa, on a reputable job, taking no leave, cutting no corners, and though 6,000 miles from home I felt entitled to assume that other people had the same ideas, and that an expatriate father would still rank as a normal human being, for administrative purposes.

I thought no more of it until the time came for him to take his entrance examination, when Eileen wrote to say that Winchester seemed to know nothing about Max at all. Had I cancelled the application?

The answer was No, of course not. I went into action, as far as I could at such long range. I was then told by his prospective housemaster, who presently emerged as one of the most elusive creatures ever to don a mortar-board, that Max's name had been crossed off his list some years earlier.

What? Why?

Well, since I had not been in touch either with the house or the school during the preceding five years, it was naturally assumed that my application had lapsed.

But good heavens, I had been in South Africa, on the High Commissioner's staff! How could I keep in touch?

Ah well. . . . It reminded me very strongly of that man who had refused to sell me a bottle of gin in 1946. *Then* I had been told: If I would keep dotting about, how could I expect to be a registered customer? Now the verdict was: Since I had not kept in close touch, as a prospective parent, the application had accordingly been cancelled.

Without saying a word about it to me? Oh, quite.

I appealed direct to the headmaster, who was then Mr Desmond Lee. His answer was courteous, kind, and adamant. Yes, it was true that Max had been entered for the school at the correct time. Yes, it was true that the housemaster had removed his name from the list of applicants, as nothing had been heard from me in the interim. (Christ, where was I supposed to be? On top of Everest?) No, it was not possible to reverse the decision. Housemasters had this absolute discretion. No, there were no other vacancies, nor any prospect of the position changing.

We thus had to look around, very quickly, but luckily we did not have to look long. My publisher, Desmond Flower, had been at Lancing (so had Father Trevor Huddleston, still pursuing me, in my private morality play, as the Conscience of Mankind). Lancing, Desmond said, was the place for Max; and Lancing it was.

It worked out very well. Lancing, though a devout establishment, concerned for the last half-century with building a school chapel which was nearer to a cathedral than many another aspirant, also took care of its transient mortals. Max grew tall, taller than I would ever be, and with brains—well, the time for comparisons was not yet.

Just as I had been good at running (the coward's solution to most of the problems of the small years), so he was good at boxing, the alternative tactic. Thus did the breed improve.

He liked the place. There was no other valid tribute, in the whole of the scholastic world.

Now his two half-brothers, aged three and aged two, all my pretty chickens in the Canadian coop, were in charge of Katie Ann Nicolson, nurse.

There are not many human beings of whom one can say: This one is as God intended, warm, generous, kind, hard-working, and efficient. Katie Nicolson came to Stone House by happy chance, selected after a simple exchange of letters before the computer-age fouled things up for good. Born, bred, and raised in the furthest Highlands, trained in Edinburgh, she was a little smiling Scots girl for whom young children had some magic attraction.

It seemed to be entirely mutual. From the first meeting, the

small nursery grew large in contentment, and even, now and
again, in good behaviour.

It had been a great relief to find her, at the first shot, since
children's nurses of such warm-hearted quality appeared to be
discontinued stock, like a missing coffee-cup. They seemed to
have become computerized themselves, and I always compared
Katie with a terrible example of the iron-souled instructress
who descended on some friends in Johannesburg. One of their
children, playing with the family dog, gave it a somewhat
intimate pinch.

'Don't touch his ballies, darling,' his mother cautioned. 'He
doesn't like it.'

The nurse, grey-uniformed like a female Guardee, was
furious. 'Madam!' she said. 'I have been teaching them *testicles!*'

Katie's charges, leased to us, were called Marc and Anthony
(what else could one christen a younger brother of Marc, except
perhaps Marc II?) Both had been born at the Civic Hospital in
Ottawa, and Marc's arrival gave rise to a favourite Ottawa joke.
His mother, when she went into hospital, noted down her
religion as Roman Catholic, which was technically true. But she
was not ardent, and when visited by the scouting priest she
declined his ministrations. Following a natural train of thought,
he asked: 'Are you married, my child?'

In Max's case, I had never been there when I wanted to be,
and never enjoyed his small years except in sessions just as
small. Now I staked my claim, as a matter of daily routine. At
noon I would stop work, or stop fooling around with a slow-
thinking typewriter, and say: 'I'll take them now, Katie,' and
shovel the small load into my study.

The seven-foot steel desk had two reliable pull-out shelves,
one on either side of the centre space. A child was planted on
each, and sat there, within reach of a guardian arm. (If I could
be scared of any fifth floor, perhaps they could be worried about
a drop of twenty-nine inches.) We then pursued an ordained
pattern of social intercourse.

'First we'll have a little think,' I said. For a couple of minutes they would stare at me, as bright as buttons. Already they knew what a think was; it was smiling silence. Then: 'Now both of you tell me a story, one at a time.' They were rather short stories, particularly Anthony's, whose command of English was unripe. Occasionally he would produce a string of unrelated syllables, whereupon the two of them would burst into roars of laughter, and I knew that Anthony must have made a very good remark indeed.

'Now I'll finish my drink,' and I did so, while they giggled at the theatrical slurping noises which were, I suppose, rather bad for nursery discipline. 'Now we'll go for a walk,' was the one after that, and the walk was always down the long slope of green lawn, to Aylmer Road and its quick-moving traffic at the bottom.

The two dogs followed us, one making heavy weather of it, the other prancing like a miniature heraldic lion in motion. One was an old, crotchety Sealyham, shortly to disgrace itself with two snarling snaps at the human race, the second of which missed Anthony's eye by less than an inch and left what looked like a life-long scar. After a flurry of blood, shock, dashes to the hospital, and rabies injections which were themselves a considerable hazard, the Sealyham, his grey hairs dishonoured, was asked to leave.

The other dog was mine: a small, sprightly, utterly neurotic French poodle called Noblesse Oblige, which could be very good company when in the mood, and a real little creep when it was not. It survived two years, and then disappeared; run over on the Aylmer Road, it was tossed into the nearest snow-drift, where it was discovered, three months later, on a sad spring morning.

On the return journey, I would say, like my father: 'I've got a bone in my leg,' and climb the last slope at a sorry limp. Then it was: 'Now we'll go for a little drive,' and at that point, stern discipline took over. This was *my* Rolls, not their rocking-horse

'*Don't* jump about. *Don't* touch the door handles. *Don't* put your feet on the seats.' These were of finest, pale-yellow

ox-hide, and smelt, for more than three years, as fresh and exciting as the new-born car itself. We drove along the Aylmer Road,
giving way, like anyone else with a grain of sense in his head,
to the dashing Quebec drivers, as far as a high-class hunting and
riding stables, known to the ribald, though not to my sheltered
children, as the Horses' Astor. Then back to the Country Club,
for *one* ice-cream, or Coke, or some other wild, fizzy, pre-lunch
stimulant.

Then it was home again, and discipline again, which might
perhaps last for the next five minutes. '*Both* wash your hands.
Both eat all your lunch. *Both* do exactly as Katie tells you.
Otherwise——' the language was already coarsening, 'there'll be
one *hell* of a row!'

Sometimes I said: 'Otherwise you will make me very sad,' and
they would look at me as if their little hearts were ready to crack.

I had time to play father, because I was on retirement leave
from my job.

By now I had been in the Information Service for very nearly
the second five-year term which I had contracted for, privately,
on that summer morning in London in 1951; and the strain was
beginning to tell, possibly on both sides.

Certainly this had nothing to do with the current High Commissioner in Canada, to whose staff I was attached as 'Counsellor
(Information)'—Lieutenant-General Sir Archibald Nye. The
enormous luck which had given me Sir Evelyn Baring as boss
in South Africa had flowered again; the new overlord was
another paragon of important virtues. But though there was
remarkable similarity between the two men—both public servants whose energy and devotion went far beyond their duty,
and perhaps beyond our deserts—yet there was remarkable
contrast also.

Baring, the aristocrat in action, had descended from above.
Archibald Nye had rammed a pathway upwards, with astonishing success.

He was a regimental sergeant-major's son, educated at a

school for the sons of N.C.O.s, and he started a long climb as a dog-soldier, a 1914 private with a rifle on his shoulder and a ferocious war to fight. He ended his military career, twenty-seven years later, as Vice-Chief of the Imperial General Staff, for a term of years which had never been more crucial for Britain: 1941-46.

He then rounded out all this with an impressive string of peace-time jobs—Governor of Madras, High Commissioner to India, and now to Canada. He was fifty-eight when I met him, sixty-one when I said good-bye.

Like Baring, he was a great man to work for; and, again like Baring, one of the few teetotallers who, as company, was ever worth a damn. The High Commission house was called Earns-cliffe, beautifully sited on the banks of the Ottawa River: a handsome old country place which had once been the home of Canada's very first Prime Minister, Sir John A. Macdonald.* To be invited there, to make up the numbers or plug a gap at a formal dinner-party, was not an office chore. It was always wholly enjoyable.

Diplomatic Ottawa was a good deal more formal and pat-terned than anything I needed to cope with in Johannesburg. The list of things one had to do on arrival, and the directives for our later behaviour, covered twenty-two foolscap pages, and ranged in subject from Curtseying (*not* to a Provincial Lieutenant-Governor) to the proper manipulation of visiting cards (bring 500 with you, as a starter): from where to seat Her Excellency's Lady-in-Waiting at a dinner party (she ranked as the wife of a Deputy Minister) to how to get hold of an Esso credit card.

The visiting card protocol was undeniably tricky, as must have been the original written instructions on how to dance the quadrille.

---

* Sir John A. was certainly in some contrast with Nye, being a dedicated drunk as well as a jugular-type politician. Once, at a rowdy political meeting, and faced with a difficult question, he bent down and was sick on the platform. But he could pass off even this sort of lapse. 'My opponents,' he said, coming up for air, 'always make me sick.'

1. On first arrival.

To introduce the new arrival and his wife their cards are sent to their equals or seniors, accompanied by the High Commissioner's cards with 'p.p.' (*pour présenter*) written on them in pencil. The procedure in detail is as follows:

(a) A man sends one card to each man shown in the Diplomatic List who is his equal or senior in rank, and to his wife. A wife sends a card only to each wife. No cards are sent by or to unmarried daughters.

(b) The cards sent to each High Commissioner's office and foreign Mission are divided into two batches. In one envelope, addressed to the Head of Mission and his wife, are sent the cards destined for them, accompanied by one of the High Commissioner's cards. In another envelope, addressed to the Mission as a whole (e.g. 'French Embassy') are sent, with one of the High Commissioner's cards, all the cards destined for other members of the Mission, with the name of the person for whom the card is intended written in pencil on the top of each card.

(c) A wife arriving after her husband has sent his cards round should send her cards similarly to wives of the officers to whom her husband has sent cards, accompanied in each case by the card of the High Commissioner's wife with 'p.p.' on it.

2. On Departure.

Cards are sent with the same distribution and with 'p.p.c.' (*pour prendre congé*) pencilled on each card. These cards are not accompanied by the High Commissioner's cards.

3. On Receipt of cards from other Missions.

'p.p.' cards received from other Missions should be returned, on the scale on which they are received (except that a woman does not return a card to a man), within a week. Nothing is written on such cards.

4. The Ottawa practice is to send all cards by post. If a card is received with a corner turned down, this indicates that it

has been left personally. It should be returned within a week,
with the corner turned down.*

5. '*Pour féliciter*' (p.f.), '*Pour remercier*' (p.r.), and '*Pour
condoler*' (p.c.) cards.

Some foreign Missions in Ottawa follow the customary
diplomatic practice of sending on appropriate occasions 'p.f.',
'p.r.' and 'p.c.' cards. 'p.f.' cards are sent by them to a Head
of Mission on the occasion of his national day, and elicit from
him in return cards marked 'p.r.'. 'p.c.' cards are s milarly
used to convey sympathy on occasions of national or personal
mourning.

Though antique, it did make one feel part of the family; and
it might be said that the average Canadian friend didn't give a
damn about visiting cards, and if the corners were turned
down would have blamed it on the dog.

The Ottawa Information Office could only be called 'Fair',
like unsatisfactory conduct in the Navy, and the accommodation
—a converted bowling alley overlooking the Colonial Coach
Lines main bus station—was not impressive. There was a first-
class man, Donald Kerr, as my deputy director: an Australian
who worked with rare, tremendous appetite and who, in the
coming expansion programme, was to prove himself a tower of
strength.

But expansion was certainly the first thing I thought of, as
soon as I looked the place over: one such office, and a staff of
twenty-four, was hardly adequate for a country of seventeen
million people and nearly four million square miles.

I was still enjoying the job very much, and the new country
was one I had always wanted to see. Sir Archibald Nye believed
strongly in the information arm of his High Commiss on. But
belief was not 100 per cent firm among my other colleagues:
not in information, not in me.

---

* This is imprecise, as I (an experienced proof-reader) felt bound to point out. You
didn't return the other chap's card; you 'returned' it by sending him one of
your own.

At the outset I was told that I was not to make any speeches or broadcasts, for at least six months, until I 'knew what to say'. I had known what to say for the last seven years in South Africa, a far trickier country, and the restriction was irksome. However, I had to turn down a round hundred of such invitations, without any valid explanation, and that made me feel a fool as well.

The Affair of the Canadian Destroyer made me feel an even bigger one.

There was a new, highly sophisticated destroyer nearing completion at Montreal, and it was thought, by a very senior man in the Ministry of Defence, that I would be interested in seeing over it. The invitation came at a party, but it was renewed on the telephone next morning, and I said that I would be delighted. The arrangements were made, and communicated to me. Then all the buttons burst.

It started with another telephone call, from our Royal Navy Liaison Mission in Ottawa. Would I come over immediately to discuss a most important matter?

The most important matter was my proposed walk round the new destroyer, and the man who interviewed me about it was really very annoyed indeed. Why had I not cleared it through his office first?

I explained that the invitation came direct from the Canadian Defence Department, that it was *their* destroyer, not ours, and that I hadn't thought it necessary to do anything but accept gratefully.

'That is *not* the way things are done here!' I was being looked at in a way I had already encountered: I might have been a sailor once, but I was only an information wallah now—and a *writer!* 'All these things have to go through this office. Damn it, we have to give you clearance! There's a total security ban on these new ships!'

'But damn it!' the vehemence was catching, '*they* asked me. It's *their* security worry, not ours. It's they who have to be satisfied about me. They know that I've had six years in the Navy, and more than seven in the information service. I must have been cleared for both. How can there be any security angle?'

'Well, there is!' he snapped. 'Anyway, we like to keep these things under control. What's going to happen if people on the High Commissioner's staff start wandering all over the place without us knowing?'

'Nothing,' I said, unwisely.

It produced a baleful response. 'Well, something *is* going to happen, in this case. Frankly, we would prefer you not to go.' And as I looked at him, mutinous in a very non-naval way, the real truth popped out. 'It's quite irregular. None of us here has been invited yet.'

I had to let it go, backing down without any argument. It was a silly, dog-in-the-manger exercise; certainly my security status must be good enough to let me walk round a nearly-finished naval ship. I had done it scores of times, and if this one had a lot of mysterious new weaponry, as was proudly claimed, I wouldn't understand the first thing about it anyway. But equally certainly, I didn't want a collision, at this sort of level, in my first month on the new job.

To our mutual embarrassment, I had to tell my Ministry of Defence friend that the visit was off. God knows what he thought. Perhaps that I couldn't really be trusted.

As time went on, it began to appear that I couldn't really be trusted in other spheres as well.

Writing a bestseller, and thereby making large sums of money in the process, was not the best pathway to advancement in the civil service. I was now earning quite a superior salary, measured by the standards of the past; when the rent allowance and the local cost-of-living differential were added, it came to £4,140 a year.

But there were also reports from time to time in the Press that my earnings outside the service, as a writer, must be something like ten times that amount. The fact could not have been endearing, though it need not have become an occasion of guilt.

A simple calculation showed that whatever I wrote, by way of official memorandum or draft despatch, was delivered practically free, while anything I produced for outside consumption earned about ten shillings a word. The contrast must have seemed irresistible. Before long my official prose, which went first to the Deputy High Commissioner, began to have a progressively rough time at Earnscliffe.

The blue pencil came to the fore, and hung poised over each paragraph. What might serve well enough for popular fiction would *not* pass scrutiny here. 'Poor construction, Monsarrat', was a phrase used on at least one occasion. 'Too many adjectives. (Verbiage.) This is far too long. (Develop.) This surely needs expansion.' And sometimes: 'I suggest you do it again.'

Not the chief editor of Cassell's, not even Alfred Knopf, would have essayed such slaughter.

There was, occasionally, some arbitrary editorship indeed. Once, when I was bringing up to date a survey of the senior members of the Press Gallery, and removed a man who had been dead for a year, he was reinstated.

It had its funny side, but it was deeply depressing nonetheless. I was beginning to think that I would never really prosper in the service, never get the sort of job I wanted; never even be a Deputy High Commissioner, with a little blue pencil in my little grey fist. The social differences between information personnel and those on the other side of the green baize door were still marked. We might be useful; but we still lived and died in the warrant officers' mess.

I could foresee a five-year term in Canada, and probably another five in India. By then I would be fifty-three, and would sweat out my last seven years at the Commonwealth Relations Office in Whitehall, reorganizing their film-strip filing system.

The willing horse so easily became the silly ass. Perhaps, with the best of motives and the worst of commonsense, I had already stayed in the service too long.

But my resignation, in the end, was triggered off by a very unlikely man, in a most unusual way.

It came during the last week of that 1955 trip to South Africa, which began in the Alien Income Tax Section of Upper Manhattan and finished up at my father-in-law's house in Plettenberg Bay, on the south coast of the Cape Province between Port Elizabeth and Cape Town.

This was a gem of a place, set back in the sandhills within sight of the beach and the sea: within sight of the old whaling station which had been the original reason for Plettenberg Bay's existence, and within sight of the hotel, which naturally belonged to my friend Soli Ornstein.

We were very content there, showing off the infant Marc to cooing Afrikaner neighbours, voyaging about in a motorized surf-boat, and eating all the fish I caught (our staple diet, meat). But by the end I, at least, was not at all content.

The crack in the blue sky came in the form of an express letter from the British High Commission in Cape Town.

This was polite, as usual, and concise, but somewhat ominous. The Commonwealth Relations Office had been in touch with them. There had been a report in a London newspaper of an interview, in which I was quoted as saying that I was about to publish a novel about race relations in South Africa.

C.R.O. was naturally concerned about this, in view of my recent term of office in that country, and felt that they should have more details on what might become a sensitive, or even a controversial matter. In short, what was this all about?

I had, of course, a perfectly good answer to this, and I made it promptly. The man in London had got it wrong, I assured the High Commissioner's office. My novel, which would not be out for at least a year, was not about South Africa—I would never have considered such a project. It was about Africa generally— African problems, African solutions, African hopes for the future.

It was set in an invented country—a mythical island, in fact— which did not bear the slightest resemblance to South Africa. South Africa indeed was scarcely mentioned, and her peculiar race-situation not at all. The book, if it took any particular

standpoint, was in praise of British colonial history and administration.

It was a detailed answer, because in all the circumstances I felt
that they, and the Commonwealth Relations Office, were entitled
to it. The reaction was speedy, and scarcely expected. In view
of the information I had given, I was told, it would be best if I
came to Cape Town as soon as possible, to discuss the matter
with our newly arrived High Commissioner.

This was a discomforting turn, for a special reason. The new
High Commissioner was Sir Percivale Liesching, who had been
the Permanent Under-Secretary at the Commonwealth Relations
Office and was now taking up his last job—a job of immense
importance, in the light of the fading British connection with
South Africa—before his retirement.

I was lucky enough to know him well, from various calls
while in London, to admire him without qualification, and to
know also that his reputation as an immensely capable administrator was founded on solid fact, and not on any artificial aids to
career-building.

He was the third in my gallery of three public servants who
deserved all their medals twice over.

It was therefore all the more worrying to have to face him
on a matter like this. I could not help feeling, also, that he had
plenty of more important things to occupy his time.

The meeting was in two parts, and grew progressively more
disturbing. Sir Percivale, an iron-grey man with a formidable
chin, gave me a drink, as he had always done before. Then he
began to ask a lot of questions, prefaced by a brief recapitulation
of the ground-rules.

I was a permanent civil servant, subject to the general proviso
that while I was in the service I would not write, for publication,
anything which made any reference, or bore any relation, to the
work I was doing or the country where I was *en poste*. On retirement, I would still be subject to the Official Secrets Act, so far
as it involved any confidential material acquired in the course
of my duties.

I was aware of this?

Yes.

So. . . . The cross-examination started, and it was, as might have been expected, a very good one.

This book of mine. He had read my letter, and he was sure that it had cleared up a lot of questions, as far as London was concerned. But there were still some further points on which he, and they, would like assurance. This mythical country of mine. It might not be South Africa. Personally he was sure that it was not. But could it be *supposed* that it was South Africa, with consequent possibilities of embarrassment?

No. The locale bore no relation to South Africa, nor did its political set-up. I did not want to write about South Africa, even if I had not known that this was out of the question. Mine was a simple, pastoral country called Pharamaul, just moving into the twentieth century. It was my own invention.

Then was it, or could it be thought to be, an *enclave* of South Africa (this was the dear old B. B. & S. file again: Bechuanaland, Basutoland, and Swaziland, which had given us all quite enough trouble already). Was it a country which, surrounded by South Africa, might be under pressure from her bigger neighbour?

No. It was not like that at all.

Then what was it like?

Did my book concern Britain's attitude towards race relations?

In that case, was it critical of South Africa?

Was it critical by implication?

Was it critical of Britain?

Was it critical because of some special knowledge which I had learned in my official capacity?

Could my views be embarrassing to the British Government?

Could they be embarrassing to *me*, presuming that I wanted to continue to be employed by the Commonwealth Relations Office?

(And I hope you will be, he was kind enough to add. But I was beginning to feel a cool draught, even in Cape Town's steamy summer heat.)

Finally: Would I then be submitting the book to the Commonwealth Relations Office before I published it?

This was a crucial point, and it had to be faced. I felt bound to answer: No, I had not thought of submitting it, because the book did not concern either my job, or C.R.O. In similar circumstances, I had never submitted *The Cruel Sea* to the Admiralty, because I knew very well that there was nothing objectionable in it, from the security point of view, even though it was assuredly based on 'knowledge acquired during service in the Royal Navy'.

Sir Percivale Liesching, bless him, could pounce very swiftly, and he did so now.

The Cruel Sea, he reminded me, had been published after the war, and at least five years after I ceased to be a naval officer. This book about *Africa* (he could smile quickly, as well as pounce) would be published while I was still a member of the Commonwealth Relations Office, and it would follow a very recent appointment to that particular part of the world. In the circumstances, C.R.O. would certainly feel happier . . .

All right, I told him. I *would* submit it, if I were still in the public service.

I was being pressured, and I knew it, and he knew it: courtesy, consideration, measured language still carried their cutting edge. That was possibly—probably—the whole point of our meeting. But I was scarcely prepared for the second stage of the interview. Liesching pressed his bell, and asked a senior member of his staff to come in.

This was someone whom I knew only from inter-office correspondence. It was clear that he did not know me, except as a potential nuisance; it was enough that he knew the reason for the summons. It was even more clear that the session had now become formal, and disciplinary, and that he was to be the witness to it. Suddenly, I did not like this at all.

My attention, Liesching said, when the third man was seated, was drawn to the Official Secrets Act. It was also drawn to my undertaking not to use any material of a confidential nature obtained in the course of my employment. While I was so employed, he must advise me that any book I wrote even remotely connected with any material I might have acquired during this employment, should be submitted to the Commonwealth Relations Office before publication. It would be better if I sent them a synopsis of my new novel, as soon as possible.

Our witness made unobtrusive notes—the most obtrusive notes of all.

I was by now rather angry, and angry with a good man, for the first time in the whole of my official life. Sir Percivale Liesching was entirely in the right: he was only doing his duty, with his customary thoroughness and honesty. If London was worried, it was up to him to convey the fact to me, beyond any argument, or any later dispute.

I could never admire him less, because of such a confrontation. I even believed, and certainly hoped, that it was not much to his taste. But the anger, the stinging wound, remained.

It was the presence of the witness, doubtless by C.R.O. directive, which got me on the raw. The implications were obvious, and enraging. *Two* people could now swear—if it came to swearing—that I had been duly warned of my dangerous course. Should I even try to twist out of it. . . .

Wouldn't those niggling bastards ever trust me? . . . Still furious, I drove back along the winding Garden Route from Cape Town to Plettenberg Bay: 300 miles of sunlit, and then moonlit, coastal landscape, over hill and dale, across small mountains, past rolling beaches—one of the most magical drives still available to man.

Eleven miles from home, I had a puncture. Eleven miles, out of 300—why couldn't my silly old father-in-law, with all those bloody servants, have his tyres checked? . . . I walked those last eleven miles, under the moon, and then the stars. There had been rumours of a wild cat, a real wild cat, a mountain lion or puma (or cougar: *Felis Concolor*, anyway) loose in the area.

There was a herd of elephants there already, wandering the

15

Knysna Forest. Every time the roadside grass stirred, or a twig snapped, I braced myself for blood and trampling, claw marks and death.

They would only match what I felt had happened to me in Cape Town.

At some point during that eleven-mile plod, which finished at 2 a.m., I made up my mind. For a whole gallery of reasons, it was obvious that I could not be a civil servant and a writer at the same time. Even if it had not been, by a fantastic margin, the more profitable task, writing was the job for me.

Next morning, fortified by sunshine and Cape brandy, I sent to Sir Percivale Liesching, without the smallest shrinkage of respect, my letter of resignation, and repeated it to Archie Nye, with the same undiminished personal regard.

It could take effect, I said, at any time convenient to them within the next year—my last bow towards duty, discipline, and the pride and pleasure I had always felt, even in such confined employment.

In reply, Liesching sent back one of the nicest letters I had ever received from anyone. Its general purpose was to say how sorry he would be if our recent interview had impelled me to resignation. It had been his duty, etc. . . . I had done valuable work in the Information Service, and it was good to hear that I would not be leaving immediately.

One of the funnier, or sadder, aspects of all this, was something which Sir Percivale Liesching did not then know (though I took good care to tell him about it later): that he himself figured prominently in *The Tribe*, as the model or prototype for Sir Hubert Godbold, the Permanent Under-Secretary of my 'Scheduled Territories Office', and the only wholly admirable character in the book.

As it turned out, I stayed on for another full year, and I tried to make it a good one. With stalwart help from Sir Archibald Nye, I was able to complete the expansion job on our information service in Canada; in fact I rammed it home up to the hilt, where it still stands—my only monument, but a better one than that stone house on the hill could ever be.

It was Nye himself who had shown me the way, about a year earlier. He came to lunch one day, when we were both temporary bachelors, with wives either visiting relatives in England or addressing women's clubs in far-off Prince Edward Island.

While we walked to and fro under the trees afterwards, he remarked that on the west coast of Canada, where he had just been on a speaking tour, no one except a few newspaper editors who were on our mailing list had ever heard of the U.K. Information Office.

I said that this, though mortifying, was more than likely. Vancouver, for example, was over 2,500 miles from Ottawa— and Vancouver didn't like Ottawa, anyway. There was no reason why they should know that we existed. Unless we were operating on the spot, they never would.

'Exactly!' He had a way of tossing his head up when he wanted to emphasize a point, and he did so now. 'So we should be there.'

'Yes.' After lunch, in my own house, I didn't say 'sir'.

'And some other places too?'

'Two or three, anyway.'

'Right!' He rubbed his hands together, as if he could smell from afar off a battlefield at least as crucial as Alamein or Tobruk. 'What I would like you to do,' he said, 'is to let me have a plan. The ideal information service, to cover the whole of Canada. With all the details—offices and costs and everything.'

'It would be very expensive,' I told him. I had been playing round with the idea for some months, and the figures, when set against our perennial, atrocious, dreary dollar situation, were awful.

'Excellent!'

It was an unusual word to hear from a civil servant, but he was an unusual civil servant. I believed the man, and therefore the word, and I went to work.

I knew exactly what I wanted to do: to improve on that

inadequate, one-office, Ottawa set-up, which simply could not cover the ground. It had its prestige link with the High Commission, and a strategic link with the Parliamentary Press Gallery, on which all Canadian newspapers and a number of foreign ones were represented; and that was about all.

The Press Gallery, in any case, was far from being adequate itself, and therefore was not all that important. It was an incestuous body; the members were much more likely to interview each other (on the lines of 'What do you think of the situation, Joe?' 'I think it's alarming, Walt,' which would then give rise to: 'Informed sources in Ottawa have expressed considerable alarm etc.') rather than to get up, go outside, and ferret out a few facts for themselves.

They also had absurd privileges, including free office-space within the House of Commons itself, free mailing rights, and a time-honoured habit of accompanying Cabinet ministers on their jaunts, in private planes, at the public expense, and thereafter writing up their benefactors' mighty deeds ('Hon. Minister of Works Opens $10 Million Dam'—a very stupid thing to do) in the nearest they could come to glowing prose.

There were some honourable exceptions, a handful of first-class men: Michael Barkway of the Toronto *Financial Times*, Blair Fraser of *Macleans*, Frank Swanson of the *Ottawa Citizen*, Patrick Nicholson of Thomson Newspapers, Ray Daniell of the *New York Times*, and Hilary Brigstocke of the London *Times*.

These were all valued friends as well as worthwhile newspaper men, though once, on a certain New Year's Eve, I did have a monumental row with Hilary Brigstocke, who charged me with hating journalists because I had once been one myself, to which I replied that I loathed journalists anyway, and did not need any personal reasons for it.

It was a fairly quotable comment from the head of the British Information Service, which Brigstocke was kind enough not to quote.

But apart from this, the Press Gallery was not the thing to concentrate on, nor was Ottawa the pivot of this enormous

country, as far as our work was concerned. A single glance at
the map showed the ludicrous gaps, which could never be filled
by duplicated press releases from Ottawa. We needed to be
there—and 'there' meant having an office, and a man, and a staff,
and a visible presence, in all the major population centres, from
the Atlantic to the Pacific.

It was an important idea because, as far as I could judge, the
Canada-British link seemed to be fading gently away, like that
South African one—though here it was not politics, nor principles, but lack of contact. The miserable wet hand of the
Treasury, intent on their penny-pinching travel restrictions (a
hopeless handicap to put upon a country trying to sell itself and
its wares), dictated that the only Britons whom Canadians ever
saw were a few civil servants, the resident mice, and after that,
travelling businessmen trying to eke out a handful of dollars as
they went their humble rounds.

The monarchy was a faraway charade; even the commonwealth tie, in which I believed passionately, seemed to be
coming unstuck, for lack of a simple, common interchange. All
the time there was an enormous, unflagging, relentless pull from
the United States, just over the border, hammered home by
newspaper, magazine, film, radio, television, and book.

We had to fight the belief that anything efficient, anything
worthwhile, whether a car, a TV set, an aircraft, a travelling
salesman, a theatrical company, a breeding bull or a political
idea, had to come from America.

There was work to be done—and the British Information
Service could at least try to do it. . . . Being cautious, I produced two plans for our expansion; one modest, and therefore
cheaper, the plan I thought the Treasury *might* buy, and a
second one, far-out, costing the earth compared with our little
Ottawa budget.

In the latter, the true ideal, I planned a chain of five information offices, covering the whole vast country: linked by tele-
printer, linked with our Trade Commissioners on the spot,
linked to Britain by firm, really efficient ties of communication.

It involved a British information 'presence' in Quebec, Montreal, Ottawa, Toronto, and Vancouver, with side-contacts to
Winnipeg and Edmonton. It was detailed, down to the last
square foot of office carpet. It would cost—and I was almost
ashamed to set down in cold print the final noughts in the total
budget.

When Archie Nye presently came back from a working leave
in London ('I had to see the old boy,' he said, and the old boy
could only be Sir Winston Churchill, now nearing retirement,
with whom he was on the best of terms) he called me up and
told me that it was all organized, and that I could go ahead. He
was almost off-hand—as off-hand as a Lieutenant-General could
ever be.

'But which one, sir?' I had to ask. I was going to be very
pleased anyway. 'Plan A?'

'Plan B.'

My normal expletive would have been inappropriate; Nye
was a lapsed Catholic, with (as was often the case) a far more
tender conscience towards blasphemy than many another upright citizen. I could only say: 'Good heavens!'

'Winston also said,' Nye continued, ' "Tell him it was a fine
book." '

I could have slain any dragon that day.

I spent the last nine months of my employment putting
together the bricks and mortar of this grand design. Donald
Kerr did nearly all the spade-work, travelling to and fro, working like the Canadian beaver itself; making contacts, leasing
premises, engaging staff, settling squabbles ('How can I work
in *Taronna*?' a girl in the registry asked, as if a move from
Ottawa to Toronto, all of 240 miles, was a matter of desperate,
last-ditch emigration), sorting out problems which, at first in-
soluble, melted like thin snow under an imported Australian sun.

When I retired, and he succeeded me as the heir to this new
empire, the promotion was so thoroughly deserved that I could
not be sad for anything lost, nor envious of anything gained, for
more than the customary period of court mourning.

Of course, there were one or two things I missed, and missed for all time. One was the sense of service which had been mine for sixteen years, ever since I was measured for my cherished blue suit in 1940. It was a large slice of a working life, but there were moments when it seemed that such a slice could never be too large; that it ought to go on for ever, or at least for the regulation forty years, without complaint and without any thought of making a change for the better.

Anyone could be rich. The reputable thing was to be devoted to duty, and honourably poor.

Another gap was the gap in awareness. As soon as I resigned, I felt out of things immediately; I had been reading telegrams and despatches and memoranda, some of them highly confidential, ever since I joined the information service, and when that source was cut off, when one was no longer 'in the know', even in the most limited sense, one felt down-graded. Now all the facts, all the interpretations, had to come from those damned newspapers.

A lot of officially acquired knowledge could never be used, nor even mentioned outside a closed door. But it had always been satisfying to hear it and to have it; to know the real reasons why a certain thing was being done one way instead of another; to be given a glimpse, through a slightly parted curtain, of the orderly, sensible, skilful, and continuing world of diplomacy.

Policy always had a reason behind it, sometimes unstated, often unmentionable until long afterwards. Now I would never know, except by guesswork, why the necessary manipulation of my life, and of tens of millions of other lives, was being so oddly conducted. I would never know anything except what I read in the Toronto *Telegram*, and the *Daily Express*, and *Newsweek*. It was a fearsome thought. From now I could only be Yours truly, Frankly Disgusted.

I missed, very much, the chance of meeting important and gifted people which even a minor diplomatic post had given me. At Earnscliffe, for example, I had met the Mountbattens, and Prime Minister Nehru of India, and Prime Minister St Laurent of Canada, and Duncan Sandys, and Alan Lennox-Boyd, and Field-Marshals Montgomery and Templer, and Lord Swinton, and possibly thirty ambassadors, from the American to the Russian, from Iceland to Indonesia. There was a certain snobbery involved in this mixed bag, but it was the snobbery of achievement, and it would never disappear while I was alive to observe and to admire.

There would never be another electric occasion like Sir Winston Churchill's last Press conference in Canada, in 1954.

He was very frail when he arrived from Washington; he was by then eighty years old, he had barely recovered from his recent stroke, and he was to resign from public life within a year. I think we all knew that Canada would never see him again, nor the world either, before very long, and the atmosphere was charged with emotion on both sides.

I shared the top table with this great man, and Sir Anthony Eden, and Sir Archibald Nye, and it was my job to put the questions to him—written questions, by his choice, which had been sent to me by the assembled correspondents.

Churchill was in wonderful form, from the very beginning, and as sharp at eighty as any two other men at forty each. He arrived late, having been delayed at a Canadian cabinet meeting; but by a curious coincidence, the clock which was a prominent feature of the conference room had stopped at exactly eleven o'clock, the time he was due.

He noticed this immediately, and he began, in that great growling voice which was still strong, though now a little quavering at the edges:

'I was about to apologize for keeping you waiting, but——' he looked up at the clock, and all our eyes followed, 'I see that, with rare delicacy——'

The rest was lost in laughter, and from then on the fun and the spectacle started. I spoke, he answered; and to be thus involved, even as a verbal postman, was a proud and memorable privilege. A friend in the Canadian Broadcasting Corporation

later gave me a recording of the entire proceedings, and it is a
treasure which I have taken good care will never be lost.*

There was one small, behind-the-scenes diversion which I
knew about. In the course of routine inquiries about his accommodation in Ottawa, the High Commissioner had asked what
the Prime Minister would prefer to drink during his visit. The
answer came back smartly, almost with the pop of a cork:

'Rhine wine at luncheon, champagne at dinner, and brandy
at all other times.'

That was the kind of thing I was going to miss.

I left the service on 20 April 1956, ten years to the day since
I had first landed at Cape Town. For a hundred different reasons,
we had decided to stay on in Canada. Though it was funny to be
free, this was a marvellous country to be free in.

3.

The great skeins of Arctic geese flew north in April on their
return journey from a chic winter in Florida or Mexico or even
South America, 4,000 miles away. One could hear them coming
from a long way off, honking endlessly like mad motorists;
then what looked like a thin smoky cloud would take shape,
and it would be these huge grey birds by the thousands and
thousands—the leaders spread out ahead in a thin questing line,
the outriders veering this way and that, the whole vast throng
changing shape and direction as if they really were clouds,
harried by the wind.

They always seemed to cross the highway between Ottawa
and Montreal at the same point, near a village called Hawkes-
bury, and it was worth getting out of the car to watch them fly
by. When they were directly overhead, one could see the great,

* An extract can be found in Appendix C.

slow-beating, weary wings flailing away without respite, one could almost lose the wild beauty and only share their exhausted labour.

Even in the short time one watched, they would have flown twenty miles across this small arc of heaven. They still had more than a thousand to go, as they faded into the northern skies, and their sound, like the sound of a faraway, ghostly pack of hounds in desperate cry, faded with them.

They were coming back to their own country, with the same prodigious determination which had taken them south last fall; and they were right.

I once wrote, for the *Daily Express*, an article on 'Why I Stayed On In Canada', instead of coming home, like a sensible chap, to enjoy the delights of the British climate, the lavish elbow-room, the handsome urban development, and the general industrious benevolence, after ten years in two assorted wildernesses.

The most cogent reason could be pared down to five words, 'Because I liked the place', but these had to be expanded, in the interests of filling one and a half columns and earning £100. Dredging about, I came up with what I thought was a fair picture of a country which would really have needed a book to describe its merits, and a good fat appendix to cover the drawbacks.

By that time, I spent most of the year living on an island in the St Lawrence River, with side-trips to Ottawa to have a bath instead of a shower; and, half-way through my account, it was from there that I took off, in the middle of the giant Seaway, two miles from the Canadian river-bank, three from the American shore-line opposite, with ship after ship romping past, under the flags of twenty different countries, a hundred yards from my stone patio.

The St Lawrence River island is simple bliss. It is in an area called the Thousand Islands (although there are more

than 1,700 of them), and I know by personal observation that
it is as lovely as any comparable part of Italy, Southern
Africa, or the deep South Pacific.

But my island and its surroundings are not unique. There
are places like it all over Canada, where you can lead the
ideal outdoor life. Here, as elsewhere, we have everything or
our own front doorstep: sailing, fishing, water-skiing, swimming: gardening in the spring, duck-shooting in the autumn.

And after autumn comes a four-month winter when skiing,
skating, and curling are readily available not more than three
or four miles away.

Canada has what I think is the perfect climate: a very hard
winter with lots of snow, but guaranteed sunshine: a short
spring to liberate the spirit: a long, hot summer: and the
most beautiful autumn in the world. We don't have any dead
Novembers or weeping Februaries (or Augusts). Instead we
have a wonderful contrast of seasons which allows me, for
instance, to work hard all winter (because my skiing days are
over), and to sail, think, work not quite so hard, and soak up
the sun all summer.

It's important to make the point that I'm not describing
the life of rich or privileged people. All these joys are
available very cheaply—if they cost anything at all—to every
Canadian family. Outboard motorboats are as common as
bicycles. The weekend skiing trip to the Laurentians, north
of Montreal, is as easy and as normal as a stroll in Hyde
Park for a Londoner.

I've travelled twice right across this country—once by air
on a speaking tour, and once on a leisurely car trip which
took about two months. The contrast of scenery is as vivid
as the contrast of seasons.

It ranges from the endless rolling wheatlands of Manitoba
to the snowy spine of the Rockies; from a soft-running salmon
river in Newfoundland to the thunderous cataracts of Niagara
Falls. There is a marvellous sense of space, particularly in the
west, which one gets in very few other countries.

I've emphasized the outdoor side of life, because Canada is basically still that kind of pioneering country: cheerful, rough and ready, suspicious of social graces. But it is no intellectual wasteland either. Last year, for example, Toronto had eight of the world's finest orchestras visiting them in the course of two months. We had Glenn Gould to play the piano, Stratford (Ontario) to stage the finest Shakespearian season in North America, and Karsh of Ottawa to raise portrait photography to the level of art.

We feel morally strong enough to entertain Red Army singers and Chinese ballet dancers, banned from the more delicate air of the United States. And the Canada Council spends a yearly budget of more than £1,000,000 in general support of the arts.

Of course, there are drawbacks. Much of the food is awful. The liquor laws are barbaric. Some of our sports are brutal; we play football for money, and ice-hockey for blood. There is a more-than-average seasonal unemployment. Our Federal affairs are conducted like some childish guessing game. But there is also a healthy if-you-don't-work-you-don't-eat outlook, which might be Canada's best re-export to the Mother Country.

Come and take a look at us. It's only six hours away—quicker and safer than driving down to Cornwall. And the sun will be shining when you get here.*

The sun must have been shining when I wrote that; it is a *little* bit on the highly coloured side, like a picture postcard of the Lake District which omits the drenching rain. But perhaps even that hopeful optimism was a product of Canada, which I certainly grew to love, and where I was to stay for fourteen years.

Fourteen years is at least one third of an adult life, using the term for that fortunate span when, with luck, one can pick and choose one's surroundings. I never thought of making any

* By courtesy of the *Daily Express*.

change until, much later, change itself compelled me to do so.

To establish truth, one should start at the lowest end of the scale, up to the hocks in muck if need be, and then climb up into the clear, breathable air, where even the most horrible swamp gives way to the hand of heaven.

It was true that Canadian politics, and politicians were a murky lot, operating in a way which would have disgraced even Liverpool civic tactics in the Thirties, and which is now outlawed by general consent of the governed and the governors.

Scandals abounded, of the most deplorable kind; they were briefly paraded, lapped up by a sanctimonious yet cynical public, and then shrugged off and forgotten. What could you expect? This was politics! Of course the bastards put their hands into the till, and for every one that was caught, you should have seen the one that got away.

Immorality only meant two things: sex and drink, the twin undoubted crimes. Immorality meant being found in the wrong bed, or drawing a cork in public. It did *not* mean cruelty, stealing from public funds, taking bribes, telling commercial or political lies, or cutting corners under the banner of Business. It certainly did not mean gross election frauds—that, once again, was only politics.

Most disconcerting of all, if a politician were caught doing something which, in Britain at least, would drive him out of public life for ever, he almost always popped up for re-election next time, smiling the smile which only a hide like a rhinoceros could muster.

Some random samplings from a horrid ragbag of misdemeanour could produce a quick and very nasty taste.

A local Controller (municipal councillor) took a regular percentage on a garbage-collecting contract; when discovered, he only said: 'Everyone does it.'

A senior member of a school board bought a piece of land cheap, declared it to be the ideal site for a new school (a decision on which he had the final vote), and sold it back to the municipality at over 100 per cent profit.

Men impersonating other voters at an election, and men giving false names or the names of the recently deceased, and other men raiding polling booths and trying to carry off ballot-boxes, were never in serious trouble with the law. If caught, they were detained at the nearest police station, and released when the voting day was over.

A Roman Catholic priest, in return for small donations to church funds, made out and signed falsely inflated 'charitable receipts', which then ranked as an income tax deduction for his parishioners. A formal complaint, but no prosecution, came from the tax authorities.

Following a local election, voters who made a solemn declaration, before the successful candidate and the parish priest, that they had voted 'the right way', were then given jobs on the public payroll.

This kind of contempt for the law slopped over into atrocious union lawlessness—illegal picketing, beating up of strike-breakers, stoning, overturning, and burning of delivery trucks, and sabotage of equipment such as tampering with the brakes or steering of company cars.

No politician would dare to denounce such tactics. Union members were reliable voters. Reliable voters were money in the bank. Anyway, it wasn't *wrong*: it was a sort of politics—the rough sort. Dig a little deeper, and you might open a can of worms.*

However, politics did *not* include communism; the 'commie' label here was as much a brand on the brow as in America, and Canadians, caught in the aspic of set attitudes, could be extraordinarily strait-laced about it.

Even to hint, for example, that there might be something in the original communist ethic ('From each according to his ability, to each according to his needs') which could spring from noble, generous impulse—that it once had a root or two in

* Politics bred its own peculiar jargon. Of a Cabinet minister who was falling into disfavour, I once heard it said: 'He's going through a process of de-band-wagonization.'

Christianity: even to hint, as I once unwisely did, that it was perhaps a good thing that the Russians had the atom bomb, because this was too awful a weapon for a one-nation monopoly, and that therefore atom spies and defectors might have done us all a brave service in striking a balance of terror—this was monstrous heresy, the equivalent in evil of hitting an old woman over the head with an iron bar.

It broke up dinner parties, sundered friendships, and caused tight lips all round, for many a long day.

But sex—now that was something really naughty. In politics and business, much was excused; in sex, nothing. A Senator who rifled the public purse could declare that he had no intention of resigning; a Cabinet minister having a brief fling in an unhallowed bed was kicked out forthwith

It was a product, probably, of Canada's 'two cultures'; the one a dour, Calvinist, 'pleasure is wrong' outlook, the other a French-Canadian, hard-line Catholicism which saw wickedness behind every hemline, and woman as the lustful seductress of high-thinking, moral man. Between the frowning Scottish elder and the peeping priest, Canada had apparently broken its frontiers and peopled its land, all without a single twinkle in the eye.

Officially, contraception was illegal, as well as sinful within the Catholic code; the police, for a change of pace after hounding the motorist, could always hound the local chemist. In the realm of mixed-up values, there was one interesting case, cited by a welfare worker. An unmarried girl became pregnant, and was mildly cross-questioned. How many times had she made love? 'About a hundred.' Why did she not use contraceptives? 'My boyfriend says they're immoral.'

More generally, it was love itself which was immoral. Canadians seemed to have an inborn horror of admitting affection for a woman; the climate of love was 'unmanly'; to be seen carrying home a bunch of flowers meant being branded as a homosexual or, at the very least, an interior decorator—a baffling reversal of the roles.

At parties, the sexes separated with the minimum delay, as they did in Australia; at one end of the room the men talked sport, at the other it was domestic topics all the way—all the way, that was, through a cosy nesting-box of cooking, sewing, washing, recipes, children, and dogs. Love was *not* a domestic topic.

Any man who dared to mingle with the wrong end of the room was a suspect, and the male eyes which bored into the back of his neck were matched by the steely glances as the women closed ranks against this loose-living maniac, and kept the conversation firmly centred on left-over fish-fingers.

A Canadian friend, in oblique reference to a rumoured love-affair of mine, pronounced his verdict: 'What I always say is, sex will get you nowhere.' The phrase could well stand for the whole joyless scene.

Sex incurred the social frown; alcohol the official one. Canada, like other outdoor nations, was a strong drinking country: somewhere between Kenya, where it was an excess almost artistic, and townee Australia, where it was gross. But Canadian authority did not recognize this aberration; or rather, they did not recognize that to make alcohol difficult to procure, and thus an occasion of sin, merely intensified the lust to get hold of it. Canadian liquor laws were grotesque.

Since drinking was sinful, it was fit only for a strict government monopoly. A thirsty man had first to buy a two-dollar 'liquor permit'. He then went to a government liquor store, wrote out his order (a bottle of Johnny Walker became '1 x 12A', and two bottles of Gordon's gin '2 x 167B'), produced it together with his permit, paid the cashier, and carried his purchase away in a brown paper bag which was as recognizable, and as vaguely disreputable, as a costermonger's cart.

In the liquor store, there was no information to be had about wine ('I'd like to try some vinn roodge,' I once heard a customer say, to which the man behind the counter replied: 'Suit yourself!'), nor the best choice of spirits. The assistants were not allowed to give advice, nor to recommend one brand

CANADIAN STRATFORD FESTIVAL, 1956
Christopher Plummer as Henry V, Ginette Letondal as Katharine

THE FIRST STRATFORD (ONTARIO) TENT THEATRE, 1953

THE PERMANENT STRATFORD FESTIVAL THEATRE, 1957

THREE JOLLY SAILORMEN
Max, N. M., and Commodore J. P. Dobson, C.B.E., D.S.C., R.D., R.N.R.,
on board the *Empress of Scotland*

'STONE HOUSE', AYLMER ROAD,
PROVINCE OF QUEBEC

THE FIRST
CONTINENTAL
BENTLEY
In Rockcliffe Park,
Ottawa

THE DRAGON YACHT *VALHALLA*
heading for a picnic on Lake St Louis, near Montreal

PLONK!
George Formby giving some ukelele instruction on board the *Empress of Scotland*. Beryl
Formby suffering on the right

THESE FOOLISH THINGS
Standing in a life-boat, in the rain, under a flowered beach umbrella, at Rockefeller Center
on Fifth Avenue, soliciting books for the U.S. Merchant Marine

over another. They could hardly be expected to know about
wine anyway, since they were low-grade civil servants, the next
off the bench, who might just as well have been sorting tax
forms or writing out car licences.

Once inside, you were on your own, part of a furtive
shuffling *clientèle* which (one could not help feeling) had no
business to be there in the first place.

Once *outside* the liquor store, you were a marked man. The
bottle had to be carried home intact. It must only be opened in
your own house, or in your hotel room. Once opened, it could
not be brought out of doors again. It must be finished in private
—perhaps the origin of the manly 'killing the bottle' drinking
session: a barbarous social tradition which persisted long after
the rules were relaxed.

It could not be drunk, with strict legality, in your own back
garden. It could not be broached at a roadside picnic park, nor
on board your own boat. In fact, it was illegal to have an opened
bottle in your possession in any public place; and equally illegal
to buy a drink, even in your own club, on any election day.

Total prohibition was still in force here and there, since to be
'wet' or 'dry' was always a matter of local option. When
Ottawa, for example, built its handsome new international airport some fifteen miles out of town, it included an equally
handsome bar for travellers and their friends.

But its shelves remained empty, and its counters deserted,
for years afterwards. By mischance, they had built the airport
in a 'dry' sub-division of the county, and only by the most
ferocious lobbying did they manage, eventually, to have the ban
lifted.

Naturally enough, this maze of rules did not stop people
drinking; it merely gave them awful drinking habits. The
bottle-killing tradition was always strong, even in civilized
Ottawa, where an hour or so of 'hard liquor' was the usual
prelude to any meal, and the tendency for one or two of the male
guests to finish dinner face downwards in the Baked Alaska was
accepted as unfortunate but inevitable.

High on the list of other things which had to be endured was local radio.

The Canadian Broadcasting Corporation, making its brave try to link the whole of Canada in some reputable sort of bond, and to take the place of the non-existent national newspaper, was one of the bright stars on the Canadian cultural scene; the two commercial radio stations, and a dozen others within range of a car, however fast it was fleeing, were at the other end of the scale, though they had the same goal of linkage.

Here the link was the sacred bond of advertising.

Sandwiched between the endless, dreary pop-sessions, the selling jingles also bashed the ear unmercifully. The key words were hammered home like the nails of Calvary. Every bleached sheet was Whiter than White. Every car was Power-Packed. Every house for sale was Gracious, every flat Exclusive. Every southern fried chicken was Finger-Lickin' Good.

Every cigarette was Cool, though some were Free and Easy on the Draw, others So Round, So Firm, So Fully Packed that it could have hurt, and others yet again, endowing the filter tip with even more sexual prowess, maintained that It's What's Up Front that Counts.

Every scent was Mysterious, every politician Sincere, every book a Daring Exposay. Every cup of coffee had Deep-Down Goodness, the product of Aged Beans. All night clubs were Intimate, all make-up Glamorous, Alluring, all laxatives Gentle yet Effective. Every little aspirin could bravely surmount the Pain Threshold; every last egg was Farmhouse Fresh; every soup Tangy, every popsicle Yummy, and every sausage Country-Style. Every medicinal relief was Fast—Fast—FAST! When it came to hair-cream, A Little Dab'll Do Ya! (but How are You Fixed for Blades?). Pepsi Hit the Spot. Every single gallon of gasoline put a Tiger in Your Tank.

Everything was New. They even had 'NEW Old Dutch Cleanser'. What my mother would have thought. . . .

Station CKOY, our busiest operator in this area, sometimes had its news bulletins sponsored by a local funeral home. Then, at the end, they gave the day's tally of corpses 'resting' on the premises, with names and ages, and detailed their visiting hours. One could almost hear a spectral voice adding: 'Big Triple Feature! Best Value in Town!'

Religion was always a strong seller. Every Sunday morning, the evangelists thundered or whined. The Rev. Alpheus Noseworthy was prominent. The Back-to-the-Bible Hour wrestled for its share of souls with the Voice of Prophecy, and both of them with the Tabernacle of Christ the King. ('We cannot solicit offerings. But remember, the Lord's work is like that rare and precious ointment—costly! Send us your thoughts! The address is . . .')

The Radio League of Mary Immaculate split the take with the Sacred Heart Shut-In Club. 'Christ was a union man!' proclaimed Norman Vincent Peale. But Billy Graham, the old pro, knew the best approach to the heart of a business community. He always signed off with a confederate smirk and: 'May the Lord bless you—real good!'*

All this rubbish was an original import from America, with whom Canada enjoyed a singular, frenetic love-hate relationship.

America was *there* all the time, the Big Brother, the pushy neighbour with ten times the population and twenty times the money. 'They're trying to take us over!' the Canadian loyalists shouted. 'Look how much of our industry they own through investment!'

'Let them take us over,' a few realists were ready to answer. 'We couldn't survive a week without their money. And they know how to *do* things!'

Somewhere in between were those who thought of themselves as Americans Minus, and blamed it on the colonial past.

It was a perennial argument, never to be resolved; it had lasted one century already, and was assuredly good for another, before the slow process of history gave its own verdict. Meanwhile, the tourists crowded in, and the visiting conventions

---

* The business world had its own gloss on the Scriptures: 'Do unto others before they do unto you.'

multiplied. Nearly every week there was a banner across the handsome front of the Chateau Laurier Hotel in Ottawa.

'Welcome Knights of Columbus!' (red fezzes, scarlet plus-fours, and white gaiters). 'Welcome American Guild of Morticians!' (very dark suits, rather cheerful faces). 'Welcome Daughters of the Revolution!' (a sea of millinery, pitched almost as high as the squawking voices). 'Welcome, Rotarians, Lions, Kiwanis, Elks, Knights of Pythias, Civitas, Associated Chambers of Commerce, American Mayors, Hibernian Lodge Brothers, Caledonian Society, United Mineworkers' Union, Boy Scouts, and Used Car Dealers of New York State.'

At most conventions, the delegates were issued with large lapel badges, inscribed, e.g., as follows: 'NAME: Charles Thompson. HOME TOWN: West Falls, Virginia. NICK-NAME: Chaz.' This enabled one to go up to a complete stranger and say: 'Hi, Chaz! How are things in West Falls?' He could then look at the opposing label, and answer: 'Hiya, Irv! As good as Minneapolis–St Paul, I'll bet!' Thus was the ice broken.

In the bar they made loud calls, accompanied by knowing sideways glances, for a 'bullshot' (vodka and beef *consommé*), hoping by this merry quip to score a hit with the wives of other delegates.

Ottawa, our small capital, kept its head in all this jungle. It could afford to. Though Montreal had the variety and the colour, and Toronto had all the money, Ottawa had the brains and the quality to match them, and that was enough for its proud citizens.

Shabby and run-down at the edges, it was still a handsome town, dominated by Parliament Hill and the Peace Tower: the home ground of the Governor-General, the Government, the Loyal Opposition, the majority of Federal civil servants, all the Federal ministries, an Old Guard of first families, and a diplomatic corps of some fifty-four embassies.

Some of these diplomats were of less than first-class quality (I can supply the name, rank, and country of origin of a certain *attaché* who sold a whole garage-full of duty-free wines and spirits, at a price half-way between what he had paid and what the market would bear, just before his transfer home). Some combined their Ottawa duty with their main appointment to Washington or the United Nations, and were hardly ever seen until the weather warmed up; and many of them put on a social splash which bore no relation to the country they were representing.

One had only to ask oneself: what sort of a man is this man when he is back in his own country?—how does he live, how do his fellow-countrymen live, how would his cultivated insolence and his almost inevitable Mercedes suit the scene, back home in the Republic of Lower Revolta?—one had only to observe, to listen, and then to wonder, in order to appreciate the absolute falsity of much of this diplomatic representation.

The ambassador of Ghana, for example (this was before his country subsided into corrupt bankruptcy, leaving the World Bank to sort out the bills), had the flower-beds surrounding his swimming-pool permanently planted with blooms to match the Ghanaian flag (red, yellow, and green)—an expensive piece of showing-off, in view of the climate; and he rode round the city in a pink Cadillac which was as relevant to the fortunes of Ghana as Stilton cheese to a poor church mouse.

True, the British Commission had a Rolls, though only after Monsarrat had a Rolls; before that, the official car was one of those funereal black Humbers which, like its South African counterpart, sometimes turned undiplomatic and broke down in inaccessible places. But damn it, at least we *built* Rolls-Royces!

Very few diplomats, with the exception of the Americans, the French, the British, and the Russians (who had just been exposed, with the help of cypher-clerk Igor Gouzenko, in a flagrant spy operation directed across the border at the United States), had anything very much to do except take care of that brisk traffic in visiting cards. Seriously under-employed, they spent their time partying, with the Latin-American contingent well to the fore, particularly at the Dance Club.

This was a winter diversion, founded (by Mrs Lester Pearson, when her husband was External Affairs Minister), 'to facilitate contact between the Diplomatic Corps and Ottawa residents'; and it had to be accepted that such contact often included fiery, non-Canadian glances, enraged husbands, and the demonstration of the Spanish Grip while dancing—the knuckles ground into the small of the female back, so that she had either to arch inwards to the embrace of her masterful partner, or accept a row of bruised vertebrae and prolonged South American sulks.

But all these individuals drew happily together on their recurrent National Days, in celebration, usually, of their freedom from the foul British yoke, and toasted the glorious future in champagne kindly made available by a recurrent British grant-in-aid.

Most of them lived in the smart, beautifully laid-out, leafy suburb of Rockliffe Park, where the price of houses, harsh enough in the rest of the city, grew steadily and vilely more expensive, and where even our British rent-allowances, wrung from a shocked Treasury, had to climb to $500 a month—then over £2,000 a year—to match the heat of the diplomatic climate.

A full day's work on the dip. circuit could include three or even four cocktail parties, where everyone moved on to their next appointment in steady droves, at a steady clip, through a steady downfall of snow, in order to meet the people they had just said good-bye to, half an hour earlier; like the animated figures of some intricate, baroque, Bavarian clock-face—except that the clock-face figures did not have to totter up successive glissades of ice, heavily sanded, which were the front doorsteps, shed their fur hats, fur coats, snow-boots, gloves, and scarves in the icy blast from the open door, and advance, beaming, upon a host and hostess who had advanced, beaming, upon *them*, the day before and possibly the day before that.

After this marathon run-up, the evening would conclude with a dinner party.

Here the food might differ (the Americans were wild about duck, as I was, the Italians concentrated on *cannelloni* and iced confections, and Earnscliffe, naturally, excelled in roast beef); but the people in attendance, as at the cocktail parties, were old and tried friends.

At my very first Ottawa dinner, given by our Deputy High Commissioner, the butler saw me to the door at the end of the evening. He helped me on with my coat and then, quietly, unobtrusively, he handed me his card.

'Any time, sir,' he murmured. 'You will find the phone number there.'

He was a senior graduate, and a very good one, of the Ottawa Servants' Pool, which supplied the sinews for this pampered circus, and were essential to it.

They were a most capable lot: a roving band of about thirty waiters and cooks, who had the expertise to march into any upper-crust house in Ottawa, organize a bar, dish up the *canapés*, hand round drinks at a steady pace, and (before one had been in residence very long) bring you the drink you wanted almost before you had passed the receiving line

If it were a dinner party, they could take care of everything, from the place-cards (in order of precedence) to the last whisky-and-soda on the stroke of eleven.

One could count on meeting them everywhere, and they became welcome friends, even accomplices in this charade. It was always good to see at least one of these hospitable faces, and to feel instantly at home on that account.

If Whitehead or Mrs Perch were on deck, for example, then all was well; the drinks would be nicely graded to the taste, the chipolata sausages and shrimp *bouchées à la reine* done to a turn; and every last glass would be dried and polished, every plate washed and stacked, every baking tin scoured clean before they left.

It gave one a sense of family, with Carruthers the aged retainer beaming round on the assembled generations. However, I knew also that it was somewhat disconcerting for the

Comptroller at Government House, Commander Jake Pemberton, to be handed a drink at a foreign cocktail party by one of his own footmen, who was picking up a little extra cash on his day off.

'He looked me straight in the eye,' Jake told me later, 'and said: "Scotch and water and *no* ice, I believe".'

Up on Parliament Hill, the true shrine of this attractive city, the Liberal Party under Mr Louis St Laurent was just starting its ninth and last year in office, to the accompaniment of giant grumbles from the waiting Conservatives and a certain yawning apathy from Canada itself.

The House of Commons of that date was not a very high-class establishment. Certainly there were a handful of stars: Mr Lester Pearson himself, and others who achieved office, and deserved it—Lionel Chevrier, Brooke Claxton, Jack Pickersgill, George Hees, Paul Martin, Davie Fulton, and Jean Lesage, who went on to become Premier of Quebec.

Just over the horizon, also, was a real old-style thunderer, John Diefenbaker, shortly to oust George Drew as Conservative leader, in the first of many such bloody battles, and to reach the highest office in the land. But when one had run down that list, there were still more than 250 MPs left; and most of them were of mediocre calibre indeed.

This made for mediocre debates, to match the dragging tail. Many of them were simply noisy slanging matches, at the level of the schoolboy argument—except that no properly supervised schoolboy would ever have been allowed to carry on like this; crude personal insults ('Sit down—you're drunk!') alternated with vicious squabbles about French-speaking Quebec, English-speaking Vancouver, and mongrel Toronto in between.

Meanwhile, the country staggered on, from year to year, from petty crisis to stage-managed storm—amateurishly run, deeply divided, only defended by benevolent America, and yet potentially so rich that it could afford to keep even this bunch of clowns in command.

It was better to avert one's eyes, and to enjoy the place and the people a hundred yards down the hill and directly opposite the Peace Tower—the Rideau Club.

Gentlemen do not talk about their clubs; even writers should refrain (though one such writer-member, an able Ottawa journalist who must have known better, did break the story of a ferocious internal battle to admit four distinguished Jews to membership—one of them being the Governor of the Bank of Canada).*

But the Rideau Club was not really like that at all. It was a memorably friendly community, housed in just the right kind of old-fashioned surroundings—sagging leather armchairs, SILENCE in the Reading Room, and a hall porter, Archie, who had started as a page-boy, survived more than forty years, and now had more than enough authority to tell a Cabinet minister, just up for membership, that he must not appear in the club on his election day.

The Rideau Club had been founded in 1865, the moving spirit being that same Prime Minister Sir John A. Macdonald, who liked to have a private waterhole within convenient reach of the House of Commons. His portrait, complete with a magnificent fur coat which I would have coveted in any day and age, looked down upon the relaxing members. It also looked down on a small collection of cronies who, since they always occupied the table under the last fluted pillar in the lounge, called themselves the Last Post.

I was a Last Poster for fourteen years, and well contented with it. Its membership changed as people left town, or went broke, or even died. But the basic corps remained, adding materially to the bar profits: a bank manager, a stockbroker, a Canadian general, an American general, a Quebec senator, two men from a sensitive branch of the U.S. Embassy a retired Royal Canadian Navy captain who now built office blocks, the

* There was really no end to this sort of nonsense. Cf. Mr Harry Oppenheimer, chairman of De Beers and of half the gold-producing companies in South Africa, who for years was debarred (or shall one say, discouraged) from membership of the Rand Club in Johannesburg.

editor of the *Ottawa Citizen*, and another writer—this writer.

When a member of the Last Post distinguished himself in any way (and how could we help it?) he was presented with a silver model of that fluted pillar—a symbol more phallic than the original exhibit itself. When I got married, for the third and last time, I received my award.

It was the first such presentation, and (I am glad to record) the tallest pillar. After that, we were inclined to skimp on the silver content and thus on the height. The later, stunted versions never quite matched my lofty eminence.

Even in this hospitable atmosphere, I had found it prudent to adjust my British accent, from the very beginning, to the one I heard all round me. It was a curious quirk of the Canadian character that they still thought the London brand of English very funny indeed; in many cases, they could not wait to go behind the nearest tree and imitate the ludicrous way one talked. Luckily, I had become used to this, from long ordeal.

I had dropped my Liverpool twang when I went to Winchester; I adjusted the resulting upper-class accent when I joined the Labour Party, and 'cum-radd' became 'com-raid'. Reverting to it when I graduated to naval officer, I had to moderate it again on arriving in South Africa—though not completely, theirs being the most atrocious brand of English spoken anywhere on the face of the globe.

Now, in Canada, I made a further compromise, to escape contempt or merriment. This was especially necessary on trips to New York, when a cab driver could not, or would not, respond to anything but a nasal trans-Atlantic drawl, coupled with a tourist-sized tip.

Up the hill again—much further up, and appropriately so— was the dominating pinnacle of Government House, and its honoured tenant, Mr Vincent Massey.

His was the first local appointment to the Governor-Generalship of Canada; a home-grown product, he had followed Field-Marshal Earl Alexander of Tunis, the last British import and a difficult man to follow in any case.

Mr Massey's former career had embraced the academic world (twenty-eight honorary degrees from various universities), a Liberal cabinet post in Canada, diplomatic appointments (he had been Canadian High Commissioner in London throughout the war, and a delegate to the League of Nations); a term as a trustee of the National Gallery and the Tate, and the presidency of Massey-Harris, which made tractors and other farm-machinery.

It was a remarkably mixed bag, and the man himself—small, spare, infinitely courteous, and of a steely will when he felt like it—was remarkable also. He had to overcome the tradition of royalty, and other competition almost as great, in the vice-regal position, as well as a certain anti-native prejudice which always made people prefer Gruyère cheese to red Cheshire, or a conductor named Jonescu to one called Jones. He had succeeded brilliantly.

But he was basically a culture man, thank God, and we could certainly use one at such a peak of eminence. Now in his seventieth year, and with a burdensome round of official duties he still had time and to spare for the liberal arts; he had been instrumental in promoting the Canada Council, the very first essay into artistic patronage by the government; and from the beginning he had been a firm friend of the fledgling Shakespeare Festival at Stratford, Ontario.

He had one other claim to fame, reported to me by an *Ottawa Journal* man who had been covering 'crowd reactions' at the State Opening of Parliament, when Mr Massey drove from Government House to Parliament Hill in a horse-drawn landau, attended by a scarlet-clad bodyguard of the Royal Canadian Mounted Police. It was, among other things, a considerable tourist attraction, and the *Journal* man found himself next door to some visiting Americans.

They asked him who the man in the carriage was, and the conversation then continued like this:

'That's Mr Massey.'

'Who's he?'

'The Governor-General of Canada.'

'Oh.'

Reporter: 'He's Raymond Massey's brother.'

Tourist (deeply impressed): 'Gee! No kidding!'

It was to go to a Government House Ball that I had at last invested in a new pair of evening tails, after my original ones (vintage 1928), though still serviceable and just good enough for a Trafalgar Day reunion, had finally to be pensioned off in their twenty-eighth year. All the time I was being measured, I seemed to hear the ghostly voice of Mr Pratt, of Pratt & Manning in Trinity Street, murmuring: 'A little more on the *lower* chest, I think.'

Then, in the good old days, they had cost fourteen guineas; now the Ottawa price was $200—about £67. But the splendid surroundings and the glittering occasion made any price worthwhile.

In the course of the evening Mr Massey, a charming and indefatigable host who seemed to spend some time with every last one of his 500 guests, discussed the forthcoming programme at the Stratford Festival, now embarking on its fourth season after three tremendously successful years.

He was a theatre *aficionado*, with a historian's spirit added.

'I think you should write a book about it,' he said, 'before some of the important early things are forgotten.'

It was as near as I was ever likely to come to a royal command, and in due course I obeyed.*

My first voyage across the whole of Canada was a straight drive of 5,075 miles (plus 500 by water across Lake Huron and Lake Superior) in that original Bentley, a Mark VI Continental by H. J. Mulliner, shaped like a Dutch cigar.

It took eight weeks, and I wrote a series of articles about it for a syndication of a dozen newspapers headed by the Montreal *Star*. However, as I was under an official ban not to be 'critical' of any aspect of Canadian life, the series was rather short on significance.

* *To Stratford With Love* (McClelland & Stewart, Toronto, 1963).

But it was an unforgettable trip, and I enjoyed it enormously, and learned a lot about Canada at first hand. In particular, its hugeness and variety, never to be comprehended by staring at a map, came home with staggering impact.

The tiny fishing village in Nova Scotia, which still gave shelter to salty schooners working on the Grand Banks *was* in the same country as the dusty, endless, prairie road, leading only to the Manitoba horizon, as straight and dull as an old school ruler.

The wonderfully engineered highway which climbed foot by foot over the Rockies, winding like a curling whiplash between enormous craggy peaks which never lost their snow-caps from one century to another, *did* lead down into a lush green valley where acres of fruit grew like wayside flowers, and the lake at its further end was blessed with water as warm and soft as the wings of the dove, and an air as gentle as an Italian sky.

I learned how men could divide this country, as fantastically as nature. Montreal traditionally loathed Toronto, and both derided Ottawa, the universal enemy, the 'talking-shop that takes all our taxes and spends them on hand-outs and ballet-shows'. To hear a man in far-west Vancouver sneering at the Frogs in Quebec was an equally melancholy experience, comparable to the way the south of England saw the north as a grim barbarian wilderness, and the north saw the south as a soft, worthless Sodom.*

I learned how this time-honoured quarrel between 'French' and 'English' Canada was still alive, and sharpening to a new kind of crisis; and how many French-Canadians, reacting with fervour instead of relapsing into spiritless, self-pitying apathy, the world of the hard-pressed, down-trodden, dull-witted *habitant*, now thought of themselves more and more as a separate nation, never to be assimilated (in spite of pious hopes and declarations) into this alien Anglo-Saxon land.

I learned, and saw, with what long-term spite this had once

---

* A typical British Columbia taunt, in this tradition, was the suggestion that the coat of arms of Canada should portray a beaver with a frog on its back.

been expressed, in some faraway year, in the City of Quebec
itself, by a man with a forgotten grudge who had carved a
statue of a golden dog. Staring gimlet-eyed into the future,
this was what he had inscribed underneath it:

> I am a dog gnawing a bone.
> While I am gnawing, I take my rest.
> But a time will come, which is not yet come,
> When I shall bite him who has bitten me.

It could be that the time was now near at hand, and that the
grudge, by no means forgotten, had only been laid by, buried,
like the bone, with a memory-marker on top.

I learned, what I had known only by family fable, that I
really had some ancestors in this part of the world.

In Rivière du Loup on the banks of the St Lawrence River
there was a small engineering works, which looked as though it
might have grown out of a garage, boldly labelled 'Monsarrat
Limited', and I was able to confirm that this was in truth a
family connection. There were still three generations of Mon-
sarrats in Rivière du Loup, I was told. They had come from
France in the old days. They were *'très gentil'*.

There was also a Charles Nicholas Monsarrat (1872–1940)
'of whom Sir Thomas Shaughnessy, the President of the Railway, speaks in the highest terms', who had been a bridge
engineer with the Canadian Pacific, and had designed at least
two fine Canadian bridges—the Jacques Cartier at Montreal,
and the Lion's Gate at Vancouver.

Down in London, Ontario, the obliging publisher of the
London Free Press, Arthur Ford, dug deep into his files
and came up with an 1856 reference to two pioneer settlers,
Charles and Mark, who had figured in the town's first business
directory.

Going even further back, he found two other candidates: an
exact namesake, Nicholas Monsarrat, born in London in 1829,
died there in 1910 (the year *I* was born); and an 1837
Lieutenant Johnny Monsarrat. 'a most facetious Irishman who

had left Ireland with considerable wealth and settled in Canada. His good dinners and jovial character made him a universal favourite.'

Très gentil indeed.

I learned about Canadian public cooking: not in Montreal, where it could be excellent, nor in Toronto, where the influx of German and Italian immigrants had brought new flavour to a stereotyped menu, but in the small towns and wayside stopping places strung out across the continent.

It was terrible: a great greasy frieze of French fries, hamburgers doused in ketchup, frankfurters *à la hot dog* (as one roadside joint in Quebec phrased it) and fried egg sandwiches. Even in the places run by the Chinese (there were lots in the west), the egg rolls had taken on a leathery North-American armour plating. Over all, over the whole vast land, hung the murmur of innumerable beans.*

I loitered as long as I could on that trip, during a third of which I was alone, and averaged less than a hundred miles a day. Woven into the articles I wrote were about twenty snapshots of sight and sound and story—one for every two hundred and fifty miles: twenty oddments, twenty things that caught the eye, or stayed in the memory far beyond the next horizon. Sometimes it was the place itself, sometimes the facts or fables associated with it.

They were all part of that diverse flavour, which left the cooking so far behind that the whole kitchen might have been some horrible eleventh province of Canada, despised, condemned, inhabited only by scullions, potboys, slaves.

In *St John's, Newfoundland*, the Tourist Development Board lent me a fishing dory to explore the harbour. This was cold and foggy at its narrow cliff-entrance, one of the trickiest to negotiate of the whole Atlantic seaboard; but warm and snug inside, with ships moving all the time, and fish by the thousand drying on open-air staging, and a line of big, hard-working,

---

* Our progress recalled the extraordinary English myth, summed up in the phrase: 'It must be a good place—all the lorry-drivers eat there.'

dirty old schooners from Spain and Portugal, deep-laden, waiting to make the return journey.

The naval dockyard where we used to lie during the war was empty; everywhere else was crowded, and busy with loading and unloading, export and import; and the biggest news was of the biggest cod ever caught in these parts (105 lb., 4ft. 6ins. long) which had just breathed its last. St John's had returned to its true nature, which was to live by the sea: a tradition stretching back to John Cabot, who first landed on the bluffs overlooking the harbour in 1497.

In *Charlottetown, Prince Edward Island,* on which Cabot *may* have landed, and Jacques Cartier (1534) *did*, and Leif Erikson (1000) *might*, was Confederation Chamber, where delegates from all the other provinces met in 1864 to wrangle, to plan, and finally to agree on a pattern for a future Canada. It was a lofty room, beautifully proportioned, with pictures and fading yellow photographs of the austere (and not so austere) Fathers of Confederation on its walls, and a commemorative plaque proclaiming, with more accuracy than most: 'They builded better than they knew.'

To *Halifax,* back in 1943, I had brought my frigate *Ettrick,* weary and bashed about after a long, hard winter crossing which left her with exactly four tons of oil (half a day's steaming) at the bottom of her tanks, in order to hand her over to the Royal Canadian Navy and get an American ship in exchange. When all the paperwork was done, her new captain had given me an informal receipt: 'Received—One Frigate.' I had never done business on that scale, before or since.

Now Halifax was peacefully thriving again, and they were building a new bridge across the harbour. At the moment, it was no more than two colossal steel towers linked by a sagging tracery of girders and wires overhead. Tradition had a curious story about this project.

Hundreds of years earlier, it was said, an old Indian (speaking apparently in English rhyming couplets) had laid a curse on the white man's bridge. Three would be built, he said, and three destroyed—the first in storm, the second in silence the third in death.

It was a fact that the first bridge was blown down by a gale, and the second collapsed without warning. The new one was the third.

Near *Amherst, Nova Scotia*, I passed a village called Economy. Later a newsman on the St John *Telegraph-Journal* told me there was another one nearby called Lower Economy, 'where things are even tougher'. I believed him.

All round the *Bay of Fundy*, a gloomy arm of the sea where fog abounded, and the tide could rise and fall fifty feet, the wrecks lay thick as rotting seaweed. Owing to that monstrous tide, Fundy fishermen were able to practise a strange variation of their craft. Their nets were hoisted up and strung on poles, somewhere near the highest water level; when the tide went out the owners walked out across the beach and took the fish down with pitch-forks.

In *St John, New Brunswick*, founded by Champlain in 1604, there was a museum with an alluring maritime section. In it was a beautiful model of the tea clipper *Star of the East*, built at this very seaport in 1853. She once sailed from London to Shanghai—15,000 miles—in 104 days, and she earned her building costs in three prosperous voyages.

St Andrew's, New Brunswick, had a memorable pioneering conception, just suited to Canada. It had been founded in 1783 by a handful of determined settlers, hard as hickory wood, who knew exactly what they wanted in life and were not going to take less.

Originally they had been living in a village called Fort George on the banks of the Penobscot River in Maine. They had always thought that the Penobscot was the boundary between Maine (America) and Nova Scotia/New Brunswick (Canada), and that they lived on the Canadian side of it. Then someone in London decided that the boundary was not the Penobscot River but the River St Croix, many miles to the eastwards, and wrote to tell them so.

16

I could just hear one of those men saying: 'Well sir, it was like this. We wanted to live in Canada, not America. Nothing against Americans—don't get me wrong. But a flag is a flag. Right? So. . . .' So they upped and moved. They took with them their wives and children, their furniture, farming tools, farm animals, hired men, linen, and stocks of food. They even moved their favourite coffee-house, plank by plank, joist by joist, brick by brick ('3,000 bricks, 1,000 feet of seasoned boards, four window frames, one panelled door' said the itemized bill) and set it up in their new home—St Andrew's-by-the-Sea.

In this town of such splendid origin, I had a nice rich friend, Murray Vaughan, who, as all rich men should, owned a 60-foot motor yacht. We had a glorious day cruising round Passamaquoddy Bay, focus of the 'Quoddy Project' of depression times, when they planned to dam the whole thing and make everyone rich (except the fishermen): and Deer Island and Campobello, where President Roosevelt had a summer home: and Grand Manan Island, and Clam Head Cove, and so back to our moorings, on exactly the same compass course as those 'Loyalists' of 1783 had used when they headed towards the unknown harbour which was to be their new home.

I had to keep reminding myself that my job was to cross Canada by car.

Fredericton, capital of New Brunswick, was a university town—serene, studious, a nice change from the 'business community' and perhaps a nice change from some other university towns now building up a head of steam in other parts of Canada. I walked round it at dusk, enjoying the calm architecture and the green lawns sloping down to the river's edge. When I got back to my hotel, I heard somewhere the sound of a piano being played.

After several false starts I tracked it down to the main convention hall—a vast room, with serried rows of vacant chairs, and now in near-total darkness. At one end of it, on stage, was a grand piano; and at the piano, a solitary figure which I presently made out to be a smallish man bending over the keyboard.

I tiptoed in and sat down near him, in the empty room. He was playing a series of Chopin waltzes, and playing them well. Half-way through, he became aware of me sitting close by, but he went on playing just the same. At the end, when the last notes of the last waltz faded, I stood up, still in darkness, while he closed the piano.

I said 'Thank you', and he answered: 'I don't often get a chance to play.'

Then we walked out of the deserted hall, by different doors. Sometimes things happened just right.

At *Hartland*, I passed the first 1,000-mile mark of the journey under a historic rural canopy, crossing 'the longest covered bridge in the world': wooden-built on pegged trestles, creaking, a slatted tunnel 1,282 feet long.

The city of *Quebec* had a fine turreted hotel, the Chateau Frontenac, perched on the steep hillside in a honeycomb of back alleys overlooking the St Lawrence, with a magnificent view of the harbour below. I wasted hours ship-watching, when I should perhaps have been scouting round for signs of anti-British subversion, or in earnest colloquy with the Anglican Bishop of Quebec, who had almost a martyr's role in this hard-core Catholic province: or paying a battlefield visit to the Heights of Abraham, where Wolfe for the British defeated Montcalm for the French, and left a permanent mark on Canadian history, and Montcalm could only leave his skull, still on view there after two hundred years.

But it was ships for me: among them a big 'Empress' liner docking (it was time I took a trip), a tanker anchoring in mid-stream, freighters and lake-boats plugging away against the current, an R.C.N. frigate hurrying somewhere (probably going on leave), and the square-cut little ferry-boat from Quebec to Levis just opposite, which ran three times every hour and had to be carefully watched.

West of *Ottawa* we discovered a new kind of hitch-hiker: not the hopeful waving type, not the thumb-jerking tyrant, not the scowling low-lifer on his way to a new job in Winnipeg, but the

Travelling Scholar. He was a young bespectacled man, sitting on his suitcase, his nose buried in a book. As each car approached, he raised his head briefly, with the faraway look of a monk who might have to leave his manuscripts to obey the refectory bell. Then he went back to his studies.

He was waiting for someone who appreciated learning, and I wished it could be me. But we could not stop, because the car was almost full of luggage, and also I had taken an oath to be hard-hearted about hitch-hikers, following a wave of knifings and hold-ups and rapes and kidnaps and general abuse of the kindly motorist. Would I have stopped, I was asked, if he had been reading one of my own books? The question did not arise.

But later he sped past us, a passenger in a faster car—or rather, a car that wanted to go faster; and a hundred miles down the highway, there he was again, having easily outstripped us, once more reading and waiting—a triumph for scholarship over all other crude approaches.

Kingston, at the head of Lake Ontario, boasted a strongpoint, Fort Henry, with a curious history. Now a tourist attraction, with a fake 'changing of the guard' ceremony to keep the cash-register busy and to give summer employment to students, it had once been real.

It had been built around 1812 to repel the Americans, who might choose this part of the border for an attack; and the fort should obviously have faced southwards down the lake. But it did not; it faced north, and its guns seemed to be pointing, not at the ships of the hated invader but inland at its own honest citizens.

The explanation was legend, but it could have been fact. It was said that Fort Henry was designed, not for Kingston, Ontario, but for Kingston, Jamaica, and that someone (no doubt a vague, myopic, old civil servant, weak on geography or too much plagued by his Colonial Office files), sent the plans to the wrong address. It was further said that the architect, having accepted these plans and built the wrong fort the wrong way round, committed suicide to avoid criminal proceedings.

True or false, Fort Henry did demonstrably face the wrong way. . . . No one could tell me why it was called Fort Henry, except a ribald man in Toronto who said that obvious y the architect's name was Henry Fort.

A long way north and west, at *Port Arthur* on the farther shores of Lake Superior, we began an entirely new leg of the journey, which a hundred years earlier had confronted other voyagers, by the thousand and ten thousand, at this same departure-point, when the whole of the unknown second half of Canada was still there before them, to be discovered, and crossed, and conquered, and enjoyed.

The next stop was three hundred miles away, and, lacking a prairie wagon to sleep in, we had to do it in one piece. This was no hardship. The scenery, at the heart of the great middle-section of the continent known as the Canadian Shield, was purely Alpine: three hundred miles of birch and fir trees, three hundred miles of small hills and welcoming valleys, strung together by an endless chain of lakes. There were more than three thousand of these in this single section of northern Ontario.

We chose one near *Kenora* called Lake-of-the-Woods, and there, at Devil's Gap Camp (access by boat only), we settled down to two days of rustic innocence modified by Canadian Pacific catering. We had a log cabin among the trees, with central heating in reserve; every passing Indian had an outboard motor clipped to his canoe. It was a world of contented compromise.

Winnipeg, by reliable Bentley speedometer, was 2,680 miles from Sydney, Cape Breton, and thus just over the half-way mark of the journey. A century ago, this traditional meeting-place of trappers and fur-traders focused on a historic crossroads in the heart of the city, the corner of Portage and Main. Like the Hudson's Bay store, it was still a civic landmark, and possibly the windiest corner in Canada.

The Legislative Building had walls of Italian marble and massive local stone; and the stone was worth a very close look. It could be seen that the surface of each cut slab enshrined

hundreds of tiny sea fossils, now open for inspection after a
million secret years. But the stone did not come from the sea-
shore as we knew it today; it had been quarried outside
Winnipeg itself.

A-top the Legislature was a fourteen-foot statue, the Golden
Boy, which like the Golden Dog of Quebec had gathered its
own legends. Originally cast in France, it had been consigned
to Canada at the outbreak of the First World War; and, caught
in a confused tide (or forgotten altogether), it was said to have
spent the entire period of 1914–18 crossing and recrossing the
seven seas.

Though this was a time of unrestricted U-boat warfare, and
there were many narrow escapes, no ship that carried the
Golden Boy ever came to harm.

The journey across the *Prairies*, over the long straight
stretches, through the enormous dusty wheatfields, past the oil-
rigs and the tiny cross-roads towns, had its own rhythm, like a
long straight sea voyage. The towns were all alike: a cluster of
one garage, one café owned and run by a Chinese family, one
general store, and a quota of grain elevators, from one to six.
These served as did the stars in a Travellers' Guide; one-
elevator towns had nothing, six-elevator towns had a hotel and
a cinema. All had the faithful, endless railway line to link them.

Every highway and mileage post hereabouts was marked by a
buffalo sign. It was a reminder of the past—a past more wicked
and wanton even than our own. The figures of the wholesale
slaughter of buffalo, the prime target of the greedy hunter in the
old days, were fantastic.

One such executioner shot three thousand in a single season;
another, when short of ready cash, would kill a dozen or so, cut
out their tongues (which fetched fifty cents in the delicacy
market), and leave the carcases rotting on the plain.

Within ten years, the enormous herds of these animals,
sometimes observed to be twenty-five miles wide by fifty miles
deep, virtually disappeared from North America.

Regina, capital of Saskatchewan, was originally called Pile of

Bones, for the same gruesome reason. This was where the buffalo skeletons were brought, by superstitious Indians who wanted to help them join their ancestors. It signified a mournful, disgusting Order of Merit: 1, the Buffalo; 2, the Indians; and the rest unplaced. It was also the tally of the graveyard, in order of arrival.

The pride of *Saskatoon* was the Western Development Museum, a kind of physical history of the west. Here was assembled some of the huge and cumbersome farm machinery which first broke open the Prairies, and ancient treadle sewing-machines to show the other side of the picture.

There were colossal steam tractors, which must have seemed like snorting monsters from another planet when they first appeared on the wheatlands. There was an old road-grading machine which needed fourteen horses to operate it, and a thresher demanding a crew of twenty-eight men. At the other end of the labouring scale was a wooden plough, designed to be drawn by a team of Doukhobor women when their menfolk were away;* and a pumping wheel powered by dogs which ran perpetually uphill. I had two candidates for this little chore at home.

In the transport section was a Stanley Steamer (1898) with the boiler discouragingly placed under the front seat; a 1903 Ford (one of the first batch of 650 Ford cars ever turned out); a Red River cart of 1883 with buffalo-hide tyres—a breed of vehicle which squeaked and creaked so noisily that it was called a Manitoba Piano; the original City of Moose Jaw horse-ambulance, which I am sure was called a lot of other things; and the Yukon Stage Sleigh, which carried freight and

* Usually in jail. The Doukhobors (the word means 'spirit-wrestlers') were an earnest, troublesome sect of Russian origin, who established various farming communities in British Columbia. From time to time, when they decided that they had accumulated too many riches on earth, they burned everything down and started afresh somewhere else. Since what they burned down, or dynamited, usually included government buildings such as schools and post-offices, and since their usual form of protest, for both sexes, was to strip naked and defy all comers to arrest them, the scene was often chaotic. Mr Diefenbaker, once faced with an audience of angry, disrobing women, said: 'You can't scare me. I was brought up on a farm.' It was thought that he lost conservative female votes by this quip.

passengers from White Horse to Dawson City, taking five days and a total of 275 horses for the 300-mile journey.

Jasper National Park, Alberta, the largest on the American continent (4,000 square miles), was a fabulous place, and tucked into one corner of it was Jasper Park Lodge, on the edge of Lac Beauvert, with cabins grouped along the lakeside under the shadow of Mt Edith Cavell. Waiters, who were college-boys on vacation, having a whale of a time with the female staff and making a fortune in tips, brought everything, from a jug of ice to a five-course meal, at express speed, on bicycles: balancing the tray in one hand, steering with the other.

We drove to a canyon, and looked down; we drove to a glacier, and looked up. One could fish, ride, swim, sail, and sleep. One could take a taxi to see the bears (25c.), but it was never necessary; little black bears were ambling all over the place, amiable and greedy at the same time. In this luxurious wilderness the whole of Canada seemed to come together in one superb package.

From *Calgary* one could see the noble foothills of the Rockies, eighty miles away. But Calgary was not at all noble; it was a raucous western wonderland, with money to burn, a welcome to match, and a brash uninhibited pride in its success.

In Calgary the hats were huge, just like the steaks, which the principal hotel listed by weight, from a sissy 7oz. snack to a double T-bone of 28oz. It had magnificent farming and ranching. It had oil gushing from every pore. It had a display of dinosaurs, and an entire village of motels, and the Calgary Stampede.

It did not sound as if the Calgary Stampede would be quite my style. When I mentioned to a friendly photographer that I thought of attending it next year, he looked me up and down, and then said: 'If I were you, I'd forget that tie.' When I asked him why, he made a brisk snipping motion, as with a pair of scissors.

Now there was only 900 miles left, across the Rockies to *Vancouver*: the most wonderful drive of the whole of my driving life. There was only one blot on this, and it was man-made, as usual: the aftermath, the brutal scars, of a forest fire in Manning Provincial Park which had destroyed 5,700 acres in one disastrous holocaust.

A single camper with a single match was said to be responsible; and they had marked the spot with a mock gallows from which was suspended the huge effigy of a cigarette. Looking round two or three entire mountain-sides, which, even after three years, still had nothing to show but scorched black earth and dead tree stumps, one would have liked to put something else up on that gallows.

At *Victoria* on Vancouver Island, 4,500 miles from where the deed was done, and on the Pacific Ocean instead of the Atlantic, I met by extreme coincidence the man to whom I had given my frigate in Halifax, ten years earlier. He was Captain W. R. Stacey, now a marine surveyor.

Victoria was flowers, flowers all the way. They greeted one, in red-white-and-blue, at the quayside; they surrounded the hotel; they hung in ornamental baskets from the lamp standards. They lined the main roads, and came to a fantastic peak in Butchart Gardens, where, sun-blessed by day, they were floodlit by night.

They seemed to grow on every available square foot of the island. It was like ending the journey on a flower-decked aircraft carrier.

I had collected, on the way, a small bouquet of odd signs in public places. When I tried them on a Canadian, back home in Ottawa, it was a total failure; he did not see the point of some, accepted others as a normal part of the scene, and wore, at the end of my recital, the look of a governess whose 'nature walk' had been a childish waste of time.

But the alien British eye had picked out:

In a park in Sydney, cautioning the public: 'To linger but not to litter, To rest but not molest, To enjoy but not to destroy.'

A newspaper in Charlottetown: 'Covers Prince Edward Island like the Dew.'

16*

In New Brunswick: 'Welcome to our city! Enjoy yourself! Police patrolled. Speed electrically timed.'

Near St John: 'Through this door walk the finest people on earth—OUR CUSTOMERS!'

Crossing the Quebec—Ontario border: 'First chance for margarine.'

Cobourg, Ont.: 'Home of Marie Dressler.'

In Saskatchewan: 'Welcome to X. Population 1,500. We love them all. Drive slowly.'

Hotel lobby in Alberta: 'Only registered guests allowed upstairs.'

High in the Rockies: 'If you MUST carve your name, use this board.'

Nelson, B.C.: 'Sorry about the next 40 miles—We ARE building you a better road.'

And back in holy Montreal: 'This elevator does not run on Ascension Day.'

It only remains to add that the car behaved faultlessly, throughout six time zones, ten provinces, and all those 5,075 miles. There were only two casualties: a windshield chipped by a flying stone on the Prairies, and an exhaust muffler which succumbed to a rock lying in the road near Edmonton.

At the start, Rolls-Royce of Canada had kindly provided me with an inclusive kit of spare parts, ranging from a dynamo to six extra shock-absorbers. I never broke its seal, nor used as much as a single washer from it. It was emotional impulse rather than commonsense which made me swap the car as soon as I got back.

Impulse, and the money to indulge it, were already adding up to something that looked like zero. But at that stage this was still difficult to discern—or to admit.

'Madam Chair, Mr Mayor,' I would begin, with practised, odious suavity, '—and may I say, sir, how reassuring it is for me to have at least one masculine supporter in this extremely feminine gathering' (Tee-hee-hee), 'distinguished guests, and ladies. I would like to start by saying what a great pleasure it is to pay a visit to——' (Get the name right) 'to see the kind of civic progress which a thriving community can make' (new electrical transformer building glimpsed on the way in from the station), 'and to enjoy your very kind hospitality' (grapefruit cocktail, individual chicken pot pie, pineapple rings with a dollop of cream cheese on top, coffee).

'As you know, I come from outer space' (Tee-hee', 'yes, from Ottawa,' (Ha-ha-ha) 'but I am proud to say that I have connections in this part of Canada.' (Sensation.) 'My great-grandfather etc. . . . However, perhaps that is only important to me.' (No, no.) 'Tonight, I want to talk to you about the role of the British Commonwealth in the world today.'

These speeches of mine, nearly all of them made under the auspices of the Canadian Club, which organized such occasions right across Canada, were limited in theme; but they could be repeated time and again, since, unless one dropped an absolute clanger, they would only be reported in the local paper, to less than 10,000 people. However, they all had to have different beginnings.

Small, mousy jokes were best; sometimes they were very small, and any reputable mouse would have felt trapped. Talking about sea-power to a Winnipeg audience, I could make the point that most Canadian sailors I met during the war seemed to come from the Prairies (true), 'either because they wanted a nice change, or because, never having seen the sea, they didn't have the sense to keep away from it.'

In Vancouver, where they prided themselves on their sunshine record, I would start with the story of the man boasting about his home town: 'We have brilliant sunshine 365 days of the year—and that's a conservative estimate.'

Toronto, full of aspiring novelists, called for: 'Out of every hundred people in a room, ninety-nine are suppressed writers and the other is a writer who ought to be suppressed.'

Anywhere in the Maritimes I was able to mention that the three Canadian corvettes in my escort group had been called

Fredericton, *Moncton*, and *Galt*, and since British corvettes were all called by the names of flowers, I had always wondered what a Fredericton looked like. Now I knew.

In Montreal there was room for a bit about the discovery of 'Monsarrat Limited', and in London, Ontario, I could give them the whole family works.

If there was really nothing to use by way of a link, I put in something vague yet inspiring about 'historic ties'. There were bound to be historic ties, even in Swift Current.

Sometimes the chairman's introduction gave me a last-minute chance. When, as occasionally happened, this was too generous ('Renowned throughout the entire world'—'Will be remembered as long as books are read'),* I countered modestly by suggesting that he too seemed well qualified for a career in the realm of fiction. Sometimes they got my name wrong, but it would have been impolite to comment on this. I was variously called Monster-rat (just as at school), Mouserat (which was a natural association of ideas), and even, a bad first shot by a flurried man, Mounterass—to our mutual embarrassment.

After these preliminary skirmishes, I had a choice of four rather dull subjects; the Commonwealth: modern sea power: economic progress in Britain (up-dated for me by the Senior Trade Commissioner, who could always produce the percentage increase in our exports of cashmere twin-sets, just by pressing his bell): and the role of an Information Service.

When fed up with this sort of thing, I talked about the life of a writer. But that was a funny speech, and not really in the line of business.

Once or twice, when the audience was mixed, I spoke partly in French. It said much for the quality of the French language as practised in Quebec, a guttural *patois* of which my Paris publisher, Georges Roditi, observed: 'They speak the French of a province which does not exist,' and which had been likened, less kindly, to the sound of a Swiss businessman making love,

---

* *Cf.* a tribute to a modern composer: 'His name will be famous when Mozart, Beethoven, and Brahms are forgotten. But not till then.'

that a local paper once reported that I spoke *'un Français presque impeccable'*. I knew that I did not.

Those particular occasions had been daunting. But I would have loathed and feared the ordeal anyway. Even though I had a script to follow (by local High Commission rule) and came to know it by heart, I was always pathologically nervous about speech-making.

Nothing did any good: neither alcohol, nor tranquillizers, nor the knowledge that it would all be over within an hour, and the conviction that it did not matter much anyway. I had only to get up before an audience to be nearly demolished by fear; my hands trembled uncontrollably; I grew breathless, and my sweat glands opened up like Niagara.

My father, to whom I confessed this cowardice, once advised me: 'Think of them as friends in your own home. Imagine you are just talking to people you know. Be natural.' That didn't do any good either; he might as well have said: 'Be six feet off the ground.' As natural as an actor in his first speaking part in his very first play, I would begin with the shakes and finish in a bath of sweat—and with an enormous, childish, exquisite sense of relief.

But I knew it would be just as awful next time; and next time might be tomorrow—or even that same evening.

The audiences, on balance, were mostly women, since the Women's Canadian Club was usually out on its own, whereas its male counterpart had to contend with a rash of competitors and a choice of half a dozen other gatherings. But between an ocean of flowered hats, and a cobbled square of bald heads, what was the difference? And why were these people, men or women, there anyway? Even without the cute introductions and the plodding propaganda themes, I often felt that the occasion was phoney, and myself with it.

The men, who made up the majority of the lunch-time meetings, were 'joiners'; and if their goal had not been the Canadian Club, with Monsarrat holding forth on the Commonwealth, then it would have been the Lions' Club, with Mr X on Selling

as a Key Factor in the Canadian Way of Life, or Rotary International, and Mr Y with some inspiring thoughts on their
motto, Service Before Self, which seemed to bear as much
relation to fact as the Metro-Goldwyn-Mayer banner, *Ars
Gratia Artis*.

With women, it was probably a matter of social pressures,
plus snobbery as an active ingredient. Anyone who was anybody went to the Canadian Club gatherings, and under such
compulsion they were ready to sit there in a comfortable,
companionable daze and listen to whatever was on the
menu, whether it was the economics of inflation or flower-
arrangement, photography or posture-control, child-care or
foreign policy in a nuclear age.

I was reminded of this when Madam Chair, reading out her
notes for future meetings before I was called upon to speak on
good old Sea Power (*their* choice), said: 'Next week we have a
real treat—a return visit from our popular friend Mrs James of
the Home Baking Circle, who will give us another of her
splendid talks on desserts, including Cream Puff Pitfalls.'
Another time it was: 'There will be no meeting next month,
which is the St Barnabas Strawberry Social.'

A reliable commentator assured me that this was in the
upper bracket of social intercourse; in more modest areas, such
as his own home town, they held Prune Socials.

It was with such competition in view that I suffered those
agonies of nervousness, and the killing schedule which sometimes went with them. I made twenty-three of these forays in
1954; once, on a brief swing through the Maritimes, I made
five speeches in four days, with forty-eight hours of train travel
sandwiched in between. Before and after the speeches, there
were the welcoming committees to be met, and the tea or
coffee parties afterwards.

These could be fierce. 'You've forgotten me, haven't you?—
now just own up!' was a familiar greeting from many an injured
woman, not at all amused by the idea of such a lapse. 'We met
three years ago at Regina! *Don't you even remember my name?*'

Once, in Newfoundland, it was even more challenging. 'Mr Monsarrat, I am going to make a frontal attack on you!' the lady said, her eyes full of the purest hatred and scorn. I murmured that I did not think my wife would like this at all, but the feeble counter-stroke was brushed aside as the feeble masculine trash it was. 'Just tell me this! Why did you say in your book that St John's was a bleak place in winter?'

I would do my best, both on and off stage. Then I would move on, smiling my Judas smile upon the next gathering, justifying the Rôle of an Information Office with stalwart, ringing phrases. But by the end, I would be feeling something less than stalwart.

Was it for this that I shook like a leaf? Was it for this that I travelled all night between Montreal and Halifax, and greeted the blizzard and the gimlet-eyed reception committee on a station platform at 6.30 in the morning? Was it for this that I ate French dressing with shreds of lettuce leaf floating on top?

Was it for this that I had to listen to one man say: 'Folks don't read much books hereabouts. But I guess it's a living, eh?' and another: 'Let's see—you're free-lancing now, aren't you?' Above all, was it doing any good?

For sometimes my best efforts fell on stony ground indeed. In Halifax, after I had just spent a brilliant, persuasive, oratorical hour demonstrating how completely independent each and every self-governing member of the Commonwealth was, especially Canada, Madam Chair rose to move a vote of thanks. She began: 'It is *so* nice for us out here in the colonies . . .'

But all these doubts and terrors and embarrassments were now past. If I chose, I need never make another speech till Judgment Day, though that one had better be the best effort of my life. This summer of 1956 I was at last free: free of the office, free of the clock, free of everything. Part of that freedom was the first love of all, sailing.

When presenting me and my crew with three of the six available trophies at the end of the 1955 racing season, the

Commodore of the Royal St Lawrence Yacht Club remarked:
'It used to be said that the three most useless objects in a
sailing-boat were an umbrella, a cow, and a naval officer. You
can't be sure of anything these days, can you?'

I could welcome the laughter, having (I thought) earned it,
and the silver cups that went with it, the hard way. But now it
was 1956, when the boat, ten years old, seemed suddenly to
have grown much older than that, and slower than she should
be, like a bride become a drudge; and, like the bride, we were
not doing so well, in any department.

Except on one rare, delicious occasion, which confounded the
bookies and was widely written off as a fluke, the Dragon
yacht *Valhalla* spent the season well down among the rats and
mice of the racing fleet.

It didn't make any difference. In sailing, nothing mattered
except doing it and enjoying it. It was the one realm where the
Olympic motto, now reduced to a bad-tempered joke, or a plain
lie: 'What counts is not the winning, but the taking part,' was
really, undeniably true.

The Royal St Lawrence Yacht Club, which was sixty-eight
years old that season, had a spectacular position on the shores of
Lac St Louis at Dorval, about ten miles west of Montreal; its
manicured lawns and treed slopes stretched down from the
highway to the edge of the lake, which was really a widening of
the main St Lawrence channel over on the far side.

It still had its original buildings, turreted, massively tim-
bered, deliciously old-fashioned; inside, the walls were lined
with yellowing photographs of old yachts, famous in their day,
the outstanding winners of fifty and sixty years ago, and with
scale models of their hulls, including the contenders for the
Seawanhaka Cup, a trophy which the club held against all
American challengers for eight years in succession at the turn
of the century.

Now the main buildings were getting shabby, flaking off,
running down, and gently falling to bits; there was also an
undeniable element of fire hazard. Already vast plans were

a-foot for rebuilding the whole place, to make it the foremost sailing club in North America. As a member of the Development Committee, I shared the current doubts as to whether we could ever raise the $450,000 necessary for this vast project. But we did.

Every Saturday morning, at the prime of the day, I would set out from Ottawa to drive the 112 miles down to Derval. A good average time for this weekly swoop was two hours; once, in a hurry, I did it in one hour and forty minutes, only to be hauled up by the Quebec police, in the last mile, for driving at 35 m.p.h. in a 30 m.p.h. zone, escorted to the police station, and delayed there till well past the starting-gun. (Fine: $20.)

It was on these trips that I completed, twice a year, a small nerve-testing chore, just to keep my hand in and to show that I still had the spark (and the childish urge to prove it): which was to push the Rolls past the 100 m.p.h. mark and held it there for a mile. There *was* one long deserted stretch of Route 2 where this was safe, and not abnormally anti-social.

At the R.S.L. I raced twice on Saturday, morning and afternoon; and spent the night in my rented room in the fire-trap of the 'dormitory house'; and raced again on Sunday morning before speeding back to Ottawa. Saturday night passed agreeably in sitting on the balcony of the men's club house.

From that superior vantage-point we watched the dusk falling, the late sailors drifting back into harbour on the tail-end of the breeze, and the St Lawrence channel lights come winking one by one out of the calm darkness; and discussed without rancour what had gone wrong on the last tack (or the first tack, or any other tack which had put us out of the running and into the ruck of tenth place out of fourteen'; and getting quietly stoned in the process.

It was a male world, for my age group at least and I relished it without regret or second thought. Racing was, as always, exciting, tiring, usually disappointing; sailing itself was still the most wonderful kind of movement in the world, and a silent, lazy, sunlit glide up-river to the great locks at Beauharnois, or

through to our neighbour lake, Lake of Two Mountains, was a
blessing not to be matched by any glittering achievement, nor
to be spoiled by any fiasco on the racing-circuit.

Those evenings afterwards were such a respite, such a release
from care, such a relief from the idiot jungle of writing, not
writing, signing cheques, paying bills, quarrelling, apologizing,
and warding off real or imagined blows, that I came to count on
them, as other men came to count on the prospect of parole
after a solid span of years in the clink.

I was a member of the Royal St Lawrence for thirteen years,
and disqualified from membership in sad and foolish circumstances, like a small nagging nightmare tacked on to the end of a
happy dream.* But that year, it was still unqualified bliss.

I had been talked into buying a Dragon by an old-time sailing
enthusiast, Mr R. C. Stevenson, a past commodore of the Royal
St Lawrence, a superb, tireless, and foxy helmsman, and a man
dedicated, in and out of season, to building up the club fleet. He
came into my Ottawa office, soon after I arrived, and suggested
that I should join his club, buy a boat, and race it at Montreal,
without any further delay.

Perhaps, he allowed, it was too late this year. But what about
the next one? And as for a boat—well, Dragons were good
boats. He had one himself. The club had seven of them already.
How about making it eight?

R. C. Stevenson was then nearly seventy, with the kind of
wild enthusiasm I had had when I was thirteen. I temporized,
being already wary of people who tried to sell me things, or
persuade me to buy them from other people, whether they were
vintage cars (say, a 1927 Hispano-Suiza with the only known
example of an electric gear-box) or a vintage Frans Hals por-

---

* When I left Canada I was immediately involved, like any other sterling area
transplant, in exchange control complications which made it very difficult to
settle any dollar debts promptly. For a year I owed the club a $20 overseas mem-
bership fee. Presently I was able to settle this, and my next year's subscription as
well; by then, however, their patience exhausted after constant reminders which
admittedly I had allowed to pile up, they had thrown me out. But darn it, I had
given them my $250 building debenture when I left!

trait, a portrait so like 'The Laughing Cavalier' that there were many people who were prepared to swear that it must be the original. Now it was a Dragon yacht. . . . To begin with, how much did Dragons cost?

'About six thousand dollars,' Mr Stevenson answered promptly. 'Then there's the freight, and a bit of customs duty as well. Then you have to truck it down to the club.' My expression must have been less than enthusiastic, because he went on: 'But why not start with a second-hand boat? Just to get the feel of it?'

'How much would that be?' I was sorry to sound such a miserable, tight-wadded young bastard, but six thousand dollars was nearly three months' living expenses.

He produced, from a bulging briefcase, a copy of the *Yachting World*, and slapped it down on my desk, folded open at a certain page. 'There's one here for £600. I guess that would be about eighteen hundred dollars. She sounds good. Champion of the Solent for three years.'

'I used to write for the *Yachting World*,' I told him, still temporizing. 'In fact they took my very first article, back in 1934.'

He beamed. 'Is that so? Well, now . . .' and I realized that I should never have brought the point up, even as a delaying measure. In some way it seemed to make me one of the family already. 'Would you like to write them, or shall I?'

Valhalla was shipped out that winter, and dipped her keel in the frigid waters of Lac St Louis the following April. Like all Dragons, she was a superbly graceful racing machine, with a 30-foot black hull shaped like the underside of a dolphin, and just as lively and swift. But there was a whole range of fresh skills to be learned, before I could make her work.

The set of her sails, for example, depended on a careful, almost mathematical tuning of the mast, which was something altogether new to me, and somehow decadent, like a velvet smoking-jacket of which the shoulders must be brushed one way and the sleeves another. Yet it quickly became apparent,

after trial and error, that unless all *Valhalla's* standing rigging
was precisely set up to allow a 40-foot mast to taper off into a
pliant curve, rather like an immensely tall bamboo shoot which
only leans against the wind, then we might as well lower the
sails and row home.

Being a racing machine, she was almost entirely useless for
anything else. People did sometimes use Dragons for overnight
cruising, living on sandwiches, sleeping on the floor-boards,
and relying on a bucket for all else; but with a cabin-top allow-
ing only four feet of headroom at the most, one had to be
enthusiastic indeed to put it to the test—or else to have
extra-maritime motives.

'There's plenty of headroom in a Dragon,' maintained a
noted club Romeo who had just got engaged, 'as long as you're
lying down.'

My motives were different, and with my devoted crew of Reg
Gillman and Andy Starke I did my best to crown them with
success. But the Dragon class was growing swiftly; there were
now fourteen of us; the competition had grown hot, the protest
flags flew to and fro like writs in the very spring of alimony; and
Valhalla, in 1956, had to try very hard to rise above double
figures in the list of those finishing the course.

There was another hazard that year, which God knows was
the same for all of us, but less of an embarrassment to hardened
skippers who, like Reg Stevenson himself, knew Lac St Louis as
intimately as the back of their horny hands. This was the building
of the St Lawrence Seaway, now nearing completion, which had
lowered the level of the lake by two or three feet, and brought
near to the surface rocks and shoals we scarcely knew had been
there.

I had seen over this vast project, which probed two thousand
miles into the very heart of the continent, the year before, and
marvelled at its man-made lakes scooped out of the solid earth,
and false islands suddenly imposed, and fresh channels cut
through virgin land, and villages submerged and other villages
transported bodily to higher ground, and the great chain of new

locks which were going to change the whole pattern of this ancient waterway for the next million years.

It was a staggering rearrangement of nature, which had taken years to plan and then to carve out; now at last the bathwater was filling up, and in the process small expendable items like lakeside cottages woke to find themselves a hundred yards from the nearest trickle of water, and sailing clubs suddenly ran out of usable space in which to hold their races.

As a consequence, everyone except the most crafty kept running aground, sometimes with a soft squelching noise as if one had steered nose-first into a nursery blancmange, sometimes with a jarring, spine-cracking thud which, when one limped back to harbour to have the boat hauled out, was found to have removed sizeable slices of lead from our shapely keel.

Dragons, built like rocks themselves, with the loving care which no moulded synthetic hull would ever call for, were tough enough. *Valhalla*, before my time, had won wild cross-Channel races in horrible steep seas and the kind of forcible winds which had wrecked the Spanish Armada. But she did draw 5ft. 11ins., like all the rest, and when the rocks now stuck up to within two feet of the surface, we became paper Dragons, and the torture was indeed Chinese.

To begin with—and this had been my first thought, when I was being conned into buying a boat—I had rather scoffed at lake sailing. It was all right, one supposed, for fair-weather mariners, who liked smooth surfaces and a picnic atmosphere, but could it ever match handling an open 14-footer in the open Irish Sea, which was the way I had been brought up? It did, and I found the fact out very quickly.

There was one race, a long 30-mile slog for the Mirage Trophy, the pride of a rival yacht club, which was sailed in the very worst weather I had ever faced in a small boat. Storms could build up and pounce very quickly on Lac St Louis; and half-way through this race I looked up from some close calculation of the next mark to see, bearing down on us from the head of the lake, a genuine 'line-squall'—a villainous purple

mass of cloud, straight as a ruler, and underneath it a wall of
creamy water building up into a horrid turmoil.

We were leading the field at the time: we might even win—it
was one of those rare, blessed days—and I hated to do anything
to spoil our chances. We had the ordinary, unreefed mainsail set,
and a big Genoa jib, and as the wind freshened we began to
move like a train. But perhaps it would be better if——

Then it hit us, and the next thing I said was: 'Get your life-
jackets on!'

It came down on us like a real blow, like a wicked fist. We
were hammered flat, in one awful instant of time, and I thought
we were gone; and there the boat stayed, for nearly ten minutes.
The jib was ripped and torn to shreds—which was just as well:
if it had held, we would have gone under foot by foot, and sunk
like a stone.

As it was, the angle of the deck was murderous, and the waves
were now pouring in, in a steady cataract. I had to keep some
tension on the mainsail; if I let it run out, it would have been in
the water, and would fill, and over we would go.

We lay there, absolutely powerless, nearly done, while the
wind screamed and bashed at us as if we were its last enemy on
the lake.

Somehow we had to get the mainsail down. This meant no
more than letting go a single ratchet; but that was below decks, at
the foot of the mast, only to be reached by crawling through two
feet of water, with the boat still pinned down at its fearful angle.

I could not do it: I had the tiller to control, a tiller nearly
wrenching my arm out of its socket, and I was hanging on to
the main sheet as well. Reg Gillman could not do it; he was
working like a crazy dog at the pump. That left Andy Starke,
whose normal job was to handle the headsails; now, with the
jib gone, he was crouched under the cabin top, sheltering from
the tearing wind and the waves slapping over us. I had to shout
at him twice: 'Let go the main halyard!' before he understood
what I wanted.

He was young, and strong, and admirably brave. First he

took off his glasses, and tucked them inside his life-jacket. Then he crawled down into the little cabin below decks, his back tight up against the cabin top.

The wind dealt us one last, extra, smashing blow while he was still imprisoned below. Then there was an enormous bang which could be felt throughout the boat, and the mainsail, which for once did not jam in its tracks, slid down with a screech, and we came slowly upright.

Andy, our saviour, reappeared, grinning. He put on his glasses again. Then he clawed his way forward, along the sluicing deck, and let go the anchor: a small miniature of courage, and pure gold, even from the rear view.

We stayed where we were for another fifteen minutes, pumping out, getting the tangle straight again, catching our breath after the astonishment of reprieve. If she had gone over in that howling wilderness it would have been a short swim in hell for us, and after that the Lachine Rapids, waiting for us downstream. We still could not see more than ten yards in any direction, so thick was the flying scud. Then the storm ripped away to leeward, and the blue sky came out, as innocent as a harlot on holiday.

Now it could be seen that the next mark was only half a mile to windward, and there wasn't another boat in sight. By God, by God, it was still possible. . . . We took down the rags of the Genoa job, and hoisted a mouldy old substitute in its place; then we hauled up the anchor, got under way, made our mark, turned for home and, while the rest of the battered fleet was still sorting itself out, won that race by a comfortable mile.

I was stiff and sore for a week afterwards. It cost us a nylon Genoa, a mainsail so warped and stretched that it could never be used again, and several moments of terror. All we got in return was a beer-mug each, of disputable pewter, labelled 'Pointe Claire Yacht Club: Mirage Trophy.' But when really in need of reassurance, I used to drink out of that beer-mug. And never again did I think of lake sailing as something for an idle summer afternoon, with parasols fluttering on the foredeck.

This year, by contrast, we limped through a sad season. New boats were coming along all the time, and, as had happened at Trearddur Bay, twenty-five years earlier, the new boats, light and dry, with sails flat as boards and all sorts of novel gadgets to work them, could out-point and out-sail the old stagers, every time.

Fresh stars emerged; and even if they were forty-year-old doctors like Sandy MacDonald, who was later to represent us in the Olympic Games, rather than fourteen-year-old younger brothers like Denys, the new wave, and its swift success, had the power to wound and to discourage.

Towards the end of the season, I decided that a brand-new Dragon was the only answer, and I ordered one from Camper & Nicolson in Gosport. She was to be called *Shearwater*, I decided, after my long-ago first corvette command, and she would incorporate, among a lot of other refinements, my third and last invention, after the variable gear and perpetual motion: the double-ended, reversible, instant-clip-on spinnaker-boom— and this time it worked!

It was a little too technical to be explained in terms of family reading, but good enough to be adopted as a standard item thereafter.

Camper & Nicolson (who, I learned years afterwards, went by the horrid *sobriquet* of 'Cami-Knicks' among a certain class of yachtsman) were to make an outstanding job of *Shearwater*; and I must admit that in placing this order I had my eye on the 1960 Olympics at Naples, though that was a deep dark secret which luckily I confided to no one except my crew. But no sooner had the contract for her been signed than *Valhalla*, as if to put me to shame for my disloyalty, won a race on which, against all the odds, I had set my heart.

This was the Windmill Point Shield, an admired trophy which we had won, with all sorts of luck, in 1955. I would have dearly loved to retain it for the second year in succession, but I did not really give ten cents for our chances. We had not won a single race that season, nor ever looked like doing so. I had already kissed the Windmill Point Shield good-bye, half-way between Ottawa and Dorval. But I still longed for it.

The wind that afternoon was light, very fluky, hard to forecast; one had to go and look for it, or guess where it would come from, *if* it came from anywhere, and then be ready for it—which boiled down to being in one particular stretch of Lac St Louis, and pointing the right way, when everyone else was somewhere quite different, and stern-first towards the winning post. That, by a glorious chance, was exactly what happened.

Half an hour after the start, every other boat in the fleet was playing around inshore, tacking to and fro among the tall trees at the edge of the lake, which for some mysterious reason often seemed able to conjure up a breeze of their own. I decided that if we were going to be thrashed, then we might as well be thrashed real good, as Dr Billy Graham would have said.

I set our course slap up the middle of the lake, against the main current, never changing tacks, never deviating from a distant mark on the shore-line ahead, under which lay our turning-buoy.

We were entirely alone. The boats inshore were tacking to and fro like mad bees, tearing each other to ribbons. All the Dragon stars—Reg Stevenson, Sandy MacDonald, Archie Cameron, Gerry Letourneau—were there. *But they were not making any more progress than we were.* We sailed placidly on up the main channel; no one bothered us: it was a private world, good enough for hopeless amateurs, of gently rippling water, of sails just filled enough to keep us on course, of a little bubbling wake which meant that we were moving, and always in the right direction.

Presently, far ahead of us, the surface of the lake ruffled, and changed colour, from pale blue to dark. It was the wind—our wind, the one I had been looking for, and only ours. No one else was placed to gain any benefit from it. I knew then that we were going to win, and an hour later we did.

Sometimes *Valhalla*, when I had her properly balanced, moved like a dream, slicing through the water as if she were skating

on gentle ice. She did so now. Gathering speed, we romped
away into the blue, still completely on our own; and by the time
the breeze reached the shore-gang, we could not be caught.
With a creaming wake we rounded Windmill Point, three
hundred yards ahead of all pursuit, and made for the finishing
line; and Max, spending his summer holidays in Canada, was
on the committee boat to see us get the gun.

Not even the drenching rain which presently blotted out the
lake, and everything on it, could spoil that moment.

'Well done!' said my friend Reg Stevenson later. He never
grudged any man anything. 'But you had no right to win, you
know. All the *reliable* breeze was inshore. It always is. You
didn't even try to cover us! By all the rules of racing . . .' He
was shaking his head, but smiling at the same time; there was a
funny side to this, and after a lifetime's fanatical competition he
could still see it very easily. 'I don't know why you want to
bother with a new boat,' he concluded. 'On her day, *Valhalla*
can't be beaten.'

'But it's only one day, out of about five months.'

'We'll take darned good care of that!'

But there was something else that summer, and every summer
in Canada, which had the true precedence: which was to sailing
as a subtle burgundy is to a lively champagne. This was the
Shakespeare Festival season down at Stratford, Ontario, a
miraculous act of faith now entering its fourth triumphant
season. I had just been elected to its Board of Governors, and I
was as pleased and proud about that as when, in the unlikely
year of 1953, I wrote that this was a project which had the
brightest future of anything of its kind in Canada, and wrote, as
well, the modest cheque which made me a Founding Patron.

It had started, like buying *Valhalla*, with a man coming into
my office with an idea to sell. He was announced as Mr Tom
Patterson of Stratford, Ontario. I had never heard of Tom
Patterson, nor of Stratford, Ont., either. But at the end of an
hour, I knew almost everything about both.

Tom Patterson was a small, diffident, bald young man with a
gleam in his eye and a mission. Such visitors were not always
welcome at the United Kingdom Information Office. I had, in
the past, already wasted acres of prime time listening to single-
minded fellow-visionaries trying to enlist my support for epic
poetry readings in caves, for a season of British Morris Dancing,
for the planting of groves of oaks in memory of Trafalgar

But Tom Patterson was of a different quality altogether.
After ten minutes, I realized that his project, crazy as it was,
had a certain wild validity. Less than an hour later, I was a
whole-hearted supporter.

Patterson was an ex-journalist who, during some war
service in Italy and elsewhere, had the luck to see a lot of
theatre and opera—a happy dividend, more readily available to
soldiers than, for example, to sailors. When he came back to his
home-town of Stratford he decided—just like that, with a snap
of the fingers and perhaps a couple of drinks—that Stratford,
even the wrong Stratford, was going to live up to its honoured
name. Whether it knew it or not, it was going to build a really
great theatre, of international quality, dedicated to the plays of
Shakespeare.

Stratford, at that time, was a rural town of 18,000 people, as
plain and prosperous as its surrounding countryside. It served
farmers, it made a little furniture and children's footwear, it
housed its citizens comfortably; it had an extra employment
bonus in the shape of a Canadian National Railways repair shop.
Apart from that, it was an absolutely typical Canadian community, unsullied by any extravagant notions of culture. There
had been no theatre there for half a century.

This was the material Tom Patterson had to work on, and in
the course of our talk I learned just how far he had got, and at
what sort of pace.

First he had taken his lunatic idea to the local council, and
told them all about it. Somehow he must have caught them off
balance, which was a talent he was able to bring to perfection
during the next five years. But even so, they did not go wild.

They voted him the sum of $125, and asked him to examine the prospects and to report back. It seemed probable that the stake, though less than princely, was $125 more than most of the city fathers thought those prospects were worth.

The measure of the man was that, on this frugal basis, he engineered a trip to England, and enlisted the support of Tyrone Guthrie. It must have been an interesting contrast in style; Guthrie, as well as being a talented and sought-after director, was six-foot-four of somewhat imperious resolution. But presently he wrote back: 'I have never before felt so convinced of the obvious practical value of anything I've been asked to be connected with,' and he promptly corralled Tanya Moiseiwitsch, Irene Worth, and Alec Guinness to join him in the enterprise.

'Of course I will do the *décor* and the costumes,' said Tanya Moiseiwitsch. 'Of course I will come and act,' said Irene Worth. 'Of course I will play Richard the Third in the opening performance,' said Alec Guinness.

'But have you collected any more money?' I asked Tom at this point.

'No, not really,' he answered. 'But Massey thinks it's a marvellous idea. And we've ordered a tent, and Tanya has already designed the stage.'

'You'd better come and have lunch.'

There were other things besides Shakespeare and Stratford which could make his eyes gleam. 'Lead on! I'm certainly hungry!'

He was indeed to meet prolonged financial troubles before the curtain went up at Stratford; hunger must have seemed the keynote, during all that mangled period when he and the handful of other enthusiasts were walking a tight-rope, beneath which yawned a cavern of indifference and spite. No one really believed in the damned thing; or rather, they believed in it in theory, and did nothing to help it in practice. There was a time when the whole undertaking, losing momentum, limped and tottered from crisis to crisis.

It became known that money was only trickling in, and as the word spread (shortage of funds was, in Canada, a worse contagion than the plague) many people involved in the project began to demand cash on the nail. There wasn't any cash, only hope, and the ludicrous dream itself. At one point, construction work on the theatre stopped entirely; even a few weeks before the opening, there was a chance that the Stratford Festival would have to be written off altogether.

Its critics and detractors, hard at work on an easy target, came very near to destroying it completely. Then, just in time, the tide turned.

There was really no reason for this, except that people such as Tyrone Guthrie, and others who had never wavered in their support, and Tom Patterson himself, all kept plugging away as if it were beyond question that the promised opening night would take place as advertised, and anyone who thought differently was not fully informed.*

Contractors who had seemed cagey and suspicious suddenly turned liberal. The financial appeal, particularly in hard-headed Toronto, began to prosper; and Stratford itself, unaccountably catching fire, subscribed a heart-warming $3.75 for every man, woman, and child within the city limits. Out of a working budget of $150,000, generous Stratford put up nearly half.

There was absolutely no reason for this either, except a sort of constructive civic contrariness. People were saying this thing was going to be a flop? Well, we'll show them. . . . It was all the more astonishing because the local paper, the Stratford *Beacon-Herald*, the only newspaper which most of the inhabitants read,

---

* One of the things at which Tyrone Guthrie certainly plugged away was pronunciation. For a long time, his large Canadian contingent of actors seemed unable to appreciate that the name 'Buckingham', as in the Duke of Buckingham, must be pronounced in the English fashion, and not as 'Bucking-HAM', the North American version. Finally he called the male members of the cast together. 'I've had enough of Bucking-HAM,' he was reported to have said. 'Now just you listen to me! You're always talking about fucking 'em, aren't you? I'm told that you're always *doing* it. Well, this chap's name is Bucking 'em. Got it?' From that moment on, their diction in this respect was faultless.

and which should have been as habit-forming as a medical prescription, was vehemently anti-Festival from the start, and had persisted in this almost until curtain time.

At the very moment, ten days before the first night, when people would be making up their minds whether to buy tickets and attend, or to let the whole silly business slide into limbo, the *Beacon-Herald* came out with an editorial headed 'AN UNHAPPY CHOICE OF PLAY'.

Elsewhere on this page today is printed the introduction to 'The Tragedy of King Richard III'. . . . The *Beacon-Herald* gives space to an obviously-needed outline of the sordid story, because of the seemingly general lack of knowledge about the major dramatic offering in the nearing Stratford Shakespearean Festival.

Having in mind that this summer's Shakespearean Festival must win strong approval and support if it is to become a permanent enterprise, the thought will not down [*sic*] that an unfortunate choice was made when 'King Richard III' was selected as the spearhead stage offering. It is definitely the most unwholesome of all Shakespeare's tragedies, and its only character of any real dramatic interest is that of Richard himself—a physically repulsive hypocrite, liar and murderer, without one redeeming feature. No modern-day criminal has yet matched in foulness this detestable villain, whose evil hypocrisies, falsehoods, and cold-blooded murders are an unbroken string from beginning to end. He occupies the stage much of the time, and there is nothing to applaud unless the audience enjoys a monstrous menu of blood-letting, with men, women and even children the victims of the rottenest recorded character in the history of the British Throne and of English 'nobility'.

Frankly, this column regrets that a deplorable character in history—one which is better forgotten at any time—is being made the centre-piece of a supposedly 'cultural' crusade. That this hideous blot on Royalty should be featured so brazenly in

this Coronation Year of 1953 seems incredibly poor judgment. Can we turn so easily from acclaiming the glories of the
Monarchy of Queen Elizabeth the Second to applaud the
murderous King Richard the Third? It is surely a pretty tall
order!

In other words: Put that nasty thing down! Don't touch it!
Don't go near it! Perhaps it *was* a pretty tall order; and it might
have been thought that after this pronouncement, which certainly
demonstrated that the art of dropping poison in the innocent ear
had not disappeared with Hamlet's uncle, the *Beacon-Herald*
would have found it impossible to reverse their stand entirely
and jump on the band-wagon.

But just in time, they saw the light; and with a display of
impudence which many an old-time snake-oil salesman might
have envied, they ran a leader headed 'WE WISH THE FESTI-
VAL SUCCESS', two days before opening night.

It was certainly adroit:

As the Stratford Shakespearean Festival opens its five-
weeks run, there is universal hope that a full measure of
success will crown this bold dramatic venture If the enthusiasm of its sponsors is matched by public support, any
remaining problems in this difficult enterprise can be overcome. It has required passionate zeal and unflagging determination to transcend the periods of crisis that challenged the
Festival promoters' faith in the practicality of their dream. . . .

It is important, then, that the widest possible support of
the Festival be cultivated—and that every care be taken to
leave only wholesome memories in the minds of all who
attend the plays. . . . The winning of broad and lasting support rests upon a demonstration that public confidence can be
reposed without stint in the utter sincerity of all who have
worked so hard to develop a new (and difficult) addition to
this community's influences towards leadership in good
living.

The *Beacon-Herald* has been frank in its editorial treatment of the Festival project. . . . We need hardly repeat that it is our sincere hope that the Festival will be an unqualified success—and that play-goers from near and far will derive pleasure and inspiration in excess of all expectations.

They did. For me, and for countless others, there had never been anything like that opening night, in a whole life-time of theatre-going; the 'monstrous menu of blood-letting' turned out to be a marvellous banquet for every conceivable palate, whether delicate or strong, jaded or innocent.

Part of the enormous excitement of the occasion was the background knowledge, common to almost everyone in the theatre, of the whole chain of crises, all the damnable headaches, which had for so long been conspiring to prevent the first night ever taking place.

These had been overcome, one after the other, by faith and energy and a persistent, dedicated will to win. It had been a very near thing, down to the last few days. But now, here were the trumpets sounding to prove victory, and to acclaim it, and to put Mr Faintheart and Mr Envy and Mr Sneerwell to shame.

A gun went off, a Shakespearean cannon, much too close, making us all jump. Then there was a doom-like note on a bell, and then, under a single diffused spotlight, Alec Guinness appeared on the balcony high above the stage.

Only it was not Alec Guinness at all; it was Richard III, in the brave scarlet finery which mocked the pitiable man within. I was not sure what I had been expecting to see, except that it should have been a vaguely familiar face: the reality, the man on the balcony, was a complete stranger, and a figure from a bad dream as well.

He was dwarfish and repellent; a humped shoulder was balanced by a drooping eye; under the red cap, the face shone with a malignant glow; beneath the rusty cloak, a leg dragged, as if unwilling to follow so misshapen a body. But, with all this, the man was a king, noble and hideous at the same time: and when he spoke, the fact was confirmed.

There is indeed such a thing as the 'thrilling voice' of fiction, and now we heard it. It flooded the theatre with the first words of the Stratford Festival, absolutely prophetic of all that was to come:

> Now is the winter of our discontent
> Made glorious summer by this sun of York.

The play was on.

It was an outstanding evening, one of the best I ever remembered. Everything helped it: great acting, splendid decoration of a quality never seen before, and a universal sense of relief and gratitude that, after all, this astonishing venture had come to full flower. It carried the whole audience with it. The tumult of applause at the end, Stratford's first standing ovation, saluted two things: a wonderful presentation, and a wonderful act of faith.

The range of that faith had been as strange and rare as its quality. The man who delayed sending in his bill for pouring the concrete foundations had shared it with Alec Guinness, who, in Coronation year, might reasonably have been expected to preside over some safe and sumptuous hit in London's West End. This, also, was part of what we were applauding. The echoes never really died away.

I had offered to write a three-article account of that Stratford opening for the *Ottawa Citizen*, as a small gift to God and Tom Patterson, and I signed off my contribution with a couple of paragraphs which it is a treat (of an obvious, I-told-you-so brand) to record:

> There is absolutely no reason why this Stratford Festival should not gather momentum, year by year, until in good time it becomes a going concern without any outside aid. Something new has been added to the Canadian theatrical

17

scene: something new, something worthwhile, something stunning in its enterprise. It is there for all to enjoy. You may readily and willingly travel miles to attend it. To go to Stratford today is more than a duty—it is a pleasure.

As an earnest of this, that first season of two plays was presently extended from five weeks to six, and sold a phenomenal 98 per cent of all the available seats.

Going to the theatre is normally a simple and even cold-blooded routine: you buy the tickets, arrive on time, plant yourself in the right seat, sit back, and say: 'Now, show me.' Going down to Stratford, in 1956, was still a pious pilgrimage; it had been so wonderful in the past three years, and to make the journey again was an avowal of trust that it would be wonderful this time also.

The occasion had now become more professional, and certainly more social. It could not be spoiled by either.

It involved a drive of 350 miles, and as usual we took it slowly; it was something to be enjoyed, to be spun out: a picnic with all the signs set fair, an act of piety which would, for a change, earn a positive reward. There was another, twentieth-century reason why the journey should not be hurried. At this point of summer, the Canadian roads, like the woods in the shooting season, were full of sporting idiots.

An Ontario farmer, plagued by stock losses, used to paint the word 'COW' on the side of all his cows, as soon as autumn came round and the guns began to roar. On the same basis, one might never get to Stratford at all, unless one crept there like a mouse in a car defensively labelled 'CAR'.

In any case, how did one want to arrive there, for the first of two nights of theatrical delight? Sweating like a pig? Shaking like a bed-spring? Prematurely drained, like a miscued lover? No one in his senses would thus betray his union. Yet it *was* something of a Canadian habit, to run all the way there, to enjoy a panting rest while the plays were on, and to run all the way back.

We had an Ottawa friend who habitually drove those three
hundred and fifty miles in half a day, after an early morning
visit to his broker's office; arrived at Stratford at 6 p.m. and
checked into his hotel; and then, fortified by a cold shower, a
fried-egg sandwich, and five dry martinis, went straight to the
theatre.

It was a horrid thought that a poet of four centuries ago, and
a hundred talented people toiling like dedicated beavers for the
past four months, had worked to give this man this owl-eyed
moment.

The last thirty miles of the Stratford journey were in odd
contrast with what was to come. The road ran straight, through
a level and featureless countryside. This was wholesome farming land, well-kept, orderly, prosperous, and dull: one of those
pockets of Canada settled by one particular brand of newcomer,
and never to lose its original *marque*. Here the settlement had
been German, and devoutly thorough, and ploddingly industrious.

From Kitchener (which had been called Berlin until 1914,
when the label grew embarrassing), the signposts read like a
catalogue inscribed by some homesick exile from the beloved
fatherland: New Hamburg, Baden, Guelph, Brunner, Breslau,
Mannheim, Wallenstein, Heidelberg. One began to wonder
whether it was part of the plot to prove that Shakespeare had
been German after all: a towering monument to Teutonic
genius which no English country bumpkin could ever have
matched.

But then nature, history, and propaganda relented. Suddenly
we were back in England, back to the Warwckshire poacher
turned actor, back to Ann Hathaway and the second-best bed.
The next signpost said Tavistock, and the next village was
called Shakespeare. After that, the next and last town was
Stratford, through which the River Avon, though pronounced
'Avvon', meandered with historic accuracy and was patrolled by
authentic swans.

We stayed at a motel, the Imperial, one of the rash of motels which had sprung up as soon as the Festival was seen to be a civic as well as an artistic sure-thing. It was run by a family, and a man, with a name as anonymous as that of some of his clients, Smith.

David Smith had already become a good friend, and his establishment was a model of what one hoped to find at the end of such a journey. But—speaking in the most general terms—I could never believe that I would like to run a motel, which must be a great strain on the patience and, occasionally, on one's sense of propriety.

By now I had stayed in hundreds of them, from Montreal to the Florida Keys: from Trois Rivières, Quebec (not too good) to Beverly Hills (not bad at all). It was in many ways an ideal, time-saving, painless-parking method of settling in after an all-day drive. But undoubtedly there were hazards connected with the profession. Many of the customers, checking into their rooms, seemed to check their rules of deportment at the same time.

People stole things from motels: not just tumblers and ash-trays, but sheets, blankets, and even rugs and radio sets. (A notice in one South Carolina establishment expressed it thus tactfully: 'Please notify the office before disconnecting this television receiver, as it is connected to the burglar alarm system.') People behaved badly in motels; there were screams in the night, raucous family disputes, the thud of falling bodies, the cries of unwilling brides; quarrels broke out over cards, over the division of the loot, over nothing at all; and above the up-roar rose the steady clink, tinkle, and crash of bottles and glasses.

Such goings-on had only directly concerned me once. This was in a motel in Saratoga, at the height of the racing season, when the most hideous disturbance was caused by a woman who, at 2 a.m., began hammering on the doors of all the fifty-six units which made up the establishment.

She was looking for her husband; it was a drama which, in this instance, could not have involved me, though judging by the uproar it had a generally traumatic effect on a number of other occupants. But I always kept my fingers crossed. Sooner or later, it seemed, the door of one of these utilitarian nests would crash open, and the Chief of Police, burly, thick-set, and leering, would burst in, shouting: 'Hold it! You're both under arrest for exceeding the legal limit!'

But at the Imperial Motel, Stratford, everything was peace and gentle relaxation and an innocent renewal of friendship: all the right preludes to enchantment.

Stratford meant real-life people as well as players, though sometimes the dividing line between the two aspects of human behaviour was thin indeed. There were some traditional visitors to the Imperial Motel, and some traditional calls to be made, before the evening became exclusively theatrical. An early caller, and a favourite one, was Douglas Campbell.

First met when he was leading the Old Vic touring company in South Africa, Douglas Campbell was now a Festival main-stay, and a fourth-season veteran of the company. Starting as the braggart-soldier Parolles in *All's Well That Ends Well*, he had progressed to a superlative performance, for two years running, in and as *Oedipus Rex*. This year—tomorrow night—he would be Falstaff in *The Merry Wives of Windsor* and it was as Falstaff, with a bit of Oedipus thrown in, and a touch of Parolles and a massive slice of Douglas Campbell as well, that he sat on the motel lawn and greeted his first customers.

Douglas was a very considerable character off stage as well as on: wearing execrable clothes, disdaining socks, he could still exude an aura of personal distinction, compounded of one-third ham actor, one-third boundless stamina, and one-third of full-grained personality. It was the stamina which enabled him to make such a call on the eve of an exhausting performance; any other actor would have been too tired, too preoccupied, too nervous, or too self-absorbed.

He was a ferocious arguer, of the sort who made it impossible not to argue back with equal vehemence. That afternoon he was doing battle over Stratford's drink laws, which did not suit his temperament, and the homosexual cult which was threatening, though briefly, a Festival take-over, and a very small, very subtle, very important, almost inexplicable piece of direction in tomorrow night's play, which did not accord with his sense of artistic purity.

But he would have argued about anything, and he preferred to. In the programme for Stratford's very first season, there had been a brief, significant notation: 'Fights arranged by Douglas Campbell.' It remained appropriate.

Yet I remembered him best of all at a moment of abject defeat in that same first season, when, as the ineffable Parolles, he had been tricked by his fellow soldiers into a shameful display of cowardice. Discovered, and disgraced for ever, he could still shrug it all away with the line: 'Captain I'll be no more.'

His manner was rueful, shamefaced, yet optimistic still; he had been knocked flat on his back, for the very first time, but after all he had resigned, he had not been sacked. . . . There would be other chances to cheat the world. He need only wait till other dupes grew on other trees.

All that, in a single phrase.

When asked about tomorrow's Falstaff, he relapsed into his Victorian actor-manager image again, and proclaimed: 'It will give me full scope, laddie!'

A spectral voice seemed to be adding: 'Four times round the world, and never missed a cue!'

Brief contact was also made with Michael Langham who, as the director of both plays that season, really was phenomenally busy, though his brand of stamina—non-physical, nervous, almost spiritual—was always enough to pull him through any occasion like this.

He had succeeded Tyrone Guthrie as Artistic Director the year before; the difficult succession—difficult because Guthrie cast a very long shadow, and deserved to—had become a personal triumph, and Michael Langham was now consolidating the foundation of a thirteen-year tenure which was to put

Stratford forever on the map, with the name hammered out in gold.

Then a small meek car drove up, and a small meek man got out, and it was Tom Patterson, the undoubted 'onlie begetter' of all this flowering. He was rather subdued, as he had a right to be; fathers, even though the child they were expecting was now their fourth, could still sweat a little as they waited for the outcome.

He was also, I knew, beginning to be depressed about his own position within the Festival. From the first heady season, when admittedly he had been given most of the credit for the venture, and a lot of people who did a lot of other work never got as much as a one-line mention in the *Beacon-Herald*, Tom had been the target of a persistent, nagging campaign, on the basis of 'After all, what did he actually *do?*' which was just beginning to build up a head of steam.

There was already a tendency to shuffle him out of the way: to find some meaningless niche with a vague title, and then demote him from there. There were variations on the theme of 'Planning Consultant' which showed a skilful effort to accord him a Festival stained-glass window without paying him any particular compliment.

He was labelled 'Founder', which was accurate, for a number of years; later he was to figure as 'Director of Public Relations' —but separate from the 'Director of Publicity', who presumably did all the spade-work. As far as I was concerned he was, then and in the future, a necessary man. He did not make the Festival, which was the work of many hands; but he did invent it. If Stratford needed a totem pole, then this small slight model with the polished dome was just right.

He was also worried about money—I never knew a year when he was not—and about his marriage, which was in process of cracking up. I knew all about that as well, having an important, somewhat grotesque connection with the turmoil which need not be detailed until Judgment Day.

Presently Tom said: 'Have you had lunch yet?'

He was the kind of man who was always asking this, even at
half past three in the afternoon.

I said that I had indeed lunched, on the way down, but if he
was hungry we could send out for something from the joint
down the road. I even produced their menu, which offered, as
usual, hot dogs and hamburgers and cheeseburgers and chicken-
in-a-basket and jumbo shrimps encased in batter and French
fries dipped in tomato ketchup.

'Or you could have a Heavenly Twin.'

'What's that?'

'*Two* hamburgers.'

'Better not. There's still the party before the show.' He grew
melancholy. 'I don't know what you think, but it seems to me
that party is beginning to get out of hand.'

We soon confirmed that this was true.

The official party before the opening had started in a small
way, at the beginning of the first season, as a matter of courtesy
on the part of the Festival Governors, in order to greet their
supporters, give the evening some kind of a starting-point, and
also to eke out the town's meagre eating and drinking facilities.
It had then been a drink-and-a-snack show, for which the
church-going wives of Stratford had baked and brewed and cut
and spread all the preceding day: a modest prelude to the real
point of the evening, and modestly priced at two dollars.

Now it had grown until it had changed its nature entirely; the
early simple ritual was now buried under an avalanche of compulsive sociality. Tickets for it had soared to six dollars per
person and, in the case of some of the guests, it looked as though
this intensive spree was the high point of their evening. They
shovelled down mounds of food; they dived into the drink as if
they would not reach another oasis for a hundred miles or more;
in one way or another, they were clearly determined to get their
six dollars' worth, or bust. Or both. It was like an orphans'
picnic, with the orphans big, glossy, and unsupervised.

This stepped-up invasion stemmed from the mother-lode of
Canadian snobbery, Toronto. Socialite Toronto, a generous sup-

porter from the beginning, was now going for Stratford in a very big way indeed. It sent along its best team, all ready and primed to do the Shakespeare bit on the right night, in the right clothes, at the right social temperature.

If one looked carefully, it became clear that these were the same people who, each November, appraised so discerningly the livestock at Canada's other big occasion, the Royal Winter Fair. However, there was a delicate piece of social distinction here. While they put on full evening dress to look at the rumps of bulls and horses, they wore dinner-jackets for the actors.

The place, the scene of the Festival party, was damnably over-crowded and noisy; that year, over seven hundred tickets had been issued, and things were chaotic from the start. The early arrivals grabbed all the available tables, and there sat for up-wards of two hours, eating like horses, drinking like lions at dusk, and watching the jostling, shoving queues of late-comers grabbing desperately for the last of the chicken salad, or trying to catch a sweating barman's eye.

The whole atmosphere was a cross between a Buckingham Palace Garden Party after royalty had left, and an Australian bar five minutes before closing time. It was the worst prelude to the evening's entertainment which could possibly be devised, and within a few years had to be abandoned—or rather, trans-ferred to *after* the performance instead of before. But tonight, it was still in full flower, and the sad frown on Tom Paterson's face as he contemplated the prospect was a charitable understatement.

And yet, and yet . . . Stratford, and all the evening before us, was still unspoilable. It began to knit together again with another prelude to our delight, the best that the Festival pro-vided: something which always put me in mind of that exquisite work of Delius which he called *A Walk to the Paradise Garden*. This was the traditional stroll along the bank of the River Avon, on the way to the theatre. It was the happiest part of the pil-grimage, and the last moment of calm before the true engage-ment.

The scene, to paraphrase Polonius, was nocturnal-pastoral.
17*

The long stretch of green sloping riverside park had somehow been preserved against building encroachment, against the demands of parking space, against all civic greed and expediency; and it might have been preserved for this moment. The weeping willow trees bent low over the water, the river glowed in the dusk, and along the opposite bank the lights were coming on one by one. The family picnic parties were packing up, and Stratford's circling swans were arching their necks as they reached for their dividend of the scraps.

A group of nuns sitting at a wooden table sedately brushed the crumbs from their habits, and gave devout thanks before rising. (But how did nuns organize an outing such as this? Did one of them, a managerial type, go round from cell to cell, asking 'Girls! Who's for Stratford?' Did the Mother Superior nominate the party? Did they forfeit the treat if they were naughty? How naughty?) Car doors slammed one by one as the occupants joined the moving throng; caught in a slow swirling tide, we advanced up the hill towards the brightly-lit theatre, completing our climb to Parnassus.

At the top, we had to make our way through another kind of audience, ticketless but not at all concerned on that account: the lesser citizens of Stratford, sitting on the railings, standing at the kerbside, watching and enjoying this outlandish invasion from another world. I sometimes wondered what they thought of us, and whether this free show was, for them, as compelling as the one we were going to see.

We might have been just as funny, for example, as the bumbling rustics in *A Midsummer Night's Dream* when viewed by sophisticated courtiers. We might not be funny at all, but simply odd, like any other kind of interloper.

Once inside the glaring foyer, all was high-class intercourse; it was the last chance for people who were so inclined to make a significant entrance, before the real actors took over. They did not let it go to waste. Dear friends who had not seen each other since the previous evening screamed their greetings across the intervening space. Toronto tycoons assumed the grand manner of patrons of the arts. Affectation took over from simplicity, and mink from both.

But soon, within the auditorium, it was awe which began to supplant everything else. The very sight of the stage—Tanya Moiseiwitsch's stark and simple apron platform, ready to be put to a thousand uses—was enough to make all amateur performances seem foolish. We settled down as quickly as we could, while the last seat-hopping extrovert gave his last loud salute to a friend, and waited, in taut expectation.

The same fanfare of trumpets sounded as in other years. The same ear-splitting cannon startled us, and the same toll of the bell gave a gentler signal. Then the lights gained strength, and brightened, and the sombre stage came alive, with people, with flaring colours, with music and voice: with—

> O for a Muse of fire that would ascend
> The brightest heaven of invention,
> A kingdom for a stage, princes to act,
> And monarchs to behold the swelling scene

and in an instant we had it all before us, in the glittering magic of *Henry V*.

It was very good indeed that year. Christopher Plummer made a noble, eloquent, and potent king, in splendid contrast with the foppish French courtiers, the first contingent of Quebec actors to decorate our stage; though his later courtship scene with Ginette Letondal* as Katharine showed him delightfully unmanned.

The boastful, mincing Dauphin was duly cut down to size when a courtier proclaimed: 'He longs to eat the English!' and the unimpressed Constable of France answered dryly: 'I think he will eat all he kills.' Agincourt was won, the cowards at home condemned, the dead mourned, and victory proclaimed with streaming banners.

It was proclaimed again the next night, when Douglas

---

* Another Quebec import of sparkling talent, and a sad suicide shortly afterwards.

Campbell stopped being Douglas Campbell, or anything else, and gave us a Falstaff so gross, so rumbustious, so sad, so funny, and so satisfying that it seemed to make the proverb forever true—that inside every fat old man was a slim young stripling yearning to escape, and that this could endure for sixty years, and still be as urgent at the end as at the beginning.

It chanced to be windy that night, and we were reminded of the drawbacks of staging a play in a tent theatre, however robust it might be. The actors had to compete for much of the time with the rattle and thud of slatting canvas. Often the whole tent creaked and laboured, like a ship under too much sail.

During a lull, two other hazards made themselves plain: the sound of police sirens wailing down the wind (Now what was it *this* time? we wondered, like any other scandalized citizens), and then a long-drawn-out train whistle, sounding so near, seeming so imperative, that it brought the play to an uneasy stop, and compelled laughter when laughter was not appropriate.

But we had our own remedy for this last interruption. At the sound, almost every occupant of the stalls turned and stared at Mr Donald Gordon, the president of Canadian National Railways, the man unfairly held to be responsible for this rude intrusion. He bore our gaze stoically; tough enough to survive the yearly prying onslaught of a Parliamentary committee of inquiry, which was dedicated to proving that C.N.R. was the worst-run outfit on the continent, he was certainly able to cope with this small by-product of consumer resistance.

But it was a fact that in all succeeding years, trains entering or leaving Stratford station did so in decorous silence.

1956 was, in any case, the last year when the Festival tent, which had served us so manfully for four seasons, made its own peculiar contribution to the drama. When it was struck, at the end of the run, it was struck for ever, and the new, permanent theatre took its place. We (this was the royal 'we' of the Board of Governors) passed the final plans and the accounts for this at a committee meeting that same week.

The project was going to be very expensive, like the new

Royal St Lawrence Yacht Club. Our first guess at the overall cost had been $984,000; now we signed for $1½ million; and this was to grow to $2¼ million before the whole thing was completed (including a hefty $400,000 for a vast, essential air-conditioning plant).

But it was promptly paid for by the customers; it stood as an enduring monument to an incredible idea; and it was in fact as handsome, efficient, and manageable as any theatre-building could hope to be.

Now, fifteen years afterwards, it attracts playgoers from all over the world; and its quality earns a dependable $1 million in ticket sales every year—which, as with an author's royalties, is a measure, not of money but of generous and contented people, who return again and again to enjoy its offerings.

Once, when I had a little spare money, or thought I had, we took over an entire local hotel and gave a mid-season party for the cast and the backstage wizards. It was to pay tribute, return thanks, for an outstanding production of *Twelfth Night* by a home-coming Tyrone Guthrie: one of the best evenings ever to be recalled, with Siobhan McKenna a handsome and graceful Viola, and Christopher Plummer, once again, playing Sir Andrew Aguecheek as a tremulous old club drunk, and at one point falling headlong through a trapdoor, like a gangling sack of potatoes, to give the Festival its loudest, longest laugh of all.

There was also Bruno Gerussi, a small, bouncy, rubbery young man with (off-stage) a ripe Chicago-gangster accent, who contributed a striking performance as the Clown Feste. It was impossible not to be achingly moved by the closing scene of this play, when Feste, to crown a happy ending led the company in successive choruses of 'The Wind and the Rain'.

Bruno, God bless him, could not sing a note, in any musical sense; he might have saluted Rex Harrison as Caruso. But he gave us pure music that night—they all did—and it was this that I wanted to celebrate.

The party was something of a riot, though the rioters behaved very well, within a theatrical framework. They were fed
till the kitchens gaped (hungry actors were as traditional as
hungry writers) and sluiced till all the wells ran dry. In return,
and without too much coaxing from the host, they sang for their
supper.

They sang—for me, for us, for a hushed, spell-bound hotel-
full of Festival friends—their song from the end of *Twelfth
Night*, with Bruno Gerussi leading, and the rest joining in one
by one. I have never forgotten, nor ever will, the eye-pricking
moment as the last chorus of that song softly died away, the
song which has always left an echo down the enchanted corridors
of time:

> A great while ago the world begun,
> With hey, ho, the wind and the rain;
> But that's all one, our play is done,
> And we'll strive to please you every day.

4.

Already it was better to keep moving, instead of sitting at
home in the cushioned well-deck of a stone frigate and pretend-
ing that 'We'll strive to please you every day' was anything but
an addled joke. That summer, in addition to all the rest, we
drove across to St Andrew's, New Brunswick, to see David
Walker (*Geordie, Harry Black*), a hermit-novelist whose other
label had once been 'Comptroller to the Viceroy of India'.

We also paid homage to Sir James Dunn, a legendary
Canadian steel tycoon, and his wife Christy (who later married
Lord Beaverbrook), and his stunning Salvador Dali painting,
Christ on the Sea Shore, to admit which an entire wall of his
house had been removed and then replaced.

We drove down the coast of Maine, wolfing 'shore dinners'

of broiled lobster and steamed clams and cracked crab by the way, to visit Willis Wing in his summer retreat at Boothbay Harbor; and then on to Fisher's Island, on Long Island Sound, where Thayer Hobson and his family were installed for the season in an area of controlled immigration so prestigious that one had to state the make of one's car before being allowed to rent a house.

'Do bring the Rolls,' Thayer had written. 'It'll look good outside the back door.' He was right. 'God damn it!' said one of our dinner hosts during the course of our stay, when the weather turned sweltering and the humidity almost unbearable. 'We left the air-conditioned Cadillacs at home!' The Texas plural was beyond reproach.

We missed the New York *première* of *The Ship That Died of Shame*, for some stupid reason which must be filed away with all the other stupid reasons why certain people, counted on to be at Point X on Day Y, are inevitably at Point Y on Day Z, and blissfully, shamefully unaware of the *gaffe*.

But now, at last, it was time for me to be a writer again: to be serious, to call a halt to all the hopped-up nonsense—or, if that was itself too silly an idea, with the merry-go-round still whirling and spinning, then at least to bob up above the tossing tide of painted animals, swinish noise, and shout: 'I am here! This is me! The well-known writer! Remember?'

The next stake in my future, which was still very important to me, was now coming up for assessment, and I had wagered, among other things, a considerable expense of spirit on the outcome.

What I had tried to do, with *The Tribe That Lost Its Head*, was what all writers try to do when they fall in love with an idea and want to marry it. They treat it with respect and cherishing care, and an almighty fear of something going wrong with it. Borrowing from *Othello* ('Speak of them as they are. Nothing extenuate, nor set down aught in malice'), they aim to tell *all* the truth, lay bare *all* the lies, and exhibit every last vestige of hope.

Having lived a long time in a troubled place, I wanted to write its story faithfully and accurately: to explain what might have gone wrong, and what could be right, and above all, what was likely to happen next.

But my troubled place was all Africa; and into a single book I had to put all the problems, perplexities, and ambitions of a whole huge continent at a moment of turmoil.

To this purpose I invented a small country, the island of Pharamaul,* and tried to make it a microcosm of that continent. I peopled it with everyone I had met, or observed, or heard about, during my seven years' African journeying: injected a sudden crisis, and let the thing rip.

Thus my small country was Colonial Africa, to start with—something already vanishing below the rim of history; then Africa waking from its sleep and stretching its muscles; then Africa on the verge of independent, viable life, and choosing a reputable pathway towards it—a moment which no longer exists, either, though it might come again, and in some cases must.

There were two themes which were very important to me: firstly, that in spite of the trend already becoming modish, there was a place for the white man in Africa, a job for him to do, and a dividend in which, as one of the advance guard, he was entitled to share; and secondly, that Britain's colonial past was nothing to be ashamed of, and in many cases had introduced, for the very first time, the pattern of tolerable life itself.

Neither of these ideas was fashionable, even then, which was another reason why they were important.

I made the colonial point by portraying most of the civil servants, past and present, as hard-working and devoted, with nothing but a medal, a dried-out body and spirit, and a derisory pension to show for it at the end; and added a few ninnies and incompetents to balance the account. The progress from pastoral slum to modest urban prosperity, with hope as the unique bequest, was there for all to see.

* Derivation: Pharos, a lighthouse, and Maula, the tribal name of the inhabitants.

I described, from half a dozen grim aspects of real life, the African dangers now looming: the appetite for cruelty, the taste for major and minor racketry, the hazards of too quick a freedom, and the readiness to revert to authoritarian rule, tribal tyranny, as an easy way out of all dilemmas.

Much of Africa, the book maintained, was far from ready for emancipation; in spite of all the screams, it was better for the 'colonial power' to leave too late rather than too soon. If it was a choice of remaining perhaps one more generation, or betraying all the past and watching it swill down the drain, then honour bound us to stay put and ride out the storm.

In a row with a group of journalists, which recalled (and not by accident) my own ill-tempered plunge into criticism in Bechuanaland, I had my 'hero', district officer David Bracken, come out flat-footed as follows:

'Yes, I do think that, man for man, at this moment of evolution, a Maula native is inferior to a white man.'

'But that's not his fault, surely?'

'*Fault?* There's no fault. It's a historical accident, and it will be corrected in due course. But it is true now.

'For Christ's sake!'—this was the same British newsman again—'I thought people like you went out with the slave trade!'

'I'm trying to be honest and realistic. It's time we took another look at this idea of complete racial equality.'

'Then you don't think a black man can do a white man's job?'

'I think that may turn out to be the twentieth century's most fatuous illusion.'

In 1956, that was still a guess.

Finally, to try to assess the future after a crisis of torment and bloodshed, I had 'Sir Hubert Godbold' speak for me:

'We have these same problems all over Africa, as you

know. . . . There's no single answer to Africa. Out of any of
our possessions or dependencies there, we can make—or try
to make—one of three things: a black dominion, a black-and-
white partnership, or a purified white enclave. . . . I think we
can write off the last alternative, as a matter of common sense.
It goes directly against the historic trend. Africa is moving
the other way. And in any case, if you inflict permanent sub-
jection on a people, telling them that not only they themselves, but their children's grandchildren, will never have any
political or economic advancement whatsoever, then there
can only be one result—an explosion.'

Godbold walked towards his desk, sat down, took a drink,
leant back. 'You and I both know these things,' he went on,
'but it's a good idea to restate them sometimes, particularly
when you are wondering what to make of some specific
country. . . . The black dominion is a perfectly feasible idea, if
the people concerned are really ready for the test of complete
independence in a very difficult world—which means, in
effect, if *we* have been there long enough. It's already emerg-
ing in Nigeria and on the Gold Coast,* as you know. My
personal view is that we have moved too fast there, but I may
well be mistaken. The most promising of all'—he emphasized
his words with a pointing finger—'is what they are trying to
do in the Central African Federation. There's the beginning,
there, of a genuine black-white partnership, with both races
sitting down side-by-side to legislate and to govern. It's
almost the only one in the world, and God prosper it! If that
Federation scheme is a success, it may serve as a pattern for
Africa as a whole, and that would be a very proud thing
indeed.'

In 1956, that was still a fair hope.
There were indications already that the book would be
banned in South Africa, for reasons a little hard to assess,

* Soon to be President Nkrumah's Republic of Ghana.

except that the idea of a black-white partnership was always unacceptable, and a black-white rape scene near the end gave partnership even more of a bad name. However, the Minister of the Interior would not have to publish his reasons, and there could be no appeal against such a verdict. Otherwise, all the omens were good.

Already the mysterious undercurrent was at work, the groundswell of advance comment which made a book sell—or sometimes killed it stone dead. The trade papers kept on mentioning it; individual booksellers already knew all about 'the new Monsarrat', like the new Alistair McMouse or the new Hammond Egges.

Cassell's first print would be 100,000 copies, and there were other marks of confidence which made up a satisfying sum—the kind of sum I now saluted, in common with the Bank of Montreal, Barclays in London and Barbados, and the Morgan Guaranty Trust in New York. On the eve of publication, it went like this:

Cassell advance	£3,600
Morrow advance	5,360
Reader's Digest (U.K.)	1,500
John Bull serial	3,150

Translation rights in Norway, Sweden, Holland, Germany, and France brought this part of the total to £16,000. On top of that, it had been sold to the American *Reader's Digest* for $80,000, of which my share would be another £14,300. It would also be a Book-of-the-Month Club alternate selection in America, if anyone there 'chose to read a work of fiction' instead of *This Hallowed Ground*, by Bruce Catton.

They would be fools, I thought, if they did not.

Of course, it could never do as well as *The Cruel Sea*, that child prodigy which no other offspring, legal or bastard, would ever catch up. By now, this had sold over three million copies, and, translated into nineteen languages, from Estonian to

Portuguese,* had in five years earned the respectable sum of £166,000 (it looked even more respectable in dollars, $465,000). It was still selling, world-wide, a comforting 100,000 copies a year.

But five years at this sort of rate had been much too fast for income-tax comfort, and the book had been the object of punitive slashing by the Inland Revenue. As a diplomat, subject to U.K. taxation, I could take no avoiding action; I just had to sit there and sweat off the pounds. It was better not to think about it, though there were moments of non-socialist frustration, even of reactionary rage. I loved my fellow men, but not to the extent of about 85 per cent of my income.

It had fathered, by proxy, a racehorse called 'The Cruel Sea' (by Seven Seas out of Heidi) which had not done nearly as well as the book (seven wins out of forty-eight races and eight years of hoof-prints). It had been translated into the sign hanging outside that pub in Hampstead. Half a dozen yachts had been registered under the name of *Compass Rose* (they were to include, two years later, one of my own, a twin-engined Chris-Craft motor-cruiser which finally signalled the abyss between sailor and driver).

Two people, both of whom I had actively loathed, got a lot of mileage out of claiming to be the originals of my two most reputable characters. A confidence-man in Australia pretended to be the author, and did very profitably until he began to masquerade as 'an English nobleman' as well. That of course was more serious, and he went to jail.

A bishop newly destined for a far-northern diocese, and thus able to sign himself, charmingly, 'Donald the Arctic' (his predecessor had been 'Archibald the Arctic'), was understood to have murmured, on learning of his appointment: 'A cruel see indeed.'

The title, in fact, had become a brand-name, and I welcomed

---

* And in Polish, under the catchy title of *Okrutne Morze, Tom I & II* (translated by Maria Boduszynska-Borowikowa), and the banner of Wydawnictwo Ministerstwa Obrony Narodowej.

the idea. Others in the same circumstances did not. I knew that
J. B. Priestley, for example, particularly disliked strangers saying to him 'Oh yes, *The Good Companions*', when he had written
so many other books and plays of which he was entitled to be
proud.

But that admirable first huge best-seller did put him plumb in
the middle of the map, at a time when he was scarcely known
outside literary London, and its echoes must have done a great
deal to keep him there for the succeeding forty years.

It seemed ungrateful to neglect, if not disown, one's early
offspring, just because the ones that came after were also tall,
beautiful, and intelligent, with the added allurement of youth.

The Tribe, I realized already, would never match my own
first explosion. But it ought to do a lot better than *Esther
Costello* (currently being filmed), and I had tried hard to make it
deserve this.

Most important of all, it was *writing*, not fooling around as a
semi-celebrity with a diarrhoea of O.K. jargon and a smooth
mike-side manner. It was the best I could do at the age of forty-
six. It was two and a half years' work, and had come out at 538
pages and 250,000 words. It was deadly serious, and lovingly
compiled; and the effort to produce it—sometimes as grim and
killing as a desert crawl, sometimes as pleasurable as playing
the piano all day—had been so utterly private and absorbed that
it had erased totally the outside world.

Just as *The Cruel Sea* had been written in warm dry Johannesburg, 6,000 feet above sea-level and about as far from it as
possible, so *The Tribe* had been written in cold sub-zero
Canada, where the only steamy jungle was the House of Commons. Happy in my clam-shell, I had scarcely noticed either.

Now the job was selling it, which could also be killing, and
also fun. Now it was time to keep two important appointments,
in London and New York, in order to find out, in these twin
tough market-places, if the second hard try was any good.

We sailed from Montreal in the *Empress of Scotland*, under

Captain J. P. Dobson, at the end of August. I had grown very fond of Dobbie (who among other things had done three years as a wartime commodore of convoys) during previous voyages: he had the liner-captain's talent, highly developed, for being as expert at social navigation (mealtime and dance floor) as he was on the bridge.

All the same, we excused ourselves from sitting at his table, on the ground that (a) I might be working, and therefore late for meals, which was not permissible, and (b) Max was sailing back with us, and might even eat with us now and again.

These were both lies, as Dobbie, a realist, knew. But as a friend he was quite ready to accept them. The fact was that the captain's table was a trap, to be avoided by all voyagers who wanted to choose their company, their daily routine, and above all their wine. Otherwise one could get stuck, for the entire duration of the voyage, with some of the dullest drips who ever put to sea.

There was sure to be a titled couple, proud as show-dogs, acid as lemon rind, empty as old balloons. There was sure to be a lone drunk woman who had a brother or an uncle on the board of directors. There was sure to be a non-stop M.P. with a pet subject (communism, wheat prices, fluoridization, the scourge of campus sex), or a soldier with a howitzer nose and camouflaged eyes, or a Toronto businessman who had made so much money out of metal window frames or plastic cups that he could not be excluded, or a minor diplomat and his major wife, returning to obscurity in furthest Europe.

Above all, there was certain to be one of the vice-presidents on the Canadian sales-and-service side of General Motors, and his wife, of whom all that could be said was that she was the wife of one of the vice-presidents on the Canadian sales-and-service side of General Motors, and had a mink stole, a jangle of jewellery, a face like a Chev radiator, a mouth like a horseshoe with the luck running out, and a conversational style like a show-off parrot, to prove it.

These were the people with whom one could be trapped, for

eight days and nights; who gave unavoidable cocktail parties twice a day, and for whom one had to give cocktail parties equally unavoidable; and who dictated, at meal-times, a deplorable pattern of non-hospitality.

If one wanted champagne at lunch (I was the only one who ever did, until I mentioned it, whereupon everyone clapped their hands), one had to buy it for ten thirsty customers. Next day one received, in return, a glass and a half of sweet Chablis to drink with roast pheasant or rack of lamb.

These were the beautiful people in the ads. . . . Feeling a swine, as usual, I decided that this was Dobbie's bad luck, not mine. We excused ourselves, and ate in selfish state at a *banquette* for six, and watched the high-ups munching flaming *crêpes suzettes* in wobbling paper hats.

The Atlantic voyage was a great pleasure, and a necessary prelude: smooth as silk, luxurious as a very good hotel, in a ship just the right size which took just the right number of days for such a crossing. We landed at Liverpool on 3 September; a man from Canadian Pacific took care of the baggage and the customs; a man from Claridge's met the boat-train at Euston, and a man from the Daimler Hire Company did all the rest. We drove sedately down town from grimy Euston to immaculate Brook Street, and dived right in.

After that, it was like *The Cruel Sea* all over again, only now I was *blasé*, and spoiled, and believed that I had earned everything that came my way: everything good, that was—the rest must be the work of envious enemies, of tiny corrupt minds, of bad luck or bad faith. But I kept notes on London and New York, because I had a feeling that it might not happen again for a long time.

Perhaps notes were all it was worth. Reflecting life, they were scrappy and disjointed: hectic and happy, embarrassing, angry, ridiculous, dull and accurate. Sour notes, discordant notes, notes as pure as choir-boys before their little pennies dropped, as magical as music under a night sky, they went like this.

CLARIDGE'S again, thank God: the best hotel in the world, and who argues? The warm welcome starts with the huge cockaded porter at the Brook Street entrance asking after the children. The fire burned brightly in the *foyer*. Met by manager, H. A. van Thuyne: after handling everything for twenty-five years, from touchy royalty to trans-Atlantic exuberance, he must know more secrets than half a dozen foreign secretaries, but he can keep them, which marks the difference. He had just had Bulganin and Khrushchev staying there. I said: 'B and K— the Heavenly Twins.' He said: 'I did not know they were related.'

He took us up in the lift: met the Oppies coming down, then a tall Indian, handsome as the devil (now where did that one spring from?), smooth as sharkskin, got into the lift after us. Spouse, a little elevated, asked: 'Who is this beautiful man?' I kept my head, said: 'Good afternoon, Mr Krishna Menon.' Menon, baffled, bowed. Van Thuyne looked straight to the front. Liftman concentrated on his boots.

Suite 418–19. Extremely elegant, just right. Flowers in room: gentle coal fire in the grate: my poker table folded discreetly in the lobby, and the bowler hat, which is London-based, hanging from a peg in the hall. Stacks of letters and messages and more flowers: Christine Campbell Thomson, Cassell's, Joan Crawford, Chas Frend, J. Metcalf plus champagne (ah, to be an advertising *Wunderkind*!), M. Pertwee ('Sucker-money in town! When do we play?') and La Vicomtesse d'Orthez—that's little Moira Lister to you. Thayer Hobson called from N.Y., very good timing, said: 'This is instead of our flowers, which Isabelle forgot.' I *love* Americans.

Some day must write a dissertation, German-style (Ph.D. thesis?—they seem to include every brand of trivial rubbish in the world), on this marvellous hotel. The social differences between the floors: as near as I can make it, Floor 2 is for solid families (interconnected suites, two or three or four bedrooms); Floor 3 is for people who like glitter (film-stars?); Floor 4, the most civilized and well-behaved; Floor 5 for rich Americanos, north and south; Floor 6 for global nuisances—ex-kings with fake 'courts', heads of state who pluck their own chickens, or have armed bodyguards with scimitars sleeping in the corridor outside. But maybe they swap all this hierarchy round from time to time, to stop people being *blasé*.

Harry Oppenheimer asked later how much a book like *The Tribe* would make, and when I said, maybe £50,000, he exclaimed, in that little bubbling voice: 'But that's fabulous!' Coming from him, rather good: they must keep £50,000 in the petty cash down at Anglo-American. Reminded me of elegant old Edmond de Rothschild in New York, sipping Dom Pérignon and saying, in an Oscar Wilde-ish way: 'Of course, we are the *poor* Rothschilds.' (Or was it Etienne de R? I know it wasn't Victor. Oh, tra la la! Memo: Never drop names which might bounce.)

THE MARVELLOUS MATURITY OF LONDON: I would rather be dead in this town than preening my feathers in heaven. John Moore fixed me up at the Savile Club, and Eric Ambler at Les A. and the Milroy (if one does have to be fixed up at Les A. and the Milroy). But discovered peerless new restaurant, the *Etoile* in Charlotte Street (Frank Rossi at the helm), marvellous food and service, waiters really would stay all night if necessary.

At midnight Johnny Metcalf said: 'No panic. It's only when they start piling the chairs on the table, with one leg in the butter-dish, that you have to worry. And they wouldn't do that here, anyway.' But his restaurant is the White Tower, down the street, Greek. He goes there for the *taramosalata*, which is smoked cod's roe *pâté*, which is a bizarre reason for going any-where—which is the best kind.

What happened to the marvellous maturity of London? Well, it's there, in every theatre, opera, play, concert: every whiff of stinking air in Regent Street: every walk down Bond Street to Asprey's: every time you say 'Send it round to Claridge's', and Claridge's shell out £400 C.O.D. and put it on the bill: every time you loiter at Speakers' Corner and hear the Irish and the

expatriate blacks and the Communist League of South Stepney
kicking the hell out of the British fascist constitution, with a
policeman standing by, half asleep: every time you see one of
those fornicating tourists taunting the sentries outside Buckingham Palace or the Horse Guards: every time you sit in the
Lobby of the House of Commons, and watch the self-important,
show-off roundabout of M.P.s, and know that it works: every
time a drunken beggar says 'Give us ten bob for a cup of tea,'
or a girl on a street-corner croaks: 'How about it, handsome—
I'm very French,' (and I'm about as handsome as Ernie Bevin,
and she as French as jellied eels): every time a bus queue waits
and waits and waits, with never a cross word: every time . . .
You hardly need to write about it. You breathe it, swallow it,
love it.

    'TRIBE' PROMOTION AND PROSPECTS. Edwin Harper
has done a slap-up job on the book: sent out 1,000 bound-proof
copies to booksellers, plus a funny-looking poster apparently
made out of reinforced sandpaper, to remind them that Africa
is sandy. (Smart, eh?) Hence that whopping advance order.
Thirty-three interviews altogether including very good one by
Marshall Pugh. He started off with authentic *Daily Mail* intro:
'The doors of Suite 418–19 at Claridge's shivered politely, and
Mr Nicholas Monsarrat entered etc.' (Get the carpenter!)

    Silly side swipe by some illiterate idiot—no, let us avoid all
possibility of identification—some mistaken purist, to the effect
that *Tribe* 'repeats the ritual for a bestseller'. There is no such
thing, and if there were, this envious hyena would be the first
to use it. Unmistakeable traces of pygmy shit here. One be-
gins to feel it's a mistake to treat these little sods as human
beans.

    Also nice Canadian Wally Reyburn of the *Toronto Telegram*
quoted me: 'When I want civilization I can always hop on a
train down to New York.' H'm. That's one which will certainly
be picked up in the old home town. Thank God such cracks can
no longer land me on the H.C.'s carpet.

    Did 'In Town Tonight' (now on TV) and BBC 'Brains

Trust', ditto, with Eric James and Arthur Calder-Marshall.
Earlier, with Marghanita Laski, charmer with intellect, Dr
Bronowski, and Prof. A. J. Ayer. (Said Johnny Metcalf: 'Unless
you know him as Freddy Ayer, you're a dead duck in this town.
And for Christ's sake, E. M. Forster is "Morgan"!') Enjoyed
'Brains Trust', but that lunch beforehand at Scott's is a killer.
How can you possibly talk sense in front of the camera
when you're gorged on Dover sole and exquisite hock
(*Johannisberger Erntebringer Riesling Spätlese*: may have got
that wrong?)

But after these sessions, everyone—my dear, but *everyone!*—
says: 'I saw you on TV last night.' One day someone will say:
'I just read a book of yours,' whereupon I shall faint dead away.
Cheered by a touching sort of tribute which gets me every
time: a group of autograph-hunters gathered under the lamp
at the corner of Brook Street and Davies Street: one of
them goes to a phone box and rings up to know when I am
coming out. Then they surge round. . . . Cold potato-pie for a
film star; but for a *writer*! . . . The marital verdict: They were
probably queers.'

Tribe reprinting already, a couple of days before publication.
But just been banned in South Africa—for which I am in mourning for more than a 10,000 sale. All sorts of people there I
wanted to read it. Now it will never get past some creep in the
Customs.

REVIEWS. Mostly excellent, including two winners in the
Sunday Times and the *Times Lit. Supp.* By God, I believe I'm
going up in the world! As usual, the good ones exhilarate and
the bad ones amuse (Dept. of Defence Mechanism, Quill Pen
Division). Some real claw-marks from the *Liverpool Post*,
etched in purest critspeak by the same man as snapped his fangs
at *The Cruel Sea*, and wrote it off as a smelly old kipper. Acid
must be habit-forming.

Another bashing from the *Daily Mail*: 'A remarkably high
level of gratuitous indecency.' (Actually that's rather hard to
achieve.) Worst one of all from Nancy Spain, friend of the

family and a true artist with the ice-pick. In *Daily Express*, headed 'OH DEAR, IT'S *HIS* HEAD HE'S LOST'. Oh dear, indeed. Quote: 'An admirable fellow' (that's because I bought the oysters at Cunningham's the week before, and her in her linoleum slacks and fisherman's jersey!) 'an admirable fellow, if only it wasn't for the awful stuff he writes. . . . One of the most repulsive books I have ever been forced to read. Such a silly, bitter, venomous book.' (Ha! The master speaks!) 'Perhaps he is working too hard. There is certainly something feverish about it.' (That's the brain-tumour or cancer bit.) 'Why not look for joy and affection and fun and games instead? There *are* such things.'

Drop dead, Spain.*

SOLD 125,000 copies in the first three weeks, and celebrated with a round of visits, an 800-mile swing round the shires. To Max at Lancing: to Camper & Nicolson at Gosport to see the new Dragon now half-built: to H.M.S. *Victory* across the bay, to pay my respects: to Brixham in Devon to see the replica of the *Mayflower*, nearly finished (I volunteered for the voyage to Plymouth, Massachusetts, but I don't think they want any other writers except skipper Alan Villiers): to Plymouth, our Plymouth, to see the helpful City Librarian, Best-Harris, and collect photostats of some old Armada prints: then back and up to John Moore's at Little Heating—politely called Kemerton Lodge, near Tewkesbury.

A merry time there: John and Lucile in great form. He's just finished another 'country wanderings' sort of book, and we scouted round for a title. Mine was *Up Fanny Hill*, rejected.†️ But we found a good one for a really specialist job, of limited appeal: *Sex Changes at the Siege of Troy*.

John at his best reading excerpts from *Decline & Fall of the Roman Empire*, can bring out Gibbon's elegant, Latinate, dead-

---

* She did so, literally, before my very eyes, on Aintree race-course eight years later: crashing in a light plane in the middle of the course, just before the Grand National. I have never again used the expression 'Drop dead'.

† In favour of the more pedestrian *Come Rain, Come Shine* (Collins, 1956).

pan humour to perfection. He found one I had never heard, about St George (our own honoured St George of England), a saint of somewhat murky background. In his early days he had been a contractor to the Roman Army, and apparently the job was not well regarded. Gibbon said: 'His occupation was menial; he made it contemptible.'

Then the real beauty about one of the ancient Popes John, a crapulent old rogue, finally overtaken by justice: 'He fed and was brought back a prisoner; the most scandalous charges were suppressed; the Vicar of Christ was only accused of piracy, murder, rape, sodomy, and incest.'

One thing sure: E. Gibbon didn't really care for Holy Mother Church. Will see John Moore again at Cheltenham Festival, where I have promised to give a lecture on Writing About the Sea. Ugh.

Then back to Woolstone to see my father, now eighty-four and blooming: then up to Nottingham to sister Felicity, and her five chattering children, and her ice-cold house. (My bedroom was 45° in the early a.m.! In Canada it is forbidden to keep dogs at this temperature.) Finally went racing at Newmarket: lost £84, but stayed very pleasurably with Mary Delamere at nearby Six Mile Bottom. She was once married to Captain Alec Cunningham-Reid, Marylebone M.P., but drifted apart in sensational style some time in the Thirties. (Big society scandal. He kept a little black Talent Book, crossed off the names one by one.)

SAW *The Caine Mutiny*, and talked to Lloyd Nolan (Captain Queeg) afterwards. Splendid performance in every respect. But thank God the U.S. Navy was not really like that at all.

WE ARE THE TARGETS OF THIEVES AND BEG-GARS. Interior decorators pile in, likewise portrait painters, bust-sculptors, people who get an (undeclared) 10 per cent cut on jewellery and clothes sold to us: begging letters enough to make you weep until you start to smell the drains instead.

One woman who has been on my payroll for years, with tales of dire woe, everything from mortgage trouble to 'an intimate

operation of which I cannot bring myself to speak', had always
signed herself Mary Ellen X. Now, in the same handwriting,
with the same range of problems, she has suddenly switched to
Drusilla X. Still a lone lorn widder woman. Her filing system
must have slipped a cog.

Man turned up at Claridge's with a transparently faked
Nelson letter. Dated 1804, it had been written with his right
hand, which he lost in 1797.

An old civil servant chum needs £250 to go into hospital.
Wretched-looking, down-and-out man who had actually been at
Winchester with me touched me for £5: said he owed it for his
Salvation Army lodgings. Another Old Wykehamist, one of
those darling prefects in my own house, wrote appealing for
half a million pounds for the Winchester College Building Fund
(not all of it from me). Superimposed on a duplicated page was a
hand-written scrawl:

> 'Dear Montserrat, You are probably the best-known O.W.
> writer of our generation' (well, spell my name right!) . . . 'I
> thought your book was technically accurate and gave the right
> atmosphere. . . . I am therefore writing to ask etc.' (How to
> win friends and influence the freed slaves.)

Men with sure-fire goldmines, men with inventions, men
with the secret of the Spanish Prisoner's Treasure (heavens,
even *I* know about that one!). A man who needed £75 to finish
a book; he knew I would understand. Just heard that the
Johannesburg stockbroker who collapsed and cried, pledged me
his Stock Exchange seat in return for a loan, did not register the
transaction which he thus knew was worthless, and then collapsed and died, will now pay out 4s. 11d. in the £; so I get
£572 for my £2,300.

Man in Australia who stole substantial sections of *The Cruel
Sea*, incorporated them in one of his own paperbacks, and was
threatened with prosecution, sent me weepy letter: not his
fault, he had been hard-pressed for time. Publisher also sent me

weepy letter, with strong flavour of crocodile; could he sell off
the rest of the edition if he paid me 'a small royalty'? Answer:
No. Destroy books. Pay £100 to the Royal National Life Boat
Institution. And *don't try it again*.

Would I like to buy Hitler's Mercedes? Would I like the
late Lord Z's steam yacht, a floating palace, A.1 at Lloyd's in
1924? Would I join party of men of sympathetic tastes, charter-
ing airplane to fly to secluded retreat on Island of Rhodes?
Would I care to be included in new universal *Who's Who*, Men
of Global Distinction, now being actively compiled in Liechten-
stein? Subscription only £25, with my name embossed in
genuine gold leaf on the cover.

Best of all, the man with the Rembrandt. He was a big bulging man with a very brisk line of talk. 'A portrait, I suppose
you'd call it. Twelve thousand pounds. Of course I haven't got
it here, it's under heavy guard, but I've brought the photograph
to show.' He unrolled a tattered print. It looked more like a
Gainsborough. 'Of course it's a genuine Rembrandt!' the man
said. 'Look at the photograph! It's been certified!' 'What?—the
portrait has been certified?' 'No, no, no—the *photograph's* been
certified.' He read out an inscription on the back ' "This is
certified as a true photograph of the portrait attributed to
Rembrandt". There you are! Can't do better than that, can
you?'

I said I didn't really want a Rembrandt. 'Well, what *do* you
want?' It was clear that I must want something, staying at
Claridge's, all that stuff in the newspapers. He thought, briefly.
'Tell you what. All these new countries—they're all starting up
their own airlines, right? Well, I've got, I mean I can *put my
hands on*, a lot of surplus R.A.F. flying boats. They'd do for a
start, wouldn't they? Twelve of them. In South Rhodesia.
They've been impounded, but *you* can get round that. I read in
the paper, you're a diplomat. There's no engines, of course.'
'Of course.' 'But I can always get you *engines*.'

I had to say No again. Undaunted: 'Didn't I read in the
paper, your wife collects old paperweights?' I said that it must

be someone else's wife. 'Well, maybe. But if you *want* paperweights——'

It seemed a shame not to buy. Not to buy from him, anyway;
we bought from everyone else. Bought three minks from
Calman Links—and that's a very expensive rhyme.

IF YOU WANT TO MAKE A SPEECH, you need never
be short of an audience. During this six weeks in London, have
received invitations from:

> Montreal Kiwanis
> Cheltenham Festival
> Foyle's Lit. Lunch
> The North Hatley Playhouse (Quebec)
> Library Association of Ottawa
> London Women's Press Club
> Rotary Club of Chesham
> The Whitefriars' Club, London
> University of Toronto Alumni Association of Owen Sound
> Nottingham & Derby Society of Chartered Accountants
> Cambridgeshire Conservative Association
> W. H. Smith Lit. Lunch, Toronto
> Toronto Chapter of the Business Paper Editors' Association.

Also: to speak at a Liverpool Beer and Cheese Tasting
Evening ('to foster the public acceptance of cheese'); and to
award the Madame Prunier Trophy (Blue Ribbon of the North
Sea) to the skipper making the largest catch of herring during
the season.

It's nice to be asked, and bliss to refuse in most cases; this is
not my area of endeavour, and never will be. But I did take on
two writing assignments which were fun: as TV Guest Critic for
three nights for the *Evening Standard*, and then to write a piece
for the *Sunday Express* on U.K./Canada relations, which, coupled
now with the freedom to say what I liked, was the most fun of all.

The TV critic job involved more organization than judgment,
plus a little bleary-eyed endurance. Had to watch all the available programmes from 7 p.m. till 11; dictate 500 words of

sparkling prose; wait till it was typed out; and then send it down by taxi to reach the *Standard* by midnight. This involved, in turn, a girl coming in from the Brook Street Agency every night at eleven, and apparently enjoying my company until midnight; on her way out she was paid by the porter downstairs. Most hotels would raise managerial eyebrows at such goings-on. All Claridge's ever said: 'The young lady is here.'

Watched a lot of trash in the twelve hours involved, with a pleasurable spark here and there. But at that time of night I was a little short on epigrams. Among the items:

The Grove Family. With all apologies to friend Michael Pertwee, who wrote it and no doubt thrives on it what terrible people! Is this grunting, snuffling, ugly clan the future pattern of England?

Vic Oliver. Used to be a great favourite, billed as 'The Aristocrat of Comedy'. But now—Roll on the Revolution!

Labour Party Conference at Blackpool. Very interesting, worth watching in every sense. 'Today's moles and screwballs may be tomorrow's Prime Ministers.'

A Night with I.T.A. Terrible ads, compared with U.S.: dull, ugly, and amateurish. How they can sell a single bar of soap to a short-sighted, stone-deaf millionaire is beyond belief.

Bob Monkhouse: 'a coy young man who looks like Liberace under a light coating of dust'.

Robin Hood. Phooey from me *and* the Sheriff of Nottingham!

Dragnet. Full marks. I was hooked on this years ago. Just give me the facts, ma'am.

The Crazy Gang. Five old gentlemen 'lumbering through a routine which really wrung its last involuntary laugh full twenty years ago. I like ruins, but I do prefer them to stand still'.

Got into deep trouble with that last remark, having under-estimated the grotesque loyalty of the British towards their old-stagers. Can only hope it comes my way in the same circum-stances.

In the Canadian article I plugged, once again, the idea that

18

our two countries were growing apart, because there was not enough exchange of ordinary people—especially of young English people, who couldn't get the currency for a trip, and after seventeen years were now a new generation of utter strangers to Canada.

More trouble over this one, particularly from the *Toronto Star* and the *Ottawa Journal*, which courteously blasted me in long editorial headed 'TOO DOLEFUL, MR MONSARRAT!', maintained that 'Canada's place in the Commonwealth is as safe and secure as ever in our history'. Sadly, don't believe it.

One other bad mark was the deplorable headline 'We Could Lose Canada Too', dreamed up by the *Sunday Express*. Mine had been 'The Dollar Curtain', which may have been a bit cute but at least was not patronizing. Canada is not ours to lose.

FILM MEN John & James Woolf ('The Wolves', as Christine called them, perhaps unfairly, though they did get *Esther Costello* for £5,000) gave me succulent lunch at Les Ambassadeurs, then produced Rolls-Royce and chauffeur to take me down to Shepperton (or Pinewood or Elstree: these British film studios are a little blurred) to watch *Esther* being filmed. Talked to American director David Miller, then to Rossano Brazzi and Joan Crawford, the two stars involved.

Rossano Brazzi a small, very good-looking, *soigné*, perfectly barbered and tailored man who could make anyone else (such as a writer, even when dressed by Strickland's of Savile Row, Hawes & Curtis, and Sulka), look and feel like a country boy in his first whip-cord suit. But reminded me of Ivor Novello—the myth of masculine appeal rather than the fact. Married to enormous, delightful wife, Lydia, whose cooking later proved exquisite and whose manner was often pure Wagnerian soprano, crossed with doting mother. Would clasp her hands, and intone: 'Ross-*ah*-no! Your feet have become wet! You will *die* in this climate!' Then build up his strength with seven different kinds of *pasta*. But he just right as handsome swine of the old school.

Joan Crawford was something else again. Her descent on

England had been the subject of usual snide newspaper comment: 'Arrived with 28 suitcases, 48 film costumes, one trunk
of suits, one trunk of furs, and a millionaire husband.' She was
just as I had pictured: tough, professional, as sweet as molasses
if she was enjoying herself, brutally indifferent if not. I think
she had the old-style Hollywood view of writers as something
between errand-boys and resident drunks. But she was excellent
in the short scene I watched being filmed: she had to cry, and
when the moment came the tears flowed readily and almost
genuinely, like Niagara switched on to meet a tourist deadline.

I complimented her afterwards. 'I can cry any time!' she declared, looking at me as if I had charged her with arrant
incompetence. 'All I have to do is hit myself twice—*here*!' She
gave herself a slap and a jab, somewhere between her sculptured
bosom and her invisible navel. Immediately, large tears rolled
down her cheeks. 'I'm a pro,' she said.

Esther ought to be a good film; has the necessary aura of
competence, prestige, and lots of money. By contrast Ealing
Studios just folded as a separate entity, without a murmur
except from sad orphans such as Charles Frend who will be
homeless. In future Ealing will be under the thumb of M.G.M.,
will share distribution with them. In practice, they are dead.
One gathers that Michael Balcon will be found floating the right
way up.

Going out to dine with Lydia and Rossano, had a slight car
crash at Hyde Park Corner; a Green Line bus ploughed into our
stationary back, giving everyone what is called 'the whiplash
effect'. Had to cancel visit to Cheltenham Festival, and the
chance to mingle with such *élite* as (wait for it) Compton
Mackenzie, John Betjeman, Richard Gordon, C. Day Lewis,
Edith Sitwell, Colin Wilson, Sir Arthur Bryant, and Ludovic
Kennedy. I never meet anybody!

On our dinner arrival, very late, Lydia Brazzi distraught, but
in her best style. 'Ross-*ah*-no! They are wounded! Come
quickly!'

Stuck in Bond Street in the sort of traffic jam which made a

taxi the most expensive residential unit in the world. I was
loudly hailed by an elegant pedestrian who was out-walking us.
It was Moura Lympany, one of the children's godmothers.
'Nicholas!' she shouted. 'Darling, I'm having a baby!' Before I
could answer, the traffic and the stalled taxi ground forwards.
'Bad luck, sir,' said the driver.

FED UP with endless feuding and screaming (What do you
have to do to win a medal? What do you do to avoid firing-
squad at dawn? How do you make sure of dawn anyway?
Prisoner was shot for his own protection) took off for Liverpool
and Trearddur Bay. (Diagnosed as 'return to womb'. Could be.
I say, porter! What's my womb number?) Away for four days,
copped in Chester for parking all night outside the Grosvenor
Hotel. No fun, but no fun anyway.

SERETSE KHAMA allowed back to Bechuanaland as
'private citizen'. Well done, that man!—and good luck to him.

PENGUIN published that other book with considerable
flapping of wings. First print of 250,000—and, from them, their
first-ever illustrated cover.

PEOPLE & PARTIES & POKER. London finished up with
a swing; there would never be another bash quite like this one
(though, after a breathing-space of eight days at sea and four in
Canada, there was still the New York circuit to come.) Johnny
Metcalf gave farewell party at his elegant shack on Charles
Street; then Moira Lister; then Cassell boardroom lunch; then
Eric Ambler at Pelham Crescent, next door to admired actor
Emlyn Williams.

Delicious chance meeting here with never-met heroine of
twenty-three years ago. Was talking with handsome-looking
woman of about forty; suddenly realized who she was—ballet
dancer Baronova, last seen as a chubbyish girl of seventeen or
eighteen, one of glamorous trio of 'little girls' (Baronova,
Riaboushinska, and Toumanova), the darlings of *Ballets Russes
de Monte Carlo* of 1933. Could hear far-off, haunting echoes of
Les Sylphides and *Présages* all the time we were talking—
which was more than an enchanted hour.

Then poker, the last of seven games, in a setting suitable to this most civilized of pastimes: play from eight till ten, a cold supper in the best tradition of Claridge's kitchens, and then on till 1 a.m. I finished about even—i.e., didn't lose more than £100 on the series.

A sprinkling of good remarks to enliven us. Michael Pertwee, talking of visit to Spanish cathedral: 'I was scared to go in: the place was full of plain-clothes nuns'; Johnny Metcalf, following up religious backchat: 'Ah, you've got to be born in the right manger'; and Monja Danischevsky, funny man of Ealing and also in mourning for its demise, though this did not show: 'They're the sort of people who have a Siamese cat and call it Oedipus.' Someone else, golfer Charles Sweeny who married Margaret Whigham in the long long ago, recounted supposed answer by Oscar Wilde, when a friend complained 'I thought you were turning over a new leaf': 'Oh yes! But I'm starting at the bottom of the page.' Did my own best with 'Pa's encore' for a second act of intercourse. Prompted no doubt by Stupid, the God of Love. In cold print, cold potato-pie again.

Cassell's gave me, by way of a farewell present, a beautiful silver statuette of a galleon under full sail, but with a female firmly planted at the helm. Once again, could be.

Claridge's bill, £1,853 for six and a half weeks. Of all creditors, they are the most welcome. Sailed Empress of Scotland, 19 October, Dobbie again, and George Formby as a stimulating fellow-voyager. We thought he should finish ship's concert with He Played his Ukelele as the Ship Went Down, but Beryl, prudent wife-manager, thought not.

New York went at shutter-like speed: now you see it, now you don't, now you don't want to, now you are cursing fate for snatching something away before it has been fully savoured. A rush job to get away from Ottawa, where eight weeks' mail had piled up, the whole water-pump system had broken down (entailing $1,035 worth of rude components such as brass nipples, female adaptors, male elbows, flexible ball sockets, and aircocks), and the Bank of Montreal was quietly steaming on top of a towering overdraft.

On the way south (total mileage, 452) broke the journey at Utica on the edge of the New York Thruway (sorry, that's how they spell it). Note: if you arrive at a motel in a Rolls, the price of a room jumps from $10 to $18. Next morning, a peerless drive down a half-section of the best road in the world: 240 miles of six-lane motorway, superbly engineered so as *not* to be boring: with carefully calculated slopes and long curves, beautiful fall colours on cunning display, the Hudson River as companion, and the Catskill Mountains as the last backdrop. (The whole highway stretches from the Pennsylvania border, south of Buffalo, to New York, 496 miles without a stop-light, a crossroads, or a check of any sort.) The 'lane discipline' was impressive; so were the cops who jumped on any offenders.

Some of this is old Indian country, with funny names as labels for the sophisticated 'service areas': Oneida, Indian Castle, Mohawk, Iroquois, Chittenango, Seneca, Canojoharie. A steady 70 m.p.h. turned this leg of the trip into a four-hour journey, and the score at the end for the use of this paragon, $4.10.

Stayed at the St Regis instead of the Pierre, which had not got the *precise* choice of suite available. But they put us on the sixteenth floor, which meant it was my turn to be choosy, and we transferred to much lower down: I simply could not stand the height, and at the first dawn had to lock myself in the bathroom so as not to jump out of the window. Don't know what's happening in this area of nerves. Domestically, they have been christened 'the vapours', but by Christ they are real.

Found that the Morrow boys had promoted the book to such good effect that it was in the best-seller list three days before publication: booksellers jumping the gun, illegal but enjoyable, involving 46,000 copies and a third printing already. (With that flying start, it reached No. 1 at a useful moment, nine days before Christmas, was then knocked out by juicy newcomer *Peyton Place*, but stayed somewhere in the tabernacle for twenty-one weeks.)

Front-page reviews in the *New York Times Book Review* and the *Chicago Sunday Tribune* (what odd items make an author's eyes shine). A real stinker, as usual, in the *New Yorker*, from their lop-sided little ball of venom who won't get a plug from me, beginning with a superior twitter: 'Those who have suspected for some time that Mr Nicholas Monsarrat fluked his literary reputation by writing *The Cruel Sea* . . . may feel confirmed in their suspicions by his new offering.' But many of the other reviews re-warmed our shrivelled cockles, particularly in the advertising department.

Eleven interviews and broadcasts, but this time no TV at all; perhaps they've gone off the boil as far as writers peddling their own books are concerned. Recorded for Doubleday Book Concert, 'Luncheon at Sardi's', and 'Breakfast with Tex and Jinx' (she the beautiful ex-film star Jinx Falkenburg). Funny way to make a living, on both sides. Party for booksellers, party by P.E.N. Club, party in Boston, lunch-party in Philadelphia given by the *Saturday Evening Post* (where I actually heard someone say: 'Let's run up the flag and see who salutes').

At the end of lunch, silence fell, and the boss, in a short speech of welcome, asked me if I had anything in mind which might suit their magazine. Off the cuff, I suggested an article, a global survey of American unpopularity, and how it could possibly be reconciled with America's supremely generous record in foreign aid. Round the table, about twenty-two pairs of eyes were watching, not me but the head man. Felt that if he smiled, everyone else would smile, say 'Sensational!' 'Oh boy!' 'Sounds just great!' He did not smile; no one saluted my little flag; after weighty silence the man said: 'I had in mind something in the fiction field.'

Willis Wing told me funny story on the train going back, one of the canon of Sam Goldwyn apocrypha. At a script conference, it was found that the name of the hero had not yet been settled. Someone said: 'Let's go for something plain. Let's call him Joe.' 'No, no!' said Goldwyn. 'Every Tom, Dick, and Harry is called Joe!'

Party down at United Nations given by old South African
External Affairs chum, 'Pot' Steward. Still called 'Pot'. How
do you learn to say 'Please call me Pot' in fifty languages?
Best thing about the U.N. is that spectacular East River view.
Then the building. Then the people. A thousand self-important,
inflated nothings still add up to zero.

But technically, not a good time to be selling books in New
York, or anywhere else on the continent. They were in the
throes of their election (Eisenhower *v.* Stevenson) and until
7 November hadn't much time for anything else. After 7 November, still arguing about what went wrong or, for the slight
majority, what went right. And the big Suez Canal row was
on, all this time: a shattering point of debate and preoccupation,
with everyone taking sides and all of them seemingly anti-
British. Even the cab-drivers wouldn't talk to the British while
the worst was going on. Self relentlessly pro-Israel, anti-Arab,
and feel likely to remain so for ever.

For a change of scene, gorgeous party given by Drue and
Jack Heinz. She sent me guest-list beforehand ('But don't
change your mind!') on very superior dark-blue notepaper from
which I learned that the Heinz family motto is *Veritatis et
Aequitatis Tenax* (roughly, Stick to truth and fair play). Her list
started strongly, and so continued:

> Greta Garbo
> Vera Zorina
> The John Roosevelts
> The David and John Rockefellers
> Sir Pierson and Lady Dixon
> Budd Schulberg
> The Jack Warners of Warner Bros.
> Santha Rama Rau
> The Oscar Hammersteins
> The Harvey Firestones
> The Gimbels
> Etc.

Couldn't swear to meeting any of these prestigious people except Etc. and Budd Schulberg, since the principal party gimmick was pink champagne flowing lavishly from a series of beautiful—well, they looked like glass tea urns as designed by someone like Fabergé, strategically placed round the apartment. Schulberg a disappointment: a little top-heavy with vast success, though his Scott Fitzgerald play, based on novel *The Disenchanted*, which we had just seen, was enough to turn anyone's head. But did enjoy session with Alastair Cooke, witty and charming man whose radio reports from America I've listened to for nearly twenty years, and before that, when he was BBC film critic in the early Thirties. He gloomy over Suez—about the only guest who was.

By contrast, the final Morrow party something of a shambles. Good start: Thayer Hobson greeted me with: 'Well, what's it like to be an avuncular, patronizing bore?' and when I queried this, though politely, as became the guest of honour, he explained: 'I just read a *rather* unfavourable review in the *Sydney Morning Herald.*' 'Didn't they say anything good?' 'Oh, sure!' Thayer pulled a slip of paper from his pocket. ' "A gorgeous hunk of novel"—how about that?' 'You better go on.' ' "Five hundred and thirty-eight pages of muscular prose, rippling with self-assurance, swollen with athletic vigour, and invincibly wooden-headed." Would you like a drink?' 'I believe I would.'

But the general style of the evening, staged at the Waldorf, grew cramped. Isabelle arrived in spirited mood, and by God she had competition. Half-way through, discovered I had become a lone bachelor. When? How? Where? Sped back to the St Regis. Only witness the doorman, who reported: 'The lady said "Grand Central Station".' You can get to a hell of a lot of places from Grand Central.

For just about the first time, in a mood of to-hell-with-all-this-why-should-an-important-evening-be-ruined?, went back to the pre-arranged dinner party and finished up watching striptease at a fearful joint a couple of doors from 21, with selected

18*

members of the Morrow board of directors and Temple Fielding, whose *Travel Guide to Europe* is tucked under every touring
American arm.

Fielding must know his way around New York as well. Three
girls joined us at our twilight table, unasked. Temp turned
round, said something to them, and they all disappeared without
trace in a matter of seconds. (That's something I would never
know how to do.) Girls on tiny stage all seemed to be huge:
with nipples as brazen as my plumber's, identical bumps and
curves, identical thigh-bruises, and identical yearning to
sit astride the back of an armchair and groan rhythmically.
Favourite costume was a curious little black velvet *cache-sexe*
with three golden balls dangling from it: these they tossed and
twirled, while their hands hovered over pneumatic breasts as if
checking the pressure, and the band played pulsating jungle
music.

But why *three* balls, emblem of distress outside every pawn-
shop? It would be wrong to identify the customers who
answered: 'Abandon hope, all ye who enter here,' and 'Con-
fucius say, man with spare ball never lose bearings,' or the
earnest punster who carefully wrote out, on the back of a menu:
'It's PAWNographic.'

Past two o'clock when we came out into the cold tired air
of 52nd Street, feeling happy and foolish: all middle-aged
acting bachelors whose wild oats had been dutifully cast on this
arid ground. Temp Fielding suggested: 'What about 21 again?'
but the mood was No. The middle-aged bachelors all had
manuscripts to write, books to publish, contracts to read, letters
to dictate, cheques to cash, answers to give, all within seven
hours.

Sam Lawrence, solicitous as usual, asked if I would be all
right. I said that I would.

5.

On a golden autumn day, we closed down a gold mine, driving 300 miles north and west to a point near Rouyn on the Quebec border to do the mysterious deed. I had no idea what ceremony it would entail, and indeed there was none; it was a party, male and boisterous, to mark the last day of a mine which had been a profitable enterprise for thirty years. My hosts were two of my favourite Ottawa friends, Brian and Barry O'Brien; and the mine in fact was the O'Brien Gold in Cadillac Township (so called after the French colonial administrator who founded Detroit in 1701 and thus fathered that motorcar.)

It had not run out of gold, as a souvenir cigarette-lighter containing lumps of glittering, gold-bearing ore later proved; but it had run out of gold at the right price. We therefore travelled in style, in a massive station-wagon full of food and drink and guns and people, to attend the obsequies. Among the party was an Ottawa artist, Robert Hyndman, whose nickname in this non-cultural society was Rembrandt. Mine, even more inaccurate, was Tolstoy. It was wild, deserted country through which we sped northwards, and the road was often a rutted, corrugated mess, recalling South Africa or even Bechuanaland under the stress of harsh weather. Now and again the tangled trees came down to the roadside and then retreated, leaving us in our vast wilderness.

Sometimes we would see, in the distance, a car with an odd shapeless mound on top of it; and when it drew near, the mound proved to be a dead moose spread-eagled on the roof, its huge antlered head balanced just over the windshield. This was the hunter's prime trophy hereabouts. The legal allotment was a strict one-to-each-customer; all of us in the car carried a Provincial Government licence headed 'Permit to shoot ONE MOOSE', and I had the feeling that one would be enough.

At dusk we stopped at a wayside garage, to fill up with petrol and to have supper. Supper was hamburgers and fried potatoes and Canadian Club whisky: as we were eating, a shot

rang out, very near, and when we trooped outside to see what
the action was we found a 'hunter' standing triumphantly over a
colossal grizzly bear, which had once been eight feet tall and
was now stretched out, stone dead, beside the garbage can it
had been robbing.

It had a savage beauty, even in death; and the ruined snout,
still pumping blood onto the tarmac, seemed as sad a piece of
destruction as could be found anywhere. But perhaps, if one
had come round the corner from an innocent visit to the backyard, and met that bear face to face, the reaction would have
been different.

We arrived very late, slept in the bunkhouse, breakfasted
enormously off fried eggs and potato fritters, and then set off
for the mine. It was a last tour for the O'Brien brothers, and
probably a sad one; the place already had a run-down, desolate
air, and we were followed everywhere by a handful of rather
grim, oldish men, the 'care and maintenance' crew who had
been seeing the gold mine into its last decline. The rest of the
miners had been laid off, for ever.

It was cold above ground, in spite of blanket-cloth wind-
breakers and fur-lined boots; and almost as cold, and dank with
neglect, when we began our descent. The echoing cavern below
was like an abandoned, ghostly crypt. We made our way along
winding galleries, up and down ladders from one level to
another, along narrow stopes in which, it seemed, one tiny
movement of the earth could embalm a man for ever, like a dead
bee in a buried hive.

Nervous about heights, I now found that I was nervous
about depths. The reaction was to turn *blasé*. I felt bound to
remind them that this was rather a shallow mine; that I had
once been down the Robinson Deep on the Rand. How deep
was that? About 9,000 feet—nearly two miles.

'All right, old timer,' said Brian O'Brien. We were all
wearing helmets with electric torches clipped to them; when a
man turned to speak, it was like an old 'tortured prisoner'
movie-routine, with the bound and blinded captive enduring the

final stages of third-degree pressure. 'All right. Now tell us about the Klondyke.'

'What's all that heavy breathing?' a beam of light behind me asked.

The heavy breathing was me; so was the smell of sweat. I could almost feel the pressure of the earth bearing down on me, and the rock wall at my back beginning to crack and tremble. Though I told them all about the gold rush of '49, and the old days with Charlie Chaplin, I was very glad to get above ground again.

In the afternoon we went moose hunting—or hunting for guinea-fowl, or rabbits, or anything: it was not clear what the bag might be. We split up as soon as we arrived on the scene: Brian in one direction, Barry and Bob Hyndman in another, myself alone, free to choose. There had been reports of a moose in the district.

'What do I do if I see one?' I asked.

'Shoot it!'

'With a twelve-bore shot gun?' A moose could be seven feet high at the withers, weigh nearly a ton, and, meeting a car head on, toss it bodily off the roadway.

'You have to let it get near enough.'

Barry O'Brien, who had been in Canadian corvettes, said: 'Call me if it comes on to blow.'

Then they left me, alone in a forest clearing with my puny gun, twelve cartridges, and a station-wagon to retreat to. But a station-wagon—even a Chrysler station-wagon—could be no match for a ton of moose in a show-off mood.

I walked around a little, penetrating the bush here and there. Nothing stirred, but I was not ambitious. I wanted to hear the whirr of wings, or the scuttle of a rabbit, and that was about all. It was lonely. There was not, I knew, a single main highway between me and the Arctic Circle. But presently there was a great crashing and trampling in the undergrowth. It drew unmistakably nearer. I slipped the safety-catch, and waited.

'Sorry,' said Brian. 'I left my cigarettes.'

As soon as he was gone, I went back into the clearing, where at least I could see what was coming: took a stiff drink, sat down on the front bumper of the car, and read one of my own reviews, of a book called *Frogman*, in an old copy of the *New York Times*. There was a softer, safer world somewhere, but it was all down south, and under-water.

As it turned out, no one shot anything, so I was not utterly disgraced. Back in the bunkhouse, the stay-at-homes woke from their drowsing round the wood stove, and went into a chorus of the Quebec version of 'For He's A Jolly Good Fellow', which was called '*Il a Gagné Ses Epaulettes*'. It did not feel like it. But the evening afterwards, and the poker, and the booze, and 'Rembrandt' immortalizing the occasion in one of his quick, funny drawings,* brought everything right again, for a brief spell of bliss.

The first swirling drifts of snow were riming the road ahead as we made our way back. The leaves, which a few days earlier had been a blaze of scarlet and orange and gold, were now drifting down to their withered grave, stripping the maple branches as bare as etchings. The sad season was upon us, and all the signals of a winter world. The geese were flying out again, honking their way joyfully towards their faraway retreat. I envied the geese.

But it was Ottawa for me: Ottawa, where all the huge chaos lay in wait, like a moose as big as the Ritz. It was 'Make Friends with Your Jeweller' Week: a good time to cast the accounts, and to plot, if I could, an up-to-date graph of what was right and what was wrong.

What was wrong started with money.

The account book showed that I had earned £236,000 since all the flurry started five years earlier. Where was it? It had certainly gone: on taxes, on living, on showing off. The era of constructive penury involved in subsisting on my dollar salary and ordering everything else from England had now

* See photograph following page 290.

passed away; I had been told, officially, that I was free to spend
my royalties, from whatever source, as and how I wished, and
the result was that I now had an overdraft of $91,000. A lot of
it was tied up in the house; a lot was not.

I had signed over eight hundred cheques that year: two a day,
fifteen a week, sixty-seven a month—whichever way one looked
at it, it was a powerful, sustained effort of writing. A sample
month's accounting, compiled with loving care and God knows
what private reservations by Mrs Macdonell, showed how this
ludicrous output had been achieved. She made it admirably
easy to read.

Day	Classification	Amount
1.	First mortgage, repayment	500.00
1.	First mortgage, interest	485.20
1.	Second mortgage, repayment	500 00
1.	Second mortgage, interest	213.19
1.	Allowance, Maria's mother	12.00
1.	Personal insurance	19.60
1.	Court order	280.00
3.	Upholstering	9.00
4.	Vaillant, groceries	141.65
4.	Electrical	5.68
4.	Medical services	7.00
4.	Delicatessen	42.60
4.	Clothing (A. J. Freiman)	11.25
4.	Taxi account	61.30
4.	Gatineau Power Company	31.58
4.	Horticultural Services	27.65
6.	Books	24.25
6.	Fish	19.17
6.	Rideau Club	8.95
6.	Ontario Motor League	17.50
6.	Canadian Club dues	4.00
6.	Fuel oil	48.20
6.	Royal St Lawrence Yacht Club	13.59

6.	Silver repairs	37.00
6.	Expert Window Cleaning Co.	20.00
6.	Carpentry	34.00
7.	Trans-Canada Airlines	26.00
9.	Cash	50.00
9.	Magazines	2.00
9.	Pastries	14.50
9.	Gasoline	5.51
9.	Hardware	96.03
9.	Decorating house (final account)	3,344.25
9.	Car repairs	12.70
11.	Cables & telegrams, C.P.R.	3.83
11.	Raffle tickets, Ottawa Press Club	5.00
11.	Cash	10.00
13.	Cash	100.00
13.	Trans-Canada Airlines (Crosby)	1,135.00
13.	Parking ticket	2.00
13.	Seeds	2.49
13.	Office supplies	4.25
13.	Milk	35.86
13.	Moving chest	6.00
13.	Flowers	19.50
13.	Cleaning	25.25
13.	Postage stamps	10.00
20.	Domestic wages	105.00
20.	Picture framing	15.00
20.	Hotel accommodation	5.00
23.	Medical services	6.00
24.	Books	15.00
24.	Cash	45.00
25.	Meat	45.15
25.	Telephone	43.95
25.	Drugs	20.02
25.	Office stationery	2.00
26.	Chair covers	664.28
26.	Meat (Canada Packers)	43.76

26.	Insurance on Rolls-Royce	170.10
27.	Carpentry	35.60
28.	Gardener	28.00
30.	Hardware	31.22
30.	Gasoline	81.00
30.	Entertainment (Café Henri Burger)	22.85
30.	Secretarial	250.00
31.	Domestic wages	400.00
31.	Cash	50.00

'Total: $9,562.89', Mrs Macdonell noted, and added a cautionary note: 'To this should be added: Interest on bank overdraft.' I knew well enough what that meant: another $600.

There was evidence of one odd leakage here, almost lost in the general sieve: $225 in cheques to 'Cash', when I never used the stuff except for haircuts and ice-cream, needed a little explanation, and never got it. Perhaps, that month, bought a lot of newspapers. There were also aspects of appeasement in this largesse. Part of the huge, smirking irony of life was that they never appeased.

Then there were taxes, taxes, taxes. There was a time when I had built up £30,000 in Tax Reserve Certificates, ready for the bite; the bite had already swallowed it whole, and was still hungry for more. Towards the end of this year, there had been added an enormous extra complication: a big income tax dispute, not between me and anyone else, but between Canada and the United Kingdom, with me in the middle, facing both ways with a stupid smile and no effective answer.

The engagement could be set out briefly, though its ramifications and its consequential miseries were to prove endless, for the next fifteen years and beyond. After I had been in Canada for three years, paying all my taxes, as a diplomat whose constructive residence was always England, to the United Kingdom, I was suddenly informed that only my diplomatic salary should have been subject to U.K. taxation; all the rest, the Canadian Department of National Revenue now claimed, should have been paid to Canada. What was I going to do about that?

All I could do was to stand quietly to one side while the point was argued. It was, after all, a dispute between Governments and their departments: God knows I had paid the taxes promptly enough, and if I had paid them into the wrong till, then that could surely be remedied.

Indeed, that was how it happened; the U.K. Government surrendered the point gracefully, and refunded most of my payments, and I was then newly assessed in Canada. The Canadians then slapped my innocent face with a penalty for three years' 'tax delinquency'—i.e., non-payment to *them*, whatever else I had done with the money—for $45,000.

In spite of the best efforts of Cooper Brothers, my new allies, this unjust decision stood, and indeed still stands. It was futile to argue that I had already paid the taxes to the U.K., and that they had accepted them, while later agreeing that they were not so entitled; futile to argue that I was not 'delinquent' in any moral sense, since I had always paid up as ordered, and could not know that I had been paying the wrong man.

The *fact* was that I had failed to put in a Canadian tax return for three years. There was, it seemed, 'no discretion'.

Down on the enormous bill, just for staying alive, went another $45,000; and down, in a private diary of despair, went the conviction that now I would never really catch up.

Just for once, it was not my fault! But try realizing a little ready cash on *that* conviction.

What was wrong continued with niggling little things, as annoying as acne when one has done nothing to deserve it. After the pump troubles came the tree troubles; an army of 'tree surgeons' had to descend upon Stone House, to lop, prune, cut down, bolster up, and generally nurse back to health many of our beautiful elms and maples, which had looked so stalwart when I bought the place and were now, it seemed, a sad and sickly grove of invalids.

Then came heating troubles, to coincide with winter; the massive boiler in the basement, which warmed the entire house and the garage, and drank a thousand dollars' worth of prime fuel oil a year, suddenly developed such a fearful fit of the staggers that most of it had to be ripped out and replaced.

Outside, in the garden, while burning off some under-brush, Dinty Moore and I between us managed to set fire to a stand of fir-trees quite near the house. They went up in flames, like quick-burning torches: menacing for one sweating afternoon, irreplaceable thereafter.

One would not rate butler-trouble among the greater social evils of our time; but we had butler-trouble, anyway. Before very long, Angus the mainstay of the household left to join a much more glamorous outfit, that of the Belgian ambassador to Washington, Baron Silvercruys. Then we had, or did not have, a candidate who got as far as outfitting himself at Moss Bros., at my expense, before deciding that he would not be happy in Canada.

Then we advertised locally for a 'Houseman'. The answer was prompt.

'I hear you're looking for a horseman,' said the confident English voice on the phone. 'Well, I'm not bad, not bad at all! Plenty of point-to-point stuff, and all that! Shall we give it a try?'

Then it was the turn of Angelo, an Italian whose passport, we presently found, described him as a labourer.

He might have been a labourer at home, but he was something short of this in Canada. His contempt for women was so absolute that he would not flush the toilet after using it; that was women's work. So was almost everything else. His most strenuous, and last, effort, was to bash up the Land-Rover in a minor collision on the Aylmer Road, after which he left the scene of the accident' to walk home.

This was a serious traffic offence in Canada, and I was visited very promptly by two RCMP constables who thought I must be the culprit and came storming up the hill to get their man.

After I had convinced them that it was Angelo, driving with my permission, who had been involved, the tension eased.

Italian injured innocence, Italian volubility, Italian tears of remorse, finally disposed of the case. But he was not quite what we had in mind as the main domestic sinew of our household, and his place was taken by Colin, an admirable young man who had previously alternated between Government House and Earnscliffe, but was finally lured in our direction. He came too late to restore order to a collapsing enterprise.

What was wrong continued and ended with the darkening domestic scene. While the wounds were still raw, I roughed out a long, well-documented piece about this era of destruction, with an acid content suitable to a writer who could no longer write what he hoped to, even in his own barred corner of the zoo: who had done his best, and beaten his brains out in the process, and felt there was blame to be shared as well as shouldered. One might as well keep the dust off the typewriter keys, somehow, anyhow. But I scrapped it.

Compassion for the once-loved person, gratitude for the always-loved past, warred with furious rage that so much had been tossed down the drain; and compassion won—as it should, if one was ever to reach heaven, or even to stay alive until, in due course, one was dead meat instead of live spirit. It would not have won in the crucifying season of 1956.

Life then was a giant sleeping-pill, an over-stimulant, a stomach pump, a mess: a yearning for the tender past, and a bleak mourning for the present which was being eaten, drunk, misted over, fouled up, hacked to pieces, and thrown away. Life was Equanil for me, the mild essential tranquillizer, on the prescription for which my doctor had written: 'Take two as necessary when flying.' How many when crawling, doctor? He did not have to tell me.

Life was a near-resident psychiatrist, and a range of funny, bitter jokes about his ministrations, and a whole new gallery of Catholic onlookers to people the clinic: 'Father Figure won't like it. Mother Fixation is not at all pleased. Brother Libido may have to leave.' Life was a Swedish masseur, twice a week, to bash us both about. We did not need a Swedish masseur, either.

Life was violence, and spells of warm happiness, and the sniping crackle of rifle-fire again. Life was a house full of nurses, a departing cook, a couple of children enthralled, as all children should be, with recurrent dramatic change. Life was snapping dogs, and snapping people.

Life was war and peace, treachery and confederate delight. Life was '*Balls!*' to end a dinner-party argument—and the dinner-party as well.

Life was savage battling, truce-lines passionately sworn to, swift betrayal, white flags presently spattered by so much flying filth that not all the multitudinous seas could make them usable again.

Life was a spectral voice from a balcony above, sliding down like sleet into the moonlight: 'You want a divorce? You'll have to be a —— good provider!'

I was a fairly good provider—everybody, however inept or wretched, can do *something*—but at this pace it would not last very long. I could not write in this turmoil; I felt I had shot my bolt with *The Tribe*, and in fact I wrote nothing except twelve short stories in the next four years. I knew already that this was going to happen, like a man, sick but sensible, who acknowledges in the most private part of his mind: 'This is more than an occasional bad turn. Aspirin is not enough. Spring may not come again. I have cancer.'

Having this cancer, the only thing to do was to shrink down very small, to count the blessings instead of all the rest, and to contemplate, with the humble, penitent eye of poverty-in-riches, what was right.

What was right seemed a very small tally, and so entirely self-centred that it lacked any pretensions to maturity. But it would have to do.

I could read other people's novels, and, living in a world
devoted to lists, I compiled a list of these also, and solemnly,
slowly set out to walk again with the men and women who in
the past had been admired companions. That autumn and winter,
I assembled and began to read:

Death of a Hero and *All Men are Enemies:* Richard Aldington.
Invitation to the Waltz and *The Weather in the Streets:*
    Rosamund Lehmann.
Europa and *Europa in Limbo:* Robert Briffault.
Number One: John Dos Passos.
A Farewell to Arms: Ernest Hemingway.
Babbitt and *Elmer Gantry:* Sinclair Lewis.
Wasteland: Jo Sinclair.
Growth of the Soil: Knut Hamsun.
The Razor's Edge: Somerset Maugham.
The Edwardians: V. Sackville-West.
The Thinking Reed: Rebecca West.
Brideshead Revisited and *A Handful of Dust:* Evelyn Waugh.
The Grapes of Wrath: John Steinbeck.

They were not all great; perhaps they were not all good;
but they were the ones which had taken the imagination when
their stars first rose, and, rising again, they brought solid
comfort from a more generous past. It was curious how some
of them went in pairs. Would there come a time when people
would re-read my books in pairs? Not at this rate.

I could listen to music, and the music I wanted to hear had
turned profoundly sad; it seemed that the hurt within could only
be matched by another man telling me his troubles, and making
them so moving, so desolate, that one ache assuaged another.
There was a secondary sadness here: the fact that I could not
write music myself. Often it seemed the only language, the
universal tongue, and the most beautiful. There could be no
dialogue to match the second movement of the *Kreutzer* Sonata,
no terrors like the fearful Witches' Sabbath nightmares of
Berlioz in *Symphonie Fantastique.*

But now it was time for the lamenting piano and the guitar, the voices of bereavement: for Chopin's *Nocturnes* or the *Andante Spianato*, for Frescobaldi and Fernando Sor, Villa-Lobos and Tarrega, for Segovia playing *Recuerdos de la Alhambra* as if all hearts were breaking all over Spain.

It was a time for opera—not gay or brittle Mozart, but sad and noble Verdi: for the throat-catching last acts of *La Forza del Destino* and *Il Trovatore*, for '*O fratei, pieta! Pieta!*' for '*Salita a Dio*'—'She has gone to God'—as Leonora died.

My two 'perfect' symphonies, the Mozart G Minor and the Brahms No 1, remained in their jackets, guests not invited to this wake. They were not sad enough. They still spoke of hope.

I could play with the two little boys, and reassure them, and myself. I could mow the lawn, and find in this repetitious chore, continuing hour after hour, another sort of music, another small accomplishment.

I could collect the letters of Admiral Lord Nelson.

By now I had fifty-two of these, assembled with reverent care over the last few years, with the help of C. R. Sawyer's in London; and if it was not the finest private collection in the world, I liked to think that it was. Usually they came on the market in ones and twos, though sometimes there was a substantial clear-out at auction, and Sawyer's went into action on my behalf.

One happy day we bought fourteen of them at Sotheby's, for a total of £1,172, and they included a rare prize, as sad as I could hope to find in the most evil hour—one of the first letters written by Nelson with his left hand, in crabbed despair, when his right had been shattered and with it, he feared, his whole future.

There was one written to Lieutenant-General John Graves Simcoe, the first Lieutenant-Governor of Upper Canada; dated 1803, it was on black-edged notepaper, Nelson being, with the utmost delicacy, in mourning for Sir William Hamilton. There were several written between 1800 and 1803 to Sir Alexander Ball, Governor of Malta after the French were ousted and the Maltese opted for British rule.

There were three from Carlisle Bay in the Barbados ('Barbarous Island') when he was the twenty-six-year-old captain of the frigate *Boreas*; and one to Lady Hamilton ('My dearest Emma. . . . Be assured that I am, etc. Nelson and Bronte').

There was the 'Plan of Attack' for Trafalgar, to be circulated to his captains, that 'band of brothers' who loved this man as much as I now did myself; and, to crown the collection, two written in the cabin of H.M.S. *Victory* on 9 and 10 October, 1805—eleven days before Trafalgar: the first to Vice-Admiral Collingwood ('My dear Coll.') and the second to Captain Blackwood of the *Euryalus*, in command of the look-out frigates off Cadiz.

To read, and to touch gently, these letters, revived the fiercest of pride and admiration. In particular, it was wonderful to note how that pitiful left-hand scrawl formed gradually into something firm and free again—like the birth of a new and even braver man. Reading them, I felt at one with the 'band of brothers', the captains of ships-of-the-line with such ringing names as *Royal Sovereign*, *Agamemnon*, *Tonnant*, *Bellerophon*, *Revenge*, *Téméraire*, and *Dreadnought*, in their hero-worship and their boundless respect.

I spent, with the same sort of pride, nearly £5,000 on these my fifty-two jewels. They were all sold, in a sudden alimony squeeze, a few years later, for £2,000; and that was a defiling day indeed.

If I could not write, I could at least plan what I hoped to write; and what I had in mind now was the longest novel ever written about the sea and about sailors; covering nearly four hundred years of maritime venture, from the Spanish Armada in 1588 to the completion of the St Lawrence Seaway—the furthest foray (2,250 miles) ever made by ships into the heart of a continent—in 1958.

I wanted to tell the story—the whole story—of what sailors had done to open up the known world: by charting its oceans, by fighting, by commerce, by the great voyages of exploration and plunder.

The book would have ships, from Spanish galleon to nuclear-
powered tanker; and men, from Drake to Captain Cook, from
Nelson to Samuel Cunard, from Pepys to Thor Heyerdahl;
and stories, from Henry Hudson's voyage in 1610 to the China
Clippers of 1840, from the *Chesapeake* versus the *Shannon* to the
Ark Royal versus U.81; from the 'Black-birding' slavers of 1807
to Samuel Plimsoll and his cattle-ships; from the pirates of
Port Royal to the last stewards' strike at Southampton.

I did not then see how the story could be told, though I was
to solve this later. What I did at this stage was to make out a
list—a list rather too long (130 books) to be detailed—of what
was absolutely essential reading before I could even make a
start; and to divide up the projected book into the necessary
sixteen chapters, in accordance with the best civil service
planning technique.

Already the pattern was quite clear in my mind:

1.	The Coward	1588
2.	Voyager	1610
3.	Pirate	1650
4.	Admiralty Clerk	1682
5.	Fisherman	1720
6.	Marine	1759
7.	Navigator	1776
8.	Navy Captain	1791
9.	Black-Birder	1807
10.	Pressed Man	1812
11.	Foremast Hand	1830
12.	Look-Out	1857
13.	Super-Cargo	1890
14.	Valiant Gunner	1914
15.	Ship-Keeper	1935
16.	The Good Acquittal	1958

I also had a 'motto' for the whole work, from *The Tempest*:
'He has suffered a sea-change, Into something rich and strange';
and a recurrent theme: 'He who commands the Sea commands

the Situation' (Themistocles, admiral of the Athenian Fleet, 480 B.C.); and I had a title. One day I would write it: all 600,000 words of it.*

Marcel Proust's *Remembrance of Things Past* was 1,307,000 words long; Tolstoy's *War and Peace* a mere 490,000. Somewhere in between. . . .

All this play-acting, minuscule endeavour, and fiddling about could always be brought up short—between the third and the fourth whisky-and-soda, the fifth and sixth cigar, Chopin's Opus 55, No 1 in F Minor and No 2 in E Flat—by the fact of non-achievement. Apart from certain dreams of happiness which had been stifled by a sackcloth pillow, other ambitions, formulated long ago in the spring of hope, and latterly swift to rise, were now fading out of sight. It was once more a case of Now you see it, Now you don't, and now I didn't see it.

Long ago I had made a list, another list, which was beginning to look as silly as a fat Lord Mayor stripped down to his mildewed chain of office and a grubby pair of shorts. It was becoming embarrassing to contemplate it, though very good for the soul to recognize and then to scrub out the ones which could never happen now.

1. To ride the winner of the Grand National.
2. To win the America's Cup (J Class).
3. To be a Member of Parliament.
4. To write a world-wide bestseller.
5. To be invited to join the Athenaeum Club.
6. To get a knighthood.
7. To win the Nobel Prize for Literature.
8. To receive the Order of Merit.

These were all honourable goals: 'A man's reach,' said Robert Browning, 'should exceed his grasp, Or what's a heaven

---

* Four years later, I promised Cassell's that it would be the one after *The Nylon Pirates* (1960). After nine other books, I re-promised them, as recently as May 1970, that it would be the one after the one after this.

for?'; but embarrassing was now the word. . . . 'Time is the dog that barks us all to hell.' and already, so early that it was ridiculous and shameful, time was running out.

Between sadness and self-pity, there was still enough spirit left—of a sort—to determine that I need not actually roll over and play dead. I would run out too.

The planned escape-route was a round-the-world trip to look at all the world's principal harbours: clearly justifiable, even to the Department of National Revenue, if I were ever to write that half-million-word *mag. op.*, *I'm a Son of a Beach* (working title).

I could still press a button, even with a wet thumb, and the answer presently came in the form of a letter from BCAC:

'We are glad to confirm that we have made travel reservations for the following itinerary:
'Ottawa/Montreal/London/Oslo/Stockholm/Copenhagen/ London/Lagos/Accra/Johannesburg/Nairobi/Karachi/ Bombay/Madras/Calcutta/Rangoon/Hong Kong/Shanghai/ Hong Kong/Tokio/Manila/Singapore/Djakarta/Australia/ Nandi/Suva/Apia/Aitutaki/Papeete/Nandi/Honolulu/ San Francisco/New York/Ottawa.'

I learned also that a visa for Tahiti cost 1,500 francs, for Japan $3.15, for the Philippines $15 (£5), and that I would have to forward my finger-prints (by courtesy of the Royal Canadian Mounted Police) if I wanted to visit President Sukarno's Indonesia.

Christmas. . . . The white stuff was here again, as certain Canadians phrased it, fearing, like superstitious Africans, to name the name of their enemy. Overnight, the snow had fallen in a soft cataract; now it stretched down from my study window to the Aylmer Road, in a broad sloping carpet, gleaming white, shining under the pale sun, reflecting ten million tiny crystals. It would be there till next spring.

We drove across the U.S. border, and thirty miles beyond to

Plattsburg on Lake Champlain, to pick up a basset-hound puppy which had been marooned at a railway depot on its way up from Connecticut. When we found it, it was small, immensely mournful, incontinent, and ravenous. Chekhov seemed the only name for it.

We sent out five hundred Christmas cards, the list being confined to our very dearest friends.

The main Christmas present was a new Plymouth, a long, not bad-looking car with far too much horse-power, painted in a young-at-heart shade technically known as Gulf Stream Blue. Driving it home, I became aware that it was overheating dramatically; presently smoke, and then flames, began to pour out from the radiator grille. I swept blindly into the nearest garage, where the young man at the pumps, not at all put out, threw open the bonnet and doused the fire with a bucket of sand. A loose fuel connection, spraying petrol onto hot metal, was the culprit.

'So that's the new Plymouth,' the young man said.

I hoped that, both as a car and a present, it would last a little longer than all this suggested.

'How was Christmas, Scrooge-wise?' someone at the club asked me. It was not bad, not bad at all. The Spirit of Christmas Past must have taken a hand, with the slam and tinkle of the cash-register to mute the clanking chains. God bless us all, said Tiny Tool.

New Year. . . . Suddenly the house was *not* full of nurses, masseurs, psychiatrists, and thunder-faced servants. Instead, all was sweetness, and light, and even love, and we were giving the party of the year on New Year's Eve.

Earlier, Mrs Macdonell had made out the final three lists of 1956: 120 first-choice guests, 45 spares as possible replacements, and an *aide-memoire* for the boss as the bits fell into place:

Address List	Completed
Invitation cards	Delivered
Invitations sent out	O.K.

Notices for driveway	Delivered
Piano	O.K. From Lawrence Freiman
Public address system	O.K. From Don Cruikshank
Band	O.K. Champ Champagne plus quintet. Contract with Musicians' Union signed.
Flood-lighting for parking area	Jerry plus electrician
Snow-plough, parking area	Dinty
Erect bandstand	Dinty
Police	1 on gate, 1 motor-cycle patrolman will check periodically
Beds for band	Ordered
Champagne	Checked
Barmen	3. Double wages for N.Y. Eve agreed
Carpets lifted	10 a.m. Dec 30
Additional glassware	Hired. We pay insurance
Coat-hangers	200 cn loan from Canadian Legion
Ice	8 × 50-lb blocks, due 5 p.m. 31.12.

After that it was easy. The fancy dress ordained was 'Old
Film Characters', and old film characters arrived by the cart-
load. There were three Keystone Cops (among them Jack
Heinz, who flew in from Pittsburgh), and two hideous versions of
Harpo Marx, plus Barry O'Brien as Groucho, champing on *my*
cigars. Israel Ambassador Michael Comay and Lawrence
Freiman, Ottawa's Selfridge and the town's most civilizing
influence as well, both came as Sheiks of Araby; Yousuf Karsh
was a sad-eyed Jackie Coogan.

The sight of my bank manager, Ted Royce, as the evil Dr Fu
Manchu was daunting; so was a certain Quebec intellectual
(anyone in this province who could dial a seven-digit phone

number was a Quebec intellectual) as Charlie Chaplin. But we had George Arliss with a kiss-curl, Theda Bara with an asp in her navel, Laurel and Hardy, a stone-faced Buster Keaton, and a Fugitive from a Chain Gang, to comfort us.

There were a few Mack Sennett bathing belles. But most of the women seemed to have taken a wild stab at Pola Negri.

The band began its eight-hour stint. Ottawa's only Bad Girl, and very welcome on that account, made her entrance, wearing the sort of Circassian slave outfit favoured by film starlets *en route* for the casting-couch. She looked very fetching, and I complimented her.

'It's my *après*-screw,' she said.

The band played on. Dinner was served. A gate-crasher, son of a U.S. diplomat, was thrown out; having pruned the guest-list till the bones showed through, I was not in the mood for immunity. At midnight the two children were brought down by Katie. Sleepy-eyed, puzzled, and then entranced, they made the rounds, Marc under his own steam, Anthony in the arms of god-mother Moura Lympany.

'Isn't it bad for them?' a Spock-minded matron inquired.

'Oh, I hope so.'

The band played on. There were only four drunks, and they could have been forecast from the form-book. People began to leave at three. Some people never left. At dawn the motor-cycle cop, making his last rounds, drove into an illuminated Christmas tree and fused all the lights. At 8 a.m. band-leader Champ Champagne laid aside his melodious, tireless, sweet-as-molasses clarinet and asked: 'Can I help you with that hair dye?'

My jet-black hair, glossy and lacquered, was still unimpaired, appropriate to the oldest living juvenile lead in the business.

Breakfast was served, and the last of the Louis Roederer (the last that I was going to provide, anyway). Champ Champagne still toiled away at my scalp, with soap and water, petrol, melted butter, and a nail-brush. It became clear that he would never succeed, and that I must remain a raven-haired beauty, well on into 1957.

Early-rising Jack Heinz, nursing a wine-glassful of chilled tomato-juice ('Oh God!' I had to tell him; 'It's *local!*') said: 'That was quite a thrash. You know, I *like* Canada!'

Late-rising Drue Heinz, wandering down later, more beautiful than any woman had a right to be at such an hour, said: 'Darling—your hair!'

Champ Champagne, still the most dedicated man of this or any other crusade, said: 'What say we try that stuff they put on locks?'

Thus, on New Year's morning, in a positive soup of symbolism, staking my claim to be the only rate-payer on the north side of the Aylmer Road who had to miss the Governor-General's New Year *Levée* because, even with the help of a Negro band-leader, he could not get the black dye out of his hair, I rested my case.

In spite of imperial elevation, I knew that it had only been a breathing-space, a dividend for which the fugitive cashier would later be held accountable. It would last as long as the blessed bubbles, and no longer. I knew also that Lord Byron, club foot, incest, brooding genius and all, still had it right:

> 'He seems
> To have seen better days, as who has not
> Who has seen yesterday.'

ACKNOWLEDGEMENTS

No blame of any sort for the result, but only my grateful appreciation, goes to the large number of people who have helped me with various queries during the eighteen months it took to write this book. I can only list their names, and add my unqualified thanks to:

Dr George Chandler, M.A., PH.D., Liverpool City Librarian: Mr St J. B. V. Harmsworth, Metropolitan Magistrate, Great Marlborough Street: the British Museum Newspaper Library: Mr Leonard Sachs: Dr Desmond Flower, M.C., of Cassell's: Mr Chappie D'Amato: the Ministry of Agriculture, Fisheries, and Food: Miss Madeleine Masson: the Department of Health and Social Security: Lieut.-Commander P. M. Marcell, R.N., Assistant Secretary to Naval Secretary, Ministry of Defence: Captain S. R. le H. Lombard Hobson, C.V.O., O.B.E., R.N.: Captain Jack Broome, D.S.C., R.N.: Mr J. A. Wright of the Library and Records Department, Foreign and Commonwealth Office: Mr Stanley Uys of the Johannesburg *Sunday Times*: Mr John Willey of Morrow's: the Editor of *Drive* Magazine: Mr Willis Wing of New York: Mr Charles Frend: Mr Edwin Harper of Cassell's: Mr R. A. Usborne: Lord Glenavy (Mr Patrick Campbell): the Rt Hon Patrick Gordon Walker, P.C., C.H., M.P.: Mr R. W. Southam of Southam Newspapers, Canada: the Photographic Section of the *Cape Times*: the Publicity Department of the Stratford (Ontario) Festival: Mrs Eileen Monsarrat: His Excellency the Rt Hon Sir Morrice James, P.C., K.C.M.G., C.V.O., M.B.E., British High Commissioner in India: Mr Marc McNeill of Canadian Pacific Steamships: Sir Percivale Liesching, G.C.M.G., K.C.B., K.C.V.O.: Mr Clarence

Paget of Pan Books: Mr Robert S. Hyndman of Ottawa: Mr
P. B. Firth, Clerk of the Course, Newmarket Racecourse:
Mr Brian O'Brien of Ottawa: and my agent, Mr John Mc-
Laughlin, for efforts far above and beyond the ten per cent scale.

My special thanks go to the following, who acted as manu-
script couriers between Malta and London: Mr Ben Perrick of
Foyle's Bookshop: Mr Hugh Willatt, Secretary-General of the
Arts Council of Great Britain, and Mrs Willatt (Evelyn Gibbs):
Mr Bill McMullan of Pan Books: Mr Graham Lord of the
Sunday Express: and Miss Ruth Cornish-Bowden.

When, in my 'acknowledgements' following Volume One of
Life is a Four-Letter Word, I paid tribute to my wife for her
essential contribution in fair-copying and proof-reading, I
received a number of letters asking how I could subject anyone
I loved to such an atrocious ordeal. I can only repeat, remorse-
fully and gratefully, that it has happened again.

N.M.

Gozo, Malta: May 1970

APPENDIX A

LILI MARLENE
(Hatchett's Version)

Out in the desert the lonely sentry stood
Thinking of Hatchetts and their lovely 'pud',
But he went to fight in Africa, in Africa, in Africa,
Met the 15th Panzers and kicked 'em in the pants sir.

They chased us from Gazala back to Alamein,
There we stopped old Gerry and cracked him once again
And even tho' we get no thanks we broke his ranks
And stopped his tanks, we are the 8th Armada the gallant
8th Armee.

Chased him up to Tunis, chased him out to sea,
Took 2,000 ships and crossed to Sicily,
First came Augusta then the rain, we fought again
And swept the plain, we are the 8th Armada the gallant
8th Armee.

On the Italian mainland we got 'em on the go,
The 5th and 8th Armadas were swimming in the Po,
Oh what a blow for the Nazi swine, we heard it
On the news at 9, a cheer for the 8th Armada, the 5th and the
8th Armee.

On to Volturno what a bloody sight,
There we saw old Gerry covered all over wih —— sh——!
Nibelwurfers and Eighty Eights, the roaring spate
We crossed in state, we are the 8th Armada the gallant
8th Armee

On to Mondragone wearing out one's tracks,
Shooting nasty Germans in their Nazi backs,
And even though we ploughed through mud and German blood,
Despite the flood, we are the 8th Armada the gallant 8th Armee.

Now the Italian mainland far away from home,
We pushed the Kesselringers miles and miles from home,
Oh what a welcome victory, a victory, a victory
For the 5th and 8th Armadas, the 5th and 8th Armee.

Out on the beach-head the gallant sentry stands,
No regrets for Hatchetts or their lovely bands,
For he went to fight in Normandy, in Normandy, in Normandy
With the boys of the Allied Armies—and the men of the
                                                    King's Navee.

Now down among his U-boats Doenitz sits and quakes,
Tried to prolong the war on propaganda fakes,
But we went and fought thro' Germany, thro' Germany,
                                                    thro' Germany
With the help of the 'military idiots' and the whole of the
                                                    Grand Armee.

Their job in Europe's finished, the boys'll soon be here,
You'll meet them in the local, queueing for 'No beer'
But that's all been sent to Germany, to Germany, to Germany,
No beer for the 8th Armada, the gallant 8th Armee.

Back in dear old England, land of hope and glore,
Just a spot of leave and off we go once more,
Chests all covered with D.F.C.s and O.B.E.s
And lots of fleas, we are the 8th Armada, the gallant 8th Armee.

BUSINESS IN GREAT WATERS
by DAVID CLIMIE

Verse

Three old sea dogs!
Three old he-dogs!
Three old jolly old sons of she-dogs!
Three old Barnacle Bills come back from sea!
Three old war dogs!
Three not four dogs!
Three old jolly old ship not shore dogs!
Three in the upper income groups are we!
For, though we never ruled the waves and we're no Captain Cooks,
We're no fools—we waived the rules,
And wrote best-selling Naval Books!

Refrain

We're three rollicking literary sailors!
Three lovable literary tars!
We wrote of war and anguish in the plain and simple language
Which the plain and simple sailors used to write upon the wall.
In the frisky Bay of Biscay when things got a little risky
I lashed myself to my shift key!
We went through quite a fair amount of action, we confess,
But where it was and when it was we none of us can guess,
For we couldn't hear the firing for the typing in the mess
While sailing on the Cruel, Cruel Sea!

I must go down to the sea again,
To the lonely days and nights;
And all I ask is a small advance
And the *John Bull* serial rights!

We're three rollicking literary sailors!
Writing of the things that sailors do.
While patrolling our Dependencies some psychopathic tendencies
Were shown by certain independent members of my crew.
I said 'Go on and mutiny—I don't care what you do to me—
It's what I need for Chapter Three.'
I can't forget the fateful day a Channel port we took;
I hoisted up a signal as we sailed around the Hook—
'England expects this day that every man will write a book'—
A book about the Cruel, Cruel Sea!

Columbus sailed the ocean blue
In fourteen hundred and ninety-two;
But on the whole we had more sport
With a publisher in every port!

We're three rollicking sailors!
Writing of the days when men were men;
For the kind of books we retail are the kind which speak in detail
Of the more engrossing biological aspects of the WREN.
Obscenity—profanity—we write of with urbanity,
And naval slang's our cup of repartee!
We can't forget the comradeship we simple sailors had;
And when the war was over—well, I guess we all felt sad—

Why don't we all sign on again?
          You must be bloody mad!
We're finished with the Cruel Cruel Sea.
          Thank God for film rights!
We're so grateful to the Kind Cruel Sea!

From *Sketches and Lyrics from INTIMACY AT 8.30* published by
Samuel French Ltd.

APPENDIX C

Extract from the transcript of Sir Winston Churchill's Press conference held on 30 June 1954 at the Canadian External Affairs Ministry in Ottawa: being the closing minutes of his last Press conference on his last visit to North America.

Question: Have you any plans for coming back to Ottawa sometime, Sir?

Sir Winston Churchill: Well I really don't wish to cut myself off from doing so by making quite needless predictions at this moment. But when I came here fifty-four years ago for the first time, your population was just over five million. Now it's just under fifteen. And all that's happened in a life—in my life. Extraordinary! Wonderful! But if I were coming back. . . . I don't think I ought to lay down any . . . any . . . limits to what your population should be. I dare say by the end of the century it may be thirty or forty million, or more, and what a wonderful thing, what a marvellous thing. What a work you are all engaged in—building up, rapidly, the life of this vast community, so free and so buoyant. This wonderful country with hitherto unmeasured possibilities, far beyond what you've already seen. A wonderful range lies before you, in the future, playing your part and serving world forces and never forgetting the old country which . . . to which you owe so much of the civilization that you enjoy and are spreading throughout the world.

We have rough times behind us and many difficulties to face in our small island with our vast population, but nothing encourages us more to face these difficulties than the increasingly friendly and loving relations which are growing up between you and us and between the other great Commonwealth states like Australia and New Zealand. It really enables us to face every problem with a feeling of confidence.

I shall not indulge in making an engagement today as to when I shall return to Canada again.

Question: Would you say, Sir, whether the spirit of the Commonwealth, which you have just described, possibly gives a solution to affairs in Asia?

Sir Winston Churchill: The wisdom of the Commonwealth and of our friends in the United States may well provide a solution to those affairs. At the same time I am bound to say I attach more importance to Europe, to what happens in Europe, than I do to what happens in China—but that's no doubt because I live there.

Sir Winston Churchill spoke with frequent pauses, and sometimes great emotion, towards the end of this forty minute Press conference, which ended happily with loud laughter.